Lecture Notes in Computer Science 4079

Commenced Publication in 1973
Founding and Former Series Editors:
Gerhard Goos, Juris Hartmanis, and Jan van Leeuwen

Sandro Etalle   Mirosław Truszczyński (Eds.)

Logic Programming

22nd International Conference, ICLP 2006
Seattle, WA, USA, August 17-20, 2006
Proceedings

 Springer

Volume Editors

Sandro Etalle
University of Twente
Department of Computer Science
P.O. Box 217, 7500AE Enschede, The Netherlands
E-mail: s.etalle@utwente.nl

Mirosław Truszczyński
University of Kentucky
Department of Computer Science
Lexington, KY 40506-0046, USA
E-mail: mirek@cs.uky.edu

Library of Congress Control Number: 2006928958

CR Subject Classification (1998): D.1.6, I.2.3, D.3, F.3, F.4

LNCS Sublibrary: SL 2 – Programming and Software Engineering

ISSN   0302-9743
ISBN-10   3-540-36635-0 Springer Berlin Heidelberg New York
ISBN-13   978-3-540-36635-5 Springer Berlin Heidelberg New York

Springer is a part of Springer Science+Business Media

springer.com

© Springer-Verlag Berlin Heidelberg 2006

Typesetting: Camera-ready by author, data conversion by Scientific Publishing Services, Chennai, India
Printed on acid-free paper   SPIN: 11799573   06/3142   5 4 3 2 1 0

Preface

This volume contains the proceedings of the 22nd International Conference on Logic Programming, ICLP 2006, held in Seattle, USA, during August 17–20, 2006. The conference was collocated with seven pre- and post-conference workshops:

- International Workshop on Applications of Logic Programming in the Semantic Web and Semantic Web Services (ALPSWS)
- Colloquium on Implementation of Constraint and LOgic Programming Systems (CICLOPS)
- International Workshop on Software Verification and Validation (SVV)
- Preferences and Their Applications in Logic Programming Systems
- Search and Logic: Answer Set Programming and SAT
- Workshop on Logic-Based Programming Environments (WLPE)
- International Workshop on Multi-Valued Logic and Logic Programming (MVLP)

ICLP 2006 and its workshops were part of the 4th Federated Logic Conference, FLoC 2006. This collocation offered ICLP 2006 attendees excellent opportunities to interact with researchers working in different but closely related areas. Other conferences that formed the program of FLoC 2006 were:

- Conference on Computer-Aided Verification (CAV)
- International Joint Conference on Automated Reasoning (IJCAR)
- IEEE Symposium on Logic in Computer Science (LICS)
- Conference on Rewriting Techniques and Applications (RTA)
- International Conference on Theory and Applications of Satisfiability Testing (SAT).

Since the first conference in Marseilles in 1982, ICLP has been the premiere international conference for disseminating research results in logic programming. The present edition of the conference received 83 submissions from 22 countries: USA (13), Spain (6), UK (6), Belgium (5), Germany (5), Italy (5), and also Arab Emirates, Australia, Brazil, Canada, China, Czech Republic, France, Hungary, Ireland, Japan, Korea, Poland, Portugal, Russia, Turkey and Venezuela. The Program Committee selected 27 papers for presentation and inclusion in the proceedings: 20 technical papers, six application papers, and one special interest paper. In addition, the program also included 17 poster presentations.

As in the past, the ICLP Program Committee selected the best paper and the best student paper. The Best Paper Award went to Martin Gebser and Torsten Schaub, for the paper "Tableaux Calculi for Answer Set Programming," while the Best Student Paper Award went to the paper "Declarative Semantics of Production Rules for Integrity Maintenance," by Luciano Caroprese, Sergio Greco, Cristina Sirangelo and Ester Zumpano.

The highlights of ICLP 2006 included invited talks by Monica Lam on the use of Datalog to analyze programs, and by Chris Welty on the Semantic Web. The program also featured an invited tutorial by Brigitte Pientka on the use of Logic Programming to design reliable software systems. Thanks to the FLoC collocation, the participants of ICLP 2006 could also attend a FLoC plenary talk by David Dill and a keynote address by David Harel.

ICLP 2006 was organized by the Association for Logic Programming (ALP), in collaboration with the FLoC 2006 Organizing Committee and the Organizing Committees of other FLoC 2006 participating conferences. ICLP 2006 was sponsored by the Association for Logic Programming, the University of Kentucky, Logical Software Solutions, New Mexico State University and, indirectly, by all sponsors of FLoC 2006: Cadence, IBM, Microsoft Research, NEC, and The John von Neumann Minerva Center for the Development of Reactive Systems. We greatly appreciate their generous support.

There are many people who contributed to the success of the conference and to whom we owe our gratitude and thanks. PC members and several other external referees provided timely and in-depth reviews of the submitted papers, and worked hard to select the best papers and posters for the conference program. Manuel Hermenegildo did a superb job representing ICLP 2006 on the FLoC 2006 Steering Committee. Christian Schulte, the Workshop Chair, and Enrico Pontelli, the Doctoral Consortium Chair, helped to enrich significantly the program of the conference. Alexander Serebrenik, the Publicity Chair, worked hard to make sure the conference was broadly publicized. Bart Demoen ran again the traditional and very successful Programming Contest. It goes without saying that the broad logic programming community contributed the most by submitting excellent technical and application papers and posters. Our special thanks go to Lengning Liu, who helped us with the preparation of the proceedings, and to developers of the EasyChair conference management system, which made our job if not *easy* then definitely easier.

August 2006   Sandro Etalle and Mirosław Truszczyński
Program Committee Co-chairs
ICLP 2006

Organization

ICLP was organized by the Association for Logic Programming.

Organizing Committee

Conference Chair	Manuel Hermenegildo(Technical University of Madrid, Spain, and University of New Mexico, USA)
Program Co-chairs	Sandro Etalle (University of Twente, The Netherlands)
	Mirosław Truszczyński (University of Kentucky, USA)
Workshop Chair	Christian Schulte (KTH - Royal Institute of Technology, Sweden)
Publicity Chair	Alexander Serebrenik (TU Eindhoven, The Netherlands)
Doctoral Consortium Chair	Enrico Pontelli (New Mexico State University, USA)

Program Committee

Maria Alpuente (Technical University of Valencia, Spain)
Krzysztof Apt (CWI and University of Amsterdam, The Netherlands)
Annalisa Bossi (University of Venice, Italy)
Veronica Dahl (Simon Fraser University, Canada)
Giorgio Delzanno (University of Genoa, Italy)
Pierre Deransart (INRIA Rocquencourt, France)
Agostino Dovier (University of Udine, Italy)
Thomas Eiter (Technical University of Vienna, Austria)
Sandro Etalle, Co-chair (University of Twente, The Netherlands)
John Gallagher (University of Roskilde, Denmark)
Michael Gelfond (Texas Tech University, USA)
Hai-Feng Guo (University of Nebraska at Omaha, USA)
Manuel Hermenegildo (Technical University of Madrid, Spain)
Tomi Janhunen (Helsinki University of Technology, Finland)
Fangzhen Lin (Hong Kong University of Science and Technology, Hong Kong)
Michael Maher (National ICT Australia, Australia)
Victor Marek (University of Kentucky, USA)
Eric Monfroy (UTFSM, Chile, and University of Nantes, France)

Stephen Muggleton (Imperial College, UK)
Brigitte Pientka (McGill University, Canada)
Maurizio Proietti (The National Research Council, Italy)
I.V. Ramakrishnan (SUNY Stony Brook, USA)
Peter van Roy (Catholic University of Louvain, Belgium)
Harald Søndergaard (The University of Melbourne, Australia)
Mirosław Truszczyński, Co-chair (University of Kentucky, USA)
German Vidal (Technical University of Valencia, Spain)
Andrei Voronkov (The University of Manchester, UK)
Roland Yap (National University of Singapore, Singapore)

Additional Referees

Elvira Albert	Wolfgang Faber	C. R. Ramakrishnan
James Bailey	Francois Fages	Maria Jose Ramirez-
Paolo Baldan	Gilberto Filè	Quintana
Marcello Baldiccini	Norman Foo	Christophe Ringeissen
Demis Ballis	Andrea Formisano	Panagiotis Rondogiannis
Chitta Baral	Rosella Gennari	Gianfranco Rossi
Maryam Bavarian	Laurent Granvilliers	Pablo Saez
Leopoldo Bertossi	Baohua Gu	Konstantinos Sagonas
Marcello Bonsangue	Remy Haemmerle	Diptikalyan Saha
Lucas Bordeaux	Didier Hoareau	Frederic Saubion
Peter Borovansky	Giovambattista Ianni	Peter Schachte
Luca Bortolussi	Yves Jaradin	Josep Silva
Sebastian Brand	Pascual Julián	Anu Singh
Torben Braner	Michael Kifer	Zoltan Somogyi
Francisco Bueno	Lengning Liu	Peter Stuckey
Daniel Cabeza	Lunjin Lu	Terry Swift
Manuel Carro	Salvador Lucas	Paul Tarau
Carlos Castro	Marco Maratea	Frank D. Valencia
Yin Chen	Massimo Marchiori	Jørgen Villadsen
Tom Chothia	Jose Morales	Alicia Villanueva
Henning Christiansen	Stephen Muggleton	Toby Walsh
Michael Codish	Catuscia Palamidessi	David S. Warren
Jesus Correas	Alessandro dal Palù	Richard Watson
Stefania Costantini	Alberto Pettorossi	Stefan Woltran
Alexander Dekhtyar	Carla Piazza	Yuanlin Zhang
Roberto Montagna	Enrico Pontelli	Chang Zhao
Gregory J. Duck	Bernie Pope	Kenny Q. Zhu
Esra Erdem	Fred Popowich	Qi Zhang
Santiago Escobar	Luis Quesada	

Table of Contents

Program Analysis

Answer-Set Programming

Special Interest Paper

Applications I

Semantics

Applications II

Poster Presentations

Doctoral Consortium Presentations

Why Use Datalog to Analyze Programs?

Monica S. Lam

Computer Science Department
Stanford University
Stanford, CA 94305
lam@stanford.edu

We use Datalog because (1) we can write program analyses easier and (2) the analyses in Datalog run faster!

As we turn to automatic program analysis to improve software reliability and security, we find it necessary to perform more complex program analyses. Specifically, if we wish to reason about heap objects, we must perform an interprocedural pointer alias analysis that distinguishes between calling contexts. This is challenging because a typical large program can have over 10^{14} calling contexts, even if we collapse all recursive cycles.

We discovered that it is possible to represent the exponentially many context-sensitive points-to relations succinctly using binary decision diagrams (BDDs). However, it took us months to make just one analysis run at speed. We automated the optimization process and implemented a system called bddbddb (BDD-Based Deductive DataBase), which uses active machine learning to translate Datalog into efficient BDD operations.

A pointer alias analysis now takes just tens of lines of Datalog code rather than thousands of lines of Java code. Pointer alias analysis by itself is not useful. So, more importantly, we can use the results of pointer alias analysis to compute the information of interest by writing a few more Datalog rules. For example, we have used this approach to find numerous vulnerabilities in large C and Java programs. The use of Datalog makes it possible for unsophisticated users to use complex context-sensitive analysis to answer some of the hard questions about their programs.

The research discussed in the talk was performed jointly with John Whaley, Ben Livshits, Michael Martin, Dzintars Avots, Michael Carbin, and Christopher Unkel. It is supported in part by the National Science Foundation under Grant No. 0326227, NSF Graduate Student Fellowships, Stanford Graduate Fellowships, and an Intel student fellowship.

S. Etalle and M. Truszczyński (Eds.): ICLP 2006, LNCS 4079, p. 1, 2006.
© Springer-Verlag Berlin Heidelberg 2006

Semantic Web: The Story of the RIFt so Far

Christopher A. Welty

IBM Watson Research Center
19 Skyline Dr.
Hawthorne, NY 10532
cawelty@frontiernet.net

Abstract. The W3C has embarked on a new standardization effort: the Rules Interchange Format (RIF). The goal of the effort has undergone several changes from the initial idea of creating a standard "rules" layer for the semantic web, and its official mission is to provide a standardized interchange for rules. This change, from creating a rule language to an interchange standard, has been driven mainly by the large number of interests the effort is trying to satisfy, which make it seem impossible to settle on a single language and potentially more feasible to design a method for interoperability. Even with this slightly less politically charged agenda, the number of interests are large, from "Business Rules", "Production Rules", "Reactive Rules", etc., to query languages, First-order logic, alethic and deontic modal logic, etc., to bayes nets, fuzzy logic, etc., to programming languages themselves. Will anything usable ever arise from this morass?

S. Etalle and M. Truszczyński (Eds.): ICLP 2006, LNCS 4079, p. 2, 2006.
© Springer-Verlag Berlin Heidelberg 2006

Overcoming Performance Barriers:
Efficient Verification Techniques
for Logical Frameworks

Brigitte Pientka

School of Computer Science
McGill University
Montreal, Canada
bpientka@cs.mcgill.ca

Abstract. In recent years, logical frameworks which support formalizing language specifications together with their meta-theory have been pervasively used in small and large-scale applications, from certifying code [2] to advocating a general infrastructure for formalizing the meta-theory and semantics of programming languages [5]. In particular, the logical framework LF [9], based on the dependently typed lambda-calculus, and light-weight variants of it like LF_i [17] have played a major role in these applications. While the acceptance of logical framework technology has grown and they have matured, one of the most criticized points is concerned with the run-time performance. In this tutorial we give a brief introduction to logical frameworks, describe its state-of-the art and present recent advances in addressing some of the existing performance issues.

1   Introduction

Logical frameworks [9] provide an experimental platform to specify, and implement formal systems together with the proofs about them. One of its applications lies in proof-carrying code, where it is successfully used to specify and verify formal guarantees about the run-time behavior of programs. More generally, logical frameworks provide an elegant language for encoding and mechanizing the meta-theory and semantics of programming languages. This idea has recently found strong advocates among programming languages researchers who proposed the POPLmark challenge, a set of benchmarks to evaluate and compare tool support to experiment with programming language design, and mechanize the reasoning about programming languages [5].

In this tutorial, we consider the Twelf system [22], an implementation of the logical framework LF [9]. Encodings in LF typically rely on ideas of higher-order abstract syntax where object variables and binders are implemented by variables and binders in the meta-language (i.e. logical framework). One of the key benefits behind higher-order abstract syntax representations is that one can avoid implementing common and tricky routines dealing with vari-

S. Etalle and M. Truszczyński (Eds.): ICLP 2006, LNCS 4079, pp. 3–10, 2006.

ables, such as capture-avoiding substitution, renaming and fresh name generation. Moreover, specifications encoded in Twelf can be executed via a higher-order logic programming language [19] thereby allowing the user to experiment with the implemented formal specifications. Higher-order logic programming as found in Twelf extends traditional first-order logic programming in three ways: First, we have a rich type system based on dependent types, which allows the user to define her own higher-order data-types and supports higher-order abstract syntax[21]. Second, we not only have a static set of program clauses, but assumptions may be introduced dynamically during proof search. Third, we have an explicit notion of proof, i.e. the logic programming interpreter does not only return an answer substitution for the free variables in the query, but the actual proof as a term in the dependently typed lambda-calculus.

These features make Twelf an ideal framework for specifying properties about programming languages and mechanizing the meta-theory about them. For this reason several projects on proof-carrying code [6,7,4] have selected it as their system of choice. The code size in the foundational proof-carrying code project [1] at Princeton ranges between 70,000 and 100,000 lines of Twelf code, which includes data-type definitions and proofs. The higher-order logic program, which is used to execute safety policies, consists of over 5,000 lines of code, and over 600 – 700 clauses. Such large specifications have put to test implementations of logical frameworks and exposed a wide range of new questions and problems. For example, the size of safety proofs in logical frameworks may be unreasonably large and validating them may take a long time. In addition, performance of logical frameworks is inadequate for rapid prototyping and large-scale experiments for two main reasons: redundant computation hampers the execution and many optimizations known and well-understood in first-order reasoning are still poorly understood in the higher-order setting.

In this tutorial, we give a brief introduction to logical frameworks and describe different algorithms to overcome some of the existing performance issues and extend its expressive power. First, we describe the central ideas behind optimizing unification in logical frameworks. In particular, we will consider eliminating unnecessary occurs-checks [26] and eliminating redundancy of some dependent type arguments [25]. Second we discuss higher-order term indexing techniques [23] which are for example used in tabled higher-order logic programming [24] to sustain performance in large-scale examples. All these algorithms are described using contextual modal type theory [15] which provides a simple clean foundation to justify and explain concisely complex higher-order issues. We will also discuss experiments with our algorithms within the logical framework Twelf which demonstrate that these optimizations taken together constitute a significant step toward exploring the full potential of logical frameworks in practical applications. Although the main focus of this work has been the logical framework Twelf, we believe the presented optimizations are applicable to any higher-order reasoning system such as λProlog [13] or Isabelle[18].

2 Optimizing Higher-Order Pattern Unification

Unification lies at the heart of logic programming, theorem proving, and type-reconstruction. Thus, its performance affects in a crucial way the global efficiency of each of these applications. This need for efficient unification algorithms has led to many investigations in the first-order setting. However, the efficient implementation of higher-order unification, especially for dependently typed λ-calculus, is still poorly understood limiting the potential impact of higher-order reasoning systems such as Twelf [22], Isabelle [18], or λProlog [13].

The most comprehensive study on efficient and robust implementation techniques for higher-order unification so far has been carried out by Nadathur and colleagues for the simply-typed λ-calculus in the programming language λProlog [14]. Higher-order unification is implemented via Huet's algorithm [10] and special mechanisms are incorporated into the WAM instruction set to support branching and postponing unification problems. To only perform an occurs-check when necessary, the compiler distinguishes between the first occurrence and subsequent occurrences of a variable and compiles them into different WAM instructions. While for the first occurrence of a variable the occurs-check may be omitted, full unification is used for all subsequent variables. This approach seems to work well in the simply-typed setting, however it is not clear how to generalize it to dependent types. In addition, it is well known, that Huet's algorithm is highly non-deterministic and requires backtracking. An important step toward efficient implementations, has been the development of higher-order pattern unification [12,20]. For this fragment, higher-order unification is decidable and deterministic. As was shown in [11], most programs written in practice fall into this fragment. Unfortunately, the complexity of this algorithm is still at best linear [27] in the sum of the sizes of the terms being unified, which is impractical for any useful programming language or practical framework.

In [26], the author and Pfenning present an abstract view of existential variables in the dependently typed lambda-calculus based on contextual modal type theory. This allows us to distinguish between existential variables, which are represented as contextual modal variables, and bound variables, which are described by ordinary variables. This leads to a simple clean framework which allows us to explain a number of features of the current implementation of higher-order unification in Twelf [22] and provides insight into several optimizations such as lowering and raising. In particular, it explains one optimization called linearization, which eliminates many unnecessary occurs-checks. Terms are compiled into linear higher-order patterns and some additional variable definitions. Linear higher-order patterns restrict higher-order patterns in two ways: First, all existential variables occur only once. Second, we impose some further syntactic restrictions on existential variables, i.e. they must be applied to *all* distinct bound variables. This is in contrast to higher-order patterns, which only require that existential variables are applied to *some* bound variables. Linear higher-order patterns can be solved with an assignment algorithm which resembles first-order unification (without the occurs check) closely and is constant time. Experimental results show that a large class of programs falls into the linear higher-order pattern fragment and can be handled with this algorithm. This leads to significant performance improvement (up to a factor of 5) in many example applications including those in the the area of proof-carrying code.

Most recently, we have explored a different optimization to higher-order unification where we skip some redundant implicit type arguments during unification [25]. Unlike our prior optimization which is restricted to proof search, skipping some redundant type arguments during unification is a general optimization and hence impacts not only the proof search performance, but also any other algorithm relying on unification such as type-reconstruction, coverage checking, termination checking etc.

Our experimental results show that although the size of redundant arguments is large and there is a substantial number of them, their impact on run-time performance is surprisingly limited (roughly 20% improvement). Our experimental results also demonstrate that optimizations such as eliminating the occurs checks are more important than previously thought. These results provide interesting insights into efficient implementations of dependently typed systems in general, and can provide guidance for future implementations.

3   Higher-Order Term Indexing

Efficient data-structures and implementation techniques play a crucial role in utilizing the full potential of a reasoning environment in real-world applications. In logic programming, for example, we need to select all clauses from the program which unify with the current goal. In tabled logic programming we memoize intermediate goals in a table and reuse their results later in order to eliminate redundant and infinite computation. Here we need to find all entries in the table such that the current goal is a variant or an instance of the table entry and re-use the associated answers. If there is no such table entry, we need to add the current goal to the table.

To address this problem, different indexing techniques have been proposed for first-order terms (see [28] for a survey), however term indexing techniques for higher-order languages are essentially non-existent thereby limiting the application and the potential impact of higher-order reasoning systems.

We have designed and implemented higher-order term indexing techniques based on substitution trees [23]. Substitution tree indexing is a highly successful technique in first-order theorem proving, which allows the sharing of common sub-expressions via substitutions. This work extends first-order substitution tree indexing [8] to the higher-order setting.

Consider specifying well-know equivalence preserving transformation in first-order logic. In this example, we must represent formulas such as $\forall x.(A(x) \wedge B)$ or $\forall x.(C \wedge D(x))$. These formulas can be represented as terms using higher-order abstract syntax. The first one corresponds to (all $\lambda x.(A\ x$ and $B)$) and the second one to (all $\lambda x.(C$ and $D\ x)$). Inspecting the terms closely, we observe that they share a lot of structure which can be described by the following skeleton: (all $\lambda x.(*_1$ and $*_2)$). We can obtain the first term by instantiating

$*_1$ with the term $(A\ x)$ and $*_2$ with the term B. Similarly we can obtain the second term by by instantiating $*_1$ with the term C and $*_2$ with the term $(D\ x)$. Note that $*_1$ and $*_2$ are instantiated with open terms which are allowed to refer to the bound variable x. Our goal is to share subexpressions even in the presence of binders and instantiate holes denoted by $*$ by replacement. How could this be done? Computing the skeleton of two terms relies on finding the most specific generalization of two terms. However in the higher-order setting, the most specific generalization of two terms may not exist in general. Moreover, retrieving all terms, which unify or match, needs to be simple and efficient – but higher-order unification is undecidable in general. Although, most specific generalizations exist for higher-order patterns and higher-order pattern unification [12,20] is decidable, experience with these algorithms demonstrates that they may not be efficient in practice [26]. Therefore, it is not obvious that they are suitable for higher-order term indexing techniques.

Instead, we use linear higher-order patterns as a basis for higher-order term indexing [26]. This allows us to reduce the problem of computing most specific generalizations for higher-order terms to an algorithm which resembles closely its first-order counterpart [23]. Contextual modal type theory provides a clean theoretical framework to describe and reason about holes and instantiations with open terms. This technique has been implemented to speed-up the execution of the tabled higher-order logic programming engine in Twelf. Experimental results demonstrate that higher-order term indexing leads to substantial performance improvements (by up to a factor of 10), illustrating the importance of indexing in general [23].

4 Conclusion

We have developed several important techniques using contextual modal type theory as a uniform framework. This allows a clean concise theoretical description which clarifies many higher-order issues related to bound variable dependencies. Moreover we have implemented and experimentally evaluated our techniques within the logical framework Twelf. Our results show that the presented techniques taken together considerably improve the performance of higher-order reasoning systems. This a first step toward exploring the full potential of logical frameworks in practice and apply it to new areas such as security and authentication [3]. However, the presented techniques are just a first step toward narrowing the performance gap between higher-order and first-order systems. There are many more optimizations which have been already proven successful in the first-order setting and we may be able to apply to higher-order languages.

Finally, the application of logical frameworks to certified code raises new question, which traditionally have not played a central role in logic programming. One of the main ideas in certified code is not only to verify that a program is safe, but also to efficiently transmit and then check the proof. In [16,29] the authors explore the novel use of higher-order logic programming for checking the correctness of a certificate. To reduce the proof size, the certificate encodes the non-deterministic choices of a higher-order logic programming interpreter as a bit-string. To reconstruct and check the proof, we rerun a deterministic higher-order logic programming interpreter guided by the certificate.

Last but not least, programming language researchers [5] have recently strongly emphasized the need for formalizing and experimenting with programming language designs. Higher-order logic programming environments are ideally suited for this kind of endeavor, since they allow high-level declarative descriptions and execution of formal specifications. Our community also has already a lot of experience in verifying meta-properties such as determinism, termination, or totality which provide valuable insights into properties of these formal specifications. Hence, we see exciting opportunities for encoding and experimenting with the meta-theory and semantics of programming languages within higher-order logic programming environments and applying logic programming technology to this domain.

References

1. Andrew Appel. Foundational proof-carrying code project. personal communication.
2. Andrew Appel. Foundational proof-carrying code. In J. Halpern, editor, *Proceedings of the 16th Annual Symposium on Logic in Computer Science (LICS'01)*, pages 247–256. IEEE Computer Society Press, June 2001. Invited Talk.
3. Andrew W. Appel and Edward W. Felten. Proof-carrying authentication. In *ACM Conference on Computer and Communications Security*, pages 52–62, 1999.
4. W. Appel and Amy P. Felty. A semantic model of types and machine instructions for proof-carrying code. In *27th ACM SIGPLAN-SIGACT Symposium on Principles of Programming Languages (POPL '00)*, pages 243–253, Jan. 2000.
5. B. Aydemir, A. Bohannon, M. Fairbairn, J. Foster, B. Pierce, P. Sewell, D. Vytiniotis, G. Washburn, S. Weirich, and S. Zdancewic. Mechanized metatheory for the masses: The poplmark challenge, 2005.
6. Andrew Bernard and Peter Lee. Temporal logic for proof-carrying code. In *Proceedings of the 18th International Conference on Automated Deduction (CADE-18)*, volume 2392 of *Lecture Notes in Artificial Intelligence*, pages 31–46, Copenhagen, Denmark, July 2002.
7. Karl Crary and Susmit Sarkar. Foundational certified code in a metalogical framework. In *19th International Conference on Automated Deduction*, Miami, Florida, USA, 2003. Extended version published as CMU technical report CMU-CS-03-108.
8. Peter Graf. Substitution tree indexing. In *Proceedings of the 6th International Conference on Rewriting Techniques and Applications, Kaiserslautern, Germany,* Lecture Notes in Computer Science (LNCS) 914, pages 117–131. Springer-Verlag, 1995.
9. Robert Harper, Furio Honsell, and Gordon Plotkin. A framework for defining logics. *Journal of the Association for Computing Machinery*, 40(1):143–184, January 1993.
10. Gérard Huet. A unification algorithm for typed λ-calculus. *Theoretical Computer Science*, 1:27–57, 1975.
11. Spiro Michaylov and Frank Pfenning. An empirical study of the runtime behavior of higher-order logic programs. In D. Miller, editor, *Proceedings of the Workshop on the λProlog Programming Language*, pages 257–271, Philadelphia, Pennsylvania, July 1992. University of Pennsylvania. Available as Technical Report MS-CIS-92-86.

12. Dale Miller. Unification of simply typed lambda-terms as logic programming. In *Eighth International Logic Programming Conference*, pages 255–269, Paris, France, June 1991. MIT Press.

13. Gopalan Nadathur and Dale Miller. An overview of λProlog. In Kenneth A. Bowen and Robert A. Kowalski, editors, *Fifth International Logic Programming Conference*, pages 810–827, Seattle, Washington, August 1988. MIT Press.

14. Gopalan Nadathur and Dustin J. Mitchell. System description: Teyjus – a compiler and abstract machine based implementation of Lambda Prolog. In H. Ganzinger, editor, *Proceedings of the 16th International Conference on Automated Deduction (CADE-16)*, pages 287–291, Trento, Italy, July 1999. Springer-Verlag LNCS.

15. Aleksandar Nanevski, Frank Pfenning, and Brigitte Pientka. A contextual modal type theory. 2005.

16. G. Necula and S. Rahul. Oracle-based checking of untrusted software. In *28th ACM Symposium on Principles of Programming Languages (POPL'01)*, pages 142–154, 2001.

17. George C. Necula and Peter Lee. Efficient representation and validation of logical proofs. In Vaughan Pratt, editor, *Proceedings of the 13th Annual Symposium on Logic in Computer Science (LICS'98)*, pages 93–104, Indianapolis, Indiana, June 1998. IEEE Computer Society Press.

18. Lawrence C. Paulson. Natural deduction as higher-order resolution. *Journal of Logic Programming*, 3:237–258, 1986.

19. Frank Pfenning. Logic programming in the LF logical framework. In Gérard Huet and Gordon Plotkin, editors, *Logical Frameworks*, pages 149–181. Cambridge University Press, 1991.

20. Frank Pfenning. Unification and anti-unification in the Calculus of Constructions. In *Sixth Annual IEEE Symposium on Logic in Computer Science*, pages 74–85, Amsterdam, The Netherlands, July 1991.

21. Frank Pfenning and Conal Elliott. Higher-order abstract syntax. In *Proceedings of the ACM SIGPLAN '88 Symposium on Language Design and Implementation*, pages 199–208, Atlanta, Georgia, June 1988.

22. Frank Pfenning and Carsten Schürmann. System description: Twelf — a meta-logical framework for deductive systems. In H. Ganzinger, editor, *Proceedings of the 16th International Conference on Automated Deduction (CADE-16)*, pages 202–206, Trento, Italy, July 1999. Springer-Verlag Lecture Notes in Artificial Intelligence (LNAI) 1632.

23. Brigitte Pientka. Higher-order substitution tree indexing. In C. Palamidessi, editor, *19th International Conference on Logic Programming, Mumbai, India*, Lecture Notes in Computer Science (LNCS 2916), pages 377–391. Springer-Verlag, 2003.

24. Brigitte Pientka. Tabling for higher-order logic programming. In *20th International Conference on Automated Deduction (CADE), Talinn, Estonia*, volume 3632 of *Lecture Notes in Computer Science*, pages 54–68. Springer, 2005.

25. Brigitte Pientka. Eliminating redundancy in higher-order unification: a lightweight approach. In U. Furbach and N. Shankar, editors, *Proceedings of the Third International Joint Conference on Automated Reasoning, Seattle, USA*, Lecture Notes in Artificial Intelligence (LNAI), page to appear. Springer-Verlag, 2006.

26. Brigitte Pientka and Frank Pfennning. Optimizing higher-order pattern unification. In F. Baader, editor, *19th International Conference on Automated Deduction, Miami, USA*, Lecture Notes in Artificial Intelligence (LNAI) 2741, pages 473–487. Springer-Verlag, July 2003.

27. Zhenyu Qian. Linear unification of higher-order patterns. In *Proceedings of TAP-SOFT'93*, pages 391–405. Springer-Verlag Lecture Notes in Computer Science (LNCS) 668, 1993.
28. I. V. Ramakrishnan, R. Sekar, and A. Voronkov. Term indexing. In Alan Robinson and Andrei Voronkov, editors, *Handbook of Automated Reasoning*, volume 2, pages 1853–1962. Elsevier Science Publishers B.V., 2001.
29. Karl Crary Susmit Sarkar, Brigitte Pientka. Small proof witnesses for lf. In Maurizio Gabbrielli and Gopal Gupta, editors, *21th International Conference on Logic Programming, Sitges, Spain*, volume 3668 of *Lecture Notes in Computer Science (LNCS)*, pages 387–401. Springer-Verlag, 2005.

Tableau Calculi for Answer Set Programming

Martin Gebser and Torsten Schaub

Institut für Informatik, Universität Potsdam, Postfach 90 03 27, D–14439 Potsdam

Abstract. We introduce a formal proof system based on tableau methods for analyzing computations made in Answer Set Programming (ASP). Our approach furnishes declarative and fine-grained instruments for characterizing operations as well as strategies of ASP-solvers. First, the granulation is detailed enough to capture the variety of propagation and choice operations of algorithms used for ASP; this also includes SAT-based approaches. Second, it is general enough to encompass the various strategies pursued by existing ASP-solvers. This provides us with a uniform framework for identifying and comparing fundamental properties of algorithms. Third, the approach allows us to investigate the proof complexity of algorithms for ASP, depending on choice operations. We show that exponentially different best-case computations can be obtained for different ASP-solvers. Finally, our approach is flexible enough to integrate new inference patterns, so to study their relation to existing ones. As a result, we obtain a novel approach to unfounded set handling based on loops, being applicable to non-SAT-based solvers. Furthermore, we identify backward propagation operations for unfounded sets.

1 Introduction

Answer Set Programming (ASP; [1]) is an appealing tool for knowledge representation and reasoning. Its attractiveness is supported by the availability of efficient off-the-shelf ASP-solvers that allow for computing answer sets of logic programs. However, in contrast to the related area of satisfiability checking (SAT), ASP lacks a formal framework for describing inferences conducted by ASP-solvers, such as the resolution proof theory in SAT-solving [2]. This deficiency led to a great heterogeneity in the description of algorithms for ASP, ranging over procedural [3,4], fixpoint [5], and operational [6,7] characterizations. On the one hand, this complicates identifying fundamental properties of algorithms, such as soundness and completeness. On the other hand, it almost disables formal comparisons among them.

We address this deficiency by introducing a family of tableau calculi [8] for ASP. This allows us to view answer set computations as derivations in an inference system: A branch in a tableau corresponds to a successful or unsuccessful computation of an answer set; an entire tableau represents a traversal of the search space. Our approach furnishes declarative and fine-grained instruments for characterizing operations as well as strategies of ASP-solvers. In fact, we relate the approaches of *assat, cmodels, dlv, nomore++, smodels*, etc. [3,4,9,7,5] to appropriate tableau calculi, in the sense that computations of an aforementioned solver comply with tableau proofs in a corresponding calculus. This provides us with a uniform proof-theoretic framework for analyzing and comparing different algorithms, which is the first of its kind for ASP.

S. Etalle and M. Truszczyński (Eds.): ICLP 2006, LNCS 4079, pp. 11–25, 2006.

Based on proof-theoretic concepts, we are able to derive general results, which apply to whole classes of algorithms instead of only specific ASP-solvers. In particular, we investigate the proof complexity of different approaches, depending on choice operations. It turns out that, regarding time complexity, exponentially different best-case computations can be obtained for different ASP-solvers. Furthermore, our proof-theoretic framework allows us to describe and study novel inference patterns, going beyond implemented systems. As a result, we obtain a loop-based approach to unfounded set handling, which is not restricted to SAT-based solvers. Also we identify backward propagation operations for unfounded sets.

Our work is motivated by the desire to converge the various heterogeneous characterizations of current ASP-solvers, on the basis of a canonical specification of principles underlying the respective algorithms. The classic example for this is DPLL [10,11], the most widely used algorithm for SAT, which is based on resolution proof theory [2]. By developing proof-theoretic foundations for ASP and abstracting from implementation details, we want to enhance the understanding of solving approaches as such. The proof-theoretic perspective also allows us to state results in a general way, rather than in a solver-specific one, and to study inferences by their admissibility, rather than from an implementation point of view.

Our work is inspired by the one of Järvisalo, Junttila, and Niemelä, who use tableau methods in [12,13] for investigating Boolean circuit satisfiability checking in the context of symbolic model checking. Although their target is different from ours, both approaches have many aspects in common. First, both use tableau methods for characterizing DPLL-type techniques. Second, using cut rules for characterizing DPLL-type split operations is the key idea for analyzing the proof complexity of different inference strategies. General investigations in propositional proof complexity, in particular, the one of satisfiability checking (SAT), can be found in [14]. From the perspective of tableau systems, DPLL is very similar to the propositional version of the KE tableau calculus; both are closely related to weak connection tableau with atomic cut (as pointed out in [15]). Tableau-based characterizations of logic programming are elaborated upon in [16]. Pearce, de Guzmán, and Valverde provide in [17] a tableau calculus for automated theorem proving in equilibrium logic, based on its 5-valued semantics. Other tableau approaches to nonmonotonic logics are summarized in [18]. Bonatti describes in [19] a resolution method for skeptical answer set programming. Operator-based characterizations of propagation and choice operations in ASP can be found in [6,7,20].

2   Answer Set Programming

Given an alphabet $\mathcal{P}$, a (normal) *logic program* is a finite set of rules of the form $p_0 \leftarrow p_1, \ldots, p_m, not\ p_{m+1}, \ldots, not\ p_n$, where $0 \leq m \leq n$ and each $p_i \in \mathcal{P}$ $(0 \leq i \leq n)$ is an *atom*. A *literal* is an atom p or its negation $not\ p$. For a rule r, let $head(r) = p_0$ be the *head* of r and $body(r) = \{p_1, \ldots, p_m, not\ p_{m+1}, \ldots, not\ p_n\}$ be the *body* of r; and let $body^+(r) = \{p_1, \ldots, p_m\}$ and $body^-(r) = \{p_{m+1}, \ldots, p_n\}$. The set of atoms occurring in a program Π is given by $atom(\Pi)$. The set of bodies in Π is $body(\Pi) = \{body(r) \mid r \in \Pi\}$. For regrouping rule bodies with the same head p, let $body(p) = \{body(r) \mid r \in \Pi, head(r) = p\}$. A program Π is *positive* if

$body^-(r) = \emptyset$ for all $r \in \Pi$. $Cn(\Pi)$ denotes the smallest set of atoms closed under positive program Π. The *reduct*, Π^X, of Π relative to a set X of atoms is defined by $\Pi^X = \{head(r) \leftarrow body^+(r) \mid r \in \Pi, \ body^-(r) \cap X = \emptyset\}$. A set X of atoms is an *answer set* of a logic program Π if $Cn(\Pi^X) = X$. As an example, consider Program $\Pi_1 = \{a \leftarrow; \ c \leftarrow not \ b, not \ d; \ d \leftarrow a, not \ c\}$ and its two answer sets $\{a, c\}$ and $\{a, d\}$.

An *assignment* A is a partial mapping of objects in a program Π into $\{T, F\}$, indicating whether a member of the *domain* of A, $dom(A)$, is true or false, respectively. In order to capture the whole spectrum of ASP-solving techniques, we fix $dom(A)$ to $atom(\Pi) \cup body(\Pi)$ in the sequel. We define $A^T = \{v \in dom(A) \mid A(v) = T\}$ and $A^F = \{v \in dom(A) \mid A(v) = F\}$. We also denote an assignment A by a set of signed objects: $\{Tv \mid v \in A^T\} \cup \{Fv \mid v \in A^F\}$. For instance with Π_1, the assignment mapping body $\emptyset$ of rule $a \leftarrow$ to T and atom b to F is represented by $\{T\emptyset, Fb\}$; all other atoms and bodies of Π_1 remain undefined. Following up this notation, we call an assignment *empty* if it leaves all objects undefined.

We define a set U of atoms as an *unfounded set* [21] of a program Π wrt a partial assignment A, if, for every rule $r \in \Pi$ such that $head(r) \in U$, either $(body^+(r) \cap A^F) \cup (body^-(r) \cap A^T) \neq \emptyset$ or $body^+(r) \cap U \neq \emptyset$. The *greatest unfounded set* of Π wrt A, denoted $GUS(\Pi, A)$, is the union of all unfounded sets of Π wrt A. *Loops* are sets of atoms that circularly depend upon one another in a program's positive atom dependency graph [3]. In analogy to external support [22] of loops, we define the *external bodies* of a loop L in Π as $EB(L) = \{body(r) \mid r \in \Pi, head(r) \in L, body^+(r) \cap L = \emptyset\}$. We denote the set of all loops in Π by $loop(\Pi)$.

3   Tableau Calculi

We describe calculi for the construction of answer sets from logic programs. Such constructions are associated with binary trees called *tableaux* [8]. The nodes of the trees are (mainly) *signed propositions*, that is, propositions preceded by either T or F, indicating an assumed truth value for the proposition. A *tableau* for a logic program Π and an initial assignment A is a binary tree such that the root node of the tree consists of the rules in Π and all members of A. The other nodes in the tree are *entries* of the form Tv or Fv, where $v \in dom(A)$, generated by extending a tableau using the rules in Figure 1 in the following standard way [8]: Given a tableau rule and a branch in the tableau such that the prerequisites of the rule hold in the branch, the tableau can be extended by adding new entries to the end of the branch as specified by the rule. If the rule is the *Cut* rule in *(m)*, then entries Tv and Fv are added as the left and the right child to the end of the branch. For the other rules, the consequent of the rule is added to the end of the branch. For convenience, the application of tableau rules makes use of two conjugation functions, t and f. For a literal l, define:

$$tl = \begin{cases} Tl & \text{if } l \in \mathcal{P} \\ Fp & \text{if } l = not \ p \text{ for a } p \in \mathcal{P} \end{cases} \qquad fl = \begin{cases} Tp & \text{if } l = not \ p \text{ for a } p \in \mathcal{P} \\ Fl & \text{if } l \in \mathcal{P} \end{cases}$$

Some rule applications are subject to provisos. (§) stipulates that $B_1, \ldots, B_m$ constitute all bodies of rules with head p. (†) requires that p belongs to the greatest unfounded set

$$\frac{p \leftarrow l_1, \ldots, l_n}{\dfrac{tl_1, \ldots, tl_n}{T\{l_1, \ldots, l_n\}}}$$

(a) Forward True Body (FTB)

$$\frac{F\{l_1, \ldots, l_i, \ldots, l_n\}}{\dfrac{tl_1, \ldots, tl_{i-1}, tl_{i+1}, \ldots, tl_n}{fl_i}}$$

(b) Backward False Body (BFB)

$$\frac{p \leftarrow l_1, \ldots, l_n}{\dfrac{T\{l_1, \ldots, l_n\}}{Tp}}$$

(c) Forward True Atom (FTA)

$$\frac{p \leftarrow l_1, \ldots, l_n}{\dfrac{Fp}{F\{l_1, \ldots, l_n\}}}$$

(d) Backward False Atom (BFA)

$$\frac{p \leftarrow l_1, \ldots, l_i, \ldots, l_n}{\dfrac{fl_i}{F\{l_1, \ldots, l_i, \ldots, l_n\}}}$$

(e) Forward False Body (FFB)

$$\frac{T\{l_1, \ldots, l_i, \ldots, l_n\}}{tl_i}$$

(f) Backward True Body (BTB)

$$\frac{FB_1, \ldots, FB_m}{Fp} \; (\S)$$

(g) Forward False Atom (FFA)

$$\frac{Tp \quad FB_1, \ldots, FB_{i-1}, FB_{i+1}, \ldots, FB_m}{TB_i} \; (\S)$$

(h) Backward True Atom (BTA)

$$\frac{FB_1, \ldots, FB_m}{Fp} \; (\dagger)$$

(i) Well-Founded Negation (WFN)

$$\frac{Tp \quad FB_1, \ldots, FB_{i-1}, FB_{i+1}, \ldots, FB_m}{TB_i} \; (\dagger)$$

(j) Well-Founded Justification (WFJ)

$$\frac{FB_1, \ldots, FB_m}{Fp} \; (\ddagger)$$

(k) Forward Loop (FL)

$$\frac{Tp \quad FB_1, \ldots, FB_{i-1}, FB_{i+1}, \ldots, FB_m}{TB_i} \; (\ddagger)$$

(l) Backward Loop (BL)

$$\frac{}{Tv \quad | \quad Fv} \; (\sharp[X])$$

(m) Cut (Cut[X])

$(\S) : body(p) = \{B_1, \ldots, B_m\}$
$(\dagger) : \{B_1, \ldots, B_m\} \subseteq body(\Pi),\ p \in GUS(\{r \in \Pi \mid body(r) \notin \{B_1, \ldots, B_m\}\}, \emptyset)$
$(\ddagger) : p \in L, L \in loop(\Pi),\ EB(L) = \{B_1, \ldots, B_m\}$
$(\sharp[X]) : v \in X$

Fig. 1. Tableau rules for answer set programming

$$a \leftarrow$$
$$c \leftarrow not\ b, not\ d$$
$$d \leftarrow a, not\ c$$

	$\boldsymbol{T}\emptyset$	(a)
	$\boldsymbol{T}a$	(c)
	$\boldsymbol{F}b$	(g)

$\boldsymbol{T}c$		$\boldsymbol{F}c$	$(Cut[atom(\Pi)])$
$\boldsymbol{T}\{not\ b, not\ d\}$	(h)	$\boldsymbol{F}\{not\ b, not\ d\}$	(d)
$\boldsymbol{F}d$	(f)	$\boldsymbol{T}d$	(b)
$\boldsymbol{F}\{a, not\ c\}$	(e)	$\boldsymbol{T}\{a, not\ c\}$	(a)

Fig. 2. Tableau of $\mathcal{T}_{smodels}$ for Π_1 and the empty assignment

induced by the rules whose bodies are not among $B_1, \ldots, B_m$. ($\ddagger$) makes sure that p belongs to a loop whose external bodies are $B_1, \ldots, B_m$. Finally, ($\sharp[X]$) guides the application of the *Cut* rule by restricting cut objects to members of X.[1] Different tableau calculi are obtained from different rule sets. When needed, this is made precise by enumerating the tableau rules. The following tableau calculi are of particular interest:

$$\mathcal{T}_{comp} = \{(a)\text{-}(h), Cut[atom(\Pi) \cup body(\Pi)]\} \tag{1}$$

$$\mathcal{T}_{smodels} = \{(a)\text{-}(i), Cut[atom(\Pi)]\} \tag{2}$$

$$\mathcal{T}_{noMoRe} = \{(a)\text{-}(i), Cut[body(\Pi)]\} \tag{3}$$

$$\mathcal{T}_{nomore++} = \{(a)\text{-}(i), Cut[atom(\Pi) \cup body(\Pi)]\} \tag{4}$$

An exemplary tableau of $\mathcal{T}_{smodels}$ is given in Figure 2, where rule applications are indicated by either letters or rule names, like (a) or $(Cut[atom(\Pi)])$. Both branches comprise Π_1 along with a total assignment for $atom(\Pi_1) \cup body(\Pi_1)$; the left one represents answer set $\{a, c\}$, the right one gives answer set $\{a, d\}$.

A branch in a tableau is *contradictory*, if it contains both entries $\boldsymbol{T}v$ and $\boldsymbol{F}v$ for some $v \in dom(A)$. A branch is *complete*, if it is contradictory, or if the branch contains either the entry $\boldsymbol{T}v$ or $\boldsymbol{F}v$ for each $v \in dom(A)$ and is closed under all rules in a given calculus, except for the *Cut* rule in *(m)*. For instance, both branches in Figure 2 are non-contradictory and complete.

For each $v \in dom(A)$, we say that entry $\boldsymbol{T}v$ (or $\boldsymbol{F}v$) can be deduced by a set $\mathcal{R}$ of tableau rules in a branch, if the entry $\boldsymbol{T}v$ (or $\boldsymbol{F}v$) can be generated from nodes in the branch by applying rules in $\mathcal{R}$ only. Note that every branch corresponds to a pair (Π, A) consisting of a program Π and an assignment A, and vice versa;[2] we draw on this relationship for identifying branches in the sequel. Accordingly, we let $D_{\mathcal{R}}(\Pi, A)$ denote the set of all entries deducible by rule set $\mathcal{R}$ in branch (Π, A). Moreover, $D_{\mathcal{R}}^*(\Pi, A)$ represents the set of all entries in the smallest branch extending (Π, A) and being closed under $\mathcal{R}$. When dealing with tableau calculi, like $\mathcal{T}$, we slightly abuse notation and write $D_{\mathcal{T}}(\Pi, A)$ (or $D_{\mathcal{T}}^*(\Pi, A)$) instead of $D_{\mathcal{T} \setminus \{(m)\}}(\Pi, A)$ (or $D_{\mathcal{T} \setminus \{(m)\}}^*(\Pi, A)$),

---

[1] The *Cut* rule ((*m*) in Figure 1) may, in principle, introduce more general entries; this would however necessitate additional decomposition rules, leading to extended tableau calculi.

[2] Given a branch (Π, A) in a tableau for Π and initial assignment A_0, we have $A_0 \subseteq A$.

thus ignoring *Cut*. We mention that $D^*_{\{(a),(c),(e),(g)\}}(\Pi, A)$ corresponds to Fitting's operator [23]. Similarly, we detail in the subsequent sections that $D^*_{\{(a)-(h)\}}(\Pi, A)$ coincides with unit propagation on a program's completion [24,25], $D^*_{\{(a),(c),(e),(g),(i)\}}(\Pi, A)$ amounts to propagation via well-founded semantics [21], and $D^*_{\{(a)-(i)\}}(\Pi, A)$ captures *smodels*' propagation [5], that is, well-founded semantics enhanced by backward propagation. Note that all deterministic rules in Figure 1 are answer set preserving; this also applies to the *Cut* rule when considering both resulting branches.

A tableau is *complete*, if all its branches are complete. A complete tableau for a program and the empty assignment such that all branches are contradictory is called a *refutation* for the program; it means that the program has no answer set, as exemplarily shown next for *smodels*-type tableaux.

Theorem 1. *Let Π be a logic program and let $\emptyset$ denote the empty assignment. Then, the following holds for tableau calculus $\mathcal{T}_{smodels}$:*

1. *Π has no answer set iff every complete tableau for Π and $\emptyset$ is a refutation.*
2. *If Π has an answer set X, then every complete tableau for Π and $\emptyset$ has a unique non-contradictory branch (Π, A) such that $X = A^T \cap atom(\Pi)$.*
3. *If a tableau for Π and $\emptyset$ has a non-contradictory complete branch (Π, A), then $A^T \cap atom(\Pi)$ is an answer set of Π.*

The same results are obtained for other tableau calculi, like $\mathcal{T}_{noMoRe}$ and $\mathcal{T}_{nomore++}$, all of which are sound and complete for ASP.

4   Characterizing Existing ASP-Solvers

In this section, we discuss the relation between the tableau rules in Figure 1 and well-known ASP-solvers. As it turns out, our tableau rules are well-suited for describing the approaches of a wide variety of ASP-solvers. In particular, we cover all leading approaches to answer set computation for (normal) logic programs. We start with SAT-based solvers *assat* and *cmodels*, then go on with atom-based solvers *smodels* and *dlv*, and finally turn to *hybrid* solvers, like *nomore++*, working on atoms as well as bodies.

SAT-based solvers. The basic idea of SAT-based solvers is to use some SAT-solver as model generator and to afterwards check whether a generated model contains an unfounded *loop*. Lin and Zhao show in [3] that the answer sets of a logic program Π coincide with the models of the *completion* of Π and the set of all *loop formulas* of Π. The respective propositional logic translation is $Comp(\Pi) \cup LF(\Pi)$, where:[3]

$$Comp(\Pi) = \{p \equiv (\bigvee_{k=1...m} \bigwedge_{l \in B_k} l) \mid p \in atom(\Pi), body(p) = \{B_1, \ldots, B_m\}\}$$
$$LF(\Pi) = \{\neg(\bigvee_{k=1...m} \bigwedge_{l \in B_k} l) \rightarrow \bigwedge_{p \in L} \neg p \mid$$
$$L \in loop(\Pi), EB(L) = \{B_1, \ldots, B_m\}\}$$

This translation constitutes the backbone of SAT-based solvers *assat* [3] and *cmodels* [4]. However, loop formulas $LF(\Pi)$ require exponential space in the worst case [26]. Thus, *assat* adds loop formulas from $LF(\Pi)$ incrementally to $Comp(\Pi)$,

---

[3] Note that a negative default literal *not p* is translated as $\neg p$.

whenever some model of $Comp(\Pi)$ not corresponding to an answer set has been generated by the underlying SAT-solver.[4] The approach of *cmodels* avoids storing loop formulas by exploiting the SAT-solver's inner backtracking and learning scheme. Despite the differences between *assat* and *cmodels*, we can uniformly characterize their model generation and verification steps. We first describe tableaux capturing the proceeding of the underlying SAT-solver and then go on with unfounded set checks.

In analogy to Theorem 1, models of $Comp(\Pi)$ correspond to tableaux of $\mathcal{T}_{comp}$.

Theorem 2. *Let Π be a logic program. Then, M is a model of $Comp(\Pi)$ iff every complete tableau of $\mathcal{T}_{comp}$ for Π and $\emptyset$ has a unique non-contradictory branch (Π, A) such that $M = A^T \cap atom(\Pi)$.*

Intuitively, tableau rules *(a)-(h)* describe unit propagation on a program's completion, represented in CNF as required by most SAT-solvers. Note that *assat* and *cmodels* introduce propositional variables for bodies in order to obtain a polynomially-sized set of clauses equivalent to a program's completion [28]. Due to the fact that atoms and bodies are represented as propositional variables, allowing both of them as branching variables in $\mathcal{T}_{comp}$ (via $Cut[atom(\Pi) \cup body(\Pi)]$; cf. (1)) makes sense.

Once a model of $Comp(\Pi)$ has been generated by the underlying SAT-solver, *assat* and *cmodels* apply an unfounded set check for deciding whether the model is an answer set. If it fails, unfounded loops whose atoms are true (so-called *terminating loops* [3]) are determined. Their loop formulas are used to eliminate the generated model. Unfounded set checks, as performed by *assat* and *cmodels*, can be captured by tableau rules *FFB* and *FL* (*(e)* and *(k)* in Figure 1) as follows.

Theorem 3. *Let Π be a logic program, let M be a model of $Comp(\Pi)$, and let $A = \{Tp \mid p \in M\} \cup \{Fp \mid p \in atom(\Pi) \setminus M\}$.*
Then, M is an answer set of Π iff $M \cap (D_{\{FL\}}(\Pi, D_{\{FFB\}}(\Pi, A)))^F = \emptyset$.

With SAT-based approaches, sophisticated unfounded set checks, able to detect unfounded loops, are applied only to non-contradictory complete branches in tableaux of $\mathcal{T}_{comp}$. Unfortunately, programs may yield exponentially many loops [26]. This can lead to exponentially many models of a program's completion that turn out to be no answer sets [29]. In view of Theorem 3, it means that exponentially many branches may have to be completed by final unfounded set checks.

Atom-based solvers. We now describe the relation between *smodels* [5] and *dlv* [9] on the one side and our tableau rules on the other side. We first concentrate on characterizing *smodels* and then sketch how our characterization applies to *dlv*.

Given that only literals are explicitly represented in *smodels'* assignments, whereas truth and falsity of bodies are determined implicitly, one might consider rewriting tableau rules to work on literals only, thereby, restricting the domain of assignments to atoms. For instance, tableau rule *FFA* (*(g)* in Figure 1) would then turn into:

$$\frac{fl_1, \ldots, fl_m}{Fp} \quad (\{r \in \Pi \mid head(r) = p, body(r) \cap \{l_1, \ldots, l_m\} = \emptyset\} = \emptyset)$$

---

[4] Note that every answer set of Π is a model of $Comp(\Pi)$, but not vice versa [27].

Observe that, in such a reformulation, one again refers to bodies by determining their values in the proviso associated with the inference rule. Reformulating tableau rules to work on literals only thus complicates provisos and does not substantially facilitate the description.[5] In [29], additional variables for bodies, one for each rule of a program, are even explicitly introduced for comparing *smodels* with DPLL. Given that propagation, even within atom-based solvers, has to consider the truth status of rules' bodies, the only saving in the computation of answer sets is limiting branching to atoms, which is expressed by $Cut[atom(\Pi)]$ in $\mathcal{T}_{smodels}$ (cf. (2)).

Propagation in *smodels* is accomplished by two functions, called *atleast* and *atmost* [5].[6] The former computes deterministic consequences by applying completion-based forward and backward propagation ((a)-(h) in Figure 1); the latter falsifies greatest unfounded sets (*WFN*; (i) in Figure 1).

The following result captures propagation via *atleast* in terms of $\mathcal{T}_{comp}$.

Theorem 4. *Let Π be a logic program and let A be an assignment such that $A^T \cup A^F \subseteq atom(\Pi)$. Let $A_S = atleast(\Pi, A)$ and $A_T = D^*_{\mathcal{T}_{comp}}(\Pi, A)$.*

If $A_S^T \cap A_S^F \neq \emptyset$, then $A_T^T \cap A_T^F \neq \emptyset$; otherwise, we have $A_S \subseteq A_T$.

This result shows that anything derived by *atleast* can also be derived by $\mathcal{T}_{comp}$ (without *Cut*). In fact, if *atleast* detects an inconsistency ($A_S^T \cap A_S^F \neq \emptyset$), then $\mathcal{T}_{comp}$ can derive it as well ($A_T^T \cap A_T^F \neq \emptyset$). Otherwise, $\mathcal{T}_{comp}$ can derive at least as much as *atleast* ($A_S \subseteq A_T$). This subsumption does not only originate from the (different) domains of assignments, that is, only atoms for *atleast* but also bodies for $\mathcal{T}_{comp}$. Rather, it is the redundant representation of rules' bodies within *smodels* that inhibits possible derivations obtained with $\mathcal{T}_{comp}$. To see this, consider rules $a \leftarrow c, d$ and $b \leftarrow c, d$ and an assignment A that contains Fa but leaves atoms c and d undefined. For such an A, *atleast* can only determine that rule $a \leftarrow c, d$ must not be applied, but it does not recognize that rule $b \leftarrow c, d$, sharing body $\{c, d\}$, is inapplicable as well. If $b \leftarrow c, d$ is the only rule with head atom b in the underlying program, then $\mathcal{T}_{comp}$ can, in contrast to *atleast*, derive Fb via *FFA* ((g) in Figure 1). A one-to-one correspondence between *atleast* and $\mathcal{T}_{comp}$ on derived atoms could be obtained by distinguishing different occurrences of the same body. However, for each derivation of *atleast*, there is a corresponding one in $\mathcal{T}_{comp}$. That is, every propagation done by *atleast* can be described with $\mathcal{T}_{comp}$.

Function *atmost* returns the maximal set of potentially true atoms, that is, $atom(\Pi) \setminus (GUS(\Pi, A) \cup A^F)$ for a program Π and an assignment A. Atoms in the complement of *atmost*, that is, the greatest unfounded set $GUS(\Pi, A)$ augmented with A^F, must be false. This can be described by tableau rules *FFB* and *WFN* ((e) and (i) in Figure 1).

Theorem 5. *Let Π be a logic program and let A be an assignment such that $A^T \cup A^F \subseteq atom(\Pi)$.*

We have $atom(\Pi) \setminus atmost(\Pi, A) = (D_{\{WFN\}}(\Pi, D_{\{FFB\}}(\Pi, A)))^F \cup A^F$.

---

[5] Restricting the domain of assignments to atoms would also disable the analysis of different *Cut* variants in Section 5.

[6] Here, *atleast* and *atmost* are taken as defined on signed propositions instead of literals [5].

Note that *smodels* adds literals $\{Fp \mid p \in atom(\Pi) \setminus atmost(\Pi, A)\}$ to an assignment A. If this leads to an inconsistency, so does $D_{\{WFN\}}(\Pi, D_{\{FFB\}}(\Pi, A))$.

We have seen that *smodels'* propagation functions, *atleast* and *atmost*, can be described by tableau rules *(a)-(i)*. By adding $Cut[atom(\Pi)]$, we thus get tableau calculus $\mathcal{T}_{smodels}$ (cf. (2)). Note that *lookahead* [5] can also be described by means of $Cut[atom(\Pi)]$: If *smodels'* lookahead derives some literal tl, a respective branch can be extended by Cut applied to the atom involved in l. The subbranch containing fl becomes contradictory by closing it under $\mathcal{T}_{smodels}$. Also, if *smodels'* propagation detects an inconsistency on tl, then both subbranches created by Cut, fl and tl, become contradictory by closing them; the subtableau under consideration becomes complete.

After having discussed *smodels*, we briefly turn to *dlv*: In contrast to *smodels'* *atmost*, greatest unfounded set detection is restricted to strongly connected components of programs' atom dependency graphs [20]. Hence, tableau rule *WFN* has to be adjusted to work on such components.[7] In the other aspects, propagation within *dlv* [6] is (on normal logic programs) similar to *smodels'* *atleast*. Thus, tableau calculus $\mathcal{T}_{smodels}$ also characterizes *dlv* very closely.

Hybrid solvers. Finally, we discuss similarities and differences between atom-based ASP-solvers, *smodels* and *dlv*, and *hybrid* solvers, working on bodies in addition to atoms. Let us first mention that SAT-based solvers, *assat* and *cmodels*, are in a sense hybrid, since the CNF representation of a program's completion contains variables for bodies. Thus, underlying SAT-solvers can branch on both atoms and bodies (via $Cut[atom(\Pi) \cup body(\Pi)]$ in $\mathcal{T}_{comp}$). The only genuine ASP-solver (we know of) explicitly assigning truth values to bodies, in addition to atoms, is *nomore++* [7].[8]

In [7], propagation rules applied by *nomore++* are described in terms of operators: $\mathcal{P}$ for forward propagation, $\mathcal{B}$ for backward propagation, $\mathcal{U}$ for falsifying greatest unfounded sets, and $\mathcal{L}$ for lookahead. Similar to our tableau rules, these operators apply to both atoms and bodies. We can thus show direct correspondences between tableau rules *(a)*, *(c)*, *(e)*, *(g)* and $\mathcal{P}$, *(b)*, *(d)*, *(f)*, *(h)* and $\mathcal{B}$, and *(i)* and $\mathcal{U}$. Similar to *smodels'* lookahead, derivations of $\mathcal{L}$ can be described by means of $Cut[atom(\Pi) \cup body(\Pi)]$. So by replacing $Cut[atom(\Pi)]$ with $Cut[atom(\Pi) \cup body(\Pi)]$, we obtain tableau calculus $\mathcal{T}_{nomore++}$ (cf. (4)) from $\mathcal{T}_{smodels}$. In the next section, we show that this subtle difference, also observed on SAT-based solvers, may have a great impact on proof complexity.

5 Proof Complexity

We have seen that genuine ASP-solvers largely coincide on their propagation rules and differ primarily in the usage of Cut. In this section, we analyze the relative efficiency of tableau calculi with different Cut rules. Thereby, we take $\mathcal{T}_{smodels}$, $\mathcal{T}_{noMoRe}$, and $\mathcal{T}_{nomore++}$ into account, all using tableau rules *(a)-(i)* in Figure 1 but applying the Cut rule either to $atom(\Pi)$, $body(\Pi)$, or both of them (cf. (2–4)). These three calculi are of particular interest: On the one hand, they can be used to describe the strategies of ASP-solvers, as shown in the previous section; on the other hand, they also represent

---

[7] However, iterated application of such a *WFN* variant leads to the same result as *(i)* in Figure 1.

[8] Complementing atom-based solvers, the *noMoRe* system [30] is rule-based (cf. $\mathcal{T}_{noMoRe}$ in (3)).

different paradigms, either atom-based, rule-based, or hybrid. So by considering these particular calculi, we obtain results that, on the one hand, are of practical relevance and that, on the other hand, apply to different approaches in general.

For comparing different tableau calculi, we use well-known concepts from *proof complexity* [14,12]. Accordingly, we measure the complexity of unsatisfiable logic programs, that is, programs without answer sets, in terms of *minimal* refutations. The size of a tableau is determined in the standard way as the number of nodes in it. A tableau calculus T is not *polynomially simulated* [14,12] by another tableau calculus T', if there is an infinite (witnessing) family $\{\Pi^n\}$ of unsatisfiable logic programs such that minimal refutations of T' for Π are asymptotically exponential in the size of minimal refutations of T for Π. A tableau calculus T is *exponentially stronger* than a tableau calculus T', if T polynomially simulates T', but not vice versa. Two tableau calculi are *efficiency-incomparable*, if neither one polynomially simulates the other. Note that proof complexity says nothing about how difficult it is to find a minimal refutation. Rather, it provides a lower bound on the run-time of proof-finding algorithms (in our context, ASP-solvers), independent from heuristic influences.

In what follows, we provide families of unsatisfiable logic programs witnessing that neither $T_{smodels}$ polynomially simulates T_{noMoRe} nor vice versa. This means that, on certain instances, restricting the *Cut* rule to either only atoms or bodies leads to exponentially greater minimal run-times of either atom- or rule-based solvers in comparison to their counterparts, no matter which heuristic is applied.

Lemma 1. *There is an infinite family* $\{\Pi^n\}$ *of logic programs such that*

  1. *the size of minimal refutations of* T_{noMoRe} *is linear in* n *and*
  2. *the size of minimal refutations of* $T_{smodels}$ *is exponential in* n.

Lemma 2. *There is an infinite family* $\{\Pi^n\}$ *of logic programs such that*

  1. *the size of minimal refutations of* $T_{smodels}$ *is linear in* n *and*
  2. *the size of minimal refutations of* T_{noMoRe} *is exponential in* n.

Family $\{\Pi_a^n \cup \Pi_c^n\}$ witnesses Lemma 1 and $\{\Pi_b^n \cup \Pi_c^n\}$ witnesses Lemma 2:

$$
\Pi_a^n = \begin{Bmatrix} x \leftarrow not\ x \\ x \leftarrow a_1, b_1 \\ \vdots \\ x \leftarrow a_n, b_n \end{Bmatrix}
\quad
\Pi_b^n = \begin{Bmatrix} x \leftarrow c_1, \ldots, c_n, not\ x \\ c_1 \leftarrow a_1 \quad\quad c_1 \leftarrow b_1 \\ \vdots \quad\quad\quad \vdots \\ c_n \leftarrow a_n \quad\quad c_n \leftarrow b_n \end{Bmatrix}
\quad
\Pi_c^n = \begin{Bmatrix} a_1 \leftarrow not\ b_1 \\ b_1 \leftarrow not\ a_1 \\ \vdots \\ a_n \leftarrow not\ b_n \\ b_n \leftarrow not\ a_n \end{Bmatrix}
$$

The next result follows immediately from Lemma 1 and 2.

Theorem 6. $T_{smodels}$ *and* T_{noMoRe} *are efficiency-incomparable.*

Given that any refutations of $T_{smodels}$ and T_{noMoRe} are as well refutations of $T_{nomore++}$, we have that $T_{nomore++}$ polynomially simulates both $T_{smodels}$ and T_{noMoRe}. So the following is an immediate consequence of Theorem 6.

Corollary 1. $T_{nomore++}$ *is exponentially stronger than both* $T_{smodels}$ *and* T_{noMoRe}.

The major implication of Corollary 1 is that, on certain logic programs, a priori restricting the Cut rule to either only atoms or bodies necessitates the traversal of an exponentially greater search space than with unrestricted Cut. Note that the phenomenon of exponentially worse proof complexity in comparison to $\mathcal{T}_{nomore++}$ does not, depending on the program family, apply to one of $\mathcal{T}_{smodels}$ or $\mathcal{T}_{noMoRe}$ alone. Rather, families $\{\Pi_a^n\}$, $\{\Pi_b^n\}$, and $\{\Pi_c^n\}$ can be combined such that both $\mathcal{T}_{smodels}$ and $\mathcal{T}_{noMoRe}$ are exponentially worse than $\mathcal{T}_{nomore++}$. For certain logic programs, the unrestricted Cut rule is thus the only way to have at least the chance of finding a short refutation. Empirical evidence for the exponentially different behavior is given in [31].

Finally, note that our proof complexity results are robust. That is, they apply to any possible ASP-solver whose proceeding can be described by corresponding tableaux. For instance, any computation of *smodels* can be associated with a tableau of $\mathcal{T}_{smodels}$ (cf. Section 4). A computation of *smodels* thus requires time proportional to the size of the corresponding tableau; in particular, the magnitude of a minimal tableau constitutes a lower bound on the run-time of *smodels*. This correlation is independent from whether an assignment contains only atoms or also bodies of a program: The size of any branch (not containing duplicate entries) is tightly bound by the size of a logic program. Therefore, exponential growth of minimal refutations is, for polynomially growing program families as the ones above, exclusively caused by the increase of necessary Cut applications, introducing an exponential number of branches.

6 Unfounded Sets

We have analyzed propagation techniques and proof complexity of existing approaches to ASP-solving. We have seen that all approaches exploit propagation techniques amounting to inferences from program completion ((a)-(h) in Figure 1). In particular, SAT-based and genuine ASP-solvers differ only in the treatment of unfounded sets: While the former apply (loop-detecting) unfounded set checks to total assignments only, the latter incorporate (greatest) unfounded set falsification (WFN; (i) in Figure 1) into their propagation. However, tableau rule WFN, as it is currently applied by genuine ASP-solvers, has several peculiarities:

A. WFN is partly redundant, that is, it overlaps with completion-based tableau rule FFA ((g) in Figure 1), which falsifies atoms belonging to singleton unfounded sets.
B. WFN deals with greatest unfounded sets, which can be (too) exhaustive.
C. WFN is asymmetrically applied, that is, solvers apply no backward counterpart.

In what follows, we thus propose and discuss alternative approaches to unfounded set handling, motivated by SAT-based solvers and results in [3]. Before we start, let us briefly introduce some vocabulary. Given two sets of tableau rules, $\mathcal{R}_1$ and $\mathcal{R}_2$, we say that $\mathcal{R}_1$ is *at least as effective* as $\mathcal{R}_2$, if, for any branch (Π, A), we have $D_{\mathcal{R}_2}^*(\Pi, A) \subseteq D_{\mathcal{R}_1}^*(\Pi, A)$. We say that $\mathcal{R}_1$ is *more effective* than $\mathcal{R}_2$, if $\mathcal{R}_1$ is at least as effective as $\mathcal{R}_2$, but not vice versa. If $\mathcal{R}_1$ is at least as effective as $\mathcal{R}_2$ and vice versa, then $\mathcal{R}_1$ and $\mathcal{R}_2$ are *equally effective*. Finally, $\mathcal{R}_1$ and $\mathcal{R}_2$ are *orthogonal*, if they are not equally effective and neither one is more effective than the other. A correspondence between two rule sets $\mathcal{R}_1 \cup \mathcal{R}$ and $\mathcal{R}_2 \cup \mathcal{R}$ means that the correspondence between $\mathcal{R}_1$ and $\mathcal{R}_2$ holds when D^* takes auxiliary rules $\mathcal{R}$ into account as well.

We start with analyzing the relation between *WFN* and *FFA*, both falsifying unfounded atoms in forward direction. The role of *FFB* ((e) in Figure 1) is to falsify bodies that positively rely on falsified atoms. Intuitively, this allows for capturing iterated applications of *WFN* and *FFA*, respectively, in which *FFB* behaves neutrally. Taking up item A above, we have the following result.

Proposition 1. *Set of rules* { *WFN, FFB* } *is more effective than* { *FFA, FFB* }.

This tells us that *FFA* is actually redundant in the presence of *WFN*. However, all genuine ASP-solvers apply *FFA* as a sort of "local" negation (e.g. *atleast* of *smodels* and operator $\mathcal{P}$ of *nomore++*) and separately *WFN* as "global" negation (e.g. *atmost* of *smodels* and operator $\mathcal{U}$ of *nomore++*). Certainly, applying *FFA* is reasonable as applicability is easy to determine. (Thus, SAT-based solvers apply *FFA*, but not *WFN*.) But with *FFA* at hand, Proposition 1 also tells us that greatest unfounded sets are too unfocused to describe the sort of unfounded sets that truly require a dedicated treatment: The respective tableau rule, *WFN*, subsumes a simpler one, *FFA*.

A characterization of *WFN*'s effect, not built upon greatest unfounded sets, is obtained by putting results in [3] into the context of partial assignments.

Theorem 7. *Sets of rules* { *WFN, FFB* } *and* { *FFA, FL, FFB* } *are equally effective.*

Hence, one may safely substitute *WFN* by *FFA* and *FL* ((k) in Figure 1), without forfeiting atoms that must be false due to the lack of (non-circular) support. Thereby, *FFA* concentrates on single atoms and *FL* on unfounded loops. Since both tableau rules have different scopes, they do not overlap but complement each other.

Proposition 2. *Sets of rules* { *FFA, FFB* } *and* { *FL, FFB* } *are orthogonal.*

SAT-based approaches provide an explanation why concentrating on cyclic structures, namely loops, besides single atoms is sufficient: When falsity of unfounded atoms does not follow from a program's completion or *FFA*, then there is a loop all of whose external bodies are false. Such a loop (called *terminating loop* in [3]) is a subset of the greatest unfounded set. So in view of item B above, loop-oriented approaches allow for focusing unfounded set computations on the intrinsically necessary parts. In fact, the more sophisticated unfounded set techniques applied by genuine ASP-solvers aim at circular structures induced by loops. That is, both *smodels'* approach, based on "source pointers" [32], as well as *dlv*'s approach, based on strongly connected components of programs' atom dependency graphs [20], can be seen as restrictions of *WFN* to structures induced by loops. However, neither of them takes loops as such into account.

Having considered forward propagation for unfounded sets, we come to backward propagation, that is, *BTA*, *WFJ*, and *BL* ((h), (j), and (l) in Figure 1). Although no genuine ASP-solver currently integrates propagation techniques corresponding to *WFJ* or *BL*, as mentioned in item C above, both rules are answer set preserving.

Proposition 3. *Let* Π *be a logic program and let* A *be an assignment. Let* $B \in$ *body*(Π) *such that* $\boldsymbol{T}B \in D_{\{WFJ\}}(\Pi, A)$ *(or* $\boldsymbol{T}B \in D_{\{BL\}}(\Pi, A)$*, respectively).*
Then, branch $(\Pi, A \cup D_{\{WFN\}}(\Pi, A \cup \{\boldsymbol{F}B\}))$ *(or* $(\Pi, A \cup D_{\{FL\}}(\Pi, A \cup \{\boldsymbol{F}B\}))$*, respectively) is contradictory.*

Both WFJ and BL ensure that falsifying some body does not lead to an inconsistency due to applying their forward counterparts. In fact, WFJ and BL are contrapositives of WFN and FL, respectively, in the same way as simpler rule BTA is for FFA.

A particularity of supporting true atoms by backward propagation is that "global" rule WFJ is more effective than "local" ones, BTA and BL. Even adding tableau rule BTB ((f) in Figure 1), for enabling iterated application of backward rules setting bodies to true, does not compensate for the global character of WFJ.

Proposition 4. *Set of rules* $\{WFJ, BTB\}$ *is more effective than* $\{BTA, BL, BTB\}$.

We conclude by discussing different approaches to unfounded set handling. Both SAT-based and genuine ASP-solvers apply tableau rules FFA and BTA, both focusing on single atoms. In addition, genuine ASP-solvers apply WFN to falsify more complex unfounded sets. However, WFN gives an overestimation of the parts of unfounded sets that need a dedicated treatment: SAT-based approaches show that concentrating on loops, via FL, is sufficient. However, the latter apply loop-detecting unfounded set checks only to total assignments or use loop formulas recorded in reaction to previously failed unfounded set checks. Such a recorded loop formula is then exploited by propagation within SAT-based solvers in both forward and backward direction, which amounts to applying FL and BL. A similar kind of backward propagation, by either WFJ or BL, is not exploited by genuine ASP-solvers, so unfounded set treatment is asymmetric. We however believe that bridging the gap between SAT-based and genuine ASP-solvers is possible by putting the concept of loops into the context of partial assignments. For instance, a loop-oriented unfounded set algorithm is described in [33].

7   Discussion

In contrast to the area of SAT, where the proof-theoretic foundations of SAT-solvers are well-understood [2,14], the literature on ASP-solvers is generally too specific in terms of algorithms or solvers; existing characterizations are rather heterogeneous and often lack declarativeness. We address this deficiency by proposing a tableau proof system that provides a formal framework for analyzing computations of ASP-solvers. To our knowledge, this approach is the first uniform proof-theoretic account for computational techniques in ASP. Our tableau framework allows to abstract away implementation details and to identify valid inferences; hence, soundness and completeness results are easily obtained. This is accomplished by associating specific tableau calculi with the approaches of ASP-solvers, rather than with their solving algorithms.

The explicit integration of bodies into assignments has several benefits. First, it allows us to capture completion-based and hybrid approaches in a closer fashion. Second, it allows us to reveal exponentially different proof complexities of ASP-solvers. Finally, even inferences in atom-based systems, like *smodels* and *dlv*, are twofold insofar as they must take program rules into account for propagation (cf. Section 4). This feature is simulated in our framework through the corresponding bodies. Although this simulation is sufficient for establishing formal results, it is worth noting that dealing with rules bears more redundancy than dealing with their bodies. Related to this, we have seen that rule-wise consideration of bodies, as for instance done in *smodels'* *atleast*, can forfeit derivations that are easily obtained based on non-duplicated bodies (cf. paragraph below Theorem 4). The tableau rules underlying atom-based and hybrid systems also reveal that the only major difference lies in the selection of program objects to branch upon.

The branching rule, Cut, has a major influence on proof complexity. It is well-known that an uncontrolled application of Cut is prone to inefficiency. The restriction of applying Cut to (sub)formulae occurring in the input showed to be an effective way to "tame" the cut [8]. We followed this by investigating Cut applications to atoms and bodies occurring in a program. The proof complexity results in Section 5 tell us that the minimal number of required Cut applications may vary exponentially when restricting Cut to either only atoms or bodies. For not a priori degrading an ASP-solving approach, the Cut rule must thus not be restricted to either only atoms or bodies. Note that these results hold for any ASP-solver (or algorithm) whose proceeding can be described by tableaux of a corresponding calculus (cf. end of Section 5).

Regarding the relation between SAT-based and genuine ASP-solvers, we have seen in Section 6 that unfounded set handling constitutes the major difference. Though both approaches, as practiced by solvers, appear to be quite different, the aims and effects of underlying tableau rules are very similar. We expect that this observation will lead to convergence of SAT-based and genuine ASP-solvers, in the sense that the next generation of genuine ASP-solvers will directly incorporate the same powerful reasoning strategies that are already exploited in the area of SAT [2].

Acknowledgments. This work was supported by DFG (SCHA 550/6-4). We are grateful to Christian Anger, Philippe Besnard, Martin Brain, Yuliya Lierler, and the anonymous referees for many helpful suggestions.

References

1. Baral, C.: Knowledge Representation, Reasoning and Declarative Problem Solving. Cambridge University Press (2003)
2. Mitchell, D.: A SAT solver primer. Bulletin of the European Association for Theoretical Computer Science **85** (2005) 112–133
3. Lin, F., Zhao, Y.: ASSAT: computing answer sets of a logic program by SAT solvers. Artificial Intelligence **157**(1-2) (2004) 115–137
4. Giunchiglia, E., Lierler, Y., Maratea, M.: A SAT-based polynomial space algorithm for answer set programming. In Delgrande, J., Schaub, T., eds.: Proceedings of the Tenth International Workshop on Non-Monotonic Reasoning. (2004) 189–196
5. Simons, P., Niemelä, I., Soininen, T.: Extending and implementing the stable model semantics. Artificial Intelligence **138**(1-2) (2002) 181–234
6. Faber, W.: Enhancing Efficiency and Expressiveness in Answer Set Programming Systems. Dissertation, Technische Universität Wien (2002)
7. Anger, C., Gebser, M., Linke, T., Neumann, A., Schaub, T.: The `nomore++` approach to answer set solving. In Sutcliffe, G., Voronkov, A., eds.: Proceedings of the Twelfth International Conference on Logic for Programming, Artificial Intelligence, and Reasoning. Springer (2005) 95–109
8. D'Agostino, M., Gabbay, D., Hähnle, R., Posegga, J., eds.: Handbook of Tableau Methods. Kluwer Academic (1999)
9. Leone, N., Faber, W., Pfeifer, G., Eiter, T., Gottlob, G., Koch, C., Mateis, C., Perri, S., Scarcello, F.: The DLV system for knowledge representation and reasoning. ACM Transactions on Computational Logic (2006) To appear.

10. Davis, M., Putnam, H.: A computing procedure for quantification theory. Journal of the ACM **7** (1960) 201–215
11. Davis, M., Logemann, G., Loveland, D.: A machine program for theorem-proving. Communications of the ACM **5** (1962) 394–397
12. Järvisalo, M., Junttila, T., Niemelä, I.: Unrestricted vs restricted cut in a tableau method for Boolean circuits. Annals of Mathematics and Artificial Intelligence **44**(4) (2005) 373–399
13. Junttila, T., Niemelä, I.: Towards an efficient tableau method for boolean circuit satisfiability checking. In Lloyd J., et al., eds.: Proceedings of the First International Conference on Computational Logic. Springer (2000) 553–567
14. Beame, P., Pitassi, T.: Propositional proof complexity: Past, present, and future. Bulletin of the European Association for Theoretical Computer Science **65** (1998) 66–89
15. Hähnle, R.: Tableaux and related methods. In Robinson, A., Voronkov, A., eds.: Handbook of Automated Reasoning. Elsevier and MIT Press (2001) 100–178
16. Fitting, M.: Tableaux for logic programming. J. Automated Reasoning **13**(2) (1994) 175–188
17. Pearce, D., de Guzmán, I., Valverde, A.: A tableau calculus for equilibrium entailment. In Dyckhoff, R., ed.: Proceedings of the Ninth International Conference on Automated Reasoning with Analytic Tableaux and Related Methods. Springer (2000) 352–367
18. Olivetti, N.: Tableaux for nonmonotonic logics. [8] 469–528
19. Bonatti, P.: Resolution for skeptical stable model semantics. J. Automated Reasoning **27**(4) (2001) 391–421
20. Calimeri, F., Faber, W., Leone, N., Pfeifer, G.: Pruning operators for answer set programming systems. Technical Report INFSYS RR-1843-01-07, Technische Universität Wien (2001)
21. van Gelder, A., Ross, K., Schlipf, J.: The well-founded semantics for general logic programs. Journal of the ACM **38**(3) (1991) 620–650
22. Lee, J.: A model-theoretic counterpart of loop formulas. In Kaelbling, L., Saffiotti, A., eds.: Proceedings of the Nineteenth International Joint Conference on Artificial Intelligence, Professional Book Center (2005) 503–508
23. Fitting, M.: Fixpoint semantics for logic programming: A survey. Theoretical Computer Science **278**(1-2) (2002) 25–51
24. Clark, K.: Negation as failure. In Gallaire, H., Minker, J., eds.: Logic and Data Bases. Plenum Press (1978) 293–322
25. Apt, K., Blair, H., Walker, A.: Towards a theory of declarative knowledge. In Minker, J., ed.: Found. of Deductive Databases and Logic Programming. Morgan Kaufmann (1987) 89–148
26. Lifschitz, V., Razborov, A.: Why are there so many loop formulas? ACM Transactions on Computational Logic (2006) To appear.
27. Fages, F.: Consistency of Clark's completion and the existence of stable models. Journal of Methods of Logic in Computer Science **1** (1994) 51–60
28. Babovich, Y., Lifschitz, V.: Computing answer sets using program completion. Draft (2003)
29. Giunchiglia, E., Maratea, M.: On the relation between answer set and SAT procedures (or, between cmodels and smodels). In Gabbrielli, M., Gupta, G., eds.: Proceedings of the Twenty-first International Conference on Logic Programming. Springer (2005) 37–51
30. Konczak, K., Linke, T., Schaub, T.: Graphs and colorings for answer set programming. Theory and Practice of Logic Programming **6**(1-2) (2006) 61–106
31. Anger, C., Gebser, M., Schaub, T.: What's a head without a body. In Brewka, G., ed.: Proceedings of the Seventeenth European Conference on Artificial Intelligence, IOS Press (2006) To appear.
32. Simons, P.: Extending and Implementing the Stable Model Semantics. Dissertation, Helsinki University of Technology (2000)
33. Anger, C., Gebser, M., Schaub, T.: Approaching the core of unfounded sets. In Dix, J., Hunter, A., eds.: Proceedings of the Eleventh International Workshop on Non-Monotonic Reasoning. (2006) To appear.

Declarative Semantics of Production Rules for Integrity Maintenance

Luciano Caroprese, Sergio Greco, Cristina Sirangelo, and Ester Zumpano

DEIS, Univ. della Calabria, 87030 Rende, Italy
{caroprese, greco, sirangelo, zumpano}@deis.unical.it

Abstract. This paper presents a declarative semantics for the maintenance of integrity constraints expressed by means of production rules. A production rule is a special form of active rule, called active integrity constraint, whose body contains an integrity constraint (conjunction of literals which must be *false*) and whose head contains a disjunction of update atoms, i.e. actions to be performed if the corresponding constraint is not satisfied (i.e. is true). The paper introduces i) a formal declarative semantics allowing the computation of founded repairs, that is repairs whose actions are specified and supported by active integrity constraint, ii) an equivalent semantics obtained by rewriting production rules into disjunctive logic rules, so that repairs can be derived from the answer sets of the logic program and finally iii) a characterization of production rules allowing a methodology for integrity maintenance.

1 Introduction

Integrity constraints are logical assertions on acceptable (or consistent) database states, and specify properties of data that need to be satisfied by valid instances of the database [1]. When constraints are violated, for example during or at the end of the execution of a transaction, the repair of the database state is usually limited to fixed reversal actions, such as rolling back the current operation or the entire transaction [6]. Moreover, since the presence of data inconsistent with respect to integrity constraints is not unusual, its management plays a key role in all the areas in which duplicate or conflicting information is likely to occur, such as database integration, data warehousing and federated databases [17,18,24]. Thus, an improved approach to constraints enforcement allows definition of compensating actions that correct violation of constraints according to a well-defined semantics *(database repairs)* or allows computing *consistent answers*. Informally, the computation of repairs is based on the insertion and deletion of tuples so that the resulting database satisfies all constraints, whereas the computation of consistent answers is based on the identification of tuples satisfying integrity constraints and matching the goal.

The following example shows a situation in which inconsistencies occur.

Example 1. Consider the relation schema $mgr(Name, Dept, Salary)$ with the functional dependency $Dept \rightarrow Name$ which can be defined through the first order formula $\forall(E_1, E_2, D, S_1, S_2) \ [mgr(E_1, D, S_1) \land mgr(E_2, D, S_2) \supset E_1 = E_2]$.

S. Etalle and M. Truszczyński (Eds.): ICLP 2006, LNCS 4079, pp. 26–40, 2006.

Consider now the inconsistent instance: $\mathcal{DB} = \{mgr(john, cs, 1000),\ mgr(frank,\ cs, 2000)\}$. A consistent (repaired) database can be obtained by applying a minimal set of update operations; in particular it admits two repaired databases: $\mathcal{DB}_1 = \{mgr(frank, cs, 2000)\}$ obtained by applying the repair $\mathcal{R}_1 = \{-mgr(john, cs, 1000)\}$ (deleting the tuple $mgr(john, cs, 1000)$) and $\mathcal{DB}_2 = \{mgr(john, cs, 1000)\}$ obtained by applying the repair $\mathcal{R}_2 = \{-mgr(frank, cs, 2000)\}$ (deleting the tuple $mgr(frank,\ cs, 2000)$).   □

The notion of integrity constraints and their automated maintenance has been investigated for many years. Several works have proposed the updating of data and knowledge bases through the use of active rules [6,7] and nonmonotonic formalisms [2,5,19,20]. Some approaches use ECA (event-condition-action) rules for checking and enforcing integrity constraints, whereas other approaches are based on simpler forms of rules, called CA (condition-action) or *production rules*, in which the event part is absent. Current DBMS languages offer the possibility of defining triggers, special ECA rules well-suited to automatically perform actions, in response to events that are taking place inside (or even outside) the database. However, the problem with active rules is the difficulty to understand the behavior of multiple triggers acting together [21,23]. Although many different proposals have been introduced over the years, at the moment there is no agreement on the integration of active functionalities with conventional database systems. A different solution based on the derivation of logic rules with declarative semantics has been recently proposed in several works. These proposals are based on the automatic generation of Datalog rules and on the computation of answer sets, from which repairs are derived [3,4,8,14,15,16,26]. All these work do not take into account the possibility to indicate the update operations making consistent the database.

This paper considers a special form of production rules called *active integrity constraints* (AIC). Active integrity constraints, recently proposed in [11], are special integrity constraints whose body consists of a conjunction of literals which should be *false* (denial constraint) and whose head contains the actions which should be performed if the body of the rule is true (i.e. the constraints defined in the body is not satisfied). AIC rules allow specification of the actions which should be performed to make the database consistent when integrity constraints are violated.

Example 2. Consider the database of Example 1 and the active constraint:

$\forall(E_1, E_2, D, S_1, S_2)[mgr(E_1, D, S_1) \wedge mgr(E_2, D, S_2) \wedge S_1 > S_2 \supset -mgr(E_1, D, S_1)]$

stating that *in case of conflicting tuples it is preferred to delete the one with greater salary*. The constraint suggests to update the database by deleting the tuple $mgr(frank, cs, 2000)$. This action, in the specific case, leads to taking into account only one of the two repairs, namely $\mathcal{R}_2$.   □

Thus, active integrity constraints are production rules expressed by means of first order logic with declarative semantics. AIC allow the computation of "preferred" repairs, that is repairs whose actions are specified explicitly and are also supported.

Contributions

The novelty of the approach here proposed consists in the definition of a formal declarative semantics for *active integrity constraints*. The new semantics allows identification, among the set of all possible repairs, of the subset of *founded repairs* whose actions are specified in the head of rules and are "supported" by the database or by other updates. The computation of founded repairs can be done by checking whether for each repair all its update atoms are founded or by rewriting the constraints into a Datalog program and then computing its stable models; the founded repairs are obtained by selecting, for each stable model, the set of "update atoms".

The paper also studies the characteristic of AIC rules and show that for each production rule r (consisting of a body defining the integrity constraint and a head containing alternative actions which should be performed if the constraint is not satisfied), update head atoms not making the conjunction of body literals, defining an integrity constraint, false with respect to the repaired database (i.e. such that the body integrity constraint is satisfied), are useless [1]. This formal result confirms the intuition that for integrity maintenance general (E)CA rules are not necessary. Therefore, active integrity constraints can be thought as special CA rules with declarative semantics whose aim is to repair the database and to help consistently answering queries over inconsistent databases. As, in the general case, the existence of founded repairs is not guaranteed the class of universally quantified constraints under a different semantics in which actions are interpreted as preference conditions on the set of possible repairs ("preferable" semantics) is also investigated. Under such a semantics every database with integrity constraints admits repairs and consistent answers.

Finally, the paper studies the computational complexity and shows that computing founded and preferred repairs and answers is not harder than computing "standard" repairs and answers.

2   Preliminaries

Familiarity with relational database theory, disjunctive logic programming and computational complexity is assumed [1,9,13,22].

Disjunctive Databases. A *(disjunctive Datalog) rule* r is a clause of the form[2]

$$\bigvee_{i=1}^{p} A_i \leftarrow \bigwedge_{j=1}^{m} B_j, \bigwedge_{j=m+1}^{n} not\ B_j, \varphi \qquad p+m+n>0 \qquad (1)$$

where $A_1, \cdots, A_p, B_1, \cdots, B_n$ are atoms of the form $p(t_1, ..., t_h)$, p is a *predicate* of arity h and the terms $t_1, ..., t_h$ are constants or variables, while φ is a conjunction of built-in atoms of the form $u\ \theta\ v$ where u and v are terms and θ is a comparison predicate.

---

[1] Under the declarative semantics here proposed.

[2] A literal can appear in a conjunction or in a disjunction at most once. The meaning of the symbols '∧' and ',' is the same.

An interpretation $\mathcal{M}$ for $\mathcal{P}$ is a model of $\mathcal{P}$ if $\mathcal{M}$ satisfies all rules in $ground(\mathcal{P})$ (the ground instantiation of $\mathcal{P}$). The (model-theoretic) semantics for a positive program $\mathcal{P}$ assigns to $\mathcal{P}$ the set of its *minimal models* $\mathcal{MM}(\mathcal{P})$, where a model $\mathcal{M}$ for $\mathcal{P}$ is minimal, if no proper subset of $\mathcal{M}$ is a model for $\mathcal{P}$. The more general *disjunctive stable model semantics* also applies to programs with (unstratified) negation [13]. Disjunctive stable model semantics generalizes stable model semantics, previously defined for normal programs [12]. For any interpretation $\mathcal{M}$, denote with $\mathcal{P}^{\mathcal{M}}$ the ground positive program derived from $ground(\mathcal{P})$ by 1) removing all rules that contain a negative literal *not A* in the body and $A \in \mathcal{M}$, and 2) removing all negative literals from the remaining rules. An interpretation $\mathcal{M}$ is a stable model of $\mathcal{P}$ if and only if $\mathcal{M} \in \mathcal{MM}(\mathcal{P}^{\mathcal{M}})$. For general $\mathcal{P}$, the stable model semantics assigns to $\mathcal{P}$ the set $\mathcal{SM}(\mathcal{P})$ of its *stable models*. It is well known that stable models are minimal models (i.e. $\mathcal{SM}(\mathcal{P}) \subseteq \mathcal{MM}(\mathcal{P})$) and that for negation free programs, minimal and stable model semantics coincide (i.e. $\mathcal{SM}(\mathcal{P}) = \mathcal{MM}(\mathcal{P})$). Observe that stable models are minimal models which are "supported", i.e. their atoms can be derived from the program.

Queries. Predicate symbols are partitioned into two distinct sets: *base predicates* (also called EDB predicates) and *derived predicates* (also called IDB predicates). Base predicates correspond to database relations defined over a given domain and they do not appear in the head of any rule; derived predicates are defined by means of rules. Given a database $\mathcal{DB}$ and a program $\mathcal{P}$, $\mathcal{P}_{\mathcal{DB}}$ denotes the program derived from the union of $\mathcal{P}$ with the facts in $\mathcal{DB}$, i.e. $\mathcal{P}_{\mathcal{DB}} = \mathcal{P} \cup \mathcal{DB}$. In the following a tuple t of a relation r will be also denoted as a fact $r(t)$. The semantics of $\mathcal{P}_{\mathcal{DB}}$ is given by the set of its stable models by considering either their union (*possibly semantics* or *brave reasoning*) or their intersection (*certain semantics* or *cautious reasoning*). A disjunctive Datalog *query* Q is a pair $(g, \mathcal{P})$ where g is a predicate symbol, called the *query goal*, and $\mathcal{P}$ is a disjunctive Datalog program. The answer to a disjunctive Datalog query $Q = (g, \mathcal{P})$ over a database $\mathcal{DB}$ (denoted by $Q(\mathcal{DB})$), under the possibly (resp. certain) semantics, is given by $\mathcal{DB}'(g)$ where $\mathcal{DB}' = \bigcup_{\mathcal{M} \in \mathcal{SM}(\mathcal{P}_{\mathcal{DB}})} \mathcal{M}$ (resp. $\mathcal{DB}' = \bigcap_{\mathcal{M} \in \mathcal{SM}(\mathcal{P}_{\mathcal{DB}})} \mathcal{M}$).

A disjunctive Datalog program $\mathcal{P}$ is said to be *semi-positive* if negation is only applied to database atoms. For a semi-positive program $\mathcal{P}$ and a database $\mathcal{DB}$, the set of stable models coincides with the set of minimal models containing as true database facts only those in $\mathcal{DB}$ (i.e. EDB database atoms not appearing in $\mathcal{DB}$ are assumed to be *false*). A (relational) query can be expressed by means of 'safe' non recursive Datalog, even though alternative equivalent languages such as relational algebra could be used as well [1,25].

3   Databases and Integrity Constraints

A database $\mathcal{DB}$ has an associated schema $\langle \mathcal{DS}, \mathcal{IC} \rangle$ defining the intentional properties of $\mathcal{DB}$: $\mathcal{DS}$ denotes the structure of the relations, while $\mathcal{IC}$ denotes the set of integrity constraints expressing semantic information over data.

3.1   Integrity Constraints

Definition 1. A (universally quantified or full) *integrity constraint* is a formula of the first order predicate calculus of the form:

$$(\forall X)[\bigwedge_{j=1}^{m} b_j(X_j), \; \varphi(X_0) \supset \bigvee_{j=m+1}^{n} b_j(X_j)]$$

where b_j ($1 \leq j \leq n$) is a predicate symbol, $\varphi(X_0)$ denotes a conjunction of built-in atoms, $X = \bigcup_{j=1}^{m} X_j$, $X_i \subseteq X$ for $i \in [0..n]$ and all existentially quantified variables appear once. □

The reason for considering constraints of the above form is that we want to consider range restricted constraints, i.e. constraints whose variables either take values from finite domains only or the exact knowledge of their values is not relevant [25]. Often our constraints will be written in a different form by moving literals from the right side to the left side and vice-versa. For instance, by rewriting the above constraint as denial we obtain:

$$(\forall X)[\bigwedge_{j=1}^{m} b_j(X_j), \; \bigwedge_{j=m+1}^{n} not \; b_j(X_j, Z_j), \; \varphi(X_0) \supset].$$

In the following we assume that the set of integrity constraints $\mathcal{IC}$ is satisfiable, that is there exists a database instance $\mathcal{DB}$ satisfying $\mathcal{IC}$. For instance, by considering constraints of the above form with $m > 0$, the constraints are satisfied by the empty database.

3.2   Repairing and Querying Inconsistent Databases

In this section the formal definition of consistent database and repair is first recalled and, then, a computational mechanism is presented that ensures selecting repairs and consistent answers for inconsistent databases.

An update atom is in the form $+a(X)$ or $-a(X)$. A ground atom $+a(t)$ states that $a(t)$ will be inserted into the database, whereas a ground atom $-a(t)$ states that $a(t)$ will be deleted from the database. Given an update atom $+a(X)$ (resp. $-a(X)$) we denote as $Comp(+a(X))$ (resp. $Comp(-a(X))$) the literal $not \; a(X)$ (resp. $a(X)$). Given a set $\mathcal{U}$ of ground update atoms we define the sets $\mathcal{U}^+ = \{a(t) \mid + a(t) \in \mathcal{U}\}$, $\mathcal{U}^- = \{a(t) \mid - a(t) \in \mathcal{U}\}$ and $Comp(\mathcal{U}) = \{Comp(\pm a(t)) \mid \pm a(t) \in \mathcal{U}\}$. We say that $\mathcal{U}$ is *consistent* if it does not contain two update atom $+a(t)$ and $-a(t)$ (i.e. if $\mathcal{U}^+ \cap \mathcal{U}^- = \emptyset$). Given a database $\mathcal{DB}$ and a consistent set of update atoms $\mathcal{U}$, we denote as $\mathcal{U}(\mathcal{DB})$ the updated database $\mathcal{DB} \cup \mathcal{U}^+ - \mathcal{U}^-$.

Definition 2. Given a database $\mathcal{DB}$ and a set of integrity constraints $\mathcal{IC}$, a *repair* for $\langle \mathcal{DB}, \mathcal{IC} \rangle$ is a consistent set of update atoms $\mathcal{R}$ such that 1) $\mathcal{R}(\mathcal{DB}) \models \mathcal{IC}$, 2) there is no consistent set of update atoms $\mathcal{U} \subset \mathcal{R}$ such that $\mathcal{U}(\mathcal{DB}) \models \mathcal{IC}$.

Repaired databases are consistent databases, derived from the source database by means of a minimal set of update operations. Given a database $\mathcal{DB}$ and a set of integrity constraints $\mathcal{IC}$, the set of all possible repairs for $\langle \mathcal{DB}, \mathcal{IC} \rangle$ is denoted as $\mathbf{R}(\mathcal{DB}, \mathcal{IC})$. Observe that the set of possible repairs in the case of constraints containing not range-restricted variables could be infinite.

Given a set of (universally quantified) constraints $\mathcal{IC}$, an integrity constraint $r \in \mathcal{IC}$ and a domain Dom, a ground instantiation of r with respect to Dom can be obtained by replacing variables with constants of Dom and eliminating the quantifier $\forall$. The set of ground instances of r is denoted by $ground(r)$, whereas $ground(\mathcal{IC}) = \bigcup_{r \in \mathcal{IC}} ground(r)$ denotes the set of ground instances of constraints in $\mathcal{IC}$. Clearly, for any set of universally quantified constraints $\mathcal{IC}$, the cardinality of $ground(\mathcal{IC})$ is polynomial in the size of the database (and in the size of Dom).

Theorem 1. *Let $\mathcal{DB}$ be a database, $\mathcal{IC}$ a set of full integrity constraints and $\mathcal{R}$ a repair for $\langle \mathcal{DB}, \mathcal{IC} \rangle$. For each $\pm a(t) \in \mathcal{R}$, let $\mathcal{R}' = \mathcal{R} - \{\pm a(t)\}$, there exists in $ground(\mathcal{IC})$ a ground integrity constraint $\phi \wedge Comp(\pm a(t)) \supset$ such that $\mathcal{R}'(\mathcal{DB}) \models \phi$.* □

The above theorem states that each update atom of a repair is necessary to satisfy at least a ground integrity constraint.

Definition 3. Given a database $\mathcal{DB}$ and a set of integrity constraints $\mathcal{IC}$, an atom A is *true* (resp. *false*) with respect to $\mathcal{IC}$ if A belongs to all repaired databases (resp. there is no repaired database containing A). The atoms which are neither *true* nor *false* are *undefined*. □

Thus, true atoms appear in all repaired databases, whereas undefined atoms appear in a non empty proper subset of repaired databases.

Definition 4. Given a database $\mathcal{DB}$ and a relational query $Q = (g, \mathcal{P})$, the *consistent answer* of the query Q on the database $\mathcal{DB}$, denoted as $Q(\mathcal{DB}, \mathcal{IC})$, gives three sets, denoted as $Q(\mathcal{DB}, \mathcal{IC})^+$, $Q(\mathcal{DB}, \mathcal{IC})^-$ and $Q(\mathcal{DB}, \mathcal{IC})^u$. These contain, respectively, the sets of g-tuples which are *true* (i.e. belonging to $\bigcap_{\mathcal{R} \in \mathbf{R}(\mathcal{DB}, \mathcal{IC})} Q(\mathcal{R}(\mathcal{DB}))$), *false* (i.e. not belonging to $\bigcup_{\mathcal{R} \in \mathbf{R}(\mathcal{DB}, \mathcal{IC})} Q(\mathcal{R}(\mathcal{DB}))$) and *undefined* (i.e. set of tuples which are neither *true* nor *false*). □

3.3   Repairing and Querying Through Stable Models

As shown in [15,16], a relational query over databases with standard constraints can be rewritten into disjunctive query over the same database without constraints. More specifically, it is obtained from the union of the non recursive Datalog query and the disjunctive rules derived from the constraints.

Given a database $\mathcal{DB}$ and a set of integrity constraints $\mathcal{IC}$, the technique derives from $\mathcal{IC}$ a disjunctive program $\mathcal{DP}(\mathcal{IC})$. The repairs for $\mathcal{DB}$ can be derived from the stable models of $\mathcal{DP}(\mathcal{IC}) \cup \mathcal{DB}$, whereas the consistent answers for a query $(g, \mathcal{P})$ can be derived from the stable models of $\mathcal{P} \cup \mathcal{DP}(\mathcal{IC}) \cup \mathcal{DB}$.

Definition 5. Let c be a (range restricted) full integrity constraint of the form

$$(\forall X)[\bigwedge_{j=1}^{m} b_j(X_j), \bigwedge_{j=m+1}^{n} not\ b_j(X_j), \varphi(X_0) \supset] \tag{2}$$

where $X = \bigcup_{j=1}^{m} X_j$ and $X_i \subseteq X$ for $i \in [0..n]$. We denote as $dj(c)$ the rule

$$\bigvee_{j=1}^{m} -b_j(X_j) \vee \bigvee_{j=m+1}^{m} +b_j(X_j) \leftarrow \bigwedge_{j=1}^{m} (b_j(X_j) \vee +b_j(X_j)), \bigwedge_{j=m+1}^{n} (not\ b_j(X_j) \vee -b_j(X_j)), \varphi(X_0)$$

Given a set $\mathcal{IC}$ of full integrity constraints, we define $\mathcal{DP}(\mathcal{IC}) = \{\ dj(c) \mid c \in \mathcal{IC}\ \} \cup \{\leftarrow -b(X), +b(X) \mid b$ is a predicate symbol$\}$.   □

In the above definition the variable X in the constraint $\leftarrow -b(X), +b(X)$ denotes a list of k distinct variables with k equal to the arity of b.

Given a database $\mathcal{DB}$, a set of full integrity constraints $\mathcal{IC}$ and a stable model $\mathcal{M}$ of $\mathcal{DP}(\mathcal{IC}) \cup \mathcal{DB}$, the set of update atoms $\mathcal{R}(\mathcal{M}) = \{\pm a(t) \mid \pm a(t) \in \mathcal{M}\}$ is a repair for $\mathcal{DB}$.

Observe that, for every database $\mathcal{DB}$, set of integrity constraints $\mathcal{IC}$, query $Q = (g, \mathcal{P})$ and repaired database $\mathcal{DB}'$ (i) each atom $A \in Q(\mathcal{DB}, \mathcal{IC})^+$ belongs to each stable model of $\mathcal{P} \cup \mathcal{DB}'$ (soundness) and (ii) each atom $A \in Q(\mathcal{DB}, \mathcal{IC})^-$ does not belong to any stable model of $\mathcal{P} \cup \mathcal{DB}'$ (completeness).

4   Active Integrity Constraints

This section presents an extension of integrity constraints that allows the specification for each constraint of the actions which can be performed to make the database consistent. For simplicity of presentation we only consider universally quantified variables, although the framework can be applied also to constraints with existentially quantified variables appearing once in body literals.

4.1   Syntax and Semantics

Definition 6. A (universally quantified) *Active Integrity Constraint* (*AIC*) is of the form

$$(\forall X)[\bigwedge_{j=1}^{m} b_j(X_j), \bigwedge_{j=m+1}^{n} not\ b_j(X_j), \varphi(X_0) \supset \bigvee_{i=1}^{p} \pm a_i(Y_i)] \tag{3}$$

where $X = \bigcup_{j=1}^{m} X_j$, $X_i \subseteq X$ for $i \in [0..n]$ and $Y_i \subseteq X$ for $i \in [1..p]$.   □

In the above definition the conditions $X = \bigcup_{j=1}^{m} X_j$, $X_i \subseteq X$ for $i \in [0..n]$ and $Y_i \subseteq X$ for $i \in [1..p]$ guarantee variables to be range restricted. Given an AIC $r = (\forall X)[\Phi \supset \Psi]$, Φ is called body of r (and is denoted by $Body(r)$), whereas Ψ is called head of r (and is denoted by $Head(r)$).

Example 3. Consider the relation manager *mgr* of Example 1. The active constraint of Example 2 states that in case of conflicting tuples (i.e. there are two managers managing the same department) we prefer to repair the database by deleting the one having a higher salary, whereas the constraint

$$\forall (E_1, E_2, D, S_1, S_2)[mgr(E_1, D, S_1), mgr(E_2, D, S_2), E_1 \neq E_2 \supset$$
$$-mgr(E_1, D, S_1) \vee -mgr(E_2, D, S_2)]$$

states that between two different managers of the same department we do not have any preference and, therefore, one of them, selected nondeterministically, can be deleted. □

AICs are constraints specifying actions which can be performed to obtain repairs. Given an AIC r of the form (3) $St(r)$ denotes the standard constraint

$$(\forall\ X)\,[\ \bigwedge_{j=1}^{m} b_j(X_j),\ \ \bigwedge_{j=m+1}^{n}\ not\ b_j(X_j),\ \varphi(X_0) \supset\ ] \tag{4}$$

derived from r by removing the head update atoms. Moreover, for a set of active integrity constraints $\mathcal{IC}$, $St(\mathcal{IC})$ denotes the corresponding set of standard integrity constraints, i.e. $St(\mathcal{IC}) = \{St(r) \mid r \in \mathcal{IC}\}$.

Definition 7. A repair for a database $\mathcal{DB}$ and a set of AICs $\mathcal{IC}$ is any repair for $\langle \mathcal{DB}, St(\mathcal{IC}) \rangle$. □

Note that not all repairs contain atoms which can be derived from the active integrity constraints. Thus, we can identify a class of repairs, called *founded*, whose actions can be "derived" from the active integrity constraints.

Example 4. Consider the database $\mathcal{DB} = \{movie(Marshall, Chicago, 2002),$ $director(Stone)\}$ and the constraint

$$\forall (D, T, A)\,[\,movie(D, T, A) \wedge not\ director(D) \supset +director(D)\,]$$

There are two feasible repairs $\mathcal{R}_1 = \{-movie(Marshall, Chicago, 2002)\}$ and $\mathcal{R}_2 = \{+director(Marshall)\}$, but only $\mathcal{R}_2$ contains updates derived from the active integrity constraint. □

In the following the definition concerning the truth value of ground atoms and ground update atoms, with respect to a database $\mathcal{DB}$, a consistent set of update atoms $\mathcal{U}$ and a founded repair are provided.

Definition 8. Given a database $\mathcal{DB}$ and a consistent set of update atoms $\mathcal{U}$, the truth value of

- a positive ground literal $a(t)$ is *true* w.r.t. $(\mathcal{DB}, \mathcal{U})$ if $a(t) \in \mathcal{U}(\mathcal{DB})$,
- a negative ground literal $not\ a(t)$ is *true* w.r.t. $(\mathcal{DB}, \mathcal{U})$ if $a(t) \notin \mathcal{U}(\mathcal{DB})$,
- a ground update atom $\pm a(t)$ is *true* w.r.t. $(\mathcal{DB}, \mathcal{U})$ if $\pm a(t) \in \mathcal{U}$,
- built-in atoms, conjunctions and disjunctions of literals is given in the standard way,
- a ground AIC $\phi \supset \psi$ is *true* w.r.t. $(\mathcal{DB}, \mathcal{U})$ if ϕ is *false* w.r.t. $(\mathcal{DB}, \mathcal{U})$. □

Definition 9. Let $\mathcal{DB}$ be a database, $\mathcal{IC}$ a set of AICs and $\mathcal{R}$ a repair for $\langle \mathcal{DB}, \mathcal{IC} \rangle$.

- A ground update atom $\pm a(t) \in \mathcal{R}$ is *founded* if there exists $r \in ground(\mathcal{IC})$ s.t. $\pm a(t)$ appears in $Head(r)$ and $Body(r)$ is *true* w.r.t. $(\mathcal{DB}, \mathcal{R} - \{\pm a(t)\})$. We say that $\pm a(t)$ is *supported* by r.
- A ground rule $r \in ground(\mathcal{IC})$ is *applied* w.r.t. $(\mathcal{DB}, \mathcal{R})$ if there exists $\pm a(t) \in \mathcal{R}$ s.t. $\pm a(t)$ appears in $Head(r)$ and $Body(r)$ is *true* w.r.t. $(\mathcal{DB}, \mathcal{R} - \{\pm a(t)\})$. We say that r *supports* $\pm a(t)$.
- $\mathcal{R}$ is *founded* if all its atoms are *founded*.
- $\mathcal{R}$ is *unfounded* if it is not founded. □

The set of founded update atoms in $\mathcal{R}$ with respect to $\langle \mathcal{DB}, \mathcal{IC} \rangle$ is denoted as $Founded(\mathcal{R}, \mathcal{DB}, \mathcal{IC})$, whereas $Unfounded(\mathcal{R}, \mathcal{DB}, \mathcal{IC}) = \mathcal{R} - Founded(\mathcal{R}, \mathcal{DB}, \mathcal{IC})$. The set of applied rules in $ground(\mathcal{IC})$ is denoted as $Applied(\mathcal{R}, \mathcal{DB}, \mathcal{IC})$, whereas $Unapplied(\mathcal{R}, \mathcal{DB}, \mathcal{IC}) = ground(\mathcal{IC}) - Applied(\mathcal{R}, \mathcal{DB}, \mathcal{IC})$. Thus, update atoms of founded repairs are inferable by means of AICs. Given a database $\mathcal{DB}$ and a set of AICs $\mathcal{IC}$, $\mathbf{FR}(\mathcal{DB}, \mathcal{IC})$ denotes the set of founded repairs for $\langle \mathcal{DB}, \mathcal{IC} \rangle$. Clearly, the set of founded repairs is contained in the set of repairs ($\mathbf{FR}(\mathcal{DB}, \mathcal{IC}) \subseteq \mathbf{R}(\mathcal{DB}, St(\mathcal{IC}))$).

Example 5. Consider the following set of AICs $\mathcal{IC}$

$$\forall (E, P, D)[\, mgr(E, P),\ prj(P, D),\ not\ emp(E, D) \supset\ +emp(E, D)\,]$$

$$\forall (E, D_1, D_2)[\, emp(E, D_1),\ emp(E, D_2),\ D_1 \neq D_2 \supset\ -emp(E, D_1) \vee -emp(E, D_2)\,]$$

The first constraint states that every manager E of a project P carried out by a department D must be an employee of D, whereas the second one says that every employee must be in only one department. Consider now the database $\mathcal{DB} = \{mgr(e_1, p_1),\ prj(p_1, d_1),\ emp(e_1, d_2)\}$. There are three repairs for $\mathcal{DB}$: $\mathcal{R}_1 = \{-mgr(e_1, p_1)\}$, $\mathcal{R}_2 = \{-prj(p_1, d_1)\}$ and $\mathcal{R}_3 = \{+emp(e_1, d_1), -emp(e_1, d_2)\}$. $\mathcal{R}_3$ is the only founded repair as only the update atoms $+emp(e_1, d_1)$ and $-emp(e_1, d_2)$ are derivable from $\mathcal{IC}$. □

Theorem 2. *Let $\mathcal{DB}$ be a database, $\mathcal{IC}$ a set of AICs and $\mathcal{R}$ a founded repair for $\langle \mathcal{DB}, \mathcal{IC} \rangle$. For each ground AIC $r = \phi \supset \psi \in Applied(\mathcal{R}, \mathcal{DB}, \mathcal{IC})$, let $\mathcal{U}$ be the set of ground update atoms appearing in ψ, then $\mathcal{U}(\mathcal{DB}) \not\models \phi$ (i.e. $\mathcal{U}(\mathcal{DB}) \models St(r)$).* □

The above theorem states that for each ground applied constraint there must be among the true update head atoms, at least one atom $\pm a(y)$ which makes the body of the active constraint false with respect to the repaired database, i.e. the body must contain a literal $Comp(\pm a(y))$. Observe that, if for each ground AIC $r = \phi \supset \psi \in ground(\mathcal{IC})$ the set $\mathcal{U}$ of ground update atoms appearing in ψ is such that $\mathcal{U}(\mathcal{DB}) \models \phi$ (i.e. $\mathcal{U}(\mathcal{DB}) \not\models St(r)$), no founded repair exists.

Corollary 1. *Given a database $\mathcal{DB}$ and a set of AICs $\mathcal{IC}$, an update atom $\pm a(t)$ can belong to a founded repair only if there exists $r \in ground(\mathcal{IC})$ such that $\pm a(t)$ appears in $Head(r)$ and $Comp(\pm a(t))$ appears in $Body(r)$.* □

Definition 10. Given a ground AIC $r = \phi \supset \psi$, $Core(r)$ denotes the ground AIC $\phi \supset \psi'$, where ψ' is obtained by deleting from ψ any update atom $\pm a(t)$ such that $Comp(\pm a(t))$ does not appear in ϕ. Given a set $\mathcal{IC}$ of AICs, $Core(\mathcal{IC}) = \{Core(r) \mid r \in ground(\mathcal{IC})\}$. □

Theorem 3. *Given a database $\mathcal{DB}$ and a set $\mathcal{IC}$ of AICs,*

$$\mathbf{FR}(\mathcal{DB}, \mathcal{IC}) = \mathbf{FR}(\mathcal{DB}, Core(\mathcal{IC})).$$

The above results (Theorem 2, Corollary 1 and Theorem 3) state that every head update atom $\pm a(t)$ not repairing the body (i.e. such that the body does not contain a literal $Comp(\pm a(t))$) is useless and can be deleted. This is an important result suggesting that active rules (with the declarative semantics here proposed), used to repair databases, should have a specific form: the head update atoms must repair the database so that the body of the active constraint is *false* (i.e. the constraint is satisfied).

Example 6. Consider the database $\mathcal{DB} = \{a, b\}$ and the set $\mathcal{IC} = \{a \supset -b, b \supset -a\}$ of AICs. The unique repair for $\langle \mathcal{DB}, \mathcal{IC} \rangle$ is $\mathcal{R} = \{-a, -b\}$, but it is not founded. Intuitively, if we apply $a \supset -b$, b is deleted from $\mathcal{DB}$, so $b \supset -a$ cannot be applied. If we apply $b \supset -a$, a is deleted from $\mathcal{DB}$, so $a \supset -b$ cannot be applied. □

From the previous results, in the following, only AICs in which for each head update atom $\pm a(t)$, there exists in the body a corresponding complementary literal $Comp(\pm a(t))$, are considered.

Theorem 4. *Let $\mathcal{DB}$ be a database, $\mathcal{IC}$ a set of AICs and $\mathcal{R}$ a founded repair for $\langle \mathcal{DB}, \mathcal{IC} \rangle$. For each $\pm a(t) \in \mathcal{R}$ there exists a ground AIC $\rho \in Core(\mathcal{IC})$ s.t. $\pm a(t)$ is the unique update atom in $\mathcal{R}$ supported by ρ.* □

Next example shows how AICs can be used to express classical hard problems.

Example 7. Graph coloring. The following set of constraints $\mathcal{IC}$ checks if the coloring of a (possibly partially colored) graph, defined by means of the relations *node* and *edge*, can be completed by using only the two colors *red* and *blue*.

$$\forall(X)[\, node(X),\ not\, col(X, red),\ not\, col(X, blue),\ not\, col(X, yellow) \supset$$
$$+col(X, red) \vee +col(X, blue)\,]$$

$$\forall(X, Y, C)[\, edge(X, Y),\ col(X, C),\ col(Y, C) \supset -col(X, C) \vee -col(Y, C)\,]$$

The two constraints state that colored nodes can be (re-)colored with one of two available colors. □

Observe that in the above example if the head update atoms are removed from the second constraint, as colored nodes cannot be re-colored, the expressed problem consists in completing the coloring of the graph. Assuming that the input graph is not colored, the classical 3-coloring problem constraints can be defined by the following constraints:

$$\forall(X)[\,node(X),\ not\,col(X,red),\ not\,col(X,blue),\ not\,col(X,yellow) \supset$$
$$+col(X,red) \vee +col(X,blue) \vee +col(X,yellow)\,]$$

$$\forall(X,Y,C)[\,edge(X,Y),\ col(X,C),\ col(Y,C) \supset\,]$$

It is worth noting that the same problem cannot be expressed using not founded repairs as a repair can also be obtained by deleting nodes from the input graph. The problem with active integrity constraints is that the existence of founded repairs, in the general case, is not guaranteed. Thus, Section 5 will present a different semantics where founded repairs can be considered as repairs which are preferable with respect to the not founded ones as they contain only actions derived from the active constraints.

4.2   Rewriting into Logic Programs

The technique introduced in [15,16] cannot be applied to AICs. Consider for instance the database $\mathcal{DB} = \{a,b\}$ and the set $\mathcal{IC}$ containing AICs $a \supset -a$ and $a,b \supset -b$. The database $\mathcal{DB}$ is inconsistent and the unique repairs is $\mathcal{R} = \{-a\}$. Moreover, the program $\mathcal{DP(IC)}$ consists of the rules $-a \leftarrow (a \vee +a)$ and $-b \leftarrow (a \vee +a), (b \vee +b)$. The program $\mathcal{DP(IC)} \cup \mathcal{DB}$ has a unique stable model $\mathcal{M} = \{-a,-b,a,b\}$ from which we derive the set of updates $\mathcal{R(M)} = \{-a,-b\}$ which is not a repair.

A different technique will now be shown which generalizes the one proposed in [15,16] so that repairs can be produced by logic programs derived from rules defining integrity constraints. It is worth noting that the presence of existentially quantified variables in negated body literals, does not allow the generation of a possibly infinite number of repairs as the logic rules derived from the rewriting of constraints are *safe* [25].

Given a set $\{ic_1, \ldots, ic_r, \ldots, ic_k\}$ of ground AICs and a ground update atom $+a(t)$ (resp. $-a(t)$), we use the following notation:

- $a^+(t,r)$ (resp. $a^-(t,r)$) means that the update $+a(t)$ (resp. $-a(t)$) is performed by ic_r. We call $a^+(t,r)$ (resp. $a^-(t,r)$) a *marked update atom*.
- $\overline{a^+}(t,r)$ (resp. $\overline{a^-}(t,r)$) means that the update $+a(t)$ (resp. $-a(t)$) is performed by a ground AIC different from ic_r.

Definition 11. Given a database $\mathcal{DB}$, a set $\mathcal{IC} = \{ic_1, \ldots, ic_k\}$ of ground AICs, and a founded repair $\mathcal{R} = \{\pm a_1(t_1), \ldots, \pm a_n(t_n)\}$ for $\langle \mathcal{DB}, \mathcal{IC} \rangle$,

- a *marked founded repair* derived from $\mathcal{R}$ is a set of marked update atoms $\mathcal{MR} = \{a_1^\pm(t_1, r_1), \ldots, a_n^\pm(t_n, r_n)\}$ s.t.
  • $\forall\, a_i^\pm(t_i, r_j) \in \mathcal{MR}$, $\pm a_i(t_i)$ is supported by ic_j,
  • $r_i \neq r_j$ for $i, j \in [1..n]$ and $i \neq j$.
- the mapping between $\mathcal{R}$ and the set of marked founded repairs derived from $\mathcal{R}$ is defined by means of a (multivalued) *marking function* γ.   □

Thus, $\gamma(\mathcal{R})$ denotes the set of marked founded repairs derived from $\mathcal{R}$ (it is here assumed that the database and the active integrity constraints are understood). We define the set of marked founded repairs for $\langle \mathcal{DB}, \mathcal{IC} \rangle$: $\mathbf{MFR}(\mathcal{DB}, \mathcal{IC}) = \bigcup_{\mathcal{R} \in \mathbf{FR}(\mathcal{DB}, \mathcal{IC})} \gamma(\mathcal{R})$.

Example 8. Consider the database $\mathcal{DB} = \{a, b\}$ and the set $\{ic_1, ic_2\} = \{a \supset -a, \ a \wedge b \supset -a\}$ of AICs. There exists only the founded repair $\mathcal{R} = \{-a\}$. As the update atom $-a$ is supported by both AICs, there are two possible marked founded repairs derived from $\mathcal{R}$: $\mathcal{MR}_1 = \{a^-(1)\}$ and $\mathcal{MR}_2 = \{a^-(2)\}$ stating, respectively, that the deletion of the atom a is associated with the first and second constraints. $\qquad \square$

The existence of at least a marked founded repair for each founded repair is guaranteed by the following corollary.

Corollary 2. *Given a database $\mathcal{DB}$ and a set $\mathcal{IC}$ of ground AICs, for each founded repair $\mathcal{R}$, $\gamma(\mathcal{R}) \neq \emptyset$.* $\qquad \square$

The following definition shows how active integrity constraints are rewritten into Datalog programs.

Definition 12. Let $\mathcal{IC}$ be a set of AICs and $\{ic_1, \ldots, ic_r, \ldots, ic_k\}$ its ground version w.r.t. a database $\mathcal{DB}$, where

$$ic_r = \bigwedge_{j=1}^{m} b_j(x_j), \ \bigwedge_{j=m+1}^{n} \text{not } b_j(x_j), \ \varphi(x_0) \supset \bigvee_{i=1}^{p} \pm a_i(y_i).$$

We define $Rew(ic_r) = Rew^0(ic_r) \cup Rew^1(ic_r) \cup Rew^2(ic_r)$, where $Rew^0(ic_r)$ is the set of rules

r.1 : $\bigvee_{i=1}^{p} a_i^{\pm}(y_i, r) \leftarrow \bigwedge_{j=1}^{m} \widetilde{b_j}(x_j, r), \bigwedge_{j=m+1}^{n} \text{not } \widetilde{b_j}(x_j, r), \ \varphi(x_0)$

r.2.j : $\widetilde{b_j}(x_j, r) \qquad \leftarrow (b_j(x_j), \text{not } \overline{b_j^-}(x_j, r)) \vee \overline{b_j^+}(x_j, r) \qquad j \in [1..n]$

r.3.i : $a_i^{\pm}(y_i, l) \qquad \leftarrow a_i^{\pm}(y_i, r), \ 1 \leq l \leq k, \ r \neq l \qquad i \in [1..p]$

$Rew^1(ic_r)$ is the set of rules

r.4 : $\qquad \leftarrow \bigwedge_{j=1}^{m} \widehat{b_j}(x_j), \ \bigwedge_{j=m+1}^{n} \text{not } \widehat{b_j}(x_j), \ \varphi(x_0)$

r.5.j : $\widehat{b_j}(x_j) \leftarrow (b_j(x_j), \text{not} - b_j(x_j)) \vee + b_j(x_j) \qquad j \in [1..n]$

and $Rew^2(ic_r)$ is the set of rules

r.6.i : $\pm a_i(y_i) \leftarrow a_i^{\pm}(y_i, r) \qquad i \in [1..p]$

r.7.i : $\qquad \leftarrow +a_i(y_i), -a_i(y_i) \ i \in [1..p].$

We define $Rew^u(\mathcal{IC}) = \bigcup_{i=1}^{k} Rew^u(ic_i)$, with $u \in \{0, 1, 2\}$, and $Rew(\mathcal{IC}) = \bigcup_{i=1}^{k} Rew(ic_i)$. $\qquad \square$

The rules in $Rew^0(\mathcal{IC})$ are used to compute stable models corresponding to sets of updates, whereas the rules in $Rew^1(\mathcal{IC})$ and in $Rew^2(\mathcal{IC})$ check that the stable models of $Rew^0(\mathcal{IC})$ define (consistent) database repairs. Intuitively, the atom $\widetilde{b}_j(x_j, r)$ states that the atom $b_j(x_j)$ is present in the database if ic_r doesn't perform any update actions, whereas the atom $\widehat{b}_j(x_j)$ expresses the fact that the atom $b_j(x_j)$ is present in the database after all update action have been performed. Rule **r.1** declares that if the constraint $St(ic_r)$ is violated before any update actions is performed by ic_r, ic_r has to perform an update action. The denial **r.4** (the original integrity constraint defined over the updated database) is added in order to guarantee that the updated database satisfies ic_r.

Proposition 1. Given a database $\mathcal{DB}$, a set $\mathcal{IC}$ of AICs, a model $\mathcal{M}$ of $\mathcal{DB} \cup Rew(\mathcal{IC})$ and an atom $a^{\pm}(t, r) \in \mathcal{M}$, $\mathcal{M}$ does not contain any atom $a^{\pm}(t, l)$ with $r \neq l$. □

Definition 13. Given an interpretation $\mathcal{M}$, we denote as $UpdateAtoms(\mathcal{M})$ the set of update atoms in $\mathcal{M}$ and as $MarkedUpdateAtoms(\mathcal{M})$ the set of marked update atoms in $\mathcal{M}$. Given a set S of interpretations, we define $UpdateAtoms(S) = \{UpdateAtoms(\mathcal{M}) \mid \mathcal{M} \in S\}$ and $MarkedUpdateAtoms(S) = \{MarkedUpdateAtoms(\mathcal{M}) \mid \mathcal{M} \in S\}$. □

Next theorem shows the equivalence between (marked) founded repairs and stable models, restricted to (marked) update atoms.

Theorem 5. *Given a database $\mathcal{DB}$ and a set $\mathcal{IC}$ of AICs*
1. **MFR**$(\mathcal{DB}, \mathcal{IC}) = MarkedUpdateAtoms(SM(Rew(\mathcal{IC}) \cup \mathcal{DB}))$,
2. **FR**$(\mathcal{DB}, \mathcal{IC}) = UpdateAtoms(SM(Rew(\mathcal{IC}) \cup \mathcal{DB}))$. □

It is worth noting that given a stable model $\mathcal{M}$ of $Rew(\mathcal{IC}) \cup \mathcal{DB}$ and a marked update atom $a^{\pm}(t, r) \in \mathcal{M}$, $\mathcal{M}$ does not contain any other atom $b^{\pm}(v, r)$ different from $a^{\pm}(t, r)$. In fact, $a^{\pm}(t, r)$ and $b^{\pm}(v, r)$ can be inferred only by the rule **r.1**, and $\mathcal{M}$ is not minimal if it contains both atoms. From this observation it follows that rule **r.1** can be rewritten using exclusive disjunction in the head, i.e.

$$\mathbf{r.1} : \bigoplus_{i=1}^{p} a_i^{\pm}(y_i, r) \leftarrow \bigwedge_{j=1}^{m} \widetilde{b}_j(x_j, r), \ \bigwedge_{j=m+1}^{n} not \ \widetilde{b}_j(x_j, r), \ \varphi(x_0)$$

Data Complexity

Theorem 6. *Let $\mathcal{DB}$ be a database and $\mathcal{IC}$ a set of active integrity constraints. The problem of checking if there exists a founded repair $\mathcal{R}$ for $\mathcal{DB}$ is Σ_2^p-complete.* □

The consistent founded answer to a relational query $Q = (g, \mathcal{P})$ over a database $\mathcal{DB}$ with active constraints $\mathcal{IC}$ (denoted by $Q(\mathcal{DB}, \mathcal{IC})$), is obtained by first computing the set **FR**$(\mathcal{DB}, \mathcal{IC})$ of founded repairs for $\mathcal{DB}$ and, then, considering the intersection $\bigcap_{\mathcal{R} \in \mathbf{FR}(\mathcal{DB}, \mathcal{IC})} Q(\mathcal{R}(\mathcal{DB}))$.

Theorem 7. *Let $\mathcal{DB}$ be a database and $\mathcal{IC}$ a set of active integrity constraints. The problem of checking whether a ground atom g belongs to all repaired databases obtained by means of founded repairs is Π_2^p-complete.* □

For single head active integrity constraints the complexity is in the first level of the polynomial hierarchy.

5   Preferred Repairs and Answers

In this section we define an approach that always permits us to obtain a consistent repaired database. In particular, we interpret the actions in the head of constraints as indication of the operations the user prefers to perform to make the database consistent.

Definition 14. Let $\mathcal{DB}$ be a database, $\mathcal{IC}$ a set of active integrity constraints and $\mathcal{R}_1, \mathcal{R}_2$ two repairs for $\mathcal{DB}$. Then, $\mathcal{R}_1$ is *preferable* to $\mathcal{R}_2$ ($\mathcal{R}_1 \sqsupset \mathcal{R}_2$) w.r.t. $\mathcal{IC}$, if $Unfounded(\mathcal{R}_1, \mathcal{DB}, \mathcal{IC}) \subset Unfounded(\mathcal{R}_2, \mathcal{DB}, \mathcal{IC})$. Moreover, $\mathcal{R}_1 \sqsupset \mathcal{R}_2$ if $\mathcal{R}_1 \sqsupseteq \mathcal{R}_2$ and $\mathcal{R}_2 \not\sqsupseteq \mathcal{R}_1$. A repair $\mathcal{R}$ is said to be *preferred* w.r.t. $\mathcal{IC}$ if there is no repair $\mathcal{R}'$ such that $\mathcal{R}' \sqsupset \mathcal{R}$. □

Example 9. Consider the integrity constraint of Example 2 with the database $\mathcal{DB} = \{mgr(john, b, 1000), mgr(frank, b, 2000), mgr(mary, c, 1000), mgr(rosy, c, 2000)\}$. There are four repairs $\mathcal{R}_1 = \{-mgr(john, b, 1000), -mgr(mary, c, 1000)\}$, $\mathcal{R}_2 = \{-mgr(john, b, 1000), -mgr(rosy, c, 2000)\}$, $\mathcal{R}_3 = \{-mgr(frank, b, 2000), -mgr(mary, c, 1000)\}$ and $\mathcal{R}_4 = \{-mgr(frank, b, 2000), -mgr(rosy, c, 2000)\}$. The order relation is $\mathcal{R}_2 \sqsupset \mathcal{R}_1$, $\mathcal{R}_3 \sqsupset \mathcal{R}_1$, $\mathcal{R}_4 \sqsupset \mathcal{R}_2$ and $\mathcal{R}_4 \sqsupset \mathcal{R}_3$. Therefore, we have only one preferred model which is also founded (namely $\mathcal{R}_4$). Assume now to also have the constraint

$$not\ mgr(rosy, c, 2000) \supset$$

declaring that the tuple $mgr(rosy, c, 2000)$ must be in $\mathcal{DB}$. In such a case we have only the two repairs $\mathcal{R}_1$ and $\mathcal{R}_3$ and the preferred one is $\mathcal{R}_3$ which is not founded. □

The relation $\sqsupset$ is a *partial order* as it is irreflexive, asymmetric and transitive. The set of preferred repairs for a database $\mathcal{DB}$ and a set of active integrity constraints $\mathcal{IC}$ is denoted by $\mathbf{PR}(\mathcal{DB}, \mathcal{IC})$. Clearly, the relation between preferred, founded and standard repairs is as follows: $\mathbf{FR}(\mathcal{DB}, \mathcal{IC}) \subseteq \mathbf{PR}(\mathcal{DB}, \mathcal{IC}) \subseteq \mathbf{R}(\mathcal{DB}, \mathcal{IC})$. The next theorem states the precise relation between preferred, founded and general repairs.

Theorem 8. *Let $\mathcal{DB}$ be a database and $\mathcal{IC}$ a set of active integrity constraints, then*

$$\mathbf{PR}(\mathcal{DB}, \mathcal{IC}) \begin{cases} = \mathbf{FR}(\mathcal{DB}, \mathcal{IC}) & if\ \mathbf{FR}(\mathcal{DB}, \mathcal{IC}) \neq \emptyset \\ \subseteq \mathbf{R}(\mathcal{DB}, \mathcal{IC}) & if\ \mathbf{FR}(\mathcal{DB}, \mathcal{IC}) = \emptyset \end{cases}$$ □

Obviously, as the existence of repairs is guaranteed, the existence of a preferred repair is guaranteed too. We conclude by presenting a result on the computational complexity of computing preferred repairs and answers.

Theorem 9. *Let $\mathcal{DB}$ be a database and $\mathcal{IC}$ a set of active integrity constraints*

1. *checking if there exists a preferred founded repair $\mathcal{R}$ for $\mathcal{DB}$ is Σ_2^p-complete;*
2. *checking whether a ground atom belongs to all preferred repairs is Π_2^p-complete.* □

The above theorem states that computing preferred repairs and answers is not harder than computing standard or founded repairs and answers.

References

1. Abiteboul S., Hull R., and Vianu V., *Foundations of Databases.* Addison-Wesley, 1994.
2. Alferes J. J., J. A. Leite, Pereira L. M., Przymusinska H., and Przymusinski T.C., Dynamic updates of non-monotonic knowledge bases. *JLP*, 45(1-3), 43–70, 2000.
3. Arenas M., Bertossi L., and Chomicki J., Consistent query answers in inconsistent databases. *Proc. PODS*, 68–79, 1999.
4. Arenas M., Bertossi L., and Chomicki J., Specifying and querying database repairs using logic programs with exceptions. *Proc. FQAS*, 27–41, 2000.
5. Baral C., Embedding revision programs in logic programming situation calculus. *Journal of Logic Programming*, 30(1), 83–97, 1997.
6. Ceri S., Widom J., Deriving Production Rules for Constraint Maintenance, *VLDB*, 566-577, 1990.
7. Chomicki J., Lobo J., and Naqvi S. A., Conflict resolution using logic programming. *IEEE TKDE*, 15(1), 244–249, 2003.
8. Chomicki J., Marcinkowski J., Minimal-change integrity maintenance using tuple deletions. *Information & Computation*, 197(1-2), 90-121, 2005.
9. Eiter T., Gottlob G., and Mannila H., Disjunctive datalog. *ACM TODS*, 22(3), 364–418, 1997.
10. Flesca, S., Greco, S., Declarative semantics for active rules, *TPLP*, 1(1), 43-69, 2001.
11. Flesca S., Greco S., Zumpano E., Active integrity constraints. *PPDP*, 98-107, 2004.
12. Gelfond M. and Lifschitz V. The stable model semantics for logic programming. *Proc. ICLPS*, 1070–1080, 1988.
13. Gelfond M. and Lifschitz V. Classical negation in logic programs and disjunctive databases. *New generation Computing*, 9(3/4), 365–385, 1991.
14. Grant J. and Subrahmanian V. S., Reasoning in inconsistent knowledge bases. *IEEE TKDE*, 7(1), 177–189, 1995.
15. Greco S., and Zumpano E., Querying Inconsistent Databases. *LPAR*, 2000.
16. Greco G., Greco S., and Zumpano E., A Logical Framework for Querying and Repairing Inconsistent Databases. *IEEE TKDE*, 15(6), 1389-1408, 2003.
17. Kifer M. and Li A., On the semantics of rule-based expert systems with uncertainty. *Proc. ICDT*, 102–117, 1988.
18. Lin J., A semantics for reasoning consistently in the presence of inconsistency. *Artificial Intelligence*, 86(1), 75–95, 1996.
19. Marek V. W., Pivkina I., and Truszczynski M., Revision programming = logic programming + integrity constraints. In *Computer Science Logic*, 73–98, 1998.
20. Marek V. W. and Truszczynski M., Revision programming. *TCS*, 190(2), 241–277, 1998.
21. May W., Ludascher B., Understanding the Global Semantics of Referential Actions using Logic Rules, *ACM TODS* 27(4), 343-397, 2002.
22. Papadimitriou, C. H., *Computational Complexity.* Addison-Wesley, 1994.
23. Paton N. W., Diaz O., Active Database Systems, *ACM Computing Surveys*, 31(1), 63-103, 1999
24. Subrahmanian V. S., Amalgamating knowledge bases. *ACM TKDE*, 19(2), 291–331, 1994.
25. Ullman J. K., *Principles of Database and Knowledge-Base Systems.* Computer Science Press, 1998.
26. Wijsen J., Condensed representation of database repairs for consistent query answering. *ICDT*, 378–393, 2003.

Modules for Prolog Revisited

Rémy Haemmerlé and François Fages

Projet Contraintes – INRIA Rocquencourt – France
`FirstName.LastName@inria.fr`

Abstract. Module systems are an essential feature of programming languages as they facilitate the re-use of existing code and the development of general purpose libraries. Unfortunately, there has been no consensual module system for Prolog, hence no strong development of libraries, in sharp contrast to what exists in Java for instance. One difficulty comes from the *call* predicate which interferes with the protection of the code, an essential task of a module system. By distinguishing the called module code protection from the calling module code protection, we review the existing syntactic module systems for Prolog. We show that no module system ensures both forms of code protection, with the noticeable exceptions of Ciao-Prolog and XSB. We then present a formal module system for logic programs with calls and closures, define its operational semantics and formally prove the code protection property. Interestingly, we also provide an equivalent logical semantics of modular logic programs without calls nor closures, which shows how they can be translated into constraint logic programs over a simple module constraint system.

1 Introduction

Module systems are an essential feature of programming languages as they facilitate the re-use of existing code and the development of general purpose libraries. Unfortunately, there has been no consensual module system for Prolog, hence no strong development of libraries, in sharp contrast to what exists in Java for instance.

One difficulty in Prolog comes from the *call* predicate which interferes with the protection of the code, an essential task of a module system. There has been therefore several proposals of module systems realizing different trade-offs between code protection and the preservation of meta-programming facilities.

In order to enforce the proper segmentation of the code, and to guarantee the semantics of the predicates defined in a library, a module system has however to strictly prevent any predicate execution not allowed by the programmer. This means that it should be possible to restrict the access to the code of a module (by predicate calls, dynamic calls, dynamic asserts or retracts, syntax modifications, global variable assignments, etc.) from extra-modular code. This property is called *code protection*.

The relationship between the calling module and the called module is however asymmetric. The *called module code protection* ensures that only the visible

S. Etalle and M. Truszczyński (Eds.): ICLP 2006, LNCS 4079, pp. 41–55, 2006.

predicates of a module can be called from outside. The *calling module code protection* should ensure that the called module does not call any predicate of the calling module, as they are not visible. The following example illustrates however the need to provide an exception to this rule with a mechanism for executing a predicate in the calling environment, which we will call a *closure*.

Example 1. The list iterator predicate `forall/2` defined below in ISO-Prolog [13], checks that every element of a list, passed in the first argument, satisfies a given property, passed as a unary predicate in the second argument:

```
forall([], _).
forall([H|T], P):- G=..[P,H], call(G), forall(T, P).
```

Such a predicate `forall` cannot be defined in a library (for lists as it should) without violating the calling module code protection, as the intended meaning of the predicate is indeed to call the predicate passed as argument in the calling module environment.

Most module systems for Prolog solve the difficulty either by abandoning any form of code protection, or by introducing *ad-hoc* mechanisms to escape from the code protection rules. Our proposal here is to keep a strict code protection discipline but distinguish closures from dynamic calls, closures being executed in the environment where they are created. From a functional perspective, a closure here is basically a lambda expression with only one parameter, i.e., that `closure(X,G,C) )` is somehow equivalent to $C = (\lambda X.G)$ and `apply(C,X)` to $C.X$. This makes it possible to define a module for lists which exports a `forall` predicate taking a closure from outside as argument.

Example 2.   `:- module(lists, [forall/2, ...]).`
```
  forall([], C).
  forall([X|T], C) :- apply(C, [X]), forall(T, C).
```

That definition of `forall` using closures instead of dynamic calls can be used from any module importing the list module, by passing to it a closure constructed from a unary predicate like `var/1` for instance:

```
:- module(foo, ...).
:- use_module(lists).
all_variables(L) :- closure([X],var(X),C), forall(L,C).
```

In this paper, we first review the main module systems for Prolog in the light of the two forms of module code protection. We show that no module system ensures both forms of code protection, with the noticeable exceptions of Ciao-Prolog and XSB.

Then we give a formal presentation of a safe module system with calls and closures. We precisely define its operational semantics and show the full code protection property.

We also provide an equivalent logical semantics for modular logic programs without calls nor closures. That semantics, obtained by translating modular logic programs into constraint logic programs over a simple constraint module system, shows how the module system can be compiled into a constraint logic program.

We then conclude on the relevance of these results to an on-going implementation of a fully bootstrapped constraint programming language, from which this work originated.

Related Work

Modularity in the context of Logic Programming has been considerably studied, and there has been some standardization attempts for ISO-Prolog [14]. Different approaches can be distinguished however.

The *syntactic approach* mainly deals with the alphabet of symbols, as a mean to partitionate large programs, safely re-use existing code and develop general purpose libraries. This approach is often chosen for its simplicity and compatibility with existing code. For instance, a constraint solver like OEFAI CLP(q,r) [12], or a Prolog implementation of the Constraint Handling Rules language CHR [24], should be portable as libraries in a modular Prolog system. Most of the current modular Prolog systems, such as SICStus [25], SWI [29], ECLiPSe [2], XSB [22], Ciao [4,7,6] for instance, fall into this category. We will focus on this approach in this paper, together with the *object-oriented approach* [19,20] which is somewhat similar.

The *algebraic approach* defines module calculi with operations over sets of program clauses [21,5,23]. They are somehow more general than the object-oriented extensions of Prolog, as they consider a great variety of operations on predicate definitions, like overriding, merging, etc. On the other hand, the greater versatility does not facilitate reasoning on large programs, and this approach has not been widely adopted.

The *logical approach* to module systems extends the underlying logic of programs. One can cite extensions with nested implications [16,17], meta-logic [3] or second order predicates [9]. Such logical modules can be created dynamically, similarly to other approaches such as Contextual Logic Programming [18,1]. Perhaps because their poor compatibility with existing code, they are also not widely used however, and will not be considered in this paper.

2   Review of Existing Syntactic Module Systems

In this section, we analyze the main syntactic module systems developed for Prolog. A reference example will be used to illustrate their peculiarities, and classify them according to the two previously introduced properties: the called module code protection and the calling module code protection.

Following ISO Prolog terminology [14], a *module* is a set of Prolog clauses associated to a unique identifier, the *module name*. The *calling context* – or simply *context* – is the name of the module from where a call is made. A *qualified goal* M:G is a classical Prolog goal G prefixed by a module name M in which it must be interpreted. A predicate is *visible* from some context if it can be called from this particular context without any qualification. A predicate is *accessible* from some context if it can be called from this particular context with or without qualification. A *meta-predicate* is a predicate that handles arguments to be interpreted as goals. Those arguments are called *meta-arguments*.

2.1 A Basic Module System

We first consider a basic module system from which the syntactic module systems of Prolog can be derived through different extensions.

In this basic system, the predicates that are *visible* in a module are either defined in the module, or *imported* from another module. In order to ensure the protection of the called module code, only the predicates explicitly *exported* in the defining module can be imported by other modules. Furthermore, the qualification of predicates is not allowed.

The basic module system thus trivially satisfies both forms of code protection properties, but is not able to modularize the predicate `forall` of example 1.

2.2 SICStus Prolog

The modules of SICStus Prolog [25] make accessible any predicate, by using qualifications. The list iterator *forall* can thus be modularized, and used simply by passing to it goals qualified with the calling module. As a consequence however, this versatile module system does not ensure any form of module code protection.

It is also possible to explicitly declare meta-predicates and meta-arguments. In that case, the non-qualified meta-arguments are qualified dynamically with the calling context of the meta-predicate. With this feature, the called module is thus able to manipulate explicitly the name of the calling module and call any predicate in the calling module.

Example 3. This example, that will be also used in the following, tests the capabilities of calling private predicates in modules.

```
:-module(library, [mycall/1]).        :- module(using, [test/0]).
                                       :- use_module(library).
p :-
  write('library:p/0  ').             p :-
                                         write('using:p/0  ').
:-meta_predicate(mycall(:)).          q :-
mycall(M:G):-                           write('using:q/0  ').
  M:p, call(M:G).                     test :-
                                        library:p, mycall(q).
```

```
| ?- using:test.
library:p/0  using:p/0  using:q/0
yes
```

The private predicate *p* of the library is called from the using module, the library correctly calls the predicate *q* of the calling module, but is also able to call the private predicate *p* of the calling module.

This module system is similar to the ones of Quintus Prolog [26] and Yap Prolog [27]. The standardization attempt of ISO-Prolog [14] is also very close in spirit, but the accessibility rules of qualified predicates have been left to the implementation.

2.3   ECLiPSe

ECLiPSe [2] introduces two mechanisms to call non visible predicates. The first is the qualified call, where only the exported predicates are accessible. The second one, which uses the construct `call(Goal)@Module`, makes any predicate accessible as with a qualified goal `Module:Goal` in SICStus Prolog. This system provides also a directive `tool/2` for adding the calling context as an extra argument to the meta-predicate. This solution has the advantage of limiting the unauthorized calls made in a unconscious way.

Example 4.

```
:- module(library, [mycall/1]).

p :-
  write('library:p/0 ').

:- tool(mycall/1,mycall/2).
mycall(G, M):-
  call(p)@M, call(G)@M.
```

```
:- module(using, [test/0]).
:- use_module(library).

p :-
  write('using:p/0 ').
q :-
  write('using:q/0 ').
test :-
  call(p)@library, mycall(q).
```

```
[eclipse 2]: using:test.
library:p/0  using:p/0  using:q/0
Yes
```

As beforehand, the system does not ensure module code protection.

2.4   SWI Prolog

For compatibility reasons, SWI accepts qualified predicates and uses the same policy as SICStus Prolog. Hence the complete system does not ensure the called module code protection. Meta-programming in SWI Prolog [29] has a slightly different semantics. For a meta-call made in the clause of a meta-predicate declared with the directive `module_transparent/1`, the calling context is the calling context of the goal that invoked the meta-predicate. Hence, by declaring the list iterator `forall/2` as a module transparent predicate, one obtains the expected behavior, since the meta-call to `G` is invoked in the module that called `forall`, i.e. in the calling module.

Nonetheless, this choice has two main disadvantages:

Example 5.

```
:-module(library, [mycall/1]).

p :-
  write('library:p/0  ').

:-module_transparent(mycall/1).
mycall(G):-
  p, call(p), call(G).
```

```
:- module(using, [test/0]).
:- use_module(library).

p :-
  write('using:p/0  ').
q :-
  write('using:q/0  ').
test :-
  mycall(q).
```

```
?- using:test.
library:p/0  using:p/0  using:q/0
Yes
```

First, a dynamic call `call(p(x))` does not behave as the static one `p(x)`. Second, the conventions for meta-predicates break the protection of the calling module code.

2.5   Logtalk

Logtalk [19,20] is not really a syntactic module system but an object-oriented extension of Prolog. Nonetheless by restricting its syntax – by forbidding parameterized objects and inheritance – one obtains a module system close to the ones studied here.

The `object/1` directive can be read as a `module/2` directive, where the public predicates are the exported predicates. Then, message sending plays the role of goal qualification. Indeed, sending the message P to the object M – which is denoted by `M::P` instead of `M:P` – calls the predicate P defined in the module M, only if P have been declared public in M. Therefore this module system ensures the protection of the called module code.

In order to deal with meta-predicates, Logtalk provides its own version of the `meta_predicate/1` directive, which can be used in a similar way to the SICStus one, with `::` used instead of `:` for declaring meta-argument. As SWI, Logtalk does not realize a module name expansion of the meta-arguments, but realize dynamic calls in a context which may be different from a static call. In this system, the dynamic context is the module (i.e. object) that sent the last message. Since the non qualified calls are not considered as messages however, it is possible to call any predicate of the calling module.

Example 6.

```
:- object(library).              :- object(using).
:- public(mycall/1).             :- public(test/0).


p :-                             p :-
   write('library:p/0 ').           write('using:p/0  ').
                                 q :-
mycall(G) :- mycall(G,p).           write('using:q/0  ').
:-metapredicate(mycall(::,::)).  test :-
mycall(G1,G2) :-                    library::mycall(q).
   call(G1), call(G2).
                                 :- end_object.
:-end_object.

| ?- using::test.
using:q/0  using:p/0
yes
```

That module system does not ensure the calling module protection.

2.6   Ciao Prolog

The module system of Ciao Prolog [4] satisfies the two forms of code protection. Only exported predicates are accessible for outside a module, and this property is checked for qualified goals. The manipulation of meta-data through the module system is possible through an advanced version of the meta_predicate/1 directive.

Before calling the meta-predicates, the system dynamically translates the meta-arguments into an internal representation containing the goal and the context in which the goal must be called. Since this translation is done before calling the meta-predicate, the system correctly selects the context in which the meta-data must be called. As far as the system does not document any predicate able to create or manipulate the internal data, the protection of the code is preserved. In this sense, Ciao Prolog does make a distinction between terms and higher-order data (i.e. goals manipulated as terms) [8].

Example 7.

```
:-module(library, [mycall/1]).    :- module(using, [test/0]).
                                  :- use_module(library).
p :- write('library:p/0  ').
                                  p :- write('using:p/0  ').
:-meta_predicate(mycall(:)).
mycall(G):-                       test :- mycall(p).
   writeq(G), write(' '), call(G).

?-  using:test.
$:('using:p') using:p/0
yes
```

The program realizes the expected behavior without compromising the called module protection, nor the calling module protection.

2.7   XSB

The module system of XSB [22] is an atom-based, rather than predicate-based, syntactic module system. This means that function symbols, as well as predicate symbols, are modularized in XSB. Similar terms constructed in different modules may thus not unify. In a module, it is possible however to import public symbols from another module, with the effect that the modules share the same symbols.

Then, the semantics of the `call/1` predicate is very simple: the meta-call of a term corresponds to the call of the predicate of the same symbol and arity as the module where the term has been created. The system fully satisfies the code protection property.

Example 8.

```
:-export mycall/1.

p(_) :-
   write('library:p/1  ').

mycall(G):-
   call(G).
```

```
:- export test/1.
:- import mycall/1 from library.

p(_) :-
   write('using:p/0  ').
test(_) :-
   mycall(p(_)).
```

```
| ?-  test(_).
using:p/0
yes
```

On the other hand, the problem of defining the visibility rules for meta-programming predicates is moved to the construction of the terms. Indeed, in XSB, the terms constructed with `=../2`, `functor/2` and `read/1` belong to the module `user`. As a consequence, in a module different from `user`, the goal `(functor(X,q,1), X=q(_))` fails, whereas `(X=q(_), functor(X,q,1))` succeeds.

3   A Safe Module System with Calls and Closures

In this section, we define a formal module system with calls and closures. We present the operational semantics of modular logic programs, and formally prove that they satisfy both forms of module code protection.

3.1 Syntax of Modular Logic Programs

For the sake of simplicity of the presentation, the following conventions are adopted. First, a simple form of closures, that abstract only one argument in an atom, is considered. Second, the syntax of constraint logic programs is chosen with some syntactic conventions to distinguish between the constraints, the closures and the other atoms within goals. Third, all goals are assumed to be explicitly qualified, thereby eliminating the need to describe the conventions used for automatically prefixing the non-qualified atoms in a clause or a goal. Fourth, all public predicates in a module are assumed to be accessible from outside, with no consideration of directives such as use_module.

The following disjoint alphabets of symbols given with their arity are considered:

- V a countable set of variables (of arity 0) denoted by $x, y \ldots$;
- Σ_F a set of constant (of arity 0) and function symbols;
- Σ_C a set of constraint predicate symbols containing $=/2$ and $true/0$;
- Σ_P a set of program predicate symbols containing $call/2$, $closure/3$ and $apply/2$;
- Σ_M a set of module names (of arity 0), noted $\mu, \nu \ldots$

Furthermore, in order to interpret *calls* and *closures*, two coercion relations, $\overset{P}{\sim} \colon \Sigma_F \times \Sigma_P$ and $\overset{M}{\sim} \colon \Sigma_F \times \Sigma_M$, are assumed to interpret function symbols as predicate symbols and module names respectively. It is worth noting that in classical Prolog systems, where function symbols are not distinguished from predicate symbols, these relations are just the identity, while here they formally relate disjoint sets.

The sets of terms, formed over V and Σ_F, of atomic constraints, formed with predicate symbols in Σ_C and terms, and of atoms, formed with predicate symbols in Σ_P and terms, are defined as usual. In addition, atoms qualified by a module name are noted $\mu \colon A$. The call predicate has two arguments, the first being the module name qualifying the second argument.

A closure $closure(x, \mu \colon A, z)$ associates to the variable z a qualified atom $\mu \colon A$ (the meta-argument) in which the variable x is abstracted. The meta-argument in a closure must be a qualified atom, i.e. not a variable as in a *call*.

Definition 1. *A **closure** is an atom of the form $closure(x, \mu : A, z)$ where x and z are variables, $\mu : A$ is a qualified atom. The **application** of a closure associated to a variable z to an argument x is the atom $apply(z, x)$.*

Definition 2. *A **modular clause** is a formula of the form*

$$A_0 \leftarrow c_1, \ldots, c_l | \kappa_1, \ldots, \kappa_n | \mu_1 : A_1, \ldots, \mu_m : A_m.$$

where the c_i's are atomic constraints, the κ_i's are closures, and the $\mu_i : A_i$'s are qualified atoms.

Definition 3. *A **module** is a tuple* $(\mu, \mathcal{D}_\mu, \mathcal{I}_\mu)$ *where* $\mu \in \Sigma_M$ *is the* name *of the module,* $\mathcal{D}_\mu$ *is a set of clauses, called the* implementation *of the module, and* $\mathcal{I}_\mu \subset \Sigma_P$ *is the set of* public *predicates, called the* interface *of the module. The predicates not in* I_μ *are called* private *in* μ. *A **modular program*** $\mathcal{P}$ *is a set of modules with distinct names.*

Definition 4. *A **modular goal** is a formula*

$$c|\langle \nu_1 - \kappa_1 \rangle, \ldots, \langle \nu_n - \kappa_n \rangle \,|\, \langle \nu_1' - \mu_1 : A_1 \rangle, \ldots, \langle \nu_m' - \mu_m : A_m \rangle$$

where c *is a set of atomic constraints, the* κ_i *'s are closures, the* $(\mu_i : A_i)$ *'s are prefixed atoms and both the* ν_i *'s and the* ν_i' *'s are module names called* calling contexts.

In the following, the construct $\langle \nu - (\kappa_1, \ldots, \kappa_n) \rangle$ denotes the sequence of closures $(\langle \nu - \kappa_1 \rangle, \ldots, \langle \nu - \kappa_n \rangle)$ and similarly for sequence of atoms with context.

3.2   Operational Semantics

Let $\mathcal{P}$ be a program defined over some constraint system $\mathcal{X}$. The transition relation $\longrightarrow$ on goals is defined as the least relation satisfying the rules in table 1, where θ is a renaming substitution with fresh variables. A successful derivation for a goal G is a finite sequence of transitions from G which ends with a goal containing only constraints (the computed answer) and closures.

Table 1. Transition relation for goals with calls and closures

Modular CSLD	$\dfrac{(\mu, \mathcal{D}_\mu, \mathcal{I}_\mu) \in \mathcal{P} \quad (\nu = \mu) \vee (p \in \mathcal{I}_\mu)}{(c|K|\gamma, \langle \nu - \mu : p(t) \rangle, \gamma') \longrightarrow (c, \boldsymbol{s} = \boldsymbol{t}, c'|K, \langle \mu - k \rangle|\gamma, \langle \mu - \beta \rangle, \gamma')}$ where $(p(\boldsymbol{s}) \leftarrow c'|k|\beta)\theta \in \mathcal{D}_\mu$ and $\mathcal{X} \models \exists (c \wedge \boldsymbol{s} = \boldsymbol{t} \wedge c')$
Call	$\dfrac{\mathcal{X} \models c \Rightarrow (s = g \wedge t = f(\boldsymbol{x})) \quad g \overset{M}{\sim} \mu \quad f \overset{P}{\sim} p}{(c|K|\gamma, \langle \nu - \nu : call(s,t) \rangle, \gamma') \longrightarrow (c, s = g, t = f(\boldsymbol{x})|K|\gamma, \langle \nu - \mu : p(\boldsymbol{x}) \rangle, \gamma')}$
Apply	$\dfrac{\mathcal{X} \models c \Rightarrow z = y}{\substack{(c|\kappa_1, \langle \mu - closure(x, \mu' : A, z) \rangle, \kappa_2|\gamma, \langle \nu - \nu : apply(y,t) \rangle, \gamma') \longrightarrow \\ (c|\kappa_1, \langle \mu - closure(x, \mu' : A, z) \rangle, \kappa_2|\gamma, \langle \nu - \mu' : A[x \backslash t] \rangle, \gamma')}}$

The *modular CSLD* resolution rule is a restriction of the classical CSLD rule for CLP [15]. The additional condition $(\nu = \mu) \vee (p \in \mathcal{I}_\mu)$ imposes that $\mu : p(t)$ can be executed only if, either the call is made from inside the module (i.e. from the calling context μ), or the predicate p is a public predicate in μ. Moreover, this rule propagates the new calling context to the closures and atoms of the selected clause body.

The *call* rule defines the operational semantics of meta-calls. It is worth noting that this transition rule does not change the calling context ν. This property is necessary to guarantee the calling module code protection. For the sake of simplicity, a *call* goal with a free variable as meta-argument has no transition. Similarly, the *call* rule does not handle the meta-call of conjunctions of atoms or constraints. Those meta-calls can nevertheless be easily emulated, by supposing $(\text{','}/2 \stackrel{R}{\sim} and/2)$ and by adding the clause $(and(x, y) \leftarrow \mu\!:\!call(x), \mu\!:\!call(y))$ to the implementation of any module μ.

The *apply* rule allows the invocation of a closure collected by a previous predicate call, as expected for instance in the example 2 for the definition of `forall`. In practice, the *apply* rule looks for the closure associated to the closure variable (formally checks the equality of variables $z = y$), and applies the closure to the argument in the closure context.

3.3   Module Code Protection

Intuitively, the called module code protection property states that only the public predicates of a module μ can be called from outside, and produce subgoals in context μ. The calling module code protection property states that the goal of a closure can only be executed in the context of creation of the closure. These properties can be formalized as follows:

Definition 5. *The operational semantics of programs satisfies the* **called module code protection** *if the reduction of a qualified atom* $\mu : p(t)$ *in a context* ν *produces qualified atoms and closures in the context* μ *only, and either* p *is public in* μ *or* $\mu = \nu$.

Definition 6. *The operational semantics of programs satisfies the* **calling module code protection** *property if the application of a closure created in context* ν *produces atoms and closures in the context* ν *only.*

Proposition 1. *The operational semantics of modular logic programs satisfies the called and calling module code protection properties.*

Proof. For the called module code protection property, let us consider the reduction of a qualified atom $\mu : p(t)$ in context ν. Only a modular CSLD or a call transition can apply, producing a goal in context μ'. In the former case, we have $\mu' = \mu$ and either $\mu = \nu$ or p public in μ. In the latter case, we have trivially $\mu = \nu = \nu'$.

For the calling module code protection property, we first remark that the transition rules do not change the context of closures, which thus remain in their context of creation. Given an application of a closure created in context ν, the transition **Apply** is the only applicable rule, and produces a goal in context ν.

4   Logical Semantics

Syntactic module systems have been criticized for their lack of logical semantics [21,23]. Here we provide modular (constraint) logic programs without calls nor closures (abbreviated MCLP), with a logical semantics based on their translation into constraint logic programs. In course, that translation describes an implementation of the module system.

To a given MCLP program $\mathcal{P}$, one can associate a simple module constraint system $\mathcal{M}$, in which the constraint $allow(\nu, \mu, p)$ that states that the predicate p of module μ can be called in module ν, is defined by the following axiom schemas:

$$\frac{\nu \in \Sigma_M \quad p \in \Sigma_P}{\mathcal{M} \models allow(\nu, \nu, p)} \qquad \frac{\nu, \mu \in \Sigma_M \quad (\mu, \mathcal{D}_\mu, \mathcal{I}_\mu) \in \mathcal{P} \quad p \in \mathcal{I}_\mu}{\mathcal{M} \models allow(\nu, \mu, p)}$$

This constraint system depends solely on the interface of the different modules that composes the program $\mathcal{P}$, and not on its implementation.

Then, MCLP programs can be given a logical semantics equivalent to their operational semantics, obtained by a simple translation of pure MCLP($\mathcal{X}$) programs into ordinary CLP($\mathcal{M}, \mathcal{X}$) programs. This translation can be used for the implementation, and shows that the module system can be viewed as simple syntactic sugar. The alphabet $\dot{\Sigma}_P$ of the associated CLP($\mathcal{M}, \mathcal{X}$) program, is constructed by associating one and only one predicate symbol $\dot{p} \in \dot{\Sigma}_P$ of arity $n + 2$ to each predicate symbol $p \in \Sigma_P$ of arity n.

Let Π be the translation of MCLP programs and goals into CLP programs over $\mathcal{M}$, defined in table 2.

Table 2. Formal translation of MCLP($\mathcal{X}$) into CLP($\mathcal{M}, \mathcal{X}$)

$$\Pi \left(\bigcup \{(\mu, \mathcal{D}_\mu, \mathcal{I}_\mu)\} \right) = \bigcup \{\Pi_\mu(\mathcal{D}_\mu)\}$$
$$\Pi (\gamma, \gamma') = \Pi (\gamma), \Pi (\gamma')$$
$$\Pi (\langle \nu - \mu : p(t) \rangle) = \dot{p}(\nu, \mu, t)$$

$$\Pi_\mu \left(\bigcup \{(A \leftarrow c|\alpha)\} \right) = \bigcup \{\Pi_\mu(A \leftarrow c|\alpha)\}$$
$$\Pi_\mu \left(p_0(t) \leftarrow c|\alpha \right) = \dot{p}_0(y, \mu, t) \leftarrow allow(\mu, y, p_0), c|\Pi_\mu(\alpha)$$
$$\Pi_\mu(A, A') = \Pi_\mu(A), \Pi_\mu(A')$$
$$\Pi_\mu(\nu : p(t)) = \dot{p}(\mu, \nu, t)$$

This translation basically adds two arguments to each predicate. The first argument is the calling context and the second is the qualification. The constraint *allow* realizes a dynamic check of accessibility. It is worth noting that for a qualified atom, the contexts are known at compile-time and the accessibility check can be done statically, thereby eliminating any overhead due to the added constraints and to the module system. On the other hand, for the *call* predicate not considered in this section, the *allow* predicate implements a dynamic check, hence with an overhead due to the added constraints.

Proposition 2 (Soundness). *Let $\mathcal{P}$ and $(c|\gamma)$ be a pure MCLP program and a pure MCLP goal*

$$if \ \left((c|\gamma) \ \xrightarrow[MCLP]{\mathcal{P}} \ (d|\gamma') \right) \ then \ \left((c|\Pi(\gamma)) \ \xrightarrow[CLP]{\Pi(\mathcal{P})} \ (d, allow(y, \mu, p), y = \nu | \Pi(\gamma')) \right)$$

for some ν, μ, p and some y is not free in d.

Proof. Let us suppose $((c|\gamma) \xrightarrow[MCLP]{\mathcal{P}} (d|\gamma'))$. Let $\langle \nu - \mu{:}p(\boldsymbol{t}) \rangle$ be the selected atom in γ. Then γ is of the form $(\gamma_1, \langle \nu - \mu{:}p(\boldsymbol{t}) \rangle, \gamma_2)$ for some γ_1 and γ_2. Hence we have $\Pi(\gamma) = (\Pi(\gamma_1), \dot{p}(\nu, \mu, \boldsymbol{t}), \Pi(\gamma_2))$. Now let $(p(\boldsymbol{s}) \leftarrow c'|\alpha)\theta$ be the selected clause in module μ. In such a case whe have, in the translation of $\mathcal{P}$, the clause $(\dot{p}(y, \mu, \boldsymbol{s})) \leftarrow c, allow(y, \mu, p)|\Pi_\mu(\alpha)) \, \theta$. We also have $d = (c, \boldsymbol{t} = \boldsymbol{s}, c')$, $X \models \exists(d)$ and $(\nu = \mu) \vee (p \in \mathcal{I})$. As $(\nu = \mu) \vee (p \in \mathcal{I})$ is true, the constraint $allow(\nu, \mu, p)$ is true in $\mathcal{M}$, hence we have $\mathcal{X}, \mathcal{M} \models \exists d'$ with $d' = (c, (\nu, \mu, \boldsymbol{t}) = (y, \mu, \boldsymbol{s}), c', allow(y, \mu, p))$. Therefore we have $((c|\Pi(\gamma)) \xrightarrow[CLP]{\Pi(\mathcal{P})} (d'|\Pi(\gamma')))$.

Lemma 1. *The functions Π_μ, and Π on goals, are injective.*

Proof. As it is the composition of injective functions, the function Π on goals is injective. For the same reason, the function Π_μ on prefixed atoms, atom sequences and clauses is injective. As Π_μ on modules is the pointwise extension of the injective function Π_μ on clauses, it is injective too.

Proposition 3 (Completeness). *Let $\mathcal{P}$ and $(c|\gamma)$ be pure MCLP program and goal*

$$if \ \left((c|\Pi(\gamma')) \ \xrightarrow[CLP]{\Pi(\mathcal{P})} \ (d|\alpha) \right) \ then \ \left((c|\gamma) \ \xrightarrow[MCLP]{\mathcal{P}} \ (d'|\gamma'') \right)$$

where $\Pi(\gamma'') = \gamma'$ and $d' = (d, allow(y, \mu, p), y = \nu)$ for some ν, μ, p and such that y is not free in d.

Proof. Because Π_μ and Π are injective, we can use their respective inverses Π_μ^{-1} and Π^{-1}. Let us suppose that $((c|\Pi(\gamma)) \xrightarrow[CLP]{\Pi(\mathcal{P})} (d|\gamma'))$. The constraint c does not contain any $allow/3$ constraint since $(c|\gamma)$ is a MCLP goal. Let $q(\boldsymbol{t})$ be the selected atom, $\Pi(\gamma)$ is of the form $(\gamma_1, q(\boldsymbol{t}), \gamma_2)$ for some γ_1 and γ_2. Hence we have $\gamma = \Pi^{-1}(\gamma_1), p(\nu, \mu, \boldsymbol{t}'), \Pi^{-1}(\gamma_2)$ with $q = \dot{p}$ and $t = (\nu, \mu, \boldsymbol{t}')$. Let $q(\boldsymbol{s}) \leftarrow c'|\beta$ be the selected clause. We have $p(\boldsymbol{s}') \leftarrow c''|\Pi_{\mu'}^{-1}(\beta)$ in the implementation of some module μ', with $\boldsymbol{s} = (y, \mu', \boldsymbol{s}')$ and $c'' = c', allow(y, \mu', p)$ where y is fresh. We have $d = (c, c'', allow(y, \mu', p), (\nu, \mu, \boldsymbol{t}') = (y, \mu', \boldsymbol{s}'))$ and $\mathcal{X}, \mathcal{M} \models \exists(d)$. Hence for $d' = (c, c'', \boldsymbol{t}' = \boldsymbol{s}')$, we have $\mathcal{X}, \mathcal{M} \models \exists(d')$. Therefore, for $\alpha = (\Pi^{-1}(\gamma_1), \Pi^{-1}(\beta), \Pi^{-1}(\gamma_2))$, we conclude that $(c|\gamma)$ can be reduced by a clause of $\mathcal{P}$ to $(d'|\gamma'')$ with $\Pi(\gamma'') = \gamma'$.

5   Conclusion

In a paper of D.H.D. Warren [28], the higher-order extensions of Prolog were questioned as they do not really provide more expressive power than meta-programming predicates. We have shown here that the situation is different in the context of modular logic programming, and that module code protection issues necessitate to distinguish between calls and closures.

The module system we propose is close to the one of Ciao Prolog in its implementation. We gave an operational semantics for modular logic programs with calls and closures , and used it to formally prove the full module code protection property. Furthermore, an equivalent logical semantics for modular logic programs without calls nor closures has been provided, showing a translation of modular logic programs into constraint logic programs. The logical semantics of modular calls and closures is currently under investigation in the framework of linear logic concurrent constraint (LCC) programming [10].

This module system has been implemented in GNU-Prolog, and has been used to port some existing code as libraries. The modularization of the Constraint Handling Rules language CHR obtained by porting a Prolog implementation [24] as a library, provides an interesting example of intensive use of the module system, as it allows the development of several layers of constraint solvers in CHR. New libraries are also developed with this module system for making a fully bootstrapped implementation of the LCC language SiLCC [11].

Acknowledgements. We are grateful to Sumit Kumar for a preliminary work he did on this topic, during his summer 2003 internship at INRIA. We thank also Emmanuel Coquery and Sylvain Soliman for valuable discussion on the subject. and Daniel de Rauglaudre and Olivier Bouissou for their comments and help in the implementation.

References

1. S. Abreu and D. Diaz. Objective: in minimum context. In *Proceedings of ICLP'2003, International Conference on Logic Programming*, Mumbai, India, 2003. MIT Press.
2. A. Aggoun and al. *ECLiPSe User Manual Release 5.2*, 1993 – 2001.
3. A. Brogi, P. Mancarella, D. Pedreschi, and F. Turini. Meta for modularising logic programming. In *META-92: Third International Workshop on Meta Programming in Logic*, pages 105–119, Berlin, Heidelberg, 1992. Springer-Verlag.
4. F. Bueno, D. C. Gras, M. Carro, M. V. Hermenegildo, P. Lopez-Garca, and G. Puebla. The ciao Prolog system. reference manual. Technical Report CLIP 3/97-1.10#5, University of Madrid, 1997-2004.
5. M. Bugliesi, E. Lamma, and P. Mello. Modularity in logic programming. *Journal of Logic Programmming*, 19/20:443–502, 1994.
6. D. Cabeza. *An Extensible, Global Analysis Friendly Logic Programming System*. PhD thesis, Universidad Politécnica de Madrid, Aug. 2004.
7. D. Cabeza and M. Hermenegildo. A new module system for Prolog. In *First International Conference on Computational Logic*, volume 1861 of *LNAI*, pages 131–148. Springer-Verlag, July 2000.
8. D. Cabeza, M. Hermenegildo, and J. Lipton. Hiord: A type-free higher-order logic programming langugae with predicate abstraction. In *Proceedings of ASIAN'04, Asian Computing Science Conference*, pages 93–108, Chiang Mai, 2004. Springer-Verlag.

9. W. Chen. A theory of modules based on second-order logic. In *The fourth IEEE. Internatal Symposium on Logic Programming*, pages 24–33, 1987.

10. F. Fages, P. Ruet, and S. Soliman. Linear concurrent constraint programming: operational and phase semantics. *Information and Computation*, 165(1):14–41, Feb. 2001.

11. R. Haemmerlé. SiLCC is linear concurrent constraint programming (doctoral consortium). In *Proceedings of International Conference on Logic Programming ICLP 2005*, Lecture Notes in Computer Science. Springer-Verlag, 2005.

12. C. Holzbaur. Oefai clp(q,r) manual rev. 1.3.2. Technical Report TR-95-09, Österreichisches Forschungsinstitut für Artificial Intelligence, Wien, 1995.

13. International Organization for Standardiztion. *Information technology – Programming languages – Prolog – Part 1: General core*, 1995. ISO/IEC 13211-1.

14. International Organization for Standardiztion. *Information technology – Programming languages – Prolog – Part 2: Modules*, 2000. ISO/IEC 13211-2.

15. J. Jaffar and J.-L. Lassez. Constraint logic programming. In *Proceedings of the 14th ACM Symposium on Principles of Programming Languages, Munich, Germany*, pages 111–119. ACM, Jan. 1987.

16. D. Miller. A logical analysis of modules in logic programming. *Journal of Logic Programming*, pages 79–108, 1989.

17. D. Miller. A proposal for modules in lambda prolog. In *Proceedings of the 1993 Workshop on Extensions to Logic Programming*, volume 798 of *Lecture Notes in Computer Science*, pages 206–221, 1994.

18. L. Monterio and A. Porto. Contextual logic programming. In *Proceedings of ICLP'1989,International Conference on Logic Programming*, pages 284–299, 1989.

19. P. Moura. Logtalk. http//www.logtalk.org.

20. P. Moura. *Logtalk - Design of an Object-Oriented Logic Programming Language*. PhD thesis, Department of Informatics, University of Beira Interior, Portugal, Sept. 2003.

21. R. A. O'Keefe. Towards an algebra for constructing logic programs. In *Symposium on Logic Programming*, pages 152–160. IEEE, 1985.

22. K. Sagonas and al. *The XSB System Version 2.5 - Volume 1: Programmer's Manual*, 1993 – 2003.

23. D. T. Sannella and L. A. Wallen. a calculus for the construction of modular Prolog programs. *Journal of Logic Programming*, pages 147–177, 1992.

24. T. Schrijvers and D. S. Warren. Constraint handling rules and table execution. In *Proceedings of ICLP'04, International Conference on Logic Programming*, pages 120–136, Saint-Malo, 2004. Springer-Verlag.

25. Swedish Institute of Computer Science. *SICStus Prolog v3 User's Manual*. The Intelligent Systems Laboratory, PO Box 1263, S-164 28 Kista, Sweden, 1991–2004.

26. Swedish Institute of Computer Science. *Quintus Prolog v3 User's Manual*. The Intelligent Systems Laboratory, PO Box 1263, S-164 28 Kista, Sweden, 2003.

27. R. R. Víctor Santos Costa, Luís Damas and R. A. Diaz. *YAP user's manual*, 1989–2000.

28. D. H. D. Warren. Higher-order extensions to Prolog: Are they needed? In *Machine Intelligence*, volume 10 of *Lecture Notes in Mathematics*, pages 441–454. 1982.

29. J. Wielemaker. *SWI Prolog 5.4.1 Reference Manual*, 1990– 2004.

A Local Algorithm for Incremental Evaluation of Tabled Logic Programs[*]

Diptikalyan Saha and C.R. Ramakrishnan

Dept. of Computer Science, Stony Brook University, Stony Brook, NY 11794
{dsaha, cram}@cs.sunysb.edu

Abstract. This paper considers the problem of efficient incremental maintenance of memo tables in a tabled logic programming system. Most existing techniques for this problem consider insertion and deletion of facts as primitive changes, and treat update as deletion of the old version followed by insertion of the new version. They handle insertion and deletion using independent algorithms, consequently performing many redundant computations when processing updates. In this paper, we present a local algorithm for handling updates to facts. The key idea is to interleave the propagation of deletion and insertion operations generated by the updates through a dynamic (and potentially cyclic) dependency graph. The dependency graph used in our algorithm is more general than that used in algorithms previously proposed for incremental evaluation of attribute grammars and functional programs. Nevertheless, our algorithm's complexity matches that of the most efficient algorithms built for these specialized cases. We demonstrate the effectiveness of our algorithm using data-flow analysis and parsing examples.

1 Introduction

Tabled resolution [4, 6, 29] and its implementations have enabled the development of applications in areas ranging from program analysis and verification [8, 20, e.g.], to object-oriented knowledge bases [32, e.g.]. Since results of computations are cached, tabling also offers the potential to incrementally compute the changes to the results when a rule or fact in the program changes. Incremental evaluation of tabled logic programs will enable us to directly derive incremental versions of different applications.

The Driving Problem. The problem of incremental evaluation of logic programs is closely related to the view maintenance problem which has been extensively researched, especially in the context of deductive databases [11, 12, e.g.]. Most of these works, including our earlier algorithms [22–24] consider changes to the program only in terms of addition and deletion of facts. An update of a fact is treated as the deletion of the old version followed by the addition of the new version, which may lead to several unnecessary evaluation steps. In contrast, techniques originally from incremental attribute-grammar evaluation [9, 21], treat update as in-place change, and propagate this change. This approach is very restrictive for logic programs, since an update may lead to additions or deletions in general. In-place update techniques for logic programs work only with non-recursive programs, and restrict the changes to "non-key attributes" [27]: i.e. the control

---

[*] This research was supported in part by NSF grants CCR-0205376 and CCR-0311512.

S. Etalle and M. Truszczyński (Eds.): ICLP 2006, LNCS 4079, pp. 56–71, 2006.

```
:- table r/2.
r(X,Y) :- e(X,Y).
r(X,Y) :- e(X,Z), r(Z,Y).

e(1,2).
e(2,3).
e(3,4).
e(4,3).
```

Calls	Answers
r(1,A)	r(1,2), r(1,3), r(1,4)
r(2,A)	r(2,3), r(2,4)
r(3,A)	r(3,4), r(3,3)
r(4,A)	r(4,3), r(4,4)

(a)   (b)

Fig. 1. Example tabled logic program (a), and its call and answer tables (b)

behavior of the program cannot change. However, these update propagation algorithms are optimal when the restrictive conditions are met.

The interesting problem then is to devise an incremental technique for processing additions, deletions as well as updates, which applies to a large class of logic programs, and yet is optimal for the class of programs handled by the in-place update algorithms. We present such a technique in this paper. We give an incremental algorithm that *interleaves* the processing of additions and deletions. When the conditions of in-place update algorithms are met, our algorithm generates matching pairs of additions and deletions which result in optimal change propagation. Our incremental algorithm naturally generalizes those for attribute evaluation [21] and functional program evaluation [1].

An Illustrative Example. Consider the evaluation of query r(1,A) over the program in Figure 1(a). In the program, r/2 defines the reachability relation over a directed graph, whose edge relation is given by e/2. The calls and answers computed by tabled resolution for this query are given in Figure 1(b).

Now consider the effect of changing fact e(2,3) to e(2,4) and treating this change as the deletion of e(2,3) followed by the addition of e(2,4). First, when e(2,3) is deleted, nodes 3 and 4 are no longer reachable from 1 or 2. Thus the answers r(2,3), r(2,4), r(1,3) and r(1,4) are deleted. Subsequently, the addition of e(2,4) makes nodes 3 and 4 again reachable from 1 and 2. Incremental processing of this addition introduces answers r(2,4), r(2,3), r(1,4) and r(1,3).

Updates may lead to deletions or additions in general making in-place update algorithms restrictive. For instance, in the above example, if fact e(2,3) is changed to e(3,2), node 2 becomes reachable from 3 and 4, and nodes 3 and 4 are no longer reachable from 1 or 2. However, a judicious interleaving of additions and deletions can simulate the effect of in-place update wherever possible. For instance, consider the above example again when e(2,3) is changed to e(2,4). Since e(2,3) is changed, we first inspect r(2,X)'s answer table and recalculate results. If we process all changes to r(2,X) first, we will stop the propagation there since there is no net change in r(2,X)'s answers. Hence r(1,3) and r(1,4) will not even be deleted.

Salient Features of Our Approach. We consider definite logic programs where facts as well as rules may be changed between two query evaluation runs. We consider an update as a delete and an insert, but select the order in which they will be processed based on the dependencies between and among the queries and computed answers. We describe data structures and algorithms to process additions bottom-up while using the information about the original queries. Section 2 introduces the data structures used for incremental processing of additions and deletions. Interleaving between the two operations is achieved by decomposing the processing of an addition or deletion into finer-grained operations, and assigning priorities to these operations. Section 3 describes the assignment of priorities and a scheduler to perform the operations in order.

The order in which the operations are performed generalizes the call-graph based orders used in previous incremental algorithms [13, e.g.] where changes are evaluated from topologically lower strongly connected components (SCCs) to higher SCCs in the call graph. As a result, our algorithm inspects the same number of answers in tables (which is a good measure of an incremental algorithm's performance) as algorithms that perform in-place updates. In particular, for non-recursive programs, the order in which operations are performed coincide with the topological order of the call dependencies. Hence our algorithm is optimal for the cases for which optimal update algorithms are known. Moreover the algorithm handles inserts, deletes and updates efficiently, even when the changes affect the control behavior of the program. We explain how our algorithm naturally generalizes incremental evaluation of attribute grammars [21] and functional programs [1] in Section 4. We also present experimental results showing the effectiveness of the algorithm in that section.

In a more general setting when the dependencies may be recursive, our algorithm interleaves insertion and deletion operations even within an SCC in the call graph. It can be shown that our schedule of operations is uniformly better than inserts-first or deletes-first schedules. Our approach is closely related to those used in several incremental program analysis techniques where change propagation is controlled by considering SCCs in a dependency graph. A detailed discussion relating this algorithm to previous work appears in Section 5. Extensions and optimizations of our technique are discussed in Section 6. A more detailed version of this paper with formal aspects of the local algorithm is available as a technical report [26].

2   Data Structures for Incremental Evaluation

We restrict our main technical development to definite logic programs. In Section 6 we describe how to extend these results to general logic programs evaluated under the well-founded semantics. We assume that definitions of only those predicates that are marked as *volatile* may be changed (i.e. with additions, deletions or updates).

In SLG resolution [6], derivations are captured as a proof forest, called *SLG forest* [5]. The SLG forest constructed when evaluating goal $r(1,X)$ over the program in Figure 2(a) is given in Figure 2(e). Each tree in the forest corresponds to a call in the call table. For a given tree of a call, each node corresponds to a step in the derivation of the call. Each edge in the SLG forest arises due to program or answer clause resolution. The leaves of a complete SLG forest of the form $G_0 :- G_1, \ldots, G_n$ represent a failed derivation; the other leaves represent successful derivations of answers. For program given in Figure 2(a) with facts in (b), the tabled call and answers are given in Figure 2(c); and the SLG forest in Figures 2(d) and (e).

Each tree in the SLG forest corresponds to a *generator*; the call associated with the root of a tree is said to be the call of that generator (denoted by *p.call* where p is the generator). Each non-root node in the SLG forest whose selected literal is either tabled or volatile corresponds to a *consumer*, defined formally as follows:

Definition 1 (Consumer). *Let $\mathcal{P}$ be a definite logic program, and F be the SLG forest constructed when evaluating a query Γ over P. Then $c = \langle p, G_0, G_1, [G_2, \ldots, G_n]\rangle$ for some $n \geq 0$ is a consumer iff the SLG tree of generator p in F has a non-root node $G_0 :- G_1, G_2, \ldots, G_n$. The set of all consumers in F is denoted by C_F.*

Note that a consumer carries more information than its corresponding non-root node in the SLG forest. For the rest of this paper we refer to the 'non-root nodes' in the SLG forest and its corresponding 'consumer' interchangeably.

For each edge (n_1, n_2) in the forest, n_1, as well as the clause or answer used in that resolution step are called the *premises* of n_2. For instance, $r(1,X):-r(1,Z),e(Z,X)$ (node c_2) and the answer $r(1,2)$ are premises to $e(2,X)$ (node c_3).

Definition 2 (Support). *A consumer $c \in C_F$ corresponding to a leaf of the SLG forest (i.e. $c = \langle \_, h, true, [] \rangle$) representing a successful derivation of an answer a (i.e. h is a variant of a) is called a* support *of the answer a, denoted as $a = c.answer$ and $c \in a.supports$.*

In Figure 2 (e), the nodes corresponding to the supports are shown as s_i. The various dependencies between the elements of SLG forests are defined below.

Generator-consumer dependencies: If p is a generator and $c = \langle \_, \_, g, \_\rangle \in C_F$ is a consumer such that p is a variant of g, we say p is the generator of the consumer c, denoted by $p = c.generator$ and $c \in p.consumers$.

Consumer-consumer dependencies: For two consumers $c, c' \in C_F$ such that c is a premise of c' we say that $c' \in c.next\_consumer$ and $c = c'.prev\_consumer$.

Answer-consumer dependencies: If an answer a is a premise of a consumer $c \in C_F$ we say that a immediately affects c ($c \in a.imm\_affects$) and c depends on a ($c.depends\_on = a$). For example, s_6 depends on f_4 and f_4 immediately affects s_6.

We assume that the set of all consumers C_F is indexed on its third (goal) component and for constant time access the above defined relations such as *consumers, generator*, etc., are maintained explicitly.

Incremental changes to the facts/rules modify the SLG forest as follows. For instance, consider the insertion of fact $e(4,6)$. Since the goal field of consumer c_5 unifies with this fact, we can add in the SLG forest a child to c_5, say s_8: a support for answer $r(1,6)$. This is a new answer to generator p_1, which gets forwarded to its consumer c_2 [$c_2 \in p_1.consumers$]. The consumption of this answer by c_2 creates a child of c_2, say $c_8 = r(1,A)$:- $e(6,A)$. No further resolution steps are possible and the evaluation stops. Note that we perform only those operations that are needed to change the original forest to include the new fact and its effects.

Now consider the deletion of fact $e(3,4)$ (f_4) from the program in Figure 2. Since the node s_6 in the SLG forest depends on f_4, that node should be deleted. Moreover, we now need to check if the corresponding answer a_3 ($r(1,4)$) is derivable using a different support *independent of* a_3. The Delete-Rederive (DRed) algorithm proposed

```
:- table r/2.
r(X,Y) :- e(X,Y).            % rule 1
r(X,Y) :- r(X,Z), e(Z,Y).    % rule 2
r(X,Y) :- d(X,Z), r(Z,Y).    % rule 3
              (a)
```

```
e(1,2). % f1
e(1,3). % f2          Call: r(1,Y)
e(2,3). % f3          Answers: r(1,2) [a₁]
e(3,4). % f4                   r(1,3) [a₂]
e(2,4). % f5                   r(1,4) [a₃]
e(4,2). % f6                   r(1,5) [a₄]
e(2,5). % f7
     (b)                       (c)
```

$[p_1]$ r(1,A) :- r(1,A). $[s_1]$ r(1,2).
$[c_1]$ r(1,A) :- e(1,A). $[s_2]$ r(1,3).
$[c_2]$ r(1,A) :- r(1,B), e(B,A). $[s_3]$ r(1,3).
$[c_3]$ r(1,A) :- e(2,A). $[s_4]$ r(1,4).
$[c_4]$ r(1,A) :- e(3,A). $[s_5]$ r(1,5).
$[c_5]$ r(1,A) :- e(4,A). $[s_6]$ r(1,4).
$[c_6]$ r(1,A) :- e(5,A). $[s_7]$ r(1,2).
$[c_7]$ r(1,A) :- d(1,B), r(B,A).
              (d)

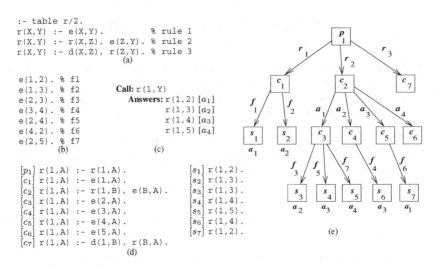

Fig. 2. Example program (a), facts (b), calls and answers (c), nodes in SLG forest (d), and SLG forest (e)

for view maintenance in deductive databases [12] computes the changes in two phases. In the first phase, answers that are derivable from the deleted fact are marked. In the second phase the marked answers that are derivable using only unmarked answers and facts are *rederived* and the marks on such answers are removed. This strategy is also used in incremental analysis such as model checking [28], pointer analysis [33], MOD analysis [34], and data-flow analysis [18]. Following this approach, we mark the support s_6 and hence the answer a_3. In the next step, node c_5 is marked since it depends on a_3. The mark on c_5 propagates to s_7, hence to answer a_1 (r(1,2)), ultimately marking nodes c_3–c_6, s_3–s_7 and answers a_1–a_4. In the second phase, since s_1 and s_2 are unmarked, we remove the marks on answers a_1 and a_2, and consequently nodes c_3–c_6, s_3–s_5, s_7 and answers a_3 and a_4.

Note that when a support is marked, the answer may still have other independent derivations. We can significantly reduce the number of markings by identifying *acyclic* supports: the nodes whose existence is independent of the answer it supports. Using acyclic supports, we can mark an answer a only when all its acyclic supports are marked. Note that the *first* support for an answer constructed by tabled resolution is acyclic; we call this as the *primary* support. We can significantly improve on the DRed strategy using primary supports, as illustrated by the following example. Let us again consider the deletion of fact e(3,4) (f_4) from the program in Figure 2. Deletion of f_4 marks s_6. Note that supports in the figure are listed in chronological order. Marking of s_6 does *not* lead to marking a_3 since its primary support s_4 is still unmarked.

The effectiveness of this heuristic can be improved if we can identify acyclic supports other than the primary support. In [23] we used *derivation lengths* to determine the acyclicity of supports. In this paper we refine and generalize this measure. First, we maintain a *call graph* that captures the dependencies between the generators in an SLG forest, and identify strongly connected components (SCCs) in the graph. If p_1 is independent of p_2 in the call graph (i.e. p_1 does not call p_2), then consumers and answers of

p_1 are independent of those of p_2. We number the SCCs in a topological order so that the independence of two generators can be determined based on their SCC numbers, denoted by $p.scc$ when p is a generator. This permits us to quickly identify independent consumers and answers irrespective of their derivation lengths. Consider again the example given in Figure 1. The call graph SCC consists of two trivial SCCs - $r(1,A)$ and $r(2,A)$ and a non-trivial SCC consists of calls $r(3,A)$ and $r(4,A)$ with SCC $r(2,A)$ topologically lower than SCC $r(1,A)$. This means that call $r(2,A)$ is independent of call $r(1,A)$ and hence we can process changes to $r(2,A)$ before propagating any changes to $r(1,A)$. Note that in this example there is no net change in the answers of $r(2,A)$ and thus we do not even process the call $r(1,A)$. Call-graph SCCs have been used before for localizing change propagation, and serve the same purpose in our algorithm.

Although processing changes within an SCC before propagating its net changes to topologically higher SCCs seems to be fruitful in some cases, it is clearly ineffective for change propagation *within* an SCC. To order change propagation within an SCC, we also associate an *ordinal* with all consumers (analogous to the derivation length) in the evaluation graph. The ordinal and SCC number attributes (*ord* and *scc*, resp.) are defined as follows:

Entity (X)	SCC number ($X.scc$)	Ordinal ($X.ord$)
Answer (a)	$p.scc$ where a is an answer of $p.call$, where p is a generator	$\{s.ord \mid s$ is the primary support of $a\}+1$
Consumer (c)	$p.scc$ where $c = \langle p, h, g, G \rangle$	$max\{c'.ord, Ord, 0\}$, where $c' = c.prev\_consumer$, $a = c.depends\_on$ and $Ord = a.ord$ if $a.scc = c.scc$ and 0 o.w.

A support s of an answer a is acyclic if $s.ord < a.ord$.

The ordinal and SCC numbers are used not only to control the propagation of markings during deletion, but also to interleave operations arising from addition of facts/rules with those from deletion. This is described in detail in the next section.

3   The Local Algorithm

In this section we present the algorithm for maintaining the SLG forest incrementally when facts/rules are added, deleted or updated. The goal of our algorithm is to confine the processing as closely as possible to the part of the SLG forest that is modified by the change. We will measure an algorithm's cost as the total number of answers taken up for processing. Updates are still treated as simultaneous deletes and inserts, but the algorithm interleaves the deletion phase of marking answers and processing of insertion such that it reduces (a) the number of answers marked for deletion and (b) the number of new answers computed only to be subsequently deleted. We illustrate some of the key features of the algorithm using the example given in Figure 2.

Comparison of Inserts-first, Deletes-first Methods.   We notice that neither inserts-first nor deletes-first strategies is uniformly better than the other. Consider the program in Figure 2 after updating fact $e(1,2)$ ($f1$) to $e(1,5)$. This is treated as deleting

$f1$ and inserting a new fact $f8 =$e$(1,5)$. If we process deletion before insertion, we would do the following: (i) mark $a1$ and $a4$ in the deletion phase; (ii) rederive $a1$ and $a4$; and finally (iii) generate $a4$ that can again be derived based on the inserted fact. On the other hand, if we process insertion before deletion we will (i) generate a new acyclic support for $a4$ (derivation based on the inserted fact is shorter than the earlier derivation of $a4$) (ii) mark $a1$ but not mark $a4$ due to presence of the new acyclic support. Thus processing insertion first is better than processing deletion first for this example.

Now consider a different change to the program in Figure 2: deleting e$(1,2)$ ($f1$) and adding e$(2,6)$ ($f9$). Processing insertion before deletion, we will (i) derive a new answer r$(1,6)$ based on r$(1,2)$ and e$(2,6)$; (ii) mark this new answer along with answers $a1$ and $a4$ in the deletion phase (due to deletion of e$(1,2)$); (iii) rederive all three answers since r$(1,2)$ has an alternative derivation. Processing deletion before insertion will mark answers $a1$ and $a4$, and rederive both. Insertion of e$(2,6)$ will generate a new answer r$(1,6)$. For this example, processing deletions first results in fewer operations than processing insertions first.

The above examples indicate that interleaving the deletion and insertion may be better. In fact, if we delete $f1$ and insert $f8$ and $f9$, it is easy to see that the best change propagation strategy will be to process the insertion of $f8$ first, deletion of $f1$ next and insertion of $f9$ last. This key idea is encoded in our algorithm, where the ordering of operations is driven by associating events with each operation and priorities with each event, and processing the events in the order of their priorities.

The Event Model.   Our algorithm is based on the event model where processing insertion of facts/answers is done using the event *consume* and processing deletion of facts is done using three events called *mark*, *may_rederive* and *rederive*. We maintain two priority queues— *ready queue* and *delay queue* for processing events. Events are scheduled only from the ready queue in increasing order of their SCC numbers; thus all events of an SCC are scheduled before processing events of topologically higher SCC. This ensures that change propagation is processed from topologically lower to higher SCCs. The delay queue consists of events that were originally scheduled but later discovered to be needed only under certain conditions; events in the delay queue may be moved back into the ready queue when these conditions are satisfied.

Within an SCC, *mark* and *consume* events have higher priority that *rederive* and *may_rederive* regardless of their ordinals. We process *mark* and *consume* events in ascending order of their ordinals. Among events with the same ordinal, a *mark* event has higher priority over a *consume* event.

Before getting into more detailed description of our algorithm we provide here the key intuition behind interleaving of *mark* and *consume* events. Note that a *mark* event overapproximates the actual answers that need to be deleted, and a *consume* event can generate a support for a new/old answer. Marking of an answer can be avoided if we can generate an acyclic support for the answer using inserted and existed answers, provided the used answers are never going to be marked. The following two requirements guide the design of our local algorithm and choice of ordinals of events and entities.

Requirement 1. *The answers used in generating a new answer or a new support should not be marked in the same incremental phase.*

process_event(e=consume(a,c))	12 is_newanswer=chk_ins_ans(p,a')
1 $c=\langle p,h,g,G\rangle$	13 if(is_newanswer)
2 $\theta=mgu(a,g)$	14 a'.ord=c'.ord+1;
3 g'=head($G\theta$) // g'=true if G is empty	15 $\forall c''\in p.consumer$
4 G'=tail($G\theta$) // G'=null if G is empty	16 if(!marked(c''))
5 a'= hθ //answer generated	17 create_event(consume(a',c''))
6 $c'=\langle p,a',g',G'\rangle$ // new consumer	18 else
7 add c' in c.next_consumer, c'.prev_consumer=c	19 delay_event(consume(a',c''))
8 add c' in a.imm_affects, c.depends_on=a	20 else
9 if(!is_empty(G)) // last subgoal of a clause	21 if($\forall c''\in(a'.supports-\{c'\})$
10 resolve_goal(c')	(c''.ord<a'.ord$\rightarrow$marked(c'')))
11 else	22 if ((c'.ord<a'.ord) &&
12 is_newanswer=chk_ins_ans(p,a)	(e.ord<a'.ord))
//checks if a' is in p.answer_table,if not inserts a'	23 delete_from_readyQ(mark(a'))
	24 else
	25 create_event(may_rederive(a'))

(a)

process_event(mark(a))	event_loop()
1 a.marked=true	1 while((SC=next_scc(CallSCC_Q))
2 $\forall c'$, same_scc(a,c'),	!=NULL)
3 move_to_delay(consume(a,c'))	2 while(!empty(READY_Q,SC))
4 $\forall c\in a.affected \wedge same\_scc(a,c)$	3 event=next_event(READY_Q,SC);
5 if(justmarked(c))	4 process_event(event)
6 $\forall a'$, move_to_delay(consume(a',c))	5 $\forall a$ such that a.scc=SC
7 if(is_leaf(c) $\wedge$ c.ord<c.answer.ord)	6 if(a.marked)
// acyclic support	/* do same operation as in mark
8 if($\forall c'\in$ c.answer.supports-$\{c\}$	event but for different scc */
9 (c'.ord< c.answer.ord$\rightarrow$ marked(c')))	
// all other acyclic supports are marked	
10 create_event(mark(c.answer))	
11 create_event(may_rederive(c.answer))	

(b)   (c)

process_event(rederive(a))	process_event(may_rederive(a))
1 a.marked=false	1 if($\exists c\in a.support$ s.t. !marked(c))
2 $\forall c$, s.t. !marked(c)	2 if($\forall c'\in$ a.support
3 move_to_ready(consume(a,c))	(c'.ord<a.ord$\rightarrow$ marked(c')))
4 $\forall c\in a.affected, same\_scc(a,c) \wedge !marked(c)$	3 a.ord=max{c''.ord $\mid$ c''$\in$
5 $\forall a'$ s.t. !a'.marked,	a.supports,!marked(c'')}+1
6 move_to_ready(consume(a',c))	4 create_event(rederive(a))
7 $\forall c \in a.affected, same\_scc(a,c)$	
8 c.ord = max(c.ord, a.ord)	
// update ordinal of consumers	

(d)   (e)

Fig. 3. Algorithms for processing Consumer Answer (a), Mark (b), Main (c), Rederive (d), May Rederive (e) events

Requirement 2. *Marking and propagation of marking of an answer should be avoided if an acyclic support of the answer is generated due to insertion of facts.*

Insertion.   Generation of a new answer or insertion of a fact/rule generates *consume* events. For instance, when an answer a is added to p's table, we generate a *consume* event for each consumer c of p. The event handler *consume*(a, c) does the work needed to extend the SLG forest when an answer or a fact (a) is consumed by a consumer (c) (Figure 3(a)). If the consumer corresponds to the last subgoal of a rule, the consumption of the answer can generate a new answer (lines 1–9, 12–19), or a new support for an existing answer (lines 1–9, 12, 13, 20–25). Otherwise (i.e. the consumer has a non-empty continuation) it generates a new consumer for the next literal of the clause.

The algorithm in Figure 4 describes processing of the new consumer. The function *call_check_insert(g)* returns the generator of g, creating a generator if one does not already exist. If a new generator were created, we perform program clause resolution by iterating through all the clauses of the program (lines 1–5). Otherwise we iterate through all answers in answer table of g, creating *consume* events for each of them (lines 7–11).

For example, insertion of fact e(1,5) [$f8$] generates the event *consume*$(f8, c1)$ which when processed produces a new acyclic support for the already existing answer $a4$ (lines 1–9, 11–13, 21–25 of Figure 3(a)). On the other hand, insertion of d(1,1) [$f9$] is consumed by the consumer $c7$ to generate a new consumer $\langle p1, r(1,Y), r(1,Y), [] \rangle$ [$c8$] (lines 1–10). Processing of consumer $c8$ by the function *resolve_goal* creates four *consume* events for $c8$ and each of the answers $a1$, $a2$, $a3$, and $a4$ in generator $p1$'s answer table.

Most of the steps of *consume* are common to traditional SLG

```
resolve_goal(c=⟨p,h,g,G⟩)
1  p'=call_check_insert(g)
2  if(is_newgenerator(p')) //g is a new call
3    ∀ rules α:-β₁,β₂ ..., βₙ s.t. (θ=mgu(g,α)!=φ)
4      c'=⟨p',gθ,β₁θ,[β₂θ,...,βₙθ]⟩
       // new consumer
5      resolve_goal(c')
6  else
7    ∀a∈p'.answer_table
8      if(!a.marked)
9        create_event(consume(a,c))
10     else
11       delay_event(consume(a,c))
12   add c in p'.consumer, p'=c.generator
13   calculate_call_graph_incrementally
```

Fig. 4. Algorithm for function *resolve_ goal*

resolution. The interesting aspects are the interaction between the effects of insertion and (possibly scheduled) deletion. For instance, when a new acyclic support c' is generated for an answer a' (line 22, first condition) whose other acyclic supports are already marked (line 21) and *mark*(a') event has been scheduled (line 22, second condition) we remove the *mark*(a') from the ready queue since a' cannot be deleted due to c', meeting Requirement 2.

Mark.   The mark event for an answer marks a given answer and propagates the effect of marking (Figure 3(b)). If an answer is marked we move all *consume* events (in the same SCC) which would consume the answer from the ready queue to the delay queue (lines 2–3). This is due to the fact that if the consumer corresponding to a *consume* event is dependent on a deleted answer then it should not be scheduled (following Requirement 1). The following definitions are used in the marking algorithm:

Definition 3 (Affected set of an answer). *A consumer c is said to be* affected *by an answer a (denoted by $c \in a.affected$) if $c.depends\_on = a$, or $c.prev\_consumer$ is affected by a.*

Definition 4 (Marked consumer). *A consumer c is marked (denoted by $marked(c)$) if either of its premises is marked. A consumer is just marked (denoted by $justmarked(c)$) if there exists one and only one answer 'a' such that a is marked and $c \in a.affected$.*

The consumers in an affected set of an answer are created due to the presence of the answer. Thus, when an answer is deleted, all its affected consumers must be deleted too. Thus when an answer a is marked we move any *consume* event associated with an affected consumer c (in the same call graph component as a) from the ready queue to the delay queue (lines 4–6). When the last acyclic support of an answer gets marked, we mark the answer and place a *may_rederive* event for it in the ready queue (lines 7–11).

Scheduling of Events. We now describe the assignment of event ordinals. Based on Requirement 1, we process a *consume(a, c)* only after processing all *mark(a')* events which can affect the consumer c. To ensure this we make the ordinal of *consume* event no less than the ordinal of its consumer. Additionally we need to ensure that a consumer does not consume an answer which can be potentially marked later on. Firstly, if an answer belongs to topologically lower SCC than its consumer's SCC, the above condition is satisfied as we process all events in components according to their increasing SCC numbering. Secondly, we ensure that a new answer generated can never be marked in the same incremental phase. The only remaining case is when the answer a in the same SCC existed before the incremental phase (function *resolve_goal*, lines 8–11), in which case it can be potentially marked. We ensure that the event is processed after a's marking is processed by making the ordinal of *consume(a, c)* event no less than $a.ord$. The SCC number of *consume(a,c)* is same as $c.scc$ and its ordinal is given by

$$\begin{cases} max\{c.ord, a.ord\} & \text{if } (same\_scc(a,c) \wedge \text{ existed\_answer}(a)) \\ c.ord & \text{otherwise} \end{cases}$$

Moreover, each of *mark(a)*, *may_rederive(a)*, and *rederive(a)* events have SCC number of $a.scc$ and an ordinal of $a.ord$. This assignment of ordinals is critical for the following two properties of the algorithm.

Property 1. If *consume(a, c)* is a scheduled event, then a is never marked in the same incremental phase.

Property 2. If a' is a new answer and s is a support for an unmarked answer generated while processing *consume(a, c)* (lines 14 and 21, Figure 3(a)) then a' and s are never marked in the same incremental phase.

The correctness of our local algorithm is based on the above two properties. Formal proofs of these properties and the correctness of the local algorithm are in [26].

Consider deleting $f1 = e(1,2)$, and inserting $f9 = e(2,6)$ and $f10 = d(1,1)$ to the example in Figure 2. This generates events $e1 = consume(f10, c7)$, $e2 = consume(f9, c3)$, $e3 = mark(a1)$, and $e4 = may\_rederive(a1)$. Although we can process event $e1$ before processing any other event (since $c7$ is not dependent on any answer), we cannot process event $e2$ before processing the mark event $e3$. This is because $c3$ depends on answer $a1$ which may be marked when $e3$ is processed. We ensure this by making a consumer's ordinal no less than that of any answer that affects it.

In the above example, using these ordinal assignments we get $e1.ord = c7.ord = 0$, $e2.ord = c3.ord = a1.ord = 1$, and $e3.ord = e4.ord = a1.ord = 1$. As all four events belong to the same SCC we process $e1$ first which generates four events $e5 = consume(a1, c8)$, $e6 = consume(a2, c8)$, $e7 = consume(a3, c8)$, and $e8 = consume(a4, c8)$. Processing the next event $e3$ moves event $e2$ and $e5$ in the delay queue and generates events $e9 = mark(a4)$ and $e10 = may\_rederive(a4)$. Event $e6$ is processed next without any effect. Event $e9$ is processed next (since it has the lowest priority with ordinal 2) which moves event $e8$ to the delay queue, followed by event $e7$. The ready queue now contains two $may\_rederive$ events ($e4$ and $e10$) and the delay queue contains $e2$, $e5$, and $e8$.

Rederivation. When processing a $may\_rederive(a)$ event, we first check whether the answer a has any unmarked supports left. Subsequently, we make all existing unmarked supports acyclic by raising the ordinal of the answer a to the maximum ordinal of its unmarked supports (Figure 3(e)). We then create $rederive(a)$ event which rederives a and propagates this further. The rederivation of a moves all $consume(a, c)$ events with an unmarked c from the delay queue to ready queue, thereby undoing the effect of marking in a's call-graph component. Furthermore, if any consumer c (in the same SCC as that of a) got unmarked due to rederivation of a then all $consume(a', c)$ events are moved from the delay queue to the ready queue provided a' is unmarked (Figure 3(e)). Rederivation of answer a also updates the ordinal of the support that contains a and belongs to the same call graph SCC as that of a.

In the above example, processing the next highest priority event $e4$ creates an event $e11 = rederive(a1)$ as the answer $a1$ has an unmarked support $s7$ which is made acyclic by updating the ordinal of $a1$ to that of $s7.ord + 1 = 3$. Processing the next event $e11$ rederives $a1$, moves the events $e2$ and $e5$ to the ready queue, updates the ordinals of supports $s3$, $s4$, and $s5$ to 3. Subsequent processing of remaining events does not reveal any other interesting property of the algorithm and is not discussed here.

Figure 3(c) shows the pseudo code for the scheduling of events. After all events of a component are processed, we propagate the effect of marked answers in the component to topologically higher components. Note that the call graph can change during the evaluation. In our algorithm call graph edges are never deleted. Hence only two types of changes in the call graph are possible: (i) the topological order of components are changed without changes in any component (Example 4.3, [26]); and (ii) components are merged into larger components (Example 4.4, [26]). We employ incremental SCC maintenance algorithm of [3, 17] to maintain the call graph SCCs. The correctness of our algorithm depends on the maintenance of an invariant between ordinal numbers of answers and supports within an SCC: that the ordinal of the primary support for an answer is lower than that of the answer itself. Note that it is possible to have an answer

$a1$ whose ordinal is lower than that of its premise answer $a2$ if $a2$ belongs to lower topological component than $a1$. Thus when multiple SCCs are merged, the ordinals of the answers and the supports needs to be redistributed within the merged component (details are omitted; see Example 4.4, [26]).

4   Results

In this section we describe the optimality of the local algorithm for incremental attribute evaluation and incremental functional program evaluation, and present experimental results on its effectiveness.

Optimal Incremental Attribute Grammar Evaluation.   In [21] Reps presented an optimal algorithm for evaluation of non-circular attribute grammars. The dependency between attribute instances are maintained using an acyclic dependency graph which remains static during the change propagation. In such cases, evaluation based on topological order is optimal: i.e. the number of evaluated attributes is of the order of number of changed attributes. The local algorithm presented in this paper shows the same optimal behavior for non-circular attribute grammar evaluation. In this case each update to an attribute instance is performed using a pair of *consume* and *mark* event. When the (acyclic) dependency between attribute instances is represented by the call graph, topological evaluation of call graph SCCs produces optimal change propagation. Otherwise, if the call graph is cyclic (e.g., for left-recursive grammars), the dependencies between answers represent attribute dependencies. In this case topological scheduling of `consume` and `mark` events allows us to obtain the desired optimal behavior.

Optimal Incremental Evaluation of Functional Programs.   We now discuss the optimality of our algorithm when the call graph is acyclic but dynamic. We encounter such graphs when evaluating functional programs (hence non-recursive dependencies) incrementally [1]. We can build an incremental functional program evaluator by writing an interpreter for pure functional programs and evaluating it using our incremental algorithm. Since the call graph is acyclic, evaluation based on topological order suffices. However, since the graph may change over time (due to different outcomes for the conditionals), [1] employs an optimal dynamic topological order maintenance algorithm [10]. When the call graph is acyclic, our incremental topological SCC maintenance algorithm converges to dynamic topological graph maintenance [1]. Thus we obtain the optimal change propagation algorithm for functional programs.

The complexity of the local algorithm for interpreting a pure functional program is no worse than the complexity of the algorithm given in [1]. A formal statement and proof about the correspondence between the local algorithm and functional program evaluation is beyond the scope of this paper. However, we formally state and prove this correspondence in [26].

Experimental Results.   We now present results of experiments aimed at measuring the effectiveness of the local algorithm as well as its overheads. The local algorithm was implemented by extending the XSB logic programming system [31] (ver. 2.7.1).

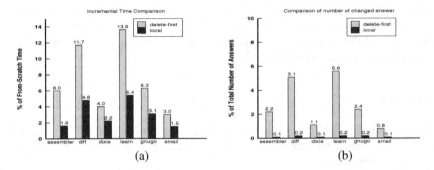

Fig. 5. Reaching Definition Analysis; Time comparison (a); Change comparison (b)

Our implementation, experimental setup, benchmark characteristics, and detailed experimental results on parsing and pointer analysis are available in [26].

We evaluated the effectiveness of the local algorithm by performing reaching definition analysis [2] of C programs which can be easily encoded as a logic program. The incremental change used in these experiments is the deletion of a statement from the C program source. In the data-flow graph, this translates to deletion of all incoming and outgoing edges from the deleted statement, and addition of flow edges from the statement's predecessors to its successors. The local algorithm is expected to perform well in this case, by confining the changes to reaching definitions to the affected region of the graph. We compare the performance of the local algorithm with the that of from-scratch evaluation and that of deletes-first strategy. The deletes-first strategy first performs all marking and rederivations due to deletion before processing insertions. Marking and rederivation phases are performed in each strongly connected component of the call-graph (in topological order) before their effect is propagated to other components in the call graph. Thus comparison of the local and the deletes-first strategy demonstrates the effectiveness of interleaving the processing of deletions and insertions.

For each benchmark we deleted 250 randomly chosen assignment statements from the source. The ratios of the average time taken and the average number of answers processed by the local algorithm and the deletes-first strategy, compared to the from-scratch strategy is shown in Figure 5. Note that the number of inserted and deleted answers is considerably less (8–20 times) for local algorithm compared to deletes-first strategy. Despite the extra overhead of maintaining event priority queues, our preliminary implementation achieves 50–70% reduction in time compared to deletes-first strategy.

In cases where deletes-first strategy is extremely fast, such as flow-insensitive pointer analysis, we notice a maximum run-time overhead of 70% for the local algorithm compared to deletes-first strategy. The local algorithm is optimal for incremental evaluation of parsing problems. In the parsing problem, the time taken for incremental evaluation depends on the position where change occurs in the input string, and some changes may require the entire parse tree to be regenerated. In such cases, when from-scratch evaluation is optimal, we observe that the local algorithm incurs a time overhead of 5% compared to from-scratch evaluation.

5   Related Work

The problem of incremental evaluation of table logic program is closely related to the problem of materialized view maintenance which has been extensively researched (see, e.g. [11, 15] for surveys) in database community. Most of the works in recursive view maintenance generate rules that are similar in spirit to those of DRed [12] and are subsumed by DRed (as compared in [11]). As described in Section 2, DRed marks an answer if any of its support is deleted, thereby over-propagating the effects of a deletion. We significantly reduce the deletion progagation by first using primary supports [22], and later, their generalization to acyclic supports [23]. The space overhead due to the support graphs is mitigated by representing them symbolically [24]. The local algorithm presented in this paper further optimizes and extends the deletion mark propagation: (i) using the effect of insertion of new facts and answers which is very useful in updates where insertion and deletion occur hand-in-hand; and (ii) by scheduling rederivation of answers in each call graph component, ensuring that topologically lower components are stabilized before the effects are propagated to a higher component. In our earlier works, incremental insertion was done by evaluating difference rules [16] (obtained by program transformation) which are evaluated top-down. In contrast, in this paper we presented a combined bottom-up algorithm to handle both insertions and deletions.

Recently, we developed an algorithm for incremental evaluation for arbitrary tabled Prolog programs including those that use Prolog built-ins, cuts, aggregation and non-stratified negation [25]. That algorithm maintained a much coarser dependency structure based on calls. The algorithm presented in this paper maintains finer grained dependency structures based on answers. The results of [25] show that answer-based approaches perform significantly better, but cannot be easily extended beyond pure programs. Moreover, as this paper shows, fine-grained dependencies are needed to achieve or at least approach optimal performance for incremental evaluation. Integrating the fine-grained local algorithm so that it can be deployed wherever applicable within the more general setting of [25] is an interesting open problem.

The idea of using SCC-reduced dependency graphs to optimize propagation of changes has been seen in various past works [7, 13, 14, 19, 30]. Among these, Hermenegildo et. al.'s works [13, 19] on re-analyzing (constraint) logic programs are closest to our work. Our event based description for modeling the main aspects of memoized logic program has been inspired by their work. These papers consider one answer pattern per call, and propagation is controlled based on the call graph. In [19] insertion events are processed in such a way that lower components are stabilized before their effect is propagated to higher ones without explicitly computing the SCCs. However, since the SCCs are themselves dynamic, the event ordering only approximates the SCC ordering. In our approach we maintain call graph SCCs explicitly, similar to [13]. However, we use event ordering to control propagation of changes *within* an SCC, leading to finer-grained interleaving between insertion and deletion operations.

6   Concluding Remarks

We presented an efficient algorithm for incrementally evaluating definite logic programs with the rules/facts of the program being changed: added, deleted, or updated. The key to the algorithm is the interleaving of insertion and deletion operations based on an order that generalizes those based on call dependency graphs. The algorithm naturally generalizes techniques that were developed in settings where dependencies are non-recursive (e.g. attribute grammars, functional programs).

The bottom-up propagation of insertions and deletions enables us to adapt our algorithm to handle programs with stratified negation, processing one stratum at a time, and processing lower strata completely before propagating its effects to the higher ones. We can also extend our technique to handle programs with non-stratified negation under the well-founded semantics as follows. With each consumer, we can keep the delay list containing negative literals [5], mark a negative literal if an answer is added to its corresponding positive literal and resolve the negated literal if all answers are deleted from the positive literal. Note that interleaving of insertion and mark propagation is essential to handle programs with non-stratified negation.

Our algorithm maintains extensive dependency information for propagation of changes. We believe that the space problem due to this can be solved by using techniques such as those used in symbolic support graphs [24].

References

1. U. A. Acar, G. E. Blelloch, and R. Harper. Adaptive functional programming. In *POPL*, pages 247–259. ACM Press, 2002.
2. A. V. Aho, R. Sethi, and J. D. Ullman. *Compilers: principles, techniques, and tools*, pages 585–718. Addison-Wesley, 1986.
3. B. Alpern, R. Hoover, B. K. Rosen, P. F. Sweeney, and F. K. Zadeck. Incremental evaluation of computational circuits. In *Symposium on Discrete algorithms*, pages 32–42, 1990.
4. R. Bol and L. Degerstadt. Tabulated resolution for well-founded semantics. In *ILPS*, 1993.
5. W. Chen, T. Swift, and D. S. Warren. Efficient implementation of general logical queries. *JLP*, 1995.
6. W. Chen and D. S. Warren. Tabled evaluation with delaying for general logic programs. *JACM*, 43(1):20–74, 1996.
7. C. L. Conway, K. S. Namjoshi, D. Dams, and S. A. Edwards. Incremental algorithms for inter-procedural analysis of safety properties. In *CAV*, volume 3576 of *LNCS*, pages 449–461, Edinburgh, Scotland, July 2005.
8. S. Dawson, C. R. Ramakrishnan, and D. S. Warren. Practical program analysis using general purpose logic programming systems — a case study. In *ACM PLDI*, pages 117–126, 1996.
9. A. Demers, T. Reps, and T. Teitelbaum. Incremental evaluation for attribute grammars with application to syntax-directed editors. In *POPL*, pages 105–116. ACM Press, 1981.
10. P. Dietz and D. Sleator. Two algorithms for maintaining order in a list. In *STOC*, pages 365–372, New York, NY, USA, 1987. ACM Press.
11. A. Gupta and I. Mumick. Maintenance of materialized views: Problems, techniques, and applications. *IEEE Data Engineering Bulletin*, 18(2):3–18, 1995.
12. A. Gupta, I. S. Mumick, and V. S. Subrahmanian. Maintaining views incrementally. In *SIGMOD*, pages 157–166, 1993.
13. M. Hermenegildo, G. Puebla, K. Marriott, and P. J. Stuckey. Incremental analysis of constraint logic programs. *ACM Trans. Program. Lang. Syst.*, 22(2):187–223, 2000.
14. L. G. Jones. Efficient evaluation of circular attribute grammars. *ACM Trans. Program. Lang. Syst.*, 12(3):429–462, 1990.
15. E. Mayol and E. Teniente. A survey of current methods for integrity constraint maintenance and view updating. In *ER Workshops*, pages 62–73, 1999.

16. R. Paige and S. Koenig. Finite differencing of computable expressions. *TOPLAS*, 4(3):402–454, 1982.
17. D. J. Pearce and P. H. J. Kelly. Online algorithms for topological order and strongly connected components. Technical report, Imperial College, London, 2003.
18. L. L. Pollock and M. L. Soffa. An incremental version of iterative data flow analysis. *IEEE Trans. Softw. Eng.*, 15(12):1537–1549, 1989.
19. G. Puebla and M. V. Hermenegildo. Optimized algorithms for incremental analysis of logic programs. In *SAS*, pages 270–284, 1996.
20. C. R. Ramakrishnan et al. XMC: A logic-programming-based verification toolset. In *CAV*, number 1855 in LNCS, pages 576–580, 2000.
21. T. Reps. Optimal-time incremental semantic analysis for syntax-directed editors. In *POPL*, pages 169–176, New York, NY, USA, 1982. ACM Press.
22. D. Saha and C. R. Ramakrishnan. Incremental evaluation of tabled logic programs. In *ICLP*, volume 2916 of *LNCS*, pages 389–406, 2003.
23. D. Saha and C. R. Ramakrishnan. Incremental and demand-driven points-to analysis using logic programming. In *PPDP*. ACM Press, 2005.
24. D. Saha and C. R. Ramakrishnan. Symbolic support graph: A space-efficient data structure for incremental tabled evaluation. In *ICLP*, volume 3668 of *LNCS*, pages 235–249, 2005.
25. D. Saha and C. R. Ramakrishnan. Incremental evaluation of tabled prolog: Beyond pure logic programs. In *PADL*, volume 3819 of *LNCS*, pages 215–229. Springer, 2006.
26. D. Saha and C. R. Ramakrishnan. A local algorithm for incremental evaluation of logic programs. Technical report, Stony Brook University, 2006. Available at http://www.lmc.cs.sunysb.edu/~dsaha/local.
27. R. Seljee and H. de Swart. Three types of redundancy in integrity checking; an optimal solution. *Journal of Data and Knowledge Eniginering*, 30:135–151, 1999.
28. O. V. Sokolsky and S. A. Smolka. Incremental model checking in the modal mu-calculus. In *CAV*, volume 818 of *LNCS*, pages 351–363, 1994.
29. H. Tamaki and T. Sato. OLDT resolution with tabulation. In *ICLP*, pages 84–98, 1986.
30. J. A. Walz and G. F. Johnson. Incremental evaluation for a general class of circular attribute grammars. In *PLDI*, pages 209–221, New York, NY, USA, 1988. ACM Press.
31. XSB. The XSB logic programming system. Available at http://xsb.sourceforge.net.
32. G. Yang and M. Kifer. FLORA: Implementing an efficient DOOD system using a tabling logic engine. In *CL 2000*, volume 1861 of *LNCS*, pages 1078–1093, 2000.
33. J. Yur, B. G. Ryder, and W. Landi. An incremental flow- and context-sensitive pointer aliasing analysis. In *ICSE*, pages 442–451, 1999.
34. J. Yur, B. G. Ryder, W. Landi, and P. Stocks. Incremental analysis of side effects for C software system. In *ICSE*, pages 422–432, 1997.

Memory Reuse for CHR

Jon Sneyers*, Tom Schrijvers**, and Bart Demoen

Dept. of Computer Science, K.U. Leuven, Belgium
{jon, toms, bmd}@cs.kuleuven.be

Abstract. Two Constraint Handling Rules compiler optimizations that drastically reduce the memory footprint of CHR programs are introduced. The reduction is the result of reusing suspension terms, the internal CHR constraint representation, and avoiding the overhead of constraint removal followed by insertion. The optimizations are defined formally and their correctness is proved. Both optimizations were implemented in the K.U.Leuven CHR system. Significant memory savings and speedups were measured on classical and well-known benchmarks.

1 Introduction

Constraint Handling Rules (CHR) [4] is a high-level programming language extension based on multi-headed committed-choice rules. Originally designed for writing constraint solvers, it is increasingly used as a general-purpose programming language. We assume the reader to be familiar with CHR [4,5,8].

Recently, we have argued [10] that every algorithm can be implemented in CHR with the best-known asymptotic time and space complexity. The proof sketch of the complexity result of [10] contains the claim that in the RAM machine simulator written in CHR, space can be reused when updating a constraint representing a RAM memory cell. In the current CHR systems this kind of space reuse is not implemented. Instead, new space is allocated for a new memory cell constraint at every update. In this paper, we present two optimizations inspired by compile-time garbage collection techniques. Both optimizations affect a large class of CHR programs, including typical constraint solvers and logical algorithms. They drastically reduce the memory footprint — and hence the task of the garbage collector. As a side effect we get considerable speedups because less instructions are executed and because a lower memory footprint improves the locality of low-level memory accesses, allowing more effective hardware caching.

Section 2 describes the space usage issue and informally explains our new optimizations that tackle it. In Section 3 we present an abstract formal framework that captures the essence of both optimizations, and we prove their correctness. Section 4 discusses implementation choices. Experimental results are presented and explained in Section 5 and we conclude in Section 6.

---

* Research funded by a Ph.D. grant of the Institute for the Promotion of Innovation through Science and Technology in Flanders (IWT-Vlaanderen). This work was also partly supported by F.W.O.-Vlaanderen (projects G.0144.03 and G.0160.02).

** Research Assistant of the Research Foundation - Flanders (F.W.O.-Vlaanderen).

S. Etalle and M. Truszczyński (Eds.): ICLP 2006, LNCS 4079, pp. 72–86, 2006.

2   Motivating Examples and Basic Ideas

Repeatedly replacing a constraint with a new one is one typical pattern that, in current CHR implementations, does not have the space complexity one might expect. The extra space can be reclaimed using garbage collection, but this comes at a cost in execution time. Indeed, CHR programmers often see that more than half of the runtime is spent on garbage collection.

Example 1. Consider the following rules, which show a frequently used pattern to implement imperative variables which can be updated destructively.

```
update(Key,NewValue), item(Key,_) <=> item(Key,NewValue).
update(_,_) <=> write('Error: key not found'), fail.
```

Internally, the following happens: if the **update/2** constraint finds the corresponding 'old' **item/2** constraint, the internal representation of that constraint (which is called the *(constraint) suspension*) is marked 'removed' and it is removed from the constraint store (the suspension becomes garbage), and then a new suspension for the 'new' **item/2** constraint is constructed and the 'new' constraint is inserted into the constraint store. As a result, the space complexity of performing n update operations on one item is not constant as one might hope for, but $O(n)$. The constraint store overhead and the construction of a new suspension can be avoided by performing the updates *in-place*. This results in a speedup and a smaller memory footprint. The above program uses only $O(1)$ space when the updates are performed in-place.

2.1   In-Place Updates

Rules representing updates have the following form:

$$C_1 \setminus C_2, c(\bar{a}), C_3 \quad \texttt{<=>} \quad G \mid B_1, c(\bar{b}), B_2.$$

When the rule is applied, we do not need to remove $c(\bar{a})$ from the constraint store and insert $c(\bar{b})$ into the constraint store. Instead, we can do a direct update on the suspension representing $c(\bar{a})$, updating the constraint arguments in-place.

However, we have to be careful if there are indexes on some argument position(s) for efficient lookups. If all indexed argument positions are the same in $\bar{a}$ and $\bar{b}$, we can avoid all constraint store overhead. Otherwise we have to remove and reinsert the constraint from the indexes on modified argument positions. In many cases, a constraint is indexed on more than one argument, i.e. when different lookup patterns are used. It pays off to do the remove/insert only on the affected indexes — without the in-place update optimization, a full remove/insert would be done.

In many programs, the updates are not as direct as in the above example.

Example 2. Consider the classical **primes** program:

```
candidate(1) <=> true.
candidate(N) <=> N>1 | M is N-1, prime(N), candidate(M).
prime(I) \ prime(J) <=> J mod I =:= 0 | true.
```

In this case, the in-place update optimization is ineffective, since there is no direct update: the second rule inserts `prime/1` constraints which can cause removal of other `prime/1` constraints by the third rule. In general there can be an arbitrary amount of intermediate computations between the removal and the insertion. To tackle this, we propose a generalization of the in-place update optimization, called *suspension reuse*.

2.2   Suspension Reuse

The suspension reuse optimization avoids constructing a new suspension for the new `item/2` constraint by maintaining a cache of old suspensions which can be reused. The time and space gains are typically smaller than in the first optimization, but this optimization has a wider applicability. It works as follows:

When a constraint is removed, its suspension is added to the cache, but it is not (yet) removed from the constraint store. The suspension is marked so it can be skipped when found later in a partner constraint lookup.

When a new constraint is added and a suspension has to be created, an old suspension is extracted from from the cache and its arguments are updated to

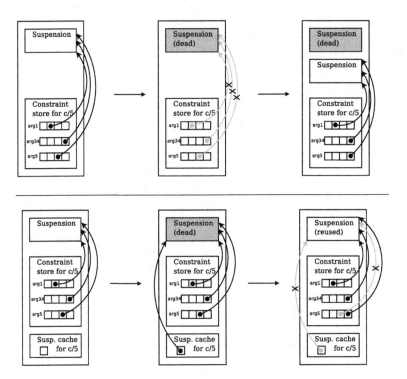

Fig. 1. Without (top) and with (bottom) the suspension reuse optimization. The memory configurations shown are: *initial situation* → *deletion* → *addition of new constraint*.

those of the new constraint. A remove/insert is done only on the indexes that are affected by modified arguments, saving some (or all) constraint-store overhead. Only when the cache is empty, a new term has to be created and a full insert has to be done. Note that it makes sense to restrict the maximum size of the cache. The mechanism is illustrated schematically in Figure 1.

3   Formal Framework

In this section we extend the operational semantics of CHR to capture the reuse of removed constraints in general (Section 3.2). By showing that this extension is equivalent to the original semantics (Section 3.3), and by formulation our optimizations as particular instances of the extension (Section 3.4), correctness follows trivially. But first we briefly recall the refined operational semantics.

3.1   The Call-Based Refined Operational Semantics ω_c

The call-based refined operational semantics ω_c [9] is one of the equivalent formulations of the refined operational semantics of CHR [3] that allows us to easily express our extension. Formally, the execution state of the ω_c semantics is the tuple $\langle G, A, S, B, T \rangle_n$ where G, A, S, B, T, and n represent (respectively) the goal, call stack, CHR store, built-in store, propagation history, and next free identity number. We use $\sigma, \sigma_0, \sigma_1, \ldots$ to denote execution states. An *identified* CHR constraint $c\#i$ is a CHR constraint c associated with some unique integer i. This number serves to differentiate among copies of the same constraint. We introduce functions $chr(c\#i) = c$ and $id(c\#i) = i$, and extend them to sequences and sets of identified CHR constraints in the obvious manner. An *occurrenced* identified CHR constraint $c\#i\!:\!j$ indicates the identified CHR constraint is being considered for matches at occurrence j of constraint c.

The *goal* G is a sequence of CHR constraints and built-in constraints. We use $\square$ to denote the empty sequence, and write it as **true** in programs. The *execution stack* A is a sequence of occurrenced identified CHR constraints. The *CHR store* S is a set of identified CHR constraints. The *built-in constraint store* B contains any built-in constraint that has been passed to the underlying solver. We assume $\mathcal{D}$ is the constraint theory for the underlying solver. The *propagation history* T is a set of sequences, each recording the identities of the CHR constraints which fired a rule, and the name of the rule itself. This is necessary to prevent trivial non-termination for propagation rules. Finally, the *next free identity* n represents the next integer which can be used to number a CHR constraint. Given an initial goal G, the initial state is $\langle G, \square, \emptyset, \emptyset, \emptyset \rangle_1$.

Transition Rules of ω_c. Execution proceeds by exhaustively applying transitions to the initial execution state until the built-in solver state is unsatisfiable or no transitions are applicable. We define transitions from state σ_0 to σ_1 as $\sigma_0 \rightarrowtail_N \sigma_1$ where N is the (shorthand) name of the transition. We let $\rightarrowtail^*$ be the reflexive transitive closure of $\rightarrowtail$ (for all names N). We let $\uplus$ denote multiset union and $+\!\!+$ denote sequence concatenation. Let $vars(o)$ be the variables in

Table 1. The call-based refined operational semantics (ω_c) of CHR

---

1. Solve: $\langle c, A, S, B, T \rangle_n \rightarrowtail_{So} \langle \Box, A, S', B', T' \rangle_{n'}$ where c is a built-in constraint. If $\mathcal{D} \models \bar{\neg}\exists_\emptyset(c \wedge B)$, then $S' = S$, $B' = c \wedge B$, $n' = n$. Otherwise ($\mathcal{D} \models \bar{\exists}_\emptyset(c \wedge B)$), where $\langle S_1, A, S, c \wedge B, T \rangle_n \rightarrowtail^* \langle \Box, A, S', B', T' \rangle_{n'}$ and $S_1 = wakeup\_policy(S, B, c)$ is a subset of S. The exact definition of the wakeup policy depends on the host-language and the specifics of the implementation. It is not important for this paper.

2a. Activate: $\langle c, A, S, B, T \rangle_n \rightarrowtail_A \langle c\#n:1, A, \{c\#n\} \uplus S, B, T \rangle_{(n+1)}$ where c is a CHR constraint which has never been active.

2b. Reactivate: $\langle c\#i, A, S, B, T \rangle_n \rightarrowtail_R \langle c\#i : 1, A, S, B, T \rangle_n$ where $c\#i$ is a CHR constraint in the store (back in the queue through **Solve**).

---

3. Drop: $\langle c\#i : j, A, S, B, T \rangle_n \rightarrowtail_{Dp} \langle \Box, A, S, B, T \rangle_n$ where $c\#i : j$ is an occurrenced active constraint and there is no such occurrence j in P.

---

4. Simplify $\langle c\#i:j, A, \{c\#i\} \uplus H_1 \uplus H_2 \uplus H_3 \uplus S, B, T \rangle_n \rightarrowtail_{Si} \langle \Box, A, S', B', T'' \rangle_{n'}$ where $\langle \theta(C), A, H_1 \uplus S, \theta \wedge B, T' \rangle_n \rightarrowtail^* \langle \Box, A, S', B', T'' \rangle_{n'}$ where the jth occurrence of CHR constraint c is d_j in rule $r \in P$ of the form $H_1' \setminus H_2', d_j, H_3' \iff g \mid C$ and there exists a matching substitution θ such that $c = \theta(d_j)$, $chr(H_x) = \theta(H_x')$ for $x \in \{1, 2, 3\}$, and $\mathcal{D} \models B \rightarrow \bar{\exists}_{vars(r)}(\theta \wedge g)$, and the tuple $h = (id(H_1) + [i] + id(H_2) + id(H_3) + [r]) \notin T$. The substitution θ must also rename apart all variables appearing only in g and C. In the intermediate transition sequence $T' = T \cup \{h\}$. If no such matching substitution exists then $\langle c\#i:j, A, S, B, T \rangle_n \rightarrowtail_{Si} \langle c\#i:j + 1, A, S, B, T \rangle_n$

---

5. Propagate $\langle c\#i : j, A, \{c\#i\} \uplus S, B_0, T_0 \rangle_{n_0} \rightarrowtail_P \langle G, A, S_k, B_k, T_k \rangle_{n_k}$ where the jth occurrence of c is d_j in rule $r \in P$ of the form $H_1', d_j, H_2' \setminus H_3' \iff g \mid C$. Let $S_0 = S \uplus \{c\#i\}$. Now assume, for $1 \leq l \leq k$ and $k \geq 0$, we have subderivations

$$\langle C_l, [c\#i:j|A], H_{1l} \uplus \{c\#i\} \uplus H_{2l} \uplus R_l, B_{l-1}, T_{l-1} \cup \{t_l\} \rangle_{n_{l-1}}$$
$$\rightarrowtail^* \langle \Box, [c\#i:j|A], S_l, B_l, T_l \rangle_{n_l}$$

where $\{c\#i\} \uplus H_{1l} \uplus H_{2l} \uplus H_{3l} \uplus R_l = S_{l-1}$ and there exists a matching substitution θ_l such that $c = \theta_l(d_j)$, $C_l = \theta_l(C)$, $chr(H_{xl}) = \theta_l(H_x')$ for $x \in \{1, 2, 3\}$, $\mathcal{D} \models B_{l-1} \rightarrow \bar{\exists}_{vars(\theta_l(r))}\theta_l(g)$, and $t_l = id(H_{1l}) + [i] + id(H_{2l}) + id(H_{3l}) + [r] \notin T_{l-1}$ where θ_l renames apart all variables only appearing in g and C (separately for each l). Furthermore, for $k + 1$ no such transition is possible. The resulting goal G is either $G = \Box$ if $\mathcal{D} \models \bar{\neg}\exists_\emptyset B_k$ (i.e. failure occurred) or $G = c\#i:j + 1$ otherwise.

---

6. Goal $\langle [c|C], A, S, B, T \rangle_n \rightarrowtail_G \langle G, A, S', B', T' \rangle_{n'}$ where $[c|C]$ is a sequence of built-in and CHR constraints and $\langle c, A, S, B, T \rangle_n \rightarrowtail^* \langle \Box, A, S', B', T' \rangle_{n'}$ and $G = \Box$ if $\mathcal{D} \models \bar{\exists}_\emptyset(\neg B')$ (i.e. calling c caused failure) or $G = C$ otherwise.

---

object o. We use $\exists_{\{v_1,\ldots,v_n\}}$ to mean $\exists v_1 \cdots \exists v_n$. We use $\bar{\exists}_V F$ to mean $\exists_{vars(F)\setminus V}$, that is quantifying all variables not in V. Table 1 lists the transitions.

The ω_c semantics allows different execution strategies: many transitions may be applicable and transitions may have different results, e.g. depending on the order in which the combinations of partner constraints are tried.

We also allow the following transition to remove redundant history tuples:
Applying this transition clearly does not affect a derivation.

> **7. CleanHistory:** $\langle G, A, S, B, T \cup \{t\}\rangle_n \rightarrowtail_{CH} \langle G, A, S, B, T\rangle_n$ if there is an identifier in t which is not the identifier of any constraint in S.

Note that the execution strategy implemented in the K.U.Leuven CHR system is an *instance* of the above semantics: In our CHR implementation, the propagation history is only checked and updated when applying a propagation rule. Simplification rules and simpagation rules cannot be applied twice to the exact same constraints, since at least one of the head constraints is removed after the first application. We can simulate this behavior by applying the **CleanHistory** transition after every constraint-removing rule. Also, in our implementation, the propagation history is maintained in a distributed way: suspensions contain history tuples added when the constraint they represent was active. As a result, when a constraint is removed and its suspension becomes garbage, the corresponding tuples are automatically removed from the propagation history. This corresponds to applying **CleanHistory** a number of times.

3.2 The Extended Call-Based Refined Operational Semantics ω_c'

We now allow the store to contain *dead* constraints, which are removed and cannot be used to match the head constraints of a rule. A dead constraint c with identifier i is denoted as $\dagger c \# i$. When X is a set of (non-dead) constraints, we write $\dagger X$ to denote $\{\dagger x \mid x \in X\}$. The *extended* call-based refined operational semantics ω_c' is obtained by extending ω_c with the transitions listed in Table 2.

3.3 Equivalence of ω_c and ω_c'

It is clear that every ω_c derivation is also a valid ω_c' derivation, since ω_c' is an extension of ω_c. We will now prove that every ω_c' derivation (denoted with $\rightarrowtail_{c'}^*$) can be mapped to an ω_c derivation (denoted with $\rightarrowtail_c^*$).

Definition 1. *Given an execution state* $\sigma = \langle G, A, S_l \uplus \dagger S_d, B, T\rangle_n$ *where* S_l *contains no dead constraints. The* **visible part** *of* σ *is* $\Psi(\sigma) = \langle chr(S_l), B\rangle$.

Definition 2. *Two execution states* σ_1 *and* σ_2 *are* **indistinguishable** *if and only if* $\Psi(\sigma_1) = \Psi(\sigma_2)$. *We denote this by* $\sigma_1 \cong \sigma_2$.

Theorem 1. *Suppose* σ_0 *is an initial execution state. If* $\sigma_0 \rightarrowtail_{c'}^* \sigma_1$, *then a* σ_2 *exists such that* $\sigma_0 \rightarrowtail_c^* \sigma_2$ *and* $\sigma_1 \cong \sigma_2$.

Proof. If the **ReuseID** transition is not used in the ω_c' derivation, we can derive σ_2 from σ_0 in ω_c by replacing every **Reuse** by a corresponding **Activate**, **Simplify'** by a corresponding **Simplify**, **Propagate'** by a corresponding **Propagate** and removing all **RemoveDead** transitions from the original $\sigma_0 \rightarrowtail_{c'}^* \sigma_1$ derivation. The only difference between σ_1 and σ_2 is in their CHR stores S_1 and S_2: it is easy to see that $S_2 \subseteq S_1$ and that $S_1 \setminus S_2$ contains only dead constraints. Hence the result trivially holds in this case.

Table 2. The additional transitions of ω_c'

2c. Reuse: $\langle c, A, \{\dagger c'\#i\} \uplus S, B, T\rangle_n \rightarrowtail_R \langle c\#n : 1, A, \{c\#n\} \uplus S, B, T\rangle_{(n+1)}$ where c is a CHR constraint which has never been active.

2d. ReuseID: $\langle c, A, \{\dagger c'\#i\} \uplus S, B, T\rangle_n \rightarrowtail_{Rid} \langle c\#i : 1, A, \{c\#i\} \uplus S, B, T\rangle_n$ where c is a CHR constraint which has never been active and $\forall t \in T : i \notin t$.

4b. Simplify': $\langle c\#i : j, A, \{c\#i\} \uplus H_1 \uplus H_2 \uplus H_3 \uplus S, B, T\rangle_n \rightarrowtail_{Si} \langle \square, A, S', B', T'''\rangle_{n'}$ where $\langle \theta(C), A, H_1 \uplus \dagger(\{c\#i\} \uplus H_1 \uplus H_2) \uplus S, \theta \wedge B, T'\rangle_n \rightarrowtail^* \langle \square, A, S', B', T'''\rangle_{n'}$ and with the other conditions as in the usual **Solve** transition.

5b. Propagate': Defined exactly as the usual **Propagate** transition, except that the series of subderivations is now

$$\langle C_l, [c\#i : j | A], H_{1l} \uplus \{c\#i\} \uplus H_{2l} \uplus \dagger H_{3l} \uplus R_l, B_{l-1}, T_{l-1} \cup \{t_l\}\rangle_{n_{l-1}}$$
$$\rightarrowtail^* \langle \square, [c\#i : j | A], S_l, B_l, T_l\rangle_{n_l}$$

---

8. RemoveDead: $\langle G, A, \{\dagger c\#i\} \uplus S, B, T\rangle_n \rightarrowtail_{RD} \langle G, A, S, B, T\rangle_n$

If the **ReuseID** transition is used r times, we compute an identifier permutation $\mu = \mu_r$ as follows. Let μ_0 be the identical permutation. We look at every **ReuseID** transition in the ω_c' derivation from σ_0 to σ_1, in order. If the k-th **ReuseID** transition is $\langle c, A, \{\dagger c'\#i\} \uplus S, B\rangle_n \rightarrowtail_{Rid} \langle c\#i : 1, A, \{c\#i\} \uplus S, B\rangle_n$, we let $\mu_k(m) = \mu_{k-1}(m)$ for all $m < n$ and $m \neq i$, $\mu_k(i) = \mu_{k-1}(n)$, and $\mu_k(m) = \mu_{k-1}(m+1)$ for all $m \geq n$. Since the reused identifier i does not occur in the propagation history (by definition of the transition), it will uniquely identify the activated constraint just like the fresh identifier n. Hence, replacing the **ReuseID** transition by a **Reuse** transition does not affect the rest of the derivation. By applying the previous case on $\sigma_0 \rightarrowtail_{c'}^* \mu(\sigma_1)$, we get a σ_2 such that $\sigma_0 \rightarrowtail_c^* \sigma_2$ and $\sigma_2 \cong \mu(\sigma_1)$. From $\sigma_2 \cong \mu(\sigma_1)$ and $\mu(\sigma_1) \cong \sigma_1$ (identifier permutations clearly do not affect the visible part) we can conclude $\sigma_1 \cong \sigma_2$. $\square$

3.4   Defining the Optimizations

Definition 3 (Suspension reuse). *Suspension reuse with maximum cache size n corresponds to the following ω_c' execution strategy: always perform the **Simplify'** and **Propagate'** transitions (instead of **Simplify** and **Propagate**), followed by **RemoveDead** transitions until there are no more than n dead constraints with the same predicate name in the store. Furthermore, the **Activate** transition is only applied when **Reuse** or **ReuseID** are not applicable.*

Definition 4 (In-place updates). *Performing an updates in-place corresponds to the following ω_c' execution strategy: if the goal is an occurrenced constraint and the corresponding rule is of the form "$C_1 \setminus C_2, c(\bar{a}), C_3$ <=> $G \mid B_1, c(\bar{b}), B_2$." (as in Section 2.1), then perform the **Simplify'** and **Propagate'** transitions (not the **Simplify** and **Propagate** transitions). In the subderivation for the rule body (as-*

suming the rule fired), the removed constraint $c(\bar{a})$ is reused in a **Reuse** *or* **ReuseID** *transition when the goal is $c(\bar{b})$.*

Both optimizations are defined as an execution strategy which instantiates the ω_c' semantics. Because of Theorem 1, this implies that the optimizations are correct with respect to the visible part of CHR.

4   Implementation

In this section we describe our implementation of the new optimizations in the K.U.Leuven CHR system [1] for hProlog [2] and discuss some of the implementation choices and complications. More information on the compilation schema used in the reference CHR system [5], on which the K.U.Leuven CHR system was based, can be found in [8] (in particular: Chapters 2, 4, 5 and 6). We intend to port the optimizations to the K.U.Leuven CHR system for SWI-Prolog.

4.1   Constraint Representation

The following internal representation is used for a constraint:

$$\texttt{suspension(ID,MState,Continuation,MHistory,C,}X_1,\dots,X_n)$$

The representation is a term with functor `suspension` and a number of fields (or arguments). Note that its arity depends on the arity of the constraint it represents. This term representation is called *constraint suspension* or *suspension* for short. The meaning of the fields is listed in Table 3.

Table 3. Meaning of the constraint suspension fields

ID	The unique constraint identifier. In practice it is an integer.
MState	The state of the suspension. It takes one of three values:
	not_stored The constraint is not yet stored. (this value is used for the *late storage* optimization)
	stored The constraint is stored in the CHR constraint store.
	removed The constraint is removed from the store.
	limbo The constraint is removed, but still in the store. (this value is used for the new optimizations)
Continuation	The continuation goal to be executed during a **ReActivate** transition. This calls the code for the first occurrence.
MHistory	Part of the propagation history.
C	The constraint functor.
$X_1,\dots,X_n$	The arguments of the constraint.

Some of the fields in the term are mutable; this is indicated with the initial capital M in their name. The other fields remain constant during the lifetime of a constraint, although we may have to update all fields when the suspension

is reused. It is possible that a constraint is removed while somewhere in the
execution stack, its suspension occurs in the iterator returned by a universal
lookup. To prevent such a removed constraint from being used later on as a
partner constraint, the `MState` field in the suspension is updated to `removed`
when a constraint is removed, and only suspensions with the field set to `stored`
are accepted as candidate partner constraints.

4.2   Suspension Reuse

In our implementation we use cache size 1, which allows easy and efficient cache
manipulation and minimal space overhead. For every constraint we maintain a
global variable, which is initialized to an atom representing an empty cache.
When a constraint is removed, the variable is checked: if it is empty, it is overwritten with the suspension term; otherwise, the usual remove is performed. In
both cases, the suspension state is set to `removed`. When a suspension term is
constructed for some constraint, the global variable is checked: if it is empty, the
usual term construction is done; otherwise the suspension in the global variable
is reused and the global variable is updated to the empty atom.

To reuse a suspension term, the fields for the constraint arguments must be
updated. The constraint functor field can be left untouched. There may be other
fields that have to be overwritten. We use the *backtrackable* hProlog built-in
`setarg/3` (modifies one argument of a term) to update suspension term fields and
`b_setval/2` (modifies a global variable) to implement the cache. Although CHR
rules are committed-choice, choice-points can be left by host-language predicates
that are called in the rule bodies or that call CHR constraints, so it is important
to use backtrackable versions of those destructive update built-ins.

Fields to Overwrite. Note that in general it requires an inspection of the
entire constraint store — which is very expensive — to check whether keeping
the old identifier is safe. For this reason our implementation uses the following
approximation: If the constraint occurs in a multi-headed propagation rule with
at least one (other) active head, the identifier field is always overwritten with a
fresh identifier (this corresponds to applying the **Reuse** transition). Otherwise,
the propagation history tuples in which the old identifier occurs are all stored
in the cached (dead) suspension. If the suspension term field storing the partial
history is updated in any part of the generated code, we overwrite it with a term
representing an empty partial history (corresponding to a (series of) **CleanHistory** transition). We can reuse the old identifier (the **ReuseID** transition), since
it no longer occurs in the propagation history.

One final subtle implementation issue is the following. If the constraint has
an active kept occurrence in a rule with a body which might cause the removal
and reuse of the active constraint, we have to make sure that we detect this at
the return from the body, so we can avoid incorrectly calling the continuation
of a removed constraint. If the active constraint is removed, but not reused, it
suffices to check the state field before calling the continuation. However, if it
is reused after removal, the state field will have reverted, rendering that check

ineffective. To solve this issue, we also check after executing the body whether the constraint identifier is unmodified. To make sure the test is effective, we never use the **ReuseID** transition for such constraints.

4.3   In-Place Updates

If all occurrences of the in-place updated constraint are passive, it suffices to update the suspension term as above and update the affected parts of the constraint store. The potentially modified arguments are determined statically by comparing the arguments of the removed head constraint and the arguments of the constraint call in the body. For every potentially affected index, we test at run-time whether the index position has changed and do a remove and reinsert from that index if it has. If the part of the body before the insertion (B_1 in Section 2.1) does not observe the removal of the updated constraint (e.g. if it is empty or a conjunction of safe host-language built-ins), then we do not have to set the MState field of the suspension to removed before executing B_1 and restore it to stored afterwards. This is related to observation analysis [9].

If there are non-passive occurrences of the updated constraint, we call the predicate for the first occurrence after the updates are performed.

There is a choice in how to do the updates if there is more than one removed head constraints or more than one body constraint with the same functor and arity. In our current implementation we simply match the i-th removed constraint with the i-th inserted constraint, which is a simple but suboptimal strategy. Consider the rule "a(A,C) \ b(A,B), b(C,D) <=> b(C,C), b(A,A)." where the constraint $b/2$ is indexed on its first argument. If b(A,B) is updated to b(A,A) and b(C,D) is updated to b(C,C), no index is affected and only two arguments have to be updated, which clearly is optimal. The simple matching strategy has two affected indexes and four arguments to be updated.

4.4   Interference with Late Storage

The late storage optimization [9] may delay the creation of a suspension term and the insertion into the constraint store, so overhead is avoided if the constraint is removed before the suspension creation or before the constraint store insertion.

Late Storage and Suspension Reuse. For the suspension reuse optimization, we want to maintain the invariant that cached suspensions are in the data structure implementing the constraint store. Hence, if a constraint is removed after its suspension term has been created but before it has been inserted into the data structure, we do not put it in the cache.

To cooperate with the late storage optimization, we delay the constraint store update until the late insertion program point. If that point is at a later occurrence than the suspension creation, we need to distinguish between a fresh suspension (which needs a full insert) and a reused suspension (which needs an in-place store update). This is done by adding a new suspension state "limbo", which mostly acts like not_stored, except at insertion and early removal. The constraint arguments are not yet updated at the point of suspension reuse, but the reused suspension's state is set to limbo. At insertion, we still have the old arguments in the suspension term, so we can compare them to the new arguments to do an in-place store update. If the constraint is removed early, i.e. before the insertion point, we have to remove the old suspension from the store.

Late Storage and In-Place Updates. Late storage also interferes with the in-place update optimization. If the suspension is not created before the first occurrence, we can not simply call the predicate for the first occurrence. The reason is that at some point in that subcomputation, a suspension might be created and the constraint might be stored *again*, which would duplicate the constraint. To solve that problem, we generate additional clauses with a different predicate name. In the additional clauses, the late storage optimization is disabled, preventing a second suspension creation and constraint insertion. Note that adding clauses can almost double the code size, which may have some negative effect on the runtime because it may affect hardware caching.

When an in-place update is performed, the old suspension is updated and the stores are updated. Without in-place updates we would remove the old constraint and call the new one. If the new constraint is removed before it is stored, the overhead of insertion and removal is avoided by late storage. Hence, without in-place updates we only do one full remove in this case. With in-place updates, we do an in-place store update (a partial remove and partial insert) followed by a full remove (of the new constraint). As a result, when late storage is involved, there is only a performance gain if the new constraint is not removed early.

5   Experimental Results

We now present an evaluation of the optimizations introduced in the previous sections. All tests were performed on a Pentium 4 (1.7 GHz) with 512 MB RAM (cpu cache size: 256 KB) running Debian GNU/Linux (kernel version 2.6.8) with a low load. We used the K.U.Leuven CHR system in hProlog 2.4.23. The benchmarks can be downloaded at [1] and some are discussed in more detail in [11]. We used a sufficiently large initial heap size so no garbage collection is performed, allowing accurate memory usage statistics. Note that in a realistic setting, a reduction in memory use implies less garbage collection, which results in further speedups. Table 4 lists the results.

We can drastically improve performance of the generated code by inlining and specializing calls to the auxiliary predicates for suspension term construction, removal, and lookup. This saves time and space, for reasons explained in [11]. We evaluate the new optimizations with inlining enabled, which means it is harder for them to look good since much of the overhead avoided by the optimizations is reduced by inlining.

5.1   Suspension Reuse

Suspension reuse introduces some runtime overhead for maintaining the suspension cache. If the dynamic behavior of the program is such that the cache is

Table 4. Benchmark results. The first column shows the benchmark name and problem size. Columns two, three and four indicate which optimizations were enabled: the abbreviations denote respectively *Inlining*, *Suspension reuse*, and *In-place updates*. The fifth column shows the relative ratio of suspension cache hits at suspension creation (only applies when suspension reuse is enabled). The next four columns list the runtime (in seconds), the total amount of (heap+trail) memory used (in 4-byte cells), and percentages indicating relative time and memory use. The last column contains some comments on case-specific properties of the optimizations: whether the (most important) in-place updated constraint has active occurrences ("active occs") for which additional clauses had to be generated ("new clauses"), the number of potentially modified indexed arguments ("index-args"), the number of in-place updates in the generated code ("inpl. upd."), and whether the propagation history ("history reset") and the constraint identifier ("new identifier") suspension fields need to be updated.

Benchmark	Inl	SR	IU	Hits	Runtime	Memory	%time	%mem	Notes
`bool_chain`					20.78	1756826	233.7%	101.6%	
(1000)	✓				8.89	1728326	100.0%	100.0%	
	✓	✓		0%	9.93	1726263	111.7%	99.9%	
`fib_heap`					7.16	61992261	141.2%	198.3%	
(dijkstra)	✓				5.07	31256958	100.0%	100.0%	active occs
(65536)	✓	✓		78%	5.39	24064894	106.3%	77.0%	new clauses
	✓		✓		5.22	29730416	103.0%	95.1%	3 index-args
	✓	✓	✓	72%	5.60	24111191	110.5%	77.1%	(4 inpl. upd.)
`inference`					0.111	160057	111.0%	111.3%	history reset
	✓				0.100	143831	100.0%	100.0%	new identifier
	✓	✓		14%	0.105	139958	105.0%	97.3%	active occs
	✓		✓		0.100	143161	100.0%	99.5%	25 index-args
	✓	✓	✓	9%	0.104	140427	104.0%	97.6%	(17 inpl. upd.)
`primes`					21.23	40924601	129.5%	100.5%	
(10000)	✓				16.39	40734620	100.0%	100.0%	
	✓	✓		50%	6.73	16138562	41.1%	39.6%	
`ram_simul`					12.41	88003112	149.7%	293.3%	
(1000000)	✓				8.29	30002947	100.0%	100.0%	
	✓	✓		100%	6.19	6002961	74.7%	20.0%	no active occs
	✓		✓		5.13	2961	61.9%	0.0%	no index-args
	✓	✓	✓	0%	5.23	2961	63.1%	0.0%	(8 inpl. upd.)
`sudoku`					130.28	112483	118.9%	121.8%	
(283576	✓				109.60	92387	100.0%	100.0%	
solutions,	✓	✓		100%	107.42	23329	98.0%	25.3%	no active occs
27 givens)	✓		✓		60.89	20515	55.6%	22.2%	no index-args
	✓	✓	✓	0%	63.65	20187	58.1%	21.9%	(3 inpl. upd.)
`union-find`					8.85	66611812	132.9%	154.9%	new identifier
(200000)	✓				6.66	43013248	100.0%	100.0%	active occs
	✓	✓		52%	5.94	32302433	89.2%	75.1%	new clauses
	✓		✓		5.14	29064918	77.2%	67.6%	3 index-args
	✓	✓	✓	0%	5.41	28664915	81.2%	66.6%	(8 inpl. upd.)
`zebra`					0.181	41904	116.0%	131.8%	
	✓				0.156	31798	100.0%	100.0%	
	✓	✓		97%	0.148	26407	94.9%	83.0%	active occs
	✓		✓		0.131	24915	84.0%	78.4%	no index-args
	✓	✓	✓	38%	0.136	24625	87.2%	77.4%	(2 inpl. upd.)

(almost) always empty at suspension creation, i.e. if there are few cache hits and many cache misses, we do not get time or memory benefits. Examples like **bool_chain** and **inference** show that the time overhead can be more than 10%. Although there are many cache hits in the **fib_heap** benchmark, the runtime still increases. This seems to be because the constraint stores used in **fib_heap** (the singleton store and the array store) provide very cheap insertion and removal. The overhead of maintaining the suspension cache and dynamically checking for affected indexes is simply higher than the cost of the avoided store operations. In the other benchmarks, suspension reuse results in a net gain in both time and space. The speedup is typically between 5 and 25 percent, but can be as high as 59%. The space reduction is more than 60% in some benchmarks.

5.2   In-Place Updates

In-place updates are not always applicable: the **bool_chain** and **primes** programs do not contain any rule of the required form. However, when they are, the time and space gains are quite impressive. In the **ram_simul** benchmark, all space usage is eliminated from the main loop, reducing the space complexity from linear to constant. In other examples, space gains are typically between 20 and 30 percent. Speedups are typically between 15 and 40 percent. There are more gains if the updated constraint has no active occurrences and if there are few indexes that are affected by the update. For example, compare the **sudoku** and **ram_simul** benchmarks to the **fib_heap** and **inference** benchmarks. In the former, no indexes are affected and there are no active occurrences, resulting in a 40% speedup and a 80% memory reduction (100% in the case of **ram_simul**). In the latter, there is a small slowdown and only a marginal reduction in memory use. Because of the active occurrences, the effect of the late storage optimization is largely lost. If almost all indexes are affected, the update that replaces the remove and insert can be as expensive as a full remove and insert.

When combining in-place updates and suspension reuse, the number of cache hits drops: many in-place updates 'steal' a hit. As a consequence, the overhead of suspension reuse often outweighs the gains if (many) in-place updates are done. A simple heuristic could be added to avoid this.

The operational CHR semantics leaves the order in which partner constraints are tried unspecified. Programs should not depend crucially on the order used in some specific CHR system. Both suspension reuse and in-place updates can affect this order. For some programs, the impact on the search space results in unexpected performance differences. An example is the **sudoku** benchmark with a different initial board setup (2 solutions, 16 givens), where in-place updates result in a *slowdown* of 46%, while suspension reuse results in a *speedup* of 64% — both effects are mostly caused by the different order. The new order can in principle be arbitrarily better or worse than the original one. Of all programs listed in Table 4, only **sudoku** and **inference** are affected. For the query instances listed in the table, the search space is unchanged or slightly bigger when the partner constraint order is modified by the optimizations. Sophisticated analyses and/or heuristics could be conceived to improve the order.

6   Conclusion

As far as we know, this is the first paper that proposes techniques specifically aimed at improving the memory footprint of CHR programs. By inlining and specializing some crucial parts of the generated code we already achieved a dramatic improvement in both time and space. However, our main contribution is twofold: we have provided a general formal framework that allows us to formulate and reason about reuse of removed constraints at an abstract level, and we have introduced two new optimizations, *in-place updates* and *suspension reuse*, and proved their correctness. We have implemented both optimizations in the K.U.Leuven CHR system, which revealed that they interfere with the existing *late storage* optimization. This interference complicates the implementation and it also decreases the effect of in-place updates. Experimental results indicate that both optimizations can cause small slowdowns in some benchmarks and big speedups in others. The memory footprint is improved in all benchmarks — sometimes only marginally, often significantly.

Related Work. This work is somewhat related to compile-time garbage collection (CTGC) [6,7]. In-place updates are related to *direct structure reuse* as defined in Chapter 9 of [6] (in the context of Mercury compilation), while suspension term reuse is related to *indirect structure reuse*. The analysis required for CTGC on arbitrary Mercury (or Prolog) programs is quite involved. Luckily, we only had to consider the particular code of the compilation schema used in the CHR compiler so we could manually specialize the CTGC liveness and reuse analyses to relatively simple conditions on the CHR program to be compiled.

In SICStus CHR, the option `already_in_heads` (which also exist as a pragma) is offered. When a body constraint is identical to one of the removed head constraints, the removal and reinsert is avoided. This roughly corresponds to the in-place update optimization, restricted to the case where none of the arguments are modified. However, the `already_in_heads` option may affect the behavior of the CHR program. The CHR programmer is responsible for verifying whether the operational semantics are preserved by the option.

Future Work. There are many possibilities to improve and extend the current implementation. For example, bigger suspension cache sizes could increase the number of cache hits. Also suspension terms could be reused even if the constraint functor is different (not only when the arity is the same). In rules with two or more in-place updates we could compute the optimal matching between removed head constraints and inserted body constraints, minimizing the number of affected indexes. It would also be interesting to investigate the impact of modifying the order in which partner constraint are tried, and perhaps mechanisms can be conceived to control and improve that order. Finally, some heuristics could be added to decide when to enable what optimizations.

References

1. The K.U.Leuven CHR system. *http://www.cs.kuleuven.be/~toms/Research/CHR/*.
2. Bart Demoen. The hProlog home page. *http://www.cs.kuleuven.be/~bmd/hProlog/*.
3. Gregory J. Duck, Peter J. Stuckey, María García de la Banda, and Christian Holzbaur. The refined operational semantics of Constraint Handling Rules. In *Proc. 20th Intl. Conf. on Logic Programming (ICLP'04)*, St-Malo, France, 2004.
4. Thom Frühwirth. Theory and practice of Constraint Handling Rules. *Journal of Logic Programming*, 37(1–3):95–138, October 1998.
5. Christian Holzbaur and Thom Frühwirth. Compiling constraint handling rules into Prolog with attributed variables. In *Proc. Intl. Conference on Principles and Practice of Declarative Programming (PPDP'99)*, pages 117–133, 1999.
6. Nancy Mazur. *Compile-time Garbage Collection for the Declarative Language Mercury*. PhD thesis, K.U.Leuven, Leuven, Belgium, May 2004.
7. Nancy Mazur, Peter Ross, Gerda Janssens, and Maurice Bruynooghe. Practical aspects for a working compile time garbage collection system for Mercury. In *Proc. 17th Intl. Conf. on Logic Programming (ICLP'01)*, Paphos, Cyprus, 2001.
8. Tom Schrijvers. *Analyses, Optimizations and Extensions of Constraint Handling Rules*. PhD thesis, K.U.Leuven, Leuven, Belgium, June 2005.
9. Tom Schrijvers, Peter Stuckey, and Gregory Duck. Abstract Interpretation for Constraint Handling Rules. In *Proceedings of the 7th Intl. Conference on Principles and Practice of Declarative Programming (PPDP'05)*, Lisbon, Portugal, July 2005.
10. Jon Sneyers, Tom Schrijvers, and Bart Demoen. The computational power and complexity of Constraint Handling Rules. In *Proc. 2nd Workshop on Constraint Handling Rules (CHR'05)*, pages 3–17, Sitges, Spain, October 2005.
11. Jon Sneyers, Tom Schrijvers, and Bart Demoen. Suspension optimization and in-place updates for optimizing CHR compilation. Technical Report CW 433, K.U.Leuven, Dept. CS, December 2005.

Overlapping Rules and Logic Variables in Functional Logic Programs*

Sergio Antoy[1] and Michael Hanus[2]

[1] Computer Science Department, Portland State University,
P.O. Box 751, Portland, OR 97207, USA
antoy@cs.pdx.edu
[2] Institut für Informatik, CAU Kiel, D-24098 Kiel, Germany
mh@informatik.uni-kiel.de

Abstract. Functional logic languages extend purely functional languages with two features: operations defined by overlapping rules and logic variables in both defining rules and expressions to evaluate. In this paper, we show that only one of these features is sufficient in a core language. On the one hand, overlapping rules can be eliminated by introducing logic variables in rules. On the other hand, logic variables can be eliminated by introducing operations defined by overlapping rules. The proposed transformations between different classes of programs not only give a better understanding of the features of functional logic programs but also may simplify implementations of functional logic languages.

1 Motivation

Functional logic languages [20] integrate the best features of functional and logic languages in order to provide a variety of programming concepts. For instance, the concepts of demand-driven evaluation and higher-order functions from functional programming can be combined with logic programming features like computing with partial information (logic variables), constraint solving, and non-deterministic search for solutions. In contrast to purely functional languages, functional logic languages allow computations with overlapping rules (i.e., more than one rule can be applied to evaluate a function call) and logic variables (i.e., unbound variables occurring in the initial expression and/or rules, also called extra variables). Operationally, these features are supported by nondeterministic computation steps.

Functional logic languages are modeled by constructor-based term rewriting systems (TRS) with narrowing as the evaluation mechanism. A crucial choice in the design of a language, both at the source level and the implementation level, is the class of rewrite systems used to model the programs. Early languages (e.g., Babel [28] and K-Leaf [19]) were modeled by weakly orthogonal, constructor-based TRSs. Larger classes are more expressive, i.e., programs in larger classes

---

* This work was partially supported by the German Research Council (DFG) grant Ha 2457/5-1 and the NSF grant CCR-0218224.

S. Etalle and M. Truszczyński (Eds.): ICLP 2006, LNCS 4079, pp. 87–101, 2006.

are textually shorter and/or conceptually simpler. Thus, modern languages, such as Curry [21,23] and $\mathcal{TOY}$ [26], are modeled by the whole class of the constructor-based rewrite systems with extra variables. However, the implementation of a language modeled by a smaller class is likely to be simpler and/or more efficient.

For the above reason, program transformation among different classes of TRSs is an interesting research subject. The goal is to transform a program in the source language into an equivalent program in a language, referred to as the *core* language, that is conceptually simpler or could be implemented more efficiently. For example, the results of [5] show that any conditional constructor-based TRS can be transformed into an unconditional overlapping inductively sequential TRS [4]. The target class is a proper subclass of the source class, a situation that leads to conceptual and practial benefits. This paper studies two transformations similar to that described in [5] and with the same intent.

The first transformation maps the overlapping inductively sequential TRS with or without extra variables into the inductively sequential TRS with extra variables. This shows that if a language allows extra variables, then, at the core level, overlapping is not necessary. Of course, at the source level overlapping is a feature that contributes to the expressiveness of a language and therefore is desirable.

The second transformation eliminates logic variables from computations within the overlapping inductively sequential TRS. By "logic variables" we mean extra variables in rewrite rules and variables, which are free or unbound, in expressions to evaluate. A somewhat unexpected, though immediate, consequence of this transformation is that the power of narrowing computations can be obtained by mere rewriting. As for the previous transformation, at the source level logic variables contribute to the expressiveness of a language and therefore are desirable.

Loosely speaking, these results can be understood as the possibility to trade in a core language logic variables for a rather disciplined form of rule overlapping and vice versa. Section 2 reviews concepts and notations used in this paper. Section 3 defines the transformation that replaces overlapping with extra variables and states its correctness. Section 4 defines the transformation that replaces logic variables with overlapping and states its correctness. Section 5 offers our conclusion. The proofs of the results presented in this paper can be found in the full version of the paper [8].

2   Preliminaries

In this section we review some term rewriting [11,18] notations and functional logic programming [20] concepts used in the remaining of this paper.

We consider a many-sorted *signature* Σ partitioned into a set $\mathcal{C}$ of *constructors* and a set $\mathcal{F}$ of (defined) *functions* or *operations*. We write $c/n \in \mathcal{C}$ and $f/n \in \mathcal{F}$ for n-ary constructor and operation symbols, respectively. Given a set of sorted variables $\mathcal{X}$, the set of well-sorted *terms* and *constructor terms* are denoted by $\mathcal{T}(\Sigma, \mathcal{X})$ and $\mathcal{T}(\mathcal{C}, \mathcal{X})$, respectively. We write $\mathcal{V}ar(t)$ for the set of all the variables occurring in a term t. A term t is *ground* if $Var(t) = \varnothing$. A term is *linear* if it does not contain multiple occurrences of a variable. A term is *operation-rooted* (*constructor-rooted*) if its root symbol is an operation (constructor). We write $\overline{o_k}$ for a sequence of objects $o_1, \ldots, o_k$.

Example 1. In the following, we write datatype declarations in Curry syntax [23], i.e., a sort S is defined by enumerating its constructors in the form

> data S = C_1 s_{11} ... s_{1a_1} | ... | C_n s_{n1} ... s_{na_n}

Thus, C_i is a constructor of sort S and arity a_i with argument sorts $s_{i1}, \ldots, s_{ia_i}$. For instance, the sorts of Boolean values and natural numbers in Peano's notation are defined as

> data Bool = True | False
> data Nat = 0 | S Nat   □

A *pattern* is a linear term of the form $f(t_1, \ldots, t_n)$ where $f/n \in \mathcal{F}$ is an operation symbol and $t_1, \ldots, t_n$ are constructor terms. A constructor-based rewrite system is a set of pairs of terms or *rewrite rules* of the form

> $l \rightarrow r$

where l is a pattern and l and r are of the same sort. An operation f is *defined* by all the rewrite rules whose left-hand side is rooted by f. A *functional logic program* is a constructor-based rewrite system. Traditionally, term rewriting systems have the additional requirement $Var(r) \subseteq Var(l)$. However, in functional logic programming variables occurring in $Var(r)$ but not in $Var(l)$, called *extra variables*, are often useful. Therefore, we allow rewrite rules with extra variables in functional logic programs. We denote the set of extra variables of a rewrite rule $l \rightarrow r$, defined as $Var(r) \backslash Var(l)$, with $\mathcal{E}var(l \rightarrow r)$.

To formally define computations w.r.t. a given program, additional notions are necessary. A *position* p in a term t is represented by a sequence of natural numbers. Positions are used to identify specific subterms. Thus, $t|_p$ denotes the *subterm* of t at position p, and $t[s]_p$ denotes the result of *replacing the subterm* $t|_p$ with the term s (see [18] for details). A *substitution* is an idempotent mapping $\sigma : \mathcal{X} \rightarrow \mathcal{T}(\Sigma, \mathcal{X})$ such that its *domain* $Dom(\sigma) = \{x \mid \sigma(x) \neq x\}$ is finite and x and $\sigma(x)$ are of the same sort for all variables x. We denote a substitution σ by the finite set $\{x \mapsto \sigma(x) \mid x \in Dom(\sigma)\}$. In particular, $\varnothing$ denotes the identity substitution. We denote by $\sigma|_V$ the restriction of a substitution σ to a set of variables V. A *(ground) constructor substitution* σ has the property that $\sigma(x)$ is a (ground) constructor term for all $x \in Dom(\sigma)$. The composition $\sigma \circ \eta$ of two substitutions is defined by $(\sigma \circ \eta)(x) = \eta(\sigma(x))$ for all variables x. Substitutions are extended to morphisms on terms in the obvious way. The *subsumption ordering* is a binary relation on terms defined by $u \leq v$ if there is a substitution σ with $\sigma(u) = v$. In this case, v is also called an *instance* of u. If, in addition, v is a (ground) constructor term, we call it *(ground) constructor instance*. If $u \leq v$ and $v \leq u$, then u and v differ only for a renaming of variables. We write $u < v$ if $u \leq v$ and $v \not\leq u$. A *unifier* of two terms s and t is a substitution

σ such that $\sigma(s) = \sigma(t)$. The unifier σ is *most general* if for any other unifier σ' there exists a substitution η with $\sigma' = \sigma \circ \eta$. Furthermore, we denote by $s \lhd t$ the most general unifier of s and t restricted to $\mathcal{V}ar(s)$.

A *rewrite step* $t \to_{p,l \to r,\eta} t'$ w.r.t. a given rewrite system $\mathcal{R}$ is defined if there are a position p in t, a rule $l \to r \in \mathcal{R}$ with fresh variables, and a substitution η with $t|_p = \eta(l)$ such that $t' = t[\eta(r)]_p$. We impose the condition on the freshness of the variables since we allow extra variables in rewrite rules. The indices in the notation of a rewrite step are omitted when inconsequential. $\xrightarrow{+}$ and $\xrightarrow{*}$ denote the transitive and reflexive-transitive closure of the relation $\to$, respectively.

Functional logic languages compute solutions of free variables occurring in expressions by instantiating these variables to constructor terms so that a rewrite step becomes applicable. The combination of variable instantiation and rewriting is called *narrowing*. Formally, $t \leadsto_\sigma t'$ is a *narrowing step* if $\sigma(t) \to_{p,l \to r,\eta} t'$ where σ is a substitution, $t|_p$ is not a variable, and $\mathcal{D}om(\eta) \subseteq \mathcal{V}ar(l)$. We denote by $t_0 \leadsto_\sigma t_n$ a sequence of narrowing steps $t_0 \leadsto_{\sigma_1} \ldots \leadsto_{\sigma_n} t_n$ with $\sigma = \sigma_1 \circ \cdots \circ \sigma_n$ (if $n = 0$ then $\sigma = \varnothing$). We omit the substitution in the notation of both narrowing steps and sequences when irrelevant to the discussion.

The requirement that $\mathcal{D}om(\eta) \subseteq \mathcal{V}ar(l)$, as in [5], ensures that no extra variable in a rule is instantiated during a narrowing step. An extra variable in a rewrite rule is generally intended as a place holder for any term, e.g., see [12] where extra variables are allowed in the conditions of rewrite rules. In constructor-based rewrite systems, a more suitable convention should allow an extra variable to stand only for constructor terms, since terms that cannot be reduced to a constructor term are intended as errors. By contrast, requiring that extra variables remain uninstantiated in a rewrite step appears as treating extra variables as constants, thus foregoing the computational power that they provide. However, when computations are performed by narrowing, particularly using an efficient strategy, it seems most sensible to avoid instantiating extra variables in the step that introduces them. The reason is that these variables become logic variables in subsequent steps and therefore may be narrowed. The advantage of instantiating them in a narrowing step after they are introduced, as opposed to instantiating them in the step that introduces them, is that the latter would have no information on choosing useful instantiations, whereas the former could instantiate them with choices useful to perform a step. In particular, efficient strategies such as [4,7] will instantiate logic variables only as far as necessary to perform needed steps. This level of specialization seems impossible to achieve at the time extra variables are introduced, unless the step introducing them performs some kind of lookahead.

For an example of the expressiveness of code using extra variables, consider the following definition (in Curry syntax) of an operation that computes the last element of a list:

```
last l | l =:= x++[e] = e   where x,e free
```

where "++" denotes the concatenation of lists. Narrowing instantiates the extra variables x and e to satisfy the equation. The instantiation of e is the result of the computation.

Narrowing is implemented by a strategy intended to limit the steps of an expression to a small set that suffices to ensure the completeness of the results. An important narrowing strategy, needed narrowing [7], is defined on the subclass of the *inductively sequential* TRSs. This class can be characterized by definitional trees [3] that are also useful to formalize and implement demand-driven narrowing strategies. Since only the left-hand sides of rules are important for the applicability of needed narrowing, the following formulation of definitional trees [4] considers patterns partially ordered by subsumption.

A *definitional tree* of an operation f is a non-empty set T of linear patterns partially ordered by subsumption having the following properties:

Leaves property: The maximal elements of T, called the *leaves*, are exactly the (variants of) the left-hand sides of the rules defining f. Non-maximal elements are also called *branches*.

Root property: T has a minimum element, called the *root*, of the form $f(x_1, \ldots, x_n)$ where $x_1, \ldots, x_n$ are pairwise distinct variables.

Parent property: If $\pi \in T$ is a pattern different from the root, there exists a unique $\pi' \in T$, called the *parent* of π (and π is called a *child* of π'), such that $\pi' < \pi$ and there is no other pattern $\pi'' \in \mathcal{T}(\Sigma, \mathcal{X})$ with $\pi' < \pi'' < \pi$.

Induction property: All the children of a pattern π differ from each other only at a common position, called the *inductive position*, which is the position of a variable in π.[1]

An operation is called inductively sequential if it has a definitional tree. Traditionally, it is also required that the rules do not contain extra variables [7]. Here, we relax this requirement: A TRS is *inductively sequential with extra variables* (*ISX*) if all its defined operations are inductively sequential. Purely functional programs and the vast majority of functions in functional logic programs are inductively sequential.

Example 2. The following operations are inductively sequential w.r.t. the datatype declarations of Example 1:

```
leq(0,x)       → True
leq(S(x),0)    → False
leq(S(x),S(y)) → leq(x,y)
cond(True,x) → x
nine → S(S(S(S(S(S(S(S(S(0)))))))))
```

The operation `smallnum` denotes a number less than ten and is defined by an ISX rule containing an extra variable x:

```
smallnum → cond(leq(x,nine),x)
```
□

Functional logic languages extend purely functional languages by allowing overlapping rules. We are interested only in a disciplined form of overlapping. Two

---

[1] There might exist distinct definitional trees of an operation. In this case one can use any tree for computing a needed narrowing step of a term since the need of the step does not depend on the selected tree.

distinct rewrite rules $l_1 \to r_1$ and $l_2 \to r_2$ are called *overlapping* if the left-hand sides l_1 and l_2 are variants of each other, i.e., they are equal by subsumption. We denote the set of all rules with the same left-hand side l by the single (meta) rule $l \to r_1 ? \cdots ? r_k$, where "?" is a meta symbol and $r_1, \ldots, r_k$ are the right-hand sides. A TRS is *overlapping inductively sequential (OIS)* if all its defined operations are inductively sequential when overlapping rules with identical left-hand sides are joined into a single rule as above. The purpose of this paper is to show that an ISX program executed by narrowing can be transformed into an OIS program executed by rewriting and vice versa, i.e., the classes ISX and OIS loosely speaking have the same expressiveness.

Next, we define the needed narrowing strategy on inductively sequential rewrite systems.

Definition 1. Let $\mathcal{R}$ be an inductively sequential TRS where each function symbol has a uniquely associated definitional tree. We define the function λ from operation-rooted terms to sets of triples (position, rule, substitution) as follows. Let $t = f(t_1, \ldots, t_n)$ be an operation-rooted term, T the definitional tree associated to f, and π a maximal pattern of T that unifies with t. Then $\lambda(t)$ is the least set satisfying

$$\lambda(t) \ni \begin{cases} (\Lambda, \pi \to r, t \lhd \pi) & \text{if } \pi \text{ is a leaf of } T \text{ and } \pi \to r \\ & \text{is a variant of a rewrite rule} \\ (q \cdot p, R, \eta \circ \sigma) & \text{if } \pi \text{ is a branch of } T, \\ & \text{where } q \text{ is the inductive position of } \pi, \\ & \eta = t \lhd \pi, \text{ and } (p, R, \sigma) \in \lambda(\eta(t|_q)) \end{cases} \qquad \square$$

In each recursive step during the computation of λ, a position and a substitution is composed with the results computed by the recursive call. Thus, each needed narrowing step can be represented as $(p_1 \cdots p_k, R, \sigma_1 \circ \cdots \circ \sigma_k)$, where $p_k = \Lambda$, p_j is an inductive position for all $j \in \{1, \ldots, k-1\}$, and σ_j a most general unifier restricted to the term variables computed in each recursive call for all $j \in \{1, \ldots, k\}$. This representation of a needed narrowing step is called its *canonical decomposition*.

Proposition 1 ([4]). *Let $\mathcal{R}$ be an overlapping inductively sequential TRS and t an operation-rooted term. If $(p, l \to r, \sigma) \in \lambda(t)$, then $t \leadsto_{p,l \to r,\sigma} \sigma(t[r]_p)$ is a needed narrowing step, also denoted by $t \stackrel{NN}{\leadsto}_{p,l \to r,\sigma} \sigma(t[r]_p)$.*

The need of the step computed by λ in Proposition 1 is *modulo the nondeterministic choice* of the right-hand side. The term t cannot be narrowed to a constructor term without a step at p with a rule $l \to r'$. However, it may be possible that $r \neq r'$.

3 Eliminating Overlapping Rules

In this section we show that using rules with multiple right-hand sides does not increase the expressiveness of a functional logic language already providing inductively sequential rewrite systems with extra variables. For this purpose, we introduce a transformation from OIS into ISX systems and prove that needed narrowing computes the same results on the original and the transformed system.

Definition 2 (Transformation from OIS into ISX). We define a transformation OE (*Overlapping Elimination*) on TRSs. Non-overlapping rewrite rules are not changed. Overlapping rewrite rules of the form $f(\overline{t_n}) \to r_1 ? \cdots ? r_k$ are replaced by a single rule $f(\overline{t_n}) \to f'(y, \overline{x_l})$ where $Var(\overline{t_n}) = \{x_1, \ldots, x_l\}$, y is a new free variable, and f' is a new function symbol defined by the new rules

$$f'(I_1, \overline{x_l}) \to r_1$$
$$\vdots$$
$$f'(I_k, \overline{x_l}) \to r_k$$

The constants I_j are the elements of a new index type defined by

```
data Ix = I₁ | ⋯ | I_k
```

In practice, one can use the same index type (e.g., natural numbers) for all the rules.   □

The transformation only adds new function and constructor symbols. Thus, every term w.r.t. the original signature is also a term w.r.t. the transformed signature. In the following, we denote the original TRS by $\mathcal{R}$ and the transformed TRS by $\mathcal{R}' = OE(\mathcal{R})$.

Example 3. Consider an operation `parent` that nondeterministically returns either the mother or the father of the argument:

```
parent(x) → mother(x) ? father(x)
```

The OE transformed program is:

```
data Iparent = I0 | I1
parent(x) → parent'(y,x)
parent'(I0,x) → mother(x)
parent'(I1,x) → father(x)
```
                                                                             □

Proposition 2. *If $\mathcal{R}$ is overlapping inductively sequential, then the transformed system $\mathcal{R}'$ is inductively sequential with extra variables.*

The transformation is correct if, loosely speaking, any result computed by the original program can be computed by the transformed program and vice versa. This concept is formulated by the next theorem. The soundness is based on the fact that any narrowing step in the original system can be simulated in the transformed system by either the same step or two consecutive steps using the introduced rules. The completeness is based on the fact that every needed narrowing step in the transformed system that introduces a function symbol not occurring in the signature of the original system is immediately followed by a needed narrowing step that removes that symbol.

Theorem 1 (Correctness of OE). *Let $\mathcal{R}$ be a OIS TRS, $\mathcal{R}' = OE(\mathcal{R})$, and t, s terms of $\mathcal{R}$. The following claims hold.*

Soundness. *If $t \overset{NN\,*}{\leadsto}_{\sigma'} s$ w.r.t. $\mathcal{R}'$, then there exists a derivation $t \overset{NN\,*}{\leadsto}_{\sigma} s$ w.r.t. $\mathcal{R}$ such that $\sigma =_{Var(t)} \sigma'$.*

Completeness. *If $t \overset{NN\,*}{\leadsto}_{\sigma} s$ w.r.t. $\mathcal{R}$, then there exists a derivation $t \overset{NN\,*}{\leadsto}_{\sigma'} s$ w.r.t. $\mathcal{R}'$ such that $\sigma =_{Var(t)} \sigma'$.*

4 Eliminating Logic Variables

In the previous section, we have shown that the class of the inductively sequential TRSs with extra variables, *ISX*, is at least as expressive as the class of the overlapping inductively sequential TRSs, *OIS*. This result is interesting because it enables us to trade in the implementation of a language the complications of overlapping, or multiple right-hand sides, for the presence of extra variables. Since we already allow extra variables in the *OIS* programs, we simply eliminate overlapping in the transformation.

In this section, we present a somewhat complementary result. We show that the overlapping inductively sequential TRSs, *without extra variables*, denoted OIS^-, are at least as expressive as the *ISX* programs. We use a transformation that eliminates unbound variables *entirely*, i.e., also from the "top-level" or initial term being evaluated. Therefore, a computation in the OIS$^-$ programs is by rewriting, not narrowing. This result is interesting because it enables us to trade in the implementation of a language the complications of narrowing, in particular the use of substitutions, for the presence of multiple right-hand sides in the program rules.

As for the *OE* transformation, a functional logic program is an overlapping inductively sequential, many sorted, constructor-based TRSs with extra variables. This time, though, our goal is to eliminate extra variables, instead of overlappings. Thus, we denote with *XE*, *extra variable elimination*, this transformation. For any sort S, we consider a constant operation, `instanceOfS`, that enumerates the values of the sort S. We call this operation a *generator* of S.

Definition 3 (`instanceOf`). Let S be a sort defined by a datatype declaration of the form

> `data` S = $C_1\ t_{11}\ \ldots\ t_{1a_1}$ | $\ldots$ | $C_n\ t_{n1}\ \ldots\ t_{na_n}$

The operation `instanceOfS` is defined by the overlapping rules

> `instanceOfS` $\rightarrow$ C_1(`instanceOft`$_{11}$,...,`instanceOft`$_{1a_1}$)
> ? $\ldots$
> ? C_n(`instanceOft`$_{n1}$,...,`instanceOft`$_{na_n}$) $\qquad\qquad$ □

If S is a *primitive* or *builtin* sort, e.g., integers or characters, then we will assume that the operation `instanceOfS` is primitive or builtin as well. However, the following example shows that generators of primitive sorts, even infinite ones, can be coded by ordinary rules.

Example 4. Suppose that a sort "tree of integers" is defined by

```
data TreeInt = Leaf | Branch Int TreeInt TreeInt
```

the generator of `TreeInt` is

```
instanceOfTreeInt
  → Leaf
  ? Branch(instanceOfInt,instanceOfTreeInt,instanceOfTreeInt)
```

Below are two plausible ordinary definitions of the generator of the integers:

```
instanceOfInt → 0 ? genNeg ? genPos
genNeg →   -1 ? genNeg - 1
genPos →    1 ? genPos + 1
```

or also

```
instanceOfInt →   gen(0)
gen(x)  →  if x>=0 then x ? gen(-(x+1))
                   else x ? gen(-x)
```

In the following, we consider only ordinary rewrite systems over algebraic datatypes. For such systems, Definition 3 immediately implies the following property of `instanceOf`.

Lemma 1 (Completeness of generators). *For every ground constructor term t of sort S, there exists a rewrite sequence of* `instanceOfS` *to t.*

The XE transformation replaces any free variable v in a term with an operation that evaluates to any value that could instantiate the variable v during a computation.

Definition 4 (Extra variable elimination). Let V be a set of (sorted) variables. Then the *instantiation substitution* IO_V is defined as

$$IO_V = \{x \mapsto \texttt{instanceOfs}_x \mid x \in V \text{ has sort } s_x\}$$

For every term t we define

$$XE(t) = IO_{Var(t)}(t) \qquad \square$$

The following lemma extends Lemma 1 to terms with variables.

Lemma 2. *For every variable x and constructor term u of the same sort, $XE(x) \xrightarrow{*} XE(u)$.*

Definition 5 (Transformation from OIS into OIS⁻). Let $\mathcal{R}$ be an *OIS* program. We define $XE(\mathcal{R}) = \mathcal{R}' \cup I$, where I defines a fresh symbol `instanceOfS` for every sort S in the signature of $\mathcal{R}$, and $l \to r'$ is a rule of $\mathcal{R}'$ iff $l \to r$ is a rule of $\mathcal{R}$ and $r' = IO_{\mathcal{E}var(l \to r)}(r)$. $\qquad \square$

Proposition 3. *If $\mathcal{R}$ is an overlapping inductively sequential TRSs, then $XE(\mathcal{R})$ is an overlapping inductively sequential TRSs without extra variables.*

To claim the correctness of the XE transformation, we need to show that, under appropriate conditions and qualifications, every computation in the original system has a corresponding computation in the transformed system and vice versa. First, we discuss the completeness of XE. We state the completeness for narrowing derivations that compute constructor substitutions.

Lemma 3 (Completeness of XE derivations). *Let $\mathcal{R}$ an OIS program. For any term t and constructor term u, if $t \overset{*}{\rightsquigarrow} u$ w.r.t. $\mathcal{R}$ where the substitution of each narrowing step is a constructor substitution, then for any ground constructor instance v of u, $XE(t) \overset{*}{\rightarrow} v$ w.r.t. $XE(\mathcal{R})$.*

The evaluation of expressions with free variables, particularly in the tradition of logic programming, produces variable bindings. These bindings are lost by the XE transformation. We will discuss how to recover this information after introducing new concepts that simplify the problem.

For narrowing derivations with arbitrary substitutions, the proof of Lemma 3 fails since `instanceOf` rewrites only to constructor terms. To extend the proof to obtain a more general result, we need to consider a variation of `instanceOf` defined as follows:

$$\texttt{instanceOf}S \;\rightarrow\; s_1(\texttt{instanceOf}t_{11}, \ldots, \texttt{instanceOf}t_{1a_1})$$
$$? \;\ldots$$
$$? \; s_n(\texttt{instanceOf}t_{n1}, \ldots, \texttt{instanceOf}t_{na_n})$$

where $\{s1, \ldots, s_n\}$ are all the signature symbols of sort S and the arguments of s_i have sorts $t_{i1}, \ldots, t_{ia_i}$. However, this extension is not relevant in practice since narrowing strategies used in functional logic languages compute only constructor substitutions [6,7].

In general, the transformation XE is not sound, i.e., there are rewrite derivations in the transformed system that have no correspondence in the original system.

Example 5. Consider the following program defining an operation that evaluates to an arbitrary even number:

```
even → x+x
```

Applying XE to this program yields:

```
even → instanceOfInt + instanceOfInt
```

Consequently, the term `even` can be evaluated as follows:

$$\texttt{even} \;\rightarrow\; \texttt{instanceOfInt} + \texttt{instanceOfInt} \overset{+}{\rightarrow} 0 + 1 \rightarrow 1 \qquad \square$$

This examples shows that all the occurrences of an `instanceOf` operation originating from the same variable should be reduced to the same value. Derivations where this condition is satisfied are called *admissible*. We will show that the XE transformation is sound for admissible derivations.

The problem in the previous example would be eliminated by having only one occurrence of `instanceOfInt`. Therefore, we introduce a notation of terms where only one occurrence is represented so that the derivation above is no longer possible. Our notation uses pairs $\langle t, \chi \rangle$ of a term t and a substitution χ which represents the term $\chi(t)$. The substitution χ will be defined as $IO_{Var(t)}$ so that it contains a single occurrence of an `instanceOf` operation for each free variable of t. An example of this representation, using the familiar `let` notation for defining substitutions, is shown in Display (1). We define rewrite steps on this representation. A redex may occur in either t or χ. Rewriting in t corresponds to standard rewriting, whereas a rewrite step in χ may correspond to a multistep [24] in $\chi(t)$ if the bound variable has several occurrences in t.

Definition 6 (Transformation to term/substitution pairs). For every term t we define $XEP(t) = \langle t, IO_{Var(t)} \rangle$. For every OIS program $\mathcal{R}$ we define $XEP(\mathcal{R}) = \mathcal{R}' \cup I$, where I is as in Definition 5, and $l \to r'$ is a rule of $\mathcal{R}'$ iff $l \to r$ is a rule of $\mathcal{R}$ and $r' = \langle r, IO_{\mathcal{E}var(l \to r)} \rangle$. $\qquad\square$

Definition 7 (Rewriting on term/substitution pairs). Let $\mathcal{R}$ be an OIS program and $XEP(\mathcal{R}) = \mathcal{R}' \cup I$. Let t be a term and $XEP(t) = \langle t, \chi \rangle$. We define a rewrite step on $XEP(t)$ as follows. $\langle t, \chi \rangle \to \langle t', \chi' \rangle$ if one of the following conditions holds:

(type-1 step) there exist a position p in t, a variant $l \to \langle r, \psi \rangle$ with fresh variables of a rule in $\mathcal{R}'$, a substitution σ such that $\mathcal{D}om(\sigma) \subseteq Var(l)$, $\sigma(l) = t|_p$, $t' = t[\sigma(r)]_p$, and $\chi' = \chi|_{Var(t')} \cup \psi$

(type-2 step) there exist a variable $v \in \mathcal{D}om(\chi)$ with $\chi(v) = $ `instanceOf`S and a rule

$$\texttt{instanceOf}S \to c(\texttt{instanceOf}S_1, \ldots, \texttt{instanceOf}S_k)$$

according to Definition 3 such that $t' = \{v \mapsto c(v_1, \ldots, v_k)\}(t)$, $\chi' = (\chi \backslash \{v \mapsto \texttt{instanceOf}S\}) \cup \{v_i \mapsto \texttt{instanceOf}S_i \mid i = 1, \ldots, k\}$ where $v_1, \ldots, v_k$ are fresh variables. $\qquad\square$

The term/substitution representation is an appealing formalism for this problem because it can be directly mapped to `let` binding constructs available in many programming languages. For instance, the transformed program of Example 5 can be coded in Curry [23] with a `let` binding as

$$\texttt{even = let x = instanceOfInt in x+x} \qquad (1)$$

The semantics of the `let` binding construct is defined in such a way that all occurrences of `let` bound variables are replaced by the same replacement [1,25] (efficiently implemented by sharing). Our notion of rewriting is a natural adaptation of this semantics.

Theorem 2 (Correctness of XEP). Let $\mathcal{R}$ be a OIS TRS, $\mathcal{R}' = XEP(\mathcal{R})$, t, s terms of $\mathcal{R}$, and $t' = XEP(t)$. Then the following claims hold.

Soundness. If $t' \xrightarrow{*} \langle v, \nu \rangle$ is a derivation w.r.t. $\mathcal{R}'$, then there exists a narrowing derivation $t \overset{*}{\leadsto} u$ w.r.t. $\mathcal{R}$ with $u \leq \nu(v)$. In particular, if $\nu(v)$ is a constructor term, then $\nu = \varnothing$ and u is a constructor term.

Completeness. *If $t \stackrel{*}{\leadsto} s$ w.r.t. $\mathcal{R}$, then there exists a derivation $t' \stackrel{*}{\rightarrow} s'$ w.r.t. $\mathcal{R}'$ such that $s' = XEP(s)$. In particular, if s is a constructor term, then there exists a derivation $t' \stackrel{*}{\rightarrow} \langle v, \varnothing \rangle$ w.r.t. $\mathcal{R}'$ for any ground constructor instance v of s.*

The proof of this theorem relies on a commutativity property of reductions and transformations. More precisely, given an ordinary term t, the result of transforming t into a term/substitution pair and reducing it is equivalent to computing some reduction sequence of t and transforming the final reduct into a term/substitution pair.

The above results show that, loosely speaking, variables and overlapping rules have the same computational power in a functional logic language. To keep track of the binding of logic variables replaced by the *XEP* transformation, we transform the initial term t of a computation into a tuple $(t, x_1, \ldots, x_n)$ where $x_1, \ldots, x_n$ are the variables of t. The evaluation of the tuple will be $(e, b_1, \ldots, b_n)$ where e is the computed value and $b_1, \ldots, b_n$ constitute the computed answer. A remaining obstacle is that bindings may contain variables whereas in our approach $b_1, \ldots, b_n$ are ground. To overcome this obstacle, one may adopt the convention that an occurrence of `instanceOf` is only evaluated if its value is necessary to perform a type-1 step. Observe that type-1 steps are never performed in $b_1, \ldots, b_n$.

The size of search space of a computation is roughly the same in both systems. In $XEP(\mathcal{R})$ an occurrence of an `instanceOf` operation is evaluated only when demanded by its context. This evaluation corresponds to a step in which some variable v is instantiated in $\mathcal{R}$. There is a small difference in favor of $\mathcal{R}$, though, which is difficult to quantify. If the evaluation of an occurrence of `instanceOf` is demanded by an incompletely defined operation, some replacement of `instanceOf` may have no corresponding binding for v.

5   Conclusion

We have presented two transformations on functional logic programs. The first transformation eliminates overlapping rules by introducing auxiliary functions and extra variables. Together with the results of [5], this transformation shows that any functional logic program can be mapped into an inductively sequential TRS with extra variables so that it can be executed by needed narrowing. Hence, the class ISX is a reasonable core language for functional logic programming. The second transformation completely eliminates logic variables from functional logic computations by replacing them with operations defined by overlapping rules. The correctness of this transformation requires the consistent evaluation of these new operations w.r.t. the logic variable occurrences. This can be achieved by sharing which is usually available in lazy languages.

The results presented in this paper provide a better understanding of the features of functional logic languages and their interactions. Although the source level of such languages extend purely functional languages by overlapping rules *and* extra variables, our results show that only one of these alternative concepts is enough for a core language.

Apart from these theoretical considerations, our results have also a practical interest since a simplified core language can reduce the implementation effort it requires. For instance, typical implementations of core languages are based on abstract machines that bridge the gap between the source level and the hardware (e.g., [9,22,27]). Usually, these machines provide instructions and data structures to support the implementation of both overlapping rules and logic variables. Our results enable the simplification of these abstract machines. For instance, specific instructions to handle computations that use overlapping rules need not be considered in an abstract machine if the *OE* transformation is applied in the compilation process. This is done in the implementations described in [15,30], although without any formal justification. Likewise, the handling of logic variables (e.g., data structures such as binding arrays and binding instructions) can be removed if the *XEP* transformation is applied. Which of the two alternatives is more convenient depends on the concrete architecture of the machine. A simplified core language can also reduce the effort to build tools for functional logic languages. For instance, recent tools for debugging functional logic programs (e.g., tracers [14], profilers [13], slicers [29]) or program optimization (e.g., partial evaluation [2]) are based on a core language that supports both overlapping rules and logic variables which could be simplified using our results. The effects that each transformation may have on the efficiency of the execution of a program are a subject for future investigation.

After submitting this paper, we received from Paco López-Fraguas a draft [17] describing a transformation substantially identical to our *XEP*. They prove theoretical results very similar to ours but within the framework of CRWL, and present some benchmarks that show that eliminating logic variables does not incur any substantial efficiency loss.

Finally, the *XEP* transformation also sheds some new light on the role of logic variables in declarative programming. It has been sometimes argued (in the functional programming community) that the instantiation of a logic variable during a computation is similar to a side effect due to its global visibility. For instance, this has led to the modeling of logic variables as references in Haskell [16]. However, our results show that the binding of a logic variable can be also interpreted as the stepwise evaluation of an operation so that the power of narrowing computations can be obtained by rewriting.

We have presented our results for a first-order many-sorted functional logic language. The extension, with standard approaches (e.g., see [10,31]), to higher-order programs presents no difficulties. The extension to polymorphically typed languages is not so obvious since the *XEP* transformation assumes that the type of each logic variable is known at compile time. This information is always available in a many-sorted TRS but could be difficult to obtain in a polymorphic functional logic language where logic variables might have an arbitrary type. In this case, one could define a specific "polymorphic" `instanceOf` operation that evaluates to values of all possible types. However, this is not practical due to an increase of the search space size and the possibility of ill-typed expressions during a computation. An appropriate solution to this problem is a topic for future research.

References

1. E. Albert, M. Hanus, F. Huch, J. Oliver, and G. Vidal. Operational Semantics for Declarative Multi-Paradigm Languages. *Journal of Symbolic Computation*, Vol. 40, No. 1, pp. 795–829, 2005.
2. E. Albert, M. Hanus, and G. Vidal. A Practical Partial Evaluator for a Multi-Paradigm Declarative Language. *Journal of Functional and Logic Programming*, Vol. 2002, No. 1, 2002.
3. S. Antoy. Definitional Trees. In *Proc. of the 3rd International Conference on Algebraic and Logic Programming*, pp. 143–157. Springer LNCS 632, 1992.
4. S. Antoy. Optimal Non-Deterministic Functional Logic Computations. In *Proc. International Conference on Algebraic and Logic Programming (ALP'97)*, pp. 16–30. Springer LNCS 1298, 1997.
5. S. Antoy. Constructor-based Conditional Narrowing. In *Proc. of the 3rd International ACM SIGPLAN Conference on Principles and Practice of Declarative Programming (PPDP 2001)*, pp. 199–206. ACM Press, 2001.
6. S. Antoy. Evaluation Strategies for Functional Logic Programming. *Journal of Symbolic Computation*, Vol. 40, No. 1, pp. 875–903, 2005.
7. S. Antoy, R. Echahed, and M. Hanus. A Needed Narrowing Strategy. *Journal of the ACM*, Vol. 47, No. 4, pp. 776–822, 2000.
8. S. Antoy and M. Hanus. Overlapping Rules and Logic Variables in Functional Logic Programs. Technical Report 0608, Christian-Albrechts-Universität Kiel, 2006.
9. S. Antoy, M. Hanus, J. Liu, and A. Tolmach. A Virtual Machine for Functional Logic Computations. In *Proc. of the 16th International Workshop on Implementation and Application of Functional Languages (IFL 2004)*, pp. 108–125. Springer LNCS 3474, 2005.
10. S. Antoy and A. Tolmach. Typed Higher-Order Narrowing without Higher-Order Strategies. In *Proc. 4th Fuji International Symposium on Functional and Logic Programming (FLOPS'99)*, pp. 335–352. Springer LNCS 1722, 1999.
11. F. Baader and T. Nipkow. *Term Rewriting and All That*. Cambridge University Press, 1998.
12. J.A. Bergstra and J.W. Klop. Conditional Rewrite Rules: Confluence and Termination. *Journal of Computer and System Sciences*, Vol. 32, No. 3, pp. 323–362, 1986.
13. B. Braßel, M. Hanus, F. Huch, J. Silva, and G. Vidal. Run-Time Profiling of Functional Logic Programs. In *Proceedings of the International Symposium on Logic-based Program Synthesis and Transformation (LOPSTR'04)*, pp. 182–197. Springer LNCS 3573, 2005.
14. B. Braßel, M. Hanus, F. Huch, and G. Vidal. A Semantics for Tracing Declarative Multi-Paradigm Programs. In *Proceedings of the 6th ACM SIGPLAN International Conference on Principles and Practice of Declarative Programming (PPDP'04)*, pp. 179–190. ACM Press, 2004.
15. B. Braßel and F. Huch. Translating Curry to Haskell. In *Proc. of the ACM SIGPLAN 2005 Workshop on Curry and Functional Logic Programming (WCFLP 2005)*, pp. 60–65. ACM Press, 2005.

16. K. Claessen and P. Ljunglöf. Typed Logical Variables in Haskell. In *Proc. ACM SIGPLAN Haskell Workshop*, Montreal, 2000.

17. J. de Dios Castro and F.J. López-Fraguas. Elimination of Extra Variables in Functional Logic Programs. Personal communication, 2006.

18. N. Dershowitz and J.-P. Jouannaud. Rewrite Systems. In J. van Leeuwen, editor, *Handbook of Theoretical Computer Science, Vol. B*, pp. 243–320. Elsevier, 1990.

19. E. Giovannetti, G. Levi, C. Moiso, and C. Palamidessi. Kernel LEAF: A Logic plus Functional Language. *Journal of Computer and System Sciences*, Vol. 42, No. 2, pp. 139–185, 1991.

20. M. Hanus. The Integration of Functions into Logic Programming: From Theory to Practice. *Journal of Logic Programming*, Vol. 19&20, pp. 583–628, 1994.

21. M. Hanus. A Unified Computation Model for Functional and Logic Programming. In *Proc. of the 24th ACM Symposium on Principles of Programming Languages (Paris)*, pp. 80–93, 1997.

22. M. Hanus and R. Sadre. An Abstract Machine for Curry and its Concurrent Implementation in Java. *Journal of Functional and Logic Programming*, Vol. 1999, No. 6, 1999.

23. M. Hanus (ed.). Curry: An Integrated Functional Logic Language (Vers. 0.8.2). Available at http://www.informatik.uni-kiel.de/~curry, 2006.

24. G. Huet and J.-J. Lévy. Computations in Orthogonal Rewriting Systems. In J.-L. Lassez and G. Plotkin, editors, *Computational Logic: Essays in Honor of Alan Robinson*, pp. 395–443. MIT Press, 1991.

25. J. Launchbury. A Natural Semantics for Lazy Evaluation. In *Proc. 20th ACM Symposium on Principles of Programming Languages (POPL'93)*, pp. 144–154. ACM Press, 1993.

26. F. López-Fraguas and J. Sánchez-Hernández. TOY: A Multiparadigm Declarative System. In *Proc. of RTA'99*, pp. 244–247. Springer LNCS 1631, 1999.

27. W. Lux and H. Kuchen. An Efficient Abstract Machine for Curry. In K. Beiersdörfer, G. Engels, and W. Schäfer, editors, *Informatik '99 — Annual meeting of the German Computer Science Society (GI)*, pp. 390–399. Springer, 1999.

28. J.J. Moreno-Navarro and M. Rodríguez-Artalejo. Logic Programming with Functions and Predicates: The Language BABEL. *Journal of Logic Programming*, Vol. 12, pp. 191–223, 1992.

29. C. Ochoa, J. Silva, and G. Vidal. Dynamic Slicing Based on Redex Trails. In *Proc. of the ACM SIGPLAN 2004 Symposium on Partial Evaluation and Program Manipulation (PEPM'04)*, pp. 123–134. ACM Press, 2004.

30. A. Tolmach, S. Antoy, and M. Nita. Implementing Functional Logic Languages Using Multiple Threads and Stores. In *Proc. of the Ninth ACM SIGPLAN International Conference on Functional Programming (ICFP'04)*, pp. 90–102. ACM Press, 2004.

31. D.H.D. Warren. Higher-order extensions to PROLOG: are they needed? In *Machine Intelligence 10*, pp. 441–454, 1982.

Towards "Propagation = Logic + Control"

Sebastian Brand[1] and Roland H.C. Yap[2]

[1] National ICT Australia, Victoria Research Lab, Melbourne, Australia
[2] School of Computing, National University of Singapore, Singapore

Abstract. Constraint propagation algorithms implement logical inference. For efficiency, it is essential to control whether and in what order basic inference steps are taken. We provide a high-level framework that clearly differentiates between information needed for controlling propagation versus that needed for the logical semantics of complex constraints composed from primitive ones. We argue for the appropriateness of our *controlled propagation* framework by showing that it captures the underlying principles of manually designed propagation algorithms, such as literal watching for unit clause propagation and the lexicographic ordering constraint. We provide an implementation and benchmark results that demonstrate the practicality and efficiency of our framework.

1 Introduction

Constraint programming solves combinatorial problems by combining search and logical inference. The latter, constraint propagation, aims at reducing the search space. Its applicability and usefulness relies on the availability of efficiently executable propagation algorithms.

It is well understood how primitive constraints, e.g. indexical constraints, and also their reified versions, are best propagated. We also call such primitive constraints *pre-defined*, because efficient, special-purpose propagation algorithms exist for them and many constraint solving systems provide implementations. However, when modelling problems, one often wants to make use of more complex constraints whose semantics can best be described as a combination of pre-defined constraints using logical operators (i.e. conjunction, disjunction, negation). Examples are constraints for breaking symmetries [FHK+02] and channelling constraints [CCLW99].

Complex constraints are beneficial in two aspects. Firstly, from a reasoning perspective, complex constraints give a more direct and understandable high-level problem model. Secondly, from a propagation perspective, the more more global scope of such constraints can allow stronger inference. While elaborate special-purpose propagation algorithms are known for many specific complex constraints (the classic example is the alldifferent constraint discussed in [Rég94]), the diversity of combinatorial problems tackled with constraint programming in practice implies that more diverse and rich constraint languages are needed.

Complex constraints which are defined by logical combinations of primitive constraints can always be decomposed into their primitive constituents and

S. Etalle and M. Truszczyński (Eds.): ICLP 2006, LNCS 4079, pp. 102–116, 2006.

Boolean constraints, for which propagation methods exist. However, decomposing in this way may

(A) cause redundant propagation, as well as
(B) limit possible propagation.

This is due to the loss of a global view: information between the constituents of a decomposition is only exchanged via shared constrained variables.

As an example, consider the implication constraint $x = 5 \rightarrow y \neq 8$ during constructive search. First, once the domain of x does not contain 5 any more, the conclusion $y \neq 8$ is irrelevant for the remainder of the search. Second, only an instantiation of y is relevant as non-instantiating reductions of the domain of y do not allow any conclusions on x. These properties are lost if the implication is decomposed into the reified constraints $(x = 5) \equiv b_1$, $(y \neq 8) \equiv b_2$ and the Boolean constraints $\text{not}(b_1, b_1')$, $\text{or}(b_1', b_2)$.

Our focus is point (A). We show how **shared control information** allows a constraint to signal others what sort of information is relevant to its propagation or that any future propagation on their part has become irrelevant to it. We address (B) to an extent by considering implied constraints in the decomposition. Such constraints may be logically redundant but not operationally so. Control flags connecting them to their respective antecedents allow us to keep track of the special status of implied constraint, so as to avoid redundant propagation steps. Our proposed control framework is naturally applicable not only to the usual tree-structure decomposition but also to those with a more complex DAG structure, which permits stronger propagation.

Our objective is to capture the *essence* of manually designed propagation algorithms, which implicitly merge the separate aspects of logic and control. We summarise this by *Propagation = Logic + Control* in the spirit of [Kow79]. The ultimate goal of our approach is a fully automated treatment of arbitrary complex constraints specified in a logic-based constraint definition language. We envisage such a language to be analogous to CLP but focused on propagation. Our framework would allow users lacking the expertise in or the time for the development of specialised propagation to rapidly prototype and refine propagation algorithms for complex constraints.

Preliminaries

Consider a finite sequence of different variables $X = x_1, \ldots, x_m$ with respective domains $D(x_1), \ldots, D(x_m)$. A **constraint** C on X is a pair $\langle S, X \rangle$. The set S is an m-ary relation and a subset of the Cartesian product of the domains, that is, $S \subseteq D(x_1) \times \ldots \times D(x_m)$. The elements of S are the **solutions** of the constraint, and m is its *arity*. We assume $m \geqslant 1$. We sometimes write $C(X)$ for the constraint and often identify C with S.

We distinguish pre-defined, **primitive** constraints, such as $x = y, x \leqslant y$, and **complex** constraints, constructed from the primitive constraints and the logical operators $\vee, \wedge, \neg$ etc. For each logical operator there is a corresponding **Boolean** constraint. For example, the satisfying assignments of $x \vee y = z$ are the solutions of the constraint $\text{or}(x, y, z)$. The **reified** version of a constraint $C(X)$

is a constraint on X and an additional Boolean variable b reflecting the truth of $C(X)$; we write it as $C(X) \equiv b$. Complex constraints can be **decomposed** into a set of reified primitive constraints and Boolean constraints, whereby new Boolean variables are introduced. For example, the first step in decomposing $C_1 \vee C_2$ may result in the three constraints $C_1 \equiv b_1$, $C_2 \equiv b_2$, and $\text{or}(b_1, b_2, 1)$.

Constraint **propagation** aims at inferring new constraints from given constraints. In its most common form, a single constraint is considered, and the domains of its variables are reduced without eliminating any solution of the constraint. If every domain is maximally reduced and none is empty, the constraint is said to be **domain-consistent** (DC). For instance, $x < y$ with $D(x) = \{1, 2\}$, $D(y) = \{1, 2, 3\}$ can be made domain-consistent by inferring the constraint $y \neq 1$, leading to the smaller domain $D(y) = \{2, 3\}$.

Decomposing a complex constraint may hinder propagation. For example, DC-establishing propagation is guaranteed to result in the same domain reductions on a constraint and its decomposition only if the constraint graph of the decomposition is a tree [Fre82]. For instance, the constraints of the decomposition of the constraint $(x > y) \wedge (x < y)$ considered in isolation do not indicate its inconsistency.

2   Logic and Control Information

A complex constraint expressed as a logical combination of primitive constraints can be decomposed into its primitive parts. However, such a naive decomposition has the disadvantage that it assigns equal relevance to every constraint. This may cause redundant reasoning to take place for the individual primitive constraints and connecting Boolean constraints. We prevent this by maintaining fine-grained control information on whether the *truth* or *falsity* of individual constraints matters. We say that a truth status of a constraint is **relevant** if it entails the truth status of some other constraint.

We focus on the disjunction operator first.

Proposition 1. *Suppose C is the disjunctive constraint $C_1 \vee C_2$. Consider the truth status of C in terms of the respective truth statuses of the individual constraints C_1, C_2.*

- *If the falsity of C is asserted then the falsity of C_1 and C_2 can be asserted.*
- *If the truth of C is asserted then the falsity of C_1 and C_2 is relevant, but not their truth.*
- *If the truth of C is queried then the truth of C_1 and C_2 is relevant, but not their falsity.*
- *If the falsity of C is queried then the falsity of only one of C_1 or C_2 is relevant, but not the their truth.*

Proof. Let the reified version of C be $(C_1 \vee C_2) \equiv b$ and its partial decomposition be $C_1 \equiv b_1$, $C_2 \equiv b_2$, $\text{or}(b_1, b_2, b)$. The following cases can occur when asserting or querying C.

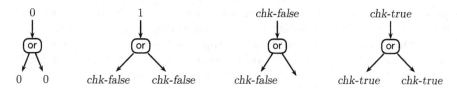

Fig. 1. Control flow through a disjunction

Case $b = 0$. Then C_1 and C_2 must both be asserted to be false.
Case $b = 1$

- Suppose C_1 is found to be true. This means that both the truth and the falsity of C_2, hence C_2 itself, have become irrelevant for the remainder of the current search. Although this simplifies the representation of C to C_1, it does not lead to any inference on it. In this sense, the truth of C_1 is useless information.
  The case of C_2 being true is analogous.
- Suppose C_1 is found to be false. This is useful information as we now must assert the truth of C_2, which may cause further inference in C_2.
  The case of C_2 being false is analogous.

Only falsity of C_1 or C_2 is information that may cause propagation. Their truth is irrelevant in this respect.

Case b **unknown.** We now assume that we know what aspect of the truth status of C is relevant: its truth or its falsity. If neither is relevant then we need not consider C, i.e. C_1 and C_2, at all. If both the truth and falsity of C are relevant, the union of the individual cases applies.

Truth of C is queried

- Suppose C_1 or C_2 is found to be true. This means that C is true, and knowing either case is therefore useful information.
- Suppose C_1 is found to be false. Then the truth of C depends on the truth of C_2. The reasoning for C_2 being false is analogous.

The truth of both C_1 and C_2 matters, but not their falsity.

Falsity of C is queried

- Suppose C_1 or C_2 is found to be true. While this means that C is true, this is not relevant since its falsity is queried.
- Suppose C_1 is found to be false. Then the falsity of C depends on the falsity of C_2. Now suppose otherwise that C_1 is queried for falsity but *not* found to be false. If C_1 is not false then C cannot be false. It is important to realise that this reasoning is independent of C_2.
  The reasoning for C_2 being false is symmetric.

In summary, to determine the falsity of C, it suffices to query the falsity of *just one* of C_1 or C_2. □

Fig. 1 shows the flow of control information through a disjunction. There, and throughout the rest of this paper, we denote a truth query by *chk-true* and a falsity query by *chk-false*.

Analogous studies on control flow can be conducted for all other Boolean operators. The case of a negated constraint is straightforward: truth and falsity swap their roles. Conjunction is entirely symmetric to disjunction due to De Morgan's law. For example, a query for falsity of the conjunction propagates to both conjuncts while a query for truth need only be propagated to one conjunct. We remark that one can apply such an analysis to other kinds of operators including non-logical ones. Thus, the cardinality constraint [HD91] can be handled within this framework.

2.1   Controlled Propagation

Irrelevant inference can be prevented by distinguishing whether the truth or the falsity of a constraint matters. This control information arises from truth information and is propagated similarly. By **controlled propagation** we mean constraint propagation that (1) conducts inference according to truth and falsity information and (2) propagates such information.

We now characterise controlled propagation for a complex constraint in decomposition. We are interested in the *effective* propagation, i. e. newly inferred constraints (such as smaller domains) on the original variables rather than on auxiliary Boolean variables. We assume that only individual constraints are propagated[1]. This is the usual case in practice.

Theorem 1 (Controlled Propagation). *Controlled and uncontrolled propagation of the constraints of the decomposition of a constraint C are equivalent with respect to the variables of C if only single constraints are propagated.* $\square$

Proof. Proposition 1 and analogous propositions for the other Boolean operators.

In the following, we explain a formal framework for maintaining and reacting to control information.

Control Store. Constraints communicate truth information by shared Boolean variables. Similarly, we think of control information being communicated between constraints by shared sets of control flags. As control flags we consider the truth status queries *chk-true*, *chk-false* and the additional flag *irrelevant* signalling **permanent irrelevance**. In this context, 'permanently' refers to subsidiary parts of the search, that is, until the next back-tracking. Note that the temporary absence of truth and falsity queries on a constraint is not the same as its irrelevance. We write

C with $\mathcal{FS}$

to mean that the constraint C can read and update the sequence of control flag sets $\mathcal{FS}$. One difference between logic and control information communication is that control flows only one way, from a producer to a consumer.

Propagating Control. A set of control flags $\mathcal{F}$ is updated by adding or deleting flags. We abbreviate the adding operation $\mathcal{F} := \mathcal{F} \cup \{f\}$ as $\mathcal{F} \cup= f$. We denote by $\mathcal{F}_1 \rightsquigarrow \mathcal{F}_2$ that from now on permanently changes to the control flags in $\mathcal{F}_1$ are reflected in corresponding changes to $\mathcal{F}_2$; e. g. an addition of f to $\mathcal{F}_1$ leads to an addition of f to $\mathcal{F}_2$.

---

[1] E. g., path-consistency enforcing propagation considers two constraints at a time.

We employ rules to specify how control information is attached to the constituents of a decomposed complex constraint, and how it propagates. The rule $A \Rightarrow B$ denotes that the conditions in A, consisting of constraints and associated control information, entail the constraints and the updates of control information specified in B. We use **delete** statements in the conclusion to explicitly remove a constraint from the constraint store once it is solved or became permanently irrelevant.

Relevance. At the core of controlled propagation is the principle that reasoning effort should be made only if it is relevant to do so, that is, if the truth or falsity of the constraint at hand is asserted or queried. We reflect this condition in the predicate

$$is\_relevant(b, \mathcal{F}) \quad := \quad \begin{aligned} & b = 1 \quad \text{or} \quad chk\text{-}true \in \mathcal{F} \quad \text{or} \\ & b = 0 \quad \text{or} \quad chk\text{-}false \in \mathcal{F}. \end{aligned} \qquad \text{(is\_rel)}$$

It applies to constraints in the form $C \equiv b$ with $\mathcal{F}$. We show later that this principle can be applied to primitive constraints.

2.2   Boolean Constraints

We again focus on disjunctive constraints. The following rule decomposes the constraint $(C_1 \vee C_2) \equiv b$ only if the relevance test is passed. In this case the shared control sets are initialised.

$$\begin{aligned} is\_relevant(b, \mathcal{F}) \quad \Rightarrow \quad & or(b, b_1, b_2) \text{ with } \langle \mathcal{F}, \mathcal{F}_1, \mathcal{F}_2 \rangle, \\ & C_1 \equiv b_1 \text{ with } \mathcal{F}_1, \mathcal{F}_1 := \varnothing, \\ & C_2 \equiv b_2 \text{ with } \mathcal{F}_2, \mathcal{F}_2 := \varnothing. \end{aligned} \qquad \text{(or}_{\text{dec}}\text{)}$$

The following rules specify how control information propagates through this disjunctive constraint in accordance with Proposition 1:

$$\begin{aligned} b = 1 \quad & \Rightarrow \quad \mathcal{F}_1 \cup= chk\text{-}false, \mathcal{F}_2 \cup= chk\text{-}false; \\ b_1 = 0 \quad & \Rightarrow \quad \mathcal{F} \rightsquigarrow \mathcal{F}_2, \text{delete } or(b, b_1, b_2); \\ b_2 = 0 \quad & \Rightarrow \quad \mathcal{F} \rightsquigarrow \mathcal{F}_1, \text{delete } or(b, b_1, b_2); \\ b_1 = 1 \quad & \Rightarrow \quad \mathcal{F}_2 \cup= irrelevant, \text{delete } or(b, b_1, b_2); \\ b_2 = 1 \quad & \Rightarrow \quad \mathcal{F}_1 \cup= irrelevant, \text{delete } or(b, b_1, b_2); \\ chk\text{-}false \in \mathcal{F} \quad & \Rightarrow \quad \mathcal{F}_1 \cup= chk\text{-}false; \qquad\qquad\qquad\qquad \text{(or}_{\text{cf}}\text{)} \\ chk\text{-}true \in \mathcal{F} \quad & \Rightarrow \quad \mathcal{F}_1 \cup= chk\text{-}true, \mathcal{F}_2 \cup= chk\text{-}true; \\ irrelevant \in \mathcal{F} \quad & \Rightarrow \quad \mathcal{F}_1 \cup= irrelevant, \mathcal{F}_2 \cup= irrelevant, \text{delete } or(b, b_1, b_2). \end{aligned}$$

In rule (or_{cf}), we arbitrarily select the first disjunct to receive $chk\text{-}false$. For comparison and completeness, here are the rules propagating truth information:

$$\begin{aligned} b_1 = 0 \quad & \Rightarrow \quad b = b_2; & \qquad b_1 = 1 \quad & \Rightarrow \quad b = 1; \\ b_2 = 0 \quad & \Rightarrow \quad b = b_1; & \qquad b_2 = 1 \quad & \Rightarrow \quad b = 1; \\ b = 0 \quad & \Rightarrow \quad b_1 = 0, b_2 = 0. & & \end{aligned}$$

Control propagation for the negation constraint $\mathsf{not}(b, b_N)$ with $\langle \mathcal{F}, \mathcal{F}_N \rangle$ is straightforward:

$$
\begin{aligned}
b = 1 \text{ or } b = 0 \text{ or } b_N = 1 \text{ or } b_N = 0 \quad &\Rightarrow \quad \text{delete } \mathsf{not}(b, b_N); \\
\textit{chk-false} \in \mathcal{F} \quad &\Rightarrow \quad \mathcal{F}_N \cup= \textit{chk-true}; \\
\textit{chk-true} \in \mathcal{F} \quad &\Rightarrow \quad \mathcal{F}_N \cup= \textit{chk-false}; \\
\textit{irrelevant} \in \mathcal{F} \quad &\Rightarrow \quad \mathcal{F}_N \cup= \textit{irrelevant}.
\end{aligned}
$$

The rules for other Boolean operators are analogous. Note that a move from binary to n-ary conjunctions or disjunctions does not affect the control flow in principle, in the same way that the logic is unaffected.

Both *chk-true* and *chk-false* can be in the control set of a constraint at the same time, as it might be in a both positive and negative context. An example is the condition of an if-then-else. On the other hand, if for instance a constraint is not in a negated context, *chk-false* cannot arise.

2.3 Primitive Constraints

Asserting and querying other primitive constraints can be controlled similarly to Boolean constraints. In particular, the relevance condition (is_rel) must be satisfied before inspecting a constraint. We furthermore deal with *irrelevant* $\in \mathcal{F}$ as expected, by not asserting the primitive constraint or by deleting it from the set of currently queried or asserted constraints.

When a query on a primitive constraint is inconclusive, it is re-evaluated whenever useful. This can be when elements from a variable domain are removed or when a bound changes. We rely on the constraint solving environment to signal such changes.

Deciding the truth or the falsity of a constraint in general is an expensive operation that requires the evaluation of every variable domain. A primitive $C(X)$ is guaranteed to be true if and only if $C(X) \subseteq D(X)$ and $C(X)$ is non-empty. C is guaranteed to be false if and only if $C(X) \cap D(X) = \varnothing$, where $X = x_1, \ldots, x_n$ and $D(X) = D(x_1) \times \ldots \times D(x_n)$. For some primitive constraints we can give complete but simpler evaluation criteria, similarly to indexicals [CD96]; see Tab. 1.

Practical constraint solving systems usually maintain domain bounds explicitly. This makes answering the truth query for equality constraints and the

Table 1. Primitive constraint queries (S is a constant set, a is a constant value)

Constraint	true if	false if
$x \in S$	$D(x) \subseteq S$	$D(x) \cap S = \varnothing$
$x = a$	$|D(x)| = 1,\ D(x) = \{a\}$	$a \notin D(x)$
$x = y$	$|D(x)| = |D(y)| = 1,\ D(x) = D(y)$	$D(x) \cap D(y) = \varnothing$
$x \leqslant y$	$\max(D(x)) \leqslant \min(D(y))$	$\min(D(x)) > \max(D(y))$

queries for ordering constraints very efficient. Furthermore, the re-evaluation of a query can be better controlled: only changes of the respective bounds are an event that makes a re-evaluation worthwhile.

3   Implied Constraints

Appropriate handling of implied constraints fits naturally into the control propagation framework. Suppose the disjunctive constraint $C_1 \vee C_2$ implies $C_\rhd$; that is, $(C_1 \vee C_2) \to C_\rhd$ is always true. Logically, $C_\rhd$ is redundant. In terms of constraint propagation, it may not be, however.

Consider the disjunction $(x = y) \vee (x < y)$, which implies $x \leqslant y$. Assume the domains are $D(x) = \{4, 5\}$, $D(y) = \{3, 4, 5\}$. Since the individual disjuncts are not false, there is no propagation from the decomposition. In order to conclude $x \leqslant y$ and thus $D(y) = \{4, 5\}$ we associate the constraint with its implied constraint.

We write a disjunctive constraint annotated with an implied constraint as

$$C_1 \vee C_2 \rhd C_\rhd.$$

To benefit from the propagation of $C_\rhd$, we could represent this constraint as $(C_1 \vee C_2) \wedge C_\rhd$. However, this representation has the shortcoming that it leads to redundant propagation in some circumstances. Once one disjunct, say, C_1, is known to be false, the other disjunct, C_2, can be imposed. The propagation of $C_\rhd$ is then still executed, however, while it is subsumed by that of C_2. It is desirable to recognise that $C_\rhd$ is operationally redundant at this point. We capture this situation by enhancing the decomposition rule (or_{dec}) as follows:

$$
\begin{aligned}
(C_1 \vee C_2 \rhd C_\rhd) &\equiv b \text{ with } \mathcal{F} \quad \Rightarrow \quad \text{or}_\rhd(b, b_1, b_2, b_\rhd) \text{ with } \langle \mathcal{F}, \mathcal{F}_1, \mathcal{F}_2, \mathcal{F}_\rhd \rangle, \\
&\qquad C_1 \equiv b_1 \text{ with } \mathcal{F}_1, \mathcal{F}_1 := \varnothing, \\
&\qquad C_2 \equiv b_2 \text{ with } \mathcal{F}_2, \mathcal{F}_2 := \varnothing, \\
&\qquad C_\rhd \equiv b_\rhd \text{ with } \mathcal{F}_\rhd, \mathcal{F}_\rhd := \varnothing.
\end{aligned}
$$

Additionally to the control rules for regular disjunctive constraints shown earlier, we now also use the following four rules:

$$
\begin{aligned}
b_\rhd = 0 &\Rightarrow b = 0; & b_1 = 0 &\Rightarrow \mathcal{F}_\rhd \cup= \textit{irrelevant}, \text{delete } \text{or}_\rhd(b, b_1, b_2, b_\rhd); \\
b = 1 &\Rightarrow b_\rhd = 1; & b_2 = 0 &\Rightarrow \mathcal{F}_\rhd \cup= \textit{irrelevant}, \text{delete } \text{or}_\rhd(b, b_1, b_2, b_\rhd).
\end{aligned}
$$

We envisage the automated discovery of implied constraints, but for now we assume manual annotation.

4   Subconstraint Sharing: From Trees to DAGs

The straightforward decomposition of complex constraints can contain unnecessary copies of the same subconstraint in different contexts. The dual constraint graph (whose vertices are the constraints and whose edges are the variables) is a tree, while often a directed acyclic graph (DAG) gives a logically equivalent but more compact representation. See, for example, CDDs [CY05].

We can apply controlled propagation to complex constraints represented in DAG form. We need to account for the multiplicity of a constraint when handling queries on it: the set of control flags now becomes a *multiset*, and in effect, we maintain *reference counters* for subconstraints. Control flags need to be properly subtracted from the control set of a constraint. For the sake of a simple example, consider the constraint $(C \vee C_1) \wedge (C \vee C_2)$. Fig. 2 shows a decomposition of it.

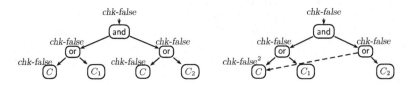

Fig. 2. Left: no sharing. Right: sharing with reference counting.

Another example is the condition in an if-then-else constraint. Opportunities for shared structures arise frequently when constraints are defined in terms of subconstraints that in turn are constructed by recursive definitions.

5   Case Studies

We examine several constraints studied in the literature and show that their decomposition benefits from controlled propagation.

Literal Watching. The DPLL procedure for solving the SAT problem uses a combination of search and inference and can be viewed as a special case of constraint programming. Many SAT solvers based on DPLL employ unit propagation with *2-literal watching*, e. g. Chaff [MMZ+01]. At any time, only changes to two literals per clause are tracked, and consideration of other literals is postponed.

Let us view a propositional clause as a Boolean constraint. We define

$$\mathsf{clause}(x_1, \dots, x_n) \quad := \quad x_1 = 1 \vee \mathsf{clause}(x_2, \dots, x_n)$$

and show in Fig. 3 the decomposition of $\mathsf{clause}(x_1, \dots, x_n)$ as a graph for controlled and uncontrolled propagation (where $D(x_i) = \{0, 1\}$ for all x_i). Both propagation variants enforce domain-consistency if the primitive equality constraints do and the variables are pairwise different. This corresponds to unit propagation.

Uncontrolled decomposition expands fully into $n - 1$ Boolean or constraints and n primitive constraints $x_i = 1$. Controlled decomposition only expands into two or constraints and the first two primitive constraints $x_1 = 1$, $x_2 = 1$. The leaf node marked $\mathsf{clause}(x_3, \dots, x_n)$ is initially not expanded as neither assertion

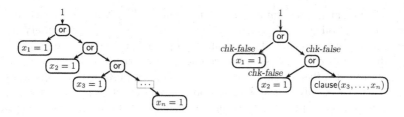

Fig. 3. Uncontrolled versus controlled decomposition of clause

nor query information is passed to it. The essence is that the first or constraint results in two *chk-false* queries to the subordinate or constraint which passes this query on to just one disjunct. This structure is maintained with respect to new information such as variable instantiations. No more than two primitive equality constraints are ever queried at a time. A reduction of inference effort as well as of space usage results.

Controlled propagation here corresponds precisely to 2-literal watching.

Disequality of Tuples. Finite domain constraint programming generally focuses on variables over the integers. Sometimes, higher-structured variable types, such as sets of integers, are more appropriate for modelling. Many complex constraints studied in the constraint community are on a sequence of variables and can thus naturally be viewed as constraining a variable whose type is tuple-of-integers. The recent study [QW05] examines how some known constraint propagation algorithms for integer variables can be lifted to higher-structured variables. One of the constraints examined is alldifferent on tuples, which requires a sequence of variables of type tuple-of-integers to be pairwise different. Its straightforward definition is

$$\mathsf{alldifferent\_tp}(\langle X_1, \ldots, X_n\rangle) := \bigwedge_{i,j\in 1,\ldots,n,\ i<j} \mathsf{different\_tp}(X_i, X_j),$$

where

$$\mathsf{different\_tp}(\langle x_1, \ldots, x_m\rangle, \langle y_1, \ldots, y_m\rangle) := \bigvee_{i\in 1,\ldots,m} x_i \neq y_i.$$

Let us examine these constraints with respect to controlled propagation. The different_tp constraint is a large disjunction, and it behaves thus like the clause constraint studied in the previous section – at most two disjuncts $x_i \neq y_i$ are queried for falsity at any time.

Deciding the falsity of a disequality constraint is particularly efficient when the primitive constraints in Tab. 1 are used, i. e. falsity of disequality when the domains are singletons. If the domains are not singletons, re-evaluation of the query is only necessary once that is the case. In contrast, a truth query for a disequality is (more) expensive as the domains must be intersected, and, if inconclusive, should be re-evaluated whenever any domain change occurred.

The alldifferent_tp constraint is a conjunction of $\binom{n}{2}$ different_tp constraints. Therefore, controlled propagation queries at most $n(n-1)$ disequality constraints for falsity at a time. Uncontrolled propagation asserts all $n(n-1)m/2$ reified disequality constraints and in essence queries truth and falsity of each. Using controlled rather than uncontrolled decomposition-based propagation for alldifferent_tp saves substantial effort without loss of effective propagation.

We remark that a specialised, stronger but non-trivial propagation algorithm for this case has been studied in [QW05]. The controlled propagation framework is then useful when specialised algorithms are not readily available, for example due to a lack of expertise or resources in the design and implementation of propagation algorithms.

Lexicographic Ordering Constraint. It is often desirable to prevent symmetries in constraint problems. One way is to add symmetry-breaking constraints such as the lexicographic ordering constraint [FHK+02]. A straightforward definition is as follows:

$$\mathsf{lex}(\langle x_1, \ldots, x_n \rangle, \langle y_1, \ldots, y_n \rangle) := x_1 < y_1$$
$$\vee$$
$$x_1 = y_1 \wedge \mathsf{lex}(\langle x_2, \ldots, x_n \rangle, \langle y_2, \ldots, y_n \rangle)$$
$$\vee$$
$$n = 0$$

With this definition, propagation of the decomposition does not always enforce domain-consistency. Consider $\mathsf{lex}(\langle x_1, x_2 \rangle, \langle y_1, y_2 \rangle)$ with the domains $D(x_1) = D(x_2) = D(y_2) = \{3..5\}$ and $D(y_1) = \{0..5\}$. Controlled decomposition results in the reified versions of $x_1 < y_1$, $x_1 = y_1$, $x_2 < y_2$ connected by Boolean constraints. None of these primitive constraints is true or false. Yet we should be able to conclude $x_1 \leqslant y_1$, hence $D(y_1) = \{3..5\}$, from the definition of lex.

The difficulty is that the naive decomposition is weaker than the logical definition because it only reasons on the individual primitive constraints. However, it is easy to see that $x_1 \leqslant y_1$ is an implied constraint in the sense of Section 3, and we can annotate the definition of lex accordingly:

$$\mathsf{lex}(\langle x_1, \ldots, x_n \rangle, \langle y_1, \ldots, y_n \rangle) := x_1 < y_1$$
$$\vee$$
$$x_1 = y_1 \wedge \mathsf{lex}(\langle x_2, \ldots, x_n \rangle, \langle y_2, \ldots, y_n \rangle)$$
$$\triangleright x_1 \leqslant y_1$$
$$\vee$$
$$n = 0$$

We state without proof that propagation of the constraints of the decomposition enforces domain-consistency on lex if the annotated definition is used.

Tab. 2 represents a trace of lex on the example used in [FHK+02], showing the lazy decomposing due to controlled propagation. We collapse several atomic inference steps and omit the Boolean constraints, and we write $v_{i..j}$ to abbreviate $v_i, \ldots, v_j$. Observe how the implied constraints $x_i \leqslant y_i$ are asserted, made irrelevant and then deleted. The derivation ends with no constraints other than $x_3 < y_3$ queried or asserted.

Table 2. An example of controlled propagation of the lex constraint

Asserted	Set of constraints queried for falsity	Variable domains				
		x_1	x_2	x_3	x_4	x_5
		y_1	y_2	y_3	x_4	y_5
$\text{lex}(\langle x_{1..5}\rangle, \langle y_{1..5}\rangle)$						
		$\{2\}$	$\{1,3,4\}$	$\{1..5\}$	$\{1..2\}$	$\{3..5\}$
		$\{0..2\}$	$\{1\}$	$\{0..4\}$	$\{0..1\}$	$\{0..2\}$
$x_1 \leqslant y_1$	$x_1 < y_1, x_1 = y_1, x_2 < y_2$					
		$\{2\}$	$\{1,3,4\}$	$\{1..5\}$	$\{1..2\}$	$\{3..5\}$
		$\{\mathbf{2}\}$	$\{1\}$	$\{0..4\}$	$\{0..1\}$	$\{0..2\}$
$x_2 \leqslant y_2$	$x_2 < y_2, x_2 = y_2, x_3 < y_3$					
		$\{2\}$	$\{\mathbf{1}\}$	$\{1..5\}$	$\{1..2\}$	$\{3..5\}$
		$\{2\}$	$\{1\}$	$\{0..4\}$	$\{0..1\}$	$\{0..2\}$
$x_3 \leqslant y_3$	$x_3 < y_3, x_3 = y_3, x_4 < y_4$					
		$\{2\}$	$\{1\}$	$\{\mathbf{1..4}\}$	$\{1..2\}$	$\{3..5\}$
		$\{2\}$	$\{1\}$	$\{\mathbf{1..4}\}$	$\{0..1\}$	$\{0..2\}$
$x_3 \leqslant y_3$	$x_3 < y_3, x_3 = y_3, x_4 = y_4, x_5 < y_5$					
		$\{2\}$	$\{1\}$	$\{1..4\}$	$\{1..2\}$	$\{3..5\}$
		$\{2\}$	$\{1\}$	$\{1..4\}$	$\{0..1\}$	$\{0..2\}$
$x_3 \leqslant y_3$	$x_3 < y_3, x_3 = y_3, x_4 = y_4, x_5 = y_5$					
		$\{2\}$	$\{1\}$	$\{1..4\}$	$\{1..2\}$	$\{3..5\}$
		$\{2\}$	$\{1\}$	$\{1..4\}$	$\{0..1\}$	$\{0..2\}$
$x_3 < y_3$						
		$\{2\}$	$\{1\}$	$\{\mathbf{1..3}\}$	$\{1..2\}$	$\{3..5\}$
		$\{2\}$	$\{1\}$	$\{\mathbf{2..4}\}$	$\{0..1\}$	$\{0..2\}$

6   Implementation and Benchmarks

We implemented a prototype of the controlled propagation framework in the CLP system ECL^{i}PS^e [WNS97], using its predicate suspension features and attributed variables to handle control information. The implementation provides controlled propagation for the basic Boolean and primitive constraints, and it handles implied constraints. Structure-sharing by a DAG-structured decomposition is not supported.

We conducted several simple benchmarks to compare controlled and uncontrolled propagation on constraint decompositions, using the clause, different_tp, alldifferent_tp and lex constraints. A benchmark consisted of finding a solution to a single constraint. For the uncontrolled propagation benchmark, the constraint was simply decomposed into built-in Boolean and primitive constraints of ECL^{i}PS^e, and implied constraints (in lex) were conjunctively added to their respective premise.

The number of variables in the respective tuple(s) was varied between five and 50. For the alldifferent_tp benchmark, we chose 20 tuples. The variables ranged over the interval $\{1..10\}$ (except for clause). Solutions to the constraints were searched by randomly selecting a variable and a value in its domain. This value was either assigned or excluded from its domain; this choice was also random. To obtain meaningful averages, every individual solution search was run a sufficient

Table 3. Benchmark results: controlled propagation (uncontrolled prop. = 100%)

	clause				different_tp				alldifferent_tp				lex			
nb. of variables	5	10	20	50	5	10	20	50	5	10	20	50	5	10	20	50
runtime (%)	100	69	50	38	88	84	67	62	66	38	23	11	138	92	69	54

number of times (typically a few 10000) so that the total computation time was roughly 15 s. Each of these runs used a new initialisation of the pseudo-random number generator resulting in a possibly different solution, while the benchmark versions (controlled vs. uncontrolled propagation) used the same initial value to obtain identical search trees. Every experiment was repeated five times. In Tab. 3, we give the relative solving time with controlled propagation, based on the corresponding uncontrolled propagation benchmark taken to be 100%.

The benchmarks show that controlling propagation can reduce the propagation time. The reduction is especially substantial for high-arity constraints. For low-arity constraints, the extra cost of maintaining control information in our implementation can outweigh the saving due to less propagation. While we have not measured the space usage of the two propagation approaches, it follows from the analyses in Section 5 that using controlled propagation for the considered constraints often also requires less space, since constraints are decomposed only when required.

We remark that efficiency was a minor concern in our high-level, proof-of-concept implementation; consequently we expect that it can be improved considerably. For example, for constraints that are in negation normal form (all constraints in our benchmark), the control flag *chk-true* is never created. A simpler subset of the control propagation rules can then be used.

7   Final Remarks

Related Work. In terms of foundations, the controlled propagation framework can be described as a refined instance of the CLP scheme (see [JM94]), by a subdivision of the set of active constraints according to their associated truth and falsity queries. Concurrent constraint programming (CCP) [Sar93], based on asserting and querying constraints, is closely related; our propagation framework can be viewed as an extension in which control is explicitly addressed and dealt with in a fine-grained way. A practical CCP-based language such as CHR [Frü98] would lend itself well to an implementation. For example, control propagation rules with delete statements can be implemented as simplification rules.

A number of approaches address the issue of propagation of complex constraints. The proposal of [BW05] is to view a constraint as an expression from which sets of inconsistent or valid variable assignments (in extension) can be computed. It focuses more on the complexity issues of achieving certain kinds of local consistencies. The work [BCP04] studies semi-automatic construction of propagation mechanisms for constraints defined by extended finite automata. An automaton is captured by signature (automaton input) constraints and state transition constraints. Signature constraints represent groups of reified primitive constraints and are considered pre-defined. They communicate with state transition constraints via constrained variables, which correspond to tuples of Boolean variables of the reified constraints in the signature constraints. Similarly to propagating the constraint in decomposition, all automata constraints are propagated independently of each other.

Controlled propagation is similar to techniques used in NOCLAUSE, a SAT solver for propositional non-CNF formulas [TBW04], which in turn lifts techniques such as 2-literal watching from CNF to non-CNF solvers. We describe here these techniques in a formal, abstract framework and integrate non-Boolean primitive constraints and implied constraints, thus making them usable for constraint propagation.

8   Conclusion

We have proposed a new framework for propagating arbitrary complex constraints. It is characterised by viewing logic and control as separate concerns. We have shown that the controlled propagation framework explains and generalises some of the principles on which efficient manually devised propagation algorithms for complex constraints are based. By discussing an implementation and benchmarks, we have demonstrated feasibility and efficiency. The practical benefits of the controlled propagation framework are that it provides *automatic* constraint propagation for *arbitrary* logical combinations of primitive constraints. Depending on the constraint, controlling the propagation can result in substantially reduced usage of time as well as space.

Our focus in this paper has been on reducing unnecessary inference steps. The complementary task of automatically identifying and enabling useful inference steps in our framework deserves to be addressed. It would be interesting to investigate if automatic reasoning methods can be used to strengthen constraint definitions, for instance by automatically deriving implied constraints.

Acknowledgements

We thank the anonymous reviewers for their comments. This paper was written while Roland Yap was visiting the Swedish Institute of Computer Science and their support and hospitality are gratefully acknowledged. The research here is supported by a NUS ARF grant.

References

[BCP04]   N. Beldiceanu, M. Carlsson, and T. Petit. Deriving filtering algorithms from constraint checkers. In Wallace [Wal04], pages 107–122.

[BW05]   F. Bacchus and T. Walsh. Propagating logical combinations of constraints. In L. P. Kaelbling and A. Saffiotti, editors, *Proc. of International Joint Conference on Artificial Intelligence (IJCAI'05)*, pages 35–40, 2005.

[CCLW99]   B. M. W. Cheng, K. M. F. Choi, J. H.-M. Lee, and J. C. K. Wu. Increasing constraint propagation by redundant modeling: An experience report. *Constraints*, 4(2):167–192, 1999.

[CD96]   P. Codognet and D. Diaz. Compiling constraints in clp(FD). *Journal of Logic Programming*, 27(3):185–226, 1996.

[CY05]   K. C. K. Cheng and R. H. C. Yap. Constrained decision diagrams. In M. M. Veloso and S. Kambhampati, editors, *Proc. of 20th National Conference on Artificial Intelligence (AAAI'05)*, pages 366–371. AAAI Press, 2005.

[FHK+02]   A. M. Frisch, B. Hnich, Z. Kiziltan, I. Miguel, and T. Walsh. Global constraints for lexicographic orderings. In P. Van Hentenryck, editor, *Proc. of 8th International Conference on Principles and Practice of Constraint Programming (CP'02)*, volume 2470 of *LNCS*, pages 93–108. Springer, 2002.

[Fre82]   E. C. Freuder. A sufficient condition for backtrack-free search. *Journal of the ACM*, 29(1):24–32, 1982.

[Frü98]   T. Frühwirth. Theory and practice of Constraint Handling Rules. *Journal of Logic Programming*, 37(1-3):95–138, 1998.

[HD91]   P. Van Hentenryck and Y. Deville. The Cardinality operator: A new logical connective for constraint logic programming. In K. Furukawa, editor, *Proc. of 8th International Conference on Logic Programming (ICLP'91)*, pages 745–759. MIT Press, 1991.

[JM94]   J. Jaffar and M. J. Maher. Constraint logic programming: A survey. *Journal of Logic Programming*, 19 & 20:503–582, 1994.

[Kow79]   R. A. Kowalski. Algorithm = Logic + Control. *Communications of the ACM*, 22(7):424–436, 1979.

[MMZ+01]   M. W. Moskewicz, C. F. Madigan, Y. Zhao, L. Zhang, and S. Malik. Chaff: Engineering an efficient SAT solver. In *Proc. of 38th Design Automation Conference (DAC'01)*, 2001.

[QW05]   C.-G. Quimper and T. Walsh. Beyond finite domains: The All Different and Global Cardinality constraints. In P. van Beek, editor, *Proc. of 11th International Conference on Principles and Practice of Constraint Programming (CP'04)*, volume 3709 of *LNCS*, pages 812–816. Springer, 2005.

[Rég94]   J.-C. Régin. A filtering algorithm for constraints of difference in csps. In *Proc. of 12th National Conference on Artificial Intelligence (AAAI'94)*, pages 362–367. AAAI Press, 1994.

[Sar93]   V. A. Saraswat. *Concurrent Constraint Programming*. MIT Press, 1993.

[TBW04]   Chr. Thiffault, F. Bacchus, and T. Walsh. Solving non-clausal formulas with DPLL search. In Wallace [Wal04], pages 663–678.

[Wal04]   M. Wallace, editor. *Proc. of 10th International Conference on Principles and Practice of Constraint Programming (CP'04)*, volume 3258 of *LNCS*. Springer, 2004.

[WNS97]   M. G. Wallace, S. Novello, and J. Schimpf. ECLiPSe: A platform for constraint logic programming. *ICL Systems Journal*, 12(1):159–200, 1997.

ACD Term Rewriting

Gregory J. Duck, Peter J. Stuckey, and Sebastian Brand

NICTA Victoria Laboratory
Department of Computer Science & Software Engineering,
University of Melbourne, Australia
{gjd, pjs, sbrand}@cs.mu.oz.au

Abstract. In this paper we introduce Associative Commutative Distributive Term Rewriting (ACDTR), a rewriting language for rewriting logical formulae. ACDTR extends AC term rewriting by adding *distribution* of conjunction over other operators. Conjunction is vital for expressive term rewriting systems since it allows us to require that multiple conditions hold for a term rewriting rule to be used. ACDTR uses the notion of a "conjunctive context", which is the conjunction of constraints that must hold in the context of a term, to enable the programmer to write very expressive and targeted rewriting rules. ACDTR can be seen as a general logic programming language that extends Constraint Handling Rules and AC term rewriting. In this paper we define the semantics of ACDTR and describe our prototype implementation.

1   Introduction

Term rewriting is a powerful instrument to specify computational processes. It is the basis of functional languages; it is used to define the semantics of languages and it is applied in automated theorem proving, to name only a few application areas.

One difficulty faced by users of term rewriting systems is that term rewrite rules are *local*, that is, the term to be rewritten occurs in a single place. This means in order to write precise rewrite rules we need to gather all relevant information in a single place.

Example 1. Imagine we wish to "program" an overloaded ordering relation for integers variables, real variables and pair variables. In order to write this the "type" of the variable must be encoded in the term[1] as in:

$$int(x) \leq int(y) \;\rightarrow\; intleq(int(x), int(y))$$
$$real(x) \leq real(y) \;\rightarrow\; realleq(real(x), real(y))$$
$$pair(x_1, x_2) \leq pair(y_1, y_2) \;\rightarrow\; x_1 \leq y_1 \vee x_1 = y_1 \wedge x_2 \leq y_2$$

In a more standard language, the type information for variables (and other information) would be kept separate and "looked up" when required.   □

---

[1] Operator precedences used throughout this paper are: $\wedge$ binds tighter than $\vee$, and all other operators, e.g. $\neg$, $=$, bind tighter than $\wedge$.

S. Etalle and M. Truszczyński (Eds.): ICLP 2006, LNCS 4079, pp. 117–131, 2006.
© Springer-Verlag Berlin Heidelberg 2006

Term rewriting systems such as constraint handling rules (CHRs) [5] and associative commutative (AC) term rewriting [3] allow "look up" to be managed straightforwardly for a single conjunction.

Example 2. In AC term rewriting the above example could be expressed as:

$$\begin{aligned} int(x) \wedge int(y) \wedge x \le y &\rightarrow int(x) \wedge int(y) \wedge intleq(x, y) \\ real(x) \wedge real(y) \wedge x \le y &\rightarrow real(x) \wedge real(y) \wedge realleq(x, y) \\ pair(x, x_1, x_2) \wedge pair(y, y_1, y_2) \wedge x \le y &\rightarrow pair(x, x_1, x_2) \wedge pair(y, y_1, y_2) \wedge \\ &\quad (x_1 \le y_1 \vee x_1 = y_1 \wedge x_2 \le y_2) \end{aligned}$$

where each rule replaces the $x \le y$ by an appropriate specialised version, in the conjunction of constraints. The associativity and commutativity of $\wedge$ is used to easily collect the required type information from a conjunction. $\qquad\square$

One difficulty remains with both AC term rewriting and CHRs. The "look up" is restricted to be over a single large conjunction.

Example 3. Given the term $int(x_1) \wedge int(y_1) \wedge pair(x, x_1, x_2) \wedge pair(y, y_1, y_2) \wedge x \le y$. Then after rewriting $x \le y$ to $(x_1 \le y_1 \vee x_1 = y_1 \wedge x_2 \le y_2)$ we could not rewrite $x_1 \le y_1$ since the types for x_1, y_1 appear in a different level.

In order to push the type information inside the disjunction we need to distribute conjunction over disjunction. $\qquad\square$

Simply adding distribution rules like

$$A \wedge (B \vee C) \rightarrow A \wedge B \vee A \wedge C \qquad (1)$$
$$A \wedge B \vee A \wedge C \rightarrow A \wedge (B \vee C) \qquad (2)$$

does not solve the problem. Rule (1) creates two copies of term A, which increases the size of the term being rewritten. Adding Rule (2) to counter this effect results in a non-terminating rewriting system.

1.1   Conjunctive Context

We address the non-termination vs. size explosion problem due to distributivity rewrite rules in a similar way to how commutativity is dealt with: by handling distributivity on the language level. We restrict ourselves to dealing with expanding distributivity of conjunction $\wedge$ over any other operator, and we account for idempotence of conjunction.[2] Thus we are concerned with distribution rules of the form

$$P \wedge f(Q_1, \ldots, Q_n) \rightarrow P \wedge f(P \wedge Q_1, \ldots, P \wedge Q_n). \qquad (3)$$

Let us introduce the conjunctive context of a term and its use in rewrite rules, informally for now. Consider a term T and the conjunction $C \wedge T$ modulo

---

[2] This means that conjunction is distributive over any function f in presence of a redundant copy of P, i.e. $P \wedge (P \wedge f(Q_1, \ldots, Q_n)) \rightarrow P \wedge f(P \wedge Q_1, \ldots, P \wedge Q_n)$. We use idempotence to simplify the RHS and derive (3).

idempotence of $\wedge$ that would result from exhaustive application of rule (3) to the superterm of T. By the *conjunctive context* of T we mean the conjunction $\mathcal{C}$.

Example 4. The conjunctive context of the boxed occurrence of x in the term

$$(x = 3) \wedge (x^2 > y \ \vee \ (\boxed{x} = 4) \wedge U \ \vee \ V) \wedge W,$$

is $(x = 3) \wedge U \wedge W$.   □

We allow a rewrite rule $P \ \rightarrow \ T$ to refer to the conjunctive context $\mathcal{C}$ of the rule head P. We use the following notation:

$$\mathcal{C} \setminus P \Longleftrightarrow T.$$

This facility provides $\wedge$-distributivity without the undesirable effects of rule (3) on the term size.

Example 5. We can express that an equality can be used anywhere "in its scope" by viewing the equality as a conjunctive context:

$$x = a \setminus x \Longleftrightarrow a.$$

Using this rule on the term of Example 4 results in

$$(x = 3) \wedge (3^2 > y \ \vee \ (3 = 4) \wedge U \ \vee \ V) \wedge W$$

without dissolving the disjunction.   □

1.2   Motivation and Applications

Constraint Model Simplification. Our concrete motivation behind associative commutative distributive term rewriting (ACDTR) is *constraint model mapping* as part of the G12 project [7]. A key aim of G12 is the mapping of solver independent models to efficient solver dependent models. We see ACDTR as the basis for writing these mappings. Since models are not flat conjunctions of constraints we need to go beyond AC term rewriting or CHRs.

Example 6. Consider the following simple constraint model inspired by the Social Golfers problem. For two groups g_1 and g_2 playing in the same week there can be no overlap in players: $maxOverlap(g_1, g_2, 0)$ The aim is to maximise the number of times the overlap between two groups is less than 2; in other words minimise the number of times two players play together in a group.

$$\text{constraint} \quad \bigwedge_{\substack{\forall w \in Weeks \\ \forall g_1, g_2 \in weeks[w] \\ g_1 < g_2}} maxOverlap(g_1, g_2, 0)$$

$$\text{maximise} \quad \sum_{\substack{\forall w_1, w_2 \in Weeks \\ \forall g_1 \in weeks[w_1] \\ \forall g_2 \in weeks[w_2] \\ g_1 < g_2}} holds(maxOverlap(g_1, g_2, 1))$$

Consider the following ACDTR program for optimising this constraint model.

$$maxOverlap(a, b, c_1) \setminus maxOverlap(a, b, c_2) \iff c_2 \geq c_1 \mid true$$
$$holds(true) \iff 1$$
$$holds(false) \iff 0$$

The first rule removes redundant $maxOverlap$ constraints. The next two rules implement partial evaluation of the $holds$ auxiliary function which coerces a Boolean to an integer.

By representing the constraint model as a giant term, we can optimise the model by applying the ACDTR program. For example, consider the trivial case with one week and two groups G_1 and G_2. The model becomes

$$maxOverlap(G_1, G_2, 0) \wedge maximise(holds(maxOverlap(G_1, G_2, 1))).$$

The subterm $holds(maxOverlap(G_1, G_2, 1))$ simplifies to 1 using the conjunctive context $maxOverlap(G_1, G_2, 0)$.   □

It is clear that pure CHRs are insufficient for constraint model mapping for at least two reasons, namely

- a constraint model, e.g. Example 6, is typically not a flattened conjunction;
- some rules rewrite functions, e.g. rules (2) and (3) rewriting function $holds$, which is outside the scope of CHRs (which rewrite constraints only).

Global Definitions. As we have seen conjunctive context matching provides a natural mechanism for making global information available. In a constraint model, structured data and constraint definitions are typically global, i.e. on the top level, while access to the data and the use of a defined constraint is local, e.g. the type information from Example 1. Another example is partial evaluation.

Example 7. The solver independent modelling language has support for arrays. Take a model having an array a of given values. It could be represented as the top-level term $array(a, [3, 1, 4, 1, 5, 9, 2, 7])$. Deeper inside the model, accesses to the array a occur, such as in the constraint $x > y + lookup(a, 3)$. The following rules expand such an array lookup:

$$array(A, Array) \setminus lookup(A, Index) \iff list\_element(Array, Index)$$
$$list\_element([X|Xs], 0) \iff X$$
$$list\_element([X|Xs], N) \iff N > 0 \mid list\_element(Xs, N - 1)$$

Referring to the respective array of the lookup expression via its conjunctive context allows us to ignore the direct context of the lookup, i.e. the true concrete constraint or expression in which it occurs.   □

Propagation Rules. When processing a logical formula, it is often useful to be able to specify that a new formula Q can be derived from an existing formula P *without consuming* P. In basic term rewriting, the obvious rule $P \iff P \wedge Q$ causes trivial non-termination. This issue is recognised in CHRs, which provide support for inference or *propagation* rules. We account for this fact and use rules of the form $P \Longrightarrow Q$ to express such circumstances.

Example 8. The following is the classic CHR `leq` program reimplemented for ACD term rewriting (we omit the basic rules for logical connectives):

$$
\begin{array}{ll}
leq(X, X) \Longleftrightarrow true & (reflexivity) \\
leq(X, Y) \setminus leq(Y, X) \Longleftrightarrow X = Y & (antisymmetry) \\
leq(X, Y) \setminus leq(X, Y) \Longleftrightarrow true & (idempotence) \\
leq(X, Y) \wedge leq(Y, Z) \Longrightarrow leq(X, Z) & (transitivity)
\end{array}
$$

These rules are almost the same as the CHR version, with the exception of the second and third rule (*antisymmetry* and *idempotence*) which generalise its original by using conjunctive context matching.   □

Propagation rules are also used for adding redundant information during model mapping.

The rest of the paper is organised as follows. Section 2 covers the standard syntax and notation of term rewriting. Section 3 defines the declarative and operational semantics of ACDTR. Section 4 describes a prototype implementation of ACDTR as part of the G12 project. Section 5 compares ACDTR with related languages. Finally, in Section 6 we conclude.

2   Preliminaries

In this section we briefly introduce the notation and terminology used in this paper. Much of this is borrowed from term rewriting [3].

We use $\mathcal{T}(\Sigma, X)$ to represent the set of all terms constructed from a set of function symbols Σ and set of variables X (assumed to be countably infinite). We use $\Sigma^{(n)} \subseteq \Sigma$ to represent the set of function symbols of arity n.

A *position* is a string (sequence) of integers that uniquely determines a subterm of a term T, where ϵ represents the empty string. We define function $T|_p$, which returns the subterm of T at position p as

$$
T|_\epsilon = T
$$
$$
f(T_1, \ldots, T_i, \ldots, T_n)|_{ip} = T_i|_p
$$

We similarly define a function $T[S]_p$ which replaces the subterm of T at position p with term S. We define the set $\mathcal{P}os(T)$ to represent the set of all *positions* of subterms in T.

An *identity* is a pair $(s, t) \in \mathcal{T}(\Sigma, X) \times \mathcal{T}(\Sigma, X)$, which is usually written as $s \approx t$. Given a set of identities E, we define $\approx_E$ to be the set of identities closed under the axioms of *equational logic* [3], i.e. symmetry, transitivity, etc.

We define the congruence class $[T]_{\approx_E} = \{S \in \mathcal{T}(\Sigma, X) | S \approx_E T\}$ as the set of terms equal to T with respect to E.

Finally, we define function $vars(T)$ to return the set of variables in T.

3 Syntax and Semantics

The syntax of ACDTR closely resembles that of CHRs. There are three types of rules of the following form:

$$
\begin{array}{ll}
(\textit{simplification}) & r @ H \iff g \mid B \\
(\textit{propagation}) & r @ H \implies g \mid B \\
(\textit{simpagation}) & r @ C \setminus H \iff g \mid B
\end{array}
$$

where r is a *rule identifier*, and *head* H, *conjunctive context* C, *guard* g and *body* B are arbitrary terms. The rule identifier is assumed to uniquely determine the rule. A program P is a set of rules.

We assume that $vars(g) \subseteq vars(H)$ or $vars(g) \subseteq vars(H) \cup vars(C)$ (for simpagation rules). The rule identifier can be omitted. If $g = true$ then the guard can be omitted.

We present the declarative semantics of ACDTR based on equational logic. First we define the set of operators that ACDTR treats specially.

Definition 1 (Operators). *We define the set of* associate commutative *operators as AC. The set AC must satisfy* $AC \subseteq \Sigma^{(2)}$ *and* $(\wedge) \in AC$.

For our examples we assume that $AC = \{\wedge, \vee, +, \times\}$. We also treat the operator $\wedge$ as *distributive* as explained below.

ACDTR supports a simple form of guards.

Definition 2 (Guards). *A* guard *is a term. We denote the set of all "true" guards as* $\mathcal{G}$, *i.e. a guard* g *is said to hold iff* $g \in \mathcal{G}$. *We assume that* $true \in \mathcal{G}$ *and* $false \notin \mathcal{G}$.

We can now define the declarative semantics for ACDTR. In order to do so we employ a special binary operator *where* to explicitly attach a conjunctive context to a term. Intuitively, the meaning of T *where* C is equivalent to that of T provided C is *true*, otherwise the meaning of T *where* C is unconstrained. For Boolean expressions, it is useful to interpret *where* as conjunction $\wedge$, therefore *where*-distribution, i.e. identity (6) below, becomes equivalent to $\wedge$-distribution (3). The advantage of distinguishing *where* and $\wedge$ is that we are not forced to extend the definition of $\wedge$ to arbitrary (non-Boolean) functions.

We denote by $\mathcal{B}$ the following set of *built-in* identities:

$$A \circ B \approx B \circ A \tag{1}$$

$$(A \circ B) \circ C \approx A \circ (B \circ C) \tag{2}$$

$$T \approx (T \text{ where } true) \tag{3}$$

$$A \wedge B \approx (A \text{ where } B) \wedge B \tag{4}$$

$$T \text{ where } (W_1 \wedge W_2) \approx (T \text{ where } W_1) \text{ where } W_2 \tag{5}$$

$$f(A_1, ..., A_i, ..., A_n) \text{ where } W \approx f(A_1, ..., A_i \text{ where } W, ..., A_n) \text{ where } W \tag{6}$$

for all $\circ \in AC$, functions $f \in \Sigma^{(n)}$, and $i \in \{1, \ldots, n\}$.

Definition 3 (Declarative Semantics for ACDTR). *The* declarative semantics *for an ACDTR program P (represented as a multiset of rules) is given
by the function* $[\![\,]\!]$ *defined as follows:*

$$
\begin{aligned}
[\![P]\!] &= \{[\![\theta(R)]\!] \mid \forall R, \theta \;.\; R \in P \wedge \theta(\mathsf{guard}(R)) \in \mathcal{G}\} \cup \mathcal{B} \\
[\![H \Longleftrightarrow g \mid B]\!] &= \exists_{vars(B)-vars(H)}(H \approx B) \\
[\![C \setminus H \Longleftrightarrow g \mid B]\!] &= \exists_{vars(B)-vars(C,H)}(H \text{ where } C \approx B \text{ where } C) \\
[\![H \Longrightarrow g \mid B]\!] &= \exists_{vars(B)-vars(H)}(H \approx H \wedge B)
\end{aligned}
$$

where function $\mathsf{guard}(R)$ *returns the guard of a rule.*

The function $[\![\,]\!]$ maps ACDTR rules to identities between the head and the
body terms, where body-only variables are existentially quantified.[3] Note that
there is a new identity for each possible binding of $\mathsf{guard}(R)$ that holds in $\mathcal{G}$.
A propagation rule is equivalent to a simplification rule that (re)introduces the
head H (in conjunction with the body B) in the RHS. This is analogous to
propagation rules under CHRs.

A simpagation rule is equivalent to a simplification rule provided the conjunctive context is satisfied.

The built-in rules $\mathcal{B}$ from Definition 3 contain identities for cre-
ating/destroying (3) and (4), combining/splitting (5), and distributing down-
wards/upwards (6) a conjunctive context in terms of the *where* operator.

The set $\mathcal{B}$ also contains identities (1) and (2) for the associative/commutative
properties of the *AC* operators.

Example 9. Consider the following ACDTR rule and the corresponding identity.

$$[\![X = Y \setminus X \Longleftrightarrow Y]\!] \quad = \quad (Y \text{ where } X = Y) \approx (X \text{ where } X = Y) \qquad (7)$$

Under this identity and using the rules in $\mathcal{B}$, we can show that $f(A) \wedge (A = B) \approx$
$f(B) \wedge (A = B)$, as follows.

$$
\begin{aligned}
&f(A) \wedge (A = B) &\approx_{(4)} \\
&(f(A) \text{ where } (A = B)) \wedge (A = B) &\approx_{(6)} \\
&(f(A \text{ where } (A = B)) \text{ where } (A = B)) \wedge (A = B) &\approx_{(7)} \\
&(f(B \text{ where } (A = B)) \text{ where } (A = B)) \wedge (A = B) &\approx_{(6)} \\
&(f(B) \text{ where } (A = B)) \wedge (A = B) &\approx_{(4)} \\
&f(B) \wedge (A = B)
\end{aligned}
$$

3.1 Operational Semantics

In this section we describe the operational semantics of ACDTR. It is based
on the theoretical operational semantics of CHRs [1,4]. This includes support
for identifiers and propagation histories, and conjunctive context matching for
simpagation rules.

---

[3] All other variables are implicitly universally quantified, where the universal quantifiers appear outside the existential ones.

Propagation History. The CHR concept of a *propagation history*, which prevents trivial non-termination of propagation rules, needs to be generalised over arbitrary terms for ACDTR. A propagation history is essentially a record of all propagation rule applications, which is checked to ensure a propagation rule is not applied twice to the same (sub)term.

In CHRs, each constraint is associated with a unique *identifier*. If multiple copies of the same constraint appear in the CHR store, then each copy is assigned a different identifier. We extend the notion of identifiers to arbitrary terms.

Definition 4 (Identifiers). *An* identifier *is an integer associated with each (sub)term. We use the notation $T\#i$ to indicate that term T has been associated with identifier i. A term T is* annotated *if T and all subterms of T are associated with an identifier. We also define function* ids(T) *to return the set of identifiers in T, and* term(T) *to return the non-annotated version of T.*

For example, $T = f(a\#1, b\#2)\#3$ is an annotated term, where ids$(T) = \{1, 2, 3\}$ and term$(T) = f(a, b)$.

Identifiers are considered separate from the term. We could be more precise by separating the two, i.e. explicitly maintain a map between $\mathcal{P}os(T)$ and the identifiers for T. We do not use this approach for space reasons. We extend and overload all of the standard operations over terms (e.g. from Section 2) to annotated terms in the obvious manner. For example, the subterm relation $T|_p$ over annotated terms returns the annotated term at position p. The exception are elements of the congruence class $[T]_{\approx_{AC}}$, formed by the AC relation $\approx_{AC}$, which we assume satisfies the following constraints.

$$A\#i \circ B\#j \approx_{AC} B\#j \circ A\#i$$
$$A\#i \circ (B\#j \circ C\#k) \approx_{AC} (A\#i \circ B\#j) \circ C\#k$$

We have neglected to mention the identifiers over AC operators. These identifiers will be ignored later, so we leave them unconstrained.

A propagation history is a set of entries defined as follows.

Definition 5 (Entries). *A propagation history entry* is of the form $(r \ @ \ E)$, *where r is a propagation rule identifier, and E is a string of identifiers. We define function* entry(r, T) *to return the propagation history entry of rule r for annotated term T as follows.*

$$
\begin{array}{lll}
\mathsf{entry}(r, T) & = (r \ @ \ \mathsf{entry}(T)) & \\
\mathsf{entry}(T_1 \circ T_2) & = \mathsf{entry}(T_1) \ \mathsf{entry}(T_2) & \circ \in AC \\
\mathsf{entry}(f(T_1, ..., T_n)\#i) & = i \ \mathsf{entry}(T_1) \ ... \ \mathsf{entry}(T_n) & \textit{otherwise}
\end{array}
$$

This definition means that propagation history entries are unaffected by associativity, but are effected by commutativity.

Example 10. Consider the annotated term $T = f((a\#1 \wedge b\#2)\#3)\#4$. We have that $T \in [T]_{\approx_{AC}}$ and $T' = f((b\#2 \wedge a\#1)\#3)\#4 \in [T]_{\approx_{AC}}$. Although T and T' belong to $[T]_{\approx_{AC}}$ they have different propagation history entries, e.g. entry$(r, T) = (r \ @ \ (4 \ 1 \ 2))$ while entry$(r, T') = (r \ @ \ (4 \ 2 \ 1))$.   □

When a (sub)term is rewritten into another, the new term is assigned a set of new unique identifiers. We define the auxiliary function $\mathsf{annotate}(\mathcal{P}, T) = T_a$ to map a set of identifiers $\mathcal{P}$ and un-annotated term T to an annotated term T_a such that $\mathsf{ids}(T_a) \cap \mathcal{P} = \emptyset$ and $|\mathsf{ids}(T_a)| = |\mathcal{P}os(T)|$. These conditions ensure that all identifiers are new and unique.

When a rule is applied the propagation history must be updated accordingly to reflect which terms are copied from the matching. For example, the rule $f(X) \Longleftrightarrow g(X, X)$ essentially clones the term matching X. The identifiers, however, are not cloned. If a term is cloned, we expect that both copies will inherit the propagation history of the original. Likewise, terms can be merged, e.g. $g(X, X) \Longleftrightarrow f(X)$ merges two instances of the term matching X. In this case, the propagation histories of the copies are also merged.

To achieve this we duplicate entries in the propagation history for each occurrence of a variable in the body that also appeared in the head.

Definition 6 (Updating History). *Define function*

$$\mathsf{update}(H, H_a, B, B_a, T_0) = T_1$$

where H and B are un-annotated terms, H_a and B_a are annotated terms, and T_0 and T_1 are propagation histories. T_1 is a minimal propagation history satisfying the following conditions:

- $T_0 \subseteq T_1$;
- $\forall p \in \mathcal{P}os(H)$ *such that $H|_p = V \in X$ (where X is the set of variables), and $\exists q \in \mathcal{P}os(B)$ such that $B|_q = V$, then define identifier renaming ρ such that $\rho(H_a|_p)$ and $B_a|_q$ are identical annotated terms. Then if $E \in T_0$ we have that $\rho(E) \in T_1$.*

Example 11. Consider rewriting the term $H_a = f((a\#1 \wedge b\#2)\#3)\#4$ with a propagation history of $T_0 = \{(r @ (1\ 2))\}$ using the rule $f(X) \Longleftrightarrow g(X, X)$. The resulting term is $B_a = g((a\#5 \wedge b\#6)\#7), (a\#8 \wedge b\#9)\#10\#11$ and the new propagation history is $T_1 = \{(r @ (1\ 2)), (r @ (5\ 6)), (r @ (8\ 9))\}$.

Conjunctive Context. According to the declarative semantics, a term T with conjunctive context C is represented as $(T\ where\ C)$. Operationally, we will never explicitly build a term containing a *where* clause. Instead we use the following function to compute the conjunctive context of a subterm on demand.

Definition 7 (Conjunctive Context). *Given an (annotated) term T and a position $p \in \mathcal{P}os(T)$, we define function $\mathsf{cc}(T, p)$ to return the conjunctive context at position p as follows.*

$$
\begin{array}{lll}
\mathsf{cc}(T, \epsilon) & = true & \\
\mathsf{cc}(A \wedge B, 1p) & = B \wedge \mathsf{cc}(A, p) & \\
\mathsf{cc}(A \wedge B, 2p) & = A \wedge \mathsf{cc}(B, p) & \\
\mathsf{cc}(f(T_1, \ldots, T_i, \ldots, T_n), ip) & = \mathsf{cc}(T_i, p) & (f \neq \wedge)
\end{array}
$$

States and Transitions. The operational semantics are defined as a set of transitions on execution states.

Definition 8 (Execution States). *An execution state is a tuple of the form* $\langle G, T, \mathcal{V}, \mathcal{P} \rangle$, *where G is a term (the* goal*), T is the* propagation history, $\mathcal{V}$ *is the set of variables appearing in the initial goal and $\mathcal{P}$ is a set of identifiers.*

We also define initial and final states as follows.

Definition 9 (Initial and Final States). *Given an initial goal G for program P, the* initial state *of G is*

$$\langle G_a, \emptyset, vars(G), \mathsf{ids}(G_a) \rangle$$

where $G_a = \mathsf{annotate}(\emptyset, G)$. A final state *is a state where no more rules are applicable to the goal G.*

We can now define the operational semantics of ACDTR as follows.

Definition 10 (Operational Semantics)

$$\langle G_0, T_0, \mathcal{V}, \mathcal{P}_0 \rangle \rightarrowtail \langle G_1, T_1, \mathcal{V}, \mathcal{P}_1 \rangle$$

1. Simplify: *There exists a (renamed) rule from P*

$$H \Longleftrightarrow g \mid B$$

such that there exists a matching substitution θ and a term G_0' such that

- $G_0 \approx_{AC} G_0'$
- $\exists p \in \mathcal{P}os(G_0') . \ G_0'|_p = \theta(H)$
- $\theta(g) \in \mathcal{G}$
- $B_a = \mathsf{annotate}(\mathcal{P}_0, \theta(B))$

Then $G_1 = G_0'[B_a]_p$, $\mathcal{P}_1 = \mathcal{P}_0 \cup \mathsf{ids}(G_1)$ and $T_1 = \mathsf{update}(H, G_0'|_p, B, B_a, T_0)$.

2. Propagate: *There exists a (renamed) rule from P*

$$r @ H \Longrightarrow g \mid B$$

such that there exists a matching substitution θ and a term G_0' such that

- $G_0 \approx_{AC} G_0'$
- $\exists p \in \mathcal{P}os(G_0') . \ G_0'|_p = \theta(H)$
- $\theta(g) \in \mathcal{G}$
- $\mathsf{entry}(r, G_0'|_p) \notin T_0$
- $B_a = \mathsf{annotate}(\mathcal{P}_0, \theta(B))$

Then $G_1 = G_0'[G_0'|_p \wedge B_a]_p$, $T_1 = \mathsf{update}(H, G_0'|_p, B, B_a, T_0) \cup \{\mathsf{entry}(r, G_0'|_p)\}$ and $\mathcal{P}_1 = \mathcal{P}_0 \cup \mathsf{ids}(G_1)$.

3. Simpagate: *There exists a (renamed) rule from P*

$$C \setminus H \Longleftrightarrow g \mid B$$

$$\langle (leq(X_1, Y_2)_3 \wedge_4 leq(Y_5, Z_6)_7 \wedge_8 \neg_9 leq(X_{10}, Z_{11})_{12}), \emptyset \rangle \rightarrowtail_{trans}$$
$$\langle (leq(X_1, Y_2)_3 \wedge_4 leq(Y_5, Z_6)_7 \wedge_{13} leq(X_{15}, Z_{16})_{14} \wedge_8 \neg_9 leq(X_{10}, Z_{11})_{12}), T \rangle \rightarrowtail_{idemp}$$
$$\langle (leq(X_1, Y_2)_3 \wedge_4 leq(Y_5, Z_6)_7 \wedge_{13} leq(X_{15}, Z_{16})_{14} \wedge_8 \neg_9 true_{17}), T \rangle \rightarrowtail_{simplify}$$
$$\langle (leq(X_1, Y_2)_3 \wedge_4 leq(Y_5, Z_6)_7 \wedge_{13} leq(X_{15}, Z_{16})_{14} \wedge_8 false_{18}), T \rangle \rightarrowtail_{simplify}$$
$$\langle (leq(X_1, Y_2)_3 \wedge_4 leq(Y_5, Z_6)_7 \wedge_{13} false_{19}), T \rangle \rightarrowtail_{simplify}$$
$$\langle (leq(X_1, Y_2)_3 \wedge_4 false_{20}), T \rangle \rightarrowtail_{simplify}$$
$$\langle (false_{21}), T \rangle$$

Fig. 1. Example derivation for the *leq* program

such that there exists a matching substitution θ and a term G'_0 such that

- $G_0 \approx_{AC} G'_0$
- $\exists p \in \mathcal{P}os(G'_0) \; . \; G'_0|_p = \theta(H)$
- $\exists D.\theta(C) \wedge D \approx_{AC} \mathsf{cc}(G'_0, p)$
- $\theta(g) \in \mathcal{G}$
- $B_a = \mathsf{annotate}(\mathcal{P}_0, \theta(B))$

Then $G_1 = G'_0[B_a]_p$, $T_1 = \mathsf{update}(H, G'_0|_p, B, B_a, T_0)$ and $\mathcal{P}_1 = \mathcal{P}_0 \cup \mathsf{ids}(G_1)$.

Example. Consider the *leq* program from Example 8 with the goal

$$leq(X, Y) \wedge leq(Y, Z) \wedge \neg leq(X, Z)$$

Figure 1 shows one possible derivation of this goal to the final state representing *false*. For brevity, we omit the $\mathcal{V}$ and $\mathcal{P}$ fields, and represent identifiers as subscripts, i.e. $T\#i = T_i$. Also we substitute $T = \{\mathtt{transitivity} @ (3\ 2\ 1\ 7\ 5\ 6)\}$.

We can state a soundness result for ACDTR.

Theorem 1 (Soundness). *If $\langle G_0, T_0, \mathcal{V}, \mathcal{P} \rangle \rightarrowtail^* \langle G', T', \mathcal{V}, \mathcal{P} \rangle$ with respect to a program P, then $[\![P]\!] \models \exists_{vars(G')-\mathcal{V}} G_0 \approx G'$*

This means that for all algebras $\mathcal{A}$ that satisfy $[\![P]\!]$, G_0 and G' are equivalent for some assignment of the fresh variables in G'.

4   Implementation

We have implemented a prototype version of ACDTR as part of the mapping language of the G12 project, called Cadmium. In this section we give an overview of the implementation details. In particular, we will focus on the implementation of conjunctive context matching, which is the main contribution of this paper.

Cadmium constructs *normalised* terms from the bottom up. Here, a *normalised* term is one that cannot be reduced further by an application of a rule. Given a goal $f(t_1, ..., t_n)$, we first must recursively normalise all of $t_1, ..., t_n$ (to say $s_1, ..., s_n$), and then attempt to find a rule that can be applied to the top-level of $f(s_1, ..., s_n)$. This is the standard execution algorithm used by many TRSs implementations.

This approach of normalising terms bottom up is complicated by the consideration of conjunctive context matching. This is because the conjunctive context of the current term appears "higher up" in the overall goal term. Thus conjunctive context must be passed top down, yet we are normalising bottom up. This means there is no guarantee that the conjunctive context is normalised.

Example 12. Consider the following ACDTR program that uses conjunctive context matching.

$$X = V \setminus X \Longleftrightarrow var(X) \wedge nonvar(V) \mid V.$$
$$one(X) \Longleftrightarrow X = 1.$$
$$not\_one(1) \Longleftrightarrow false.$$

Consider the goal $not\_one(A) \wedge one(A)$, which we expect should be normalised to $false$. Assume that the sub-term $not\_one(A)$ is selected for normalisation first. The conjunctive context for $not\_one(A)$ (and its subterm A) is $one(A)$. No rule is applicable, so $not\_one(A)$ is not reduced.

Next the subterm $one(A)$ is reduced. The second rule will fire resulting in the new term $A = 1$. Now the conjunctive context for the first term $not\_one(A)$ has changed to $A = 1$, so we expect that A should be rewritten to the number 1. However $not\_one(A)$ has already being considered for normalisation.   □

The current Cadmium prototype solves this problem by re-normalising terms when and if the conjunctive context "changes". For example, when the conjunctive context $one(A)$ changes to $A = 1$, the term $not\_one(X)$ will be renormalised to $not\_one(1)$ by the first rule.

The general execution algorithm for Cadmium is shown in Figure 2. Function normalise takes a term T, a substitution θ, a conjunctive context CC and a Boolean value Ch which keeps track of when the conjunctive context of the current subterm has changed. If $Ch = true$, then we can assume the substitution θ maps variables to normalised terms. For the initial goal, we assume θ is empty, otherwise if we are executing a body of a rule, then θ is the matching substitution.

Operationally, normalise splits into three cases depending on what T is. If T is a variable, and the conjunctive context has changed (i.e. $Ch = true$), then $\theta(T)$ is no longer guaranteed to be normalised. In this case we return the result of renormalising $\theta(T)$ with respect to CC. Otherwise if $Ch = false$, we simply return $\theta(T)$ which must be already normalised. If T is a conjunction $T_1 \wedge T_2$, we repeatedly call normalise on each conjunct with the other added to the conjunctive context. This is repeated until a fixed point (i.e. further normalisation does not result in either conjunct changing) is reached, and then return the result of apply_rule on the which we will discuss below. This fixed point calculation accounts for the case where the conjunctive context of a term changes, as shown in Example 12. Otherwise, if T is any other term of the form $f(T_1, ..., T_n)$, construct the new term T' by normalising each argument. Finally we return the result of apply_rule applied to T'.

The function call apply_rule(T',CC) will attempt to apply a rule to normalised term T' with respect to conjunctive context CC. If a matching rule is found,

```
normalise(T,θ,CC,Ch)
    if is_var(T)
        if Ch
            return normalise(θ(T),θ,CC,false)
        else
            return θ(T)
    else if T = T₁ ∧ T₂
        do
            T₁' := T₁
            T₂' := T₂
            T₁ := normalise(T₁',θ,T₂' ∧ CC,true)
            T₂ := normalise(T₂',θ,T₁' ∧ CC,true)
        while T₁ ≠ T₁' ∧ T₂ ≠ T₂'
        return apply_rule(T₁' ∧ T₂',CC)
    else
        T = f(T₁,...,Tₙ)
        T' := f(normalise(T₁,θ,CC,Ch), ..., normalise(Tₙ,θ,CC,Ch))
    return apply_rule(T',CC)
```

Fig. 2. Pseudo code of the Cadmium execution algorithm

then the result of normalise($B,\theta,CC,false$) is returned, where B is the (re-named) rule body and θ is the matching substitution. Otherwise, T' is simply returned.

5   Related Work

ACDTR is closely related to both TRS and CHRs, and in this section we compare the three languages.

5.1   AC Term Rewriting Systems

The problem of dealing with associative commutative operators in TRS is well studied. A popular solution is to perform the rewriting modulo some permutation of the AC operators. Although this complicates the matching algorithm, the problem of trivial non-termination (e.g. by continually rewriting with respect to commutativity) is solved.

ACDTR subsumes ACTRS (Associative Commutative TRS) in that we have introduced distributivity (via simpagation rules), and added some "CHR-style" concepts such as identifiers and propagation rules.

Given an ACTRS program, we can map it to an equivalent ACDTR program by interpreting each ACTRS rule $H \rightarrow B$ as the ACDTR rule $H \Longleftrightarrow B$. We can now state the theorem relating ACTRS and ACDTR.

Theorem 2. *Let P be an ACTRS program and T a ground term, then $T \rightarrow^* S$ under P iff $\langle T_a, \emptyset, \emptyset, \mathsf{ids}(T_a) \rangle \rightarrowtail^* \langle S_a, \emptyset, \emptyset, \mathcal{P} \rangle$ under $\alpha(P)$ (where $T_a = \mathsf{annotate}$ $(\emptyset, T)$) for some $\mathcal{P}$ and $\mathsf{term}(S_a) = S$.*

5.2 CHRs and CHR$^\vee$

ACDTR has been deliberately designed to be an extension of CHRs. Several CHR concepts, e.g. propagation rules, etc., have been adapted.

There are differences between CHRs and ACDTR. The main difference is that ACDTR does not have a "built-in" or "underlying" solver, i.e. ACDTR is not a constraint programming language. However it is possible to encode solvers directly as rules, e.g. the simple *leq* solver from Example 8. Another important difference is that CHRs is based on predicate logic, where there exists a distinction between predicate symbols (i.e. the names of the constraints) and functions (used to construct terms). ACDTR is based on equational logic between terms, hence there is no distinction between predicates and functions (a predicate is just a Boolean function). To overcome this, we assume the existence of a set $\mathcal{P}red$, which contains the set of function symbols that are Boolean functions. We assume that $AC \cap \mathcal{P}red = \{\wedge^{(2)}\}$.

The mapping between a CHR program and an ACDTR program is simply $\alpha(P) = P \cup \{X \wedge true \Longleftrightarrow X\}$. [4] However, we assume program P is restricted as follows:

- rules have no guards apart from implicit equality guards; and
- the only built-in constraint is *true*

and the initial goal G is also restricted:

- G must be of the form $G_0 \wedge ... \wedge G_n$ for $n > 0$;
- Each G_i is of the form $f_i(A_0, ..., A_m)$ for $m \geq 0$ and $f_i \in \mathcal{P}red$;
- For all $p \in \mathcal{P}os(A_j), 0 \leq j \leq m$ we have that if $A_j|_p = g(B_0, ..., B_q)$ then $g^{(q)} \notin AC$ and $g^{(q)} \notin \mathcal{P}red$.

These conditions disallow predicate symbols from appearing as arguments in CHR constraints.

Theorem 3. *Let P be a CHR program, and G an initial goal both satisfying the above conditions, then $\langle G, \emptyset, true, \emptyset \rangle_1^{\mathcal{V}} \rightarrowtail \langle \emptyset, S, true, T \rangle_i^{\mathcal{V}}$ (for some T, i and $\mathcal{V} = vars(G)$) under the theoretical operational semantics [4] for CHRs iff $\langle G_a, \emptyset, \mathcal{V}, \mathsf{ids}(G_a) \rangle \rightarrowtail \langle S_a, T', \mathcal{V}, \mathcal{P} \rangle$ (for some T', $\mathcal{P}$) under ACDTR, where $\mathsf{term}(S_a) = S_1 \wedge ... \wedge S_n$ and $S = \{S_1 \# i_1, ..., S_n \# i_n\}$ for some identifiers $i_1, ..., i_n$.*

We believe that Theorem 3 could be extended to include CHR programs that extend an underlying solver, provided the rules for handling tell constraints are added to the ACDTR program. For example, we can combine rules for rational tree unification with the *leq* program from Example 8 to get a program equivalent to the traditional *leq* program under CHRs.

ACDTR generalises CHRs by allowing other operators besides conjunction inside the head or body of rules. One such extension of CHRs has been studied before, namely CHR$^\vee$ [2] which allows disjunction in the body. Unlike ACDTR,

---

[4] There is one slight difference in syntax: CHRs use ',' to represent conjunction, whereas ACDTR uses '$\wedge$'.

which manipulates disjunction syntactically, $CHR^\vee$ typically finds solutions using backtracking search.

One notable implementation of $CHR^\vee$ is [6], which has an operational semantics described as an and/or $(\wedge/\vee)$ tree rewriting system. A limited form of conjunctive context matching is used, similar to that used by ACDTR, based on the knowledge that conjunction $\wedge$ distributes over disjunction $\vee$. ACDTR generalises this by distributing over all functions.

6   Future Work and Conclusions

We have presented a powerful new rule-based programming language, ACDTR, that naturally extends both AC term rewriting and CHRs. The main contribution is the ability to match a rule against the conjunctive context of a (sub)term, taking advantage of the distributive property of conjunction over all possible functions. We have shown this is a natural way of expressing some problems, and by building the distributive property into the matching algorithm, we avoid non-termination issues that arise from naively implementing distribution (e.g. as rewrite rules).

We intend that ACDTR will become the theoretical basis for the Cadmium constraint mapping language as part of the G12 project [7]. Work on ACDTR and Cadmium is ongoing, and there is a wide scope for future work, such as confluence, termination and implementation/optimisation issues.

References

1. S. Abdennadher. Operational semantics and confluence of constraint propagation rules. In Gert Smolka, editor, *Proceedings of the Third International Conference on Principles and Practice of Constraint Programming*, LNCS 1330, pages 252–266. Springer-Verlag, 1997.
2. S. Abdennadher and H. Schütz. $CHR^\vee$: A flexible query language. In *International conference on Flexible Query Answering Systems*, number 1495 in LNCS, pages 1–14, Roskilde, Denmark, 1998. Springer-Verlag.
3. F. Baader and T. Nipkow. *Term rewriting and all that*. Cambridge Univ. Press, 1998.
4. G. Duck, P. Stuckey, M. Garcia de la Banda, and C. Holzbaur. The refined operational semantics of constraint handling rules. In B. Demoen and V. Lifschitz, editors, *Proceedings of the 20th International Conference on Logic Programming*, LNCS 3132, pages 90–104. Springer-Verlag, September 2004.
5. T. Frühwirth. Theory and practice of constraint handling rules. *Journal of Logic Programming*, 37:95–138, 1998.
6. L. Menezes, J. Vitorino, and M. Aurelio. A High Performance $CHR^\vee$ Execution Engine. In *Second Workshop on Constraint Handling Rules*, Sitges, Spain, 2005.
7. P.J. Stuckey, M. Garcia de la Banda, M. Maher, K. Marriott, J. Slaney, Z. Somogyi, M. Wallace, and T. Walsh. The G12 project: Mapping solver independent models to efficient solutions. In M. Gabrielli and G. Gupta, editors, *Proceedings of the 21st International Conference on Logic Programming*, number 3668 in LNCS, pages 9–13. Springer-Verlag, 2005.

Detecting Determinacy in Prolog Programs

Andy King[1], Lunjin Lu[2], and Samir Genaim[3]

[1] University of Kent, Canterbury, CT2 7NF, UK
[2] Oakland University, Rochester, MI 48309, USA
[3] Universidad Politécnica de Madrid, Spain

Abstract. In program development it is useful to know that a call to a
Prolog program will not inadvertently leave a choice-point on the stack.
Determinacy inference has been proposed for solving this problem yet the
analysis was found to be wanting in that it could not infer determinacy
conditions for programs that contained cuts or applied certain tests to
select a clause. This paper shows how to remedy these serious deficiencies.
It also addresses the problem of identifying those predicates which can
be rewritten in a more deterministic fashion. To this end, a radically new
form of determinacy inference is introduced, which is founded on ideas
in ccp, that is capable of reasoning about the way bindings imposed by
a rightmost goal can make a leftmost goal deterministic.

1 Introduction

Understanding the determinacy behaviour of a logic program is important in program development. To this end, determinacy inference [13] has been proposed as an analysis for inferring conditions on goals that are sufficient to assure determinacy. The key difference between determinacy checking [12,14,16] and determinacy inference is that the former verifies that a given goal will generate at most one answer at most once (if it yields any at all) whereas the latter infers, in a single application of the analysis, a class of goals that are deterministic. In addition to ensuring the determinacy of the initial goal, the conditions inferred by [13] ensure the determinacy of each intermediate atomic sub-goal that is invoked whilst solving the initial goal. Therefore, any call that satisfies its determinacy condition cannot (unintentionally) leave a choice-point on the stack.

Determinacy inference is most insightful when it infers a class of calls that differs from what the programmer expects. If the class is smaller than expected, then either the predicate is unintentionally non-deterministic (i.e. buggy), or the analysis is insufficiently precise. If the class is larger than anticipated, then either the predicate possesses properties that the programmer overlooked (i.e. subtle sub-goal interactions that induce determinacy), or it has been coded incorrectly. Alas, determinacy inference was found to be insufficiently precise for programs which used the cut to enforce determinacy. This is because determinacy conditions are derived from conditions, known as mutual exclusion conditions, that are sufficient to ensure that at most one clause of a predicate can derive an answer to a call. These conditions are derived by analysing the constraints that

S. Etalle and M. Truszczyński (Eds.): ICLP 2006, LNCS 4079, pp. 132–147, 2006.
© Springer-Verlag Berlin Heidelberg 2006

arise in the different clauses of a predicate. Cuts are often introduced so as to avoid applying a test in a clause whose outcome is predetermined by a test in an earlier clause. The absence of such a test prevented a mutual exclusion condition from being inferred. This paper shows that, although this problem may appear insurmountable, that determinacy inference can be elegantly extended to support cuts. The paper also reports how the machinery used to infer mutual exclusion conditions can be refined so as to reason about tests that operate, not on the arguments of a clause, but sub-terms of the arguments. This is also key to inferring accurate mutual exclusion conditions for realistic programs.

As well as enhancing an existing analysis, the paper introduces a new form of determinacy inference. To illustrate the contribution, consider the database:

```
q(a).   q(b).   r(a).
```

and compound goal q(X), r(X) which is not dissimilar to a number of goals that we have found in existing programs [19]. The compound goal generates at most one answer, no matter how it is called, due to the way the bindings generated by the rightmost sub-goal constrain the leftmost sub-goal. The analysis of [13] would only infer that the goal is deterministic if called with X ground. Yet the vacuous groundness condition of *true* is sufficient for the goal to be determinate (even though it employs backtracking). The value in knowing that the goal is actually determinate is that it alerts the programmer to *where* the program can be improved. If the programmer can verify that the determinacy conditions hold (which is often straightforward) then the goal can be executed under a once meta-call without compromising correctness. Equivalently, the goal could be replaced with q(X), r(X), !. Either approach would remove any choicepoints that remain unexplored and thereby eliminate a performance bug. Alternatively, the programmer might observe that the goal can be reordered to obtain r(X), q(X) which will not generate any choice-points at all (though such a reordering might compromise termination).

The new form of determinacy inference reported in this paper can locate these opportunities for optimisation when it is used in conjunction with the existing analysis [13]. The new form of analysis can detect determinacy in the presence of right-to-left flow of bindings; the existing analysis cannot. Hence, any discrepancy between the results of the two analyses identifies a goal that is deterministic, yet could possibly leave choice-points on the stack. Such goals warrant particularly close scrutiny. Without this form of pinpointing, it would be necessary to manually inspect large numbers of non-deterministic predicates.

One technical contribution is in the way the new analysis is realised using suspension inference [4]. The intuition is to add delay declarations to the program so that a goal can only be selected if no more than one clause in the matching predicate can generate an answer. The sub-goals r(X) and q(X) are thus selected when, respectively, the groundness conditions of *true* and X are satisfied. Suspension inference then deduces that the condition *true* is sufficient for the compound goal not to suspend. A correctness result reported in the paper shows that non-suspension conditions can then be reinterpreted as determinacy conditions. In addition to its use in debugging, the analysis has application in the burgeoning area of semi-offline program specialisation (see the discussion in section 6). The paper is organised as follows. Section 2 presents a worked example that illustrates the new form of determinacy inference. Section 3 explains the main correctness result. (The proofs and all the supporting lemmata are all given in [6]). Sections 4 and 5 explain how to support cuts and tests between the sub-terms of arguments. Sections 6 surveys the related work.

2   Worked Example

Since the correctness argument is necessarily theoretical, this section illustrates the key ideas in the new approach to determinacy inference by way of an example:

```
(1) rev([],[]).
(2) rev([X|Xs],Ys) :- rev(Xs,Zs), app(Zs,[X],Ys).

(3) app([],X,X).
(4) app([X|Xs],Ys,[X|Zs]) :- app(Xs,Ys,Zs).
```

2.1   The Common Ground

The chief novelty in the previous approach to determinacy inference [13] was in the way success patterns for the individual clauses of a predicate were used to infer mutual exclusion conditions for a call to that predicate. The new analysis builds on these mutual exclusion conditions. Such a condition, when satisfied by a call, ensures that no more than one clause of the matching predicate can lead to a successful derivation. To illustrate, consider characterising the success patterns with an argument-size analysis in which size is measured as list-length:

$$(1)\ \mathtt{rev}(x_1, x_2)\ :-\ x_1 = 0,\ x_2 = 0.$$
$$(2)\ \mathtt{rev}(x_1, x_2)\ :-\ x_1 \geq 1,\ x_1 = x_2.$$

$$(3)\ \mathtt{app}(x_1, x_2, x_3)\ :-\ x_1 = 0,\ x_2 \geq 0,\ x_2 = x_3.$$
$$(4)\ \mathtt{app}(x_1, x_2, x_3)\ :-\ x_1 \geq 1,\ x_2 \geq 0,\ x_1 + x_2 = x_3.$$

An algorithm that takes, as input, success patterns and produces, as output, mutual exclusion conditions is detailed in our previous paper [13]. Rather than repeating the algorithm, we give the intuition of how rigidity relates to mutual exclusion. If a call $\mathtt{rev}(x_1, x_2)$ succeeds with x_1 bound to a rigid list, then so does a new call $\mathtt{rev}(x_1, x_2)$ to the new version of the predicate in which x_1 is bound to the length of the list. Hence, if the original clause succeeds with the original clause (1), then so does the new call to the new version of that clause. The presence of the constraint $x_1 = 0$ in the new clause implies that the argument x_1 of the new call was initially zero. The new clause (2) cannot then also succeed because of the constraint $x_1 \geq 1$. Hence the original clause (2) cannot also succeed with the original call. The argument follows in the other direction, hence the rigidity condition x_1 on the original call is sufficient for mutual exclusion. By similar reasoning, the rigidity of x_2 is also sufficient hence the combined condition $x_1 \vee x_2$ is also a mutual exclusion condition. Repeating this argument for $\mathsf{app}(x_1, x_2, x_3)$ yields $x_1 \vee (x_2 \wedge x_3)$ [13].

2.2   The Problem

The value of mutual exclusion conditions is that if all sub-goals encountered whilst solving a goal satisfy their conditions, then the goal is deterministic [13]. This motivates the application of backward analysis [5] which infers conditions on goals which ensure that a given set of assertions are not violated. By adding assertions that check calls meet their mutual exclusion conditions, the backward analysis will infer conditions on goals that assure determinacy. To illustrate backward analysis, consider clause (2) on the previous page. Since [X] is rigid, it is enough for $d_2 = \mathsf{Zs} \vee \mathsf{Ys}$ to hold for $\mathsf{app}(\mathsf{Zs},[\mathsf{X}],\mathsf{Ys})$ to satisfy its condition. By inspecting the success patterns of rev it follows that after the sub-goal $\mathsf{rev}(\mathsf{Xs},\mathsf{Zs})$ the rigidity property $f_1 = \mathsf{Xs} \wedge \mathsf{Zs}$ holds. Thus, if the condition $f_1 \rightarrow d_2$ holds before the sub-goal, then $(f_1 \rightarrow d_2) \wedge f_1$, hence d_2, holds after the sub-goal, and thus the mutual exclusion condition for $\mathsf{app}(\mathsf{Zs},[\mathsf{X}],\mathsf{Ys})$ is satisfied. Since $d_1 = \mathsf{Xs} \vee \mathsf{Zs}$ is the mutual exclusion condition for the $\mathsf{rev}(\mathsf{Xs},\mathsf{Zs})$, $d_1 \wedge (f_1 \rightarrow d_2) = (\mathsf{Xs} \vee \mathsf{Zs})$ guarantees that both sub-goals of the body satisfy their conditions when encountered. To satisfy this condition, it is enough for [X|Xs] to be rigid, that is, for rev to be called with a rigid first argument.

The astute reader will notice that rev is determinate when called with a rigid second argument. To see this, observe that each answer to $\mathsf{rev}(\mathsf{Xs}, \mathsf{Zs})$ will instantiate Zs to a list of different size. Now consider executing the compound goal $\mathsf{app}(\mathsf{Zs},[\mathsf{X}],\mathsf{Ys})$, $\mathsf{rev}(\mathsf{Xs}, \mathsf{Zs})$ with Ys rigid. The rigidity of Ys ensures that $\mathsf{app}(\mathsf{Zs},[\mathsf{X}],\mathsf{Ys})$ is deterministic and thus Zs has at most one solution of fixed size. This, in turn, guarantees that $\mathsf{rev}(\mathsf{Xs}, \mathsf{Zs})$ can yield at most one answer, hence the compound goal is deterministic. (Actually, rev gives one answer and then loops in this mode, though this does not compromise determinacy and such goals can always be executed under once without compromising correctness). It is therefore disappointing that [13] only discovers one deterministic mode.

2.3   The Solution

The two deterministic modes stem from different flows of bindings between the sub-goals. This motivates an analysis that considers different schedulings of sub-goals and selects a sub-goal only when its mutual exclusion condition is satisfied. In effect, mutual exclusion conditions are interpreted as delay conditions like so:

```
delay rev(X, Y) until rigid_list(X) ; rigid_list(Y).
rev([],[]).
rev([X|Xs],Ys) :- rev(Xs,Zs), app(Zs,[X],Ys).
delay app(X, Y, Z) until rigid_list(X) ; (rigid_list(Y) , rigid_list(Z)).
app([],X,X).
app([X|Xs],Ys,[X|Zs]) :- app(Xs,Ys,Zs).
```

The delay declarations, which are reminiscent of Gödel syntax, block rev and app goals until combinations of their arguments are bound to rigid lists. Suspension inference [4] (which can be considered to be a black-box) is then applicable to this transformation of the original program and, for this derived program, can infer classes of initial goals which cannot lead to suspending states. For these initial goals, the program cannot reduce to a state that only contains suspending sub-goals, that is, sub-goals which violate their mutual exclusion conditions. Since each sub-goal satisfies its condition when executed, the computation is deterministic. Furthermore, executing any such initial goal under left-to-right selection (and we conjecture any selection) will also generate at most one answer [6] — it may not terminate but again this will not undermine determinacy. Applying suspension inference [4] to the above program yields the rigidity conditions of $x_1 \vee x_2$ and $x_1 \vee (x_2 \wedge x_3)$ for $\mathtt{rev}(x_1, x_2)$ and $\mathtt{app}(x_1, x_2, x_3)$ respectively, as desired. Note that the delay conditions are not left in the program after analysis; they are only introduced for the purpose of applying suspension inference.

3   The Semantics and the Transformation

This section builds toward stating a result which explains how suspension inference can be applied to realise determinacy inference. Rather unusually, the result relates three different semantics. Firstly, a semantics that maps a single call to a Prolog program to a multiset of possible answers. This semantics is rich enough to observe non-determinacy. Secondly, a semantics for success patterns which can express the concept of a mutual exclusion condition. Thirdly, a semantics for ccp that is rich enough for observing non-suspension. In order to express the transformation of a Prolog program, all three semantics have been formulated in terms of a common language syntax and a common computational domain of constraints. This domain is detailed in section 3.1. The semantics (which themselves possess a number of novel features) are presented in sections 3.2 and 3.3. Finally the transformation and the result itself is presented in section 3.4.

3.1   Computational Domain of Constraints

The computational domain is a set of constraints Con that is ordered by an entailment (implication) relation $\models$. The set Con is assumed to contain equality constraints of the form $\boldsymbol{x} = \boldsymbol{y}$ where $\boldsymbol{x}$ and $\boldsymbol{y}$ are vectors of variables. Syntactically different constraints may entail one another and therefore a relation $\equiv$ is introduced to express equivalence which is defined by $\theta_1 \equiv \theta_2$ iff $\theta_1 \models \theta_2$ and $\theta_2 \models \theta_1$. Since we do not wish to distinguish between constraints that are semantically equivalent but syntactically different, we base our semantics on a domain of equivalence classes Con/$\equiv$ in which a class is denoted by $[\theta]_\equiv$ where θ is a representative member of the class. This domain is ordered by $[\theta_1]_\equiv \models [\theta_2]_\equiv$ iff $\theta_1 \models \theta_2$. The domain is assumed to come equipped with a conjunction operation $[\theta_1]_\equiv \wedge [\theta_2]_\equiv$ and a projection operation $\overline{\exists}_{\boldsymbol{x}}([\theta]_\equiv)$ where $\boldsymbol{x}$ is a vector of variables, both of which are assumed to posses normal algebraic properties [18].

The former conjoins constraints whereas the latter hides information in $[\theta]_\equiv$ that pertains to variables not contained within x.

Equality constraints such as $x = y$ provide a way of connecting the actual arguments x of a call with the formal arguments y of the matching procedure. However, equality is doubly useful since, when combined with projection, it provides a way of renaming constraints — an action which is inextricably linked with parameter passing. To systematically substitute each variable in x with its corresponding variable in y within the constraint $[\theta]_\equiv$ it is sufficient to compute $\overline{\exists}_y(\overline{\exists}_x([\theta]_\equiv) \wedge [x = y]_\equiv)$ provided that $\text{var}(x) \cap \text{var}(y) = \emptyset$. Since renaming is commonplace, we introduce an abbreviation — $\rho_{x,y}([\theta]_\equiv)$ — which is defined $\rho_{x,y}([\theta]_\equiv) = \overline{\exists}_y(\overline{\exists}_x([\theta]_\equiv) \wedge [x = y]_\equiv)$ if $\text{var}(x) \cap \text{var}(y) = \emptyset$ and $\rho_{x,y}([\theta]_\equiv) = \rho_{z,y}(\rho_{x,z}([\theta]_\equiv))$ otherwise, where z is a vector of fresh variables. Note that $\rho_{x,y}([\theta]_\equiv)$ removes any variables that are not renamed.

Although the domain of equivalence classes $\text{Con}/\equiv$ and its associated operators is adequate for the purposes of constructing the three semantics, it is actually simpler to work within a domain of sets of constraints where each set is closed under implication [18]. This domain is $\wp^\downarrow(\text{Con}) = \{\Theta \subseteq \text{Con} \mid \downarrow\Theta = \Theta\}$ where $\downarrow\Theta = \{\theta_1 \in \text{Con} \mid \exists\theta_2 \in \Theta.\theta_1 \models \theta_2\}$. The crucial point is that operations over $\text{Con}/\equiv$ can be simulated within $\wp^\downarrow(\text{Con})$ which has a less complicated structure. For example, consider the conjunction $[\theta_1]_\equiv \wedge [\theta_2]_\equiv$ for some $\theta_1, \theta_2 \in \text{Con}$. If $\Theta_i = \downarrow\{\theta_i\}$ for $i = 1, 2$ then the conjunction can be modeled by just $\Theta_1 \cap \Theta_2$ since $[\theta_1]_\equiv \wedge [\theta_2]_\equiv = [\theta]_\equiv$ iff $\theta \in \Theta_1 \cap \Theta_2$. The projection and renaming operators straightforwardly lift to closed sets of constraints by $\overline{\exists}_x(\Theta) = \downarrow\{\overline{\exists}_x([\theta]_\equiv) \mid \theta \in \Theta\}$ and $\rho_{x,y}(\Theta) = \downarrow\{\rho_{x,y}([\theta]_\equiv) \mid \theta \in \Theta\}$.

3.2   Multiset and Success Set Semantics for Prolog Programs

To express the transformation that maps a Prolog program into a concurrent program, it is helpful to express both classes of program within the same language. Thus we adopt concurrent constraint programming (ccp) [18] style in which a program P takes the form $P ::= \epsilon | p(x) :- A | P_1.P_2$ where A is an agent that is defined by $A ::= \text{ask}(\Theta) \rightarrow A | \text{tell}(\Theta) | A_1, A_2 | \sum_{i=1}^{n} A_i | p(x)$ and $\Theta \in \wp^\downarrow(\text{Con})$ and throughout x denotes a vector of distinct variable arguments. A Prolog program is merely a program devoid of agents of the form $\text{ask}(\Theta) \rightarrow A$. In the concurrent setting, $\text{ask}(\Theta) \rightarrow A$ blocks A until the constraint store Φ entails the ask constraint Θ, that is, $\Phi \subseteq \Theta$. In both settings, the agent $\text{tell}(\Theta)$ updates the store from Φ to $\Phi \cap \Theta$ by imposing the constraints Θ. In a Prolog program, the composition operator "," is interpreted as a sequencing operator which induces left-to-right control, whereas in a concurrent program, the same operator is interpreted as parallel composition. For both classes of program $\sum_{i=1}^{n} A_i$ is an explicit choice operator which systematically searches all A_i agents for answers. This represents the most radical departure from classic Prolog but it is a useful construction because, without loss of generality, all predicates can be assumed to be defined with exactly one definition of the form $p(x) :- A$.

The rationale of the multiset semantics is to capture whether an answer does not occur, occurs exactly once or occurs multiply to a given query. In order to make the semantics as simple as possible, the semantics maps a call, not to an arbitrary multiset of answers, but to a restricted class of multisets in which no element occurs more than twice. This restriction still enables non-determinacy to be observed but assures that the equations that define the multiset semantics have a least solution and therefore that the semantics is well-defined.

Before we proceed to the semantics, we need to clarify what is meant by a multiset of answers and how such multisets can be manipulated and written. A multiset of answers is an element in the space $\wp(\mathsf{Con}) \to \{0, 1, 2\}$, that is, a map which details how many times, if any, that an answer can arise. Henceforth we shall let $\widehat{\mathsf{Con}}$ abbreviate this set of maps. Multiset union over $\widehat{\mathsf{Con}}$ is defined by $M_1 \widehat{\cup} M_2 = \lambda\Theta.\min(M_1(\Theta) + M_2(\Theta), 2)$. Thus if an element occurs singly in both M_1 and M_2 then it occurs twice in $M_1 \widehat{\cup} M_2$. However, if it occurs singly in M_1 and twice in M_2 then it occurs twice in $M_1 \widehat{\cup} M_2$. Henceforth, to simplify the presentation, we write $\wr\wr$ for the multiset $\lambda\Theta.0$ and $\wr\Psi, \Phi, \Phi\wr$, for instance, for $\lambda\Theta.$if $\Theta = \Psi$ then 1 else (if $\Theta = \Phi$ then 2 else 0). Furthermore, we adopt multiset comprehensions with the interpretation that the predicate $\Theta\widehat{\in}M$ succeeds once/twice iff Θ occurs once/twice in M. For example, if $M' = \wr\Theta, \Theta, \Phi\wr$ then $\wr\Psi \cup \Omega \mid \Omega\widehat{\in}M'\wr = \wr\Psi \cup \Theta, \Psi \cup \Theta, \Psi \cup \Phi\wr$.

The multiset semantics is a mapping of type $\mathsf{Age}_P \to \wp(\mathsf{Con}) \to \widehat{\mathsf{Con}}$ where Age_P denotes the set of agents that can be constructed from calls to predicates defined within P. The intuition is that, for a given agent $A \in \mathsf{Age}_P$, the multiset semantics maps a closed set Φ to a multiset of closed sets that detail all the possible answers to A given the input Φ.

Definition 1. The mapping $\mathcal{M}_P : \mathsf{Age}_P \to \wp(\mathsf{Con}) \to \widehat{\mathsf{Con}}$ is the least solution to the following system of recursive equations:

$$\mathcal{M}_P[\![\mathsf{tell}(\Phi)]\!](\Theta) = \text{if } \Phi \cap \Theta = \emptyset \text{ then } \wr\wr \text{ else } \wr\Phi \cap \Theta\wr$$
$$\mathcal{M}_P[\![A_1, A_2]\!](\Theta) = \widehat{\cup}\wr\mathcal{M}_P[\![A_2]\!](\Phi) \mid \Phi\widehat{\in}\mathcal{M}_P[\![A_1]\!](\Theta)\wr$$
$$\mathcal{M}_P[\![\textstyle\sum_{i=1}^{n} A_i]\!](\Theta) = \widehat{\cup}\wr\mathcal{M}_P[\![A_i]\!](\Theta)\wr_{i=1}^{n}$$
$$\mathcal{M}_P[\![p(\boldsymbol{x})]\!](\Theta) = \wr\Theta \cap \rho_{y,x}(\Phi) \mid \Phi \in \mathcal{M}_P[\![A]\!](\rho_{x,y}(\Theta))\wr \text{ where } p(\boldsymbol{y}) :- A \in P$$

Example 1. Let $\Theta_a = \downarrow\{x = a\}$ and $\Theta_b = \downarrow\{x = b\}$ and consider the program $P = \{q(x) :- \sum_{i=1}^{3} A_i, r(x) :- \mathsf{tell}(\Theta_a), p(x) :- q(x), r(x)\}$ where $A_1 = \mathsf{tell}(\Theta_a)$ and $A_2 = A_3 = \mathsf{tell}(\Theta_b)$ which builds on the example in the introduction. The closed set Con can be used to express unconstrained input, hence:

$$\mathcal{M}_P[\![p(\boldsymbol{x})]\!](\mathsf{Con}) = \wr\Theta_a\wr \qquad \mathcal{M}_P[\![p(\boldsymbol{x})]\!](\Theta_a) = \wr\Theta_a\wr \; \mathcal{M}_P[\![p(\boldsymbol{x})]\!](\Theta_b) = \wr\wr$$
$$\mathcal{M}_P[\![q(\boldsymbol{x})]\!](\mathsf{Con}) = \wr\Theta_a, \Theta_b, \Theta_b\wr \; \mathcal{M}_P[\![q(\boldsymbol{x})]\!](\Theta_a) = \wr\Theta_a\wr \; \mathcal{M}_P[\![q(\boldsymbol{x})]\!](\Theta_b) = \wr\Theta_b, \Theta_b\wr$$
$$\mathcal{M}_P[\![r(\boldsymbol{x})]\!](\mathsf{Con}) = \wr\Theta_a\wr \qquad \mathcal{M}_P[\![r(\boldsymbol{x})]\!](\Theta_a) = \wr\Theta_a\wr \; \mathcal{M}_P[\![r(\boldsymbol{x})]\!](\Theta_b) = \wr\wr$$

Although the multiset semantics applies the left-to-right goal selection, it does not apply the top-down clause selection. This does not mean that it cannot observe non-determinacy because, in general, if a call has $n \geq 2$ answers for some input in Prolog then it has at least $m \geq n$ answers for the same input in the multiset semantics as is illustrated below.

Example 2. Consider a program consisting of the clause $p(x) :- x = [\_|y], p(y)$ followed by $p(x) :- x = []$. Because of top-down clause selection, $p(x)$ will loop in Prolog, ie. return no answers, if invoked with x unconstrained. In our presentation, the Prolog program as rendered as a program P consisting of one definition $p(x) :- \sum_{i=1}^{2} A_i$ where $A_1 = \mathsf{tell}(\downarrow\{x = [\_|y]\}), p(y)$ and $A_2 = \mathsf{tell}(\downarrow\{x = []\})$. Then $\mathcal{M}_P[\![p(x)]\!](\mathsf{Con}) = \{\Theta_i \mid i \geq 0\}$ where $\Theta_i = \downarrow\{x = [x_1, \ldots, x_i]\}$ and the semantics observes that $p(x)$ is not determinate when x is unconstrained.

The following success set semantics is the most conventional. It pins down the meaning of a success pattern which underlies the concept of mutual exclusion.

Definition 2. The mapping $\mathcal{S}_P : \mathsf{Age}_P \to \wp^{\downarrow}(\mathsf{Con})$ is the least solution to the following system of recursive equations:

$$\mathcal{S}_P[\![\mathsf{tell}(\Phi)]\!] = \Phi$$
$$\mathcal{S}_P[\![A_1, A_2]\!] = \mathcal{S}_P[\![A_1]\!] \cap \mathcal{S}_P[\![A_2]\!]$$
$$\mathcal{S}_P[\![\textstyle\sum_{i=1}^{n} A_i]\!] = \cup\{\mathcal{S}_P[\![A_i]\!]\}_{i=1}^{n}$$
$$\mathcal{S}_P[\![p(x)]\!] = \rho_{y,x}(\mathcal{S}_P[\![A]\!]) \text{ where } p(y) :- A \in P$$

3.3   Concurrency Semantics for ccp Programs

To state the key correctness result, it is necessary to introduce a concurrency semantics for verifying the absence of suspending agents. Whether suspensions manifest themselves or not depends on the quiescent (resting) state of the store, which motivates the following semantics that was inspired by the elegant quiescent state semantics that has been advocated for ccp [18].

Definition 3. The mapping $\mathcal{Q}_P : \mathsf{Age}_P \to \wp(\wp^{\downarrow}(\mathsf{Con}) \times \{0,1\})$ is the least solution to the following system of recursive equations:

$$\mathcal{Q}_P[\![\mathsf{ask}(\Phi) \to A]\!] = \{\langle \Theta, 1 \rangle \mid \downarrow\Theta = \Theta \wedge \Theta \not\subseteq \Phi\} \cup \{\langle \Theta, b \rangle \in \mathcal{Q}_P[\![A]\!] \mid \Theta \subseteq \Phi\}$$
$$\mathcal{Q}_P[\![\mathsf{tell}(\Phi)]\!] = \{\langle \Theta, 0 \rangle \mid \downarrow\Theta = \Theta \wedge \Theta \subseteq \Phi\}$$
$$\mathcal{Q}_P[\![A_1, A_2]\!] = \{\langle \Theta, b_1 \vee b_2 \rangle \mid \langle \Theta, b_i \rangle \in \mathcal{Q}_P[\![A_i]\!]\}$$
$$\mathcal{Q}_P[\![\textstyle\sum_{i=1}^{n} A_i]\!] = \cup\{\mathcal{Q}_P[\![A_i]\!]\}_{i=1}^{n}$$
$$\mathcal{Q}_P[\![p(x)]\!] = \{\langle \Theta, b \rangle \mid \downarrow\Theta = \Theta \wedge \langle \Phi, b \rangle \in \mathcal{Q}_P[\![A]\!] \wedge \rho_{y,x}(\Phi) = \exists_x(\Theta)\}$$
$$\text{where } p(y) :- A \in P$$

Since quiescent state semantics are not as well known as perhaps they should be within the world of program analysis, we provide some commentary on the recursive equations. The semantics expresses the resting points of an agent [18] and tags each constraint set with either 1 or 0 to indicate whether or not an agent contains a suspending sub-agent (in the latter case the agent has successfully terminated). Consider, for instance, the agent $\mathsf{ask}(\Phi) \to A$ and the closed set Θ. If $\Theta \not\subseteq \Phi$ then the agent suspends in Θ, and hence quiesces, and thus the pair $\langle \Theta, 1 \rangle$ is included in the set of quiescent states of the agent. Otherwise, if $\Theta \subseteq \Phi$ and $\langle \Theta, b \rangle$ is a quiescent state of A then $\langle \Theta, b \rangle$ is also a quiescent state of $\mathsf{ask}(\Phi) \to A$. Any set Θ such that $\Theta \subseteq \Phi$ is a succeeding quiescent state of the agent $\mathsf{tell}(\varPhi)$. A compound agent A_1, A_2 quiesces under $\varTheta$ iff $\varTheta$ is a quiescent set of both A_1 and A_2. The set $\varTheta$ is tagged as suspending iff either A_1 or A_2 suspend in $\varTheta$. The branching agent $\sum_{i=1}^{n} A_i$ inherits quiescent states from each of its sub-agents. Finally, an agent $p(x)$ that invokes an agent A via a definition $p(y) :- A$ inherits quiescent states from A by the application of projection and renaming. The intuition is that the variables x and y act as windows on the sets of constraints associated with $p(x)$ and A in that they hide information not pertaining to x and y respectively. If these projected sets coincide under renaming and the set for A is quiescent, then the set for $p(x)$ is also quiescent.

Example 3. Continuing with the agents A_1, A_2 and A_3 introduced in example 1:

$$\mathcal{Q}_P[\![\textstyle\sum_{i=1}^{3} A_i]\!] = \{\langle \varTheta, 0 \rangle \mid \varTheta \subseteq \varTheta_a \vee \varTheta \subseteq \varTheta_b\}$$
$$\mathcal{Q}_P[\![\mathsf{ask}(\varTheta_a) \to \textstyle\sum_{i=1}^{3} A_i]\!] = \{\langle \varTheta, 1 \rangle \mid \varTheta \not\subseteq \varTheta_a\} \cup \{\langle \varTheta, 0 \rangle \mid \varTheta \subseteq \varTheta_a\}$$

The second agent can either suspend with $\varTheta \not\subseteq \varTheta_a$ or succeed with $\varTheta \subseteq \varTheta_a$.

3.4　Transforming a Prolog Program into a ccp Program

Recall that the transformation introduces delay declarations to predicates which suspend a call until its mutual exclusion condition is satisfied. This idea is expressed in a transformation that maps each call $p(x)$ to a guarded version $\mathsf{ask}(\varTheta) \to p(x)$ where $\varTheta$ is set of constraints that enforce mutual exclusion. Recall too that the mutual exclusion conditions are derived from success patterns; the success set semantics provides a multiset of possible answers $\langle\!\langle \varTheta_1, \ldots, \varTheta_n \rangle\!\rangle$ for each call $p(x)$ and the mutual exclusion analysis then derives a condition for $p(x)$ — a constraint $\varPhi$ — which, if satisfiable with one $\varTheta_i$, is not satisfiable with any another $\varTheta_j$. This mutual exclusion property is expressed by the function $\mathsf{mux} : \widehat{\mathsf{Con}} \to \wp(\mathsf{Con})$ which represents the analysis component that derives the mutual exclusion conditions from the success patterns. With these concepts in place, the transformation is defined thus:

Definition 4. Let $\mathcal{S}_P[\![A_i]\!] \subseteq \varTheta_i$ and suppose mux satisfies the property that if $\mathsf{mux}(\langle\!\langle \varTheta_i \rangle\!\rangle_{i=1}^{n}) = \varPhi$ and $\varPhi \cap \varTheta_i \neq \emptyset$ then $\varPhi \cap \varTheta_j = \emptyset$ for all $i \neq j$. Then

$$T[\![\mathsf{tell}(\varPhi)]\!] = \mathsf{tell}(\varPhi)$$
$$T[\![P_1.P_2]\!] = T[\![P_1]\!].T[\![P_2]\!] \qquad T[\![A_1, A_2]\!] = T[\![A_1]\!], T[\![A_2]\!]$$
$$T[\![p(x) :- A]\!] = p(x) :- T[\![A]\!] \qquad T[\![\textstyle\sum_{i=1}^{n} A_i]\!] = \mathsf{ask}(\mathsf{mux}(\langle\!\langle \varTheta_i \rangle\!\rangle_{i=1}^{n})) \to \textstyle\sum_{i=1}^{n} T[\![A_i]\!]$$
$$T[\![p(x)]\!] = p(x)$$

The key result is stated below. It asserts that if $p(x)$ is invoked in the transformed program with the constraint $\varOmega$ imposed, and $p(x)$ cannot reduce to a suspending state, then calling $p(x)$ in the original program — again with $\varOmega$ imposed — will produce at most one answer and generate that answer at most once.

Theorem 1. Suppose $\langle \varPi, 1 \rangle \notin \mathcal{Q}_{T[\![P]\!]}[\![\mathsf{tell}(\varOmega), p(x)]\!]$ for all $\varPi \in \wp(\mathsf{Con})$. Then $|\mathcal{M}_P[\![p(x)]\!](\varOmega)| \leq 1$.

4   The Cut, Non-monotonicity and Incorrectness

The technique for inferring mutual exclusion conditions [13] is not sensitive to the clause ordering. This does not compromise correctness but, due to the presence of cut, the inferred conditions may be overly strong. To avoid refining the semantics and deriving a new analysis, this section shows how the procedure which computes the mutual exclusion conditions can be refined to accommodate this pruning operator.

The correctness of the analysis is founded on theorem 1 which, in turn, is a consequence of a series of monotonicity results that follows from the definition of the multiset semantics. Alas, the cut is a source of non-monotonicity as is illustrated by the r predicate:

```
r(X, Y) :- X = a, !, Y = b.          p(X, Y) :- q(X), r(X, Y).
r(X, Y) :- atomic(X).                q(a).
                                     q(b).
```

If r(X, Y) is called under the binding $\{X \mapsto b\}$ then the downward closure of the set of computed answers is $\Theta_1 = \downarrow \{X = b\}$. However, if r(X, Y) is called with a more general binding – the empty substitution – the downward closure of the set of answers is $\Theta_2 = \downarrow \{X = a, Y = b\}$. The predicate is non-monotonic because $\Theta_1 \not\subseteq \Theta_2$. The predicate p illustrates the significance of monotonicity in that it shows how non-monotonicity can undermine correctness. To see this, consider applying suspension inference in which the r(X, Y) goals are never delayed but q(X) goals are only selected when X is ground. Suspension inference [4] would infer the vacuous condition of *true* for p(X, Y) since the compound goal q(X), r(X, Y) can be scheduled in right-to-left order without incurring a suspension. However, this inference is unsafe, since the call p(X, Y) yields two answers.

One may think that the problem of non-monotonicity is insurmountable but correctness can be recovered by ensuring that the mutual exclusion conditions enforce monotonicity. The observation is that the occurrence of a cut in a clause cannot compromise monotonicity if any calls (typically tests) that arise before the cut are invoked with ground arguments. The idea is thus to strengthen the condition so as to ensure this. For example, r(X, Y) is monotonic if X is ground. The justification of this tactic is that in top-down clause selection, if a clause containing a cut succeeds, then any following clause is not considered. This behaviour can be modelled by adding negated calls to each clause that follows the cut (which is sound due to groundness [11]). Consider, for example, the following predicate:

```
part([], _, [], []).
part([X | Xs], M, [X | L], G) :- X =< M, !, part(Xs, M, L, G).
part([X | Xs], M, L, [X | G]) :- part(Xs, M, L, G).
```

For the sake of inferring mutual exclusion conditions, observe that the negation of X =< M can be inserted into the last clause since this clause is reached only if the test fails. Then, due to the negated test, the second and third clauses are mutually exclusive if the groundness condition $x_1 \wedge x_2$ holds where x_i describes the groundness of the i'th argument. It is not necessary to reason about cut to deduce that the first and second clauses are mutually exclusive if $x_1 \vee x_3$ holds. Likewise, a mutual exclusion condition for the first and third clause is $x_1 \vee x_4$. The cumulative mutual exclusion condition for the whole predicate is therefore $(x_1 \vee x_3) \wedge (x_1 \vee x_4) \wedge (x_1 \wedge x_2) = x_1 \wedge x_2$. Finally, note that when mechanising this approach, it is not actually necessary to insert the negated calls to deduce the grounding requirements; the negated tests were introduced merely to justify the tactic. Finally, applying this technique to r yields the condition x_1.

5   Experimental Results

An analyser has been constructed in SICStus 3.10.0 in order to assess the scalability of determinacy inference, study precision issues and investigate whether suspension inference can actually discover bugs. The analyser can be used through a web interface located at http://www.cs.kent.ac.uk/~amk/detweb.html. The analyser is composed of five components: (1) an argument-size analysis and (2) a depth-k analysis both of which infer success patterns for each clause; (3) an analysis which infers mutual exclusion conditions from the success patterns; (4) a suspension inference which computes determinacy conditions; and (5) a backward analysis [13] that infers determinacy conditions by only considering the left-to-right flow of bindings.

Table 1 summarises the results of four analysis experiments on a range of Prolog programs. The S column is the size of the program measured in the number of predicates. The A, B, C and D columns present the number of deterministic modes inferred for four different types of analysis. To compare against previous work [13], column A details the number of modes inferred using a form of inference that only considers the left-to-right flow of bindings [13] and mutual exclusion conditions derived without consideration of the cut, using a classic depth-k analysis. Column B details the number of deterministic modes inferred using suspension inference [4]. Column C refines this analysis by considering cut in the inference of the mutual exclusion conditions. Column D applies a more refined form of depth-k success pattern analysis to further upgrade the mutual exclusion conditions. The entries marked with a + indicate that the analysis improves on its predecessor in either inferring more modes or inferring more refined modes. Note that a predicate that will contribute 2, say, to the mode count if it is deterministic in 2 modes where both modes do not include the other; this explains why the number of modes can exceed the number of predicates.

The + entries in the B column indicate at least one moding improvement that follows from basing determinacy inference on suspension inference. By scanning the outputs of the analyses for a predicate whose modes differ between the two runs, the programmer can locate a suspicious predicate, ie., a predicate that could silently leave a choice-point on the stack. Such a predicate is determinate, but it is only determinate for some mode because of the way the bindings imposed by a goal on the right constrain a goal on the left. If this were not so, then left-to-

file	S	T	A	B	C	D %	file	S	T	A	B	C	D %
aircraft	237	2240	241	241	+241	+241 47	lee-route	13	20	14	14	+14	+14 69
asm	45	160	45	45	+45	+45 57	life	11	20	11	11	+11	11 72
boyer	26	40	33	33	+33	33 19	nand	93	400	93	93	93	+93 60
browse	16	20	16	16	+16	16 62	nbody	48	120	48	48	+48	+49 35
bryant	32	140	33	33	33	+33 75	neural	39	50	50	+52	52	52 43
btree	10	10	10	+10	+14	+18 0	peep	21	120	24	24	24	24 71
chat-80	435	9710	588	588	588	+592 51	press	51	150	56	56	56	+56 64
cp	158	730	239	239	239	+240 50	qplan	44	230	51	51	+52	52 31
circuit	5	10	8	+9	9	9 0	queens	16	20	16	16	+16	+17 37
conman	32	130	32	32	+32	32 78	read	42	130	43	43	43	+43 52
c2	8	0	8	8	+8	8 25	reducer	41	140	42	42	+42	+43 26
cr	6	0	9	+9	9	9 0	robot	26	30	29	+29	+30	+30 38
cw	11	20	13	13	+13	13 9	sccl	17	150	17	17	17	17 88
cs-r	36	370	36	36	36	36 75	sdda	33	70	33	+33	+33	+34 60
dcg	15	20	21	+21	21	21 6	serialize	7	20	9	9	+9	+9 0
dialog	30	20	33	33	+33	+33 33	sieve	6	10	6	6	+6	6 0
disj-r	31	50	31	31	31	31 48	sim	103	960	103	103	103	+105 64
ili	58	220	62	62	+63	63 46	sv	125	2280	131	131	+131	131 60
im	24	50	33	33	+33	33 41	sa	71	120	72	72	+72	72 33
inorder	2	0	2	+2	2	2 0	trs	35	3800	35	35	+35	35 57
kalah	45	70	46	46	46	+46 46	tsp	23	10	23	+23	+27	27 21

Fig. 1. Relative precision experiments: (**A**) using [13]; (**B**) using suspension inference; (**C**) adding cut logic to (B); and (**D**) adding decorated depth-k to (C) using the following name abbreviations c2 = connected2, cp = chat-parser, cr = courses-rules, cw = crypt-wamcc, im = ime-v2-2-1, sa = simple-analyzer and sv = sim-v5-2

right form of determinacy inference [13] would have also deduced this mode. Such a predicate could either be rewritten or executed under once for this particular mode. Note that to apply this form of debugging it is not necessary for the programmer to appreciate how the analysis works; the analysers collaborate and merely suggest where the programmer should focus their effort.

The columns C and D quantify how techniques for synthesising the mutual exclusion conditions impact on the overall precision. The + entries in column C confirm that reasoning about cut is important. The D column assesses the impact of applying an enriched form of depth-k analysis in the success pattern analysis that underpins the inference of the mutual exclusion conditions. To illustrate the refinement, consider the merge predicate that arises within mergesort program that can again be found at the above URL. If depth-1 analysis is enriched to track constraints between the variables in a truncated term, then the following success patterns are obtained for the three recursive clauses of merge:

```
merge([A|B],[C|D],[A|E]) :- A < C
merge([A|B],[C|D],[A|E]) :- A = C
merge([A|B],[C|D],[C|E]) :- A > C
```

From these success patterns, it can be deduced that the groundness of the first and second arguments is sufficient for mutual exclusion. This condition cannot be inferred unless the depth-k analysis additionally tracks constraints. The $+$ entries in the D column suggest that this refinement is generally useful. Such improvements may appear incremental, but our work suggests that it is only by combining all these techniques that determinacy inference becomes truly useful.

The T column is a comment on performance since it records the time required to perform all components of an analysis on a 1.4 GHz PC equipped with 640 MByte of memory, running Linux 2.6.15-2. Little variance was observed between the running times of the four analyses — even between A and B which employ different fixpoint engines. The column marked % represents the proportion of the predicates in the program for which a determinacy mode could not be inferred using analysis D. Further investigation is required to determine what fraction of these are actually non-determinate.

Space does not permit us to fully report our work on enhancing argument size analysis for determinacy inference, except to note that techniques devised in termination analysis for inferring norms [2,7] permit more general mutual exclusion conditions to be inferred. Consider, for example, a predicate that succeeds when its single argument is a list of lists. Such a predicate (named traverse) can be found at the above URL. This predicate traverses the outer list, calling an auxiliary predicate to check that each element is also a list. By using an argument size analysis based on the term-size norm, it is possible to show that the predicate is deterministic if called with a ground argument. When the program is decorated with types, however, type-based norms enable this determinacy condition to be relaxed to a rigid list of rigid lists.

Finally, a number of anomalies were discovered during the experimental evaluation. For example, the exp(N,X,Y) predicate [19, Figure 3.5] which realises the function that binds Y to X raised to the power of N, is non-deterministic for $N > 0$ and $X = 0$. These bugs were found by scanning programs for predicates that attempted to realise functions for which no modes could be inferred.

6   Related Work

The new analysis reported in this paper also has applications in the new area of semi-online program specialisation [10]. In this scheme, the usual static versus dynamic classification that is used within classic binding-time analysis is refined by adding an additional binding-type semi. As well as always unfolding a static call and never unfolding a dynamic call, the unfolding decision for a semi call is postponed until specialisation time. Determinacy inference fits into this scheme because it provides a way of annotating calls with lightweight unfolding conditions, ie., determinacy conditions. Furthermore, it is not difficult to refine determinacy inference so as to annotate semi calls with conditions that select the clause with which to unfold the call. The net result is more aggressive unfolding. Determinacy inference might also have a role in parallelisation since determinacy can be used as the basis for exploiting a form of and-parallelism

[17]. Any discrepancy in the modes inferred with the two forms of determinacy inference pinpoints a predicate that is a good candidate for being rewritten, possibly by reordering goals, so that each call to the atoms in body of the clauses is deterministic, irrespective of the bindings imposed by the other calls. This would open up more opportunities for parallelisation.

Dawson *et al.* [3] extract determinacy information from a logic program by applying a program transformation that simultaneously describes both success pattern constraints and constraints from the calling context. These constraints are then added to each clause without compromising the correctness of the program, so as to reduce backtracking. The authors state that "if the clause conditions of a predicate are pairwise non-unifiable, we infer that the predicate is determinate whenever the input arguments are sufficiently ground". However, to assure determinacy, it is also necessary to ensure that any calls invoked within the body of a clause are themselves deterministic. Ensuring this property leads onto the consideration of various computation rules, and the topic of this paper.

Goal-dependent analysis can be used to ensure that each sub-goal of a given goal cannot succeed with more than one clause of a predicate [12]. The key step is to detect whether two different clauses for a predicate are mutually exclusive with respect to the calling patterns of the predicate. Work on determinacy checking (rather determinacy inference) that is of particular note is that by Braem *et al.* [1] who present an analysis that given a calling mode for a predicate, infers bounds on the number of solutions that can be produced by a call in a given mode. In the context of partial evaluation, Sahlin [16] presents a determinacy analysis that can detect whether if a given goal fail, succeeds once, twice or more times, or whether it possibly loops. Mogensen [14] provides a semantically justified reconstruction of the work of Sahlin [16] based on a denotational semantics for Prolog programs with cut. Quite independently, Le Charlier *et al.* [8] developed a denotational sequence-based abstract interpretation framework for Prolog that can, among other things, be instantiated to obtain Sahlin's [16] determinacy analysis. Interestingly, in partial evaluation, delay declarations are sometimes used to postpone the unfolding of goals until they become sufficiently deterministic [9] which hints at the transformation at the heart of this paper. Further afield, Mercury supports a rich class of determinism categories — det, semidet, multi, nondet and failure — which are used to categorise how many times each mode to a predicate or function can succeed. Signature declarations can also be used in PAN [15] to detect unintended backtracking. Finally, the early literature on functional dependencies is reviewed in [20, Chapter 5].

7   Conclusions

This paper has shown how determinacy inference can be improved by transforming the problem to an analysis problem in concurrency. The paper shows that this approach is flexible enough to handle the cut and accurate enough to locate non-determinacy problems in existing programs.

Acknowledgments. We thank John Gallagher, Manual Hermenegildo, Michael Leuschel and Fred Mesnard for discussions on determinacy inference. This work was funded, in part, by NSF grants CCR-0131862 and INT-0327760, the EPSRC grant EP/C015517 and the Royal Society joint project grant 2005/R4-JP.

References

1. C. Braem, B. Le Charlier, S. Modar, and P. Van Hentenryck. Cardinality Analysis of Prolog. In M. Bruynooghe, editor, *International Symposium on Logic Programming*, pages 457–471. MIT Press, 1994.
2. M. Bruynooghe, M. Codish, J. Gallagher, S. Genaim, and W. Vanhoof. Termination Analysis through Combination of Type Based Norms. *ACM Transactions on Programming Languages and Systems*, To appear.
3. S. Dawson, C. R. Ramakrishnan, I. V. Ramakrishnan, and R. C. Sekar. Extracting Determinacy in Logic Programs. In *International Conference on Logic Programming*, pages 424–438. MIT Press, 1993.
4. S. Genaim and A. King. Goal-independent Suspension Analysis for Logic Programs with Dynamic Scheduling. In P. Degano, editor, *European Symposium on Programming*, volume 2618 of *LNCS*, pages 84–98. Springer-Verlag, 2003.
5. A. King and L. Lu. A Backward Analysis for Constraint Logic Programs. *Theory and Practice of Logic Programming*, 2(4–5):517–547, 2002.
6. A. King, L. Lu, and S. Genaim. Determinacy Inference by Suspension Inference. Technical Report 2-05, Computing Laboratory, University of Kent, CT2 7NF, 2005. http://www.cs.kent.ac.uk/pubs/2005/2262/.
7. V. Lagoon and P. J. Stuckey. A Framework for Analysis of Typed Logic Programs. In *International Symposium on Functional and Logic Programming*, volume 2024 of *LNCS*, pages 296–310. Springer-Verlag, 2001.
8. B. Le Charlier, S. Rossi, and P. Van Hentenryck. Sequence-based abstract interpretation of Prolog. *Theory and Practice of Logic Programming*, 2:25–84, 2002.
9. M. Leuschel. Personal Communication on Partial Evaluation, April 2005.
10. M. Leuschel, J. Jørgensen, W. Vanhoof, and M. Bruynooghe. Offline Specialisation in Prolog Using a Hand-Written Compiler Generator. *Theory and Practice of Logic Programming*, 4(1):139–191, 2004.
11. J. W. Lloyd. *Foundations of Logic Programming*. Springer-Verlag, 1987.
12. P. López-García, F. Bueno, and M. Hermenegildo. Determinacy Analysis for Logic Programs Using Mode and Type information. In *Logic-Based Program Synthesis and Transformation*, volume 3573 of *LNCS*, pages 19–35. Springer-Verlag, 2005.
13. L. Lu and A. King. Determinacy Inference for Logic Programs. In M. Sagiv, editor, *European Symposium on Programming*, volume 3444 of *LNCS*, pages 108–123. Springer-Verlag, 2005.
14. T. Mogensen. A Semantics-Based Determinacy Analysis for Prolog with Cut. In *Ershov Memorial Conference*, volume 1181 of *LNCS*, pages 374–385. Springer-Verlag, 1996.
15. M. Müller, T. Glaß, and K. Stroetmann. Pan - The Prolog Analyzer (Short system description). In *Static Analysis Symposium*, volume 1145 of *LNCS*, pages 387–388. Springer-Verlag, 1996.
16. D. Sahlin. Determinacy Analysis for Full Prolog. In *Partial Evaluation and Semantics Based Program Manipulation*, pages 23–30, 1991. SIGPLAN Notices 26(9).

17. V. Santos Costa, D. H. D. Warren, and R. Yang. Andorra-I Compilation. *New Generation Computing*, 14(1):3–30, 1996.
18. V. A. Saraswat, M. C. Rinard, and P. Panangaden. Semantic Foundations of Concurrent Constraint Programming. In *Principles of Programming Languages*, pages 333–352. ACM Press, 1991.
19. E. Shapiro and L. Sterling. *The Art of Prolog*. MIT Press, 1994.
20. J. Zobel. *Analysis of Logic Programs*. PhD thesis, Department of Computer Science, University of Melbourne, Parkville, Victoria 3052, 1990.

Collapsing Closures

Xuan Li[1], Andy King[2], and Lunjin Lu[1]

[1] Oakland University, Rochester, MI 48309, USA
[2] University of Kent, Canterbury, CT2 7NF, UK

Abstract. A description in the Jacobs and Langen domain is a set of sharing groups where each sharing group is a set of program variables. The presence of a sharing group in a description indicates that all the variables in the group can be bound to terms that contain a common variable. The expressiveness of the domain, alas, is compromised by its intractability. Not only are descriptions potentially exponential in size, but abstract unification is formulated in terms of an operation, called closure under union, that is also exponential. This paper shows how abstract unification can be reformulated so that closures can be collapsed in two senses. Firstly, one closure operation can be folded into another so as to reduce the total number of closures that need to be computed. Secondly, the remaining closures can be applied to smaller descriptions. Therefore, although the operation remains exponential, the overhead of closure calculation is reduced. Experimental evaluation suggests that the cost of analysis can be substantially reduced by collapsing closures.

1 Introduction

The philosophy of abstract interpretation is to simulate the behaviour of a program without actually running it. This is accomplished by replacing each operation in the program with an abstract analogue that operates, not on the concrete data, but a description of the data. The methodology applied in abstract interpretation is first to focus on the data, that is, pin down the relationship between the concrete data and a description, and then devise abstract operations that preserve this relationship. This amounts to showing that if the input to the abstract operation describes the input to the concrete operation, then the output of the abstract operation faithfully describes the output of the concrete operation. When this methodology is applied in logic programming, the focus is usually on the operation of abstract unification since this is arguably the most complicated domain operation. The projection operation, that merely removes information from a description, is rarely a major concern.

In this paper, we revisit the projection operation of the classic set-sharing domain and we argue that the complexity of the abstract unification ($amgu$) operation can be curbed by the careful application of a reformulated projection operation. The computational problem at the heart of $amgu$ is the closure under union operation [14] that operates on sharing abstractions which are constructed

S. Etalle and M. Truszczyński (Eds.): ICLP 2006, LNCS 4079, pp. 148–162, 2006.

from sets of sharing groups. Each sharing group is, in turn, a set of program variables. Closure under union operation repeatedly unions together sets of sharing groups, drawn from a given sharing abstraction, until no new sharing group can be obtained. This operation is inherently exponential, hence the interest in different, and possibly more tractable, encodings of set-sharing [8,10]. However, even the most creative and beautiful set-sharing encoding proposed thus far [8], does not entirely finesse the complexity of closure under union; closure under union simply manifests itself in the form of a different (and equally non-trivial) closure operator [18].

Our work was motivated by the observation that often a set-sharing analysis will calculate a series of closures that involve variables that appear in the body of a clause, only for these variables to be later eliminated when the resulting set-sharing description is restricted to those variables that occur in the head. It seems somewhat unsatisfactory that information — which is often expensive to derive — is simply thrown away. Ideally, closure operations should only be applied to variables that appear within the head of a clause. This paper shows that this ideal can be realised by reformulating abstract unification so that it can be applied in a two stage process: a phase that precedes projection (of quadratic complexity) and a phase that is applied after projection (of exponential complexity). This tactic collapses closure calculations in two important respects. Firstly, it reduces the number of variables that participate in closure calculations since there are typically fewer variables in the head of the clause than the whole of the clause. This is important because the cost of closure is related to the number of sharing groups that it operates over and this, in turn, is exponential in the number of variables in scope. Secondly, it turns out that when closure calculation is applied after projection, then the closures that arise from different unifications in the body of a clause, frequently collapse to a single closure operation. Thus, not only is the complexity of each closure operation lessened, but the total number of closure operations is also reduced.

The paper is structured as follows: Section 2 introduces the key ideas with a familiar example. Section 3 reports the main correctness results (the proofs themselves are given in the technical report [15]). Section 4 details the experimental evaluation. Section 5 reviews the related work and finally Section 6 concludes.

2   Motivating Example

This section illustrates the basic ideas behind the analysis in relation to a familiar example — the append program that is listed below:

```
append(Xs,Ys,Zs) :- Xs = [], Ys = Zs.
append(Xs,Ys,Zs) :- Xs = [X|Vs], Zs = [X|Ws], append(Vs,Ys,Ws).
```

The behaviour of the program can be captured with a T-operator that is sensitive to aliasing between the arguments of atoms [4,11]. Such an operator can be iteratively applied to obtain the following series of interpretations:

$$I_0 = \emptyset$$
$$I_1 = \{\texttt{append}(Xs, Ys, Zs) \text{ :- } \theta_1\} \quad \text{where } \theta_1 = \{Xs \mapsto [\,], Ys \mapsto Zs\}$$
$$I_2 = \{\texttt{append}(Xs, Ys, Zs) \text{ :- } \theta_2\} \cup I_1 \quad \text{where } \theta_2 = \{Xs \mapsto [X], Zs \mapsto [X|Ys]\}$$
$$I_3 = \{\texttt{append}(Xs, Ys, Zs) \text{ :- } \theta_3\} \cup I_2 \quad \text{where}$$
$$\theta_3 = \{Xs \mapsto [X, Y], Zs \mapsto [X, Y|Ys]\}$$

$$\vdots$$

$$I_i = \{\texttt{append}(Xs, Ys, Zs) \text{ :- } \theta_i\} \cup I_{i-1} \text{ where}$$
$$\theta_i = \{Xs \mapsto [X_1, \ldots, X_{i-1}], Zs \mapsto [X_1, \ldots, X_{i-1}|Ys]\}$$

Each interpretation I_i is a set of atoms each of which is constrained by a substitution. The limit of the sequence (and the least fixpoint of the T operator) is the interpretation $I = \{\texttt{append}(Xs, Ys, Zs) \text{ :- } \theta_i \mid i \in \mathbb{N}\}$ which is an infinite set. It therefore follows that I cannot be finitely computed by applying iteration.

2.1   Set-Sharing Abstract Domain

The analysis problem is to finitely compute a set-sharing abstraction of the limit I. To apply abstract interpretation to this problem, it is necessary to detail how a substitution, and more generally a set of substitutions, can be described by a set-sharing abstraction. A set-sharing abstraction for a substitution θ is constructed from a set of sharing groups: one sharing group $occ(\theta, y)$ for each variable $y \in \mathcal{V}$ drawn from the universe of variables $\mathcal{V}$. The sharing group $occ(\theta, y)$ is defined by $occ(\theta, y) = \{x \in \mathcal{V} \mid y \in var(\theta(x))\}$ and therefore contains exactly those variables which are bound by θ to terms that contain the variable y. In the particular case of θ_3 it follows that:

$$occ(\theta_3, Xs) = \emptyset \qquad\qquad occ(\theta_3, X) = \{X, Xs, Zs\}$$
$$occ(\theta_3, Ys) = \{Ys, Zs\} \qquad occ(\theta_3, Y) = \{Y, Xs, Zs\}$$
$$occ(\theta_3, Zs) = \emptyset \qquad\qquad occ(\theta_3, y\,) = \{y\} \text{ where } y \notin \{Xs, Ys, Zs, X, Y\}$$

Since the number of sharing groups for any θ is itself infinite, the abstraction map $\alpha_{\mathcal{X}}(\theta)$ is parameterised by a set of program variables $\mathcal{X}$ and defined so that $\alpha_{\mathcal{X}}(\theta) = \{occ(\theta, y) \cap \mathcal{X} \mid y \in \mathcal{V}\}$. If $\mathcal{X}$ is finite, it follows that $\alpha_{\mathcal{X}}(\theta)$ is finite. For example, if $\mathcal{X} = \{Xs, Ys, Zs\}$ then $\alpha_{\mathcal{X}}(\theta_3) = \{\emptyset, \{Xs, Zs\}, \{Ys, Zs\}\}$. The abstraction map $\alpha_{\mathcal{X}}(\theta_3)$ still records useful information: it shows that Xs and Zs can share, and similarly that Ys and Zs can share.

The domain construction is completed by lifting $\alpha_{\mathcal{X}}$ to subsets of Sub where Sub is the computational domain of substitutions. This is achieved by defining $\alpha_{\mathcal{X}} : \wp(Sub) \rightarrow Sharing_{\mathcal{X}}$ where $Sharing_{\mathcal{X}} = \wp(\wp(\mathcal{X}))$ and $\alpha_{\mathcal{X}}(\Theta) = \cup_{\theta \in \Theta} \alpha_{\mathcal{X}}(\theta)$. The concretisation map $\gamma_{\mathcal{X}} : Sharing_{\mathcal{X}} \rightarrow \wp(Sub)$ specifies which substitutions are represented by a set-sharing abstraction and is defined thus $\gamma_{\mathcal{X}}(S) = \{\theta \in Sub \mid \alpha_{\mathcal{X}}(\theta) \subseteq S\}$. (Note that an alternative definition for this domain is $Sharing_{\mathcal{X}} = \{S \mid \emptyset \in S \wedge S \subseteq \wp(\mathcal{X})\}$ since for any $\theta \in Sub$ there always exists $y \in \mathcal{V}$ such that $occ(\theta, y) \cap \mathcal{X} = \emptyset$, whence $\emptyset \in \alpha_{\mathcal{X}}(\theta)$.)

2.2 Set-Sharing Domain Operations

The concretisation mapping $\gamma_{\mathcal{X}}$ pins down the meaning of a set-sharing abstraction and thereby provides a criteria for constructing and then judging the correctness of an abstract version of the T operator. Successive interpretations J_i generated by this operator are deemed to be correct iff for each constrained atom $\mathtt{append}(Xs, Ys, Zs) \mathtt{:-} \theta \in I_i$ there exists $\mathtt{append}(Xs, Ys, Zs) \mathtt{:-} S \in J_i$ such that $\theta \in \gamma_{\mathcal{X}}(S)$. To illustrate the problems of tractability in this operator (that stem from closure under union), the discussion focusses on the computation of the interpretation J_3; the preceding iterates are listed below:

$$J_0 = \emptyset$$
$$J_1 = \{\mathtt{append}(Xs, Ys, Zs) \mathtt{:-} S_{J_1}\} \qquad \text{where } S_{J_1} = \{\emptyset, \{Ys, Zs\}\}$$
$$J_2 = \{\mathtt{append}(Xs, Ys, Zs) \mathtt{:-} S_{J_2}\} \cup J_1 \text{ where}$$
$$S_{J_2} = \{\emptyset, \{Xs, Zs\}, \{Xs, Ys, Zs\}, \{Ys, Zs\}\}$$
$$J_3 = J_2$$

Note that $\{Xs, Ys, Zs\} \in S_{J_2}$ but $\{Xs, Ys, Zs\} \notin \alpha_{\mathcal{X}}(\theta_i)$ for any $i \in \mathbb{N}$. This is symptomatic of the imprecision incurred by working in an abstract rather than the concrete setting. Notice too that the absence of the sharing group $\{Xs, Ys\}$ from S_{J_2} asserts that Xs and Ys can only share if there is sharing between Xs and Zs and likewise sharing between Ys and Zs.

A single application of the abstract T operator takes, as input, an interpretation J_i and produces, as output, an interpretation J_{i+1}. J_{i+1} is obtained as the union of the two interpretations: one interpretation generated by each clause in the program acting on J_i. Applying the first and second clauses to J_2 yield $\{\mathtt{append}(Xs, Ys, Zs) \mathtt{:-} S_{J_1}\}$ and $\{\mathtt{append}(Xs, Ys, Zs) \mathtt{:-} S_{J_2}\}$ respectively which, when combined, give $J_3 = J_2$. To illustrate how these interpretations are computed, consider the application of the second clause.

Computation is initiated with a set-sharing abstraction for the identity substitution ε with $\mathcal{X}$ assigned to the variables of the clause $\mathcal{X} = \{Vs, Ws, X, Xs, Ys, Zs\}$. This initial description is $S_0 = \alpha_{\mathcal{X}}(\varepsilon) = \{\emptyset, \{Vs\}, \{Ws\}, \{X\}, \{Xs\}, \{Ys\}, \{Zs\}\}$. Next, S_0 is progressively instantiated by firstly, simulating the unification $Xs = [X|Vs]$ with input S_0 to obtain output S_1; then secondly, solving $Zs = [X|Ws]$ in the presence of S_1 to give S_2; then thirdly, adding the bindings imposed by the body atom $\mathtt{append}(Vs, Ys, Ws)$ to S_2 to obtain a description that characterises the whole clause. Each of these steps is outlined below:

– The abstract unification operation $S_1 = amgu(Xs, [X|Vs], S_0)$ of Jacobs and Langen [14] provides a way of simulating concrete unification with set-sharing abstractions. The algorithm satisfies the correctness criteria that if $\theta_0 \in \gamma_{\mathcal{X}}(S_0)$ and $\delta \in mgu(\theta_0(X), \theta_0([X|Vs]))$ then $\theta_1 = \delta \circ \theta_0 \in \gamma_{\mathcal{X}}(S_1)$ where $mgu(t_1, t_2)$ denotes the set of most general unifiers for the terms t_1 and t_2. The algorithm is formulated in terms of three auxiliary operations: relevance operation $rel(o, S)$ where o is any syntactic object, the cross union $T_1 \uplus T_2$ of two descriptions T_1 and T_2, and closure under union $cl(S)$. The relevance mapping is defined by $rel(o, S) = \{G \in S \mid var(o) \cap G \neq \emptyset\}$

where $var(o)$ is the set of variables contained in the syntactic object o. The mapping $rel(o, S)$ thus returns those sharing groups G of S which share a variable with o. Cross union is defined by $T_1 \uplus T_2 = \{G \cup H \mid G \in T_1 \wedge H \in T_2\}$ and thus computes the union of all the pairs of sharing groups in the cross-product $T_1 \times T_2$. The closure $cl(S)$ is defined as the least superset of S satisfies the closure property that if $G \in cl(S)$ and $H \in cl(S)$ then $G \cup H \in cl(S)$. With these operations in place, abstract unification can be defined thus $amgu(t_1, t_2, S) = (S \backslash (T_1 \cup T_2)) \cup cl(T_1 \uplus T_2)$ where $T_i = rel(t_i, S)$. (This definition is actually a reformulation [10] of the classic definition [14] that is better suited to illustrate our purposes). In the particular case of $S_1 = amgu(Xs, [X|Vs], S_0)$ it follows that:

$$T_1 = rel(Xs, S_0) = \{\{Xs\}\}$$
$$T_2 = rel([X|Vs], S_0) = \{\{Vs\}, \{X\}\}$$
$$T_1 \uplus T_2 = \{\{Vs, Xs\}, \{X, Xs\}\}$$
$$cl(T_1 \uplus T_2) = \{\{Vs, Xs\}, \{Vs, X, Xs\}, \{X, Xs\}\}$$

and hence $S_1 = \{\emptyset, \{Vs, Xs\}, \{Vs, X, Xs\}, \{Ws\}, \{X, Xs\}, \{Ys\}, \{Zs\}\}$.

- Repeating this process for $S_2 = amgu(Zs, [X|Ws], S_1)$ yields $S_2 = \{\emptyset, \{Vs, Ws, X, Xs, Zs\}, \{Vs, X, Xs, Zs\}, \{Vs, Xs\}, \{Ws, X, Xs, Zs\}, \{Ws, Zs\}, \{X, Xs, Zs\}, \{Ys\}\}$.

- Next, the bindings imposed by the body atom append(Vs, Ys, Ws) need to be added to S_2. The technical problem is that these bindings are recorded in J_2, not in terms of append(Vs, Ys, Ws), but in terms of a renaming of the atom, that is, append(Xs, Ys, Zs). (This problem manifests itself because, in theory, interpretations are defined as sets of constrained atoms where each constrained atom represents a set of constrained atoms that are equivalent under variable renaming [4,11].) This problem is resolved, in practise, by extending S_2 to give $S_3 = S_2 \cup \{\{\underline{Xs}, \underline{Zs}\}, \{\underline{Ys}, \underline{Zs}\}, \{\underline{Xs}, \underline{Ys}, \underline{Zs}\}\}$ where $\underline{Xs}$, $\underline{Ys}$ and $\underline{Zs}$ are fresh variables. Then a series of abstract unifications are applied which are interleaved with projection operations to incrementally remove the freshly introduced variables. This strategy proceeds thus: $S_4 = amgu(Vs, \underline{Xs}, S_3)$, $S_5 = S_4 \upharpoonright (\mathcal{X} \backslash \{\underline{Xs}\})$, $S_6 = amgu(Ys, \underline{Ys}, S_5)$, $S_7 = S_6 \upharpoonright (\mathcal{X} \backslash \{\underline{Ys}\})$, $S_8 = amgu(Ws, \underline{Zs}, S_7)$ and $S_9 = S_8 \upharpoonright (\mathcal{X} \backslash \{\underline{Zs}\})$. The projection operation $\upharpoonright$ is defined $S \upharpoonright Y = \{G \cap Y \mid G \in S\}$ and eliminates all variables from S other than those drawn from Y. Projection preserves correctness since $\gamma_{\mathcal{X}}(S) \subseteq \gamma_{\mathcal{X}}(S \upharpoonright Y)$. This strategy computes the following descriptions for $S_4, \ldots, S_9$:

$$S_4 = \{\emptyset, \{\underline{Xs}, \underline{Ys}, \underline{Zs}, Vs, Ws, X, Xs, Zs\}, \{\underline{Xs}, \underline{Ys}, \underline{Zs}, Vs, X, Xs, Zs\},$$
$$\{\underline{Xs}, \underline{Ys}, \underline{Zs}, Vs, Xs\}, \{\underline{Xs}, \underline{Zs}, Vs, Ws, X, Xs, Zs\},$$
$$\{\underline{Xs}, \underline{Zs}, Vs, X, Xs, Zs\}, \{\underline{Xs}, \underline{Zs}, Vs, Xs\}, \{\underline{Ys}, \underline{Zs}\},$$
$$\{Ws, X, Xs, Zs\}, \{Ws, Zs\}, \{X, Xs, Zs\}, \{Ys\}\}$$
$$S_5 = \{\emptyset, \{\underline{Ys}, \underline{Zs}, Vs, Ws, X, Xs, Zs\}, \{\underline{Ys}, \underline{Zs}, Vs, X, Xs, Zs\},$$
$$\{\underline{Ys}, \underline{Zs}, Vs, xs\}, \{\underline{Zs}, Vs, Ws, X, Xs, Zs\}$$
$$\{\underline{Zs}, Vs, X, Xs, Zs\}, \{\underline{Zs}, Vs, Xs\}, \{\underline{Ys}, \underline{Zs}\},$$
$$\{Ws, X, Xs, Zs\}, \{Ws, Zs\}, \{X, Xs, Zs\}, \{Ys\}\}$$

$$\vdots$$

$$S_8 = \{\emptyset, \{\underline{Zs}, Vs, Ws, X, Xs, Ys, Zs\}, \{\underline{Zs}, Vs, Ws, Xs, Ys, Zs\},$$
$$\{\underline{Zs}, Vs, Ws, X, Xs, Zs\}, \{\underline{Zs}, Vs, Ws, Xs, Zs\},$$
$$\{\underline{Zs}, Ws, X, Xs, Ys, Zs\}, \{\underline{Zs}, Ws, Ys, Zs\}, \{X, Xs, Zs\}\}$$
$$S_9 = \{\emptyset, \{Vs, Ws, X, Xs, Ys, Zs\}, \{Vs, Ws, Xs, Ys, Zs\},$$
$$\{Vs, Ws, X, Xs, Zs\}, \{Vs, Ws, Xs, Zs\},$$
$$\{Ws, X, Xs, Ys, Zs\}, \{Ws, Ys, Zs\}, \{X, Xs, Zs\}\}$$

It should be noted that in these steps, abstract matching can be substituted for abstract unification. This can improve both the precision and the efficiency [13] but does not reduce the overall number of closures.

The description S_9 expresses the bindings imposed on the variables of the whole clause as a result of the unification and the body atom. The restriction $S_{10} = S_9 \upharpoonright \{Xs, Ys, Zs\} = \{\emptyset, \{Xs, Zs\}, \{Xs, Ys, Zs\}, \{Ys, Zs\}\}$ then describes these bindings solely in term of the variables in the head. Since S_{10} coincides with S_{J_2} it follows that a fixpoint has been reached and therefore J_2 faithfully describes the limit interpretation I. The observation that motivated this work is that this application of the abstract T operator alone, requires 5 closure calculations to compute S_1, S_2, S_4, S_6 and S_8 each of which are non-trivial descriptions that are defined over at least 6 variables. Yet the objective is merely to compute S_{10} which is necessarily defined over just 3 variables.

2.3   Reformulating Set-Sharing Domain Operations

One solution to the problem of calculating closures is to not compute them immediately, but defer evaluation until a more propitious moment, that is, when the descriptions contain less variables. Consider again the definition $amgu(t_1, t_2, S) = (S \setminus (T_1 \cup T_2)) \cup cl(T_1 \uplus T_2)$. Instead of computing $cl(T_1 \uplus T_2)$, the strategy is to tag all the groups within $T_1 \uplus T_2$ with an identifier — a unique number — that identifies those groups that participate in a particular closure. The tags are retained until head projection whereupon they are used to activate closure calculation. Then the tags are discarded. This idea leads to an abstract unification operator that is defined $amgu'(t_1, t_2, n, S) = (S \setminus (T_1 \cup T_2)) \cup tag(T_1 \uplus' T_2, n)$ where the descriptions S, T_1, T_2 are enriched with tagging information and n is a new tag that distinguishes those groups generated from $T_1 \uplus' T_2$. Formally, descriptions are drawn from a domain $Sharing'_{\mathcal{X}} = \wp(\wp(\mathcal{X}) \times \wp(\mathbb{N}))$ since, in general, a sharing group can own several tags. (Elements of this domain are only used for intermediate calculations and the infinite nature of $Sharing'_{\mathcal{X}}$ does not compromise termination.) The tagging operation $tag(S, n)$ inserts a tag n into each group in S and thus $tag(S, n) = \{\langle G, N \cup \{n\}\rangle \mid \langle G, N\rangle \in S\}$. Over this new domain, cross union is redefined $T_1 \uplus' T_2 = \{\langle G \cup H, N \cup M\rangle \mid \langle G, N\rangle \in T_1 \wedge \langle H, M\rangle \in T_2\}$. Note that rel can be used without adaption.

Now reconsider the computation of J_3 using the second clause. The initial description is again $S'_0 = \{\emptyset, \{Vs\}, \{Ws\}, \{X\}, \{Xs\}, \{Ys\}, \{Zs\}\}$ but with the interpretation that an untagged group G is actually syntactic sugar for a pair $\langle G, \emptyset \rangle$ that is equipped with an empty set of tags. Then $S_0' \in Sharing_\mathcal{X}'$. Each application of abstract unification is required to introduce a fresh identifier and these are chosen to be 1 and 2 when computing S_1' and S_2'. Computation unfolds as follows:

- Applying $S_1' = amgu'(Xs, [X|Vs], 1, S_0')$ it follows that:

$$T_1 = rel(Xs, S_0') = \{\{Xs\}\}$$
$$T_2 = rel([X|Vs], S_0') = \{\{Vs\}, \{X\}\}$$
$$T_1 \uplus' T_2 = \{\{Vs, Xs\}, \{X, Xs\}\}$$
$$tag(T_1 \uplus' T_2, 1) = \{\langle \{Vs, Xs\}, \{1\}\rangle, \langle \{X, Xs\}, \{1\}\rangle\}$$

hence $S_1' = \{\emptyset, \langle \{Vs, Xs\}, \{1\}\rangle, \{Ws\}, \langle \{X, Xs\}, \{1\}\rangle, \{Ys\}, \{Zs\}\}$.
- Repeating this strategy for $S_2' = amgu'(Zs, [X|Ws], 2, S_1')$ yields:

$$T_1 = rel(Zs, S_1') = \{\{Zs\}\}$$
$$T_2 = rel([X|Ws], S_1') = \{\{Ws\}, \langle \{X, Xs\}, \{1\}\rangle\}$$
$$T_1 \uplus' T_2 = \{\{Ws, Zs\}, \langle \{X, Xs, Zs\}, \{1\}\rangle\}$$
$$tag(T_1 \uplus' T_2, 2) = \{\langle \{Ws, Zs\}, \{2\}\rangle, \langle \{X, Xs, Zs\}, \{1, 2\}\rangle\}$$

thus $S_2' = \{\emptyset, \langle \{Vs, Xs\}, \{1\}\rangle, \langle \{Ws, Zs\}, \{2\}\rangle, \langle \{X, Xs, Zs\}, \{1, 2\}\rangle, \{Ys\}\}$. The identifiers 1 and 2 indicate which groups participate in which closures. The group $\{X, Xs, Zs\}$ is tagged with $\{1, 2\}$ since it is involved in both closures. Note that, unlike before, $|S_2'| < |S_1'| < |S_0'|$.
- The bindings from the body atom are added by again extending S_2' to $S_3' = S_2' \cup \{\{\underline{Xs}, \underline{Zs}\}, \{\underline{Ys}, \underline{Zs}\}, \{\underline{Xs}, \underline{Ys}, \underline{Zs}\}\}$. The interwoven unification and projection steps are modified by introducing fresh identifers and by redefining projection so that $S \restriction' Y = \{\langle G \cap Y, N\rangle \mid \langle G, N\rangle \in S\}$. Hence $S_4' = amgu'(Vs, \underline{Xs}, 3, S_3')$, $S_5' = S_4' \restriction' (\mathcal{X} \setminus \underline{Xs})$, $S_6' = amgu(Ys, \underline{Ys}, 4, S_5')$, $S_7' = S_6' \restriction' (\mathcal{X} \setminus \underline{Ys})$, $S_8' = amgu'(Ws, \underline{Zs}, 5, S_7')$ and $S_9' = S_8' \restriction' (\mathcal{X} \setminus \underline{Zs})$ which generates the following sequence of descriptions:

$$S_4' = \{\emptyset, \langle \{\underline{Xs}, \underline{Zs}, Vs, Xs\}, \{1, 3\}\rangle, \langle \{\underline{Xs}, \underline{Ys}, \underline{Zs}, Vs, Xs\}, \{1, 3\}\rangle,$$
$$\{\underline{Ys}, \underline{Zs}\}, \langle \{Ws, Zs\}, \{2\}\rangle, \langle \{X, Xs, Zs\}, \{1, 2\}\rangle, \{Ys\}\}$$
$$S_5' = \{\emptyset, \langle \{\underline{Zs}, Vs, Xs\}, \{1, 3\}\rangle, \langle \{\underline{Ys}, \underline{Zs}, Vs, Xs\}, \{1, 3\}\rangle,$$
$$\{\underline{Ys}, \underline{Zs}\}, \langle \{Ws, Zs\}, \{2\}\rangle, \langle \{X, Xs, Zs\}, \{1, 2\}\rangle, \{Ys\}\}$$
$$S_6' = \{\emptyset, \langle \{\underline{Zs}, Vs, Xs\}, \{1, 3\}\rangle, \langle \{\underline{Ys}, \underline{Zs}, Vs, Xs, Ys\}, \{1, 3, 4\}\rangle,$$
$$\langle \{\underline{Ys}, \underline{Zs}, Ys\}, \{4\}\rangle, \langle \{Ws, Zs\}, \{2\}\rangle, \langle \{X, Xs, Zs\}, \{1, 2\}\rangle\}$$
$$S_7' = \{\emptyset, \langle \{\underline{Zs}, Vs, Xs\}, \{1, 3\}\rangle, \langle \{\underline{Zs}, Vs, Xs, Ys\}, \{1, 3, 4\}\rangle,$$
$$\langle \{\underline{Zs}, Ys\}, \{4\}\rangle, \langle \{Ws, Zs\}, \{2\}\rangle, \langle \{X, Xs, Zs\}, \{1, 2\}\rangle\}$$
$$S_8' = \{\emptyset, \langle \{\underline{Zs}, Vs, Xs, Ws, Zs\}, \{1, 2, 3, 5\}\rangle, \langle \{\underline{Zs}, Ys, Ws, Zs\}, \{2, 4, 5\}\rangle,$$
$$\langle \{\underline{Zs}, Vs, Xs, Ys, Ws, Zs\}, \{1, 2, 3, 4, 5\}\rangle, \langle \{X, Xs, Zs\}, \{1, 2\}\rangle\}$$
$$S_9' = \{\emptyset, \langle \{Vs, Xs, Ws, Zs\}, \{1, 2, 3, 5\}\rangle, \langle \{Ys, Ws, Zs\}, \{2, 4, 5\}\rangle,$$
$$\langle \{Vs, Xs, Ys, Ws, Zs\}, \{1, 2, 3, 4, 5\}\rangle, \langle \{X, Xs, Zs\}, \{1, 2\}\rangle\}$$

Computing $S_{10}' = S_9' \restriction' \mathcal{X} \setminus \{Xs, Ys, Zs\}$ restricts S_9' to those variables in the head of the clause which yields the description $S_{10}' = \{\emptyset, \langle \{Xs, Zs\}, \{1, 2, 3, 5\}\rangle, \langle \{Xs, Zs\}, \{1, 2, 3, 4, 5\}\rangle, \langle \{Ys, Zs\}, \{2, 4, 5\}\rangle, \langle \{Xs, Zs\}, \{1, 2\}\rangle\}$. Now, only the pending closures remain to be evaluated.

2.4 Evaluating Pending Closures

The pending closures can be activated by applying a closure operation $cl(S, i)$ for each identifier i contained within S. The operation $cl(S, i)$ is a form of closure under union that is sensitive to i in the sense that it only merges two pairs $\langle G, I \rangle$ and $\langle H, J \rangle$ when both I and J contain the identifier i. The merge of these pairs is defined as $\langle G \cup H, I \cup J \rangle$ so that merge combines both the sharing groups and the tagging sets. Like classic closure, $cl(S, i)$ performs repeatedly merging until no new element can be generated. To express this process, $cl(S, i)$ is formulated in terms of $cl_K(S) = S \cup \{\langle G \cup H, I \cup J \rangle \mid \{\langle G, I \rangle, \langle H, J \rangle\} \subseteq S \wedge I \cap J \cap K \neq \emptyset\}$ where $K \subseteq \mathbb{N}$. Then $cl(S, i)$ can be defined as the limit of a sequence $cl(S, i) = \cup_{j=0}^{\infty} S_j$ where $S_0 = S$, $S_j = cl_{\{i\}}(S_{j-1})$. For instance, continuing with the example $S'_{10} = \{\emptyset, \langle \{Xs, Zs\}, \{1, 2, 3, 5\} \rangle, \langle \{Xs, Zs\}, \{1, 2, 3, 4, 5\} \rangle, \langle \{Ys, Zs\}, \{2, 4, 5\} \rangle, \langle \{Xs, Zs\}, \{1, 2\} \rangle\}$, then $cl_{\{4\}}(S'_{10}) = S'_{10} \cup \{\langle \{Xs, Ys, Zs\}, \{1, 2, 3, 4, 5\} \rangle\}$. In fact, in this case, no further applications of $cl_{\{4\}}$ are required for before convergence is obtained and $cl(S'_{10}, 4) = cl_{\{4\}}(S'_{10})$. In general, $cl(S, i)$ will only need to be applied a finite number of times before convergence is reached.

Applying the closure operator $cl(S, i)$ is sufficient to evaluate the closure that is delimited by i; a single application of $cl(S, i)$ is not sufficient to active all the pending closures. Therefore $cl(S, i)$ is itself iteratively applied by computing the sequence of descriptions $T_0 = S$ and $T_i = cl(T_{i-1}, i)$ that culminates in T_n where n is understood to be the maximal identifier of S. Henceforth, let $cl'(S) = T_n$. Returning to the running example, $cl'(S'_{10}) = \{\emptyset, \langle \{Xs, Ys, Zs\}, \{1, 2, 4, 5\} \rangle, \{Xs, Ys, Zs\}, \{1, 2, 3, 4, 5\} \rangle, \langle \{Xs, Zs\}, \{1, 2, 3, 5\} \rangle, \langle \{Xs, Zs\}, \{1, 2, 3, 4, 5\} \rangle, \langle \{Ys, Zs\}, \{2, 4, 5\} \rangle, \langle \{Xs, Zs\}, \{1, 2\} \rangle\}$.

2.5 Collapsing Closures: The Duplicated Group Rule

The remaining tags can be eliminated with $untag(S) = \{G \mid \langle G, N \rangle \in S\}$. Composing and then applying these two operations to S'_{10} gives $untag(cl'(S'_{10})) = \{\{Xs, Ys, Zs\}, \{Xs, Zs\}, \{Ys, Zs\}\}$ as desired. Although this is an advance — closure calculations have been collapsed to range over the variables of the head rather than the clause — it does not exploit the fact that the closure calculations for different identifiers can be collapsed into a single computation.

To see this, observe that S'_{10} contains three pairs $\langle G, N_1 \rangle$, $\langle G, N_2 \rangle$ and $\langle G, N_3 \rangle$ where $G = \{Xs, Zs\}$, $N_1 = \{1, 2\}$, $N_2 = \{1, 2, 3, 5\}$ and $N_2 = \{1, 2, 3, 4, 5\}$. The pairs $\langle G, N_1 \rangle$ and $\langle G, N_2 \rangle$ are redundant since $N_1 \subseteq N_3$ and $N_2 \subseteq N_3$. Removing these pairs from S'_{10} yields the description $S'_{11} = \{\emptyset, \langle \{Xs, Zs\}, \{1, 2, 3, 4, 5\} \rangle, \langle \{Ys, Zs\}, \{2, 4, 5\} \rangle\}$ which compromises neither correctness nor precision since $untag(cl'(S'_{10})) = untag(cl'(S'_{11}))$. Actually, the underlying principle is not that of eliminating a pair that shares a common group with another pair whose identifiers subsume it, but rather that all pairs which share a common group can merged into single pair. In this particular case of S'_{10}, the three pairs can be combined into the single pair $\langle G, N_1 \cup N_2 \cup N_3 \rangle$ that subsumes them all; S'_{10} merely illustrates the special case of when $N_1 \cup N_2 \cup N_3 = N_3$. In general, if $\{\langle G, N \rangle, \langle G, M \rangle\} \subseteq S$, $N \cap M \neq \emptyset$ and $S' = (S \setminus \{\langle G, N \rangle, \langle G, M \rangle\}) \cup \{\langle G, N \cup M \rangle\}$ then $untag(cl'(S)) =$

$untag(cl'(S'))$. Henceforth this equivalence will be referred to as the duplicated group rule.

2.6   Collapsing Closures: The Uniqueness Rule

Further reductions can be applied. Since the identifiers 1 and 3 occur in just one pair, it follows that these identifiers can be immediately removed from S'_{11} to obtain $S'_{12} = \{\emptyset, \langle\{Xs, Zs\}, \{2, 4, 5\}\rangle, \langle\{Ys, Zs\}, \{2, 4, 5\}\rangle\}$ whilst preserving the relationship $untag(cl'(S'_{10})) = untag(cl'(S'_{12}))$. This strategy of removing those identifiers that occur singly will henceforth be called the uniqueness rule.

2.7   Collapsing Closures: The Covering Rule

Moreover, identifier 2 always occurs within a set of identifiers that also contains 4. In this sense 4 is said to cover 2. The value of this concept is that if one identifier is covered by another, then the first identifier is redundant. Since 5 covers both 2 and 4, then both 2 and 4 are redundant and can be removed from S'_{12} to obtain $S'_{13} = \{\emptyset, \langle\{Xs, Zs\}, \{5\}\rangle, \langle\{Ys, Zs\}, \{5\}\rangle\}$ whilst again preserving $untag(cl'(S'_{10})) = untag(cl'(S'_{13}))$. This form of reduction will be called the covering rule. The key point is that by applying these three rules S'_{10} can be simplified to S'_{13} which only requires one application $cl(S'_{13}, 5)$ followed by $untag$ to evaluate the remaining closure. This results in $untag(cl(S'_{13}, 5)) = \{\emptyset, \{Xs, Zs\}, \{Ys, Zs\}, \{Xs, Ys, Zs\}\}$ as required; the same result as classic set-sharing is derived but with a significant reduction in closure calculation.

3   Equivalence Results

This section reports some new equivalence results which show that neither closure collapsing nor delaying closure evaluation incur a precision loss over classic set-sharing. The results are summarised in sections 3.1 and 3.2 respectively.

3.1   Equivalence Rules for Collapsing Closures

The closure operator $cl'(S)$ applies $cl(S, i)$ for each identifier i to evaluate each pending closure in turn. This offers a sequential model for computing $cl'(S)$. The following result provides an alternative parallel model for closure evaluation.

Proposition 1. $cl'(S) = \cup_{i=0}^{\infty} S_i$ where $S_0 = S$ and $S_{i+1} = cl_{\mathbb{N}}(S_i)$.

The force of this result is twofold. Firstly, it can save passing over S multiply, once for each identifier. Secondly, it provides a way for arguing correctness of the three collapsing rules. For pedagogical reasons, these rules were introduced in terms of the sequential model of $cl'(S)$ evaluation, yet they are still applicable in the parallel setting. This is because the cost of closure calculation is dominated by the cost of the underlying set operations and therefore any reduction in the number or size of these sets is useful. For completeness, the rules are formally stated below, complete with a counter-example which illustrates the need for the $M \cap N \neq \emptyset$ condition in the duplicated group rule.

Proposition 2 (duplicated group rule). Suppose $\langle G, M \rangle \in S$, $\langle G, N \rangle \in S$ and $M \cap N \neq \emptyset$. Then $untag(cl'(S)) = untag(cl'(S'))$ where:

$$S' = (S \setminus \{\langle G, M \rangle, \langle G, N \rangle\}) \cup \{\langle G, M \cup N \rangle\}$$

Example 1. The following values of S and S' illustrate the necessity of the $N \cap M \neq \emptyset$ condition in the duplicated group rule. This condition bars the pairs $\langle \{y\}, \{1\} \rangle$ and $\langle \{y\}, \{2\} \rangle$ within S from being merged to obtain S'. Merging looses equivalence since $\{x, y, z\} \in untag(cl'(S'_3))$ but $\{x, y, z\} \notin untag(cl'(S_3))$.

$$S = \{\langle \{x\}, \{1\} \rangle, \langle \{y\}, \{1\} \rangle, \langle \{y\}, \{2\} \rangle, \langle \{z\}, \{2\} \rangle\}$$
$$S_1 = cl(S, 1) = \{\langle \{x\}, \{1\} \rangle, \langle \{x, y\}, \{1\} \rangle, \langle \{y\}, \{1\} \rangle, \langle \{y\}, \{2\} \rangle, \langle \{z\}, \{2\} \rangle\}$$
$$S_2 = cl(S_1, 2) = \{\langle \{x\}, \{1\} \rangle, \langle \{x, y\}, \{1\} \rangle, \langle \{y\}, \{1\} \rangle, \langle \{y\}, \{2\} \rangle, \langle \{y, z\}, \{2\} \rangle,$$
$$\langle \{z\}, \{2\} \rangle\}$$
$$S_3 = untag(S_2) = \{\{x\}, \{x, y\}, \{y\}, \{y, z\}, \{z\}\}$$

$$S' = \{\langle \{x\}, \{1\} \rangle, \langle \{y\}, \{1, 2\} \rangle, \langle \{z\}, \{2\} \rangle\}$$
$$S'_1 = cl(S', 1) = \{\langle \{x\}, \{1\} \rangle, \langle \{x, y\}, \{1, 2\} \rangle, \langle \{y\}, \{1, 2\} \rangle, \langle \{z\}, \{2\} \rangle\}$$
$$S'_2 = cl(S'_2, 2) = \{\langle \{x\}, \{1\} \rangle, \langle \{x, y\}, \{1, 2\} \rangle, \langle \{x, y, z\}, \{1, 2\} \rangle, \langle \{y\}, \{1, 2\} \rangle,$$
$$\langle \{y, z\}, \{1, 2\} \rangle, \langle \{z\}, \{2\} \rangle\}$$
$$S'_3 = untag(S'_2) = \{\{x\}, \{x, y\}, \{x, y, z\}, \{y\}, \{y, z\}, \{z\}\}$$

Proposition 3 (uniqueness rule). Suppose $\langle G, N \rangle$ is the only element of S for which $n \in N$. Then $untag(cl'(S)) = untag(cl'(S'))$ where:

$$S' = (S \setminus \{\langle G, N \rangle\}) \cup \{\langle G, N \setminus \{n\} \rangle\}$$

Proposition 4 (covering rule). Suppose that $n \neq m$ and that if $n \in N$ and $\langle G, N \rangle \in S$ then $m \in N$. Then $untag(cl'(S)) = untag(cl'(S'))$ where:

$$S' = \{\langle G, N \setminus \{n\} \rangle \mid \langle G, N \rangle \in S\}$$

3.2   Equivalence of Pending Closures

This paper proposes the general strategy of delaying closure evaluation until a time when the pending closures can be evaluated over fewer variables. This technique of procrastination is founded on lemma 1. The first result stated in the lemma explains how $amgu'$ is basically a reformulation of $amgu$ that postpones the closure calculation (providing its input is closed); in the $amgu$ closure arises within the operator whereas in the $amgu'$ closure is applied after the operator. The second result states a circumstance in which a closure can be avoided; that it is not necessary to apply $amgu'$ to an S' that is closed, ie. it is not necessary to compute $cl'(S')$, providing that the result of the $amgu'$ is then closed. The strength of these two results is that they can be composed to show that only one single closure need be applied at the end of a sequence of $amgu'$ applications. This leads to the main result — theorem 1 — which is stated immediately after the lemma. The condition in the lemma on i asserts that i is a fresh tag.

Lemma 1. Suppose that $i \notin I$ for all $\langle G, I \rangle \in S'$. Then

- if $cl'(S') = S'$ then $untag(cl(amgu'(s, t, i, S'), i)) = amgu(s, t, untag(S'))$
- $cl'(amgu'(s, t, i, S')) = cl'(amgu'(s, t, i, cl'(S')))$

Example 2. Let $t = f(y, z)$ and $S' = \{\langle\{v\}, \{1\}\rangle, \langle\{x\}, \emptyset\rangle, \langle\{y\}, \{1\}\rangle, \langle\{z\}, \emptyset\rangle\}$.
Then $cl'(S') = \{\langle\{v\}, \{1\}\rangle, \langle\{v, y\}, \{1\}\rangle, \langle\{x\}, \emptyset\rangle, \langle\{y\}, \{1\}\rangle, \langle\{z\}, \emptyset\rangle\}$ and

$$amgu(x, t, untag(cl'(S'))) = \{\{v\}, \{v, x, y\}, \{v, x, y, z\}, \{x, y\}, \{x, y, z\}, \{x, z\}\}$$
$$amgu'(x, t, 2, cl'(S')) = \{\langle\{v\}, \{1\}\rangle, \langle\{v, x, y\}, \{1, 2\}\rangle,$$
$$\langle\{x, y\}, \{1, 2\}\rangle, \langle\{x, z\}, \{2\}\rangle\}$$
$$cl(amgu'(x, t, 2, cl'(S')), 2) = \{\langle\{v\}, \{1\}\rangle, \langle\{v, x, y\}, \{1, 2\}\rangle, \langle\{v, x, y, z\}, \{1, 2\}\rangle,$$
$$\langle\{x, y\}, \{1, 2\}\rangle, \langle\{x, y, z\}, \{1, 2\}\rangle, \langle\{x, z\}, \{2\}\rangle\}$$
$$cl'(amgu'(x, t, 2, cl'(S'))) = \{\langle\{v\}, \{1\}\rangle, \langle\{v, x, y\}, \{1, 2\}\rangle, \langle\{v, x, y, z\}, \{1, 2\}\rangle,$$
$$\langle\{x, y\}, \{1, 2\}\rangle, \langle\{x, y, z\}, \{1, 2\}\rangle, \langle\{x, z\}, \{2\}\rangle\}$$
$$amgu'(x, t, 2, S') = \{\langle\{v\}, \{1\}\rangle, \langle\{x, y\}, \{1, 2\}\rangle, \langle\{x, z\}, \{2\}\rangle\}$$
$$cl'(amgu'(x, t, 2, S')) = \{\langle\{v\}, \{1\}\rangle, \langle\{v, x, y\}, \{1, 2\}\rangle, \langle\{v, x, y, z\}, \{1, 2\}\rangle,$$
$$\langle\{x, y\}, \{1, 2\}\rangle, \langle\{x, y, z\}, \{1, 2\}\rangle, \langle\{x, z\}, \{2\}\rangle\}$$

Theorem 1. Let $s_1 = t_1, \ldots, s_n = t_n$ be a sequence of syntactic equations and

$$S_0 = S \qquad S_i = amgu(s_i, t_i, S_{i-1})$$
$$S_0' = \{\langle G, \emptyset \rangle \mid G \in S\} \qquad S_i' = amgu'(s_i, t_i, i, S_{i-1}')$$

Then $untag(cl'(S_n')) = S_n$.

Example 3. Consider the equations $s_1 = t_1$ and $s_2 = t_2$ where $(s_1 = t_1) = (w = f(x, y))$ and $(s_2 = t_2) = (x = z)$, $S_0 = \alpha_{\mathcal{X}}(\varepsilon)$ and $\mathcal{X} = \{w, x, y, z\}$. Then

$$S_0 = \{\{w\}, \{x\}, \{y\}, \{z\}\} \qquad S_0' = \{\langle\{w\}, \emptyset\rangle, \langle\{x\}, \emptyset\rangle, \langle\{y\}, \emptyset\rangle, \langle\{z\}, \emptyset\rangle\}$$
$$S_1 = \{\{w, x\}, \{w, y\}, \{w, x, y\}, \{z\}\} \qquad S_1' = \{\langle\{w, x\}, \{1\}\rangle, \langle\{w, y\}, \{1\}\rangle, \langle\{z\}, \emptyset\rangle\}$$
$$S_2 = \{\{w, x, y, z\}, \{w, x, z\}, \{w, y\}\} \qquad S_2' = \{\langle\{w, x, z\}, \{1, 2\}\rangle, \langle\{w, y\}, \{1\}\rangle\}$$

Therefore $cl'(S_2') = \{\langle\{w, x, y, z\}, \{1, 2\}\rangle, \langle\{w, x, z\}, \{1, 2\}\rangle, \langle\{w, y\}, \{1\}\rangle\}$ and $untag(cl'(S_2')) = \{\{w, x, y, z\}, \{w, x, z\}, \{w, y\}\} = S_2$ as theorem 1 predicts.

Theorem 1 can be taken further to obtain corollary 1 by exploiting the property that projection $\upharpoonright'$ distributes over closure cl'. The force of this result — that is formally stated in proposition 5 — is that if the set of variables Y is smaller than $var(S')$ then $cl'(S' \upharpoonright' Y)$ is cheaper to compute than $cl'(S') \upharpoonright Y$.

Proposition 5. $cl'(S') \upharpoonright' Y = cl'(S' \upharpoonright' Y)$ where $Y \subseteq \mathcal{V}$

Corollary 1. Let $s_1 = t_1, \ldots, s_n = t_n$ be a sequence of syntactic equations and

$$S_0 = S \qquad S_i = amgu(s_i, t_i, S_{i-1})$$
$$S_0' = \{\langle G, \emptyset \rangle \mid G \in S\} \qquad S_i' = amgu'(s_i, t_i, i, S_{i-1}')$$

Then $untag(cl'(S_n' \upharpoonright' Y')) = S_n \upharpoonright Y$.

Example 4. Continuing with example 3, suppose that the objective is to compute $S_2 \upharpoonright Y$ where $Y = \{x, y\}$. The corollary asserts $S_2 \upharpoonright Y = untag(cl'(S_2' \upharpoonright' Y))$ and $cl'(\{\{\langle\{x\}, \{1, 2\}\rangle, \langle\{y\}, \{1\}\rangle\}\}) = \{\langle\{x\}, \{1, 2\}\rangle, \langle\{x, y\}, \{1, 2\}\rangle, \langle\{y\}, \{1\}\rangle\}$ whence $untag(cl'(S_2' \upharpoonright' Y)) = \{\{x\}, \{x, y\}, \{y\}\}$. Indeed, from example 3 it can be seen that $S_2 \upharpoonright Y = \{\{x\}, \{x, y\}, \{y\}\}$.

4   Implementation

In order to assess the usefulness of collapsing closures, both classic set-sharing [14] and set-sharing with closure collapsing have been implemented in Sicstus 3.8.6. To obtain a credible comparison, both techniques were implemented, wherever possible, with the same data-structures and code. Both forms of set-sharing were integrated into a goal-independent (bottom-up) fixpoint engine and a goal-dependent (bottom-up) analyser that applied a magic transform [12] to collect call and answer patterns. Both frameworks track set-sharing alone, ie., they do not trace sharing as one component of a product domain [9]. This was partly to isolate the impact of collapsing on set-sharing from the effect of other domains (quantifying these interactions even for more conventional forms of sharing is a long study within itself [3]) and partly as an experiment in worst-case sharing. The rationale was that if closure collapsing had little impact in this scenario, then it would not warrant investigating how the technique can be composed with other domains. Both frameworks also computed strongly connected components (SCCs) of the call-graph so as to stratify the fixpoint into a series of fixpoints that stabilise on one SCC before moving onto another [12].

Table 1 summaries the four analysis combinations — goal-dependent versus goal-independent and classic set-sharing versus set-sharing with collapsing — for the series of common benchmark programs. As a sanity check of the theory, success patterns derived by two forms of goal-independent analysis were verified to be equivalent; likewise the call and answer patterns computed with collapsing coincided exactly with those generated by classic set-sharing. The column labeled T indicates the time in milliseconds required to compute the fixpoint on 2.4 GHz PC equipped with 512 MBytes running Windows XP. The variance in timings between different runs of all analyses was found to be negligible. For set-sharing with collapsing, the timings were generated using sequential closure evaluation. The dashed columns indicate that a timeout was exceeded. The column labeled N records the total number of closure operations that were required (closures over one group are counted as zero). The column labeled S reports the average number of sharing groups that participate in a closure calculation and the column labeled M gives the maximal number of groups that participated in a closure.

The T columns suggest that collapsing closures is potentially useful, though actual speedup will depend on the actual implementation, the overarching fixpoint framework and the underlying machine. The N, S and M columns present a more abstract view of closure collapsing and suggest that the speedup stems from reduced sharing groups manipulation; both the number of closures are reduced (due to the three simplification rules) and the complexity of each closure is reduced (closures are applied to fewer and smaller sharing groups). Interestingly, collapsing is not uniformly faster as is witnessed, by browse and conman, for goal-independent and goal-dependent analysis. This is because S is very small for these programs (2 or 3) even without collapsing. Therefore the overhead of manipulating data-structures that are sets of pairs of sets (rather than merely

Table 1. Classic set-sharing versus set-sharing with collapsing

	goal-independent							goal-dependent							
	collapsed				classic				collapsed				classic			
file	T	N	S	M	T	N	S	M	T	N	S	M	T	N	S	M
8puzzle	47	31	7	12	2281	77	83	255	78	1	2	2	78	3	2	2
ann	2734	200	6	69	11661	806	14	336	5564	615	3	12	5812	2916	7	33
asm	172	247	2	9	140	563	4	42	937	500	5	148	20701	2299	10	484
boyer	31	110	2	7	47	233	3	64	218	251	4	27	453	740	5	112
browse	32	43	2	4	16	132	2	7	62	52	3	7	31	206	3	8
conman	1187	32	2	3	1235	136	3	8	1906	93	2	4	1813	326	2	16
crip	438	132	8	113	6766	946	15	216	5093	560	8	258	25483	3917	14	304
cry_mult	5907	39	4	13	6219	201	6	32	12500	48	2	7	13016	460	9	32
cs_r	2687	149	25	274	–	–	–	–	516	32	2	8	3250	204	37	240
disj_r	110	45	9	25	8500	321	24	240	219	16	2	3	94	105	2	6
dnf	2	0	0	0	2	28	2	3	31	6	2	2	16	44	2	3
draw	78	28	2	5	281	192	2	6	172	9	2	2	78	25	2	3
ga	203	47	11	50	672	141	12	187	1422	105	12	212	11966	348	15	580
gauss	16	13	3	7	15	81	3	26	47	27	5	17	94	190	5	88
kalah	78	62	3	11	250	204	8	84	141	7	2	6	109	25	7	63
life	516	33	3	7	547	114	6	32	1532	18	3	9	1500	77	3	14
lookup	2	7	2	4	2	34	4	8	15	8	3	4	2	52	3	8
matrix	8	12	2	5	3	54	2	12	63	67	3	21	63	265	4	48
math	31	45	3	6	31	216	3	12	46	43	3	10	31	210	3	24
maze	10	9	2	3	8	14	2	3	31	1	2	2	15	3	2	2
nbody	938	93	3	18	7344	267	18	1022	5641	489	6	94	–	–	–	–
peep	125	333	3	15	329	619	5	108	5077	1576	6	44	17174	3752	10	704
peg	16	7	3	5	63	62	10	75	15	2	4	5	31	49	8	24
plan	62	73	4	26	300	193	8	108	249	178	4	18	499	769	6	112
press	266	293	5	28	641	801	7	70	1937	1184	5	45	6156	4137	8	168
qsort	15	2	3	4	16	12	2	6	16	1	2	2	16	42	2	5
queens	2	2	3	4	2	18	2	6	16	0	0	0	16	0	0	0
robot	63	49	2	10	63	179	4	24	265	203	4	19	281	669	5	32
ronp	47	35	7	31	640	185	13	87	297	137	10	32	2438	660	15	96
rotate	2	4	3	4	2	18	2	6	16	19	5	8	16	82	4	16
shape	31	8	9	14	328	77	28	64	63	32	6	14	672	220	21	64
tictactoe	63	54	6	9	12796	96	100	510	94	1	2	2	62	2	2	2
treeorder	32	28	6	17	469	102	11	120	734	154	8	87	14157	628	17	360
tsp	219	76	3	68	1156	239	10	88	407	253	2	18	187	628	3	28
yasmm	4614	9	3	8	–	–	–	–	19716	40	9	24	–	–	–	–

sets of sets) is not repaid by a commensurate reduction in closure calculation. However, if S is large — which happens more often in goal-independent analysis — then the speedup from collapsing closures can be considerable. For example, collapsing requires only 63 milliseconds for tictactoe for goal-independent analysis. Although these results are promising, they are not conclusive and future work will quantify the impact of parallel closure evaluation and investigate collapsing in the context of combined domains [9] and other frameworks [5,7].

5   Related Work

Independence information has many applications in logic programming that include occurs-check reduction [19], automatic parallelisation [17] and finite-tree analysis [1]. Set-sharing analysis [14], as opposed to pair-sharing analysis [19], has particularly attracted much attention. This is because researchers have been repeatedly drawn to the algebraic properties of the domain since these offer tantalising opportunities for implementation. For example, Bagnara et al. [2] observe that set-sharing is redundant when the objective is to detect pairs of independent variables. A sharing group G is redundant with respect to a set-sharing abstraction S iff S contains the pair sharing information that G encodes. The value of redundancy is that it reduces the complexity of abstract unification to a quadratic operation. As a response to this work, Bueno et al. [6] argue that the redundancy assumption is not always valid. Our work adds to this debate by showing the closures are not always as expensive as one might expect.

Another thread of promising work is in representing set-sharing with Boolean functions [10]. In this approach, closure under union is reformulated as a closure operator that maps one function to the smallest function that contains it which can be represented as conjunction of propositional Horn clauses. This operator, though elegant, is non-trivial [18]. Nevertheless, this encoding is advantageous since ROBDDs [18] provide a canonical representation for Boolean functions which enables memoisation to be applied to avoid repeated closure calculation.

The most commonly deployed tactic for reducing the number of closure calculations is to combine set-sharing with other abstract domains [3,9] that can be used to determine whether closure calculation is actually unnecessary. This is not merely a computational tactic, but also a way to improve precision. Although it seems straightforward to integrate groundness with closure collapsing, future work will address the issue of how to fuse linearity [3,9] with this tactic.

The work reported in this paper is hinted at by a recent paper of the authors [16] that endeavors to compute closures in an entirely lazy fashion. Each unevaluated closure is represented by a clique — a set of program variables — that augments a standard set-sharing abstractions. Alas, the advantage of this approach is compromised by the way cliques interact with projection operation to loose precision. By way of contrast, this paper shows that projection is a catalyst for collapsing closures which leads to a simpler tactic for avoiding work.

6   Conclusions

Two issues govern the efficiency of set-sharing analysis: the number of sharing groups that participate in each closure operation and the total number of closures that are applied. This paper proposes a new tactic for reducing the overhead of closure calculation based on postponing closures until a propitious moment when they can be applied on less variables. This collapses the size of closures whilst collapsing one closure calculation into another. The resulting analysis is as precise as classic set-sharing analysis.

Acknowledgments. This work was funded by NSF grants CCR-0131862 and INT-0327760, EPSRC grant EP/C015517 and the Royal Society grant 2005/R4-JP.

References

1. R. Bagnara, R. Gori, P. Hill, and E. Zaffanella. Finite-Tree Analysis for Constraint Logic-Based Languages. *Information and Computation*, 193(2):84–116, 2004.
2. R. Bagnara, P. Hill, and E. Zaffanella. Set-Sharing is Redundant for Pair-Sharing. *Theoretical Computer Science*, 277(1-2):3–46, 2002.
3. R. Bagnara, E. Zaffanella, and P. Hill. Enhanced Sharing Analysis Techniques: A Comprehensive Evaluation. *Theory and Practice of Logic Programming*, 5, 2005.
4. A. Bossi, M. Gabbrielli, G. Levi, and M. Martelli. The *s*-Semantics Approach: Theory and Applications. *The Journal of Logic Programming*, 19:149–197, 1994.
5. M. Bruynooghe. A Practical Framework for the Abstract Interpretation of Logic Programs. *The Journal of Logic Programming*, 10(2):91–124, 1991.
6. F. Bueno and M. García de la Banda. Set-Sharing Is Not Always Redundant for Pair-Sharing. In *Symposium on Functional and Logic Programming*, volume 2998 of *LNCS*, pages 117–131. Springer-Verlag, 2004.
7. M. Codish. Efficient Goal Directed Bottom-Up Evaluation of Logic Programs. *The Journal of Logic Programming*, 38(3):355–370, 1999.
8. M. Codish, V. Lagoon, and F. Bueno. An Algebraic Approach to Sharing Analysis of Logic Programs. *The Journal of Logic Programming*, 42(2):111–149, 2000.
9. M. Codish, A. Mulkers, M. Bruynooghe, M. García de la Banda, and M. Hermenegildo. Improving Abstract Interpretations by Combining Domains. *ACM TOPLAS*, 17(1):28–44, 1995.
10. M. Codish, H. Søndergaard, and P. Stuckey. Sharing and Groundness Dependencies in Logic Programs. *ACM TOPLAS*, 21(5):948–976, 1999.
11. M. Falaschi, G. Levi, C. Palamidessi, and M. Martelli. Declarative Modeling of the Operational Behavior of Logic Languages. *Theoretical Computer Science*, 69(3):289–318, 1989.
12. J. Gallagher. A Bottom-Up Analysis Toolkit. Technical Report 95-016, Department of Computer Science, University of Bristol, 1995. (Invited paper at WAILL).
13. W. Hans and S. Winkler. Aliasing and Groundness Analysis of Logic Programs through Abstract Interpretation and its Safety. Technical Report Nr. 92-27, RWTH Aachen, Lehrstuhl für Informatik II Ahornstraße 55, W-5100 Aachen, 1992.
14. D. Jacobs and A. Langen. Static Analysis of Logic Programs for Independent And-Parallelism. *The Journal of Logic Programming*, 13(2&3):291–314, 1992.
15. X. Li, A. King, and L. Lu. Correctness of Closure Collapsing. Technical Report 2-06, University of Kent, 2006. http://www.cs.kent.ac.uk/pubs/2006/2370.
16. X. Li, A. King, and L. Lu. Lazy Set-Sharing. In *Symposium on Functional and Logic Programming*, volume 3945 of *LNCS*, pages 177–191. Springer-Verlag, 2006.
17. K. Muthukumar and M. Hermenegildo. Compile-Time Derivation of Variable Dependency Using Abstract Interpretation. *The Journal of Logic Programming*, 13(2-3):315–347, 1992.
18. P. Schachte and H. Søndergaard. Closure Operators for ROBDDs. In *Verification, Model Checking and Abstract Interpretation*, volume 3855 of *LNCS*, pages 1–16. Springer-Verlag, 2006.
19. H. Søndergaard. An Application of Abstract Interpretation of Logic Programs: Occur Check Reduction. In *European Symposium on Programming*, volume 213 of *LNCS*, pages 327–338. Springer-Verlag, 1986.

Reduced Certificates for Abstraction-Carrying Code*

Elvira Albert[1], Puri Arenas[1], Germán Puebla[2], and Manuel Hermenegildo[2,3]

[1] Complutense University of Madrid
{elvira, puri}@sip.ucm.es
[2] Technical University of Madrid
{german, herme}@fi.upm.es
[3] University of New Mexico
herme@unm.edu

Abstract. *Abstraction-Carrying Code* (ACC) has recently been proposed as a framework for mobile code safety in which the code supplier provides a program together with an *abstraction* whose validity entails compliance with a predefined safety policy. The abstraction plays thus the role of safety certificate and its generation is carried out automatically by a fixed-point analyzer. The advantage of providing a (fixed-point) abstraction to the code consumer is that its validity is checked in a *single pass* of an abstract interpretation-based checker. A main challenge is to reduce the size of certificates as much as possible while at the same time not increasing checking time. We introduce the notion of *reduced certificate* which characterizes the subset of the abstraction which a checker needs in order to validate (and re-construct) the *full certificate* in a single pass. Based on this notion, we instrument a generic analysis algorithm with the necessary extensions in order to identify the information relevant to the checker. We also provide a correct checking algorithm together with sufficient conditions for ensuring its completeness. The experimental results within the CiaoPP system show that our proposal is able to greatly reduce the size of certificates in practice.

1 Introduction

Proof-Carrying Code (PCC) [16] is a general framework for mobile code safety which proposes to associate safety information in the form of a *certificate* to programs. The certificate (or proof) is created at compile time by the *certifier* on the code supplier side, and it is packaged along with the code. The consumer which receives or downloads the (untrusted) code+certificate package can then run a *checker* which by an efficient inspection of the code and the certificate can

---

* This work was funded in part by the Information Society Technologies program of the European Commission, Future and Emerging Technologies under the IST-15905 *MOBIUS* project, by the MEC project TIN-2005-09207 *MERIT*, and the CAM project S-0505/TIC/0407 *PROMESAS*. Manuel Hermenegildo is also supported by the Prince of Asturias Chair in Information Science and Technology at UNM.

S. Etalle and M. Truszczyński (Eds.): ICLP 2006, LNCS 4079, pp. 163–178, 2006.

verify the validity of the certificate and thus compliance with the safety policy. The key benefit of this approach is that the task of the consumer is reduced to checking, a procedure that should be much simpler, efficient, and automatic than generating the original certificate. Abstraction-Carrying Code (ACC) [2] has been recently proposed as an enabling technology for PCC in which an *abstraction* (or abstract model of the program) plays the role of certificate. An important feature of ACC is that not only the checking, but also the generation of the abstraction is carried out automatically, by a fixed-point analyzer. Both the analysis and checking algorithms are always parametric on the abstract domain, with the resulting genericity. This allows proving a wide variety of properties by using the large set of abstract domains that are available, well understood, and with already developed proofs for the correctness of the corresponding abstract operations. This is one of the fundamental advantages of ACC.[1]

In this paper, we consider analyzers which construct a *program analysis graph* which is an abstraction of the (possibly infinite) set of states explored by the concrete execution. To capture the different graph traversal strategies used in different fixed-point algorithms we use the *generic* description of [10], which generalizes the algorithms used in state-of-the-art analysis engines. Essentially, the certification/analysis carried out by the supplier is an iterative process which repeatedly traverses the analysis graph until a fixpoint is reached. The analysis information inferred for each call is stored in the *answer table* [10]. In the original ACC framework, the final *full* answer table constitutes the certificate. Since this certificate contains the fixpoint, a single pass over the analysis graph is sufficient to validate it on the consumer side. It should be noted that while the ACC framework and our work here are applied at the source-level, and in existing PCC frameworks the code supplier typically packages the certificate with the *object* code rather than with the *source* code (both are untrusted), this is without loss of generality because both the ideas in the ACC approach and in our current proposal can also be applied to bytecode.

One of the main challenges for the practical uptake of ACC (and related methods) is to produce certificates which are reasonably small. This is important since the certificate is transmitted together with the untrusted code and, hence, reducing its size will presumably contribute to a smaller transmission time. Also, this reduces the storage cost for the certificate. Nevertheless, a main concern when reducing the size of the certificate is that checking time is not increased as a consequence. In principle, the consumer could use an analyzer for the purpose of generating the whole fixpoint from scratch, which is still feasible since analysis is automatic. However, this would defeat one of the main purposes of ACC, which is to reduce checking time. The objective of this paper is to characterize the smallest subset of the abstraction which must be sent within a certificate –and

---

[1] The coexistence of several abstract domains in our framework is somewhat related to the notion of *models* to capture the security-relevant properties of code, as addressed in the work on Model-Carrying Code [22].However, their combination has not been studied which differs from our idea of using combinations of (high-level) abstract domains, which is already well understood.

which still guarantees a single pass checking process– and to design an ACC scheme which generates and validates such reduced certificates.

Fixpoint compression is being used in different contexts and tools. For instance, in the Astrée analyzer [8], only one abstract element by head of loop is kept for memory usage purposes. In the PCC scheme, the basic idea in order to compress a certificate is to store only the analysis information which the checker is not able to reproduce by itself [12]. With this purpose, Necula and Lee [17] designed a variant of LF, called LF_i, in which certificates discard all the information that is redundant or that can be easily synthesized. Also, Oracle-based PCC [18] aims at minimizing the size of certificates by providing the checker with the minimal information it requires to perform a proof. Tactic-based PCC [3] aims at minimizing the size of certificates by relying on large reasoning steps, or tactics, that are understood by the checker. Finally, this general idea has also been deployed in lightweight byte-code verification [20] where the certificate, rather than being the whole set of frame types (FT) associated to each program point is reduced by omitting those (local) program point FTs which correspond to instructions without branching *and* which are lesser than the final FT (fixpoint). Our proposal for ACC is at the same time more general (because of the parametricity of the ACC approach) and carries the reduction further because it includes only in the certificate those calls in the analysis graph (including both branching an non branching instructions) required by the checker to re-generate the certificate in one pass.

2   A General View of Abstraction-Carrying Code

We assume the reader is familiar with abstract interpretation (see [7]) and (Constraint) Logic Programming (C)LP (see, e.g., [14] and [13]). A certifier is a function certifier : $Prog \times ADom \times AInt \mapsto ACert$ which for a given program $P \in Prog$, an abstract domain $D_\alpha \in ADom$ and a safety policy $I_\alpha \in AInt$ generates a certificate $Cert_\alpha \in ACert$, by using an abstract interpreter for D_α, which entails that P satisfies I_α. In the following, we denote that I_α and $Cert_\alpha$ are specifications given as abstract semantic values of D_α by using the same α. The basics for defining such certifiers (and their corresponding checkers) in ACC are summarized in the following six points and Equations:

Approximation. We consider an *abstract domain* $\langle D_\alpha, \sqsubseteq \rangle$ and its corresponding *concrete domain* $\langle 2^D, \subseteq \rangle$, both with a complete lattice structure. Abstract values and sets of concrete values are related by an *abstraction* function $\alpha : 2^D \to D_\alpha$, and a *concretization* function $\gamma : D_\alpha \to 2^D$. An abstract value $y \in D_\alpha$ is a *safe approximation* of a concrete value $x \in D$ iff $x \in \gamma(y)$. The concrete and abstract domains must be related in such a way that the following holds [7] $\forall x \in 2^D : \gamma(\alpha(x)) \supseteq x$ and $\forall y \in D_\alpha : \alpha(\gamma(y)) = y$. In general $\sqsubseteq$ is induced by $\subseteq$ and α. Similarly, the operations of *least upper bound* ($\sqcup$) and *greatest lower bound* ($\sqcap$) mimic those of 2^D in a precise sense.

Analysis. We consider the class of *fixed-point semantics* in which a (monotonic) semantic operator, S_P, is associated to each program P. The meaning of the program, $[\![P]\!]$, is defined as the least fixed point of the S_P operator, i.e., $[\![P]\!] = \mathrm{lfp}(S_P)$. If S_P is continuous, the least fixed point is the limit of an iterative process involving at most ω applications of S_P starting from the bottom element of the lattice. Using abstract interpretation, we can usually only compute $[\![P]\!]_\alpha$, as $[\![P]\!]_\alpha = \mathrm{lfp}(S_P^\alpha)$. The operator S_P^α is the abstract counterpart of S_P.

$$\mathsf{analyzer}(P, D_\alpha) = \mathrm{lfp}(S_P^\alpha) = [\![P]\!]_\alpha \qquad (1)$$

Correctness of analysis ensures that $[\![P]\!] \in \gamma([\![P]\!]_\alpha)$.

Verification Condition. Let $Cert_\alpha$ be a safe approximation of P. If an abstract safety specification I_α can be proved w.r.t. $Cert_\alpha$, then P satisfies the safety policy and $Cert_\alpha$ is a valid certificate:

$$Cert_\alpha \text{ is } a \text{ valid certificate for } P \text{ w.r.t. } I_\alpha \text{ if } Cert_\alpha \sqsubseteq I_\alpha \qquad (2)$$

Certifier. Together, equations (1) and (2) define a certifier which provides program fixpoints, $[\![P]\!]_\alpha$, as certificates which entail a given safety policy, i.e., by taking $Cert_\alpha = [\![P]\!]_\alpha$.

Checking. A checker is a function $\mathsf{checker} : Prog \times ADom \times ACert \mapsto bool$ which for a program $P \in Prog$, an abstract domain $D_\alpha \in ADom$ and a certificate $Cert_\alpha \in ACert$ checks whether $Cert_\alpha$ is a fixpoint of S_P^α or not:

$$\mathsf{checker}(P, D_\alpha, Cert_\alpha) \text{ returns } true \text{ iff } (S_P^\alpha(Cert_\alpha) \equiv Cert_\alpha) \qquad (3)$$

Verification Condition Regeneration. To retain the safety guarantees, the consumer must regenerate a trustworthy verification condition –Equation 2– and use the incoming certificate to test for adherence of the safety policy.

$$P \text{ is trusted iff } Cert_\alpha \sqsubseteq I_\alpha \qquad (4)$$

A fundamental idea in ACC is that, while analysis –equation (1)– is an iterative process, checking –equation (3)– is guaranteed to be done in a single pass over the abstraction.

3   Generation of Certificates in ACC

This section recalls ACC and the notion of full certificate in the context of (C)LP [2]. For concreteness, we build on the algorithms of CiaoPP [9].

   Algorithm 1 has been presented in [10] as a generic description of a fixed-point algorithm which generalizes those used in state-of-the-art analysis engines, such as the one in CiaoPP [9]. In order to analyze a program, traditional (goal dependent) abstract interpreters for (C)LP programs receive as input, in addition to the program P and the abstract domain D_α, a set $S_\alpha \in AAtom$ of Abstract Atoms (or *call patterns*). Such call patterns are pairs of the form $A : CP$ where A is a procedure descriptor and CP is an abstract substitution (i.e., a condition of the run-time bindings) of A expressed as $CP \in D_\alpha$. For brevity, we sometimes

Algorithm 1. Generic Analyzer for Abstraction-Carrying Code

```
 1: function ANALYZE_F(S, Ω)
 2:     for A : CP ∈ S do
 3:         add_event(newcall(A : CP), Ω)
 4:     while E := next_event(Ω) do
 5:         if E := newcall(A : CP) then new_call_pattern(A : CP, Ω)
 6:         else if E := updated(A : CP) then add_dependent_rules(A : CP, Ω)
 7:         else if E := arc(R) then process_arc(R, Ω)
 8:     return answer table
```

9: **procedure** NEW_CALL_PATTERN($A : CP, \Omega$)
10:     **for all** rule $A_k : -B_{k,1}, \ldots, B_{k,n_k}$ **do**
11:         $CP_0 :=$ Aextend$(CP, vars(\ldots, B_{k,i}, \ldots))$; $CP_1 :=$ Arestrict$(CP_0, vars(B_{k,1}))$
12:         add_event($arc(A_k : CP \Rightarrow [CP_0]\ B_{k,1} : CP_1), \Omega$)
13:     add $A : CP \mapsto \bot$ to answer table

14: **procedure** PROCESS_ARC($H_k : CP_0 \Rightarrow [CP_1]\ B_{k,i} : CP_2, \Omega$)
15:     **if** $B_{k,i}$ is not a constraint **then**
16:         add $H_k : CP_0 \Rightarrow [CP_1]\ B_{k,i} : CP_2$ to dependency arc table
17:         $W := vars(A_k, B_{k,1}, \ldots, B_{k,n_k})$; $CP_3 :=$ get_answer$(B_{k,i} : CP_2, CP_1, W, \Omega)$
18:     **if** $CP_3 \neq \bot$ and $i \neq n_k$ **then**
19:         $CP_4 :=$ Arestrict$(CP_3, vars(B_{k,i+1}))$;
20:         add_event($arc(H_k : CP_0 \Rightarrow [CP_3]\ B_{k,i+1} : CP_4), \Omega$)
21:     **else if** $CP_3 \neq \bot$ and $i = n_k$ **then**
22:         $AP_1 :=$ Arestrict$(CP_3, vars(H_k))$; insert_answer_info($H : CP_0 \mapsto AP_1, \Omega$)

23: **function** GET_ANSWER($L : CP_2, CP_1, W, \Omega$)
24:     **if** L is a constraint **then return** Aadd(L, CP_1)
25:     **else** $AP_0 :=$ lookup_answer$(L : CP_2, \Omega)$; $AP_1 :=$ Aextend(AP_0, W)
26:         **return** Aconj(CP_1, AP_1)

27: **function** LOOKUP_ANSWER($A : CP, \Omega$)
28:     **if** there exists a renaming σ s.t.$\sigma(A : CP) \mapsto AP$ in answer table **then**
29:         **return** $\sigma^{-1}(AP)$
30:     **else** add_event($newcall(\sigma(A : CP)), \Omega$) where σ is renaming s.t. $\sigma(A)$ in base
         form; **return** $\bot$

31: **procedure** INSERT_ANSWER_INFO($H : CP \mapsto AP, \Omega$)
32:     $AP_0 :=$ lookup_answer$(H : CP)$; $AP_1 :=$ Alub(AP, AP_0)
33:     **if** $AP_0 \neq AP_1$ **then**
34:         add $(H : CP \mapsto AP_1)$ to answer table ;
35:         add_event($updated(H : CP), \Omega$)

36: **procedure** ADD_DEPENDENT_RULES($A : CP, \Omega$)
37:     **for all** arc of the form $H_k : CP_0 \Rightarrow [CP_1]\ B_{k,i} : CP_2$ in graph **where** there
         exists renaming σ s.t. $A : CP = (B_{k,i} : CP_2)\sigma$ **do**
38:         add_event($arc(H_k : CP_0 \Rightarrow [CP_1]\ B_{k,i} : CP_2), \Omega$)

omit the subscript α in the algorithms. The analyzer of Algorithm 1 constructs an *and–or graph* [4] (or analysis graph) for S_α which is an abstraction of the (possibly infinite) set of (possibly infinite) execution paths (and-or trees) explored by the concrete execution of initial the calls described by S_α in P. The program analysis graph is implicitly represented in the algorithm by means of two global data structures, the *answer table* and the *dependency arc table*, both initially empty.

- The answer table contains entries of the form $A : CP \mapsto AP$ where A is always a base form.[2] Informally, its entries should be interpreted as "the answer pattern for calls to A satisfying precondition (or call pattern) CP meets postcondition (or answer pattern), AP."
- A dependency arc is of the form $H_k : CP_0 \Rightarrow [CP_1] \, B_{k,i} : CP_2$. This is interpreted as follows: if the rule with H_k as head is called with description CP_0 then this causes the i-th literal $B_{k,i}$ to be called with description CP_2. The remaining part CP_1 is the program annotation just before $B_{k,i}$ is reached and contains information about all variables in rule k.

Intuitively, the analysis algorithm is a graph traversal algorithm which places entries in the answer table and dependency arc table as new nodes and arcs in the program analysis graph are encountered. To capture the different graph traversal strategies used in different fixed-point algorithms, a *prioritized event queue* is used. We use $\Omega \in QHS$ to refer to a *Queue Handling Strategy* which a particular instance of the generic algorithm may use. Events are of three forms:

- *newcall*$(A : CP)$ which indicates that a new call pattern for literal A with description CP has been encountered.
- *arc*$(H_k : \_ \Rightarrow [\_] \, B_{k,i} : \_)$ which indicates that the rule with H_k as head needs to be (re)computed from the position k, i.
- *updated*$(A : CP)$ which indicates that the answer description to call pattern A with description CP has been changed.

The functions add_event and next_event respectively push an event to the priority queue and pop the event of highest priority, according to Ω. The algorithm is defined in terms of four abstract operations on the domain D_α:

- Arestrict(CP, V) performs the abstract restriction of a description CP to the set of variables in the set V, denoted $vars(V)$;
- Aextend(CP, V) extends the description CP to the variables in the set V;
- Aadd(C, CP) performs the abstract operation of conjoining the actual constraint C with the description CP;
- Aconj(CP_1, CP_2) performs the abstract conjunction of two descriptions;
- Alub(CP_1, CP_2) performs the abstract disjunction of two descriptions.

More details on the algorithm can be found in [10,19]. Let us briefly explain its main procedures. The algorithm centers around the processing of events on the priority queue, which repeatedly removes the highest priority event (Line 4) and calls the appropriate event-handling function (L5-7). The function new_call_pattern initiates processing of all the rules for the definition of the internal literal A, by adding arc events for each of the first literals of these rules (L12). Initially,

---

[2] Program rules are assumed to be normalized: only distinct variables are allowed to occur as arguments to atoms. Furthermore, we require that each rule defining a predicate p has identical sequence of variables $x_{p_1}, \ldots x_{p_n}$ in the head atom, i.e., $p(x_{p_1}, \ldots x_{p_n})$. We call this the *base form* of p.

the answer for the call pattern is set to $\bot$ (L13). The procedure process_arc performs the core of the analysis. It performs a single step of the left-to-right traversal of a rule body. If the literal $B_{k,i}$ is not a constraint (L15), the arc is added to the dependency arc table (L16). Atoms are processed by function get_answer. Constraints are simply added to the current description (L24). In the case of literals, the function lookup_answer first looks up an answer for the given call pattern in the answer table (L28) and if it is not found, it places a *newcall* event (L30). When it finds one, then this answer is extended to the variables in the rule the literal occurs in (L25) and *conjoined* with the current description (L26). The resulting answer (L17) is either used to generate a new arc event to process the next literal in the rule, if $B_{k,i}$ is not the last one (L18); otherwise, the new answer is computed by insert_answer_info. This is the part of the algorithm more relevant to the generation of reduced certificates. The new answer for the rule is *combined* with the current answer in the table (L32). If the fixpoint for such call has not been reached, then the answer table entry is updated with the combined answer (L34) and an updated event is added to the queue (L35). The purpose of such an update is that the function add_dependent_rules (re)processes those calls which depend on the call pattern $A : CP$ whose answer has been updated (L37). This effect is achieved by adding the arc events for each of its dependencies (L38). Note that dependency arcs are used for efficiency: they allow us to start the reprocessing of a rule from the body atom which actually needs to be recomputed due to an update rather than from the leftmost atom.

The following definition corresponds to the essential idea in the ACC framework –equations (1) and (2)– of using a static analyzer to generate the certificates. The analyzer corresponds to Algorithm 1 and the certificate is the *full* answer table.

Definition 1 (full certificate). *We define function* CERTIFIER_F:*Prog* $\times$ *ADom* $\times$ *AAtom* $\times$ *AInt* $\times$ *QHS* $\mapsto$ *ACert which takes* $P \in Prog$, $D_\alpha \in ADom$, $S_\alpha \in AAtom$, $I_\alpha \in AInt$, $\Omega \in QHS$ *and returns as* full certificate, FCert $\in ACert$, *the answer table computed by* ANALYZE_F(S_α, Ω) *for* P *in* D_α *if* FCert $\sqsubseteq I_\alpha$.

4   Abstraction-Carrying Code with Reduced Certificates

The key observation in order to reduce the size of certificates is that certain entries in a certificate may be *irrelevant*, in the sense that the checker is able to reproduce them by itself in a single pass. The notion of *relevance* is directly related to the idea of recomputation in the program analysis graph. Intuitively, given an entry in the answer table $A : CP \mapsto AP$, its fixpoint may have been computed in several iterations from $\bot$, AP_0, $AP_1, \ldots$ until AP. For each change in the answer, an event updated$(A : CP)$ is generated during the analysis. The above entry is relevant in a certificate (under some strategy) when its updates force the recomputation of other arcs in the graph which *depend* on $A : CP$ (i.e., there is a dependency from it in the table). Thus, unless $A : CP \mapsto AP$ is included in the (reduced) certificate, a single-pass checker which uses the same strategy as the code producer will not be able to validate the certificate.

4.1   The Notion of Reduced Certificate

According to the above intuition, we are interested in determining when an entry in the answer table has been "updated" during the analysis and such changes affect other entries. However, there are two special types of updated events which can be considered "irrelevant". The first one is called a *redundant update* and corresponds to the kind of updates which force a redundant computation. We write $DAT|_{A:CP}$ to denote the set of arcs of the form $H : CP_0 \Rightarrow [CP_1]B : CP_2$ in the current dependency arc table such that they depend on $A : CP$ with $A : CP = (B : CP_2)\sigma$ for some renaming σ.

Definition 2 (redundant update). *Let $P \in Prog$, $S_\alpha \in AAtom$ and $\Omega \in QHS$. We say that an event* updated$(A : CP)$ *which appears in the event queue during the analysis of P for S_α is* redundant *w.r.t. Ω if, when it is generated, $DAT|_{A:CP} = \emptyset$.*

In the following section we propose a slight modification to the analysis algorithm in which redundant updates are never introduced in the priority queue, and thus they never enforce redundant recomputation. The proof of correctness for this modification can be found in [1].

The second type of updates which can be considered irrelevant are *initial updates* which, under certain circumstances, are generated in the first pass over an arc. In particular, we do not take into account updated events which are generated when the answer table contains $\perp$ for the updated entry. Note that this case still corresponds to the first traversal of any arc and should not be considered as a reprocessing.

Definition 3 (initial update). *In the conditions of Def. 2, we say that an event* updated$(A : CP)$ *which appears in the event queue during the analysis of P for S_α is* initial *for Ω if, when it is generated, the answer table contains $A : CP \mapsto \perp$.*

Initial updates do not occur in certain very optimized algorithms, like the one in [19]. However, they are necessary in order to model generic graph traversal strategies. In particular, they are intended to *resume* arcs whose evaluation has been *suspended*.

Definition 4 (relevant update). *In the conditions of Def. 2, we say that an event* updated$(A : CP)$ *is* relevant *iff it is not initial nor redundant.*

The key idea is that those answer patterns whose computation has introduced relevant updates should be available in the certificate.

Definition 5 (relevant entry). *In the conditions of Def. 2 we say that the entry $A : CP \mapsto AP$ in the answer table is* relevant *for Ω iff there has been at least one relevant event* updated$(A : CP)$ *during the analysis of P for S_α.*

The notion of *reduced certificate* allows us to remove irrelevant entries from the answer table and produce a smaller certificate which can still be validated in one pass.

Definition 6 (reduced certificate). *In the conditions of Def. 2, let* FCert= ANALYZE_F(S_α, Ω) *for P and* S_α*. We define the* reduced certificate, RCert, *as the set of relevant entries in* FCert *for* Ω.

Example 1. Consider the Ciao version of procedure rectoy, taken from [21]:

```
rectoy(N,M) :- N = 0, M = 0.
rectoy(N,M) :- N1 is N-1, rectoy(N1,R), M is N1+R.
```

Assume the call pattern rectoy(N, M) : $\{$N/int$\}$ which indicates that external calls to rectoy are performed with an integer value, int, in the first argument N. It holds that FCert = rectoy(N, M) : $\{$N/int$\} \mapsto \{$N/int, M/int$\}$ (the steps performed by ANALYZE_F are detailed in [1]). Assume now that we use a strategy $\Omega \in QHS$ which assigns the highest priority to redundant updates and selects the rules for rectoy in the textual order. For this strategy, the unique entry in FCert is not relevant as there has been no relevant updated event in the queue. Therefore, the reduced certificate for our example is empty (and, with the techniques of the next section, our checker is able to reconstruct the fixpoint in a single pass from this empty certificate). In contrast, lightweight bytecode verification [21] sends, together with the program, the reduced *non-empty* certificate $cert = (\{30 \mapsto (\epsilon, rectoy \cdot int \cdot int \cdot int \cdot \bot)\}, \epsilon)$, which states that at program point 30 the stack does not contain information (first occurrence of ϵ),[3] and variables N, M and R have type *int*, *int* and $\bot$. The need for sending this information is because rectoy, implemented in Java, contains an *if*-branch (equivalent to the branching for selecting one of our two clauses for rectoy). Thus *cert* has to inform the checker that it is possible for variable R at point 30 to be undefined, if the *if* condition does not hold. Note that this program is therefore an example of how our approach improves on state-of-the-art PCC techniques by reducing the certificate further while still keeping the checking process one-pass.   □

4.2   Generation of Certificates Without Irrelevant Entries

In this section, we proceed to instrument the analyzer of Algorithm 1 with the extensions necessary for producing reduced certificates, as defined in Def. 6. The resulting analyzer ANALYZE_R is presented in Algorithm 2. It uses the same procedures of Algorithm 1 except for the new definitions of add_dependent_rules and insert_answer_info. The differences with respect to the original definition are:

1. *We count the number of relevant updates for each call pattern.* To do this, we associate with each entry in the answer table a new field "u" whose purpose is to identify relevant entries. Concretely, u indicates the number of

---

[3] The second occurrence of ϵ indicates that there are no backwards jumps.

Algorithm 2. ANALYZE_R: Analyzer instrumented for Certificate Reduction

1: **procedure** ADD_DEPENDENT_RULES$(A : CP, \Omega)$
2:     $(AP, u) =$ get_from_answer_table$(A : CP)$
3:     set_in_answer_table$(A(u + 1) : CP \mapsto AP)$
4:     **for all** arc of the form $H_k : CP_0 \Rightarrow [CP_1] \ B_{k,i} : CP_2$ in graph **where** there exists renaming σ s.t. $A : CP = (B_{k,i} : CP_2)\sigma$ **do**
5:         add_event$(arc(H_k : CP_0 \Rightarrow [CP_1] \ B_{k,i} : CP_2), \Omega)$

6: **procedure** INSERT_ANSWER_INFO$(H : CP \mapsto AP, \Omega)$
7:     $AP_0 :=$ lookup_answer$(H : CP, \Omega)$
8:     $AP_1 :=$ Alub(AP, AP_0)
9:     **if** $AP_0 \neq AP_1$ **then**   % updated required
10:         **if** $AP_0 = \bot$ **then**
11:             **if** $DAT|_{H:CP} \neq \emptyset$ **then** $u = 0$ % non redundant initial update
12:             **else** $u = 1$ % redundant initial update
13:         **else** $(u, \_)=$get_from_answer_table$(H : CP)$ % not initial update
14:         **if** $DAT|_{H:CP} \neq \emptyset$ **then** add_event$(updated(H : CP))$
15:         set_in_answer_table$(H(u) : CP \mapsto AP_1)$

updated events processed for the entry. u is initialized when the (unique and first) initial updated event occurs for a call pattern. The initialization of u is different for redundant and initial updates as explained in the next point. When the analysis finishes, if $u > 1$, we know that at least one reprocessing has occurred and the entry is thus relevant. The essential point to note is that u has to be increased when the event is actually *extracted* from the queue (L3) and not when it is *introduced* in it (L14). The reason for this is that when a non-redundant, updated event is introduced, if the priority queue contains an identical event, then the processing is performed only once. Therefore, our counter must not be increased.

2. *We do not generate redundant updates.* Our algorithm does not introduce redundant updated events (L14). However, if they are initial (and redundant) they have to be counted as if they had been introduced and processed and, thus, the next update over them has to be considered always relevant. This effect is achieved by initializing the u-value with a higher value ("1" in L12) than for initial updates ("0" in L11). Indeed, the value "0" just indicates that the initial updated event has been introduced in the priority queue but not yet processed. It will be increased to "1" once it is extracted from the queue. Therefore, in both cases the next updated event over the call pattern will increase the counter to "2" and will be relevant.

In Algorithm 2, a call $(u, AP)=$get_from_answer_table$(A : CP)$ looks up in the answer table the entry for $A : CP$ and returns its u-value and its answer AP. A call set_in_answer_table$(A(u) : CP \mapsto AP)$ replaces the entry for $A : CP$ with the new one $A(u) : CP \mapsto AP$.

Proposition 1. *Let* $P \in Prog$, $D_\alpha \in ADom$, $S_\alpha \in AAtom$, $\Omega \in QHS$. *Let* FCert *be the answer table computed by* ANALYZE_R(S_α, Ω) *for* P *in* D_α. *Then, an entry* $A(u) : CP_A \mapsto AP \in$ FCert *is relevant iff* $u > 1$.

Note that, except for the control of relevant entries, $\text{ANALYZE\_F}(S_\alpha, \Omega)$ and $\text{ANALYZE\_R}(S_\alpha, \Omega)$ have the same behavior and they compute the same answer table (see [1] for details). We use function remove_irrelevant_answers which takes a set of answers of the form $A(u) : CP \mapsto AP \in \mathsf{FCert}$ and returns the set of answers $A : CP \mapsto AP$ such that $u > 1$.

Definition 7 (certifier). *We define the function* $\text{CERTIFIER\_R}: Prog \times ADom \times AAtom \times AInt \times QHS \mapsto ACert$, *which takes* $P \in Prog$, $D_\alpha \in ADom$, $S_\alpha \in AAtom$, $I_\alpha \in AInt$, $\Omega \in QHS$. *It returns as certificate,* $\mathsf{RCert}=$remove_irrelevant_answers(FCert), *where* $\mathsf{FCert}=\text{ANALYZE\_R}(S_\alpha, \Omega)$, *if* $\mathsf{FCert} \sqsubseteq I_\alpha$.

5   Checking Reduced Certificates

In the ACC framework for full certificates the checking algorithm [2] uses a specific graph traversal strategy, say Ω_C. This checker has been shown to be very efficient but in turn its design is not generic with respect to this issue (in contrast to the analysis design). This is not problematic in the context of full certificates since, even if the certifier uses a strategy Ω_A which is different from Ω_C, it is ensured that all valid certificates get validated in one pass by that specific checker. This result does not hold any more in the case of reduced certificates. In particular, *completeness* of checking is not guaranteed if $\Omega_A \neq \Omega_C$. This occurs because though the answer table is identical for all strategies, the subset of redundant entries depends on the particular strategy used. The problem is that, if there is an entry $A : CP \mapsto AP$ in FCert such that it is relevant w.r.t. Ω_C but it is not w.r.t. Ω_A, then a single pass checker will fail to validate the RCert generated using Ω_A. Therefore, it is essential in this context to design generic checkers which are not tied to a particular graph traversal strategy. Upon agreeing on the appropriate parameters,[4] the consumer uses the particular instance of the generic checker resulting from application of such parameters.

It should be noted that the design of generic checkers is also relevant in light of current trends in verified analyzers (e.g., [11,6]), which could be transferred directly to the checking end. In particular, since the design of the checking process is generic, it becomes feasible in ACC to use automatic program transformers to specialize a certified (specific) analysis algorithm in order to obtain a certified checker with the same strategy while preserving correctness and completeness.

The following definition presents a generic checker for validating reduced certificates. In addition to the genericity issue discussed above, an important difference with the checker for full certificates [2] is that there are certain entries which are not available in the certificate and that we want to reconstruct and output in checking. The reason for this is that the safety policy has to be tested

---

[4] In a particular application of our framework, we expect that the graph traversal strategy is agreed a priori between consumer and producer. But, if necessary (e.g., the consumer does not implement this strategy), then it could be sent along with the transmitted package.

Algorithm 3. Generic Checker for Reduced Certificates CHECKING_R

1: **procedure** INSERT_ANSWER_INFO($H : CP \mapsto AP, \Omega$)
2:    $AP_0 :=$ lookup_answer($H : CP, \Omega$); $AP_1 :=$ Alub(AP, AP_0)
3:    (IsIn,AP')=look_fixpoint($H : CP$,RCert)
4:    **if** IsIn and Alub(AP, AP') $\neq AP'$ **then return** Error   % error of type a)
5:    **if** $AP_0 \neq AP_1$ **then**   % updated required
6:       **if** $AP_0 = \bot$ **then**
7:          **if** $DAT|_{H:CP} \neq \emptyset$ **then** $u = 0$; add_event(updated($H : CP$), Ω)
8:          **else** $u = 1$
9:       **else** $(u, \_)$=get_from_answer_table($H : CP$)
10:         **if** $DAT|_{H:CP} \neq \emptyset$ and $u = 1$ **then return** Error   % error of type b)
11:         **if** IsIn and $AP_0 = \bot$ **then** $AP_1 = AP'$
12:         set_in_answer_table($H(u) : CP \mapsto AP_1$)

13: **function** LOOK_FIXPOINT($A : CP$,RCert)
14:    **if** $\exists$ a renaming σ such that $\sigma(A : CP \mapsto AP) \in$ RCert **then**
15:       **return** (True,$\sigma^{-1}(AP)$)
16:    **else return** (False,$\bot$)

---

w.r.t. the full answer table –Equation (2). Therefore, the checker must reconstruct, from RCert, the answer table returned by ANALYZE_F, FCert, in order to test for adherence to the safety policy –Equation (4). Note that reconstructing the answer table does not add any additional cost compared to the checker in [2], since the full answer table also has to be created in [2].

Definition 8 (checker for reduced certificates). *Function* CHECKING_R *is defined as function* ANALYZE_R *with the following modifications:*

1. *It receives* RCert *as an additional input parameter.*
2. *It may fail to produce an answer table. In that case it issues an* Error.
3. *Function* insert_answer_info *is replaced by the new one in Algorithm 3.*

Function CHECKER_R *takes* $P \in Prog$, $D_\alpha \in ADom$, $S_\alpha \in AAtom$, $\Omega \in QHS$, RCert $\in ACert$ *and returns the result of* CHECKING_R($S_\alpha, \Omega,$ RCert) *for* P *in* D_α.

Let us briefly explain the differences between Algorithms 2 and 3. First, the checker has to detect (and issue) two sources of errors:

a) The answer in the certificate is more precise than the one obtained by the checker (L4). This is the traditional error in ACC and means that the certificate and program at hand do not correspond to each other.
b) Recomputation is required. This should not occur during checking, i.e., only initial updates should be generated (L7) by the checker.[5] This second type of error corresponds to situations in which a relevant update is needed in order to obtain an answer (it cannot be obtained in one pass). This is detected in L10 prior to introducing the (non redundant) update if u is already 1.

---

[5] Initial updates are not needed in the particular instance of the checker of [2] because the strategy is fixed. They are needed to model a generic checker though.

The second difference is that the entries $A : CP \mapsto AP'$ stored in RCert have to be added to the answer table, after the initial updated event for $A : CP$ occurs, in order to detect errors of type a) above. In particular, L11 and L12 add the fixpoint AP' stored in RCert to the answer table together with the corresponding u-value (same value as in Algorithm 2).

The following theorem ensures that if CHECKER_R validates a certificate (i.e., it does not return Error), then the re-constructed answer table is a fixpoint. This implies that any certificate which gets validated by the checker is indeed a valid one.

Theorem 1 (correctness). *Let $P \in Prog$, $D_\alpha \in ADom$, $S_\alpha \in AAtom$, $I_\alpha \in AInt$ and $\Omega_A, \Omega_C \in QHS$. Let* FCert= CERTIFIER_F*$(P, D_\alpha, S_\alpha, I_\alpha, \Omega_A)$ and* RCert= CERTIFIER_R*$(P, D_\alpha, S_\alpha, I_\alpha, \Omega_A)$. If* CHECKER_R*$(P, D_\alpha, S_\alpha, I_\alpha,$* RCert*, $\Omega_C)$ does not issue an* Error*, then it returns* FCert*.*

The following theorem (completeness) provides sufficient conditions under which a checker is guaranteed to validate reduced certificates which are actually valid.

Theorem 2 (completeness). *Let $P \in Prog$, $D_\alpha \in ADom$, $S_\alpha \in AAtom$, $I_\alpha \in AInt$ and $\Omega_A \in QHS$. Let* FCert= CERTIFIER_F*$(P, D_\alpha, S_\alpha, I_\alpha, \Omega_A)$ and* RCert$_{\Omega_A}$ = CERTIFIER_R*$(P, D_\alpha, S_\alpha, I_\alpha, \Omega_A)$. Let $\Omega_C \in QHS$ be such that* RCert$_{\Omega_C}$ = CERTIFIER_R*$(P, D_\alpha, S_\alpha, I_\alpha, \Omega_C)$ and* RCert$_{\Omega_A}$ $\supseteq$ RCert$_{\Omega_C}$. Then,* CHECKER_R *$(P, D_\alpha, S_\alpha, I_\alpha,$* RCert$_{\Omega_A}$*, $\Omega_C)$ returns* FCert *and does not issue an* Error*.*

Obviously, if $\Omega_C = \Omega_A$ then the checker is guaranteed to be complete. Additionally, a checker using a different strategy Ω_C is also guaranteed to be complete as long as the certificate reduced w.r.t Ω_C is equal to or smaller than the certificate reduced w.r.t Ω_A. Furthermore, if the certificate used is full, the checker is complete for any strategy. Note that if RCert$_{\Omega_A}$ $\not\supseteq$ RCert$_{\Omega_C}$, CHECKER_R with the strategy Ω_C may fail to validate RCert$_{\Omega_A}$, which is indeed valid for the program under Ω_A.

6   Discussion and Experimental Evaluation

As we have illustrated throughout the paper, the gain of the reduction is directly related to the number of *updates* (or iterations) performed during analysis. Clearly, depending on the graph traversal strategy used, different instances of the generic analyzer will generate reduced certificates of different sizes. Significant and successful efforts have been made during recent years towards improving the efficiency of analysis. The most optimized analyzers actually aim at reducing the number of updates necessary to reach the final fixpoint [19]. Interestingly, our framework greatly benefits from all these advances, since the more efficient analysis is, the smaller the corresponding reduced certificates are. We have implemented a generator and a checker of reduced certificates in CiaoPP. Both the analysis and checker use the optimized depth-first new-calling QHS of [19].

Table 1. Size of Reduced Certificates and Checking Time

	Size	Certificate Size			Checking Time		
Program	**Source**	**FCert**	**RCert**	**F/R**	$\mathbf{C}_F$	$\mathbf{C}_R$	$\mathbf{C}_F/\mathbf{C}_R$
aiakl	1555	3090	1616	1.912	85	86	0.991
bid	4945	5939	883	6.726	46	49	0.943
browse	2589	1661	941	1.765	18	20	0.929
deriv	957	288	288	1.000	50	28	1.806
grammar	1598	1259	40	31.475	15	14	1.042
hanoiapp	1172	2325	880	2.642	30	28	1.049
occur	1367	1098	666	1.649	20	19	1.085
progeom	1619	2148	40	53.700	20	15	1.351
qsortapp	664	2355	650	3.623	20	21	0.990
query	2090	531	40	13.275	18	12	1.436
rdtok	13704	6533	2659	2.457	57	58	0.986
rectoy	154	167	40	4.175	8	8	1.079
serialize	987	1779	1129	1.576	27	27	1.022
zebra	2284	4058	40	101.450	123	125	0.979
Overall				3.35			1.06

In Table 1 we study two crucial points for the practicality of our proposal: the size of the reduced vs. full certificates and the relative efficiency of checking reduced certificates. As mentioned before, the algorithms are parametric w.r.t. the abstract domain. In our experiments we use the *sharing+freeness* [15] abstract domain, that is very useful for reasoning about instantiation errors, a crucial aspect for the safety of logic programs. The system is implemented in Ciao 1.13 [5] with compilation to bytecode. The experiments have been performed on a Pentium 4 (Xeon) at 2 Ghz and 4 Gb RAM, running GNU Linux FC-2, 2.6.9.

The set of benchmarks used is the same as in [10,2], where they are described in more detail. The column **Source** shows the size in bytes of the source code. The size in bytes of the certificates is showed in the next set of columns. **FCert** and **RCert** contain the size of the full and reduced certificate, respectively, for each benchmark and they are compared in column **(F/R)**. Our results show that the reduction in size is very significant in all cases. It ranges from 101.45 in *zebra* (RCert is indeed empty –the size of an empty certificate is, in this case, 40 bytes since it includes information about the abstract domain used for generating the certificate– whereas FCert is 4058) to 1 for *deriv* (both certificates have the same size). The final part of the table compares the checking time both when full and reduced certificates are used. Execution times are given in milliseconds and measure *runtime*. They are computed as the arithmetic mean of five runs. For each benchmark, $\mathbf{C}_F$ and $\mathbf{C}_R$ are the times for executing CHECKER_F and CHECKER_R, respectively. The column $\mathbf{C}_F/\mathbf{C}_R$ compares both checking times. It can be seen that the efficiency of CHECKER_R is very similar to that of CHECKER_F in most cases. The last row (Overall) summarizes the results for the different benchmarks using a weighted mean, where the weight is the actual checking time for each benchmark. Overall, certificates are reduced by a factor of 3.35 and the checker for reduced certificates is slightly faster, with an overall speedup of 1.06.

References

1. E. Albert, P. Arenas, G. Puebla, and M. Hermenegildo. Reduced Certificates for Abstraction-Carrying Code. Technical Report CLIP8/2005.0, Technical University of Madrid (UPM), School of Computer Science, UPM, October 2005.
2. E. Albert, G. Puebla, and M. Hermenegildo. Abstraction-Carrying Code. In *Proc. of LPAR'04*, number 3452 in LNAI, pages 380–397. Springer-Verlag, 2005.
3. D. Aspinall, S. Gilmore, M. Hofmann, D. Sannella, and I. Stark. Mobile resource guarantees for smart devices. In G. Barthe, L. Burdy, M. Huisman, J.-L. Lanet, and T. Muntean, editors, *Proceedings of CASSIS'04*, LNCS. Springer, 2004. To appear.
4. M. Bruynooghe. A Practical Framework for the Abstract Interpretation of Logic Programs. *Journal of Logic Programming*, 10:91–124, 1991.
5. F. Bueno, D. Cabeza, M. Carro, M. Hermenegildo, P. López-García, and G. Puebla (Eds.). The Ciao System. Reference Manual (v1.13). Technical report, School of Computer Science (UPM), 2006. Available at http://clip.dia.fi.upm.es/Software/Ciao/.
6. D. Cachera, T. Jensen, D. Pichardie, and V. Rusu. Extracting a Data Flow Analyser in Constructive Logic. In *Proc. of ESOP 2004*, volume LNCS 2986, pages 385 – 400, 2004.
7. P. Cousot and R. Cousot. Abstract Interpretation: a Unified Lattice Model for Static Analysis of Programs by Construction or Approximation of Fixpoints. In *Proc. of POPL'77*, pages 238–252, 1977.
8. P. Cousot, R. Cousot, J. Feret, L. Mauborgne, A. Miné, D. Monniaux, and X. Rival. The astrée analyser. In *Proc. ESOP 2005*, pages 21–30. Springer LNCS 3444, 2005.
9. M. Hermenegildo, G. Puebla, F. Bueno, and P. López-García. Integrated Program Debugging, Verification, and Optimization Using Abstract Interpretation (and The Ciao System Preprocessor). *Science of Computer Programming*, 58(1–2):115–140, October 2005.
10. M. Hermenegildo, G. Puebla, K. Marriott, and P. Stuckey. Incremental Analysis of Constraint Logic Programs. *ACM TOPLAS*, 22(2):187–223, March 2000.
11. G. Klein and T. Nipkow. Verified bytecode verifiers. *Theoretical Computer Science*, 3(298):583–626, 2003.
12. Xavier Leroy. Java bytecode verification: algorithms and formalizations. *Journal of Automated Reasoning*, 30(3-4):235–269, 2003.
13. J.W. Lloyd. *Foundations of Logic Programming*. Springer, second, extended edition, 1987.
14. Kim Marriot and Peter Stuckey. *Programming with Constraints: An Introduction*. The MIT Press, 1998.
15. K. Muthukumar and M. Hermenegildo. Combined Determination of Sharing and Freeness of Program Variables Through Abstract Interpretation. In *1991 International Conference on Logic Programming*, pages 49–63. MIT Press, June 1991.
16. G. Necula. Proof-Carrying Code. In *Proc. of POPL'97*, pages 106–119. ACM Press, 1997.

17. G.C. Necula and P. Lee. Efficient representation and validation of proofs. In *Proceedings of LICS'98*, page 93. IEEE Computer Society, 1998.
18. G.C. Necula and S.P. Rahul. Oracle-based checking of untrusted software. In *Proceedings of POPL'01*, pages 142–154. ACM Press, 2001.
19. G. Puebla and M. Hermenegildo. Optimized Algorithms for the Incremental Analysis of Logic Programs. In *Proc. of SAS'96*, pages 270–284. Springer LNCS 1145, 1996.
20. E. Rose and K. Rose. Java access protection through typing. *Concurrency and Computation: Practice and Experience*, 13(13):1125–1132, 2001.
21. K. Rose, E. Rose. Lightweight bytecode verification. In *OOPSLA Workshop on Formal Underpinnings of Java*, 1998.
22. R. Sekar, V.N. Venkatakrishnan, S. Basu, S. Bhatkar, and D. DuVarney. Model-carrying code: A practical approach for safe execution of untrusted applications. In *Proc. of SOSP'03*, pages 15–28. ACM, 2003.

Proving Properties of Constraint Logic Programs by Eliminating Existential Variables

Alberto Pettorossi[1], Maurizio Proietti[2], and Valerio Senni[1]

[1] DISP, University of Roma Tor Vergata, Via del Politecnico 1, I-00133 Roma, Italy
pettorossi@disp.uniroma2.it, senni@disp.uniroma2.it
[2] IASI-CNR, Viale Manzoni 30, I-00185 Roma, Italy
proietti@iasi.rm.cnr.it

Abstract. We propose a method for proving first order properties of constraint logic programs which manipulate finite lists of real numbers. Constraints are linear equations and inequations over reals. Our method consists in converting any given first order formula into a stratified constraint logic program and then applying a suitable unfold/fold transformation strategy that preserves the perfect model. Our strategy is based on the elimination of existential variables, that is, variables which occur in the body of a clause and not in its head. Since, in general, the first order properties of the class of programs we consider are undecidable, our strategy is necessarily incomplete. However, experiments show that it is powerful enough to prove several non-trivial program properties.

1 Introduction

It has been long recognized that program transformation can be used as a means of proving program properties. In particular, it has been shown that unfold/fold transformations introduced in [4,20] can be used to prove several kinds of program properties, such as equivalences of functions defined by recursive equation programs [5,9], equivalences of predicates defined by logic programs [14], first order properties of predicates defined by stratified logic programs [15], and temporal properties of concurrent systems [7,19]. In this paper we consider stratified logic programs *with constraints* and we propose a method based on unfold/fold transformations to prove first order properties of these programs.

The main reason that motivates our method is that transformation techniques may serve as a way of eliminating *existential variables* (that is, variables which occur in the body of a clause and not in its head) and the consequent quantifier elimination can be exploited to prove first order formulas. Quantifier elimination is a well established technique for theorem proving in first order logic [18] and one of its applications is Tarski's decision procedure for the theory of the field of reals. However, no quantifier elimination method has been developed so far to prove formulas within theories defined by constraint logic programs, where the constraints are themselves formulas of the theory of reals. Consider, for instance, the following constraint logic program which defines the membership relation for finite lists of reals:

S. Etalle and M. Truszczyński (Eds.): ICLP 2006, LNCS 4079, pp. 179–195, 2006.
© Springer-Verlag Berlin Heidelberg 2006

Member: $member(X, [Y|L]) \leftarrow X = Y$ $member(X, [Y|L]) \leftarrow member(X, L)$

Suppose we want to show that every finite list of reals has an upper bound, i.e.,

$$\varphi :\quad \forall L \, \exists U \, \forall X \, (member(X, L) \rightarrow X \leq U)$$

Tarski's quantifier elimination method cannot help in this case, because the membership relation is not defined in the language of the theory of reals. The transformational technique we propose in this paper, proves the formula φ in two steps. In the first step we transform φ into clause form by applying a variant of the Lloyd-Topor transformation [11], thereby deriving the following clauses:

$Prop_1$: 1. $prop \leftarrow \neg p$ 3. $q(L) \leftarrow list(L) \wedge \neg r(L, U)$
          2. $p \leftarrow list(L) \wedge \neg q(L)$ 4. $r(L, U) \leftarrow X > U \wedge list(L) \wedge member(X, L)$

where $list(L)$ holds iff L is a finite list of reals. The predicate $prop$ is equivalent to φ in the sense that $M(Member) \models \varphi$ iff $M(Member \cup Prop_1) \models prop$, where $M(P)$ denotes the perfect model of a stratified constraint logic program P. In the second step, we eliminate the existential variables by extending to constraint logic programs the techniques presented in [16] in the case of definite logic programs. For instance, the existential variable X occurring in the body of the above clause 4, is eliminated by applying the unfolding and folding rules and transforming that clause into the following two clauses: $r([X|L], U) \leftarrow X > U \wedge list(L)$ and $r([X|L], U) \leftarrow r(L, U)$. By iterating the transformation process, we eliminate all existential variables and we derive the following program which defines the predicate $prop$:

$Prop_2$: 1. $prop \leftarrow \neg p$ 2'. $p \leftarrow p_1$ 3'. $p_1 \leftarrow p_1$

Now, $Prop_2$ is a propositional program and has a *finite* perfect model, which is $\{prop\}$. Since all transformations we have made can be shown to preserve the perfect model, we have that $M(Member) \models \varphi$ iff $M(Prop_2) \models prop$ and, thus, we have completed the proof of φ.

The main contribution of this paper is the proposal of a proof method for showing that a closed first order formula φ holds in the perfect model of a stratified constraint logic program P, that is, $M(P) \models \varphi$. Our proof method is based on program transformations which eliminate existential variables.

The paper is organized as follows. In Section 2 we consider a class of constraint logic programs, called *lr-programs* (*lr* stands for lists of reals), which is Turing complete and for which our proof method is fully automatic. Those programs manipulate finite lists of reals with constraints which are linear equations and inequations over reals. In Section 3 we present the transformation strategy which defines our proof method and we prove its soundness. Due to the undecidability of the first order properties of *lr-programs*, our proof method is necessarily incomplete. Some experimental results obtained by using a prototype implementation are presented in Section 5. Finally, in Section 6 we discuss related work in the field of program transformation and theorem proving.

2   Constraint Logic Programs over Lists of Reals

We assume that the reals are defined by the usual structure $\mathcal{R} = \langle R, 0, 1, +, \cdot, \leq \rangle$. In order to specify programs and formulas, we use a *typed* first order language [11] with two types: (i) *real*, denoting the set of reals, and (ii) *list of reals* (or *list*, for short), denoting the set of finite lists of reals.

We assume that every element of R is a constant of type *real*. A term p of type *real* is defined as: $p ::= a \mid X \mid p_1 + p_2 \mid a \cdot X$, where a is a real number and X is a variable of type *real*. We also write aX, instead of $a \cdot X$. A term of type *real* will also be called a *linear polynomial*. An *atomic constraint* is a formula of the form: $p_1 = p_2$, or $p_1 < p_2$, or $p_1 \leq p_2$, where p_1 and p_2 are linear polynomials. We also write $p_1 > p_2$ and $p_1 \geq p_2$, instead of $p_2 < p_1$ and $p_2 \leq p_1$, respectively. A *constraint* is a finite conjunction of atomic constraints. A *first order formula over reals* is a first order formula constructed out of atomic constraints by using the usual connectives and quantifiers (i.e., $\neg, \wedge, \vee, \rightarrow, \exists, \forall$). By $F_{\mathcal{R}}$ we will denote the set of first order formulas over reals. A term l of type *list* is defined as: $l ::= L \mid [\,] \mid [p\,|\,l]$, where L is a variable of type *list* and p is a linear polynomial. A term of type *list* will also be called a *list*. An *atom* is a formula of the form $r(t_1, \ldots, t_n)$ where r is an n-ary predicate symbol (with $n \geq 0$ and $r \notin \{=, <, \leq\}$) and, for $i = 1, \ldots, n$, t_i is either a linear polynomial or a list. An atom is *linear* if each variable occurs in it at most once. A *literal* is either an atom (i.e., a positive literal) or a negated atom (i.e., a negative literal). A *clause* C is a formula of the form: $A \leftarrow c \wedge L_1 \wedge \ldots \wedge L_m$, where: (i) A is an atom, (ii) c is a constraint, and (iii) $L_1, \ldots, L_m$ are literals. A is called the *head* of the clause, denoted $hd(C)$, and $c \wedge L_1 \wedge \ldots \wedge L_m$ is called the *body* of the clause, denoted $bd(C)$. A *constraint logic program over lists of reals*, or simply a *program*, is a set of clauses. A program is *stratified* if no predicate depends negatively on itself [2]. Given a term or a formula f, $vars(f)$ denotes the set of variables occurring in f. Given a clause C, a variable V is said to be an *existential variable* of C if $V \in vars(bd(C)) - vars(hd(C))$.

The *definition* of a predicate p in a program P, denoted by $Def(p, P)$, is the set of the clauses of P whose head predicate is p. The *extended definition* of p in P, denoted by $Def^*(p, P)$, is the union of the definition of p and the definitions of all predicates in P on which p depends (positively or negatively). A program is *propositional* if every predicate occurring in the program is 0-ary. Obviously, if P is a propositional program then, for every predicate p, $M(P) \models p$ is decidable.

Definition 1 (*lr*-program). Let X denote a variable of type *real*, L a variable of type *list*, p a linear polynomial, r_1 and r_2 two predicate symbols, and c a constraint. An *lr-clause* is a clause defined as follows:

head term: $h ::= X \mid [\,] \mid [X|L]$
body term: $b ::= p \mid L$
lr-clause: $C ::= r_1(h_1, \ldots, h_k) \leftarrow c$
             $\mid r_1(h_1, \ldots, h_k) \leftarrow c \wedge r_2(b_1, \ldots, b_m)$
             $\mid r_1(h_1, \ldots, h_k) \leftarrow c \wedge \neg r_2(b_1, \ldots, b_m)$

where: (i) $vars(p) \neq \emptyset$, (ii) $r_1(h_1, \ldots, h_k)$ is a linear atom, and (iii) clause C has no existential variables. An *lr-program* is a finite set of *lr*-clauses. $\square$

We assume that the following *lr*-clauses belong to every *lr*-program (but we will omit them when writing *lr*-programs):

$list([\;]) \leftarrow$ $list([X|L]) \leftarrow list(L)$

The specific syntactic form of *lr*-programs is required for the automation of the transformation strategy we will introduce in Section 3. Here is an *lr*-program:

P_1: $sumlist([\;], Y) \leftarrow Y = 0$
     $sumlist([X|L], Y) \leftarrow sumlist(L, Y - X)$
     $haspositive([X|L]) \leftarrow X > 0$
     $haspositive([X|L]) \leftarrow haspositive(L)$

The following definition introduces the class of programs and formulas which can be given in input to our proof method.

Definition 2 (Admissible Pair). Let P be an *lr*-program and φ a closed first order formula with no other connectives and quantifiers besides $\neg$, $\wedge$, and $\exists$. We say that $\langle P, \varphi \rangle$ is an *admissible pair* if: (i) every predicate symbol occurring in φ and different from $\leq, <, =$, also occurs in P, (ii) every predicate of arity n (> 0) occurring in P and different from $\leq, <, =$, has at least one argument of type *list*, and (iii) for every proper subformula σ of φ, if σ is of the form $\neg\psi$, then either σ is a formula in $F_{\mathcal{R}}$ or σ has a free occurrence of a variable of type *list*. $\square$

Conditions (ii) and (iii) of Definition 2 are needed to guarantee the soundness of our proof method (see Theorem 3).

Example 1. Let us consider the above program P_1 defining the predicates *sumlist* and *haspositive*, and the formula

π : $\forall L \forall Y ((sumlist(L, Y) \wedge Y > 0) \rightarrow haspositive(L))$

which expresses the fact that if the sum of the elements of a list is positive then the list has at least one positive member. This formula can be rewritten as:

π_1 : $\neg \exists L \exists Y (sumlist(L, Y) \wedge Y > 0 \wedge \neg haspositive(L))$

The pair $\langle P_1, \pi_1 \rangle$ is admissible. Indeed, the only proper subformula of π_1 of the form $\neg\psi$ is $\neg haspositive(L)$ and the free variable L is of type *list*. $\square$

In order to define the semantics of our logic programs we consider $\mathcal{LR}$-interpretations where: (i) the type *real* is mapped to the set of reals, (ii) the type *list* is mapped to the set of lists of reals, and (iii) the symbols $+, \cdot, =, <, \leq, [\;]$, and $[\_|\_]$ are mapped to the usual corresponding operations and relations on reals and lists of reals. The semantics of a stratified logic program P is assumed to be its *perfect $\mathcal{LR}$-model* $M(P)$, which is defined similarly to the perfect model of a stratified logic program [2,12,17] by considering $\mathcal{LR}$-interpretations, instead of Herbrand interpretations. Note that for every formula $\varphi \in F_{\mathcal{R}}$, we have that $\mathcal{R} \models \varphi$ iff for any $\mathcal{LR}$-interpretation $\mathcal{I}$, $\mathcal{I} \models \varphi$.

Now we present a transformation, called *Clause Form Transformation*, that allows us to derive stratified logic programs starting from formulas, called *state-

ments, of the form: $A \leftarrow \beta$, where A is an atom and β is a typed first order formula. Our transformation is a variant of the transformation proposed by Lloyd and Topor in [11]. When applying the Clause Form Transformation, we will use the following well known property which guarantees that existential quantification and negation can always be eliminated from first order formulas on reals.

Lemma 1 (Variable Elimination). *For any formula* $\varphi \in F_{\mathcal{R}}$ *there exist* n (≥ 0) *constraints* $c_1, \ldots, c_n$ *such that:* (i) $\mathcal{R} \models \forall(\varphi \leftrightarrow (c_1 \vee \ldots \vee c_n))$, *and* (ii) *every variable in* $vars(c_1 \vee \ldots \vee c_n)$ *occurs free in* φ.

In what follows we write $C[\gamma]$ to denote a formula where the subformula γ occurs as an *outermost conjunct*, that is, $C[\gamma] = \gamma_1 \wedge \gamma \wedge \gamma_2$ for some (possibly empty) conjunctions γ_1 and γ_2.

Clause Form Transformation

Input: A statement S whose body has no other connectives and quantifiers besides $\neg$, $\wedge$, and $\exists$. *Output*: A set of clauses denoted $CFT(S)$.

(*Step* A) Starting from S, repeatedly apply the following rules A.1–A.5 until a set of clauses is generated.

(A.1) If $\gamma \in F_{\mathcal{R}}$ and γ is *not* a constraint, then replace $A \leftarrow C[\gamma]$ by the n statements $A \leftarrow C[c_1], \ldots, A \leftarrow C[c_n]$, where $c_1 \vee \ldots \vee c_n$, with $n \geq 0$, is a disjunction of constraints which is equivalent to γ. (The existence of such a disjunction is guaranteed by Lemma 1 above.)

(A.2) If $\gamma \notin F_{\mathcal{R}}$ then replace $A \leftarrow C[\neg\neg\gamma]$ by $A \leftarrow C[\gamma]$.

(A.3) If $\gamma \wedge \delta \notin F_{\mathcal{R}}$ then replace the statement $A \leftarrow C[\neg(\gamma \wedge \delta)]$ by the two statements $A \leftarrow C[\neg newp(V_1, \ldots, V_k)]$ and $newp(V_1, \ldots, V_k) \leftarrow \gamma \wedge \delta$, where $newp$ is a new predicate and $V_1, \ldots, V_k$ are the variables which occur free in $\gamma \wedge \delta$.

(A.4) If $\gamma \notin F_{\mathcal{R}}$ then replace the statement $A \leftarrow C[\neg \exists V \gamma]$ by the two statements $A \leftarrow C[\neg newp(V_1, \ldots, V_k)]$ and $newp(V_1, \ldots, V_k) \leftarrow \gamma$, where $newp$ is a new predicate and $V_1, \ldots, V_k$ are the variables which occur free in $\exists V \gamma$.

(A.5) If $\gamma \notin F_{\mathcal{R}}$ then replace $A \leftarrow C[\exists V \gamma]$ by $A \leftarrow C[\gamma\{V/V_1\}]$, where V_1 is a new variable.

(*Step* B) For every clause $A \leftarrow c \wedge G$ such that $L_1, \ldots, L_k$ are the variables of type *list* occurring in G, replace $A \leftarrow c \wedge G$ by $A \leftarrow c \wedge list(L_1) \wedge \ldots \wedge list(L_k) \wedge G$.

Example 2. The set $CFT(prop_1 \leftarrow \pi_1)$, where π_1 is the formula given in Example 1, consists of the following two clauses:

D_2 : $prop_1 \leftarrow \neg new_1$

D_1 : $new_1 \leftarrow Y > 0 \wedge list(L) \wedge sumlist(L, Y) \wedge \neg haspositive(L)$

(The subscripts of the names of these clauses follow the bottom-up order in which they will be processed by the UF_{lr} strategy we will introduce below.) $\square$

By construction, we have that if $\langle P, \varphi \rangle$ is an admissible pair and *prop* is a new predicate symbol, then $P \cup CFT(prop \leftarrow \varphi)$ is a stratified program. The Clause Form Transformation is correct with respect to the perfect $\mathcal{LR}$-model semantics, as stated by the following theorem.

Theorem 1 (Correctness of CFT). *Let $\langle P, \varphi \rangle$ be an admissible pair. Then, $M(P) \models \varphi$ iff $M(P \cup CFT(prop \leftarrow \varphi)) \models prop$.*

In general, a clause in $CFT(prop \leftarrow \varphi)$ is *not* an *lr*-clause because, indeed, existential variables may occur in its body. The clauses of $CFT(prop \leftarrow \varphi)$ are called *typed-definitions*. They are defined as follows.

Definition 3 (Typed-Definition, Hierarchy). A *typed-definition* is a clause of the form: $r(V_1, \ldots, V_n) \leftarrow c \wedge list(L_1) \wedge \ldots \wedge list(L_k) \wedge G$ where: (i) $V_1, \ldots, V_n$ are distinct variables of type *real* or *list*, and (ii) $L_1, \ldots, L_k$ are the variables of type *list* that occur in G. A sequence $\langle D_1, \ldots, D_n \rangle$ of typed-definitions is said to be a *hierarchy* if for $i = 1, \ldots, n$, the predicate of $hd(D_i)$ does not occur in $\{bd(D_1), \ldots, bd(D_i)\}$. □

One can show that given a closed formula φ, the set $CFT(prop \leftarrow \varphi)$ of clauses can be ordered as a hierarchy $\langle D_1, \ldots, D_n \rangle$ of typed-definitions such that $Def(prop, \{D_1, \ldots, D_n\}) = \{D_k, D_{k+1}, \ldots, D_n\}$, for some k with $1 \leq k \leq n$.

3   The Unfold/Fold Proof Method

In this section we present the transformation strategy, called UF_{lr} (Unfold/Fold strategy for *lr*-programs), which defines our proof method for proving properties of *lr*-programs. Our strategy applies in an automatic way the transformation rules for stratified constraint logic programs presented in [8]. In particular, the UF_{lr} strategy makes use of the definition introduction, (positive and negative) unfolding, (positive) folding, and constraint replacement rules. (These rules extend the ones proposed in [6,12] where the unfolding of a clause with respect to a negative literal is not permitted.)

Given an admissible pair $\langle P, \varphi \rangle$, let us consider the stratified program $P \cup CFT(prop \leftarrow \varphi)$. The goal of our UF_{lr} strategy is to derive a program *TransfP* such that $Def^*(prop, TransfP)$ is propositional and, thus, $M(TransfP) \models prop$ is decidable. We observe that, in order to achieve this goal, it is enough that the derived program *TransfP* is an *lr*-program, as stated by the following lemma, which follows directly from Definition 1.

Lemma 2. *Let P be an lr-program and p be a predicate occurring in P. If p is 0-ary then $Def^*(p, P)$ is a propositional program.*

As already said, the clauses in $CFT(prop \leftarrow \varphi)$ form a hierarchy $\langle D_1, \ldots, D_n \rangle$ of typed-definitions. The UF_{lr} strategy consists in transforming, for $i = 1, \ldots, n$, clause D_i into a set of *lr*-clauses. The transformation of D_i is performed by applying the following three substrategies, in this order: (i) *unfold*, which unfolds D_i with respect to the positive and negative literals occurring in its body, thereby deriving a set Cs of clauses, (ii) *replace-constraints*, which replaces the constraints appearing in the clauses of Cs by equivalent ones, thereby deriving a new set Es of clauses, and (iii) *define-fold*, which introduces a set *NewDefs* of new typed-definitions (which are not necessarily *lr*-clauses) and folds all clauses in

Es, thereby deriving a set *Fs* of *lr*-clauses. Then each new definition in *NewDefs* is transformed by applying the above three substrategies, and the whole UF_{lr} strategy terminates when no new definitions are introduced. The substrategies *unfold*, *replace-constraints*, and *define-fold* will be described in detail below.

The UF_{lr} Transformation Strategy

Input: An *lr*-program P and a hierarchy $\langle D_1, \ldots, D_n \rangle$ of typed-definitions.
Output: A set *Defs* of typed-definitions including $D_1, \ldots, D_n$, and an *lr*-program *TransfP* such that $M(P \cup Defs) = M(TransfP)$.

$TransfP := P$; $Defs := \{D_1, \ldots, D_n\}$;
for $i = 1, \ldots, n$ **do** $InDefs := \{D_i\}$;
    while $InDefs \neq \emptyset$ **do** $unfold(InDefs, TransfP, Cs)$; $replace\text{-}constraints(Cs, Es)$;
    $define\text{-}fold(Es, Defs, NewDefs, Fs)$;
    $TransfP := TransfP \cup Fs$; $Defs := Defs \cup NewDefs$; $InDefs := NewDefs$;
    end-while;
    eval-props: for each predicate p such that $Def^*(p, TransfP)$ is propositional,
    if $M(TransfP) \models p$ **then** $TransfP := (TransfP - Def(p, TransfP)) \cup \{p \leftarrow\}$
                    else $TransfP := (TransfP - Def(p, TransfP))$
end-for

Our assumption that $\langle D_1, \ldots, D_n \rangle$ is a hierarchy ensures that, when transforming clause D_i, for $i = 1, \ldots, n$, we only need the clauses obtained after the transformation of $D_1, \ldots, D_{i-1}$. These clauses are those of the current value of *TransfP*.

The following *unfold* substrategy transforms a set *InDefs* of typed-definitions by first applying the unfolding rule with respect to each positive literal in the body of a clause and then applying the unfolding rule with respect to each negative literal in the body of a clause. In the sequel, we will assume that the conjunction operator $\wedge$ is associative, commutative, idempotent, and with neutral element *true*. In particular, the order of the conjuncts will *not* be significant.

The *unfold* Substrategy

Input: An *lr*-program *Prog* and a set *InDefs* of typed-definitions.
Output: A set *Cs* of clauses.

Initially, no literal in the body of a clause of *InDefs* is marked as 'unfolded'.
Positive Unfolding: **while** there exists a clause C in *InDefs* of the form
$H \leftarrow c \wedge G_L \wedge A \wedge G_R$, where A is an atom which is not marked as 'unfolded' **do**
Let $C_1: K_1 \leftarrow c_1 \wedge B_1, \ldots, C_m: K_m \leftarrow c_m \wedge B_m$ be all clauses of program *Prog* (where we assume $vars(Prog) \cap vars(C) = \emptyset$) such that, for $i = 1, \ldots, m$, (i) there exists a most general unifier ϑ_i of A and K_i, and (ii) the constraint $(c \wedge c_i)\vartheta_i$ is satisfiable. Let U be the following set of clauses:
$$U = \{(H \leftarrow c \wedge c_1 \wedge G_L \wedge B_1 \wedge G_R)\vartheta_1, \ldots, (H \leftarrow c \wedge c_m \wedge G_L \wedge B_m \wedge G_R)\vartheta_m\}$$
Let W be the set of clauses derived from U by removing all clauses of the form
    $H \leftarrow c \wedge G_L \wedge A \wedge \neg A \wedge G_R$

Inherit the markings of the literals in the body of the clauses of W from those of C, and mark as 'unfolded' the literals $B_1\vartheta_1, \ldots, B_m\vartheta_m$;
$InDefs := (InDefs - \{C\}) \cup W$;
end-while;
Negative Unfolding: **while** there exists a clause C in *InDefs* of the form
$H \leftarrow c \wedge G_L \wedge \neg A \wedge G_R$, where $\neg A$ is a literal which is not marked as 'unfolded' **do**
Let $C_1: K_1 \leftarrow c_1 \wedge B_1, \ldots, C_m: K_m \leftarrow c_m \wedge B_m$ be all clauses of program *Prog* (where we assume that $vars(Prog) \cap vars(C) = \emptyset$) such that, for $i = 1, \ldots, m$, there exists a most general unifier ϑ_i of A and K_i. By our assumptions on *Prog* and on the initial value of *InDefs*, and as a result of the previous *Positive Unfolding* phase, we have that, for $i = 1, \ldots, m$, B_i is either the empty conjunction *true* or a literal and $A = K_i\vartheta_i$. Let U be the following set of statements:
$$U = \{H \leftarrow c \wedge d_1\vartheta_1 \wedge \ldots \wedge d_m\vartheta_m \wedge G_L \wedge L_1\vartheta_1 \wedge \ldots \wedge L_m\vartheta_m \wedge G_R \mid$$
(i) for $i = 1, \ldots, m$, either $(d_i = c_i$ and $L_i = \neg B_i)$ or $(d_i = \neg c_i$ and $L_i = true)$, and (ii) $c \wedge d_1\vartheta_1 \wedge \ldots \wedge d_m\vartheta_m$ is satisfiable$\}$
Let W be the set of clauses derived from U by applying as long as possible the following rules:
- remove $H \leftarrow c \wedge G_L \wedge \neg true \wedge G_R$ and $H \leftarrow c \wedge G_L \wedge A \wedge \neg A \wedge G_R$
- replace $\neg\neg A$ by A, $\neg(p_1 \leq p_2)$ by $p_2 < p_1$, and $\neg(p_1 < p_2)$ by $p_2 \leq p_1$
- replace $H \leftarrow c_1 \wedge \neg(p_1 = p_2) \wedge c_2 \wedge G$ by $H \leftarrow c_1 \wedge p_1 < p_2 \wedge c_2 \wedge G$
$$H \leftarrow c_1 \wedge p_2 < p_1 \wedge c_2 \wedge G$$

Inherit the markings of the literals in the body of the clauses of W from those of C, and mark as 'unfolded' the literals $L_1\vartheta_1, \ldots, L_m\vartheta_m$;
$InDefs := (InDefs - \{C\}) \cup W$;
end-while;
$Cs := InDefs$.

Negative Unfolding is best explained through an example. Let us consider a program consisting of the clauses $C: H \leftarrow c \wedge \neg A$, $A \leftarrow c_1 \wedge B_1$, and $A \leftarrow c_2 \wedge B_2$. The negative unfolding of C w.r.t. $\neg A$ gives us the following four clauses:

$H \leftarrow c \wedge \neg c_1 \wedge \neg c_2$	$H \leftarrow c \wedge \neg c_1 \wedge c_2 \wedge \neg B_2$
$H \leftarrow c \wedge c_1 \wedge \neg c_2 \wedge \neg B_1$	$H \leftarrow c \wedge c_1 \wedge c_2 \wedge \neg B_1 \wedge \neg B_2$

whose conjunction is equivalent to $H \leftarrow c \wedge \neg((c_1 \wedge B_1) \vee (c_2 \wedge B_2))$.

Example 3. Let us consider the program-property pair $\langle P_1, \pi_1 \rangle$ of Example 1. In order to prove that $M(P_1) \models \pi_1$, we apply the UF_{lr} strategy starting from the hierarchy $\langle D_1, D_2 \rangle$ of typed-definitions of Example 2. During the first execution of the body of the for-loop of that strategy, the *unfold* substrategy is applied, as we now indicate, by using as input the program P_1 and the set $\{D_1\}$ of clauses.

Positive Unfolding. By unfolding clause D_1 w.r.t. $list(L)$ and then unfolding the resulting clauses w.r.t. $sumlist(L, Y)$, we get:

C_1: $new_1 \leftarrow Y > 0 \wedge list(L) \wedge sumlist(L, Y-X) \wedge \neg haspositive([X|L])$

Negative Unfolding. By unfolding clause C_1 w.r.t. $\neg haspositive([X|L])$, we get:

C_2: $new_1 \leftarrow Y > 0 \wedge X \leq 0 \wedge list(L) \wedge sumlist(L, Y-X) \wedge \neg haspositive(L)$ $\square$

The correctness of the *unfold* substrategy follows from the fact that the positive and negative unfoldings are performed according to the rules presented in [8]. The termination of that substrategy is due to the fact that the number of literals which are not marked as 'unfolded' and which occur in the body of a clause, decreases when that clause is unfolded. Thus, we have the following result.

Lemma 3. *Let Prog be an lr-program and let InDefs be a set of typed-definitions such that the head predicates of the clauses of InDefs do not occur in Prog. Then, given the inputs Prog and InDefs, the unfold substrategy terminates and returns a set Cs of clauses such that $M(Prog \cup InDefs) = M(Prog \cup Cs)$.*

The *replace-constraints* substrategy derives from a set Cs of clauses a new set Es of clauses by applying equivalences between existentially quantified disjunctions of constraints. We use the following two rules: *project* and *clause split*.

Given a clause $H \leftarrow c \wedge G$, the *project* rule eliminates all variables that occur in c and do not occur elsewhere in the clause. Thus, *project* returns a new clause $H \leftarrow d \wedge G$ such that $\mathcal{R} \models \forall((\exists X_1 \ldots \exists X_k\, c) \leftrightarrow d)$, where: (i) $\{X_1, \ldots, X_k\} = vars(c) - vars(\{H, G\})$, and (ii) $vars(d) \subseteq vars(c) - \{X_1, \ldots, X_k\}$. In our prototype theorem prover (see Section 5), the *project* rule is implemented by using a variant of the Fourier-Motzkin Elimination algorithm [1].

The *clause split* rule replaces a clause C by two clauses C_1 and C_2 such that, for $i = 1, 2$, the number of occurrences of existential variables in C_i is less than the number of occurrences of existential variables in C. The clause split rule applies the following property, which expresses the fact that $\langle \mathcal{R}, \leq \rangle$ is a linear order: $\mathcal{R} \models \forall X \forall Y (X < Y \vee Y \leq X)$. For instance, a clause of the form $H \leftarrow Z \leq X \wedge Z \leq Y \wedge G$, where Z is an existential variable occurring in the conjunction G of literals and X and Y are not existential variables, is replaced by the two clauses $H \leftarrow Z \leq X \wedge X < Y \wedge G$ and $H \leftarrow Z \leq Y \wedge Y \leq X \wedge G$. The decrease of the number of occurrences of existential variables guarantees that we can apply the clause split rule a finite number of times only.

The *replace-constraints* Substrategy
Input: A set Cs of clauses. *Output*: A set Es of clauses.

• *Introduce Equations.* (A) From Cs we derive a new set R_1 of clauses by applying as long as possible the following two rules, where p denotes a linear polynomial which is not a variable, and Z denotes a fresh new variable:
(R.1) $H \leftarrow c \wedge G_L \wedge r(\ldots, p, \ldots) \wedge G_R$ is replaced by
$\qquad H \leftarrow c \wedge Z = p \wedge G_L \wedge r(\ldots, Z, \ldots) \wedge G_R$
(R.2) $H \leftarrow c \wedge G_L \wedge \neg r(\ldots, p, \ldots) \wedge G_R$ is replaced by
$\qquad H \leftarrow c \wedge Z = p \wedge G_L \wedge \neg r(\ldots, Z, \ldots) \wedge G_R$
(B) From R_1 we derive a new set R_2 of clauses by applying to every clause C in R_1 the following rule. Let C be of the form $H \leftarrow c \wedge G$. Suppose that $\mathcal{R} \models \forall (c \leftrightarrow (X_1 = p_1 \wedge X_n = p_n \wedge d))$, where: (i) $X_1, \ldots, X_n$ are existential variables of C, (ii) $vars(X_1 = p_1 \wedge \ldots \wedge X_n = p_n \wedge d) \subseteq vars(c)$, (iii) $\{X_1, \ldots, X_n\} \cap vars(\{p_1, \ldots, p_n, d\}) = \emptyset$. Then we replace C by $H \leftarrow X_1 = p_1 \wedge \ldots \wedge X_n = p_n \wedge d \wedge G$.
• *Project.* We derive a new set R_3 of clauses by applying to every clause in R_2 the *project* rule.

- *Clause Split.* From R_3 we derive a new set R_4 of clauses by applying as long as possible the following rule. Let C be a clause of the form $H \leftarrow c_1 \wedge c_2 \wedge c \wedge G$ (modulo commutativity of $\wedge$). Let E be the set of existential variables of C. Let $X \in E$ and let d_1 and d_2 be two inequations such that $\mathcal{R} \models \forall((c_1 \wedge c_2) \leftrightarrow (d_1 \wedge d_2))$. Suppose that: (i) $d_1 \wedge d_2$ is of one of the following six forms:

$$X \leq p_1 \wedge X \leq p_2 \qquad\qquad X \leq p_1 \wedge X < p_2 \qquad\qquad X < p_1 \wedge X < p_2$$
$$p_1 \leq X \wedge p_2 \leq X \qquad\qquad p_1 \leq X \wedge p_2 < X \qquad\qquad p_1 < X \wedge p_2 < X$$

and (ii) $(vars(p_1) \cup vars(p_2)) \cap E = \emptyset$.
Then C is replaced by the following two clauses: C_1: $H \leftarrow d_1 \wedge p_1 < p_2 \wedge c \wedge G$ and C_2: $H \leftarrow d_2 \wedge p_2 \leq p_1 \wedge c \wedge G$, and then each clause in $\{C_1, C_2\}$ with an unsatisfiable constraint in its body is removed.

- *Eliminate Equations.* From R_4 we derive the new set Es of clauses by applying to every clause C in R_4 the following rule. If C is of the form $H \leftarrow X_1 = p_1 \wedge \ldots \wedge X_n = p_n \wedge d \wedge G$ where $\{X_1, \ldots, X_n\} \cap vars(\{p_1, \ldots p_n, d\}) = \emptyset$, then C is replaced by $(H \leftarrow d \wedge G)\{X_1/p_1, \ldots, X_n/p_n\}$.

The transformation described at Point (A) of *Introduce Equations* allows us to treat all polynomials occurring in the body of a clause in a uniform way as arguments of constraints. The transformation described at Point (B) of *Introduce Equations* identifies those existential variables which can be eliminated during the final *Eliminate Equations* transformation. That elimination is performed by substituting, for $i = 1, \ldots, n$, the variable X_i by the polynomial p_i.

Example 4. By applying the *replace-constraints* substrategy, clause C_2 of Example 3 is transformed as follows. By introducing equations we get:
C_3: $new_1 \leftarrow Y > 0 \wedge X \leq 0 \wedge Z = Y - X \wedge list(L) \wedge sumlist(L, Z) \wedge \neg haspositive(L)$
Then, by applying the *project* transformation, we get:
C_4: $new_1 \leftarrow Z > 0 \wedge list(L) \wedge sumlist(L, Z) \wedge \neg haspositive(L)$ □

The correctness of the *replace-constraints* substrategy is a straightforward consequence of the fact that the *Introduce Equations, Project, Clause Split,* and *Eliminate Equations* transformations are performed by using the rule of *replacement based on laws* presented in [8]. The termination of *Introduce Equations* and *Eliminate Equations* is obvious. The termination of *Project* is based on the termination of the specific algorithm used for variable elimination (e.g., Fourier-Motzkin algorithm). As already mentioned, the termination of *Clause Split* is due to the fact that at each application of this transformation the number of occurrences of existential variables decreases. Thus, we get the following lemma.

Lemma 4. *For any program Prog and set $Cs \subseteq Prog$ of clauses, the replace-constraints substrategy with input Cs terminates and returns a set Es of clauses such that $M(Prog) = M((Prog - Cs) \cup Es)$.*

The *define-fold* substrategy eliminates all existential variables in the clauses of the set Es obtained after the *unfold* and *replace-constraints* substrategies. This elimination is done by folding all clauses in Es that contain existential variables. In order to make these folding steps we use the typed-definitions in *Defs* and, if necessary, we introduce new typed-definitions which we add to the set *NewDefs*.

The *define-fold* Substrategy.
Input: A set *Es* of clauses and a set *Defs* of typed-definitions.
Output: A set *NewDefs* of typed-definitions and a set *Fs* of *lr*-clauses.

Initially, both *NewDefs* and *Fs* are empty.
for each clause C: $H \leftarrow c \wedge G$ in *Es* **do**
if C is an *lr*-clause **then** $Fs := Fs \cup \{C\}$ **else**
- *Define*. Let E be the set of existential variables of C. We consider a clause *NewD* of the form $newp(V_1, \ldots, V_m) \leftarrow d \wedge B$ constructed as follows:
(1) let c be of the form $c_1 \wedge c_2$, where $vars(c_1) \cap E = \emptyset$ and for every atomic constraint a occurring in c_2, $vars(a) \cap E \neq \emptyset$; let $d \wedge B$ be the most general (modulo variants) conjunction of constraints and literals such that there exists a substitution ϑ with the following properties: (i) $(d \wedge B)\vartheta = c_2 \wedge G$, and (ii) for each binding V/p in ϑ, V is a variable not occurring in C, $vars(p) \neq \emptyset$, and $vars(p) \cap E = \emptyset$;
(2) *newp* is a new predicate symbol;
(3) $\{V_1, \ldots, V_m\} = vars(d \wedge B) - E$.
NewD is added to *NewDefs*, unless in *Defs* there exists a typed-definition D which is equal to *NewD*, modulo the name of the head predicate, the names of variables, equivalence of constraints, and the order and multiplicity of literals in the body. If such a clause D belongs to *Defs* and no other clause in *Defs* has the same head predicate as D, then we assume that $NewD = D$.
- *Fold*. Clause C is folded using clause *NewD* as follows:
$Fs := Fs \cup \{H \leftarrow c_1 \wedge newp(V_1, \ldots, V_m)\vartheta\}$.
end-for

Example 5. Let us consider the clause C_4 derived at the end of Example 4. The *Define* phase produces a typed-definition which is a variant of the typed-definition D_1 introduced at the beginning of the application of the strategy (see Example 2). Thus, C_4 is folded using clause D_1, and we get the clause:

   C_5: $new_1 \leftarrow new_1$

Let us now describe how the proof of $M(P_1) \models \pi_1$ proceeds. The program *TransfP* derived so far consists of clause C_5 together with the clauses defining the predicates *list*, *sumlist*, and *haspositive*. Thus, $Def^*(new_1, TransfP)$ consists of clause C_5 only, which is propositional and, by *eval-props*, we remove C_5 from *TransfP* because $M(TransfP) \not\models new_1$. The strategy continues by considering the typed definition D_2 (see Example 2). By unfolding D_2 with respect to $\neg new_1$ we get the final program *TransfP*, which consists of the clause $prop_1 \leftarrow$ together with the clauses for *list*, *sumlist*, and *haspositive*. Thus, $M(TransfP) \models prop_1$ and, therefore, $M(P_1) \models \pi_1$.   □

The proof of correctness for the *define-fold* substrategy is more complex than the proofs for the other substrategies. The correctness results for the unfold/fold transformations presented in [8] guarantee the correctness of a folding transformation if each typed-definition used for folding is unfolded w.r.t. a positive literal during the application of the UF_{lr} transformation strategy. The fulfillment of this condition is ensured by the following two facts: (1) by the definition of an admissible pair and by the definition of the Clause Form Transformation, each typed-definition has at least one positive literal in its body (indeed, by Condition (iii) of Definition 2 each negative literal in the body of a typed-definition has at least one variable of type *list* and, therefore, the body of the typed-definition has at least one *list* atom), and (2) in the *Positive Unfolding* phase of the *unfold* substrategy, each typed-definition is unfolded w.r.t. all positive literals.

Note that the set *Fs* of clauses derived by the *define-fold* substrategy is a set of *lr*-clauses. Indeed, by the *unfold* and *replace-constraints* substrategies, we derive a set *Es* of clauses of the form $r(h_1, \ldots, h_k) \leftarrow c \wedge G$, where $h_1, \ldots, h_k$ are head terms (see Definition 1). By folding we derive clauses of the form $r(h_1, \ldots, h_k) \leftarrow c_1 \wedge newp(V_1, \ldots, V_m)\vartheta$, where $vars(c_1 \wedge newp(V_1, \ldots, V_m)\vartheta) \subseteq vars(r(h_1, \ldots, h_k))$, and for $i = 1, \ldots, m$, $vars(V_i\vartheta) \neq \emptyset$ (by the conditions at Points (1)–(3) of the *Define* phase). Hence, all clauses in *Fs* are *lr*-clauses.

The termination of the *define-fold* substrategy is obvious, as each clause is folded at most once. Thus, we have the following result.

Lemma 5. *During the UF_{lr} strategy, if the define-fold substrategy takes as inputs the set Es of clauses and the set Defs of typed-definitions, then this substrategy terminates and returns a set NewDefs of typed-definitions and a set Fs of lr-clauses such that $M(TransfP \cup Es \cup NewDefs) = M(TransfP \cup Fs \cup NewDefs)$.*

By using Lemmata 3, 4, and 5 we get the following correctness result for the UF_{lr} strategy.

Theorem 2. *Let P be an lr-program and $\langle D_1, \ldots, D_n \rangle$ a hierarchy of typed-definitions. Suppose that the UF_{lr} strategy with inputs P and $\langle D_1, \ldots, D_n \rangle$ terminates and returns a set Defs of typed-definitions and a program TransfP. Then: (i) TransfP is an lr-program and (ii) $M(P \cup Defs) = M(TransfP)$.*

Now, we are able to prove the soundness of the unfold/fold proof method.

Theorem 3 (Soundness of the Unfold/Fold Proof Method). *Let $\langle P, \varphi \rangle$ be an admissible pair and let $\langle D_1, \ldots, D_n \rangle$ be the hierarchy of typed-definitions obtained from prop $\leftarrow \varphi$ by the Clause Form Transformation. If the UF_{lr} strategy with inputs P and $\langle D_1, \ldots, D_n \rangle$ terminates and returns a program TransfP, then:*

$$M(P) \models \varphi \quad iff \quad (prop \leftarrow) \in TransfP$$

Proof. By Theorem 1 and Point (ii) of Theorem 2, we have that $M(P) \models \varphi$ iff $M(TransfP) \models prop$. By Point (i) of Theorem 2 and Lemma 2 we have that $Def^*(prop, TransfP)$ is propositional. Since the last step of the UF_{lr} strategy is an application of the *eval-props* transformation, we have that $Def^*(prop, TransfP)$ is either the singleton $\{prop \leftarrow\}$, if $M(TransfP) \models prop$, or the empty set, if $M(TransfP) \not\models prop$. □

4   A Complete Example

As an example of application of our transformation strategy for proving properties of constraint logic programs we consider the *lr*-program *Member* and the property φ given in the Introduction. The formula φ is rewritten as follows:

$$\varphi_1: \ \neg\exists L \,\neg\exists U \,\neg\exists X \,(X > U \wedge member(X, L))$$

The pair $\langle Member, \varphi_1 \rangle$ is admissible. By applying the Clause Form Transformation starting from the statement $prop \leftarrow \varphi_1$, we get the following clauses:

$D_4: \ prop \leftarrow \neg p$ $D_2: \ q(L) \leftarrow list(L) \wedge \neg r(L, U)$
$D_3: \ p \leftarrow list(L) \wedge \neg q(L)$ $D_1: \ r(L, U) \leftarrow X > U \wedge list(L) \wedge member(X, L)$

where $\langle D_1, D_2, D_3, D_4 \rangle$ is a hierarchy of typed-definitions. Note that the three nested negations in φ_1 generate the three atoms p, $q(L)$, and $r(L, U)$ with their typed-definitions D_3, D_2, and D_1, respectively. The arguments of p, q, and r are the free variables of the corresponding subformulas of φ_1. For instance, $r(L, U)$ corresponds to the subformula $\exists X \,(X > U \wedge member(X, L))$ which has L and U as free variables. Now we apply the UF_{lr} strategy starting from the program *Member* and the hierarchy $\langle D_1, D_2, D_3, D_4 \rangle$.

- *Execution of the for-loop with $i = 1$.* We have: $InDefs = \{D_1\}$. By unfolding clause D_1 w.r.t. the atoms $list(L)$ and $member(X, L)$ we get:

  1.1 $r([X|T], U) \leftarrow X > U \wedge list(T)$
  1.2 $r([X|T], U) \leftarrow Y > U \wedge list(T) \wedge member(Y, T)$

No replacement of constraints is performed. Then, by folding clause 1.2 using D_1, we get:

  1.3 $r([X|T], U) \leftarrow r(T, U)$

After the *define-fold* substrategy the set Fs of clauses is $\{1.1, 1.3\}$, and at this point the program *TransfP* is *Member* $\cup \{1.1, 1.3\}$. No new definitions are introduced and, thus, $InDefs = \emptyset$ and the while-loop terminates. *eval-props* is not performed because the predicate r is not propositional.

- *Execution of the for-loop with $i = 2$.* We have: $InDefs = \{D_2\}$. We unfold clause D_2 w.r.t. $list(L)$ and $\neg r(L, U)$. Then we introduce the new definition:

  2.1 $q_1(X, T) \leftarrow X \leq U \wedge list(T) \wedge \neg r(T, U)$

and we fold using clause 2.1 (no constraint replacement is performed). We get:

  2.2 $q([\,]) \leftarrow$
  2.3 $q([X|T]) \leftarrow q_1(X, T)$

Since $NewDefs = InDefs = \{2.1\}$ we execute again the body of the while-loop. By unfolding clause 2.1 w.r.t. $list(T)$ and $\neg r(T, U)$, we get:

2.4 $q_1(X, [\ ]) \leftarrow$
2.5 $q_1(X, [Y|T]) \leftarrow X \leq U \wedge Y \leq U \wedge list(T) \wedge \neg r(T, U)$

By applying *replace-constraints*, clause 2.5 generates the following two clauses:

2.5.1 $q_1(X, [Y|T]) \leftarrow X > Y \wedge X \leq U \wedge list(T) \wedge \neg r(T, U)$
2.5.2 $q_1(X, [Y|T]) \leftarrow X \leq Y \wedge Y \leq U \wedge list(T) \wedge \neg r(T, U)$

By folding clauses 2.5.1 and 2.5.2 using clause 2.1, we get:

2.6 $q_1(X, [Y|T]) \leftarrow X > Y \wedge q_1(X, T)$
2.7 $q_1(X, [Y|T]) \leftarrow X \leq Y \wedge q_1(Y, T)$

At this point the program *TransfP* is *Member* $\cup \{1.1, 1.3, 2.2, 2.3, 2.4, 2.6, 2.7\}$. No new definitions are introduced and, thus, the while-loop terminates. *eval-props* is not performed because the predicates q and q_1 are not propositional.
• *Execution of the for-loop with* $i = 3$. We have: *InDefs* $= \{D_3\}$. By unfolding clause D_3 w.r.t. *list*(L) and $\neg q(L)$, we get:

3.1 $p \leftarrow list(T) \wedge \neg q_1(X, T)$

No replacement of constraints is performed. The following new definition:

3.2 $p_1 \leftarrow list(T) \wedge \neg q_1(X, T)$

is introduced. Then by folding clause 3.1 using clause 3.2, we get:

3.3 $p \leftarrow p_1$

Since *NewDefs* $=$ *InDefs* $= \{3.2\}$ we execute again the body of the while-loop. By unfolding clause 3.2 w.r.t. *list*(T) and $\neg q_1(X, T)$, we get:

3.4 $p_1 \leftarrow X > Y \wedge list(T) \wedge \neg q_1(X, T)$
3.5 $p_1 \leftarrow X \leq Y \wedge list(T) \wedge \neg q_1(Y, T)$

Since the variable Y occurring in the constraints $X > Y$ and $X \leq Y$ is existential, we apply the *project* rule to clauses 3.4 and 3.5 and we get the following clause:

3.6 $p_1 \leftarrow list(T) \wedge \neg q_1(X, T)$

This clause can be folded using clause 3.2, thereby deriving the following clause:

3.7 $p_1 \leftarrow p_1$

Clauses 3.3 and 3.7 are added to *TransfP*. Since the predicates p and p_1 are both propositional, we execute *eval-props*. We have that: (i) $M(TransfP) \not\models p_1$ and (ii) $M(TransfP) \not\models p$. Thus, clauses 3.3 and 3.7 are removed from *TransfP*. Hence, *TransfP* $=$ *Member* $\cup \{1.1, 1.3, 2.2, 2.3, 2.4, 2.6, 2.7\}$.
• *Execution of the for-loop with* $i = 4$. We have: *InDefs* $= \{D_4\}$. By unfolding clause D_4 w.r.t. $\neg p$, we get the clause: *prop* $\leftarrow$
This clause shows that, as expected, property φ holds for any finite list of reals.

5   Experimental Results

We have implemented our proof method by using the MAP transformation system [13] running under SICStus Prolog on a 900MHz Power PC. Constraint satisfaction and entailment were performed using the clp(r) module of SICStus. Our prototype has automatically proved the properties listed in the following table, where the predicates *member*, *sumlist*, and *haspositive* are defined as shown in Sections 1 and 2, and the other predicates have the following meanings: (i) $ord(L)$ holds iff L is a list of the form $[a_1, \ldots, a_n]$ and for $i = 1, \ldots, n-1$, $a_i \leq a_{i+1}$, (ii) $sumzip(L, M, N)$ holds iff L, M, and N are lists of the form $[a_1, \ldots, a_n]$, $[b_1, \ldots, b_n]$, and $[a_1 + b_1, \ldots, a_n + b_n]$, respectively, and (iii) $leqlist(L, M)$ holds iff L and M are lists of the form $[a_1, \ldots, a_n]$ and $[b_1, \ldots, b_n]$, respectively, and for $i = 1, \ldots, n$, $a_i \leq b_i$. We do not write here the *lr*-programs which define the predicates $ord(L)$, $sumzip(L, M, N)$, and $leqlist(L, M)$.

Property	Time
$\forall L \, \exists M \, \forall Y \, (member(Y, L) \rightarrow Y \leq M)$	140 ms
$\forall L \, \forall Y \, ((sumlist(L, Y) \wedge Y > 0) \rightarrow haspositive(L))$	170 ms
$\forall L \, \forall Y \, ((sumlist(L, Y) \wedge Y > 0) \rightarrow \exists X (member(X, L) \wedge X > 0))$	160 ms
$\forall L \, \forall M \, \forall N \, ((ord(L) \wedge ord(M) \wedge sumzip(L, M, N)) \rightarrow ord(N))$	160 ms
$\forall L \, \forall M \, ((leqlist(L, M) \wedge sumlist(L, X) \wedge sumlist(M, Y)) \rightarrow X \leq Y)$	50 ms

6   Related Work and Conclusions

We have presented a method for proving first order properties of constraint logic programs based on unfold/fold program transformations, and we have shown that the ability of unfold/fold transformations to eliminate existential variables [16] can be turned into a useful theorem proving method. We have provided a fully automatic strategy for the class of *lr*-programs, which are programs acting on reals and finite lists of reals, with constraints as linear equations and inequations over reals. The choice of lists is actually a simplifying assumption we have made and we believe that the extension of our method to any finitely generated data structure is quite straightforward. However, the use of constraints over the reals is an essential feature of our method, because quantifier elimination from constraints is a crucial subprocedure of our transformation strategy.

The first order properties of *lr*-programs are undecidable (and not even semidecidable), because one can encode every partial recursive function as an *lr*-program without list arguments. As a consequence our proof method is necessarily incomplete. We have implemented the proof method based of program transformation and we have proved some simple, yet non-trivial, properties. As the experiments show, the performance of our method is encouraging.

Our method is an extension of the method presented in [15] which considers logic programs without constraints. The addition of constraints is a very relevant feature, because it provides more expressive power and, as already mentioned, we may use special purpose theorem provers for checking constraint satisfaction and for quantifier elimination. Our method can also be viewed as an extension of other techniques based on unfold/fold transformations for proving equivalences of predicates [14,19], and indeed, our method can deal with a class of first order formulas which properly includes equivalences.

Some papers have proposed transformational techniques to prove propositional temporal properties of finite and/or infinite state systems (see, for instance, [7,10,19]). Since propositional temporal logic can be encoded in first order logic, in principle these techniques can be viewed as instances of the unfold/fold proof method presented here. However, it should be noted that the techniques described in [7,10,19] have their own peculiarities because they are tailored to the specific problem of verifying concurrent systems.

Finally, we think that a direct comparison of the power of our proof method with that of traditional theorem provers is somewhat inappropriate. The techniques used in those provers are very effective and are the result of a well established line of research (see, for instance, [3] for a survey on the automation of mathematical induction). However, our approach has its novelty and is based on principles which have not been explored in the field of theorem proving. In particular, the idea of making inductive proofs by unfold/fold transformations for eliminating quantifiers, has not yet been investigated within the theorem proving community.

References

1. K. R. Apt. *Principles of Constraint Programming.* Cambridge Univ. Press, 2003.
2. K. R. Apt and R. N. Bol. Logic programming and negation: A survey. *Journal of Logic Programming,* 19, 20:9–71, 1994.
3. A. Bundy. The automation of proof by mathematical induction. In *Handbook of Automated Reasoning,* volume I, pages 845–911. North Holland, 2001.
4. R. M. Burstall and J. Darlington. A transformation system for developing recursive programs. *Journal of the ACM,* 24(1):44–67, January 1977.
5. B. Courcelle. Equivalences and transformations of regular systems – applications to recursive program schemes and grammars. *Theor. Comp. Sci.,* 42:1–122, 1986.
6. S. Etalle and M. Gabbrielli. Transformations of CLP modules. *Theoretical Computer Science,* 166:101–146, 1996.
7. F. Fioravanti, A. Pettorossi, and M. Proietti. Verifying CTL properties of infinite state systems by specializing constraint logic programs. In *Proceedings VCL'01, Florence, Italy,* pages 85–96. University of Southampton, UK, 2001.
8. F. Fioravanti, A. Pettorossi, and M. Proietti. Transformation rules for locally stratified constraint logic programs. In *Program Development in Computational Logic,* LNCS 3049, pages 292–340. Springer, 2004.
9. L. Kott. The McCarthy's induction principle: 'oldy' but 'goody'. *Calcolo,* 19(1):59–69, 1982.
10. M. Leuschel and T. Massart. Infinite state model checking by abstract interpretation and program specialization. In A. Bossi, editor, *Proceedings of LOPSTR '99, Venice, Italy,* LNCS 1817, pages 63–82. Springer, 1999.
11. J. W. Lloyd. *Foundations of Logic Programming.* Springer, 1987. 2nd Edition.

12. M. J. Maher. A transformation system for deductive database modules with perfect model semantics. *Theoretical Computer Science*, 110:377–403, 1993.
13. The MAP System. http://www.iasi.cnr.it/~proietti/system.html.
14. A. Pettorossi and M. Proietti. Synthesis and transformation of logic programs using unfold/fold proofs. *Journal of Logic Programming*, 41(2&3):197–230, 1999.
15. A. Pettorossi and M. Proietti. Perfect model checking via unfold/fold transformations. In *Proc. CL 2000, London, UK*, LNAI 1861, pp. 613–628. Springer, 2000.
16. M. Proietti and A. Pettorossi. Unfolding-definition-folding, in this order, for avoiding unnecessary variables in logic programs. *Theor. Comp. Sci.*, 142(1):89–124, 1995.
17. T. C. Przymusinski. On the declarative semantics of stratified deductive databases and logic programs. In J. Minker, editor, *Foundations of Deductive Databases and Logic Programming*, pages 193–216. Morgan Kaufmann, 1987.
18. M. O. Rabin. Decidable theories. In Jon Barwise, editor, *Handbook of Mathematical Logic*, pages 595–629. North-Holland, 1977.
19. A. Roychoudhury, K. Narayan Kumar, C. R. Ramakrishnan, I. V. Ramakrishnan, and S. A. Smolka. Verification of parameterized systems using logic program transformations. In *Proc. TACAS 2000*, LNCS 1785, pp. 172–187. Springer, 2000.
20. H. Tamaki and T. Sato. Unfold/fold transformation of logic programs. In S.-Å. Tärnlund, ed., *Proceedings of ICLP '84*, pages 127–138, Uppsala, Sweden, 1984.

Justifications for Logic Programs Under Answer Set Semantics

Enrico Pontelli and Tran Cao Son

Dept. Computer Science
New Mexico State University
{epontell, tson}@cs.nmsu.edu

Abstract. The paper introduces the notion of *off-line justification* for Answer Set Programming (ASP). Justifications provide a graph-based explanation of the truth value of an atom w.r.t. a given answer set. The notion of justification accounts for the specifics of answer set semantics. The paper extends also this notion to provide justification of atoms *during* the computation of an answer set (*on-line justification*), and presents an integration of on-line justifications within the computation model of SMODELS. Justifications offer a basic data structure to support methodologies and tools for *debugging* answer set programs. A preliminary implementation has been developed in ASP − PROLOG.

1 Introduction

Answer set programming (ASP) is a programming paradigm [13,19] based on logic programming under answer set semantics [9]. ASP is *highly declarative*; to solve a problem P, we specify it as a logic program $\pi(P)$ whose answer sets correspond one-to-one to solutions of P, and can be computed using an answer set solver. ASP is also attractive because of its numerous building block results (see, e.g., [4]).

A source of difficulties in ASP lies in the lack of *methodologies* for program understanding and debugging. The declarative and the hands-off execution style of ASP leave a programmer with nothing that helps in explaining the behavior of the programs, especially for unexpected outcomes of the computation (e.g., incorrect answer sets).

Although ASP is syntactically close to Prolog, the execution model and the semantics are sufficiently different to make debugging techniques developed for Prolog impractical. E.g., traditional *trace-based* debuggers [17] (e.g., Prolog four-port debuggers), used to trace the entire proof search tree (paired with execution control mechanisms, like spy points and step execution), are cumbersome in ASP, since:

- Trace-based debuggers provide the entire search sequence, including failed paths, which are irrelevant in understanding specific elements of an answer set.
- The process of computing answer sets is bottom-up, and the determination of the truth value of one atom is intermixed with the computation of other atoms; a direct tracing makes it hard to focus on what is relevant to one particular atom.
- Tracing repeats previously performed executions, degrading debugging performance.

In this paper, we address these issues by elaborating the concept of *off-line justification* for ASP. This notion is an evolution of the concept of *justification*, proposed to justify

S. Etalle and M. Truszczyński (Eds.): ICLP 2006, LNCS 4079, pp. 196–210, 2006.

truth values in tabled Prolog [17,14]. Intuitively, an off-line justification of an atom w.r.t. an answer set is a graph encoding the reasons for the atom's truth value. This notion can be used to explain the presence or absence of an atom in an answer set, and provides the basis for building a *justifier* for answer set solvers.

The notion of off-line justification is helpful when investigating the content of one (or more) answer sets. When the program does not have answer sets, a different type of justification is needed. We believe it is impractical to rely on a single justification structure to tackle this issue; we prefer, instead, to provide the programmer with a *dynamic* data structure that will help him/her discover the sources of inconsistencies. The data structure we propose is called *on-line justification*, and it provides justifications with respect to a *partial* and/or *inconsistent* interpretation. The intuition is to allow the programmer to interrupt the computation (e.g., at the occurrence of certain events, such as assignment of a truth value to a given atom) and to use the on-line justification to explore the motivations behind the content of the partial interpretation (e.g., why a given atom is receiving conflicting truth values). We describe a *generic* model of on-line justification and a version specialized to the execution model of SMODELS [19]. The latter has been implemented in ASP − PROLOG [8].

Related work: Various approaches to logic program debugging have been investigated (a thorough comparison is beyond the limited space of this paper). As discussed in [14], 3 main phases can be considered in understanding/debugging a logic program. *(1) Program instrumentation and execution:* assertion-based debugging (e.g., [16]) and algorithmic debugging [18] are examples of approaches focused on this first phase. *(2) Data Collection:* focuses on *extracting* from the execution data necessary to understand it, as in event-based debugging [3] and explanation-based debugging [7,12]. *(3) Data Analysis:* focuses on reasoning on data collected during the execution. The proposals dealing with automated debugging (e.g., [3]) and execution visualization are approaches focusing on this phase of program understanding.

The notion of *Justification* has been introduced in [17,14,20] to support understanding and debugging of Prolog programs. Justification is the process of generating evidence, in terms of high-level proofs based on the answers (or models) produced during the computation. Justification plays an important role in manual and automatic verification, by providing a *proof description* if a given property holds; otherwise, it generates a *counter-example*, showing where the violation/conflict occurs in the system. The justification-based approach focuses on the last two phases of debugging—collecting data from the execution and presenting them in a meaningful manner. Justifications are focused only on parts of the computation relevant to the justified item. Justifications are fully automated and do not require user interaction (as in declarative debugging).

Our work shares some similarities with the proposals that employ graph structures to guide computation of answer sets (e.g., [1,6]), although they use graphs for program representation, instead of using graphs to justify an execution.

2   Preliminary Definitions

In this paper, we focus on a logic programming language with negation as failure—e.g., the language of SMODELS without weight constraints [19].

The Language: Let $\Sigma_P = \langle \mathcal{F}, \Pi \rangle$ be a signature, where $\mathcal{F}$ is a finite set of constants and Π is a finite set of predicate symbols. In particular, we assume that $\top$ (stands for *true*) and $\bot$ (stands for *false*) are zero-ary predicates in Π. A *term* is a constant of $\mathcal{F}$. An atom is of the form $p(t_1, \ldots, t_n)$ where $p \in \Pi$, and $t_1, \ldots, t_n$ are terms. In this paper, we deal with normal logic programs, i.e., logic programs that can make use of both positive and negation-as-failure literals. A literal is either an atom (*Positive Literal*) or *not a* where a is an atom (*NAF Literal*). We will identify with $\mathcal{A}$ the set of all atoms, and with $\mathcal{L}$ the set of all literals. Our focus is on ground programs, as current ASP engines operate on ground programs. Nevertheless, programmers can write non-ground programs, and each rule represents the set of its ground instances.

A rule is of the form $h \; :- \; b_1, \ldots, b_n$ where h is an atom and $\{b_1, \ldots, b_n\} \subseteq \mathcal{L}$. Given a rule r, we denote h with $head(r)$ and we use $body(r)$ to denote $\{b_1, \ldots, b_n\}$. We denote with $pos(r) = body(r) \cap \mathcal{A}$ and with $neg(r) = \{a \mid (not \; a) \in body(r)\}$. $NANT(P)$ denotes the atoms which appear in NAF literals in P—i.e., $NANT(P) = \{a \in \mathcal{A} \mid \exists r \in P. \, a \in neg(r)\}$.

Answer Set Semantics and Well-Founded Semantics: A *possible interpretation* (or *p-interpretation*) I is a pair $\langle I^+, I^- \rangle$, where $I^+ \cup I^- \subseteq \mathcal{A}$. For a p-interpretation I, we will use the notation I^+ and I^- to denote its two components. A *(three-valued) interpretation* I is a possible interpretation $\langle I^+, I^- \rangle$ where $I^+ \cap I^- = \emptyset$. I is a *complete interpretation* if $I^+ \cup I^- = \mathcal{A}$. For two p-interpretations I and J, $I \sqsubseteq J$ iff $I^+ \subseteq J^+$ and $I^- \subseteq J^-$. A positive literal a is satisfied by I ($I \models a$) if $a \in I^+$. A NAF literal *not a* is satisfied by I ($I \models not \; a$) if $a \in I^-$. A set of literals S is satisfied by I ($I \models S$) if I satisfies each literal in S. The notion of satisfaction is extended to rules and programs as usual.

For an interpretation I and a program P, the *reduct* of P w.r.t. I (P^I) is the program obtained from P by deleting *(i)* each rule r such that $neg(r) \cap I^+ \neq \emptyset$, and *(ii)* all NAF literals in the bodies of the remaining clauses. A complete interpretation I is an *answer set* [9] of P if I^+ is the least Herbrand model of P^I [2]. We will denote with $WF_P = \langle WF_P^+, WF_P^- \rangle$ the (unique) *well-founded model* [2] of program P (we omit its definition for lack of space).

Interpretations and Explanations: Let P be a program and I be an interpretation. An atom a is *true* (*false*, or *unknown*) in I if $a \in I^+$, ($a \in I^-$, or $a \notin I^+ \cup I^-$). *not a* is true (*false*, *unknown*) in I if $a \in I^-$, ($a \in I^+$, $a \notin I^+ \cup I^-$). We will denote with $atom(\ell)$ the atom on which the literal ℓ is constructed.

We will now introduce some notations that we will use in the rest of the paper. The graphs used to explain will refer to the truth value assigned to an atom; furthermore, as we will see later, we wish to encompass those cases where an atom may appear as being both true and false (e.g., a conflict during construction of an answer set). For an atom a, we write a^+ to denote the fact that the atom is true, and a^- to denote the the fact that a is false. We will call a^+ and a^- the *annotated* versions of a; furthermore, we will define $atom(a^+) = a$ and $atom(a^-) = a$. For a set of atoms S, $S^p = \{a^+ \mid a \in S\}$, $S^n = \{a^- \mid a \in S\}$, and $not \; S = \{ not \; a \mid a \in S\}$. In building the notion of justification, we will deal with labeled, directed graphs, called *e-graphs*.

Definition 1 (Explanation Graph). *For a program P, a labeled, directed graph* (N, E) *is called an* Explanation Graph *(or* e-graph*) if*

- $N \subseteq \mathcal{A}^p \cup \mathcal{A}^n \cup \{assume, \top, \bot\}$ *and*
- E *is a set of tuples of the form* (p, q, s), *with* $p, q \in N$ *and* $s \in \{+, -\}$;
- *the only sinks in the graph are: assume,* $\top$, *and* $\bot$;
- *for every* $b \in N \cap \mathcal{A}^p$, $(b, assume, -) \notin E$ *and* $(b, \bot, -) \notin E$;
- *for every* $b \in N \cap \mathcal{A}^n$, $(b, assume, +) \notin E$ *and* $(b, \top, +) \notin E$;
- *for every* $b \in N$, *if* $(b, l, s) \in E$ *for some* $l \in \{assume, \top, \bot\}$ *and* $s \in \{+, -\}$ *then* (b, l, s) *is the only outgoing edge originating from* b.

Edges labeled $'+'$ are called *positive* edges, while those labeled $'-'$ are called *negative* edges. A path in an e-graph is *positive* if it contains only positive edges, while a path is negative if it contains at least one negative edge. We will denote with $(n_1, n_2) \in E^{*,+}$ the fact that there is a positive path from n_1 to n_2 in the given e-graph. The above definition allows us to define the notion of a support set of a node in an e-graph.

Definition 2. *Given an e-graph* $G = (N, E)$ *and a node* $b \in N \cap (\mathcal{A}^p \cup \mathcal{A}^n)$,
- $support(b, G) = \{atom(c) \mid (b, c, +) \in E\} \cup \{ not\ atom(c) \mid (b, c, -) \in E\}$, *if for every* $\ell \in \{assume, \top, \bot\}$ *and* $s \in \{+, -\}$, $(b, \ell, s) \notin E$;
- $support(b, G) = \{\ell\}$ *if* $(b, \ell, s) \in E$ *if* $\ell \in \{assume, \top, \bot\}$ *and* $s \in \{+, -\}$.

The *local consistent explanation* describes one step of justification for a literal. Note that our notion of local consistent explanation is similar in spirit, but different in practice from the analogous definition used in [17,14]. It describes the possible local reasons for the truth/falsity of a literal. If a is true, the explanation contains those bodies of the rules for a that are satisfied by I. If a is false, the explanation contains sets of literals that are false in I and they falsify all rules for a.

Definition 3 (Local Consistent Explanation). *Let* b *be an atom,* J *a possible interpretation,* A *a set of atoms* (assumptions)*, and* $S \subseteq A \cup\ not\ A \cup \{assume, \top, \bot\}$ *a set of literals. We say that*

- S *is a local consistent explanation (LCE) of* b^+ *w.r.t.* (J, A), *if* $S \cap A \subseteq J^+$ *and* $\{c \mid\ not\ c \in S\} \subseteq J^- \cup A$, $b \in J^+$, *and*
  - $S = \{assume\}$, *or*
  - *there is a rule* r *in* P *such that* $head(r) = b$ *and* $S = body(r)$; *for convenience, we write* $S = \{\top\}$ *to denote the case where* $body(r) = \emptyset$.
- S *is a local consistent explanation of* b^- *w.r.t.* (J, A) *if* $S \cap A \subseteq J^- \cup A$ *and* $\{c \mid\ not\ c \in S\} \subseteq J^+$, $b \in J^- \cup A$, *and*
  - $S = \{assume\}$; *or*
  - S *is a minimal set of literals such that for every rule* $r \in P$, *if* $head(r) = b$, *then* $pos(r) \cap S \neq \emptyset$ *or* $neg(r) \cap \{c \mid\ not\ c \in S\} \neq \emptyset$; *for convenience, we write* $S = \{\bot\}$ *to denote the case* $S = \emptyset$.

We will denote with $LCE_P^p(b, J, A)$ the set of all the LCEs of b^+ w.r.t. (J, A), and with $LCE_P^n(b, J, A)$ the set of all the LCEs of b^- w.r.t. (J, A).

Example 1. Let P be the program:

$$a \; :- \; f, not \; b. \qquad b \; :- \; e, not \; a. \qquad e \; :- \; .$$
$$f \; :- \; e. \qquad d \; :- \; c, e. \qquad c \; :- \; d, f.$$

This program has the answer sets $M_1 = \langle \{f, e, b\}, \{a, c, d\} \rangle$ and $M_2 = \langle \{f, e, a\}, \{c, b, d\} \rangle$. We have: $LCE_P^n(a, M_1, \emptyset) = \{\{ \; not \; b\}\}$, $LCE_P^p(b, M_1, \emptyset) = \{\{e, \quad not \quad a\}\}$, $LCE_P^p(e, M_1, \emptyset) = \{\{\top\}\}$, $LCE_P^p(f, M_1, \emptyset) = \{\{e\}\}$, $LCE_P^n(d, M_1, \emptyset) = \{\{c\}\}$, $LCE_P^n(c, M_1, \emptyset) = \{\{d\}\}$. □

An e-graph is a general structure that can be used to explain the truth value of a, i.e., a positive (negative) e-graph represents a possible explanation for a being true (false). To select an e-graph as an acceptable explanation, we need two additional components: the current interpretation (J) and the collection (A) of elements that have been introduced in the interpretation without any "supporting evidence". An e-graph based on (J, A) is defined next.

Definition 4 ((J, A)-Based Explanation Graph). *Let P be a program, J a possible interpretation, A a set of atoms, and b an element in $A^p \cup A^n$. A (J, A)-based explanation graph $G = (N, E)$ of b is an e-graph such that*

- *every node $c \in N$ is reachable from b;*
- *for every $c \in N \setminus \{assume, \top, \bot\}$, $support(c, G)$ is an LCE of c w.r.t. (J, A).*

Definition 5. *A (J, A)-based e-graph (N, E) is safe if $\forall b^+ \in N$, $(b^+, b^+) \notin E^{*,+}$.*

Example 2. Consider the e-graphs in Figure 1, for the program of Example 1. We have that none of the e-graphs of a^+ ((i) and (ii)) is a $(M_1, \{c, d\})$-based e-graph of a^+ but both are $(M_2, \{b, c, d\})$-based e-graph of a^+. On the other hand, the e-graph of c^+ (iii) is neither a $(M_1, \{c, d\})$-based nor $(M_2, \{b, c, d\})$-based e-graph of c^+, while the e-graph of c^- (iv) is an a $(M_1, \{c, d\})$-based and a $(M_2, \{b, c, d\})$-based e-graph of c^-.

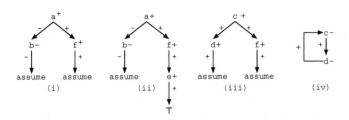

Fig. 1. Sample (J, A)-based Explanation Graphs

3 Off-Line Justifications for ASP

Off-line justifications are employed to motivate the truth value of an atom w.r.t. a given (complete) answer set. If M is an answer set and WF_P the well-founded model of P, then it is known that, $WF_P^+ \subseteq M^+$ and $WF_P^- \subseteq M^-$ [2]. Furthermore, we observe that the content of M is uniquely determined by the truth values assigned to certain atoms in $V = NANT(P) \setminus (WF_P^+ \cup WF_P^-)$, i.e., atoms that appear in negative literals and are not determined by the well-founded model. In particular, we are interested in those subsets of V with the following property: if all the elements in the subset are assumed to be false, then the truth value of all other atoms in $\mathcal{A}$ is uniquely determined. We call these subsets the *assumptions* of the answer set.

Definition 6 (Pre-Assumptions). *Let P be a program and M be an answer set of P. The* pre-assumptions *of P w.r.t. M (denoted by $\mathcal{PA}_P(M)$) are defined as:*
$$\mathcal{PA}_P(M) = \{a \mid a \in NANT(P) \wedge a \in M^- \wedge a \notin (WF_P^+ \cup WF_P^-)\}$$

The negative reduct of a program P w.r.t. a set of atoms A is a program obtained from P by forcing all the atoms in A to be false.

Definition 7 (Negative Reduct). *Let P be a program, M an answer set of P, and $A \subseteq \mathcal{PA}_P(M)$ a set of atoms. The* negative reduct *of P w.r.t. A, denoted by $NR(P, A)$, is the set of rules: $P \setminus \{ r \mid head(r) \in A\}$.*

Definition 8 (Assumptions). *Let P be a program and M an answer set of P. An* assumption *w.r.t. M is a set of atoms A such that: (1) $A \subseteq \mathcal{PA}_P(M)$, and (2) the well-founded model of $NR(P, A)$ is equal to M—i.e., $WF_{NR(P,A)} = M$. We will denote with $Ass(P, M)$ the set of all assumptions of P w.r.t. M. A* minimal assumption *is an assumption that is minimal w.r.t. properties (1) and (2).*

We can observe that the set $Ass(P, M)$ is not empty, since $\mathcal{PA}_P(M)$ is an assumption.

Proposition 1. *Given an answer set M of P, the well-founded model of $NR(P, \mathcal{PA}_P (M))$ is equal to M.*

We will now specialize e-graphs to the case of answer sets, where only false elements can be used as assumptions.

Definition 9 (Off-line Explanation Graph). *Let P be a program, J a partial interpretation, A a set of atoms, and b an element in $\mathcal{A}^p \cup \mathcal{A}^n$. An* off-line explanation graph *$G = (N, E)$ of b w.r.t. J and A is a (J, A)-based e-graph of b satisfying the following conditions: there exists no $p^+ \in N$ such that $(p^+, assume, +) \in E$, and if $(p^-, assume, -) \in E$ then $p \in A$. $\mathcal{E}(b, J, A)$ denotes the set of all off-line explanation graphs of b w.r.t. J and A.*

Definition 10 (Off-line Justification). *Let P be a program, M an answer set, $A \in Ass(P, M)$, and $a \in \mathcal{A}^p \cup \mathcal{A}^n$. An* off-line justification *of a w.r.t. M and A is an element (N, E) of $\mathcal{E}(a, M, A)$ which is safe. $\mathcal{J}_P(a, M, A)$ contains all off-line justifications of a w.r.t. M and A.*

If M is an answer set and $a \in M^+$ ($a \in M^-$), then G is an off-line justification of a w.r.t. M, A iff G is an off-line justification of a^+ (a^-) w.r.t. M, A.

Justifications are built by assembling items from the LCEs of the various atoms and avoiding the creation of positive cycles in the justification of true atoms. Also, the justification is built on a chosen set of assumptions (A), whose elements are all assumed false. In general, an atom may admit multiple justifications, even w.r.t. the same assumptions. The following lemma shows that elements in WF_P can be justified without negative cycles and assumptions.

Lemma 1. *Let P be a program, M an answer set, and WF_P the well-founded model of P. Each atom has an off-line justification w.r.t. M and $\emptyset$ without negative cycles.*

From the definition of assumption and from the previous lemma we can infer that a justification free of negative cycles can be built for every atom.

Proposition 2. *Let P be a program and M an answer set. For each atom a, there is an off-line justification w.r.t. M and $M^- \setminus WF_P^-$ which does not contain negative cycles.*

Proposition 2 underlines an important property—the fact that all true elements can be justified in a non-cyclic fashion. This makes the justification more natural, reflecting the non-cyclic process employed in constructing the minimal answer set (e.g., using the iterations of T_P) and the well-founded model (e.g., using the characterization in [5]). This also gracefully extends a similar nice property satisfied by the justifications under well-founded semantics used in [17]. Note that the only cycles possibly present in the justifications are positive cycles associated to (mutually dependent) false elements—this is an unavoidable situation due the semantic characterization in well-founded and answer set semantics (e.g., unfounded sets [2]).

Example 3. Let us consider the program in Example 1. We have that $NANT(P) = \{b, a\}$. The assumptions for this program are: $Ass(P, M_1) = \{\{a\}\}$ and $Ass(P, M_2) = \{\{b\}\}$. The off-line justifications for atoms in M_1 w.r.t. M_1 and $\{a\}$ are shown in Fig. 2.

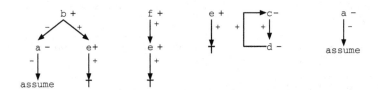

Fig. 2. Off-line Justifications w.r.t. M_1 and $\{a\}$ for b, f, e, c and a (left to right)

4   On-Line Justifications for ASP

In this section, we introduce the concept of on-line justification, which is generated *during* the computation of an answer set and allows us to justify atoms w.r.t. an incomplete interpretation (an intermediate step in the construction of the answer set). The concept of on-line justification is applicable to computation models that construct answer sets in an incremental fashion (e.g., [19,11,1])—where we can view the computation as a sequence of steps, each associated to a partial interpretation. We will focus, in particular, on computation models where the progress towards the answer set is monotonic.

Definition 11 (General Computation). *Let P be a program. A general computation is a sequence $M_0, M_1, \ldots, M_k$, such that (i) $M_0 = \langle \emptyset, \emptyset \rangle$, (ii) $M_0, \ldots, M_{k-1}$ are* *partial interpretations, and* (iii) $M_i \sqsubseteq M_{i+1}$ *for* $i = 0, \ldots, k - 1$. *A* general complete computation *is a computation* $M_0, \ldots, M_k$ *such that* M_k *is an answer set of P*.

We do not require M_k to be a partial interpretation, as we wish to model computations that can also fail (i.e., $M_k^+ \cap M_k^- \neq \emptyset$).

Our objective is to associate some form of justification to each intermediate step M_i of a general computation. Ideally, we would like the justifications associated to each M_i to explain truth values in the "same way" as in the final off-line justification. Since the computation model might rely on "guessing" some truth values, M_i might not contain sufficient information to develop a valid justification for each element in M_i. We will identify those atoms for which a justification can be constructed given M_i. These atoms describe a p-interpretation $D_i \sqsubseteq M_i$. The computation of D_i is defined based on the two operators Γ and Δ, which will respectively compute D_i^+ and D_i^-.

Let us start with some preliminary definitions. Let P be a program and I be a p-interpretation. A set of atoms S is called a *cycle w.r.t. I* if for every $a \in S$ and $r \in P$ such that $head(r) = a$, we have that $pos(r) \cap I^- \neq \emptyset$ or $neg(r) \cap I^+ \neq \emptyset$ or $pos(r) \cap S \neq \emptyset$. We can prove that, if I is an interpretation, S is a cycle w.r.t. I and M is an answer set with $I \sqsubseteq M$ then $S \subseteq M^-$. The set of cycles w.r.t. I is denoted by $cycles(I)$. For every element $e \in \mathcal{A}^p \cup \mathcal{A}^n$, let $PE(e, I)$ be the set of LCEs of e w.r.t. I and $\emptyset$.

Let P be a program and $I \sqsubseteq J$ be two p-interpretations. We define

$$\Gamma_I(J) = I^+ \cup \{head(r) \in J^+ \mid I \models body(r)\}$$
$$\Delta_I(J) = I^- \cup \{a \in J^- \mid PE(a^-, I) \neq \emptyset\} \cup \bigcup \{S \mid S \in cycles(I), S \subseteq J^-\}$$

Intuitively, for $I \sqsubseteq J$, we have that $\Gamma_I(J)$ (resp. $\Delta_I(J)$) is a set of atoms that have to be true (resp. false) in every answer set extending J, if J is a partial interpretation. In particular, if I is the set of *"justifiable"* literals (literals for which we can construct a justification) and J is the result of the current computation step, then we have that $\langle \Gamma_I(J), \Delta_I(J) \rangle$ is a new interpretation, $I \sqsubseteq \langle \Gamma_I(J), \Delta_I(J) \rangle \sqsubseteq J$, whose elements are all *"justifiable"*. Observe that it is not necessarily true that $\Gamma_I(J) = J^+$ and $\Delta_I(J) = J^-$. This reflects the practice of guessing literals and propagating these guesses in the computation of answer sets, implemented by several solvers.

We are now ready to specify how the set D_i is computed. Let J be a p-interpretation.

$$\Gamma^0(J) = \Gamma_\emptyset(J) \qquad \Delta^0(J) = \mathcal{P}\mathcal{A}_P(J) \cup \Delta_\emptyset(J)$$
$$\Gamma^{i+1}(J) = \Gamma_{I_i}(J) \qquad \Delta^{i+1}(J) = \Delta_{I_i}(J) \qquad \text{where } I_i = \langle \Gamma^i(J), \Delta^i(J) \rangle$$

Let

$$\Gamma(J) = \bigcup_{i=0}^{\infty} \Gamma^i(J) \quad \text{and} \quad \Delta(J) = \bigcup_{i=0}^{\infty} \Delta^i(J)$$

Because $\Gamma^i(J) \subseteq \Gamma^{i+1}(J) \subseteq J^+$ and $\Delta^i(J) \subseteq \Delta^{i+1}(J) \subseteq J^-$ (recall that $I \sqsubseteq J$), we know that both $\Gamma(J)$ and $\Delta(J)$ are well-defined. We can prove the following:

Proposition 3. *For a program P, we have that:*

- Γ *and* Δ *maintain the consistency of J, i.e., if J is an interpretation, then* $\langle \Gamma(J), \Delta(J) \rangle$ *is also an interpretation;*

- Γ and Δ are monotone w.r.t the argument J, i.e., if $J \sqsubseteq J'$ then $\Gamma(J) \subseteq \Gamma(J')$ and $\Delta(J) \subseteq \Delta(J')$;
- $\Gamma(WF_P) = WF_P^+$ and $\Delta(WF_P) = WF_P^-$; and
- if M is an answer set of P, then $\Gamma(M) = M^+$ and $\Delta(M) = M^-$.

Definition 12 (On-line Explanation Graph). *Let P be a program, A a set of atoms, J a p-interpretation, and $a \in \mathcal{A}^p \cup \mathcal{A}^n$. An on-line explanation graph $G = (N, E)$ of a w.r.t. J and A is a (J, A)-based e-graph of a.*

Observe that, if J is an answer set and A a set of assumption, then any off-line e-graph of a w.r.t. J and A is also an on-line e-graph of a w.r.t. J and A.

Observe that $\Gamma^0(J)$ contains the facts of P that belong to J^+ and $\Delta^0(J)$ contains the atoms without defining rules and atoms belonging to positive cycles of P. As such, it is easy to see that for each atom a in $\langle \Gamma^0(J), \Delta^0(J) \rangle$, we can construct an e-graph for a^+ or a^- whose nodes belong to $(\Gamma^0(J))^p \cup (\Delta^0(J))^n$. Moreover, if $a \in \Gamma^{i+1}(J) \setminus \Gamma^i(J)$, an e-graph with nodes (except a^+) belonging to $(\Gamma^i(J))^p \cup (\Delta^i(J))^n$ can be constructed; and if $a \in \Delta^{i+1}(J) \setminus \Delta^i(J)$, an e-graph with nodes belonging to $(\Gamma^{i+1}(J))^p \cup (\Delta^{i+1}(J))^n$ can be constructed. This leads to the following lemma.

Lemma 2. *Let P be a program, J a p-interpretation, and $A = \mathcal{P}\mathcal{A}_P(J)$. It holds that*

- *for each atom $a \in \Gamma(J)$ (resp. $a \in \Delta(J)$), there exists a safe off-line e-graph of a^+ (resp. a^-) w.r.t. J and A;*
- *for each atom $a \in J^+ \setminus \Gamma(J)$ (resp. $a \in J^- \setminus \Delta(J)$) there exists an on-line e-graph of a^+ (resp. a^-) w.r.t. J and A.*

Let us show how the above proposition can be used in defining a notion called *on-line justification*. To this end, we associate to each partial interpretation J a snapshot $S(J)$:

Definition 13. *Given a p-interpretation J, a snapshot of J is a tuple $S(J) = \langle Off(J), On(J), \langle \Gamma(J), \Delta(J) \rangle \rangle$, where*

- *for each a in $\Gamma(J)$ (resp. a in $\Delta(J)$), $Off(J)$ contains exactly one safe positive (negative) off-line e-graph of a^+ (resp. a^-) w.r.t. J and $\mathcal{P}\mathcal{A}_P(J)$;*
- *for each $a \in J^+ \setminus \Gamma(J)$ (resp. $a \in J^- \setminus \Delta(J)$), $On(J)$ contains exactly one on-line e-graph of a^+ (resp. a^-) w.r.t. J and $\mathcal{P}\mathcal{A}_P(J)$.*

Definition 14. (On-line Justification) *Given a computation $M_0, \ldots, M_k$, an on-line justification of the computation is a sequence of snapshots $S(M_0), S(M_1), \ldots, S(M_k)$.*

Remark 1. Observe that the monotonicity of the computation allows us to avoid re-computing Γ and Δ from scratch at every step. In particular, when computing the fix-point we can start the iterations from $\Gamma_{\langle \Gamma(M_i), \Delta(M_i) \rangle}$ and $\Delta_{\langle \Gamma(M_i), \Delta(M_i) \rangle}$ and looking only at the elements of $\langle M_{i+1}^+ \setminus \Gamma(M_i), M_{i+1}^- \setminus \Delta(M_i) \rangle$. Similarly, the computation of $Off(M_{i+1})$ can be made incremental, by simply adding to $Off(M_{i+1})$ the off-line e-graphs for the elements in $\Gamma(M_{i+1}) \setminus \Gamma(M_i)$ and $\Delta(M_{i+1}) \setminus \Delta(M_i)$. Note that these new off-line graphs can be constructed reusing the off-line graphs already in $Off(M_i)$.

Example 4. Let us consider the program P containing

$$s :- a, not\ t.   \quad a :- f, not\ b.   \quad b :- e, not\ a.   \quad e :-   \quad f :- e.$$

Two possible general computations of P are

$$M_0^1 = \langle \{e, s\}, \emptyset \rangle   \quad M_1^1 = \langle \{e, s, a\}, \{t\} \rangle   \quad M_2^1 = \langle \{e, s, a, f\}, \{t, b\} \rangle$$
$$M_0^2 = \langle \{e, f\}, \emptyset \rangle   \quad M_1^2 = \langle \{e, f\}, \{t\} \rangle   \quad M_2^2 = \langle \{e, f, b, a\}, \{t, a, b, s\} \rangle$$

The first computation is a complete computation leading to an answer set of P while the second one is not. An on-line justification for the first computation is given next:

$$S(M_0^1) = \langle X_0, Y_0, \langle \{e\}, \emptyset \rangle \rangle$$
$$S(M_1^1) = \langle X_0 \cup X_1, Y_0 \cup Y_1, \langle \{e\}, \{t\} \rangle \rangle$$
$$S(M_2^1) = \langle X_0 \cup X_1 \cup X_3, \emptyset, M_1^2 \rangle$$

where $X_0 = \{(\{e^+, \top\}, \{(e^+, \top, +)\})\}$, $Y_0 = \{(\{s^+, assume\}, \{(s^+, assume, +)\})\}$, $X_1 = \{(\{t^-, \bot\}, \{(t^-, \bot, -)\})\}$, $Y_1 = \{\{a^+, assume\}, \{(a^+, assume, +)\})\}$, and X_3 is a set of off-line justifications for s, a, f, and b (omitted due to lack of space).   □

We can relate the on-line justifications and off-line justifications as follows.

Lemma 3. *Let P be a program, J an interpretation, and M an answer set such that $J \sqsubseteq M$. For each atom a, if (N, E) is a safe off-line e-graph of a^+ (a^-) w.r.t. J and $J^- \cap \mathcal{PA}_P(M)$ then it is an off-line justification of a^+ (a^-) w.r.t. M and $\mathcal{PA}_P(M)$.*

Proposition 4. *Let $M_0, \ldots, M_k$ be a general complete computation and $S(M_0), \ldots, S(M_k)$ be an on-line justification of the computation. Then, for each atom $a \in M_k^+$ (resp. $a \in M_k^-$), the e-graph of a^+ (resp. a^-) in $S(M_k)$ is an off-line justification of a^+ (resp. a^-) w.r.t. M_k and $\mathcal{PA}_P(M)$.*

5 SMODELS **On-Line Justifications**

The notion of on-line justification presented in the previous section is very general, to fit the needs of different models of computation. In this section, we specialize the notion of on-line justification to a specific computation model—the one used in SMODELS [19]. This allows us to define an incremental version of on-line justification—where the steps performed by SMODELS are used to guide the construction of the justification.

We begin with an overview of the algorithms employed by SMODELS. The choice of SMODELS was dictated by availability of its source code and its elegant design. The following description has been adapted from [10,19]; although more abstract than the concrete implementation, and without various optimizations (e.g., heuristics, lookahead), it is sufficiently faithful to capture the spirit of our approach, and to guide the implementation (see Sect. 5.3).

5.1 An Overview of SMODELS' Computation

We propose a description of the SMODELS algorithms based on a composition of state-transformation operators. In the following, we say that an interpretation I does not satisfy the body of a rule r (or $body(r)$ is false in I) if $(pos(r) \cap I^-) \cup (neg(r) \cap I^+) \neq \emptyset$.

ATLEAST **Operator:** The *AtLeast* operator is used to expand a partial interpretation I in such a way that each answer set M of P that "agrees" with I (i.e., the elements in I have the same truth value in M) also agrees with the expanded interpretation.

Given a program P and a partial interpretation I, we define the following operators $AL_P^1, \ldots, AL_P^4$:

Case 1. if $r \in P$, $head(r) \notin I^+$, $pos(P) \subseteq I^+$ and $neg(P) \subseteq I^-$ then
$$AL_P^1(I)^+ = I^+ \cup \{head(r)\} \text{ and } AL_P^1(I)^- = I^-.$$

Case 2. if $a \notin I^+ \cup I^-$ and $\forall r \in P.(head(r) = a \Rightarrow body(r) \text{ is false in } I)$, then
$$AL_P^2(I)^+ = I^+ \text{ and } AL_P^2(I)^- = I^- \cup \{a\}.$$

Case 3. if $a \in I^+$ and r is the only rule in P with $head(r) = a$ and whose body is not false in I then, $AL_P^3(I)^+ = I^+ \cup pos(r)$ and $AL_P^3(I)^- = I^- \cup neg(r)$.

Case 4. if $a \in I^-$, $head(r) = a$, and $(pos(r) \setminus I^+) \cup (neg(r) \setminus I^-) = \{b\}$ then,
$$AL_P^4(I)^+ = I^+ \cup \{b\} \text{ and } AL_P^4(I)^- = I^- \text{ if } b \in neg(r)$$
$$AL_P^4(I)^- = I^- \cup \{b\} \text{ and } AL_P^4(I)^+ = I^+ \text{ if } b \in pos(r).$$

Given a program P and an interpretation I, $AL_P(I) = AL_P^i(I)$ if $AL_P^i(I) \neq I$ and $\forall j < i. \, AL_P^j(I) = I$ $(1 \leq i \leq 4)$; otherwise, $AL_P(I) = I$.

ATMOST **Operator:** The *AtMost$_P$* operator recognizes atoms that are defined exclusively as mutual positive dependences (i.e., "positive loops")—and falsifies them. Given a set of atoms S, the operator AM_P is defined as $AM_P(S) = S \cup \{head(r) \,|\, r \in P \wedge pos(r) \subseteq S\}$.

Given an interpretation I, the $AtMost_P(I)$ operator is defined as $AtMost_P(I) = \langle I^+, I^- \cup \{p \in \mathcal{A} \,|\, p \notin \bigcup_{i \geq 0} S_i\}\rangle$ where $S_0 = I^+$ and $S_{i+1} = AM_P(S_i)$.

CHOOSE **Operator:** This operator is used to randomly select an atom that is unknown in a given interpretation. Given a partial interpretation I, *choose$_P$* returns an atom of $\mathcal{A}$ such that $choose_P(I) \notin I^+ \cup I^-$ and $choose_P(I) \in NANT(P) \setminus (WF_P^+ \cup WF_P^-)$.

SMODELS COMPUTATION: Given an interpretation I, we define the transitions:

$I \mapsto_{AL^c} I'$	If $I' = AL_P^c(I)$, $c \in \{1, 2, 3, 4\}$
$I \mapsto_{atmost} I'$	If $I' = AtMost_P(I)$
$I \mapsto_{choice} I'$	If $I' = \langle I^+ \cup \{choose_P(I)\}, I^-\rangle$ or $I' = \langle I^+, I^- \cup \{choose_P(I)\}\rangle$

We use the notation $I \mapsto I'$ to indicate that there is an $\alpha \in \{AL^1, AL^2, AL^3, AL^4, atmost, choice\}$ such that $I \mapsto_\alpha I'$. A SMODELS computation is a general computation $M_0, M_1, \ldots, M_k$ such that $M_i \mapsto M_{i+1}$.

The SMODELS system imposes constraints on the order of application of the transitions. Intuitively, the SMODELS computation is shown in the algorithms of Figs. 3-4.

Example 5. Consider the program of Example 1. A possible computation of M_1 is:[1]

$$\langle \emptyset, \emptyset \rangle \qquad \mapsto_{AL^1} \langle \{e\}, \emptyset \rangle \qquad \mapsto_{AL^1} \langle \{e, f\}, \emptyset \rangle \qquad \mapsto_{atmost}$$
$$\langle \{e, f\}, \{c, d\} \rangle \mapsto_{choice} \langle \{e, f, b\}, \{c, d\} \rangle \mapsto_{AL^2} \langle \{e, f, b\}, \{c, d, a\} \rangle$$

---

[1] We omit the steps that do not change the interpretation.

```
function smodels(P):
    S = ⟨∅, ∅⟩;
loop
    S = expand(P, S);
    if (S⁺ ∩ S⁻ ≠ ∅) then
        fail;
    if (S⁺ ∪ S⁻ = 𝒜) then
        success(S);
    pick either   % non-deterministic choice
        S⁺ = S⁺ ∪ {choose(S)}  or
        S⁻ = S⁻ ∪ {choose(S)}
endloop;
```

```
function expand(P, S):
loop
    S' = S;
    repeat
        S = ALₚ(S);
    until (S = ALₚ(S));
    S = AtMost(P, S);
    if (S' = S) then return (S);
endloop;
```

Fig. 3. Sketch of *smodels*

Fig. 4. Sketch of *expand*

5.2   Constructing On-Line Justifications in SMODELS

We can use knowledge of the specific steps performed by SMODELS to guide the construction of an on-line justification. Let us consider the step $M_i \mapsto_\alpha M_{i+1}$ and let us consider the possible $\mapsto_\alpha$. Let $S(M_i) = \langle E_1, E_2, D \rangle$ and $S(M_{i+1}) = \langle E_1', E_2', D' \rangle$. Obviously, $S(M_{i+1})$ can always be computed by computing $D' = \langle \Gamma(M_{i+1}), \Delta(M_{i+1}) \rangle$ and updating E_1 and E_2. As discussed in Remark 1, D' can be done incrementally. Regarding E_1' and E_2', observe that the e-graphs for elements in $\langle \Gamma^k(M_{i+1}), \Delta^k(M_{i+1}) \rangle$ can be constructed using the e-graphs constructed for elements in $\langle \Gamma^{k-1}(M_{i+1}), \Delta^{k-1}(M_{i+1}) \rangle$ and the rules involved in the computation of $\langle \Gamma^k(M_{i+1}), \Delta^k(M_{i+1}) \rangle$. Thus, we only need to update E_1' with e-graphs of elements of $\langle \Gamma^k(M_{i+1}), \Delta^k(M_{i+1}) \rangle$ which do not belong to $\langle \Gamma^{k-1}(M_{i+1}), \Delta^{k-1}(M_{i+1}) \rangle$. Also, E_2' is obtained from E_2 by removing the e-graphs of atoms that "move" into D' and adding the e-graph $(a^+, assume, +)$ (resp. $(a^-, assume, -)$) for $a \in M_{i+1}^+$ (resp. $a \in M_{i+1}^-$) not belonging to D'.

- $\boxed{\alpha \equiv choice:}$ let p be the atom chosen in this step. If p is chosen to be true, then we can use the graph $G_p = (\{a^+, assume\}, \{(a^+, assume, +)\})$ and the resulting snapshot is $S(M_{i+1}) = \langle E_1, E_2 \cup \{G_p\}, D \rangle$—$D$ is unchanged, since the structure of the computation (in particular the fact that an *expand* has been done before the choice) ensures that p will not appear in the computation of D. If p is chosen to be false, then we will need to add p to D^-, compute $\Gamma(M_{i+1})$ and $\Delta(M_{i+1})$ (using the optimization as discussed in Remark 1), and update E_1 and E_2 correspondingly; in particular, p belongs to $\Delta(M_{i+1})$ and $G_p = (\{a^-, assume\}, \{(a^-, assume, -)\})$ is added to E_1.

- $\boxed{\alpha \equiv atmost:}$ in this case, $M_{i+1} = \langle M_i^+, M_i^- \cup AtMost(P, M_i) \rangle$. The computation of $S(M_{i+1})$ is performed as from definition. In particular, observe that if $\forall c \in AtMost(P, M_i)$ we have that $LCE_P^n(c^-, D, \emptyset) \neq \emptyset$ then the computation can be started from $\Gamma(M_i)$ and $\Delta(M_i) \cup AtMost(P, M_i)$.

- $\boxed{\alpha \equiv AL^1:}$ let p be the atom dealt with in this step and let r be the rule employed. We have that $M_{i+1} = \langle M_i^+ \cup \{p\}, M_i^- \rangle$. If $D \models body(r)$ then $S(M_{i+1})$ can be computed from the definition (and starting from $\Gamma(M_i) \cup \{p\}$ and $\Delta(M_i)$); in particular, an off-line graph for p^+, G_p, will be added to E_1 and such graph will be constructed using the rule r and the e-graphs in E_1. Otherwise, $S(M_{i+1}) = \langle E_1, E_2 \cup \{G^+(p, r, \Sigma)\}, D\rangle$, where $G^+(p, r, \Sigma)$ is the e-graph of p^+ constructed using rule r and using the e-graphs in $\Sigma = E_1 \cup E_2$ (note that all elements in $body(r)$ have an e-graph in $E_1 \cup E_2$).

○ $\boxed{\alpha \equiv AL^2\text{:}}$ let p be the atom dealt with in this step. In this case $M_{i+1}=\langle M_i^+, M_i^- \cup \{p\}\rangle$. If there exists $\gamma \in LCE_P^n(p, D, \emptyset)$ then $S(M_{i+1})$ can be computed from the definition (starting from $\Gamma(M_i)$ and $\Delta(M_i)\cup\{p\}$; observe that the graph of p^- can be constructed starting with $\{(p^-, a^-, +) \mid a \in \gamma\} \cup \{(p^-, b^+, -) \mid not\ b \in \gamma\})$. Otherwise, given an arbitrary $\psi \in LCE_P^n(p, M_i, \emptyset)$, we can build an e-graph G_p for p^- such that $\psi = support(b, G_p)$ and the graphs $E_1 \cup E_2$ are used to describe the elements of γ, and $S(M_{i+1}) = \langle E_1, E_2 \cup \{G_p\}, D\rangle$.

○ $\boxed{\alpha \equiv AL^3\text{:}}$ let r be the rule used in this step and let $p = head(r)$. Then $M_{i+1} = \langle M_i^+\cup pos(r), M_i^-\cup neg(r)\rangle$ and $S(M_{i+1})$ is computed according to the definition. Observe that the e-graph G_p for p^+ (added to E_1 or E_2) for $S(M_{i+1})$ will be constructed using $body(r)$ as $support(p, G_p)$, and using the e-graphs in $E_1\cup E_2\cup\Sigma$ for some $\Sigma \subseteq \{(a^+, assume, +) \mid a \in pos(r)\}\cup\{(a^-, assume, -) \mid a \in neg(r)\}$.

○ $\boxed{\alpha \equiv AL^4\text{:}}$ let r be the rule processed and let b the atom detected in the body. If $b \in pos(r)$, then $M_{i+1} = \langle M_i^+, M_i^- \cup \{p\}\rangle$ and $S(M_{i+1})$ is computed using the definition. Analogously, if $b \in neg(r)$ then $M_{i+1} = \langle M_i^+ \cup \{b\}, M_i^-\rangle$ and $S(M_{i+1})$ is computed using the definition.

Example 6. Let us consider the computation of Example 5. A sequence of snapshots is (we provide only the edges of the graphs and combine e-graphs of different atoms):

	E_1	E_2	D
$S(M_0)$	$\emptyset$	$\emptyset$	$\emptyset$
$S(M_1)$	$\{(e^+, \top, +)\}$	$\emptyset$	$\langle\{e\}, \emptyset\rangle$
$S(M_2)$	$\{(e^+, \top, +), (f^+, e^+, +)\}$	$\emptyset$	$\langle\{e, f\}, \emptyset\rangle$
$S(M_3)$	$\left\{\begin{array}{l}(e^+, \top, +), \{f^+, e^+, +) \\ (d^-, c^-, +), (c^-, d^-, +)\end{array}\right\}$	$\emptyset$	$\langle\{e, f\}, \{c, d\}\rangle$
$S(M_4)$	$\left\{\begin{array}{l}(e^+, \top, +), \{f^+, e^+, +) \\ (d^-, c^-, +), (c^-, d^-, +)\end{array}\right\}$	$\{(b^+, assume, +)\}$	$\langle\{e, f\}, \{c, d\}\rangle$
$S(M_5)$	$\left\{\begin{array}{l}(e^+, \top, +), \{f^+, e^+, +), \\ (d^-, c^-, +), (c^-, d^-, +), \\ (a^-, assume, -), \\ (b^+, e^+, +), (b^+, a^-, -)\end{array}\right\}$	$\emptyset$	$\langle\{e, f, b\}, \{c, d, a\}\rangle$

5.3 Discussion

The description of SMODELS on-line justifications we proposed is clearly more abstract than the concrete implementation—e.g., we did not address the use of lookahead, the use of heuristics, and other optimizations introduced in SMODELS. We also did not address the extensions available in SMODELS (e.g., choice rules). All these elements can be handled in the same spirit of what described here, and they would require more space than available in this paper; all these elements *have been addressed* in the implementation of SMODELS on-line justification.

The notions of justification proposed here is meant to represent the basic data structure on which debugging strategies for ASP can be developed. We have implemented both the off-line and the on-line justifications within the $ASP - PROLOG$ system [8]. $ASP - PROLOG$ allows the construction of Prolog programs (in CIAO Prolog) which include modules written in ASP (the SMODELS flavor of ASP). The SMODELS engine has been modified to extract, during the computation, a compact footprint of the execution, i.e., a trace of the key events (corresponding to the transitions described in Sect. 5) with links to the atoms and rules involved. The modifications of the trace are trailed to support backtracking. Parts of the justification are built on the fly, while others (e.g., certain cases of AL^3 and AL^4) are delayed until the justification is requested.

To avoid imposing the overhead of justification construction on every computation, the programmer has to specify what ASP modules require justifications, using an additional argument (justify) in the module import declaration:

```
:- use_asp(⟨module_name⟩, ⟨file_name⟩, ⟨parameters⟩ [,justify]).
```

On-line justifications are integrated in the ASP debugging facilities of $ASP - PROLOG$—which provide predicates to set breakpoints on the execution of an ASP module (e.g., triggered by assignments of a truth value to a certain atom) and to step through execution. Off-line justifications are always available.

$ASP - PROLOG$ provides the predicate model/1 to retrieve answer sets of an ASP module—it retrieves them in the order they are computed by SMODELS, and it returns the current one if the computation is still in progress. The main predicate to access the justification is justify/1 which retrieves a CIAO Prolog object [15] containing the justification; i.e., ?- my_asp:model(Q), Q:justify(J). will assign to J the object containing the justification relative to the answer set Q of the ASP module my_asp. Each justification object provides the following predicates: node/1 which succeeds if the argument is one of the nodes in the justification graph, edge/3 which succeeds if the arguments correspond to the components of one of the edges in the graph, and draw/1 which will generate a graphical drawing of the justification for the given atom (using the *uDrawGraph* application). For example,

```
?- my_asp:model(Q),Q:justify(J),findall(e(X,Y),J:edge(p,X,Y),L).
```

will collect in L all the edges supporting p in the justification graph (for answer set Q).

6   Conclusion

In this paper we provided a generalization of the notion of *justification* (originally designed for Prolog with SLG-resolution [17]), to suit the needs of ASP. The notion, named *off-line justification*, offers a way to understand the motivations for the truth value of an atom within a specific answer set, thus making it easy to analyze answer sets for program understanding and debugging. We also introduced *on-line justifications*, which are meant to justify atoms *during* the computation of an answer set. The structure of an on-line justification is tied to the specific steps performed by a computational model for ASP (specifically, the computation model adopted by SMODELS). An on-line justification allows a programmer to inspect the reasons for the truth value of an atom at the moment such value is determined while constructing an answer set. These data structures provide a foundation for the construction of tools to debug ASP.

The process of computing and presenting justifications has been embedded in the ASP-Prolog system [8], thus making justifications a first-class citizen of the language. This allows the programmer to use Prolog to manipulate justifications as standard Prolog terms. A preliminary implementation can be found at www.cs.nmsu.edu/~okhatib/asp_prolog.html.

As future work, we propose to complete the implementation, refine the definition of on-line justification to better take advantage of SMODELS, and develop a complete debugging and visualization environment for ASP based on these data structures.

Acknowledgments

The research has been partially supported by NSF grants CNS-0454066, HRD-0420407, and CNS-0220590.

References

1. C. Anger et al. The nomore++ Approach to Answer Set Solving. *LPAR*, Springer, 2005.
2. K. Apt, R. Bol. Logic Programming and Negation: A Survey. *J. Log. Program.* 19/20, 1994.
3. M. Auguston. Assertion Checker for the C Programming Language. *AADEBUG*, 2000.
4. C. Baral. *Knowledge Representation, Reasoning, and Declarative Problem Solving.* Cambridge University Press, 2003.
5. S. Brass et al. Transformation-based bottom-up computation of the well-founded model. *TPLP*, 1(5):497–538, 2001.
6. S. Costantini et al. On the Equivalence and Range of Applicability of Graph-based Representations of Logic Programs. *Information Processing Letters*, 84(5):241–249, 2002.
7. M. Ducassé. Opium: an Extendable Trace Analyzer for Prolog. *J. Logic Progr.*, 39, 1999.
8. O. Elkhatib et al. A System for Reasoning about ASP in Prolog. *PADL*, Springer, 2004.
9. M. Gelfond, V. Lifschitz. The Stable Model Semantics for Logic Programs. *ILPS*, 1988.
10. E. Giunchiglia and M. Maratea. On the Relation between Answer Set and SAT Procedures. In *ICLP*, Springer Verlag, 2005.
11. N. Leone et al. The DLV System. In *JELIA*, Springer Verlag, 2002.
12. S. Mallet, M. Ducasse. Generating Deductive Database Explanations. *ICLP*, MIT, 1999.
13. V.W. Marek and M. Truszczyński. Stable Models and an Alternative Logic Programming Paradigm. *The Logic Programming Paradigm*, Springer Verlag, 1999.
14. G. Pemmasani et al. Online Justification for Tabled Logic Programs. *FLOPS*, 2004.
15. A. Pineda. Object-oriented programming library O'Ciao. TR 6/99.0, UPM Madrid, 1999.
16. G. Puebla, F. Bueno, M.V. Hermenegildo. A Framework for Assertion-based Debugging in Constraint Logic Programming. In *LOPSTR*, Springer Verlag, 1999.
17. A. Roychoudhury et al. Justifying Proofs Using Memo Tables. *PPDP*, ACM Press, 2000.
18. E. Shapiro. Algorithmic Program Diagnosis. In *POPL*, ACM Press, 1982.
19. P. Simons et al. Extending and Implementing the Stable Model Semantics. *Artif. Intell.*, 138(1-2), 2002.
20. G. Specht. Generating Explanation Trees even for Negation in Deductive Databases. *Workshop on Logic Programming Environments*, 8–13, Vancouver, 1993.

Generality Relations
in Answer Set Programming

Katsumi Inoue[1] and Chiaki Sakama[2]

[1] National Institute of Informatics
2-1-2 Hitotsubashi, Chiyoda-ku, Tokyo 101-8430, Japan
ki@nii.ac.jp
[2] Department of Computer and Communication Sciences, Wakayama University
Sakaedani, Wakayama 640-8510, Japan
sakama@sys.wakayama-u.ac.jp

Abstract. This paper studies generality relations on logic programs. Intuitively, a program P_1 is *more general* than another program P_2 if P_1 gives us more information than P_2. In this paper, we define various kinds of generality relations over nonmonotonic programs in the context of *answer set programming*. The semantic properties of generality relations are investigated based on domain theory, and both a minimal upper bound and a maximal lower bound are constructed for any pair of logic programs. We also introduce the concept of *strong generality* between logic programs and investigate its relationships to strong equivalence. These results provide a basic theory to compare the degree of incompleteness between nonmonotonic logic programs, and also have important applications to inductive logic programming and multi-agent systems.

1 Introduction

Nonmonotonic logic programs, or logic programs with negation as failure and/or disjunctions, are useful for representing incomplete knowledge and partial information. To judge whether two logic programs represent the same knowledge, the notion of *equivalence* has recently become important in logic programming [7,6]. Another useful measure to compare the amount of information brought by logic programs is the concept of *generality*. Intuitively, a logic program P_1 is considered *more general* than another logic program P_2 if P_1 gives us more information than P_2.

The generality notion is important in the field of *inductive logic programming*, and basic studies have been done in this context [10,8,9] for *monotonic* logic programs, which can be defined as subsets of first-order clausal theories. Model theoretically, given two monotonic programs P_1 and P_2, the situation that P_1 is more general than P_2 is represented as $P_1 \models P_2$, that is, P_1 entails P_2, which means that every model of P_1 is also a model of P_2. For instance, the program $\{\, p \leftarrow \,\}$ is more general than the program $\{\, p \leftarrow q \,\}$.

In the context of *nonmonotonic* logic programs, however, relatively little attention is given to generality relations although the equivalence notion has been

S. Etalle and M. Truszczyński (Eds.): ICLP 2006, LNCS 4079, pp. 211–225, 2006.
© Springer-Verlag Berlin Heidelberg 2006

studied in depth. Let us intuitively define that, for two nonmonotonic programs P_1 and P_2, P_1 is more general than P_2 if P_1 entails more information than P_2 under the canonical model semantics (e.g., *answer set semantics* [3]). Unfortunately, there is a difficulty in this definition such that a nonmonotonic program generally has multiple canonical models. This is contrasted to a monotonic program that has a unique canonical model or an "extension" as the logical consequences of the program. For instance, consider two nonmonotonic programs:

$$P_1 : \; p \leftarrow not\, q\,,$$
$$P_2 : \; p \leftarrow not\, q\,,$$
$$q \leftarrow not\, p\,.$$

Here, P_1 has the single answer set $\{p\}$ and P_2 has two answer sets $\{p\}$ and $\{q\}$. If we reason *skeptically* and draw conclusions from the intersection of all answer sets, P_1 entails p but P_2 entails nothing. As a result, P_1 is considered more informative and more general than P_2. By contrast, if we reason *credulously* and draw conclusions from the union of all answer sets, P_2 is considered more informative than P_1. Thus, the result depends on the type of inference.

In this paper, we study a theory to compare the degree of incomplete information brought by nonmonotonic logic programs in the framework of *answer set programming*. By the above discussion, it is more appropriate to focus on the whole collection of answer sets of a program than on the set of literals entailed from it. Then, to compare the information contents of two logic programs, it is natural to directly compare the collections of answer sets of the two programs. For this purpose, *domain theory* [11,16,4], which studies orderings over the powerset of a domain, is particularly convenient. There are at least two reasonable philosophies to judge that one description is more informative than another description in domain theory. Suppose, for example, that there are three descriptions about the contents of a bag, which are represented by the following logic programs:

$$P_1 : \; red\_fruit\,;\; yellow\_fruit \leftarrow \,,$$
$$P_2 : \; cherry\,;\; strawberry \leftarrow \,,$$
$$red\_fruit \leftarrow cherry\,,$$
$$red\_fruit \leftarrow strawberry\,,$$
$$P_3 : \; cherry\,;\; banana\,;\; purple\_fruit \leftarrow \,,$$
$$red\_fruit \leftarrow cherry\,,$$
$$yellow\_fruit \leftarrow banana\,.$$

Then, P_2 is more informative than P_1 in the sense that both *cherry* and *strawberry* provide further restrictions on the contents by ruling out the possibility of *yellow_fruit* as well as other *red_fruit* like *apple*, for example. We will represent this situation as $P_2 \models^\sharp P_1$ meaning that, for each answer set S of P_2, there is an answer set T of P_1 such that $T \subseteq S$. The relation $\models^\sharp$ is called the *Smyth ordering*. On the other hand, P_3 is more informative than P_1 in the sense that P_3 provides a further enumeration of positive assertions which does not rule out the possibility of *purple_fruit* like *grape*, for example. We will represent this situation as $P_3 \models^\flat P_1$ meaning that, for each answer set T of P_1, there is an answer set S of P_3 such that $T \subseteq S$. The relation $\models^\flat$ is called the *Hoare ordering*. Then, both a minimal upper bound and a maximal lower bound are constructed for any pair of logic programs with respect to each generality ordering. We will also relate these two generality orderings with the generality relations with respect to skeptical and credulous entailment, respectively. Furthermore, we will introduce the concept of *strong generality* between logic programs and investigate its relationship to *strong equivalence* [6].

The rest of this paper is organized as follows. After introducing basic concepts of answer set programming and domain theory, Section 2 presents a theory of generality in logic programs. Section 3 examines minimal upper and maximal lower bounds of logic programs with respect to generality orderings, and discusses how to compute logic programs whose answer sets exactly correspond to those bounds. Section 4 relates the generality relations with skeptical and credulous entailment in answer set programming. Section 5 defines the notion of strong generality and relates it with strong equivalence of logic programs. Section 6 discusses applications of generality relations to *inductive logic programming* and *multi-agent systems* as well as related work.

2 Generality Relations over Answer Sets

2.1 Extended Disjunctive Programs

A *program* considered in this paper is an *extended disjunctive program* (EDP) which is a set of *rules* of the form:

$$L_1 ; \cdots ; L_l \leftarrow L_{l+1}, \ldots, L_m, \textit{not } L_{m+1}, \ldots, \textit{not } L_n \quad (n \geq m \geq l \geq 0) \quad (1)$$

where each L_i is a literal, *not* is *negation as failure* (NAF), and ";" represents disjunction. The left-hand side of a rule is the *head*, and the right-hand side is the *body*. A rule is *disjunctive* if its head contains more than one literal. A rule is an *integrity constraint* if its head is empty, and is a *fact* if its body is empty. An EDP is called an *extended logic program* (ELP) if $l \leq 1$ for each rule (1). A program is *NAF-free* if every rule contains no *not*, i.e., $m = n$ for each rule (1). A program with variables is semantically identified with its ground instantiation.

In this paper, we consider the *answer set semantics* for EDPs [3]. Let *Lit* be the set of all ground literals in the language of programs. A set $S (\subseteq \textit{Lit})$ *satisfies* a ground rule of the form (1) if $\{L_{l+1}, \ldots, L_m\} \subseteq S$ and $\{L_{m+1}, \ldots, L_n\} \cap S = \emptyset$ imply $L_i \in S$ for some i $(1 \leq i \leq l)$. Let P be an NAF-free EDP. Then, a set $S(\subseteq \textit{Lit})$ is an *answer set* of P if S is a minimal set such that

1. S satisfies every rule from the ground instantiation of P,
2. $S = \textit{Lit}$ if S contains a pair of *complementary literals*, L and $\neg L$.

Next, let P be any EDP and $S \subseteq \textit{Lit}$. For every rule of the form (1) in the ground instantiation of P, the rule $L_1 ; \cdots ; L_l \leftarrow L_{l+1}, \ldots, L_m$ is included in the

NAF-free program P^S iff $\{L_{m+1}, \ldots, L_n\} \cap S = \emptyset$. Then, S is an *answer set* of P if S is an answer set of P^S. The set of all answer sets of P is written as $A(P)$. An answer set is *consistent* if it is not *Lit*. A program P is *consistent* if it has a consistent answer set; otherwise, P is *inconsistent*. An inconsistent program is called *contradictory* if it has the single answer set *Lit*, and is called *incoherent* if it has no answer set.

We will see that the following two notions of equivalence are important to develop a theory of generality in answer set programming.

Definition 2.1. Let P and Q be programs. P and Q are *weakly equivalent* if $A(P) = A(Q)$ holds. On the other hand, P and Q are *strongly equivalent* [6] if for any logic program R, $A(P \cup R) = A(Q \cup R)$ holds.

For example, $P = \{p \leftarrow not\,q, \quad q \leftarrow not\,p\}$ and $Q = \{p; q \leftarrow \}$ are weakly equivalent, but not strongly equivalent.

2.2 Ordering on Powersets

We first recall some mathematical definitions about domains [4]. A *pre-order* $\sqsubseteq$ is a binary relation which is reflexive and transitive. A pre-order $\sqsubseteq$ is a *partial order* if it is also anti-symmetric. A *pre-ordered set* (resp. *partially ordered set*; *poset*) is a set D with a pre-order (resp. partial order) $\sqsubseteq$ on D.

For any pre-ordered set $\langle D, \sqsubseteq \rangle$, a poset is induced over the equivalence classes of D. That is, for any element $X \in D$, define the equivalence class as

$$[X] = \{Y \in D \mid Y \sqsubseteq X, \ X \sqsubseteq Y\}.$$

The equivalence relation partitions D into a set of disjoint equivalence classes. Introducing the relation $\preceq$ on the set of these equivalence classes as:

$$[X] \preceq [Y] \quad \text{if} \ \ X \sqsubseteq Y,$$

the relation $\preceq$ becomes a partial order on the set.

For any set D, let $\mathcal{P}(D)$ be the powerset of D. Given a poset $\langle D, \sqsubseteq \rangle$ and $X, Y \in \mathcal{P}(D)$, the *Smyth order* is defined as

$$X \models^\sharp Y \quad \text{iff} \ \ \forall x \in X \, \exists y \in Y. \, y \sqsubseteq x \,,$$

and the *Hoare order* is defined as

$$X \models^\flat Y \quad \text{iff} \ \ \forall y \in Y \, \exists x \in X. \, y \sqsubseteq x \,.$$

The relations $\models^\sharp$ and $\models^\flat$ are pre-orders on $\mathcal{P}(D)$. Note that the orderings $\models^\sharp$ and $\models^\flat$ are slightly different from the standard ones: we allow the empty set $\emptyset \ (\in \mathcal{P}(D))$ as the top element $\top^\sharp$ in $\langle \mathcal{P}(D), \models^\sharp \rangle$ and the bottom element $\bot^\flat$ in $\langle \mathcal{P}(D), \models^\flat \rangle$. This is because we will associate $\emptyset$ with the class of incoherent programs so that we enable comparison of all classes of EDPs.

Example 2.1. Consider the poset $\langle \mathcal{P}(\{p, q\}), \subseteq \rangle$. Then, we have $\{\{p, q\}\} \models^\sharp \{\{p\}\}$ and $\{\{p\}\} \models^\sharp \{\{p\}, \{q\}\}$, and hence $\{\{p, q\}\} \models^\sharp \{\{p\}, \{q\}\}$. On the other hand, $\{\{p, q\}\} \models^\flat \{\{p\}, \{q\}\}$ but $\{\{p\}, \{q\}\} \models^\flat \{\{p\}\}$. Note that both $\{\emptyset, \{p\}\} \models^\sharp \{\emptyset, \{q\}\}$ and $\{\emptyset, \{q\}\} \models^\sharp \{\emptyset, \{p\}\}$ hold, indicating that $\models^\sharp$ is not a partial order.

In the following, we assume a poset $\langle D, \sqsubseteq \rangle$ such that the domain $D = \mathcal{P}(Lit)$ is the family of subsets of Lit, i.e., the class of sets of literals in the language and the partial-order $\sqsubseteq$ is the subset relation $\subseteq$. Then, the Smyth and Hoare orderings are defined on $\mathcal{P}(\mathcal{P}(Lit))$, which enables us to order sets of literals or sets of answer sets. In particular, both $\langle \mathcal{P}(\mathcal{P}(Lit)), \models^\sharp \rangle$ and $\langle \mathcal{P}(\mathcal{P}(Lit)), \models^\flat \rangle$ are pre-ordered sets. Moreover, if we associate an EDP P with its set of answer sets $A(P)$, the ordering on the EDPs becomes possible as follows.

Definition 2.2. Given the poset $\langle \mathcal{P}(Lit), \subseteq \rangle$ and two programs P, Q that are constructed in the same language with Lit, we define:

$$P \models^\sharp Q \quad \text{if} \quad A(P) \models^\sharp A(Q),$$
$$P \models^\flat Q \quad \text{if} \quad A(P) \models^\flat A(Q).$$

We say that P is *more $\sharp$-general* (resp. *more $\flat$-general*) than Q if $P \models^\sharp Q$ (resp. $P \models^\flat Q$).

Intuitively, $\sharp$-generality and $\flat$-generality reflect the following situations. $P \models^\sharp Q$ means that any answer set of P is more (or equally) informative than some answer set of Q. On the other hand, $P \models^\flat Q$ means that any answer set of Q is less (or equally) informative than some answer set of P. When both P and Q have single answer sets, it is obvious that $P \models^\sharp Q$ iff $P \models^\flat Q$. The notion of $\sharp$-generality has been introduced in [5] such that Q is defined to be *weaker* than P if $P \models^\sharp Q$, although properties of this ordering have never been deeply investigated so far.

Both $\sharp$-generality and $\flat$-generality are naturally connected to the notion of weak equivalence in answer set programming.

Theorem 2.1. *Let P and Q be EDPs. Then, the following three are equivalent:*

(1) $P \models^\sharp Q$ *and* $Q \models^\sharp P$;
(2) $P \models^\flat Q$ *and* $Q \models^\flat P$;
(3) P *and* Q *are weakly equivalent.*

Proof. We prove (1)$\Leftrightarrow$(3) but (2)$\Leftrightarrow$(3) can be proved in the same way.

$P \models^\sharp Q$ and $Q \models^\sharp P$
iff $\forall S \in A(P) \exists T \in A(Q). T \subseteq S$ and $\forall T \in A(Q) \exists S \in A(P). S \subseteq T$
iff $\forall S \in A(P) \exists T \in A(Q) \exists S' \in A(P). S' \subseteq T \subseteq S$ and $\forall T \in A(Q) \exists S \in A(P) \exists T' \in A(Q). T' \subseteq S \subseteq T$
iff $\forall S \in A(P) \exists T \in A(Q). T = S$ and $\forall T \in A(Q) \exists S \in A(P). S = T$ (because for any two answer sets $S, T \in A(P)$, $S \subseteq T$ implies $S = T$ by the fact that $A(P)$ is an anti-chain on the poset $\langle \mathcal{P}(Lit), \subseteq \rangle$)
iff $\forall S \in A(P). S \in A(Q)$ and $\forall T \in A(Q). T \in A(P)$
iff $A(P) \subseteq A(Q)$ and $A(Q) \subseteq A(P)$ iff $A(P) = A(Q)$. $\qquad \square$

By Theorem 2.1, for any EDP P, every EDP in the equivalence class $[P]$ induced by the pre-order $\models^\sharp$ or $\models^\flat$ is weakly equivalent to P.

Example 2.2. Consider the following programs:

$$P_1 : p \leftarrow not\, q,$$
$$P_2 : p \leftarrow not\, q,$$
$$q \leftarrow not\, p,$$
$$P_3 : p\,;\, q \leftarrow ,$$
$$P_4 : p\,;\, q \leftarrow ,$$
$$p \leftarrow q,$$
$$q \leftarrow p.$$

Then, $P_4 \models^\sharp P_1 \models^\sharp P_2$, and $P_4 \models^\flat P_2 \models^\flat P_1$ (see Example 2.1). P_2 and P_3 are weakly equivalent, and thus $P_2 \models^\sharp P_3 \models^\sharp P_2$ and $P_2 \models^\flat P_3 \models^\flat P_2$.

3   Minimal Upper and Maximal Lower Bounds

In this section, we show that both a minimal upper bound and a maximal lower bound of any pair of logic programs exist with respect to generality orderings, and discuss how to compute logic programs whose answer sets exactly correspond to those bounds. Those bounds are important in the theory of generalization and specialization in inductive logic programming [10]. In the following, let $\mathcal{EDP}$ be the class of all EDPs which can be constructed in the language.

Proposition 3.1. *Both $\langle \mathcal{EDP}, \models^\sharp \rangle$ and $\langle \mathcal{EDP}, \models^\flat \rangle$ are pre-ordered sets.*

For notational convenience, we denote the $\sharp$- or $\flat$-generality relation as $\models^{\sharp/\flat}$ when distinction between $\sharp$- and $\flat$-general orderings is not important. In what follows, we consider the problem to find a *minimal upper bound* (mub) and a *maximal lower bound* (mlb) of given two programs P_1 and P_2. Because $\langle \mathcal{EDP}, \models^{\sharp/\flat} \rangle$ is only a pre-ordered set, there is no unique minimal/maximal bound in general. In Section 3.2, however, it is shown that the *least upper bound* (lub) and the *greatest lower bound* (glb) can be constructed for the equivalence classes $[P_1]$ and $[P_2]$ under these orderings.

3.1   Mub and Mlb in Smyth and Hoare Orderings

In this section, we suppose that $P_1, P_2 \in \mathcal{EDP}$.

Definition 3.1. A program $Q \in \mathcal{EDP}$ is an *upper bound* of P_1 and P_2 in $\langle \mathcal{EDP}, \models^{\sharp/\flat} \rangle$ if $Q \models^{\sharp/\flat} P_1$ and $Q \models^{\sharp/\flat} P_2$. An upper bound Q is an *mub* of P_1 and P_2 in $\langle \mathcal{EDP}, \models^{\sharp/\flat} \rangle$ if for any upper bound Q', $Q \models^{\sharp/\flat} Q'$ implies $Q' \models^{\sharp/\flat} Q$.

On the other hand, $Q \in \mathcal{EDP}$ is a *lower bound* of P_1 and P_2 in $\langle \mathcal{EDP}, \models^{\sharp/\flat} \rangle$ if $P_1 \models^{\sharp/\flat} Q$ and $P_2 \models^{\sharp/\flat} Q$. A lower bound Q is an *mlb* of P_1 and P_2 in $\langle \mathcal{EDP}, \models^{\sharp/\flat} \rangle$ if for any lower bound Q', $Q' \models^{\sharp/\flat} Q$ implies $Q \models^{\sharp/\flat} Q'$.

In the following, for any set X, let $min(X) = \{\, x \in X \mid \neg \exists y \in X.\, y \subset x \,\}$ and $max(X) = \{\, x \in X \mid \neg \exists y \in X.\, x \subset y \,\}$. We often denote $min\, X$ and $max\, X$ by omitting (). For two sets of literals $S, T \subseteq Lit$, we define

$$S \uplus T = \begin{cases} S \cup T, & \text{if } S \cup T \text{ does not contain a pair of complementary literals;} \\ Lit, & \text{otherwise.} \end{cases}$$

Theorem 3.1. (1) *An EDP Q is an mub of P_1 and P_2 in $\langle \mathcal{EDP}, \models^\sharp \rangle$ iff*

$$A(Q) = min\{\, S \uplus T \mid S \in A(P_1),\ T \in A(P_2) \,\}.$$

(2) *An EDP Q is an mlb of P_1 and P_2 in $\langle \mathcal{EDP}, \models^\sharp \rangle$ iff*

$$A(Q) = min(A(P_1) \cup A(P_2)).$$

(3) *An EDP Q is an mub of P_1 and P_2 in $\langle \mathcal{EDP}, \models^\flat \rangle$ iff*

$$A(Q) = max(A(P_1) \cup A(P_2)).$$

(4) *An EDP Q is an mlb of P_1 and P_2 in $\langle \mathcal{EDP}, \models^\flat \rangle$ iff*

$$A(Q) = max\{\, S \cap T \mid S \in A(P_1),\ T \in A(P_2) \,\}.$$

Proof. Because of the space limitation, we prove (1) and (2) only, but the proof of (3) and (4) can be constructed in a similar way to that of (2) and (1), respectively.

(1) Q is an upper bound of P_1 and P_2 in $\langle \mathcal{EDP}, \models^\sharp \rangle$ iff $Q \models^\sharp P_1$ and $Q \models^\sharp P_2$ iff $\forall S \in A(Q)\, \exists T_1 \in A(P_1).\, T_1 \subseteq S$ and $\forall S \in A(Q)\, \exists T_2 \in A(P_2).\, T_2 \subseteq S$ iff $\forall S \in A(Q)\, \exists T_1 \in A(P_1)\, \exists T_2 \in A(P_2).\, T_1 \cup T_2 \subseteq S.$ (*)

Now, suppose that $A(Q)$ is given as $min\{T_1 \uplus T_2 \mid T_1 \in A(P_1),\ T_2 \in A(P_2)\}$. This Q is an upper bound of P_1 and P_2 because (*) is satisfied. If Q is contradictory, then $A(Q) = \{Lit\}$. Then, for any $T_1 \in A(P_1)$ and any $T_2 \in A(P_2)$, $T_1 \uplus T_2 = Lit$, that is, $T_1 \cup T_2$ is inconsistent. In this case, Q is an mub. Else if Q is incoherent, then $A(Q) = \emptyset$. Then, for any $T_1 \in A(P_1)$ and any $T_2 \in A(P_2)$, $T_1 \uplus T_2$ is undefined, and thus, $A(P_1) = \emptyset$ or $A(P_2) = \emptyset$. That is, either P_1 or P_2 is incoherent. In this case, Q is an mub too.

Next, consider the case that Q is consistent. Suppose further that Q is not an mub. Then, there is $Q' \in \mathcal{EDP}$ such that (i) Q' is an upper bound of P_1 and P_2, (ii) $Q \models^\sharp Q'$, and (iii) $Q' \not\models^\sharp Q$. Here, (ii) and (iii) imply that $A(Q) \neq A(Q')$ by Theorem 2.1. Because $A(Q) \neq \{Lit\}$, it holds that, for any $S \in A(Q)$, $S = T_1 \uplus T_2 = T_1 \cup T_2$ for some $T_1 \in A(P_1)$ and $T_2 \in A(P_2)$. For this S, there is an answer set $S' \in A(Q')$ such that $S' \subseteq S$ by (ii) and that $S' = T_3 \cup T_4$ for some $T_3 \in A(P_1)$ and $T_4 \in A(P_2)$ by (i) and (*). Hence, $T_3 \cup T_4 \subseteq T_1 \cup T_2$. By the minimality of $A(Q)$ with respect to the operation min, it must be $T_3 \cup T_4 = T_1 \cup T_2$, and thus $S' = S$. Hence, $A(Q) \subseteq A(Q')$. By $A(Q) \neq A(Q')$, there is $U \in A(Q')$ such that $U \notin A(Q)$. Again, $U = T' \cup T''$ for some $T' \in A(P_1)$ and $T'' \in A(P_2)$ by (i) and (*). However, there must be some $V \in A(Q)$ such that $V \subseteq U$ by the construction of $A(Q)$ and the minimality of $A(Q)$ with respect to the operation min. Because $U \notin A(Q)$, $V \subset U$ holds. However, by $Q \models^\sharp Q'$, there is $U' \in A(Q')$ such that $U' \subseteq V$ and hence $U' \subset U$. This contradicts the fact that $A(Q')$ is an anti-chain. Therefore, Q is an mub of P_1 and P_2.

(2) Q is a lower bound of P_1 and P_2 in $\langle \mathcal{EDP}, \models^\sharp \rangle$ iff $P_1 \models^\sharp Q$ and $P_2 \models^\sharp Q$ iff $\forall S \in A(P_1)\, \exists T \in A(Q).\, T \subseteq S$ and $\forall S \in A(P_2)\, \exists T \in A(Q).\, T \subseteq S$ iff $\forall S \in A(P_1) \cup A(P_2)\, \exists T \in A(Q).\, T \subseteq S.$ (**)

Now, suppose that $A(Q) = min(A(P_1) \cup A(P_2))$. This Q is a lower bound of P_1 and P_2 because (**) is satisfied. If Q is contradictory, then $A(Q) = \{Lit\}$ and both P_1 and P_2 are contradictory. In this case, Q is an mlb. Else if Q is incoherent, then $A(Q) = \emptyset$ and both P_1 and P_2 are incoherent. In this case, Q is an mlb too. Else if Q is consistent, suppose further that Q is not an mlb. Then, there is a lower bound $Q' \in \mathcal{EDP}$ of P_1 and P_2 such that $Q' \models^\sharp Q$ and $A(Q) \neq A(Q')$ by the same argument as the proof of (1). By $Q' \models^\sharp Q$, for any $T' \in A(Q')$, there is $T \in A(Q)$ such that $T \subseteq T'$. By this and the fact that Q' is a lower bound of P_1 and P_2, we have that $\forall S \in A(P_1) \cup A(P_2) \, \exists T' \in A(Q') \, \exists T \in A(Q). \, T \subseteq T' \subseteq S$. By the minimality of $A(Q)$ with respect to the operation min, it must be $T' = T$, and thus $A(Q') \subseteq A(Q)$. By $A(Q) \neq A(Q')$, there is $V \in A(Q)$ such that $V \notin A(Q')$. Since $V \in A(P_1) \cup A(P_2)$ by the construction of $A(Q)$, there must be some $U \in A(Q')$ such that $U \subseteq V$ by (**). Because $V \notin A(Q')$, $U \subset V$ holds. However, by $Q' \models^\sharp Q$, there is $V' \in A(Q)$ such that $V' \subseteq U$ and thus $V' \subset V$. This contradicts the fact that $A(Q)$ is an anti-chain. Therefore, Q is an mlb of P_1 and P_2. $\square$

Example 3.1. Consider P_1, P_2 and P_4 in Example 2.2, where $A(P_1) = \{\{p\}\}$, $A(P_2) = \{\{p\}, \{q\}\}$ and $A(P_4) = \{\{p, q\}\}$. Because $P_4 \models^\sharp P_2$, an mub (resp. mlb) of P_2 and P_4 in $\langle \mathcal{EDP}, \models^\sharp \rangle$ is P_4 (resp. P_2). Correspondingly, $min\{T_1 \uplus T_2 \mid T_1 \in A(P_2), \, T_2 \in A(P_4)\} = min\{\{p, q\}\} = A(P_4)$ and $min(A(P_2) \cup A(P_4)) = min\{\{p\}, \{q\}, \{p, q\}\} = \{\{p\}, \{q\}\} = A(P_2)$. Similarly, an mub (resp. mlb) of P_2 and P_4 in $\langle \mathcal{EDP}, \models^\flat \rangle$ is P_4 (resp. P_2). Correspondingly, $max(A(P_2) \cup A(P_4)) = max\{\{p\}, \{q\}, \{p, q\}\} = \{\{p, q\}\} = A(P_4)$ and $max\{T_1 \cap T_2 \mid T_1 \in A(P_2), \, T_2 \in A(P_4)\} = max\{\{q\}, \{p\}\} = A(P_2)$.

Consider further the program $P_5 = \{q \leftarrow not\, p\}$, where $A(P_5) = \{\{q\}\}$. Then, P_4 is an mub of P_1 and P_5 in $\langle \mathcal{EDP}, \models^\sharp \rangle$ because $min\{T_1 \uplus T_2 \mid T_1 \in A(P_1), \, T_2 \in A(P_5)\} = min\{\{p, q\}\} = A(P_4)$. Also, P_2 is an mlb of P_1 and P_5 in $\langle \mathcal{EDP}, \models^\sharp \rangle$ and is an mub of P_1 and P_5 in $\langle \mathcal{EDP}, \models^\flat \rangle$ because $min(A(P_1) \cup A(P_5)) = max(A(P_1) \cup A(P_5)) = \{\{p\}, \{q\}\} = A(P_2)$. Finally, $P_6 = \emptyset$ is an mlb of P_1 and P_5 in $\langle \mathcal{EDP}, \models^\flat \rangle$ because $max\{T_1 \cap T_2 \mid T_1 \in A(P_1), \, T_2 \in A(P_5)\} = max\{\emptyset\} = A(P_6)$.

Note that any contradictory program Q is an mub of $\{p \leftarrow \}$ and $\{\neg p \leftarrow \}$ because $A(Q) = min\{T_1 \uplus T_2 \mid T_1 = \{p\}, \, T_2 = \{\neg p\}\} = min\{Lit\} = \{Lit\}$.

3.2   Lub and Glb on Equivalence Classes

Now, we can construct a poset from the pre-order set $\langle \mathcal{EDP}, \models^{\sharp/\flat} \rangle$ in the usual way as follows. For any program $P \in \mathcal{EDP}$, consider the equivalence class:

$$[P] = \{Q \in \mathcal{EDP} \mid A(Q) = A(P)\},$$

and then define the relation $\succeq^\sharp$ as:

$$[P] \succeq^\sharp [Q] \quad \text{if} \quad P \models^\sharp Q.$$

We denote the equivalence classes from $\langle \mathcal{EDP}, \models^\sharp \rangle$ as $\mathbf{P}^\sharp$. The relation $\succeq^\flat$ and the equivalence classes $\mathbf{P}^\flat$ are defined in the same way, and we write $\succeq^{\sharp/\flat}$ and

$\mathbf{P}^{\sharp/\flat}$ to represent two cases together. Then, the relation $\succeq^{\sharp/\flat}$ is a partial order on $\mathbf{P}^{\sharp/\flat}$.

Proposition 3.2. *The poset* $\langle \mathbf{P}^{\sharp/\flat}, \succeq^{\sharp/\flat} \rangle$ *constitutes a complete lattice.*

Proof. We prove for $\langle \mathbf{P}^{\sharp}, \succeq^{\sharp} \rangle$. For EDPs P_1 and P_2, consider an EDP P_3 such that $A(P_3) = min\{S \uplus T \mid S \in A(P_1),\ T \in A(P_2)\}$. Then, $[P_3]$ becomes the lub of $[P_1]$ and $[P_2]$ by Theorem 3.1 (1). On the other hand, let P_4 be an EDP such that $A(P_4) = min(A(P_1) \cup A(P_2))$. Then, $[P_4]$ becomes the glb of $[P_1]$ and $[P_2]$ by Theorem 3.1 (2). The top element $\top^{\sharp}$ of $\langle \mathbf{P}^{\sharp}, \succeq^{\sharp} \rangle$ is the class of incoherent EDPs and the bottom element $\bot^{\sharp}$ of $\langle \mathbf{P}^{\sharp}, \succeq^{\sharp} \rangle$ is $[\emptyset]$.

The result for $\langle \mathbf{P}^{\flat}, \succeq^{\flat} \rangle$ can be shown in a similar manner except that the top element $\top^{\flat}$ of $\langle \mathbf{P}^{\flat}, \succeq^{\flat} \rangle$ is the class of contradictory EDPs and the bottom element $\bot^{\flat}$ of $\langle \mathbf{P}^{\flat}, \succeq^{\flat} \rangle$ is the class of incoherent EDPs.   □

3.3 Computing Mubs and Mlbs

Theorem 3.1 presents that, given two EDPs P_1 and P_2, there are mubs and mlbs of P_1 and P_2 in $\langle \mathcal{EDP}, \models^{\sharp/\flat} \rangle$. We briefly discuss how to actually construct those EDPs whose answer sets are given as such in a finite domain.

Incidentally, composing programs corresponding to the four cases in Theorem 3.1 has been studied in a series of work by Sakama and Inoue [13,14,15]. In [13], both a program Q such that $A(Q) = A(P_1) \cup A(P_2)$ and a program R such that $A(R) = A(P_1) \cap A(P_2)$ have been composed, where Q is called *generous coordination* of P_1 and P_2 and R is called *rigorous coordination* of P_1 and P_2. Thus, Theorem 3.1 (2) and (3) correspond to generous coordination. On the other hand, [14] produces *composition* of P_1 and P_2, which is a program Q whose answer sets are exactly given as $min\{T_1 \uplus T_2 \mid T_1 \in A(P_1),\ T_2 \in A(P_2)\}$ in Theorem 3.1 (1). The final case (4) in Theorem 3.1 is considered in [15] as *maximal consensus* among P_1 and P_2. The algorithms in [13,14,15] compose such EDPs in time polynomial to the numbers of answer sets and rules in two programs.

There is also a direct and exponential-time algorithm to construct a program that has exactly the given collection of answer sets. Given a set of answer sets $\{S_1, \ldots, S_m\}$, first compute the disjunctive normal form (DNF) $S_1 \vee \cdots \vee S_m$, then convert it into the conjunctive normal form (CNF) $R_1 \wedge \cdots \wedge R_n$. The set of facts $\{R_1 \leftarrow, \ldots, R_n \leftarrow \}$ then has the answer sets $\{S_1, \ldots, S_m\}$. This DNF-CNF transformation produces disjunctive facts only. This is the case even that the given two programs are ELPs, i.e., programs with no disjunction. Technically, the resulting program P is *head-cycle-free*, that is, it contains no positive cycle through disjuncts appearing in the head of a disjunctive rule [1]. Then, P can be converted to an ELP by shifting disjuncts in the head of a rule to the body as NAF-literals in every possible way as leaving one in the head.

4   Generality Relations Relative to Entailment

In traditional studies on generality in first-order clausal theories, the amount of information brought by a program has been measured by the set of logical formulas entailed by the program. That is, given two monotonic programs P and Q, P is considered more general than Q if P logically entails more formulas than Q [8]. On the other hand, we have defined the two notions of generality for nonmonotonic programs in terms of answer sets. Here, we will connect the generality relations over answer sets with skeptical and credulous entailment in answer set programming. As a result, we will see that our notions of two generality orderings are also reasonable from the viewpoint of entailment relations.

We first review skeptical and credulous entailment in answer set programming.

Definition 4.1. Let P be a program and L a literal. Then, L is a *skeptical consequence* of P if L is included in every answer set of P. L is a *credulous consequence* of P if L is included in some answer set of P. The set of skeptical (resp. credulous) consequences of P is denoted as $skp(P)$ (resp. $crd(P)$).

Proposition 4.1. *If P is a consistent program, then*

$$skp(P) = \bigcap_{S \in A(P)} S, \qquad crd(P) = \bigcup_{S \in A(P)} S.$$

If P is incoherent, then $skp(P) = Lit$ and $crd(P) = \emptyset$. If P is contradictory, then $skp(P) = crd(P) = Lit$.

Example 4.1. Consider P_2 and P_4 in Example 2.2, where $A(P_2) = \{\{p\}, \{q\}\}$ and $A(P_4) = \{\{p, q\}\}$. Then, $crd(P_2) = crd(P_4) = skp(P_4) = \{p, q\}$, and $skp(P_2) = \emptyset$.

The orderings relative to skeptical and credulous entailment relations between two programs are defined as follows.

Definition 4.2. Let P and Q be EDPs. Then, we write:

$$P \models_{skp} Q \ \text{ if } \ skp(Q) \subseteq skp(P),$$
$$P \models_{crd} Q \ \text{ if } \ crd(Q) \subseteq crd(P).$$

We say P is *more general than Q under skeptical entailment* if $P \models_{skp} Q$. Likewise, P is *more general than Q under credulous entailment* if $P \models_{crd} Q$.

For notational convenience, we write $P \models_{s/c} Q$ when distinction between skeptical and credulous entailment is not important.

Proposition 4.2. *The relation $\models_{s/c}$ is a pre-order on $\mathcal{EDP}$.*

As in the case of $\sharp/\flat$-generality relations, the pre-order set $\langle \mathcal{EDP}, \models_{s/c} \rangle$ is turned into a poset as follows. For any program $P \in \mathcal{EDP}$ and the equivalence class

$$[P]_s = \{ Q \in \mathcal{EDP} \mid P \models_{skp} Q, \ Q \models_{skp} P \},$$

we define

$$[P]_s \succeq_{skp} [Q]_s \ \text{ if } \ P \models_{skp} Q,$$

and denote the equivalence classes from $\langle \mathcal{EDP}, \models_{skp} \rangle$ as $\mathbf{P}_{skp}$. The relation $\succeq_{crd}$ and the equivalence classes $\mathbf{P}_{crd}$ are defined in the same way, and we write $\succeq_{s/c}$ and $\mathbf{P}_{s/c}$ to represent two cases together. Then, the relation $\succeq_{s/c}$ is a partial order on $\mathbf{P}_{s/c}$.

Proposition 4.3. *The poset* $\langle \mathbf{P}_{s/c}, \succeq_{s/c} \rangle$ *constitutes a complete lattice.*

Proof. We prove for $\langle \mathbf{P}_{skp}, \succeq_{skp} \rangle$. The result for $\langle \mathbf{P}_{crd}, \succeq_{crd} \rangle$ is shown in a similar manner. For programs P_1 and P_2, there is a program P_3 such that $skp(P_3) = skp(P_1) \cup skp(P_2)$. (An instance of such a program is $P_3 = \{ L \leftarrow \ | \ L \in skp(P_1) \cup skp(P_2) \}$.) Then, $[P_3]_s$ becomes the lub of $[P_1]_s$ and $[P_2]_s$. On the other hand, for programs P_1 and P_2, there is a program P_4 such that $skp(P_4) = skp(P_1) \cap skp(P_2)$. Then, $[P_4]_s$ becomes the glb of $[P_1]_s$ and $[P_2]_s$. The top element of $\langle \mathbf{P}_{skp}, \succeq_{skp} \rangle$ is the class of incoherent EDPs and the bottom element of $\langle \mathbf{P}_{skp}, \succeq_{skp} \rangle$ is $[\emptyset]$. $\qquad\square$

Now, we relate the $\sharp$- and $\flat$-generality relations with the generality relations under skeptical and credulous entailment.

Theorem 4.1. *Let P and Q be EDPs. Then, the following two hold.*

(1) *If $P \models^{\sharp} Q$ then $P \models_{skp} Q$.*
(2) *If $P \models^{\flat} Q$ then $P \models_{crd} Q$.*

Proof. (1) Assume that $P \models^{\sharp} Q$. If P is inconsistent, then $skp(P) = Lit$ and thus $P \models_{skp} Q$. Suppose that P is consistent and $L \in skp(Q)$. Then, $L \in T$ for every answer set $T \in A(Q)$. By $P \models^{\sharp} Q$, for any $S \in A(P)$, there is an answer set $T' \in A(Q)$ such that $T' \subseteq S$. Since $L \in T'$, $L \in S$ too. That is, $L \in skp(P)$. Hence, $P \models_{skp} Q$.

(2) Assume that $P \models^{\flat} Q$. If P is incoherent, then P is in the bottom element of $\langle \mathbf{P}^{\flat}, \succeq^{\flat} \rangle$, and hence Q is too. Then, $crd(P) = crd(Q) = \emptyset$ and thus $P \models_{crd} Q$. Else if P is contradictory, then $crd(P) = Lit$ and thus $P \models_{crd} Q$. Suppose that P is consistent and $L \in crd(Q)$. Then, $L \in T$ for some answer set $T \in A(Q)$. By $P \models^{\flat} Q$, there is an answer set $S \in A(P)$ such that $T \subseteq S$. Hence, $L \in S$ and thus $L \in crd(P)$. That is, $P \models_{crd} Q$. $\qquad\square$

Theorem 4.1 tells us that, (1) the more $\sharp$-general a program is, the more it entails skeptically, and that (2) the more $\flat$-general a program is, the more it entails credulously. That is, the Smyth and Hoare orderings over programs reflect the amount of information by skeptical and credulous entailment, respectively. The converse of each property in Theorem 4.1 does not hold in general.

Example 4.2. For Example 4.1, $P_4 \models^{\sharp} P_2$ and $P_4 \models^{\flat} P_2$. Correspondingly, $skp(P_2) \subset skp(P_4)$ and $crd(P_2) = crd(P_4)$, which verify Theorem 4.1.

On the other hand, $crd(P_2) = crd(P_4)$ also implies $P_2 \models_{crd} P_4$, but $P_2 \not\models^{\flat} P_4$. Similarly, for the program $P_6 = \emptyset$, we have $skp(P_6) = \emptyset = skp(P_2)$. Then, $P_6 \models_{skp} P_2$, but $P_6 \not\models^{\sharp} P_2$.

By Theorem 4.1, the relation $\models^{\sharp/\flat}$ is a *refinement* of the relation $\models_{s/c}$, respectively. Comparing these two kinds of ordering relations, we claim that $\models^{\sharp/\flat}$ is more useful than $\models_{s/c}$ as generality criteria. This is because each equivalence class $[P] \in \mathbf{P}^{\sharp/\flat}$ is the set of programs which are weakly equivalent to P (Theorem 2.1), although there is no such a simple property for the equivalence classes $\mathbf{P}_{s/c}$. For Example 4.2, $crd(P_2) = crd(P_4)$ but $A(P_2) \neq A(P_4)$, and $skp(P_2) = skp(P_6)$ but $A(P_2) \neq A(P_6)$.

The next theorem presents interesting relationships between mubs/mlbs under the generality $\models^{\sharp/\flat}$ and skeptical/credulous entailment.

Lemma 4.1. *Let P_1 and P_2 be EDPs.*

(1) *If Q is an mub of P_1 and P_2 in $\langle \mathcal{EDP}, \models^{\sharp} \rangle$ then $skp(Q) = skp(P_1) \uplus skp(P_2)$.*
(2) *If Q is an mlb of P_1 and P_2 in $\langle \mathcal{EDP}, \models^{\sharp} \rangle$ then $skp(Q) = skp(P_1) \cap skp(P_2)$.*
(3) *If Q is an mub of P_1 and P_2 in $\langle \mathcal{EDP}, \models^{\flat} \rangle$ then $crd(Q) = crd(P_1) \cup crd(P_2)$.*
(4) *If Q is an mlb of P_1 and P_2 in $\langle \mathcal{EDP}, \models^{\flat} \rangle$ then $crd(Q) = crd(P_1) \cap crd(P_2)$.*

Proof. An mub/mlb of two programs under each ordering is given by Theorem 3.1. Then, (1) can be proved by [14, Proposition 3.5(2)], (2) can be proved by [13, Proposition 3.1-1(b)], (3) can be proved by [13, Proposition 3.1-1(a)], and (4) can be proved by [15, Proposition 5(3)]. □

Theorem 4.2. *Let P_1 and P_2 be EDPs.*

(1) *An mub of P_1 and P_2 in $\langle \mathcal{EDP}, \models^{\sharp} \rangle$ is an mub of P_1 and P_2 in $\langle \mathcal{EDP}, \models_{skp} \rangle$.*
(2) *An mlb of P_1 and P_2 in $\langle \mathcal{EDP}, \models^{\sharp} \rangle$ is an mlb of P_1 and P_2 in $\langle \mathcal{EDP}, \models_{skp} \rangle$.*
(3) *An mub of P_1 and P_2 in $\langle \mathcal{EDP}, \models^{\flat} \rangle$ is an mub of P_1 and P_2 in $\langle \mathcal{EDP}, \models_{crd} \rangle$.*
(4) *An mlb of P_1 and P_2 in $\langle \mathcal{EDP}, \models^{\flat} \rangle$ is an mlb of P_1 and P_2 in $\langle \mathcal{EDP}, \models_{crd} \rangle$.*

Proof. Each mub/mlb of P_1 and P_2 in $\langle \mathcal{EDP}, \models_{s/c} \rangle$ satisfies each equation (1) to (4) in Lemma 4.1. Then each property holds by Lemma 4.1. □

5   Strong Generality Relations over Logic Programs

In the previous sections, we have seen that the relation $\models^{\sharp/\flat}$ is useful for determining the degree of generality of EDPs. However, because $\sharp/\flat$-generality is determined solely by the answer sets of each program, sometimes the criteria is not suitable for applications in dynamic domains. For example, for ELPs $P = \{p \leftarrow not\, q\}$ and $Q = \{p \leftarrow q\}$, we have $P \models^{\sharp} Q$. Then, adding $R = \{q \leftarrow \}$ to both programs makes the results in reverse order, i.e., $Q \cup R \models^{\sharp} P \cup R$. In this section, we will thus introduce context-sensitive notions of generality.

Definition 5.1. Let P and Q be programs. P is *strongly more $\sharp$-general than Q* (written $P \trianglerighteq^{\sharp} Q$) if $P \cup R \models^{\sharp} Q \cup R$ for any program R. Similarly, P is *strongly more $\flat$-general than Q* (written $P \trianglerighteq^{\flat} Q$) if $P \cup R \models^{\flat} Q \cup R$ for any program R.

We write $\trianglerighteq^{\sharp/\flat}$ to represent both $\trianglerighteq^{\sharp}$ and $\trianglerighteq^{\flat}$ together. It is easy to see that strong $\sharp/\flat$-generality implies $\sharp/\flat$-generality.

Proposition 5.1. *Let P and Q be EDPs. If $P \trianglerighteq^{\sharp/\flat} Q$ then $P \models^{\sharp/\flat} Q$.*

Strong $\sharp/\flat$-generality can be contrasted with the notion of strong equivalence [6] in answer set programming. In fact, we have the following correspondence between strong generality and strong equivalence.

Theorem 5.1. *Let P and Q be EDPs. Then, the following three are equivalent:*

(1) $P \trianglerighteq^{\sharp} Q$ and $Q \trianglerighteq^{\sharp} P$;

(2) $P \trianglerighteq^{\flat} Q$ and $Q \trianglerighteq^{\flat} P$;

(3) P and Q are strongly equivalent.

Proof. $P \trianglerighteq^{\sharp/\flat} Q$ and $Q \trianglerighteq^{\sharp/\flat} P$

iff $P \cup R \models^{\sharp/\flat} Q \cup R$ and $Q \cup R \models^{\sharp/\flat} P \cup R$ for any program R

iff $P \cup R$ and $Q \cup R$ are weakly equivalent for any program R (by Theorem 2.1)

iff P and Q are strongly equivalent.   □

Example 5.1. Consider the four EDPs in Example 2.2. Then, $P_1 \trianglerighteq^{\sharp} P_2 \trianglerighteq^{\sharp} P_3$ holds. However, $P_4 \ntrianglerighteq^{\sharp} P_1$ (take $R = \{ q \leftarrow p \}$ then $P_1 \cup R$ is incoherent while $P_4 \cup R = P_4$, hence $P_4 \cup R \nmodels^{\sharp} P_1 \cup R$), $P_4 \ntrianglerighteq^{\sharp} P_2$ (take $R' = \{ q \leftarrow p, \ p \leftarrow q \}$ then $P_2 \cup R'$ is incoherent while $P_4 \cup R' = P_4$, hence $P_4 \cup R' \nmodels^{\sharp} P_2 \cup R'$), $P_3 \ntrianglerighteq^{\sharp} P_2$ (take R' above then $P_2 \cup R'$ is incoherent while $P_3 \cup R'$ is consistent, hence $P_3 \cup R' \nmodels^{\sharp} P_2 \cup R'$), and $P_4 \ntrianglerighteq^{\sharp} P_3$ (take $R'' = \{ \ \leftarrow not\, p, \ \ \leftarrow not\, q \}$ then $P_3 \cup R''$ is incoherent while $P_4 \cup R''$ is consistent, hence $P_4 \cup R'' \nmodels^{\sharp} P_3 \cup R''$).

On the other hand, $P_3 \trianglerighteq^{\flat} P_2 \trianglerighteq^{\flat} P_1$ holds under the relation $\trianglerighteq^{\flat}$.

In Example 5.1, the two weakly equivalent programs P_2 and P_3 are not strongly equivalent, and then $P_2 \trianglerighteq^{\sharp} P_3$ but $P_3 \ntrianglerighteq^{\sharp} P_2$. This fact can be intuitively explained as follows. $P_2 = \{ p \leftarrow not\, q, \ q \leftarrow not\, p \}$ is more informative than $P_3 = \{ p; q \leftarrow \ \}$ in the sense that the derivation of p (or q) depends on the absence of q (or p) in P_2. However, no such information is obtained in P_3 so that we have a chance to extend the contents by adding $R' = \{ q \leftarrow p, \ p \leftarrow q \}$ to P_3, which is impossible for P_2. On the other hand, under the relation $\trianglerighteq^{\flat}$, we have $P_3 \trianglerighteq^{\flat} P_2$ but $P_2 \ntrianglerighteq^{\flat} P_3$. This is because any incoherent program becomes a top element $\top^{\sharp}$ under $\trianglerighteq^{\sharp}$, while it is a bottom element $\bot^{\flat}$ under $\trianglerighteq^{\flat}$. In this regard, the next proposition gives a necessary condition for strong generality.

Proposition 5.2. *Let P and Q be EDPs.*

(1) *If $P \trianglerighteq^{\sharp} Q$ then $A(Q \cup R) = \emptyset$ implies $A(P \cup R) = \emptyset$ for any EDP R.*

(2) *If $P \trianglerighteq^{\flat} Q$ then $A(P \cup R) = \emptyset$ implies $A(Q \cup R) = \emptyset$ for any EDP R.*

Proposition 5.3. *Both $\langle \mathcal{EDP}, \trianglerighteq^{\sharp} \rangle$ and $\langle \mathcal{EDP}, \trianglerighteq^{\flat} \rangle$ are pre-ordered sets.*

As in the case of $\sharp/\flat$-generality relations, from the pre-order set $\langle \mathcal{EDP}, \trianglerighteq^{\sharp/\flat} \rangle$, a poset can be induced over the equivalence classes as usual. This poset also constitutes a complete lattice, but we omit the detail in this paper.

6 Discussion

Theories of generality relations over first-order clauses have been studied in the field of *inductive logic programming* [8,9,10]. These studies mainly focus on the generality relationship between two individual clauses and a generality order is introduced over a set of clauses. By contrast, we considered generality relations between *programs*. Moreover, the main contribution of this paper is a theory of generality relations in *nonmonotonic logic programs*, which contain incomplete information. The generality theory developed in this paper is useful for comparing the amount of information between such programs. To our best knowledge, there has never been a study on generality relations over nonmonotonic logic programs except [12]. Sakama [12] introduces an ordering over default theories and nonmonotonic logic programs. He orders ELPs based on a ten-valued logic, which is different from the domain-theoretic appraoch in this paper.

Computing mubs and mlbs of two programs in this paper is closely related to coordination, composition and consensus in *multi-agent systems*, which have been studied by Sakama and Inoue [13,14,15] (see Section 3.3). *Coordination* [13] is realized by accomodating different beliefs of individual agents. This is done by collecting answer sets of each program. On the other hand, *composition* [14] is realized by merging different answer sets of each programs, and *consensus* [15] is realized by extracting common beliefs from different answer sets of each program. The results of this paper indicate that our generalization theory can serve as a theoretical ground for formalizing social behavior of multiple agents.

The Smyth and Hoare orderings were proposed in domain theory, which is concerned with mathematical structures to formalize the denotational semantics of programming languages [11,16,4]. The recursive, concurrent and nondeterministic nature of programming constructs have been modeled on these order-theoretic powerdomains. In this viewpoint, answer set programming also imposes non-determinism, and we thus regard that domain theory is suitable to analyze structural properties of answer sets. However, there is only a few work on domain-theoretic foundations on logic programming, and in particular, no one has proposed a domain-theoretic method to compare the amount of information brought by a logic program. Zhang and Rounds [17] represent the semantics of disjunctive logic programs on Scott's information systems using Smyth powerdomain. In contrast to our work, Zhang and Rounds are concerned with the semantics of individual programs, and do not consider comparison of multiple programs in powerdomains. Eiter *et al.* [2] have proposed a framework for comparing programs with respect to binary relations on powersets of the *projected* answer sets of the programs, but relations in their framework are limited to equivalence and inclusion, and generality is not taken into account.

Finally, it should be noted that our framework to compare programs in Section 2.2 is farily general, so that its applicability is not only limited to answer set programming. In fact, $A(P)$ for a program P in Definition 2.2 can be given by any semantics of P as long as it is defined as a subset of *Lit*.

Several issues are left open. Because we have developed the theory of generality relations from the semantical viewpoint, exploring the syntactical counterpart is an important future topic. For example, construction of a more (or less) (strongly) $\sharp/\flat$-general program of a given program by a syntactical manipulation is useful for generalizing or specializing a program in inductive logic programming. For another issue, strong generality in the current form seems too strong, and it must be meaningful to relax its context-dependent generality condition from one with respect to all EDPs to one with respect to a subclass of EDPs.

References

1. R. Ben-Eliyahu and R. Dechter. Propositional semantics for disjunctive logic programs. *Annals of Mathematics and Artificial Intelligence*, 12(1):53–87, 1994.
2. T. Eiter, H. Tompits, and S. Woltran. On solution correspondences in answer-set programming. In: *Proceedings of the 19th International Joint Conference on Artificial Intelligence*, pp. 97–102, 2005.
3. M. Gelfond and V. Lifschitz. Classical negation in logic programs and disjunctive databases. *New Generation Computing*, 9:365–385, 1991.
4. C. A. Gunter and D. S. Scott. Semantic Domains. In: J. van Leeuwen (ed.), *Handbook of Theoretical Computer Science*, Vol. B, pp. 633–674, North-Holland, 1990.
5. K. Inoue and C. Sakama. Disjunctive explanations. In: *Proceedings of the 18th International Conference on Logic Programming*, Lecture Notes in Computer Science, 2401, pp. 317–332, Springer, 2002.
6. V. Lifschitz, D. Pearce and A. Valverde. Strongly equivalent logic programs. *ACM Transactions on Computational Logic*, 2:526–541, 2001.
7. M. J. Maher. Equivalence of logic programs. In: J. Minker (ed.), *Foundations of Deductive Databases and Logic Programming*, pp. 627–658, Morgan Kaufmann, 1988.
8. T. Niblett. A study of generalization in logic programs. In: *Proceedings of the 3rd European Working Sessions on Learning (EWSL-88)*, pp. 131–138, Pitman, 1988.
9. S.-H. Nienhuys-Cheng and R. de Wolf. *Foundations of inductive logic programming*. Lecture Notes in Artificial Intelligence, 1228, Springer, 1997.
10. G. D. Plotkin. A note on inductive generalization. In: B. Meltzer and D. Michie (eds.), *Machine Intelligence* 5, pp. 153–63, Edinburgh University Press, 1970.
11. G. D. Plotkin. A powerdomain construction. *SIAM Journal of Computing*, 5:452–287, 1976.
12. C. Sakama. Ordering default theories and nonmonotonic logic programs. *Theoretical Computer Science*, 338:127–152, 2005.
13. C. Sakama and K. Inoue. Coordination between logical agents. In: *Post-proceedings of the 5th International Workshop on Computational Logic in Multi-Agent Systems*, Lecture Notes in Artificial Intelligence, 3487, pp. 161–177, Springer, 2005.
14. C. Sakama and K. Inoue. Combining answer sets of nonmonotonic logic programs. In: *Post-proceedings of the 6th International Workshop on Computational Logic in Multi-Agent Systems*, Lecture Notes in Artificial Intelligence, 3900, pp. 320–339, Springer, 2006.
15. C. Sakama and K. Inoue. Constructing consensus logic programs. Submitted for publication, 2006.
16. M. B. Smyth. Power domains. *Journal of Computer and System Sciences*, 16:23–36, 1978.
17. G. Q. Zhang and W. C. Rounds. Semantics of logic programs and representation of Smyth powerdomain. In: K. Keimel *et al* (eds.), *Proceedings of the 1st International Symposium on Domain Theory*, pp. 151–181, Kluwer, 2001.

Cooperating Answer Set Programming

Davy Van Nieuwenborgh[1,*], Stijn Heymans[2], and Dirk Vermeir[1]

[1] Dept. of Computer Science
Vrije Universiteit Brussel, VUB
Pleinlaan 2, B1050 Brussels, Belgium
{dvnieuwe, dvermeir}@vub.ac.be
[2] Digital Enterprise Research Institute (DERI)
University of Innsbruck, Austria
stijn.heymans@deri.org

Abstract. We present a formalism for logic program cooperation based on the answer set semantics. The system consists of independent logic programs that are connected via a sequential communication channel. When presented with an input set of literals from its predecessor, a logic program computes its output as an answer set of itself, enriched with the input.

It turns out that the communication strategy makes the system quite expressive: essentially a sequence of a fixed number of programs n captures the complexity class Σ_n^P, i.e. the n-th level of the polynomial hierarchy. On the other hand, unbounded sequences capture the polynomial hierarchy $\mathcal{PH}$. These results make the formalism suitable for complex applications such as hierarchical decision making and preference-based diagnosis on ordered theories. In addition, such systems can be realized by implementing an appropriate control strategy on top of existing solvers such as DLV or SMODELS, possibly in a distributed environment.

1 Introduction

In *answer set programming* (see e.g. [2]) a logic program is used to describe the requirements, that must be fulfilled by the solutions to a problem. The models (answer sets) of the program, usually defined through (a variant of) the stable model semantics [18], then correspond to the solutions of the problem. This technique has been successfully applied in problem areas such as planning [20], configuration and verification [23], diagnosis [9], . . .

In this paper we use the answer set semantics to formalize a framework in which programs cooperate to obtain a solution that is acceptable to all and cannot unilaterally be improved upon. E.g., when a company has to make up an emergency evacuation plan for a building, one of the employees will make up a strategy that could be implemented for that building. However, as she is probably not aware of all current regulations about such strategies, her solution is forwarded to the emergency services, e.g. the police or the fire brigade, who will try to improve her plan so it conforms to all legal requirements. This adapted, legal version of the received starting plan is

---

* Supported by the Flemish Fund for Scientific Research (FWO-Vlaanderen).

S. Etalle and M. Truszczyński (Eds.): ICLP 2006, LNCS 4079, pp. 226–241, 2006.

then send back to the employee who verifies its feasibility. If the verification fails, the communication starts all over again by the employee sending a new possible plan to the emergency services. In the other case, i.e. the adapted plan is successfully verified by the employee, it is presented to the firm's management which will try to improve it to obtain e.g. a cheaper one. Again, this cheaper alternative is sent back to the emergency services for verification, and eventually also to the employee, to check its feasibility.

We develop a framework of cooperating programs that is capable of modeling hierarchical decision problems like the one above. To this end, we consider a sequence of programs $\langle P_i \rangle_{i=1,\ldots n}$. Intuitively, a program P_i communicates the solutions it finds acceptable to the next program P_{i+1} in the hierarchy. For such a P_i-acceptable solution S, the program P_{i+1} computes a number of solutions that it thinks improve on S. If one of these P_{i+1} improvements S' of S is also acceptable to P_i, i.e. S' can be successfully verified by P_i, the original S is rejected as an acceptable solution by the program P_{i+1}. On the other hand, if P_{i+1} has no improvements for S, or none of them are also acceptable to P_i, S is accepted by P_{i+1}. It follows that a solution that is acceptable to all programs must have been proposed by the starting program P_1.

It turns out that such sequences of programs are rather expressive. More specifically, we show not only that arbitrary complete problems of the polynomial hierarchy can be solved by such systems, but that such systems can capture the complete polynomial hierarchy, the latter making them suitable for complex applications.

Problems located at the first level of the polynomial hierarchy can be directly solved using answer set solvers such as DLV [16] or SMODELS [22]. On the second level, only DLV is left to perform the job directly. However, by using a "guess and check" fixpoint procedure, SMODELS can indirectly be used to solve problems at the second level [4, 15]. Beyond the second level, there are still some interesting problems. E.g., the most expressive forms of diagnostic reasoning, i.e. subset-minimal diagnosis on disjunctive system descriptions [13] or preference-based diagnosis on ordered theories [27], are located at the third level of the polynomial hierarchy, as are programs that support sequences of weak constraints[1] on disjunctive programs. For these problems, and problems located even higher in the polynomial hierarchy, the framework presented in this paper provides a means to effectively compute solutions for such problems, using SMODELS or DLV for each program in the sequence to compute better solutions. E.g., to solve the problems mentioned before on the third level, it suffices to write three well-chosen programs and to set up an appropriate control structure implementing the communication protocol sketched above.

The remainder of the paper is organized as follows. In Section 2, we review the answer set semantics and present the definitions for cooperating program systems. Further, we illustrate how such systems can be used to elegantly express common problems. Section 3 discusses the complexity and expressiveness of the proposed semantics, while Section 4 compares it with related approaches from the literature. Finally, we conclude and give some directions for further research in Section 5. Due to space restrictions, proofs have been omitted, but they can be found in [25].

---

[1] A weak constraint is a constraint that is "desirable" but may be violated if there are no other options.

2   Cooperating Programs

We give some preliminaries concerning the answer set semantics for logic programs [2]. A *literal* is an atom a or a negated atom $\neg a$. For a set of literals X, we use $\neg X$ to denote $\{\neg l \mid l \in X\}$ where $\neg\neg a = a$. When $X \cap \neg X = \emptyset$ we say X is *consistent*. An *extended literal* is a literal or a *naf-literal* of the form *not* l where l is a literal. The latter form denotes negation as failure. For a set of extended literals Y, we use Y^- to denote the set of ordinary literals underlying the naf-literals in Y, i.e. $Y^- = \{l \mid not\ l \in Y\}$. Further, we use *not* X to denote the set $\{not\ l \mid l \in X\}$. An extended literal l is true w.r.t. X, denoted $X \models l$ if $l \in X$ in case l is ordinary, or $a \notin X$ if $l = not\ a$ for some ordinary literal a. As usual, $X \models Y$ iff $\forall l \in Y \cdot X \models l$.

A *rule* is of the form $\alpha \leftarrow \beta$ where[2] α is a finite set of literals, β is a finite set of extended literals and $|\alpha| \leq 1$. Thus the *head* of a rule is either an atom or empty. A countable set of rules is called a *(logic) program*. The *Herbrand base* $\mathcal{B}_P$ of a program P contains all atoms appearing in P. The set of all literals that can be formed with the atoms in P, denoted by $\mathcal{L}_P$, is defined by $\mathcal{L}_P = \mathcal{B}_P \cup \neg\mathcal{B}_P$. Any consistent subset $I \subseteq \mathcal{L}_P$ is called an *interpretation* of P.

A rule $r = \alpha \leftarrow \beta$ is *satisfied* by an interpretation I, denoted $I \models r$, if $I \models \alpha$ and $\alpha \neq \emptyset$, whenever $I \models \beta$, i.e. if r is *applicable* ($I \models \beta$), then it must be *applied* ($I \models \alpha \cup \beta \wedge \alpha \neq \emptyset$). Note that this implies that a *constraint*, i.e. a rule with empty head ($\alpha = \emptyset$), can only be satisfied if it is not applicable ($I \not\models \beta$). For a program P, an interpretation I is called a *model* of P if $\forall r \in P \cdot I \models r$, i.e. I satisfies all rules in P. It is a minimal model of P if there is no model J of P such that $J \subset I$.

A *simple program* is a program without negation as failure. For simple programs P, we define an *answer set* of P as a minimal model of P. On the other hand, for a program P, i.e. a program containing negation as failure, we define the *GL-reduct* [18] for P w.r.t. I, denoted P^I, as the program consisting of those rules $\alpha \leftarrow (\beta \backslash not\ \beta^-)$ where $\alpha \leftarrow \beta$ is in P and $I \models not\ \beta^-$. Note that all rules in P^I are free from negation as failure, i.e. P^I is a simple program. An interpretation I is then an *answer set* of P iff I is a minimal model of the GL-reduct P^I.

Example 1. Consider the following program P about diabetes.

$$diabetes \leftarrow \qquad thirsty \leftarrow \qquad \neg sugar \leftarrow diabetes$$
$$cola\_light \leftarrow thirsty, not\ cola \qquad cola \leftarrow thirsty, not\ \neg sugar, not\ cola\_light$$

One can check that P has $I = \{diabetes, thirsty, \neg sugar, cola\_light\}$ as its single answer set. Indeed, the rule $cola \leftarrow thirsty, not\ \neg sugar, not\ cola\_light$ is removed to obtain the reduct P^I of P as $\neg sugar \in I$, i.e. the rule can never become applicable. Further, the rule $cola\_light \leftarrow thirsty, not\ cola$ is kept as $cola\_light \leftarrow thirsty$ in P^I. Clearly, the reduct P^I so obtained has I as its minimal model.

In the present framework, it is assumed that all programs "communicate using the same language", i.e. the Herbrand bases of the programs are all subsets of some set of atoms $\mathcal{PL}$ (and $\mathcal{L}_{\mathcal{PL}} = \mathcal{PL} \cup \neg\mathcal{PL}$). Because programs will receive input from other programs

---

[2] As usual, we assume that programs have already been grounded.

that influence their reasoning, we do not want any unintentional implicit interferences between the input of the program and the produced output. E.g., a program should be able to compute for an input containing a, an output containing $\neg a$ or containing neither a nor $\neg a$. For this purpose, we will also use a mirror language $\mathcal{PL}'$ of $\mathcal{PL}$, where we use $l' \in \mathcal{L}_{\mathcal{PL}'}$ to denote the mirror version of a literal $l \in \mathcal{L}_{\mathcal{PL}}$ and we have that $l'' = l \in \mathcal{L}_{\mathcal{PL}}$. The notation is extended to sets, i.e. $X' = \{l' \mid l \in X\}$.

Intuitively, a program will receive input in the language $\mathcal{L}_{\mathcal{PL}}$, do some reasoning with a program over $\mathcal{L}_{\mathcal{PL}} \cup \mathcal{L}_{\mathcal{PL}'}$ and it will only communicate the part over $\mathcal{L}_{\mathcal{PL}'}$ to the other programs, i.e. an input literal $l \in \mathcal{L}_{\mathcal{PL}}$ can only appear in the output as $l' \in \mathcal{L}_{\mathcal{PL}'}$ if the program explicitly provides rules for this purpose.

Definition 1. *For a language $\mathcal{PL}$, a **cooperating program** P is a program such that $\mathcal{B}_P \subseteq \mathcal{PL} \cup \mathcal{PL}'$. For such a program P and a set of literals $I \subseteq \mathcal{L}_{\mathcal{PL}}$, called the **input**, we use $P(I)$ to denote the program $P \cup \{l \leftarrow \mid l \in I\}$.*

*An interpretation $S \subseteq \mathcal{L}_{\mathcal{PL}}$ is called an **output** w.r.t. the input I, or an **improvement** by P of I, iff there exists an answer set M of $P(I)$ such that $S = (M \cap \mathcal{L}_{\mathcal{PL}'})'$.*

We use $\mathcal{AS}(P, I)$ to denote the set of all outputs of P w.r.t. input I.

Example 2. Take $\mathcal{PL} = \{sugar, cola, cola\_light, hypoglycemia, diabetes, thirsty\}$ and consider the following program P, where we use the notation **keep** $\{a_1, \ldots, a_n\}$, to denote the set of rules $\{a_i' \leftarrow a_i \mid 1 \leq i \leq n\}$, i.e. to denote that part of the input that can be literally copied to the output,

$$\textbf{keep } \{thirsty, hypoglycemia, diabetes\}$$
$$cola\_light' \leftarrow thirsty, not\ sugar', not\ cola'$$
$$cola' \leftarrow thirsty, not\ \neg sugar', not\ cola\_light'$$
$$\neg sugar' \leftarrow diabetes, not\ hypoglycemia$$
$$sugar' \leftarrow hypoglycemia$$

Intuitively, the above program only copies the part of the input concerning hypoglycemia, diabetes and thirsty, because these are the only possible non-critical input literals. Other possible input literals, like e.g. *cola* or *cola_light*, will be recomputed in function of the availability (or not) of certain input literals.

Let $I_1 = \emptyset$, $I_2 = \{thirsty, hypoglycemia\}$ and $I_3 = \{thirsty, diabetes, cola\}$ be three inputs. One can check that P has only one output $S_1 = \emptyset$ w.r.t. I_1. For both I_2 and I_3 there is an improvement $S_2 = I_2 \cup \{sugar, cola\}$ and $S_3 = \{thirsty, diabetes, \neg sugar, cola\_light\}$, respectively. Note the necessity of the mirror language to obtain the latter result.

A single cooperating program is not a very powerful instrument. However, connecting a number of such programs together reveals their real capabilities. To keep things simple we will use, in what follows, cooperating program systems of linearly connected programs.

Formally, a cooperating program system is a linear sequence of cooperating programs $P_1, \ldots, P_n$, where P_1 is the source program, i.e. the program that starts all communication. Solutions for such systems are inductively defined by the notion of acceptance. Intuitively, a solution S is accepted by the source program P_1 if it recognizes S

as an improvement of the empty input; and a successor program P_i, $1 < i \leq n$, accepts S if it has no improvement on S that can be verified by the previous program P_{i-1} to be acceptable to it.

Definition 2. *Let $\mathcal{PL}$ be a language. A **cooperating program system** is a sequence $\langle P_i \rangle_{i=1,\ldots n}$ of n cooperating programs over $\mathcal{PL}$.*
    *The set of **acceptable interpretations** $\mathcal{AC}(P_i)$ for a cooperating program P_i, $1 \leq i \leq n$, is inductively defined as follows:*

- $\mathcal{AC}(P_1) = \mathcal{AS}(P_1, \emptyset)$
- *for $i > 1$,*

$$\mathcal{AC}(P_i) = \{S \in \mathcal{AC}(P_{i-1}) \mid \forall T \in \mathcal{AS}(P_i, S) \cdot T \neq S \Rightarrow T \notin \mathcal{AC}(P_{i-1})\}$$

*An interpretation $S \subseteq \mathcal{L}_{\mathcal{PL}}$ that is acceptable to P_n, i.e. $S \in \mathcal{AC}(P_n)$, is called a **global answer set** for the cooperating program system.*

Note that the above definition allows for an output interpretation S of P_{i-1} to be accepted by a program P_i even if $P_i \cup S$ has no answer sets. This fits the intuition that the answer sets of $P_i \cup S$ are to be considered as improvements upon S. Hence, if P_i cannot be used to provide such an improvement, $P_i \cup S$ should not have any answer sets, and S should be accepted by P_i.

Example 3. Consider the job selection procedure of a company. The first cooperating program P_1 establishes the possible profiles of the applicants together with a rule stating the belief that inexperienced employees are ambitious. Thus, each answer set[3] of the program below corresponds with a possible applicant's profile.

$$male' \oplus female' \leftarrow \qquad old' \oplus young' \leftarrow$$
$$experienced' \oplus inexperienced' \leftarrow \qquad ambitious' \leftarrow inexperienced'$$

The decision on which applicant gets the job goes through a chain of decision makers. First, the human resources department constructs a cooperating program P_2 that implements company policy which stipulates that experienced persons should be preferred upon inexperienced ones. Therefore, the program passes through all of its input, except when it encounters a profile containing *inexperienced*, which it changes to *experienced*, intuitively implementing that an applicant with the same profile but *experienced* instead of *inexperienced*, would be preferable. Further, as we tend to prefer *experienced* people, for which nothing about being *ambitious* is known, we do not have any rule in P_2 containing *ambitious*, such that the literal is dropped from the input if present.

$$\textbf{keep } \{male, female, old, young, experienced\}$$
$$experienced' \leftarrow inexperienced$$

On the next level of the decision chain, the financial department reviews the remaining candidates. As young and inexperienced persons tend to cost less, it has a strong desire to hire such candidates, which is implemented in the following cooperating program P_3.

---

[3] In the rest of the paper we will use rules of the form $a \oplus b \leftarrow$ to denote the set of rules $\{a \leftarrow not\ b \ ; \ b \leftarrow not\ a\}$.

$$\mathbf{keep} \ \{ male, female, young, inexperienced \}$$
$$ambitious' \leftarrow inexperienced'$$
$$inexperienced' \leftarrow young, experienced$$
$$young' \leftarrow old, inexperienced$$
$$young' \leftarrow old, experienced, not \ old'$$
$$old' \leftarrow old, experienced, not \ young'$$
$$inexperienced' \leftarrow old, experienced, not \ experienced'$$
$$experienced' \leftarrow old, experienced, not \ inexperienced'$$
$$\leftarrow old', experienced'$$

Intuitively, this program handles the four possible cases: when the input profile is from a young and inexperienced person, the input is passed without modification indicating that this cannot be improved upon. On the other hand, if only one of the properties is not as desired, e.g. *young* and *experienced*, then the only improvement would be a profile containing both *young* and *inexperienced*. Finally, a profile containing *old* and *experienced* has three possible improvements: the last 5 rules ensure that the improvements proposed by P_3 will contain *young* or *inexperienced*, or both.

Finally, the management has the final call in the selection procedure. As the current team of employees is largely male, the management prefers the new worker to be a woman, as described by the next program P_4, which is similar to P_2.

$$\mathbf{keep} \ \{ female, old, young, experienced, inexperienced, ambitious \}$$
$$female' \leftarrow male$$

One can check that P_1 has eight answer sets (improvements on $\emptyset$), that are thus acceptable to it. However, only four of these are acceptable to P_2, i.e.

$$M_1 = \{ experienced, male, young \} \ ,$$
$$M_2 = \{ experienced, male, old \} \ ,$$
$$M_3 = \{ experienced, female, young \} \ ,$$
$$M_4 = \{ experienced, female, old \} \ ,$$

which fits the company policy to drop inexperienced ambitious people. E.g., feeding $M_5 = \{ inexperienced, female, young, ambitious \}$ as input to P_2 yields one answer set M_3, which is also acceptable to P_1 making M_5 unacceptable for P_2. Similarly, when P_3 is taken into account, only M_1 and M_3 are acceptable. Considering the last program P_4 yields a single global answer set, i.e. M_3, which fits our intuition that, if possible, a woman should get the job.

Note that rearranging the programs gives, in general, different results. E.g., interchanging P_2 with P_3 yields M_5 as the only global answer set.

3 Complexity

We briefly recall some relevant notions of complexity theory (see e.g. [2] for a nice introduction). The class $\mathcal{P}$ ($\mathcal{NP}$) represents the problems that are deterministically (non-deterministically) decidable in polynomial time, while $co\mathcal{NP}$ contains the problems whose complements are in $\mathcal{NP}$. The polynomial hierarchy, denoted $\mathcal{PH}$, is made up of three classes of problems, i.e. Δ_k^P, Σ_k^P and Π_k^P, $k \geq 0$, which are defined as follows:

1. $\Delta_0^P = \Sigma_0^P = \Pi_0^P = \mathcal{P}$; and
2. $\Delta_{k+1}^P = \mathcal{P}^{\Sigma_k^P}$, $\Sigma_{k+1}^P = \mathcal{NP}^{\Sigma_k^P}$, $\Pi_{k+1}^P = co\Sigma_{k+1}^P$.

The class $\mathcal{P}^{\Sigma_k^P}$ ($\mathcal{NP}^{\Sigma_k^P}$) represents the problems decidable in deterministic (nondeterministic) polynomial time using an oracle for problems in Σ_k^P. The class $\mathcal{PH}$ is defined by $\mathcal{PH} = \bigcup_{k=0}^{\infty} \Sigma_k^P$. Finally, the class $PSPACE$ contains the problems that can be solved deterministically by using a polynomial amount of memory and unlimited time.

To prove hardness for the above complexity classes[4], we will use validity checking of quantified boolean formulas. A quantified boolean formula (QBF) is an expression of the form $Q_1 X_1 Q_2 X_2 \ldots Q_k X_k \cdot G$, where $k \geq 1$, G is a Boolean expression over the atoms of the pairwise nonempty disjoint sets of variables $X_1, \ldots, X_k$ and the Q_i's, for $i = 1, \ldots, k$ are alternating quantifiers from $\{\exists, \forall\}$. When $Q_1 = \exists$, the QBF is k-existential, when $Q_1 = \forall$ we say it is k-universal. We use $QBF_{k,\exists}$ ($QBF_{k,\forall}$) to denote the set of all valid k-existential (k-universal) QBFs. Deciding, for a given k-existential (k-universal) QBF ϕ, whether $\phi \in QBF_{k,\exists}$ ($\phi \in QBF_{k,\forall}$) is a Σ_k^P-complete (Π_k^P-complete) problem. When we drop the bound k on the number of quantifiers, i.e. considering $QBF_\exists = \bigcup_{i \in \mathbb{N}} QBF_{i,\exists}$, we have a hard problem for $PSPACE$.

The following results shed some light on the complexity of the global answer set semantics for linear combinations of cooperating programs.

First, we consider the case where the length of the sequence of cooperating programs is fixed by some number n.

Theorem 1. *Given a cooperating program system $\langle P_i \rangle_{i=1,\ldots,n}$, with n fixed, and a literal $l \in \mathcal{L}_{PL}$, the problem of deciding whether there exists a global answer set containing l is Σ_n^P-complete. On the other hand, deciding whether every global answer set contains l is Π_n^P-complete.*

Proof Sketch. Membership Σ_n^P: It is shown, by induction, in [25] that checking whether an interpretation $S \subseteq \mathcal{L}_{PL}$ is not acceptable to P_n, i.e. $S \notin \mathcal{AC}(P_n)$, is in Σ_{n-1}^P. The main result follows by

- guessing an interpretation $S \subseteq \mathcal{L}_{PL}$ such that $S \ni l$; and
- checking that it is not the case that $S \notin \mathcal{AC}(P_n)$.

As the latter is in Σ_{n-1}^P, the problem itself can be done by an $\mathcal{NP}^{\Sigma_{n-1}^P}$ algorithm, i.e. the problem is in Σ_n^P.

Hardness Σ_n^P: To prove hardness, we provide a reduction of deciding validity of QBFs by means of a cooperating program system. Let $\phi = \exists X_1 \forall X_2 \ldots Q X_n \cdot G \in QBF_{n,\exists}$, where $Q = \forall$ if n is even and $Q = \exists$ otherwise. We assume, without loss of generality [24], that G is in disjunctive normal form, i.e. $G = \bigvee_{c \in C} c$ where C is a set of sets of literals over $X_1 \cup \ldots \cup X_n$ and each $c \in C$ has to be interpreted as a conjunction.

---

[4] Note that this does not hold for the class $\mathcal{PH}$ for which no complete, and thus hard, problem is known unless $\mathcal{P} = \mathcal{NP}$.

In what follows, we use P^i to denote the set rules

- **keep** $\{x , \neg x \mid x \in X_j \wedge 1 \leq j < i\}$,
- $\{x' \leftarrow not \neg x' ; \neg x' \leftarrow not \, x' \mid x \in X_j \wedge i \leq j \leq n\}$, and
- $\{sat' \leftarrow c' \mid c \in C\}$.

Further, we use $P_\forall^i$ and $P_\exists^i$ to denote the programs $P_\forall^i = P^i \cup \{ \leftarrow sat' ; \leftarrow not \, sat\}$ and $P_\exists^i = P^i \cup \{ \leftarrow not \, sat' ; \leftarrow sat\}$ respectively.

The cooperating program system $\langle P_i \rangle_{i=1,\ldots,n}$ corresponding to ϕ is defined as:

- P_1 contains the rules $\{x' \leftarrow not \neg x' ; \neg x' \leftarrow not \, x' \mid x \in X_j \wedge 1 \leq j \leq n\}$ and $\{sat' \leftarrow c' \mid c \in C\}$;
- if n is even, then $P_i = P_\forall^{n+2-i}$ when i even and $P_i = P_\exists^{n+2-i}$ when $i > 1$ odd;
- if n is odd, then $P_i = P_\exists^{n+2-i}$ when i even and $P_i = P_\forall^{n+2-i}$ when $i > 1$ odd.

Obviously, the above construction can be done in polynomial time. Intuitively, P_1 has answer sets for every possible combination of the X_i's and if such a combination makes G valid, then the corresponding answer set also contains the atom sat. The intuition behind the program $P_\forall^i$ is that it tries to disprove, for the received input, the validity of the corresponding $\forall$, i.e. for a given input combination over the X_j's making G satisfied, the program $P_\forall^i$ will try to find a combination, keeping the X_j's with $j < i$ fixed, making G false. On the other hand, the program $P_\exists^i$ will try to prove the validity of the corresponding $\exists$, i.e. for a given combination making G false it will try to compute a combination, keeping the X_j's with $j < i$ fixed, making G satisfied.

Instead of giving the formal proof for the above construction, we give a feel on how the construction works by means of an example and refer the reader to [25] for the actual proof.

Consider

$$\phi = \exists x \cdot \forall y \cdot \exists z \cdot (x \wedge \neg y \wedge z) \vee (y \wedge \neg z) .$$

The cooperating program P_1 contains the rules

$$
\begin{array}{llll}
x' \leftarrow not \neg x' & \neg x' \leftarrow not \, x' & y' \leftarrow not \neg y' & \neg y' \leftarrow not \, y' \\
z' \leftarrow not \neg z' & \neg z' \leftarrow not \, z' & sat' \leftarrow x', \neg y', z' & sat' \leftarrow y', \neg z'
\end{array}
$$

We have 8 possible outputs for $P_1(\emptyset)$, i.e. $I_1 = \{x, y, z\}$, $I_2 = \{x, y, \neg z, sat\}$, $I_3 = \{x, \neg y, z, sat\}$, $I_4 = \{x, \neg y, \neg z\}$, $I_5 = \{\neg x, y, z\}$, $I_6 = \{\neg x, y, \neg z, sat\}$, $I_7 = \{\neg x, \neg y, z\}$ and $I_8 = \{\neg x, \neg y, \neg z\}$. Clearly, these are all acceptable interpretations for P_1.

The second cooperating program P_2 is defined by $P_\exists^3$ and thus contains the rules

$$
\begin{array}{llll}
\textbf{keep}(\{x, \neg x, y, \neg y\}) \leftarrow & z' \leftarrow not \neg z' & \neg z' \leftarrow not \, z' & sat' \leftarrow x', \neg y', z' \\
& \leftarrow sat & \leftarrow not \, sat' & sat' \leftarrow y', \neg z'
\end{array}
$$

Feeding I_1 to P_2 yields I_2 as the single output. As I_2 is an acceptable interpretation to P_1, I_1 cannot be acceptable to P_2, i.e. $I_1 \notin \mathcal{AC}(P_2)$. On the other hand, for the input I_2, the program P_2 has no outputs, as the input contains sat, which makes the constraint $\leftarrow sat$ unsatisfied. As a result, I_2 is acceptable to P_2, i.e. $I_2 \in \mathcal{AC}(P_2)$. In case of the input I_7, P_2 is not able to derive sat' with the given input, yielding that $\leftarrow not\ sat'$ can never be satisfied and thus P_2 will not produce any outputs for I_7, again yielding that I_7 will be acceptable to P_2.

One can check in similar ways that $AC(P_2)$ contains 5 interpretations, i.e. $AC(P_2) = \{I_2, I_3, I_6, I_7, I_8\}$. It is not difficult to see that for each of these acceptable solutions it holds that $\exists z \cdot (x \wedge \neg y \wedge z) \vee (y \wedge \neg z)$ when x and y are taken as in the interpretation iff the literal sat is contained in that interpretation.

The third and final cooperating program P_3 is given by $P_\forall^2$ and contains the rules

$$\mathbf{keep}(\{x, \neg x\}) \leftarrow$$

$$
\begin{array}{llll}
y' \leftarrow not\ \neg y' & \neg y' \leftarrow not\ y' & \leftarrow not\ sat & sat' \leftarrow x', \neg y', z' \\
z' \leftarrow not\ \neg z' & \neg z' \leftarrow not\ z' & \leftarrow sat' & sat' \leftarrow y', \neg z'
\end{array}
$$

When providing P_3 with the input I_2, we have two outputs, i.e. I_1 and I_4. However, neither $I_1 \in AC(P_2)$ nor $I_2 \in AC(P_2)$, yielding that I_2 is an acceptable solution to P_3. Intuitively, P_3 accepts the input I_2 as it cannot disprove $\forall y \cdot \exists z \cdot (x \wedge \neg y \wedge z) \vee (y \wedge \neg z)$ for the chosen truth value of x in I_2. In a similar way one can check that also $I_3 \in AC(P_3)$.

On the other hand, feeding P_3 with I_6, we get the outputs $\{I_5, I_7, I_8\}$. This time, both $I_7 \in AC(P_2)$ and $I_8 \in AC(P_2)$, implying that I_6 is not acceptable to P_3. Further, using I_7 or I_8 as an input to P_3, results in no outputs, making them both acceptable to P_3. As a result, $AC(P_3) = \{I_1, I_3, I_7, I_8\}$, which are also the global answer sets of the system.

Now, one can check that for each global answer set in $AC(P_3)$ it holds that $\forall y \cdot \exists z \cdot (x \wedge \neg y \wedge z) \vee (y \wedge \neg z)$ for x taken as in the interpretation iff the literal sat is contained in that global answer set. From this it follows that ϕ is valid iff there exists a global answer set $I \in AC(P_3)$ such that $sat \in I$. In our example, I_2 is such a global answer set and one can check that ϕ holds when we assume x is true.

Π_n^P-*completeness:* To show this result, we consider in [25] the complement decision problem and show that it is Σ_n^P-complete, from which the result follows.   □

While the previous result handles the cases where the number of programs in the sequence is fixed, we can generalize the results to arbitrary sequences.

Theorem 2. *Given a cooperating program system* $\langle P_i \rangle_{i=1,\ldots,n\in\mathbb{N}}$ *and a literal* $l \in \mathcal{L}_{\mathcal{PL}}$, *the problem of deciding whether there exists a global answer set containing* l *is PSPACE-complete.*

Proof Sketch. Membership PSPACE: Intuitively, each program in the sequence needs the space to represent a single answer set, while the system itself needs the space to represent a global answer set. Now, the algorithm will place a possible solution in the latter allocated space, and will use the former allocated space to check acceptability for the different programs in the sequence. Thus, an algorithm for a sequence of n programs, needs maximum $n + 1$ times the space to represent an answer set, which is clearly polynomial in space, from which membership to *PSPACE* follows.

Hardness PSPACE: Clearly, the hardness proof of Theorem 1 can be generalized to validity checking of arbitrary quantified boolean formula, from which hardness readily follows.   □

While the previous results describe the complexity of reasoning with the presented framework, they don't give a clear picture on the expressiveness of the system, i.e. whether each problem that belongs to a certain complexity class can be expressed in the framework. The reason therefore is that a formalism F being complete for a particular class only implies that each instance of a problem in that class can be reduced in polynomial time to an instance of F such that the yes/no answer is preserved. However, completeness does not imply that the polynomial time reduction itself from an instance of the problem to an instance in F is expressible in F[5].

In this context, one says that a formalism *captures* a certain complexity class iff the formalism is in the class and every problem in that class can be expressed in the formalism. The latter part is normally proved by taking an arbitrary expression in a normal (or general) form[6] for the particular complexity class and by showing that it can be expressed in the formalism.

By using the results from [14, 12], the following normal form for the complexity class Σ_k^P, with $k \geq 2$, can be obtained. First, we have to consider a signature $\sigma = (O, F, P)$, with O finite and $F = \emptyset$, i.e. we do not allow function symbols. A finite database over σ is any finite subset of the Herbrand Base over σ. Secondly, we have three predicates that do not occur in P, i.e. *succ, first* and *last*. Enumeration literals are literals over the signature $(O, \emptyset, \{succ, first, last\})$ that satisfy the conditions:

- *succ* describes an enumeration of the elements in O; and
- *first* and *last* contain the first and last element in the enumeration respectively.

Intuitively, *succ* is a binary predicate such that $succ(x, y)$ means that y is the successor of x. Further, *first* and *last* are unary predicates.

A collection S of finite databases over the signature $\sigma = (O, \emptyset, P)$ is in Σ_k^P iff there is a second order formula of the form

$$\phi = Q_1 U_{1,\ldots,m_1}^1 Q_2 U_{1,\ldots,m_2}^2 \cdots Q_k U_{1,\ldots,m_k}^k \exists \overline{x} \cdot \theta_1(\overline{x}) \vee \cdots \vee \theta_l(\overline{x}) \ ,$$

where $Q_i = \exists$ if i is odd, $Q_i = \forall$ if i is even, $U_{1,\ldots,m_i}^i$ $(1 \leq i \leq k)$ are finite sets of predicate symbols and $\theta_i(\overline{x})$ $(1 \leq i \leq l)$ are conjunctions of enumeration literals or literals involving predicates in $P \cup \{U_{1,\ldots,m_1}^1, U_{1,\ldots,m_2}^2, \ldots, U_{1,\ldots,m_k}^k\}$ such that for any finite database w over σ, $w \in S$ iff w satisfies ϕ.

Again, we first consider the case in which the number of programs in the sequence is fixed by a number $n \in \mathbb{N}$.

Theorem 3. *The global answer set semantics for cooperating program systems with a fixed number n of programs captures Σ_n^P.*

Proof Sketch. Membership Σ_n^P: The result follows directly from the membership part of the proof of Theorem 1.

---

[5] A good example of this fact is the query class *fixpoint*, which is $PTIME$-complete but cannot express the simple query $even(R)$ to check if $|R|$ is even. See e.g. [7, 2] for a more detailed explanation on the difference between completeness and expressiveness (or capturing).

[6] A normal (or general) form of a complexity class is a form in which every problem in the class can be expressed. Note that not every complexity class necessarily has a general form.

Capture Σ_n^P: This proof is a generalization of the technique used in the hardness proof of Theorem 1. Further, the construction of the programs, especially the first program, is based on the proof of Theorem 6.3.2. in [2], where it is shown that disjunctive logic programming under the brave semantics captures Σ_2^P.

However, we first have to consider the case where $n = 1$ separately, as the general form discussed above only holds for $n \geq 2$. It is easy to see that the global answer set semantics for cooperating systems of a single program coincides with the classical answer set semantics, for which capturing of $\Sigma_1^P = \mathcal{NP}$ is already proven in the literature (e.g. in [2]).

To prove that any problem of Σ_n^P, with $n \geq 2$, can be expressed in a cooperating program system of n programs under the global answer set semantics, we have to show a construction of such a system $\langle P_i \rangle_{i=1,\ldots,n}$ such that a finite database w satisfies the formula

$$\phi = \exists U^1_{1,\ldots,m_1} \forall U^2_{1,\ldots,m_2} \cdots Q_n U^n_{1,\ldots,m_n} \exists \overline{x} \cdot \theta_1(\overline{x}) \vee \cdots \vee \theta_l(\overline{x}) \ ,$$

with everything defined as in the general form for Σ_n^P described before, iff $\langle P_i \rangle_{i=1,\ldots,n}$ has a global answer set containing *sat*.

The first program[7] P_1 in the sequence contains, beside the facts that introduce the database w (as w'), the following rules:

- For the enumeration of the predicates $U^1_{1,\ldots,m_1}, U^2_{1,\ldots,m_2}, \ldots, U^n_{1,\ldots,m_n}$, we have the rules:

$$U_k^{i\,\prime}(\overline{w_k^i}) \leftarrow not \ \neg U_k^{i\,\prime}(\overline{w_k^i}) \qquad\qquad \neg U_k^{i\,\prime}(\overline{w_k^i}) \leftarrow not \ U_k^{i\,\prime}(\overline{w_k^i})$$

  for $1 \leq i \leq n$ and $1 \leq k \leq m_i$.
- To introduce the linear ordering, we need a set of rules similar to the ones used in Section 2.1.13. of [2] (see the technical report [25] for a detailed description). This set of rules has the property that when a linear ordering is established, the literal *linear'* is derived.
- To check satisfiability, we use the rules

$$sat' \leftarrow \theta_i{}'(\overline{x}), linear'$$

  for $1 \leq i \leq l$.

The other programs of the sequence are defined, similar to the hardness proof of Theorem 1, by using two skeletons $P_\forall^i$ and $P_\exists^i$. First, both skeletons have the following set of rules P^i in common

- **keep** $\{ U_k^j(\overline{w_k^j}), \neg U_k^j(\overline{w_k^j}) \mid (1 \leq j < i) \wedge (1 \leq k \leq m_i) \}$,
- **keep** $\{facts\ of\ the\ linear\ ordering\}$,
- **keep** w ,
- $\{ U_k^{j\,\prime}(\overline{w_k^j}) \leftarrow not \neg U_k^{j\,\prime}(\overline{w_k^j}) ; \ \neg U_k^{j\,\prime}(\overline{w_k^j}) \leftarrow not \ U_k^{j\,\prime}(\overline{w_k^j}) \mid$
$\qquad\qquad\qquad\qquad (i \leq j \leq n) \wedge (1 \leq k \leq m_i) \}$, and

---

[7] For clarity, we will use non-grounded rules, but we assume that the reader is familiar with obtaining the grounded versions of non-grounded rules.

$-\{sat' \leftarrow \theta_i{}'(\overline{x}), linear' \mid 1 \leq i \leq l\}$.

Now, we define the programs $P_\forall^i$ and $P_\exists^i$ as $P_\forall^i = P^i \cup \{ \leftarrow sat' ; \leftarrow not\ sat\}$ and $P_\exists^i = P^i \cup \{ \leftarrow not\ sat' ; \leftarrow sat\}$ respectively.

Besides P_1, the remaining programs in the sequence are defined by:

- if n is even, then $P_i = P_\forall^{n+2-i}$ when i even and $P_i = P_\exists^{n+2-i}$ when $i > 1$ odd;
- if n is odd, then $P_i = P_\exists^{n+2-i}$ when i even and $P_i = P_\forall^{n+2-i}$ when $i > 1$ odd.

It is not difficult to see (similar to the hardness proof of Theorem 1) that the above constructed program will only generate, for a given input database w, global answer sets that contain *sat* iff ϕ is satisfied.   □

When we drop the fixed length of the sequence, the above result can be easily generalized to arbitrary cooperating program systems.

Corollary 1. *The global answer set semantics for cooperating program systems captures[8] $\mathcal{PH}$, i.e. the polynomial hierarchy.*

The above result yields that the presented framework is able to encode each problem in the polynomial hierarchy in a modular way, making the framework useful for complex knowledge reasoning tasks, e.g. involving multiple optimization steps.

4   Relationships to Other Approaches

In [5], answer set optimization (ASO) programs are presented. Such ASO programs consist of a generator program and a sequence of optimizing programs. To perform the optimization, the latter programs use rules similar to ordered disjunction [3], i.e. rules of the form $c_1 < \cdots < c_n \leftarrow \beta$ which intuitively read: when β is true, making c_1 true is the most preferred option and only when c_1 cannot be made true, the next best option is to make c_2 true, ... Solutions of the generator program that are optimal w.r.t. the first optimizing program and, among those, are optimal w.r.t. the second optimizing program, and so on, are called preferred solutions for the ASO program.

The framework of ASO programming looks very similar to our approach, i.e. just consider the generator program as program P_1 and the optimizing programs as programs $P_2, \ldots, P_n$. However, ASO programs are far more limited w.r.t. their expressiveness, due to the syntactical and semantical restrictions of the optimizing programs in comparison to our approach where arbitrary programs can be used to do the optimization. It turns out that the expressiveness of an ASO program does not depend on the length of the sequence of optimizing programs: it is always Σ_2^P-complete. Hence ASO programs can be captured by the presented cooperating program systems in this paper using a pair of programs. The construction of these two programs simulating ASO programs is subject to further research.

Weak constraints were introduced in [6] as a relaxation of the concept of a constraint. Intuitively, a weak constraint is allowed to be violated, but only as a last resort, meaning that one tries to minimize the number of violated constraints. Additionally, weak constraints are allowed to be hierarchically layered by means of a sequence of sets of weak

---

[8] Note that while the semantics captures $\mathcal{PH}$, it can never be complete for it as the hierarchy would than collapse.

constraints. Intuitively, one first chooses the answer sets that minimize the number of violated constraints in the first set of weak constraints in the sequence, and then, among those, one chooses the answer sets that minimize the number of violated constraints in the second set, etc.

Again, this approach can be seen as a kind of cooperating programming system. The complexity of such a system, independent of the number of sets of weak constraints, is at most Δ_3^P-complete. Thus, using the presented cooperating programming system from Section 2, a sequence of three programs suffice to capture the most expressive form of that formalism.

The framework developed in this paper can be seen as a more general version of the idea presented in [15], where a guess and a check program are combined into a single disjunctive program such that the answer sets of this program coincide with the solutions that can be obtained from the guess program and successfully checked by the check program. The approach in this paper allows to combine a guess program and multiple check programs, which each have to be applied in turn, into a single cooperating system such that the global answer sets correspond to solutions that can be guessed by the guess program and subsequently verified by the check programs.

In [26, 19], hierarchies of preferences on a single program are presented. The preferences are expressible on both the literals and the rules in that program. It is shown that for a sequence of n preference relations the complexity of the system is Σ_{n+1}^P-complete. The semantics proposed in Section 2 is a generalization of that approach: instead of using one global program with a sequence of preferences expressed on that program, we use a sequence of, in general, different programs, thus allowing a separate optimizing strategy for each individual program. To capture a hierarchy of n preference relations, we need $n + 1$ cooperating programs: the first one will correspond with the global program, while the rest will correspond to the n preference relations. The system described in Example 3 can be seen as a translation of such a preference hierarchy. Intuitively, the program P_2 describes the preference relation $experienced < inexperienced$, while P_3 implements the relation $young < old$; $inexperienced < experienced$. Finally, P_4 corresponds to the single preference $female < male$. This also suggests that the present framework may be useful to encode, in a unified way, sequential communication between programs supporting different higher level language constructs such as preference orders.

Updates of logic programs [1, 10] can be seen as a form of sequential communication. However, the approaches presented in the literature are limited to solving problems located in the first or second level of the polynomial hierarchy.

[21] presents composition of logic programs as a way to solve decision making in agent systems. Intuitively, for two programs P_1 and P_2 the system tries to compute a program P such that each answer set S of P is of the form $S = S_1 \cup S_2$ (or $S = S_1 \cap S_2$), where S_1 and S_2 are answer sets of P_1 and P_2 respectively. Clearly, this approach can be extended to sequences of programs, but it is different from the one presented in this paper in the sense that we apply each program in the sequence in turn, while all programs in the former approach are applied at once in the composed program P'. This explains why the complexity of the former semantics remains the same as that of the underlying answer set semantics.

Finally, the concept of cooperation for decision making is also used in other areas than answer set programming, e.g. in the context of concurrent or distributed theorem-proving [8, 17]. In [17], the idea is to split up and distribute a set of axioms and a theory among a number of agents that each derive new knowledge to prove the theory (using only the part of the knowledge they received) and who communicate their newly derived knowledge to the other agents in the system. [8] handles the same problem in a different way, i.e. each agent has its own strategy to prove the theory and after an amount of time the results of the cooperating agents are evaluated. If an agent scored badly during this evaluation, the system can decide to replace it with a new agent having another proof strategy. In the end, one wants to obtain a team of agents that performs best to solve the given problem.

5   Conclusions and Directions for Further Research

We presented a framework suitable for solving hierarchical decision problems using logic programs that cooperate via a sequential communication channel. The resulting semantics turns out to be rather expressive, as it essentially covers the polynomial hierarchy, thus enabling further complex applications. E.g., the framework could be used to develop implementations for diagnostic systems at the third level of the polynomial hierarchy [11, 13, 27].

Future work comprises the development of a dedicated implementation of the approach, using existing answer set solvers, e.g. DLV [16] or SMODELS [22], possibly in a distributed environment. Such an implementation will use a control structure that communicates candidate solutions between consecutive programs. When a program P_i receives a solution S from P_{i-1}, it attempts to compute an improvement S'. If no such S' exists, S is acceptable to P_i and is communicated to P_{i+1}. Otherwise, S' is send back to P_{i-1}, who verifies its acceptability (for P_{i-1}). If it is, P_i starts over to check if it can (or cannot) improve upon S'. On the other hand, when S' is not acceptable to P_{i-1}, P_i generates another improvement and starts over again. For efficiency, each program can hold some kind of success- and failure list containing solutions that have already been tested for acceptability and were either accepted or rejected.

In the context of an implementation, it is also interesting to investigate which conditions a program has to fulfill in order for it not to lift the complexity up with one level in the polynomial hierarchy, yielding possible optimizations of the computation and communication process.

Finally, we plan to look into a broader class of communication structures, e.g. a tree or, more generally, a (strict) partial ordering of programs, or even cyclic structures.

References

[1] J. J. Alferes, L. J. A., L. M. Pereira, H. Przymusinska, and T. C. Przymusinski. Dynamic logic programming. In *Proceedings of the 6th International Conference on Principles of Knowledge Representation and Reasoning*, pages 98–111. Morgan Kaufmann, 1998.

[2] C. Baral. *Knowledge Representation, Reasoning and Declarative Problem Solving*. Cambridge Press, 2003.

[3] G. Brewka. Logic programming with ordered disjunction. In *Proceedings of the 18th National Conference on Artificial Intelligence and Fourteenth Conference on Innovative Applications of Artificial Intelligence*, pages 100–105. AAAI Press, 2002.

[4] G. Brewka, I. Niemela, and T. Syrjanen. Implementing ordered disjunction using answer set solvers for normal programs. In *European Conference, JELIA 2002*, volume 2424 of *LNAI*, pages 444–455, Cosenza, Italy, September 2002. Springer.

[5] G. Brewka, I. Niemelä, and M. Truszczynski. Answer set optimization. In G. Gottlob and T. Walsh, editors, *IJCAI*, pages 867–872. Morgan Kaufmann, 2003.

[6] F. Buccafurri, N. Leone, and P. Rullo. Strong and weak constraints in disjunctive datalog. In *Proceedings of the 4th International Conference on Logic Programming (LPNMR '97)*, pages 2–17, 1997.

[7] E. Dantsin, T. Eiter, G. Gottlob, and A. Voronkov. Complexity and expressive power of logic programming. *ACM Computing Surveys*, 33(3):374–425, 2001.

[8] J. Denzinger and M. Kronenburg. Planning for distributed theorem proving: The teamwork approach. In *Advances in Artificial Intelligence, 20th Annual German Conference on Artificial Intelligence (KI-96)*, volume 1137 of *LNCS*, pages 43–56. Springer, 1996.

[9] T. Eiter, W. Faber, N. Leone, and G. Pfeifer. The diagnosis frontend of the dlv system. *AI Communications*, 12(1-2):99–111, 1999.

[10] T. Eiter, M. Fink, G. Sabbatini, and H. Tompits. Considerations on updates of logic programs. In *European Workshop, JELIA 2000*, volume 1919 of *Lecture Notes in Artificial Intelligence*, pages 2–20, Malaga, Spain, September–October 2000. Springer Verlag.

[11] T. Eiter and G. Gottlob. The complexity of logic-based abduction. *Journal of the Association for Computing Machinery*, 42(1):3–42, 1995.

[12] T. Eiter, G. Gottlob, and Y. Gurevich. Normal forms for second-order logic over finite structures, and classification of np optimization problems. *Annals of Pure and Applied Logic*, 78(1-3):111–125, 1996.

[13] T. Eiter, G. Gottlob, and N. Leone. Abduction from logic programs: Semantics and complexity. *Theoretical Computer Science*, 189(1-2):129–177, 1997.

[14] T. Eiter, G. Gottlob, and H. Mannila. Adding disjunction to datalog. In *Proceedings of the Thirteenth ACM SIGACT-SIGMOD-SIGART Symposium on Principles of Database Systems*, pages 267–278. ACM Press, 1994.

[15] T. Eiter and A. Polleres. Towards automated integration of guess and check programs in answer set programming. In V. Lifschitz and I. Niemelä, editors, *LPNMR*, volume 2923 of *LNCS*, pages 100–113, Fort Lauderdale, FL, USA, January 2004. Springer.

[16] W. Faber and G. Pfeifer. dlv homepage. http://www.dbai.tuwien.ac.at/proj/dlv/.

[17] M. Fisher. An open approach to concurrent theorem-proving. *Parallel Processing for Artificial Intelligence*, 3, 1997.

[18] M. Gelfond and V. Lifschitz. The stable model semantics for logic programming. In *Logic Programming, Proceedings of the Fifth International Conference and Symposium*, pages 1070–1080, Seattle, Washington, August 1988. The MIT Press.

[19] S. Heymans, D. Van Nieuwenborgh, and D. Vermeir. Hierarchical decision making by autonomous agents. In *Logics in Artificial Intelligence, 9th European Conference, Proceedings, JELIA 2004*, volume 3229 of *LNCS*, pages 44–56. Springer, 2004.

[20] V. Lifschitz. Answer set programming and plan generation. *Journal of Artificial Intelligence*, 138(1-2):39–54, 2002.

[21] C. Sakama and K. Inoue. Coordination between logical agents. In *Proceedings of the 5th International Workshop on Computational Logic in Multi-Agent Systems (CLIMA-V)*, volume 3487 of *Lecture Notes in Artificial Intelligence*, pages 161–177. Springer, 2005.

[22] P. Simons. smodels homepage. http://www.tcs.hut.fi/Software/smodels/.

[23] T. Soininen and I. Niemelä. Developing a declarative rule language for applications in product configuration. In *Proceedings of the First International Workshop on Practical Aspects of Declarative Languages (PADL '99)*, LNCS, San Antonio, Texas, 1999. Springer.

[24] L. Stockmeyer and A. Meyer. Word problems requiring exponential time. In *Proceedings of the 5th ACM Symposium on Theory of Computing (STOC '73)*, pages 1–9, 1973.

[25] D. Van Nieuwenborgh, S. Heymans, and D. Vermeir. Cooperating answer set programming. Technical report. Vrije Universiteit Brussel, Dept. of Computer Science, 2006, http://tinf2.vub.ac.be/˜dvnieuwe/iclp2006technical.ps.

[26] D. Van Nieuwenborgh, S. Heymans, and D. Vermeir. On programs with linearly ordered multiple preferences. In B. Demoen and V. Lifschitz, editors, *Proceedings of 20th International Conference on Logic Programming (ICLP 2004)*, number 3132 in LNCS, pages 180–194. Springer, 2004.

[27] D. Van Nieuwenborgh and D. Vermeir. Ordered programs as abductive systems. In *Proceedings of the APPIA-GULP-PRODE Conference on Declarative Programming (AGP2003)*, pages 374–385, Regio di Calabria, Italy, 2003.

Predicate Introduction Under Stable and Well-Founded Semantics*

Johan Wittocx, Joost Vennekens, Maarten Mariën, Marc Denecker, and Maurice Bruynooghe

Department of Computer Science, K.U. Leuven, Belgium
{johan, joost, maartenm, marcd, maurice}@cs.kuleuven.be

Abstract. This paper studies the transformation of "predicate introduction": replacing a complex formula in an existing logic program by a newly defined predicate. From a knowledge representation perspective, such transformations can be used to eliminate redundancy or to simplify a theory. From a more practical point of view, they can also be used to transform a theory into a normal form imposed by certain inference programs or theorems, e.g., through the elimination of universal quantifiers. In this paper, we study when predicate introduction is equivalence preserving under the stable and well-founded semantics. We do this in the algebraic framework of "approximation theory"; this is a fixpoint theory for non-monotone operators that generalizes all main semantics of various non-monotone logics, including Logic Programming, Default Logic and Autoepistemic Logic. We prove an abstract, algebraic equivalence result and then instantiate this abstract theorem to Logic Programming under the stable and well-founded semantics.

1 Introduction

This paper studies the transformation of "predicate introduction" for Logic Programming. By this, we mean the introduction of a new predicate in order to be able to simplify the expressions in the bodies of certain rules. To motivate our interest in this transformation, we consider a simplified version of a program that occurs in [1]. In this paper, a logic program (under the stable semantics) is constructed to capture the meaning of theories in the action language $\mathcal{AL}$. In particular, *static causal laws* of the following form are considered: "P is caused if $P_1, \ldots, P_N$". Here, P, $P_1, \ldots, P_N$ are propositional symbols. In its Logic Programming translation, such a causal law R is represented by the following set of facts: $\{Head(R,P), Prec(R,1,P_1), \ldots, Prec(R,N,P_N), NbOfPrec(R,N)\}$. (Throughout this paper, we use the notational convention that predicates, functions, and constant symbols start with an upper case letter, while variables are all lower case.).

Now, the meaning in $\mathcal{AL}$ of such a law is that whenever all of $P_1, \ldots, P_N$ hold, then so must P. Using the predicate $Holds/1$ to describe which propositions

---

* Works supported by FWO-Vlaanderen, IWT-Vlaanderen, and by GOA/2003/08.

S. Etalle and M. Truszczyński (Eds.): ICLP 2006, LNCS 4079, pp. 242–256, 2006.

hold, this can be captured by the following rule (we use $\Leftarrow$ to represent material implication and $\leftarrow$ for the "rule construct" of Logic Programming):

$$\forall p \; Holds(p) \leftarrow \exists r \; Head(r,p) \wedge \forall i \forall q \; Prec(r,i,q) \Rightarrow Holds(q). \tag{1}$$

This rule contains universal quantifiers in its body. Even though it is possible to define both stable and well-founded semantics for such programs, current model generation systems such as ASSAT, SModels or DLV cannot handle this kind of rules. As such, we would like to eliminate this quantifier. The well-known Lloyd-Topor transformation [12] suggests introducing a new predicate, $BodyNotSat/1$, to represent the negation of the subformula $\phi = \forall i \forall q \; Prec(r,i,q) \Rightarrow Holds(q)$. Because $\neg\phi = \exists i \exists q \; Prec(r,i,q) \wedge \neg Holds(q)$, we would then get:

$$\forall p, r \; Holds(p) \leftarrow Head(r,p) \wedge \neg BodyNotSat(r).$$
$$\forall r, i, q \; BodyNotSat(r) \leftarrow Prec(r,i,q) \wedge \neg Holds(q). \tag{2}$$

This transformation preserves equivalence under the (two-valued) completion semantics [12]. However, for stable or well-founded semantics, this is not the case. For instance, consider the $\mathcal{AL}$ theory $\mathcal{A} = \{P \text{ is caused if } Q; \; Q \text{ is caused if } P\}$. In the original translation (1), neither P nor Q holds; in the second version (2), however, we obtain (ignoring the $Head/2$ and $Prec/3$ atoms for clarity):

$$Holds(P) \leftarrow \neg BodyNotSat(R_1).$$
$$BodyNotSat(R_1) \leftarrow \neg Holds(Q).$$
$$Holds(Q) \leftarrow \neg BodyNotSat(R_2). \tag{3}$$
$$BodyNotSat(R_2) \leftarrow \neg Holds(P).$$

Under the stable semantics, this program has two models: $\{Holds(P), Holds(Q)\}$ and $\{BodyNotSat(R_1), BodyNotSat(R_2)\}$. As such, even though it might look reasonable at first, the Lloyd-Topor transformation does not preserve stable (or well-founded) models in this case.

Predicate introduction under the stable and well-founded semantics was considered by Van Gelder [15]. That paper, however, imposes strong restrictions on how newly introduced predicates can be defined. In particular, recursive definitions of such a new predicate are not allowed. However, the ability to introduce recursively defined new predicates can be very useful; indeed, it is precisely in this way that [1] manages to eliminate the universal quantifier in (1). Concretely, a predicate $AllPrecHold(r)$ is introduced to replace ϕ in (1), resulting in:

$$\forall r, p \; Holds(p) \leftarrow Head(r,p) \wedge AllPrecHold(r). \tag{4}$$

This predicate is then defined in terms of another new predicate, $AllFrom(r,i)$, that means that the preconditions $i, i+1, \ldots, n$ of a rule r with n preconditions are satisfied. We then define this predicate by the following recursion:

$$\forall r, n \; AllPrecHold(r) \leftarrow AllFrom(r,1).$$
$$\forall r, n, q \; AllFrom(r,n) \leftarrow Prec(r,n,q) \wedge Holds(q) \wedge AllFrom(r,n+1). \tag{5}$$
$$\forall r, n, q \; AllFrom(r,n) \leftarrow Prec(r,n,q) \wedge Holds(q) \wedge NbOfPrec(r,n).$$

In this paper, we prove a generalization of Van Gelder's result, that shows that this translation is indeed equivalence preserving.

We can easily prove this result in a general form, by using the algebraic framework of *approximation theory* [3] (see also Section 2.1). This is a fixpoint theory for arbitrary (non-monotone) operators that generalizes all main semantics of various non-monotone logics, including Logic Programming, Default Logic and Autoepistemic Logic. It allows properties of these different semantics for all of these logics to be studied in a uniform way. The central result of this paper (Section 3) is an abstract, algebraic fixpoint theorem, that allows us to relate the stable and well-founded models of an original theory to those of the transformed theory. In Section 4, we instantiate this result to Logic Programming under the well-founded and stable model semantics, thereby generalizing the earlier result by Van Gelder [15]. In particular, our result also applies to recursively defined new predicates. In Section 5, we discuss some applications of this result, including a general way of eliminating universal quantifiers by introducing recursively defined predicates. This offers an alternative for the corresponding step from the Lloyd-Topor transformation, which is only valid under completion semantics.

2   Preliminaries

In this section, we introduce some important concepts from approximation theory and show how these can be used to capture the stable and well-founded semantics for several Logic Programming variants.

2.1   Approximation Theory

We use the following notations. Let $\langle L, \leq \rangle$ be a complete lattice. A fixpoint of an operator $O : L \to L$ on L is an element $x \in L$ for which $x = O(x)$; a prefixpoint of O is an x such that $x \geq O(x)$. If O is monotone, then it has a unique least fixpoint x, which is also its unique least prefixpoint. We denote this x by $\mathrm{lfp}(O)$.

Our presentation of approximation theory is based on [3,5]. We consider the square L^2 of the domain of some lattice L. We will denote such an element as $(x\ y)$. We introduce the following projection functions: for a tuple $(x\ y)$, we denote by $[(x\ y)|$ the first element x of this pair and by $|(x\ y)]$ the second element y. The obvious point-wise extension of $\leq$ to L^2 is called the *product order* on L^2, which we also denote by $\leq$: i.e., for all $(x\ y), (x'\ y') \in L^2$, $(x\ y) \leq (x'\ y')$ iff $x \leq x'$ and $y \leq y'$. An element $(x\ y)$ of L^2 can be seen as approximating certain elements of L, namely those in the (possibly empty) interval $[x, y] = \{z \in L \mid x \leq z$ and $z \leq y\}$. Using this intuition, we can derive a second order, the *precision order* $\leq_p$, on L^2: for each $(x\ y), (x'\ y') \in L^2, (x\ y) \leq_p (x'\ y')$ iff $x \leq x'$ and $y' \leq y$. Indeed, if $(x\ y) \leq_p (x'\ y')$, then $[x, y] \supseteq [x', y']$, i.e., $(x'\ y')$ approximates fewer elements than $(x\ y)$. It can easily be seen that $\langle L^2, \leq_p \rangle$ is also a lattice. The structure $\langle L^2, \leq, \leq_p \rangle$ is the *bilattice* corresponding to L. If $\langle L, \leq \rangle$ is complete, then so are $\langle L^2, \leq \rangle$ and $\langle L^2, \leq_p \rangle$. Elements $(x\ x)$ of L^2 are called *exact*. The set of exact elements forms a natural embedding of L in L^2.

Approximation theory is based on the study of operators which are monotone w.r.t. $\leq_p$. Such operators are called *approximations*. An approximation A *approximates* an operator O on L if for each $x \in L$, $A(x\ x)$ contains $O(x)$, i.e. $[A(x\ x)] \leq O(x) \leq |A(x\ x)]$. An exact approximation is one which maps exact elements to exact elements, i.e., for all $x \in L$, $[A(x\ x)] = |A(x\ x)]$. Each exact approximation A approximates a unique operator O on L, namely the one that maps each $x \in L$ to $[A(x\ x)] = |A(x\ x)]$. An approximation A is *symmetric* if $\forall (x\ y) \in L^2$, if $A(x\ y) = (x'\ y')$ then $A(y\ x) = (y'\ x')$. A symmetric approximation is exact.

For an approximation A on L^2, we define the operator $[A(\cdot\ y)]$ on L that maps an element $x \in L$ to $[A(x\ y)]$, i.e. $[A(\cdot\ y)] = \lambda x.[A(x\ y)]$, and $|A(x\ \cdot)]$ that maps an element $y \in L$ to $|A(x\ y)]$. These operators are monotone. We define an operator $C_A^{\downarrow}$ on L, called the *lower stable operator* of A, as $C_A^{\downarrow}(y) = \text{lfp}([A(\cdot\ y)])$. We also define the *upper stable operator* $C_A^{\uparrow}$ of A as $C_A^{\uparrow}(x) = \text{lfp}(|A(x\ \cdot)])$. Note that if A is symmetric, both operators are identical. We define the *stable operator* $C_A : L^2 \mapsto L^2$ of A by $C_A(x\ y) = (C_A^{\downarrow}(y)\ C_A^{\uparrow}(x))$. Because both $C_A^{\downarrow}$ and $C_A^{\uparrow}$ are anti-monotone, C_A is $\leq_p$-monotone.

An approximation A defines a number of different fixpoints: the least fixpoint of A is called its *Kripke-Kleene fixpoint*, fixpoints of its stable operator C_A are *stable fixpoints* and the least fixpoint of C_A is called the *well-founded fixpoint* of A. In [3,5], it was shown that all main semantics of Logic Programming, Autoepistemic Logic and Default Logic can be characterized in terms of these fixpoints. In the next section, the case of Logic Programming is recalled.

2.2   Rule Sets and Logic Programming Semantics

We define a logical formalism generalizing Logic Programming and several of its extensions. An *alphabet* Σ consists of a set Σ^o of object symbols, a set Σ^f of function symbols, and a set Σ^p of predicate symbols. Note that we make no formal distinction between variables and constants; both will simply be called *object symbols*. The formalism considered here in this paper is that of *rule sets* Δ. A rule set consists of rules of the form:

$$\forall \boldsymbol{x} P(\boldsymbol{t}) \leftarrow \phi.$$

Here, P is a predicate symbol, $\boldsymbol{x}$ a tuple of variables, $\boldsymbol{t}$ a tuple of terms, and ϕ a first-order logic formula. We say that Δ is a rule set over alphabet Σ if Σ contains all symbols occurring free in Δ. For a rule r of the above form, the atom $P(\boldsymbol{t})$ is called the *head* of r, while ϕ is known as its *body*. Predicates that appear in the head of a rule are *defined by* Δ; the other ones are *open*. We denote the set of defined predicates by $Def(\Delta)$ and that of all open ones by $Op(\Delta)$.

We now define a class of semantics for such rule sets. We interpret an alphabet Σ by a Σ-*structure* or Σ-*interpretation*. Such a Σ-interpretation I consists of a domain $dom(I)$, an interpretation of the object symbols c of Σ by domain elements, an interpretation of each function symbol f/n of Σ by an n-ary function on D, and an interpretation of each predicate symbol P/n by an n-ary relation on $dom(I)$. A *pre-interpretation* of Σ is an interpretation of $\Sigma^o \cup \Sigma^f$. If the alphabet Σ is clear from the context, we often omit this from our notation. For any symbol $\sigma \in \Sigma$, we denote by σ^I the interpretation of σ by I. Similarly, for a term t we denote the interpretation of t by t^I and we also extend this notation to tuples $\boldsymbol{t}$ of terms. For a structure I, an object symbol x, and a $d \in dom(I)$, we denote by $I[x/d]$ the interpretation J with the same domain as I, that interprets x by d and coincides with I on everything else. We also extend this notation to tuples $\boldsymbol{x}$ and $\boldsymbol{d}$. We define a truth order $\leq$ on Σ-interpretations by $I \leq J$ if I and J coincide on all object and function symbols and $P^I \subseteq P^J$ for each $P \in \Sigma^p$.

A feature of stable and well-founded semantics of Logic Programming is that positive and negative occurrences of atoms in rule bodies are treated very differently. The following non-standard truth evaluation function captures this.

Definition 1. *Let ϕ be a formula. Let I and J be structures, which coincide on their domain D and their interpretation of both the object and function symbols. We now define when a formula ϕ is satisfied in the pair $(I\ J)$, denoted $(I\ J) \models \phi$, by induction over the size of ϕ:*

- *$(I\ J) \models P(\boldsymbol{t})$ iff $I \models P(\boldsymbol{t})$, i.e., $\boldsymbol{t}^I \in P^I$;*
- *$(I\ J) \models \neg\phi$ iff $(J\ I) \not\models \phi$;*
- *$(I\ J) \models \phi \vee \psi$ iff $(I\ J) \models \phi$ or $(I\ J) \models \psi$;*
- *$(I\ J) \models \exists x\ \phi(x)$ iff there is a $d \in dom(I)$, such that $(I[x/d]\ J[x/d]) \models \phi(x)$.*

Observe that evaluating the negation connective $\neg$ switches the roles of I and J. Hence, this is the standard evaluation except that positively occurring atoms in ϕ are interpreted by I, while negatively occurring atoms in ϕ are interpreted by J. This evaluation function has a natural explanation when we view a pair $(I\ J)$ as an approximation, i.e., when I is seen as a lower estimate and J as an upper estimate of some interpretation I'. When $I \leq I' \leq J$, positive occurrences of atoms are underestimated by using I and negative occurrences of atoms are overestimated by using J. It follows that $(I\ J) \models \phi$ implies $I' \models \phi$. Or, if $(I\ J) \models \phi$, then ϕ is certainly true in every approximated interpretation, while if $(I\ J) \not\models \phi$, then ϕ is possibly false. Vice versa, when computing whether $(J\ I) \models \phi$, positively occurring atoms are overestimated and negatively occurring ones are underestimated. Hence, if $(J\ I) \not\models \phi$, then ϕ is certainly false in approximated interpretations. Combining both observations, ϕ is certainly true in any structure in $[I, J]$ if $(I\ J) \models \phi$, certainly false if $(J\ I) \not\models \phi$ and possibly true, possibly false if $(I\ J) \not\models \phi$ and $(J\ I) \models \phi$. There is a strong link with four-valued logic. Indeed, pairs $(I\ J)$ (sharing domains and interpretations of object and function symbols) correspond to four-valued interpretations, and the above non-standard truth evaluation is equivalent to standard four-valued truth evaluation. More precisely, the four-valued valuation $\phi^{(I\ J)}$ of a formula ϕ is:

$$\phi^{(I\ J)} = \mathbf{t} \text{ iff } (I\ J) \models \phi \text{ and } (J\ I) \models \phi; \ \phi^{(I\ J)} = \mathbf{f} \text{ iff } (I\ J) \not\models \phi \text{ and } (J\ I) \not\models \phi;$$
$$\phi^{(I\ J)} = \mathbf{u} \text{ iff } (I\ J) \not\models \phi \text{ and } (J\ I) \models \phi; \ \phi^{(I\ J)} = \mathbf{i} \text{ iff } (I\ J) \models \phi \text{ and } (J\ I) \not\models \phi.$$

From now on, for a formula $\phi(\boldsymbol{x})$ and a tuple $\boldsymbol{d}$ of domain elements, we will write $(I\ J) \models \phi(\boldsymbol{d})$ instead of $(I[\boldsymbol{x}/\boldsymbol{d}]\ J[\boldsymbol{x}/\boldsymbol{d}]) \models \phi(\boldsymbol{x})$.

Given a set of predicates P, the class of all $(\Sigma^o \cup \Sigma^f \cup P)$-structures that extend some fixed pre-interpretation F is denoted as L_P^F. For the order $\leq$, L_P^F is a complete lattice. Given a pair of interpretations for the open predicates $(O_1 \; O_2)$ in $(L_{Op(\Delta)}^F)^2$, we will now define an immediate consequence operator $T_\Delta^{(O_1 \; O_2)}$ on pairs of interpretations of the defined predicates, i.e., on $(L_{Def(\Delta)}^F)^2$. The definition below is an alternative formalization of the standard four-valued immediate consequence operator [9].

Definition 2. *Let Δ be a rule set and $(O_1, O_2) \in (L_{Op(\Delta)}^F)^2$. We define a function $U_\Delta^{(O_1 \; O_2)}$ from $(L_{Def(\Delta)}^F)^2$ to $L_{Def(\Delta)}^F$ as: $U_\Delta^{(O_1 \; O_2)}(I \; J) = I'$, where for each defined predicate P/n, for each $\boldsymbol{d} \in dom(F)^n$, $\boldsymbol{d} \in P^{I'}$ iff there exists a rule $(\forall \boldsymbol{x} \; P(\boldsymbol{t}) \leftarrow \phi(\boldsymbol{x})) \in \Delta$ and an $\boldsymbol{a} \in dom(F)^n$, such that $((O_1 \cup I) \; (O_2 \cup J)) \models \phi(\boldsymbol{a})$ and $\boldsymbol{t}^{F[\boldsymbol{x}/\boldsymbol{a}]} = \boldsymbol{d}$. We define the operator $T_\Delta^{(O_1 \; O_2)}$ on $(L_{Def(\Delta)}^F)^2$ as $T_\Delta^{(O_1 \; O_2)}(I \; J) = (U_\Delta^{(O_1 \; O_2)}(I \; J) \; U_\Delta^{(O_2 \; O_1)}(J \; I))$.*

It can be shown that every $T_\Delta^{(O_1 \; O_2)}$ is an approximation of the well-known 2-valued immediate consequence operator T_Δ^O, which can be defined as $T_\Delta^O(I) = [T_\Delta^{(O \; O)}(I \; I)]$. Because $T_\Delta^{(O_1 \; O_2)}$ is an approximation, it has a stable operator $C_{T_\Delta^{(O_1 \; O_2)}}$. The *well-founded model* $(W_1 \; W_2)$ of Δ given $(O_1 \; O_2)$ is the least fixpoint of this stable operator. Similarly, a structure $S \in L_{Def(\Delta)}^F$ is a *stable model* of Δ given $(O_1 \; O_2)$ iff S is a fixpoint of this stable operator. If Δ is a logic program, then $Op(\Delta) = \emptyset$ and O_1, O_2 coincide with the Herbrand pre-interpretation F. In this case C_{T_Δ} is symmetric and the upper and lower stable operators are identical to the well-known Gelfond-Lifschitz operator $\mathcal{GL}_\Delta$ [10].

A rule set Δ is *monotone* iff every $T_\Delta^{(O_1 \; O_2)}$ is a monotone operator (w.r.t. the product order $\leq$). For such rule sets, the well-founded model of Δ given some $(O_1 \; O_2)$ can be shown to coincide with $\mathrm{lfp}(T_\Delta^{(O_1 \; O_2)})$, which is also the unique stable model for Δ given $(O_1 \; O_2)$. A rule set Δ is *positive* iff no defined predicate appears negatively in a rule body of Δ. Such rule sets are always monotone.

We now introduce the following notions of the models of a rule set. In this definition, we use the notation $(I \; J)|_\Pi$ where Π is a set of predicate symbols, to indicate the restriction of I and J to the symbols in Π.

Definition 3. *Let Δ be a rule set and F a pre-interpretation. Let S_1, S_2, W_1, W_2 be Σ-structures that extend F. The pair $(W_1 \; W_2)$ is a model of Δ under the well-founded semantics, denoted $(W_1 \; W_2) \models_w \Delta$ iff $(W_1 \; W_2)|_{Def(\Delta)}$ is the well-founded model of Δ under $(W_1 \; W_2)|_{Op(\Delta)}$. The pair $(S_1 \; S_2)$ is a model of Δ under the stable model semantics, denoted $(S_1 \; S_2) \models_s \Delta$ iff $S_1|_{Def(\Delta)} = S_2|_{Def(\Delta)}$ and $S_1|_{Def(\Delta)}$ is a stable model of Δ under $(S_1 \; S_2)|_{Op(\Delta)}$.*

Using the above definitions, we can now characterize stable and well-founded semantics of the following extensions of Logic Programming:

- Normal Logic Programming: bodies are conjunctions of literals, no open predicates, F is the Herbrand pre-interpretation.

- Abductive Logic Programming: the same, except that *abducible* predicates are open, and their interpretation is arbitrary.
- Deductive Databases, and its extension AFP [15]: intensional predicates are defined, extensional database predicates are open but interpreted by the database O.
- LP-functions [11]: rule bodies are conjunctions of literals, open and defined predicates, interpretation of open predicates is arbitrary.
- ID-logic [6]: a model of a definition Δ is any 2-valued well-founded model of Δ.

The results of the following sections are applicable to all these formalisms.

3   Fixpoint Extension

We want to study the following transformation. We start out with a rule set Δ in some alphabet Σ and then introduce a set of new symbols Σ_n, e.g., the two predicates *AllPrecHold* and *AllFrom* from the example in the introduction. We then use these new predicates to form a new definition Δ' over alphabet $\Sigma' = \Sigma \cup \Sigma_n$. In order to study such transformations in an algebraic setting, we will assume two complete lattices $\langle L_1, \leq_1 \rangle$ and $\langle L_2, \leq_2 \rangle$. Here, L_1 can be thought of as consisting of the interpretations for the original alphabet Σ, while L_2 represents the interpretations for the additional new alphabet Σ_n. We will need to prove a result concerning the stable and well-founded models of Δ', which means that we will need to work with pairs of interpretations of Σ'. As such, in our algebraic setting, we consider the square $(L_1 \times L_2)^2$ of the Cartesian product $L_1 \times L_2$, which is isomorphic to the Cartesian product $L_1^2 \times L_2^2$ of the squares of these lattices. We denote pairs $P = ((x\ u)\ (y\ v))$ of this latter Cartesian product by $\begin{pmatrix} x\ u \\ y\ v \end{pmatrix}$, where $(x\ u) \in L_1^2$ and $(y\ v) \in L_2^2$. We introduce the following projection functions: by $[P|$ we denote the pair $\begin{pmatrix} x \\ y \end{pmatrix}$, by $|P]$ the pair $\begin{pmatrix} u \\ v \end{pmatrix}$, by $\lceil P \rceil$ the pair $(x\ u)$, by $\lfloor P \rfloor$ the pair $(y\ v)$, by $\lfloor P \rfloor$ the element y, by $\lceil P \rceil$ the element x, by $\lfloor P \rfloor$ the element u, and by $\lfloor P \rfloor$ the element v.

Now, we want relate the stable and well-founded fixpoints of the operator T_Δ of the original definition Δ to those of the new operator $T_{\Delta'}$. Algebraically, we consider an approximation A on the square L_1^2 of the original lattice L_1 and an approximation B on the extended lattice $L_1^2 \times L_2^2$. We now impose some conditions to ensure a correspondence between the stable fixpoints of A and B.

The main idea behind these conditions is the following. By introducing a new predicate into our original definition Δ, we have added an additional "indirection". For instance, in the original version Δ of our example, we had the formula $\forall i, q\ Prec(r, i, q) \Rightarrow Holds(q)$, that could be evaluated in order to check whether all preconditions q of rule r were satisfied. This could be done by the T_Δ-operator in a single step. In our new definition Δ', however, every application of $T_{\Delta'}$ only checks whether a single precondition is satisfied. Intuitively, to match the effect of a single application of T_Δ to some pair (X, Y) of interpretations of the alphabet of Δ, we have to iterate $T_{\Delta'}$ long enough for the truth assignments of (X, Y) to propagate throughout all of the new symbols of Δ'. Nevertheless, the end result of this iteration of $\mathcal{T}_{\Delta'}$ should coincide with the result of the single application of $\mathcal{T}_{\Delta}$. We need some more notation to formalize this intuition.

Given the operator B on $L_1^2 \times L_2^2$ and a pair $(x\ u) \in L_1^2$, we define the operator $B^{(x\ u)}$ on L_2^2 as $\lambda(y\ v).\lfloor B\left(\begin{smallmatrix} x & u \\ y & v \end{smallmatrix}\right)\rfloor$. Conversely, given a pair $(y\ v) \in L_2^2$, we define the operator $B_{(y\ v)}$ on L_1^2 as $\lambda(x\ u).\lceil B\left(\begin{smallmatrix} x & u \\ y & v \end{smallmatrix}\right)\rceil$. We say that B is L_2-monotone iff for each $(x\ u) \in L_1^2$ and $(y\ v) \le (y'\ v') \in L_2^2$, $B\left(\begin{smallmatrix} x & u \\ y & v \end{smallmatrix}\right) \le B\left(\begin{smallmatrix} x & u \\ y' & v' \end{smallmatrix}\right)$. If B is L_2-monotone, then every operator $B^{(x\ u)}$ is monotone. The least fixpoint $lfp(B^{(x\ u)})$ of such an operator is now an important concept. Indeed, if we are extending a definition Δ with some new predicates Σ_n, then this least fixpoint will tell us what can be obtained by iteratively applying (only) the rules for Σ_n.

Definition 4 (Fixpoint extension). *Let B be an approximation on $L_1^2 \times L_2^2$ and A an approximation on L_1^2. B is a* fixpoint extension *of A iff*

- *B is L_2-monotone;*
- *For all $x, u \in L_1$, $B_{lfp(B^{(x\ u)})}(x\ u) = A(x\ u)$.*

The main algebraic result of this paper is that fixpoint extension preserves both stable and well-founded fixpoints.

Theorem 1 (Fixpoint extension). *Let B be a fixpoint extension of A. $\left(\begin{smallmatrix} x & u \\ y & v \end{smallmatrix}\right)$ is a fixpoint of the stable operator $\mathcal{C}_B$ iff $(x\ u)$ is a fixpoint of the stable operator $\mathcal{C}_A$ and $(y\ v) = lfp(B^{(x\ u)})$. Moreover, if $(x\ u)$ is the well-founded fixpoint of A and $(y\ v) = lfp(B^{(x\ u)})$, then the well-founded fixpoint of B is precisely $\left(\begin{smallmatrix} x & u \\ y & v \end{smallmatrix}\right)$.*

To prove this theorem, we first study some of the properties of B and $lfp(B^{(x\ u)})$. First, we establish that $B^{(x\ u)}$ can be split in two independent parts.

Lemma 1. *Let B be L_2-monotone. Then for all $y, v \in L_2$, $B^{(x\ u)}(y\ v) = (B_1^{(x\ u)}(y)\ B_2^{(x\ u)}(v))$, where the operators $B_1^{(x\ u)}$ and $B_2^{(x\ u)}$ on L_2 are defined as $B_1^{(x\ u)}(y) = \lfloor B^{(x\ u)}(y\ \top)\rfloor$ and $B_2^{(x\ u)}(v) = \lceil B^{(x\ u)}(\top\ v)\rceil$.*

Proof. For $B_1^{(x\ u)}$, it suffices to show that, for all $y, v \in L_2$, $B^{(x\ u)}(y\ v)$ and $B^{(x\ u)}(y\ \top)$ agree on the first component of the result, i.e., $\lfloor B\left(\begin{smallmatrix} x & u \\ y & v \end{smallmatrix}\right)\rfloor = \lfloor B\left(\begin{smallmatrix} x & u \\ y & \top \end{smallmatrix}\right)\rfloor$. Similarly, for B_2 there must be agreement on the second component, i.e., for all $y, v \in L_2$: $\lfloor B\left(\begin{smallmatrix} x & u \\ y & v \end{smallmatrix}\right)\rfloor = \lfloor B\left(\begin{smallmatrix} x & u \\ \top & v \end{smallmatrix}\right)\rfloor$. We will only prove the equality for $B_1^{(x\ u)}$; the proof of the second equality is analogous.

First, we note that $\left(\begin{smallmatrix} x & u \\ y & v \end{smallmatrix}\right) \ge_p \left(\begin{smallmatrix} x & u \\ y & \top \end{smallmatrix}\right)$. By $\le_p$-monotonicity of B, this implies that $\lfloor B\left(\begin{smallmatrix} x & u \\ y & v \end{smallmatrix}\right)\rfloor \ge \lfloor B\left(\begin{smallmatrix} x & u \\ y & \top \end{smallmatrix}\right)\rfloor$. Secondly, we also note that $\left(\begin{smallmatrix} x & u \\ y & v \end{smallmatrix}\right) \le \left(\begin{smallmatrix} x & u \\ y & \top \end{smallmatrix}\right)$. By L_2-monotonicity of B, this implies that $\lfloor B\left(\begin{smallmatrix} x & u \\ y & v \end{smallmatrix}\right)\rfloor \le \lfloor B\left(\begin{smallmatrix} x & u \\ y & \top \end{smallmatrix}\right)\rfloor$. Combining these two inequalities gives the desired result.

The stable operator $\mathcal{C}_B$ of an approximation B is defined in terms of its lower and upper stable operators $C_B^{\downarrow}$ and $C_B^{\uparrow}$. We show the following relation between these operators and the operators $B_1^{(x\ u)}$ and $B_2^{(x\ u)}$ from Lemma 1.

Lemma 2. *If $\left(\begin{smallmatrix} x \\ y \end{smallmatrix}\right) = C_B^{\downarrow}\left(\begin{smallmatrix} u \\ v \end{smallmatrix}\right)$, then $y = lfp(B_1^{(x\ u)})$. If $\left(\begin{smallmatrix} u \\ v \end{smallmatrix}\right) = C_B^{\uparrow}\left(\begin{smallmatrix} x \\ y \end{smallmatrix}\right)$, then $v = lfp(B_2^{(x\ u)})$.*

Proof. We only prove the first implication; the proof of the second one is analogous. Let $z = \text{lfp}(B_1^{(x\ u)})$. We will show that $y = z$. We start by showing that $z \leq y$. By definition of C_B, $\left(\begin{smallmatrix} x \\ y \end{smallmatrix}\right) = \lceil B\left(\begin{smallmatrix} x & u \\ y & v \end{smallmatrix}\right)\rceil$. In particular, $y = B_1^{(x\ u)}(y)$, i.e., y is a fixpoint of $B_1^{(x\ u)}$. Because z was chosen to be the least fixpoint of this operator, $z \leq y$. Now, we prove that $y \leq z$. Because $z \leq y$, it is the case that $\left(\begin{smallmatrix} x & u \\ z & v \end{smallmatrix}\right) \leq \left(\begin{smallmatrix} x & u \\ y & v \end{smallmatrix}\right)$. By L_2-monotonicity of B, this implies that $B\left(\begin{smallmatrix} x & u \\ z & v \end{smallmatrix}\right) \leq B\left(\begin{smallmatrix} x & u \\ y & v \end{smallmatrix}\right)$ and, in particular, $\lceil B\left(\begin{smallmatrix} x & u \\ z & v \end{smallmatrix}\right)\rceil \leq \lceil B\left(\begin{smallmatrix} x & u \\ y & v \end{smallmatrix}\right)\rceil = x$. Because z is a fixpoint of $B_1^{(x\ u)}$, we also have that $\lfloor B\left(\begin{smallmatrix} x & u \\ z & v \end{smallmatrix}\right)\rfloor = z$. As such, $\lceil B\left(\begin{smallmatrix} x & u \\ z & v \end{smallmatrix}\right)\rceil \leq \left(\begin{smallmatrix} x \\ z \end{smallmatrix}\right)$ or, in other words, $\left(\begin{smallmatrix} x \\ z \end{smallmatrix}\right)$ is a prefixpoint of $\lceil B\left(\begin{smallmatrix} x & \cdot \\ \cdot & v \end{smallmatrix}\right)\rceil$. Because the least fixpoint $\left(\begin{smallmatrix} x \\ y \end{smallmatrix}\right)$ of this operator is also its least prefixpoint, $\left(\begin{smallmatrix} x \\ y \end{smallmatrix}\right) \leq \left(\begin{smallmatrix} x \\ z \end{smallmatrix}\right)$; in particular, $y \leq z$.

In order to prove the correspondence between well-founded fixpoints, we will also need to take the precision order into account.

Lemma 3. $\forall x, x', u, u' \in L_1$, $(x\ u) \leq_p (x'\ u')$ iff $\left(\begin{smallmatrix} x & & u \\ & \text{lfp}(B^{(x\ u)}) & \end{smallmatrix}\right) \leq_p \left(\begin{smallmatrix} x' & & u' \\ & \text{lfp}(B^{(x'\ u')}) & \end{smallmatrix}\right)$.

Proof. It is clear that the right hand side of this equivalence directly implies the left. Let x, x', u, u' be as above and let $(y\ v) = \text{lfp}(B^{(x\ u)})$ and $(y'\ v') = \text{lfp}(B^{(x'\ u')})$. It suffices to show that $(y\ v) \leq_p (y'\ v')$. We first show that $y \leq y'$. By Lemma 1, $y = \text{lfp}(B_1^{(x\ u)})$. Because this implies that y is also the least prefixpoint of $B_1^{(x\ u)}$, it now suffices to show that y' is a prefixpoint of $B_1^{(x\ u)}$ as well, i.e., that $y' \geq B_1^{(x\ u)}(y')$. Because for any w, $\left(\begin{smallmatrix} x' & u' \\ y' & w \end{smallmatrix}\right) \geq_p \left(\begin{smallmatrix} x & u \\ y' & w \end{smallmatrix}\right)$, we have that $y' = \lfloor B\left(\begin{smallmatrix} x' & u' \\ y' & w \end{smallmatrix}\right)\rfloor \geq \lfloor B\left(\begin{smallmatrix} x & u \\ y' & w \end{smallmatrix}\right)\rfloor = B_1^{(x\ u)}(y')$.

We now show that $v \geq v'$. By Lemma 1, $v' = \text{lfp}(B_2^{(x'\ u')})$. This implies that v' is also the least prefixpoint of $B_2^{(x'\ u')}$ and, therefore, it suffices to show that $v \geq B_2^{(x'\ u')}(v)$. Because for any z, $\left(\begin{smallmatrix} x' & u' \\ z & v \end{smallmatrix}\right) \geq_p \left(\begin{smallmatrix} x & u \\ z & v \end{smallmatrix}\right)$, we have that: $B_2^{(x'\ u')}(v) = \lfloor B\left(\begin{smallmatrix} x' & u' \\ z & v \end{smallmatrix}\right)\rfloor \leq \lfloor B\left(\begin{smallmatrix} x & u \\ z & v \end{smallmatrix}\right)\rfloor = v$.

Proof (of Theorem 1). We first show that if $\left(\begin{smallmatrix} x & u \\ y & v \end{smallmatrix}\right)$ is a fixpoint of C_B, then $(x\ u)$ is a fixpoint of C_A and $(y\ v)$ is $\text{lfp}(B^{(x\ u)})$. By definition, $\left(\begin{smallmatrix} x & u \\ y & v \end{smallmatrix}\right)$ is a fixpoint of C_B iff $\left(\begin{smallmatrix} x \\ y \end{smallmatrix}\right) = C_B^{\downarrow}\left(\begin{smallmatrix} u \\ v \end{smallmatrix}\right)$ and $\left(\begin{smallmatrix} u \\ v \end{smallmatrix}\right) = C_B^{\uparrow}\left(\begin{smallmatrix} x \\ y \end{smallmatrix}\right)$. By Lemma 2, if this is the case, then $y = \text{lfp}(B_1^{(x\ u)})$ and $v = \text{lfp}(B_2^{(u\ x)})$. As such $(y\ v) = \text{lfp}(B^{(x\ u)})$. Because B is an extension of A, we now have that $\lceil B\left(\begin{smallmatrix} x & u \\ y & v \end{smallmatrix}\right)\rceil = A(x\ u)$.

To prove the other direction, let $(x\ u) = C_A(x\ u)$ and let $(y\ v)$ be $\text{lfp}(B^{(x\ u)})$. We need to show that $\left(\begin{smallmatrix} x & u \\ y & v \end{smallmatrix}\right)$ is a fixpoint of C_B, i.e., that $\left(\begin{smallmatrix} x \\ y \end{smallmatrix}\right) = C_B^{\downarrow}\left(\begin{smallmatrix} u \\ v \end{smallmatrix}\right)$ and $\left(\begin{smallmatrix} u \\ v \end{smallmatrix}\right) = C_B^{\uparrow}\left(\begin{smallmatrix} x \\ y \end{smallmatrix}\right)$. We only show that $\left(\begin{smallmatrix} x \\ y \end{smallmatrix}\right) = C_B^{\downarrow}\left(\begin{smallmatrix} u \\ v \end{smallmatrix}\right)$; the proof of the other equality is analogous. First, note that $\lceil B\left(\begin{smallmatrix} x & u \\ y & v \end{smallmatrix}\right)\rceil = \lceil A(x\ u)\rceil = x$ and $\lfloor B\left(\begin{smallmatrix} x & u \\ y & v \end{smallmatrix}\right)\rfloor = B_1^{(x\ u)}(y) = y$. Hence, $\lceil B\left(\begin{smallmatrix} x & u \\ y & v \end{smallmatrix}\right)\rceil = \left(\begin{smallmatrix} x \\ y \end{smallmatrix}\right)$, i.e., $\left(\begin{smallmatrix} x \\ y \end{smallmatrix}\right)$ is a fixpoint of $\lceil B\left(\begin{smallmatrix} \cdot & u \\ \cdot & v \end{smallmatrix}\right)\rceil$. It now suffices to show that $\left(\begin{smallmatrix} x \\ y \end{smallmatrix}\right)$ is the *least* such fixpoint. Assume that $\left(\begin{smallmatrix} a \\ b \end{smallmatrix}\right)$ is such that $\lceil B\left(\begin{smallmatrix} a & u \\ b & v \end{smallmatrix}\right)\rceil = \left(\begin{smallmatrix} a \\ b \end{smallmatrix}\right)$ and $\left(\begin{smallmatrix} a \\ b \end{smallmatrix}\right) \leq \left(\begin{smallmatrix} x \\ y \end{smallmatrix}\right)$. We show that $\left(\begin{smallmatrix} a \\ b \end{smallmatrix}\right) \geq \left(\begin{smallmatrix} x \\ y \end{smallmatrix}\right)$. Let $(b'\ c) = \text{lfp}(B^{(a\ u)})$. Because b is a fixpoint of $B_1^{(a\ u)}$, $b' \leq b$ and therefore $\left(\begin{smallmatrix} a & u \\ b' & c \end{smallmatrix}\right) \leq_p \left(\begin{smallmatrix} a & u \\ b & c \end{smallmatrix}\right)$.

By Lemma 3, the fact that $a \leq x$ implies that $c \geq v$. Consequently, we have that $\begin{pmatrix} a & u \\ b & c \end{pmatrix} \leq_p \begin{pmatrix} a & u \\ b & v \end{pmatrix}$ and, therefore, by $\leq_p$-monotonicity of B:

$$[A(a\ u)] = \lceil B\begin{pmatrix} a & u \\ b' & c \end{pmatrix} \rceil \leq \lceil B\begin{pmatrix} a & u \\ b & c \end{pmatrix} \rceil \leq \lceil B\begin{pmatrix} a & u \\ b & v \end{pmatrix} \rceil = a$$

Hence, a is a prefixpoint of $[A(\cdot\ u)]$. Because x is the least such prefixpoint, $x \leq a$ and, therefore, $x = a$. As such, by Lemma 2, we now have that $y = lfp(B_1^{(x\ u)}) = lfp(B_1^{(a\ u)})$ and, because b is a fixpoint of $B_1^{(a\ u)}$, $y \leq b$. As we already have that $b \leq y$, this implies that $b = y$.

The fact that $\begin{pmatrix} u \\ v \end{pmatrix} = C_B^\uparrow \begin{pmatrix} x \\ y \end{pmatrix}$ can be shown in the same way.

Given this one-to-one correspondence between stable fixpoints of A and those of B, the correspondence between the well-founded fixpoint of A and that of B follows directly from Lemma 3.

4 Application to Rule Sets

In this section, we use the algebraic results of Section 3 to derive a concrete equivalence theorem for rule sets. Recall that we are interested in transformations from some original rule set Δ over an alphabet Σ into a new rule set Δ' over an alphabet $\Sigma' \supseteq \Sigma$. More concretely, Δ' is the result of replacing a subformula $\phi(\boldsymbol{x})$ of some rule of Δ by a new predicate $P(\boldsymbol{x})$ and adding a new rule set δ to Δ to define this new predicate P. We will denote the result of replacing (some fixed set of occurrences of) $\phi(\boldsymbol{x})$ in Δ by $P(\boldsymbol{x})$ as $\Delta[\phi(\boldsymbol{x})/P(\boldsymbol{x})]$, i.e., $\Delta' = \Delta[\phi(\boldsymbol{x})/P(\boldsymbol{x})] \cup \delta$. We will assume that $\Sigma \cap Def(\delta)$ is empty. Note that Δ' may contain new open atoms.

We now impose some criteria to ensure that, for certain interpretations O of the open predicates of Δ', the operator $T_{\Delta'}^{(O\ O)}$ is a fixpoint extension of $T_{\Delta}^{(O\ O)}$. We state our theorem for the set C of all structures that extend O to Σ'.

Theorem 2 (Predicate introduction). *Let Δ be a rule set and let Δ' be the result of replacing some positive occurrences of $\phi(\boldsymbol{x})$ by $P(\boldsymbol{x})$ defined in δ, as outlined above. If the following conditions are satisfied:*

1. *δ is a monotone rule set;*
2. *for all $I, J \in C$ such that $(I\ J) \models_s \delta$: $\forall \boldsymbol{a} \in D^n$, $P(\boldsymbol{a})^{(I\ J)} = \phi(\boldsymbol{a})^{(I\ J)}$;*

then for all I, J in C, $(I\ I)|_\Sigma \models_s \Delta$ iff $(I\ I) \models_s \Delta'$ and $(I\ J)|_\Sigma \models_w \Delta$ iff $(I\ J) \models_w \Delta'$.

Observe that because δ is monotone, we could have equivalently used $\models_w$ instead of $\models_s$ in condition 2. To see that this theorem applies to our example from the introduction, let δ be the rules given in (5). Clearly, δ is positive. Now, if we restrict our attention to those interpretations O for $Open(\Delta')$ that actually correspond to $\mathcal{AL}$-rules[1], then it is easy to see that for all $r \in dom(O)$, $AllPrecHold(r)^{(I\ J)}$ iff $\phi(r)^{(I\ J)}$. As such, Condition 2 is satisfied.

---

[1] More specifically, for every r there should be a unique n such that $(r, n) \in NbOfPrec^O$ and for every $1 \leq i \leq n$ there should a unique q such that $(r, i, q) \in Prec^O$.

Proof (of Theorem 2). Let $L = \{I|_{Def(\Delta)} \mid I \in C\}$ and $L' = \{I|_{Def(\delta)} \mid I \in C\}$. Now, C is isomorphic to $L \times L'$. Let T be $T_\Delta^{(O\ O)} : L^2 \to L^2$ and T' be $T_{\Delta'}^{(O\ O)} : (L \times L')^2 \to (L \times L')^2$. It suffices to prove that T' is a fixpoint extension of T, i.e., that (1) T' is L'-monotone and (2) $\left\lceil T'_{\text{lfp}(T'^{(I\ J)})}(I\ J) \right\rceil = T(I\ J)$ for any $I, J \in L$.

We first show (1). Let $(I\ J) \in L^2$ and $(I'_1\ J'_1) \leq (I'_2\ J'_2) \in L'^2$. We have to prove the inequality $T'\left(\begin{smallmatrix} I & J \\ I'_1 & J'_1 \end{smallmatrix}\right) \leq T'\left(\begin{smallmatrix} I & J \\ I'_2 & J'_2 \end{smallmatrix}\right)$. By the monotonicity of δ, we have $\left\lfloor T'\left(\begin{smallmatrix} I & J \\ I'_1 & J'_1 \end{smallmatrix}\right) \right\rfloor = T_\delta^{(I\ J)}(I'_1\ J'_1) \leq T_\delta^{(I\ J)}(I'_2\ J'_2) = \left\lfloor T'\left(\begin{smallmatrix} I & J \\ I'_2 & J'_2 \end{smallmatrix}\right) \right\rfloor$. For a predicate $Q \in Def(\Delta)$ and domain elements $\boldsymbol{a}$, such that $\left\lceil T'\left(\begin{smallmatrix} I & J \\ I'_1 & J'_1 \end{smallmatrix}\right) \right\rceil \models Q(\boldsymbol{a})$, there exist a rule $\forall \boldsymbol{x}\ Q(\boldsymbol{t}) \leftarrow \psi(\boldsymbol{x})$ and domain elements $\boldsymbol{d}$ such that $\boldsymbol{t}^{O[\boldsymbol{x}/\boldsymbol{d}]} = \boldsymbol{a}$. Then $\left(\begin{smallmatrix} I & J \\ I'_1 & J'_1 \end{smallmatrix}\right) \models \psi(\boldsymbol{d})$. Since P only occurs positively in ψ, this implies $\left(\begin{smallmatrix} I & J \\ I'_2 & J'_2 \end{smallmatrix}\right) \models \psi(\boldsymbol{d})$. Hence, also in this case $Q(\boldsymbol{a}) \in \left\lceil T'\left(\begin{smallmatrix} I & J \\ I'_2 & J'_2 \end{smallmatrix}\right) \right\rceil$. For $Q(\boldsymbol{a})$ such that $\left\lceil T'\left(\begin{smallmatrix} I & J \\ I'_1 & J'_1 \end{smallmatrix}\right) \right\rceil \models Q(\boldsymbol{a})$, an analogous proof can be given to complete our proof of L'-monotonicity.

We now show (2). Let $(I'\ J') = \text{lfp}(T'^{(I\ J)})$. Then $(I'\ J') = \text{lfp}(T_\delta^{(I \cup O\ J \cup O)})$, and, therefore, by the monotonicity of δ, $\left(\begin{smallmatrix} I & J \\ I' & J' \end{smallmatrix}\right) \models_s \delta$. Denoting $I_2 = \left(\begin{smallmatrix} I \\ I' \end{smallmatrix}\right)$ and $J_2 = \left(\begin{smallmatrix} J \\ J' \end{smallmatrix}\right)$, we then have by condition 2 that $\forall \boldsymbol{c} \in D^n\ P(\boldsymbol{c})^{(I_2\ J_2)} = \phi(\boldsymbol{c})^{(I_2\ J_2)}$, hence $(I_2\ J_2) \models P(\boldsymbol{c})$ iff $(I_2\ J_2) \models \phi(\boldsymbol{c})$.

We also have that $\left\lceil T(I\ J) \right\rceil \models Q(\boldsymbol{a})$ iff Δ contains a rule $\forall \boldsymbol{x}\ Q(\boldsymbol{t}) \leftarrow \psi(\boldsymbol{x})$ and domain elements $\boldsymbol{d}$ exist such that $\boldsymbol{t}^{O[\boldsymbol{x}/\boldsymbol{d}]} = \boldsymbol{a}$ and $(I\ J) \models \psi(\boldsymbol{d})$. The corresponding rule in Δ' is $\forall \boldsymbol{x}\ Q(\boldsymbol{t}) \leftarrow \psi'(\boldsymbol{x})$. Consequently, $(I_2\ J_2) \models \psi(\boldsymbol{d})$ iff $(I_2\ J_2) \models \psi'(\boldsymbol{d})$. The proof for a $Q(\boldsymbol{a})$ such that $\left\lfloor T(I\ J) \right\rfloor \models Q(\boldsymbol{a})$ is analogous.

Condition 2 of Theorem 2 requires us to check a four-valued equivalence between $P(\boldsymbol{x})$ as defined by δ and the original formula $\phi(\boldsymbol{x})$. One might wonder whether this is really necessary, i.e., whether it would suffice to check only the following two-valued equivalence:

$$\text{For all } I \in C \text{ such that } (I\ I) \models_s \delta : \forall \boldsymbol{a} \in D^n, I \models P(\boldsymbol{a}) \text{ iff } I \models \phi(\boldsymbol{a}). \tag{6}$$

In general, this is not the case. For instance, consider an attempt to replace in $\Delta = \{R \leftarrow Q \vee \neg Q.\ Q \leftarrow \neg Q.\}$ the formula $\phi = Q \vee \neg Q$ by a new predicate P, defined by a definition $\delta = \{P.\}$. The above equivalence and all other conditions of Theorem 2 would then be satisfied, but the well-founded model of $\Delta' = \{R \leftarrow P.\ P.\ Q \leftarrow \neg Q.\}$ is $(\{R, P\}\ \{R, P, Q\})$, while that of Δ is $(\{\}\ \{R, Q\})$.

The four-valued way of interpreting formulas is an integral part of both stable and well-founded semantics. Therefore, it makes sense that, as the above example shows, a four-valued equivalence is required in order to preserve either of these semantics. In practice, however, this should not pose too much of a problem, since most common transformations from classical logic, e.g. the De Morgan and distributivity laws, are still equivalence preserving in the four-valued case.

5   Applications and Related Work

The kind of transformations considered in this paper have a long history in Logic Programming. In particular, we consider three related investigations:

- Lloyd and Topor [12] introduced transformations that preserve equivalence under the 2-valued completion semantics. It is well-known that these transformations do not preserve equivalence under the well-founded or stable model semantics. As such, our result can be seen as an attempt to provide Lloyd-Topor-like transformations for these semantics.
- Van Gelder [15] presented a logic of alternating fixpoints to generalize the well-founded semantics to arbitrary rule bodies. In the same paper, he established the result given below as Theorem 3. We discuss the relation of our work with this result in Section 5.1
- The "Principle of Partial Evaluation" (PPE) was introduced by Dix in a study of properties for classifying Logic Programming semantics [7]. As we discuss in Section 5.2, this principle has a strong relation with our work.

More recently, there has been a lot of work in Answer Set Programming on the topic of strong equivalence. In general, the transformations we considered here do not preserve strong equivalence, because they are specific to a particular rule set. To illustrate, our result shows that $\Delta = \{P \leftarrow \neg Q.\ Q \leftarrow Q.\}$ is equivalent to $\Delta' = \{P \leftarrow R.\ R \leftarrow \neg Q.\ Q \leftarrow Q.\}$. However, Δ and Δ' are not strongly equivalent. For instance, if we consider the additional rule $Q \leftarrow \neg R$, it is easy to see that the stable models of $\Delta \cup \{Q \leftarrow \neg R.\}$ and $\Delta' \cup \{Q \leftarrow \neg R.\}$ are different.

5.1   Predicate Extraction and Eliminating ∀

The following result is due to Van Gelder:

Theorem 3 ([15]). *Let Δ be a rule set containing a rule $r = \forall \boldsymbol{x}\ P(\boldsymbol{t}) \leftarrow \psi$. Let $\phi(\boldsymbol{y})$ be an existentially quantified conjunction of literals, and let Q be a new predicate symbol. If $\phi(\boldsymbol{y})$ is a positive subformula of ψ, then Δ is equivalent under the stable and well-founded semantics to the rule set Δ', that results from replacing $\phi(\boldsymbol{y})$ in r by $Q(\boldsymbol{y})$ and adding the rule $\forall \boldsymbol{y}\ Q(\boldsymbol{y}) \leftarrow \phi(\boldsymbol{y})$ to Δ.*

Because the rule set $\delta = \{\forall \boldsymbol{y}\ Q(\boldsymbol{y}) \leftarrow \phi(\boldsymbol{y}).\}$ clearly satisfies the conditions of Theorem 2, Van Gelder's theorem follows directly from ours. This result provides a theoretical justification for the common programming practice of *predicate extraction*: replacing a subformula that occurs in multiple rules by a new predicate to make the program more concise and more readable. In [14], predicate extraction is considered to be an important *refactoring* operation (i.e., an equivalence preserving transformation to improve maintainability) for Logic Programming.

Our result extends Van Gelder's theorem by allowing the new predicate Q to be defined by an additional rule set δ, instead of allowing only the definition $\{\forall \boldsymbol{y}\ Q(\boldsymbol{y}) \leftarrow \phi(\boldsymbol{y}).\}$. In particular, *recursive* definitions of Q are also allowed. This significantly increases the applicability of the theorem. Indeed, as we already illustrated in the introduction, it allows us to eliminate certain universal quantifiers. The general idea behind this method is that we can replace a universal quantifier by a recursion over some total order on the domain.

Definition 5 (Domain iterator). *Let C be a set of Σ-structures with domain D. Let $First/1$, $Next/2$ and $Last/1$ be predicate symbols of Σ. The triple*

$\langle First, Next, Last \rangle$ is a domain iterator in C iff for each structure $S \in C$: $Next^S$ is a total order on D, with a minimal element f and a maximal element l such that $First^S = \{f\}$ and $Last^S = \{l\}$.

Given such a domain iterator $It = \langle First, Next, Last \rangle$, we can introduce the following rule set δ_ϕ^{It} to define a new predicate $Forall(\boldsymbol{x})$ as a replacement for some $\phi(\boldsymbol{x}) = \forall y \; \psi(\boldsymbol{x}, y)$:

$$\forall \boldsymbol{x}, y \; Forall(\boldsymbol{x}) \leftarrow First(y) \wedge AllFrom(\boldsymbol{x}, y).$$
$$\forall \boldsymbol{x}, y, y' \; AllFrom(\boldsymbol{x}, y) \leftarrow \psi(\boldsymbol{x}, y) \wedge Next(y, y') \wedge AllFrom(\boldsymbol{x}, y'). \quad (7)$$
$$\forall \boldsymbol{x}, y \; AllFrom(\boldsymbol{x}, y) \leftarrow \psi(\boldsymbol{x}, y) \wedge Last(y).$$

The following result is obtained from Theorem 2. Due to space limitations, we omit a formal proof.

Theorem 4 ($\forall$ elimination). *Let Δ be a rule set and $\phi(\boldsymbol{x})$ be a formula of the form $\forall y \; \psi(\boldsymbol{x}, y)$, that appears only positively in the bodies of rules of Δ. For a set of structures C with finite domain, if It is a domain iterator, then $\Delta[\phi/Forall] \cup \delta_\phi^{It}$ is equivalent to Δ under stable and well-founded semantics.*

In this theorem, we assume a total order on the entire domain and this same order can be used to eliminate all universally quantified formulas, that satisfy the condition of the theorem. This is not precisely what happened in our example. Indeed, there, the universally quantified formula $\phi(\boldsymbol{x})$ was of the form: $\forall \boldsymbol{y} \; \Psi_1(\boldsymbol{x}, \boldsymbol{y}) \Rightarrow \Psi_2(\boldsymbol{x}, \boldsymbol{y})$. Using the above theorem, we would replace $\phi(\boldsymbol{x})$ by a recursion that says that the implication $\Psi_1(\boldsymbol{x}) \Rightarrow \Psi_2(\boldsymbol{x})$ must hold for every element in the domain. However, in our original version of this example, we actually replaced $\phi(\boldsymbol{x})$ by a recursion which says that for all $\boldsymbol{y}$ that satisfy $\Psi_1(\boldsymbol{x}, \boldsymbol{y})$ (i.e., for all i, q such that $Prec(r, i, q)$) the consequent $\Psi_2(\boldsymbol{x}, \boldsymbol{y})$ (i.e., $Holds(q)$) is satisfied. This is a more fine-grained approach, which we can also prove in general. A *restricted iterator* for $\boldsymbol{y}$ of $\psi_1(\boldsymbol{x}, \boldsymbol{y})$ in a structure I is a triple of predicates $\langle First(\boldsymbol{x}, \boldsymbol{y}), Next(\boldsymbol{x}, \boldsymbol{y}, \boldsymbol{y}'), Last(\boldsymbol{x}, \boldsymbol{y}) \rangle$, such that for every tuple $\boldsymbol{d}$ of elements of the domain D of I, $\langle First(\boldsymbol{d}, \boldsymbol{y}), Next(\boldsymbol{d}, \boldsymbol{y}, \boldsymbol{y}'), Last(\boldsymbol{d}, \boldsymbol{y}) \rangle$ is an iterator over $\{\boldsymbol{e} \in D^n \mid I \models \Psi_1(\boldsymbol{d}, \boldsymbol{e})\}$.

Given such a restricted iterator, we can define the following replacement $Forall(\boldsymbol{x})$ for $\phi(\boldsymbol{x})$:

$$\forall \boldsymbol{x}, \boldsymbol{y} \; Forall(\boldsymbol{x}) \leftarrow First(\boldsymbol{x}, \boldsymbol{y}) \wedge AllFrom(\boldsymbol{x}, \boldsymbol{y}).$$
$$\forall \boldsymbol{x}, \boldsymbol{y}, \boldsymbol{y}' \; AllFrom(\boldsymbol{x}, \boldsymbol{y}) \leftarrow \Psi_2(\boldsymbol{x}, \boldsymbol{y}) \wedge Next(\boldsymbol{x}, \boldsymbol{y}, \boldsymbol{y}') \wedge AllFrom(\boldsymbol{x}, \boldsymbol{y}').$$
$$\forall \boldsymbol{x}, \boldsymbol{y} \; AllFrom(\boldsymbol{x}, \boldsymbol{y}) \leftarrow \Psi_2(\boldsymbol{x}, \boldsymbol{y}) \wedge Last(\boldsymbol{x}, \boldsymbol{y}).$$

Again, Theorem 2 can be used to show that $\phi(\boldsymbol{x})$ can be replaced by $Forall(\boldsymbol{x})$.

5.2   Principle of Partial Evaluation

In a series of papers that gave properties by which major Logic Programming semantics could be classified, Dix introduced the "Principle of Partial Evaluation"

(PPE) [7]. The PPE basically states that a positive occurrence of P can be "unfolded", i.e., replaced by the definition of P. Here, we recall the weak version of this property.

Definition 6 (Weak PPE [7]). *Let Δ be a ground rule set, and let an atom P occur only positively in Δ. Let $P \leftarrow \varphi_1, ..., P \leftarrow \varphi_N$ be all the rules with head P, and assume that none of the φ_i contains P. We denote by Δ_P the rule set obtained from Δ by deleting all rules with head P and replacing each rule "Head $\leftarrow P \wedge \psi$" containing P by the rules:*

$$Head \leftarrow \varphi_1 \wedge \psi. \quad ... \quad Head \leftarrow \varphi_N \wedge \psi. \tag{8}$$

The weak principle of partial evaluation *states that there is a 1-1 correspondence between models of Δ_P and models of Δ (with removal of $\{P, \neg P\}$).*

Using Theorem 2, we can show that the stable and well-founded semantics exhibit this property: we rewrite (8) as "Head $\leftarrow (\varphi_1 \vee \cdots \vee \varphi_N) \wedge \psi$". The replacement $\delta = \{P \leftarrow \varphi_1 \vee \cdots \vee \varphi_N.\}$ then satisfies all conditions of Theorem 2.

In the (non-weak) PPE, P can occur recursively, but then its definition has to be present both before and after the transformation (i.e., the rules with head P are not deleted), making the precise relation with our result unclear. The Generalized PPE is obtained from the PPE by allowing P to have arbitrary occurrences in Δ, and not forcing every occurrence of P to be replaced. It is shown in [8] that the stable and well-founded semantics satisfy (G)PPE.

6   Conclusion and Future Work

In this paper, we have only considered the application of Theorem 1 to Logic Programming. However, due to the general, algebraic nature of this result, it can easily be more widely applied. Indeed, all of the main semantics for Autoepistemic Logic and Default Logic can also be given a natural characterization in terms of approximation theory [4]. As such, Theorem 1 can directly be applied to prove similar equivalences for these logics. There, too, such results are useful. For instance, [13] already stresses the importance of being able to replace certain modal subformulas in Autoepistemic Logic by new propositional symbols. Even though Autoepistemic Logic is beyond the scope of this paper, Theorem 1 could be used to prove the correctness of such transformations.

This paper is part of a larger research effort to develop a general "toolkit" of useful theorems in approximation theory. The aim of this project is to isolate important properties of knowledge representation logics and try to characterize these in the framework of approximation theory. In this paper, we have done this for predicate introduction. In [17], we did the same for certain modularity properties, proving an algebraic theorem that generalizes a number of known theorems for Logic Programming, Autoepistemic Logic, and Default Logic.

References

1. Marcello Balduccini and Michael Gelfond. Diagnostic reasoning with A-Prolog. *TPLP*, 3(4-5):425–461, 2003.
2. Marc Denecker. Extending classical logic with inductive definitions. In J. Lloyd et al., editor, *First International Conference on Computational Logic (CL'2000)*, volume 1861 of *Lecture Notes in Artificial Intelligence*, July 2000. Springer.
3. Marc Denecker, Victor Marek, and Mirosław Truszczyński. Approximating operators, stable operators, well-founded fixpoints and applications in nonmonotonic reasoning. In J. Minker, editor, *Logic-based Artificial Intelligence*, chapter 6, pages 127–144. Kluwer Academic Publishers, 2000.
4. Marc Denecker, Victor Marek, and Mirosław Truszczyński. Uniform semantic treatment of default and autoepistemic logics. In *Seventh International Conference on Principles of Knowledge Representation and Reasoning (KR'2000)*, pages 74–84, Breckenridge, April 11-15 2000. Morgan Kaufman.
5. Marc Denecker, Victor Marek, and Mirosław Truszczyński. Uniform semantic treatment of default and autoepistemic logics. *Artificial Intelligence*, 143(1):79–122, 2003.
6. Marc Denecker and Eugenia Ternovska. A logic of non-monotone inductive definitions and its modularity properties. In *Seventh International Conference on Logic Programming and Nonmonotonic Reasoning (LPNMR'7)*, 2004.
7. Jürgen Dix. A classification theory of semantics of normal logic programs: II. weak properties. *Fundam. Inform.*, 22(3):257–288, 1995.
8. Jürgen Dix and Martin Müller. Partial evaluation and relevance for approximations of stable semantics. In Zbigniew W. Ras and Maria Zemankova, editors, *ISMIS*, volume 869 of *Lecture Notes in Computer Science*, pages 511–520. Springer, 1994.
9. Melvin Fitting. Fixpoint semantics for logic programming - a survey. *Theoretical Computer Science*, 278:25–51, 2002.
10. Michael Gelfond and Vladimir Lifschitz. The stable model semantics for logic programming. In *International Joint Conference and Symposium on Logic Programming (JICSLP'88)*, pages 1070–1080. MIT Press, 1988.
11. Michael Gelfond and Halina Przymusinska. Towards a theory of elaboration tolerance: Logic programming approach. *Journal on Software and Knowledge Engineering*, 6(1):89–112, 1996.
12. J.W. Lloyd and R.W. Topor. Making Prolog more expressive. *Journal of Logic Programming*, 1(3):225–240, 1984.
13. V. Wiktor Marek and Mirosław Truszczyński. Autoepistemic logic. *J. ACM*, 38(3):588–619, 1991.
14. Tom Schrijvers and Alexander Serebrenik. Improving Prolog programs: Refactoring for prolog. In Bart Demoen and Vladimir Lifschitz, editors, *ICLP*, volume 3132 of *Lecture Notes in Computer Science*, pages 58–72. Springer, 2004.
15. Allen Van Gelder. The alternating fixpoint of logic programs with negation. *Journal of Computer and System Sciences*, 47(1):185–221, 1993.
16. Allen Van Gelder, Kenneth A. Ross, and John S. Schlipf. The well-founded semantics for general logic programs. *Journal of the ACM*, 38(3):620–650, 1991.
17. J. Vennekens, D. Gilis, and M. Denecker. Splitting an operator: Algebraic modularity results for logics with fixpoint semantics. *ACM Transactions on computational logic (TOCL)*, 2006. To appear.

Improving the ISO Prolog Standard
by Analyzing Compliance Test Results

Péter Szabó[1] and Péter Szeredi[2]

[1] Budapest University of Technology and Economics,
Department of Computer Science and Information Theory,
H-1117 Hungary, Budapest, Magyar tudósok körútja 2
pts@szit.bme.hu
http://www.inf.bme.hu/~pts/
[2] Budapest University of Technology and Economics,
Department of Computer Science and Information Theory,
H-1117 Hungary, Budapest, Magyar tudósok körútja 2
szeredi@szit.bme.hu
http://www.cs.bme.hu/~szeredi/

Abstract. Part 1 of the ISO Prolog standard (ISO/IEC 13211) published in 1995 covers the core of Prolog, including syntax, operational semantics, streams and some built-in predicates. Libraries, DCGs, and global mutables are current standardization topics. Most Prolog implementations provide an ISO mode in which they adhere to the standard.

Our goal is to improve parts of the Prolog standard already published by finding and fixing ambiguities and missing details. To do so, we have compiled a suite of more than 1000 test cases covering part 1, and ran it on several free and commercial Prolog implementations. In this study we summarize the reasons of the test case failures, and discuss which of these indicate possible flaws in the standard.

We also discuss test framework and test case development issues specific to Prolog, as well as some portability issues encountered.

1 Introduction

This paper describes work on testing standards compliance of several Prolog implementations. Part 1 of the Prolog standard [9] and a related textbook [3] have been available for about ten years. By now all major implementations declare that they are standards compliant. In spite of this we have found that there are lots of minor and medium importance details that are interpreted differently by the implementations tested. In a few cases this is due to ambiguities in the standard, in lots of other cases there is a clear deviation from the standard. We believe that even minor discrepancies can make porting Prolog programs very difficult, and to advocate full adherence we have developed an appropriate test framework, described in this paper.

The main goal of this work is to improve interoperability of Prolog code, by clarifying standards compliance of major implementations and pinpointing sources of non-conformance. Even if the implementations remain unchanged,

S. Etalle and M. Truszczyński (Eds.): ICLP 2006, LNCS 4079, pp. 257–269, 2006.

these results can help in developing compatibility layers to support interoperability. In long term we hope that our test framework will contribute to the wider and more precise acceptance of the standard.

The paper is structured as follows. Section 2 gives an overview of the Prolog implementations used and tested in this work. Section 3 describes the architecture of the test framework. In section 4 we present the results of the testing, including some basic statistics, a brief analysis of common failures and proposals for standard improvement. Section 5 discusses related work, while in Section 6 we present some conclusions and plans for future work.

2   Implementations Tested

It was our goal to test many different implementations, in order to identify as many problems as possible. Although we focused on free implementations, we included a commercial one (SICStus) as well. All the implementations are in active use today (and most of them are under active development), save aprolog. We did not want to test new or experimental implementations, the first versions of all of those we tested appeared at least 9 years ago.

These are the implementations we have run the tests on:

SICStus 3.12.3. The original test suite and framework was developed at SICS in an effort to make SICStus [8] ISO-compliant, so it was natural to keep it included as well. We have run the tests in the ISO mode of SICStus – the other, legacy mode is going to be dropped in version 4, anyway. Development of SICStus started in 1984, more than 10 years before the Prolog standard was published.

SWI-Prolog 5.4.7. SWI-Prolog [11,12] is one of most popular, actively developed, free Prolog implementations. It also has an ISO and a legacy mode – the tests have been run in ISO mode. We had to turn garbage collection off, because otherwise the application aborted because of a failed assertion in the middle of the tests. SWI-Prolog exists since about 1990.

YAP 5.0.1. YAP [10] is also an actively developed free implementation. It also has an ISO mode, but we rather disabled it, because the application crashes when we try to consult a new source file in ISO mode. YAP has been available since 1989.

gprolog 1.2.16. GNU Prolog [5,6] is also a free, WAM-based implementation with a native code compiler. Although the latest release is from September 2002, there is still activity on the mailing list. GNU Prolog appeared in 1996, one year after the standard.

Ciao-Prolog 1.10p6. Ciao [2] is a free implementation actively developed by researchers, with a lot of advanced static analysis tools (e.g. type checking, instantiation analysis and partial evaluation) integrated. Ciao-Prolog was released in 1995.

aprolog 1.22. aprolog is an unpublished, minimalistic, very slow standard Prolog implementation by Miklós Szeredi for educational purposes only. It lacks a module system, a WAM implementation, a garbage collector, cyclic term unification, line number reporting for exceptions and unbounded integer arithmetics. The reason we use it is that it has been developed with standards in mind – only ISO Prolog, nothing more. And it is also a demonstration that even simple implementations can be standards compliant. Although aprolog was written in 1997, some of the built-in predicate implementations date back to as far as 1984 – 11 years before the standard came out.

When we tried to port the framework to XSB (version 2.7.1), we faced the *need too many registers* error when trying to assert a fact with too complicated arguments (i.e. try `asserta(t([a(b),a(b),...,a(b)]))` with a list of more than 260 elements). A major rewrite might thus be necessary for an XSB port.

We are not planning to port the framework to other implementations by hand, but we are designing a generic approach, that autodetects as much as possible about the new Prolog system, thus adding the correct port to a new implementation (or a new version) will be easier and faster.

3   Test Suite and Framework

This section describes the structure of the software. We first deal with the test cases and then give an outline of the framework.

3.1   Test Suite Design

Our test suite consists of 1012 test cases, each corresponding to a section in the standard. Each test case has the following properties:

meta-information. Identifier (series : number), author, relevant section number of the ISO standard, dangerousness indication, irrelevancy conditions;

goal. To be executed;

environment. In which the goal is executed: files to create, Prolog source files to load, Prolog flags to alter, cleanup code after running goal;

expectations. Which determine whether the test run is OK or not. The following outcomes can be expected: success (with possible constraints on variable substitutions of each solution), failure, exception (with possible constraints on the exception term). There is a macro expansion facility in the expectations, so they can be written to be more compact and consistent.

Here is an example test case:

```
test_case(strprop:2, iso_doc, %8.11.8.4         % meta-information
    stream_property(S, output),                  % goal
    {[S <-- FOut ], [S <-- COut], ...},          % expectations
    [ pre((open(bar, write, FOut),               % environ-
      current_output(COut))), clean(bar)]).      %     ment
```

The meaning of test case *strprop:2* is the following. This is a test case whose goal is taken from the ISO standard section 8.11.8.4. The test case verifies that if we open an output stream (FOut), then *stream_property/2* has to enumerate it as well as the current output stream. The curly braces signify that the enumeration order is not significant, and ... signifies that there might be more solutions. It is possible to prescribe an order using square brackets instead of curly braces.

Some of the tests are dangerous: they hang the process (i.e. they cause segmentation violation, infinite loop or infinite memory allocation) in some implementations, but work fine in others. The reason of the hanging is clear in some cases (e.g. the unification X=f(X) can hang a Prolog implementation if it does not support unification of STO ("subject to occurs-check") terms), but sometimes there is a bug in the Prolog implementation, and the process hangs for no apparent reason. (Testing *halt/1* is also dangerous, because *halt/1* aborts the whole Prolog process, including the framework.) When the standards allows a hang in a particular case, we call the test case *irrelevant*, otherwise we call the test case *dangerous*. The test case can also be *irrelevant* if it does not hang the process, but it can be skipped for other reasons; for example, integers are bounded in some implementations, but unbounded in others, and tests that check for an *int_overflow* error must be skipped in unbounded implementations.

The framework accepts *implementation aspect declarations*, based on which the framework can decide whether a test is *irrelevant* with respect to an implementation. And even when a test is relevant, its expectations can be made dependent on the declarations. Currently declarations are not used as much as they could be: for example, a lot of tests fail, because predicate indicators in exceptions are not module qualified the same way in all Prolog implementations – and the test suite expects the SICStus way. The solution would be to introduce a new declaration for this aspect, and make the corresponding test cases use it. Declarations could also be used to have *dangerous* tests skipped; currently they have to be commented out by hand in the test suite.

The test contains tests from various sources:

iso_doc. These test cases come directly from the standard [9]. The description of each built-in predicate contains an *Examples* section with goals and a natural language expectation for each goal, which describes what should happen when the goal is called. We kept the original goals, and formalized the expectations so the test case can be automatically validated. In addition to these, the informal examples and tables in the chapters about syntax and control constructs were also converted to test cases.

eddbali. The executable specification of Prolog ([4], see below) has some test cases included. We have added them in our test suite, except for those having equivalent counterparts in the *iso_doc* part.

sics. The test cases here were added by the authors during the development of the ISO mode of SICStus Prolog.

pts. We added these recently, after we have run the test suite on 6 Prolog implementations.

3.2   Test Framework Architecture

The test framework, which runs in the same Prolog process as the tests themselves, considers test cases in the test suite in the order they are defined, and computes the test result for each of them. Possible test results are *dangerous, irrelevant, failed* and *OK*. Test results are logged, and the log file is later processed by a Perl script for statistics generation and validation of whether all test cases were considered. If some of the test cases were *missing*, this could be a sign that the Prolog process crashed in the middle.

Tests declared *dangerous* are ignored. If the irrelevancy condition of the test case with respect to the Prolog implementation is met, the test is considered *irrelevant* and it is skipped. Otherwise, the environment of the test is prepared, the test goal is run, the expectations are checked, the cleanup code is run. The test is considered *OK* if the expectations are fulfilled, otherwise it has *failed*. For *failed* tests, the outcome expected and the outcome received are also logged.

The test cases, the contents of all files and Prolog programs needed by the tests and the macro definitions are collected in a single Prolog source file as facts. The implementation language of the test framework is also Prolog: there is a big system-independent part (in standard Prolog), and there are helper files for each system: the *main* file, which loads all other files, contains the implementation aspect declarations, and provides some nonstandard functionality (such as *abolish_static/1*) using implementation-specific predicates; and the *utils* file, which implements a compatibility layer providing some utility predicates (such as *append/3* and *term_variables/2*). If possible, the utility predicates are loaded from a built-in module. Other software components are the Perl script that creates the statistics from the log files, and a Makefile that invokes the implementations with the appropriate arguments to run the tests.

The software, including our test framework and test suite can be obtained from `http://www.inf.bme.hu/~pts/stdprolog/`. Currently it needs a UNIX system with Perl, GNU Make and the Prolog implementations installed.

4   Test Results

We have run the test suite on the implementations, getting a log file for each run. The log files contained detailed information about each test case, including the description of the failures. In this chapter we present the statistics resulting from the log file, and the conclusions we made from from the failures, including improvement possibilities for the both the standard and its implementations.

4.1   Statistics and Evaluation Concerns

The statistics depicted on Table 1 were generated by a script from the test results log file. The number of failed tests, however, should not be used as a quantitative measure for the standards conformance of the implementation. That is because multiple failures can be caused by a single reason. It is also obvious why SICStus passes almost all the tests: the ISO mode of SICStus and the original version of the test suite have been developed by the same team. It is also not a surprise that aprolog fails in a few cases only: aprolog has been written from the ground up to be ISO compliant. The other implementations have quite a lot of failed test cases. That's quite reasonable, because they have not been designed with the standard in mind, but they have been patched after the standard came out.

Table 1. ISO compliance test statistics of 1012 test cases

system	version	#OK	#failed	#dangerous	#irrelevant
SICStus	3.12.3	1010	1	0	1
aprolog	1.22	996	7	0	9
gprolog	1.2.16	929	67	7	9
SWI-Prolog	5.4.7	816	158	8	30
YAP	5.0.1	632	363	7	10
Ciao-Prolog	1.10p6	541	454	7	10

Many implementations (SICStus, SWI-Prolog, YAP, gprolog and Ciao-Prolog) have two modes: an ISO mode and a backwards compatible mode. In the ISO mode, they try to follow the ISO standard as much as possible, while backwards compatible mode violates the ISO standard if necessary in order to run legacy Prolog programs. We ran our test suite with ISO mode enabled, if possible. gprolog has ISO mode only.

We do not know of any Prolog implementations that provide a strict ISO mode in which they disable non-ISO built-in predicates, and refuse all extensions, i.e. constructs forbidden by the standard. For example [1], the standard requires that an operator atom can be operand only if enclosed in parentheses, e.g. "X= <" should be changed to "X=(<)". Many Prolog implementations, including SICStus and aprolog allow both constructs. This can be considered a syntactical extension to the standard. We accept both in our test cases. Another example: section 6.3.4.3 of the standard forbids an infix and a postfix operator to have the same name. On the other hand, some Prolog implementations allow this, which can also be considered as an extension. However, when the standard explicitly says that a specific error must be thrown in a specific case, implementations must respect this, and our test cases validate each of these error conditions.

There is an *Errors* section for each built-in predicate in the standard. The standard does not specify the order in which these are checked (see section 7.12), so our test cases accept any error if more than one is appropriate.

4.2   Errors and Other Flaws Found in the Standard

We will present typos and inconsistencies and ambiguity in the standard, revealed by the failed test cases.

Sometimes the standard itself is inconsistent. For example, the expression evaluation *Examples* in 9.1.7 have error terms which are missing from section 7.9.2c (which enumerates all possible errors during expression evaluation). Our test cases respect 7.9.2c and expect `type_error(evaluable, F/N)`.

The *Examples* in 9.1.7 contain several other errors and typos, for example they expect 0 is 7/35 to be true – which is presumably a typo, and the intended call is 0 is 7//35. We have fixed those test cases in our test suite.

Section 7.8.3.4 has a bad example, too. It expects call((write(3),3)) to emit a 3, which contradicts the specification of *call/1*, which clearly states that an error should be thrown because (write(3),3) is not callable.

Section 8.14.2.4 is not clear enough whether write_canonical(.) and write _canonical([1]) must put single quotes around their dots (currently some implementations do, others do not). The general rule states that the output must be able to be read back unambiguously, but in this case the ambiguity depends on the context, i.e. the the writing of layout characters after the dot in the future.

The standard does not specify what to do with non-ASCII characters in the Prolog code. For example, should it be possible to load a Prolog source file containing X = á? A straightforward solution would be to adopt Unicode, and to make the byte ↔ character transformation of a text stream specifiable in Prolog (e.g. using stream flags).

4.3   Suggested Additions to the Standard

Part 1 of the standard [9] leaves a lot of features open, while part 2 deals with modules. The standardization of libraries, DCGs, and global mutables is underway. There are other features in existing Prolog implementations to be considered, for example tabling and coroutines using call blocking/freezing. Most Prolog systems today, however, provide an implementation of these features, but since there is no definitive standard to do them in a uniform way, each system implements them differently. In this subsection we will present the nonstandard features we used in our test framework.

We believe that more power should be granted to the programmer when querying and manipulating the predicate database. This includes a decent *predicate_property/2* built-in, which can report whether a predicate is built-in, static, private etc. There should also be a way to unload a Prolog source file, including the ability to abolish the static predicates defined in it (*abolish_static/1*).

There should also be a set of standard modules (such as *lists* and *terms*). As of now, many Prolog systems already have these, but with a different syntax.

Although modules are documented in part 2 of the standard, most implementations ignore that. When a predicate indicator is reported in an error (e.g. *type_error*), its module qualification is not consistent. This should be clarified in the new standard.

The standard should also specify how to assert, query and retract predicates in modules other than the current one.

If the behaviour of the toplevel had been specified in the standard, testing would have been much easier and safer, because we could treat the Prolog implementation as a black box, and implement the testing framework in a different process, or we could have run the tests and the framework in a different Prolog implementation.

As of now, most Prolog systems provide an ISO mode in which they follow the ISO standard more precisely, but there is no standard way to activate this mode with a single call. Moreover, some implementations crash soon after ISO mode has been activated. Others just change the set of visible predicates, but they do not adjust the semantics of the predicates to make them ISO conforming. In some implementations, Prolog flags must be adjusted one-by-one to make the implementation more ISO-compatible. As a solution to this, a new Prolog flag should be defined which controls whether the system runs in ISO mode or not. For example, the *iso* flag with the `true` value, or the *language* flag with the `iso` value. If the standard introduced a strict ISO mode, a flag should be defined for this, too. For the Prolog implementations with a command line interface, the standard should prescribe a command line option (such as `--iso`) which enables ISO mode at startup. Activating ISO mode would have the following effects: all ISO predicates would be made visible, the semantics of some predicates would be changed to be ISO conforming, existing predicates would be forced to detect error conditions according to ISO, and to throw ISO conforming exception terms, Prolog flags would be reset to their ISO default values etc.

Section 7.8.9.4 could clarify what to do when an uncaught exception is encountered and thus a "*system_error*" happens. We suggest printing the original exception to *user_error*, and then returning control to the toplevel, or – if no interactive toplevel exists – exiting from the Prolog process.

Since the primary goal of Prolog standardization is to make Prolog programs more portable across implementations, a standard library should be defined. There are many features (such as the lists and terms modules, predicates for manipulating the file system, predicates for TCP/IP communication, capturing stream output to a string, timeouts, blackboard/flag predicates, predicate mode and/or type declarations, suspended execution with coroutines and CLP(FD)) already present in multiple Prolog implementations, but because of the small differences in the load and invocation syntaxes and in the semantics, it not possible to write a portable Prolog program using these widely available features, without inserting implementation-specific code for each supported implementation.

In order to help the work of adding these common features to the standard (and also to help Prolog programmers write portable code), a compatibility library could be developed, which provides an implementation-independent interface for these features, and maps all its publicly available predicates to implementation-specific calls.

4.4   Common Failures in Implementations

We will discuss the typical reasons that made multiple test cases fail. The discussion covers the areas in which implementations should be improved, without going into details about which test case failed in which implementation. These details can be found in the test results log available from the web page of our software.

Some Prolog implementations still use the old, Edinburgh semantics of the caret, i.e., they look for the caret in the middle of the 2nd argument of *setof/3* and *bagof/3*.

There are problems with stream properties returned by *stream_property/2*. It is common that standard properties are missing or the default values for `user_output` etc. are not compliant.

Some implementations do not make a proper distinction between the end-of-stream and past-end-of-stream states. Some of them even allow reading the EOF indicator after the past-end-of-stream.

There are also some typos in error terms, e.g. `type_error(atom,...)` is reported instead of `type_error(atomic,...)`.

It is a common mistake in some implementations that they mix throwing *existence_error* and *domain_error* when an invalid stream term is passed to them. Sometimes *stream* and *stream_or_alias* are confused in the error term. The standard is always clear, however, about what and when should be thrown.

In some implementations it is possible to open inherently unrepositionable files (such as UNIX character devices) with `reposition(true)`.

In some implementations *stream_property/2* returns the alias *user_input*, which is not a stream-term, in its first argument. A similar problem is that *current_predicate/1* returns built-in predicates.

When a stream error is reported, the stream term associated with the call is not copied properly, e.g. 42 is indicated instead of `'$stream'(42)`.

Some implementations confuse character code lists (codes) and character atom lists (chars), e.g. *atom_codes/2* returns an atom list instead of a code list.

The standard is always clear about what culprit should be reported in *type_error* messages. For example, `call((true,3))` must report `type_error(callab le, (true,3))` instead of `type_error(callable, 3)`. But some implementations prefer to report the latter, more specific culprit. Our test suite has an implementation aspect declaration for this. There is a similar problem of reporting a *type_error* when the tail of the 2nd argument of *write_term/2* is not a list. Another similar case is that `myop` should not be part of the error triggered by `op(100,xfx,[myop,',',])`.

Some Prolog flags or flag values are missing in some implementations, e.g. the flag *unknown* cannot have value *warning*. Sometimes the default value of the flag does not match the defaults prescribed in section 7.11 of the standard. Sometimes they have *false* instead of *off* etc.

There are a lot of problems in arithmetic error reporting. Some implementations make `+inf is 1/0`, `nan is sqrt(-1)` or `-inf is log(0)` true – all of which must have thrown an *evaluation_error* according to the standard. Sometimes an implementation fails to report an *int_overflow*, and the addition of two large integers succeed.

The result of `X is 7//-3` depends on the rounding function used (see in section 9.1.3.1) and thus it is implementation-specific: X becomes either -2 or -4. On the contrary, the semantics of the operations *mod* and *rem* are unambiguous, but some implementations get the sign of the result wrong.

All integer operations must throw an error if they do not receive integer arguments (e.g. X is 1.0>>2). However, sometimes they just convert the float they receive to an integer.

Most arithmetic operations can return either an integer or a float – but rounding operations such as float and truncate have a specific return type (defined in section 9.1.6). Some implementations, however, do not respect this, and have 7.0 is floor(7.4) instead of 7 is floor(7.4).

Although this is not a validity but a reliability issue, we have to mention the dangerous tests here: those that hang particular Prolog implementations. We have found segmentation violations, infinite loops and infinite memory allocations, none of which should ever happen when running Prolog code. Sometimes we could not even identify a specific test case or set of test cases which created the danger, for example when the Prolog process died with a failed assertion in the middle of the garbage collection. But most of the time, the problem was caused by a single test case, which we found and declared dangerous in that implementation. For example, atom_concat(A,A,AA) triggered a bug in the native-language code of *atom_concat/3* in one of the implementations when *A* was an atom already of maximum length, and the bug caused the process to emit a segmentation violation. In another case, we could identify that testing *abolish/1* causes instability, but none of the individual test cases made the process crash.

We have found many similar fundamental flaws (dangerous or not) in the error handling code of the built-in predicates in many implementations. Section 7.12.1 is perfectly clear about what to do when an error happens: the call has to be replaced by an appropriate call to *throw/1*. On the contrary implementations tend to throw the wrong error, just fail, print an error message and then fail, or even crash – none of which is conforming.

Although full stop (.) marks the end of a term only if it is followed by a layout character, the layout character must not be consumed by *read/1* (see section 8.14.1.4). Some implementations do consume it, however.

There are many problems with *read/1*, e.g. some implementations cannot read write(0'\') or quoted atoms as structure names such as 'is'(1,2). Some implementations have problems reading terms when *char_conversion/2* is in effect.

The standard expects *read/1* to throw a *representation_error* when a limit (such as maximum atom length) is exceeded. However, some implementations throw *syntax_error* instead.

Some implementations allow an atom to contain zero-coded characters (e.g. '\000\'), and they can even read those from text streams.

number_chars/2 in some implementations has problems ignoring whitespace in the beginning of the number.

clause/2 in some implementations returns a preprocessed predicate body for dynamic predicates. Not only calls get module qualification, but calls to built-in predicates are also replaced to calls to implementation-specific, hidden predicates.

5   Related Work

We have gathered tests from various sources when compiling our test suite, see Subsection 3.1 for the details. The ISO working group X3J17 dedicated to improve the Prolog standard has also published a test suite [7] of 570 test cases. Most of them are directly copied from the standard, similarly as our 675 iso_doc test cases.

[1] suggested that the ISO Prolog standard was not taken seriously, and most implementations were not compliant. We believe that a test suite like ours, which works in multiple Prolog implementations can reveal many specific problems, which implementors can focus on if they strive for standards compliance. We are planning to publish a detailed technical report and notify the implementors about the failures we have found.

The standard has a formal semantics in its appendix. This semantics is formalized such a way that the specification can be executed – thus we can get a completely compliant implementation. The text of the appendix, the executable specification and an executor implementation in Prolog is available separately [4]. The executable specification, as it is now, is very inefficient, and it also has some limitations and bugs, see section 2.5 of [4].

6   Conclusion and Future Work

A good programming language standard makes writing portable programs possible – provided that the standard covers all the features used by the program, and that implementations conform to the standard. Validation tests can reveal weak spots of the standard and also problems in the implementations. We have written a test framework and compiled a test suite in order to explore the areas in which the Prolog standard and its implementations can be improved. We have analyzed the test results, classified the reasons why some cases failed, identified common problems and even some weaknesses of the Prolog standard. It was not our goal to fix the problems, but to attract attention of the implementors and the creators of the standard to them.

Our test suite covers most other test collections available ([9,4,7]), and our test framework has been ported to several Prolog implementations, thus it can be considered general.

It is our primary goal to cooperate with the standard designers and Prolog implementors. We are planning to improve and extend the test suite, and port the test framework to as many implementations as possible. But in order to get others involved into our work, first we have to polish the framework and document it properly. First we are planning to publish a technical report for the implementors, with the failed tests documented in detail, so they can start fixing the problems.

Currently it is hard to port the framework to a new Prolog implementation: the programmer has to adjust a lot of settings and write helper predicates after a careful study of the Prolog implementation – and they do not get proper feedback if they do it wrong. To help this, we are working on an autodetection mechanism similar to GNU autoconf, and we're also writing a porting tutorial.

More *implementation aspect declarations* should be added instead of commenting out test cases. It is important to have as many declarations as possible, because they can eliminate a lot of false non-compliance messages at once, and they can also reduce the risk of dangerous test cases. Most declarations should be auto-detected instead of being specified manually.

The handling of dangerous tests should be improved. It should be possible to declare an implementation-specific danger level for each test case, and the framework would skip that test or run it in a separated process time- and memory-constrained if necessary. (This would also make the effect of an uncaught exception testable.) Semi-automatic tools should be developed to help the programmer find the dangerous test cases.

The test framework ignores module qualification when it validates dynamic clause bodies or error culprits. However, in some cases this is not precise enough, for example in the example of section 8.9.3.4, the call to retract((foo(A) :- A,call(A))) might have to be replaced by retract((foo(A) :- A,call(user: A))) in order to succeed when the clause foo(X) :- call(X), call(X) is asserted. That's because asserting involves module qualification, which transforms the clause to foo(X) :- call(user:X), call(user:X) .

The effects of some tests are hard to describe in the current framework (e.g. when both cyclic terms and module qualification is involved). This should be improved.

Some Prolog implementations have problems parsing the test suite, even when it is in functional notation, e.g. some of them cannot parse 0'\' as an integer constant. To help this, the framework should have its own, standard compliant reimplementation of read/2, and it should use this to read the test case clauses.

As the standard develops, and possibly new parts get added, the test suite has to be extended correspondingly. It would be useful if the standard itself had a formal test suite in its appendix, in addition to the informal *Examples* for each built-in predicate.

References

1. Roberto Bagnara. Is the ISO Prolog standard taken seriously? *The Association for Logic Programming Newsletter*, 12(1):10–12, February 1999. URL http://www.cs.unipr.it/~bagnara/Papers/Abstracts/ALPN99a.
2. F. Bueno, D. Cabeza, M. Carro, M. Hermenegildo, P. López-García, and G. Puebla. *The Ciao System. Reference Manual (V1.10)*. School of Computer Science, Technical University of Madrid (UPM), 2004. URL http://clip.dia.fi.upm.es/Software/Ciao/.
3. Laurent Cervoni, Abdelali Ed-Dbali, and Pierre Deransart. *Prolog: Reference Manual*. Springer, 1996.
4. Pierre Deransart and AbdelAli Ed-Dbali. Executable specification for Standard Prolog. URL http://www.uc.pt/logtalk/links.html, Download URL ftp://ftp-lifo.univ-orleans.fr/pub/Users/eddbali/SdProlog, 5 July 1996.

5. Daniel Diaz and Philippe Codognet. GNU Prolog: Beyond compiling Prolog to C. *Lecture Notes in Computer Science*, 1753:81–92, 2000.
6. Daniel Diaz and Philippe Codognet. The GNU Prolog system and its implementation. In *ACM Symposium on Applied Computing (2)*, volume 1, pages 728–732, 19–21 March 2000.
7. Jonathan Hodgson. Validation test suite for ISO standard conformance. URL http://www.sju.edu/~jhodgson/x3j17.html, 2 October 1998.
8. Intelligent Systems Laboratory, SICS, PO Box 1263, S-164 28 Kista, Sweden. *SICStus Prolog User's Manual (for version 3.12.3)*, October 2005. URL http://www.sics.se/sicstus/docs/3.12.3/html/sicstus.html/.
9. ISO. *ISO/IEC 13211-1. International Standard, Invormation technology – Programming languages – Prolog – Part 1: General core*, 1 edition, 1995.
10. V. Santos-Costa, L. Damas, R. Reis, and R. Azevedo. *The Yap Prolog User's Manual*. Universidade do Porto and COPPE Sistemas, 2006. URL http://www.ncc.up.pt/~vsc/Yap/.
11. Jan Wielemaker. An overview of the SWI-Prolog programming environment. In Fred Mesnard and Alexander Serebenik, editors, *Proceedings of the 13th International Workshop on Logic Programming Environments*, pages 1–16, Heverlee, Belgium, December 2003. Katholieke Universiteit Leuven. CW 371.
12. Jan Wielemaker. *SWI-Prolog 5.6.4 Reference Manual*. Human-Computer Studies, 2006. URL http://gollem.science.uva.nl/SWI-Prolog/Manual/.

TOAST: Applying Answer Set Programming to Superoptimisation

Martin Brain, Tom Crick, Marina De Vos, and John Fitch

Department of Computer Science
University of Bath
Bath BA2 7AY, UK
{mjb, tc, mdv, jpff}@cs.bath.ac.uk

Abstract. Answer set programming (ASP) is a form of declarative programming particularly suited to difficult combinatorial search problems. However, it has yet to be used for more than a handful of large-scale applications, which are needed to demonstrate the strengths of ASP and to motivate the development of tools and methodology. This paper describes such a large-scale application, the TOAST (Total Optimisation using Answer Set Technology) system, which seeks to generate optimal machine code for simple, acyclic functions using a technique known as superoptimisation. ASP is used as a scalable computational engine to handle searching over complex, non-regular search spaces, with the experimental results suggesting that this is a viable approach to the optimisation problem and demonstrates the scalability of a variety of solvers.

1 Introduction

Answer set programming (ASP) is a relative new technology, with the first computation tools only appearing in the late 1990s [1,2]. Initial studies have demonstrated [3] that it has potential in many areas, including automatic diagnostics [4,5], agent behaviour and communication [6], security engineering [7] and information integration [8]. However, larger production-scale applications are comparatively scarce. One of the few examples of such a system is the *USA-Advisor* decision support system [5] for the NASA Space Shuttle. It modelled a complex domain in a concise way; although of great significance to the field it is, in computational terms, relatively small. The only large and difficult programs most answer set solvers have been tested on are synthetic benchmarks; thus it is not yet known how well these algorithms and implementations scale.

This paper investigates the possibility of using ASP technology to generate optimal machine code for simple functions. Modern compilers only provide code improvements via a range of approximations rather than generating truly optimal code; none of these existing techniques, or approaches to creating new techniques, are likely to change the current state of play.

An approach to generating optimal code sequences is called superoptimisation [9]. One of the main bottlenecks in this process is the size of the space of possible instruction sequences, with most superoptimising implementations relying on brute force searches to locate candidate sequences and then approximate equivalence verification.

From an ASP perspective, the TOAST project provides a large-scale, real-world application, with certain programs containing more than a million ground rules. From a

S. Etalle and M. Truszczyński (Eds.): ICLP 2006, LNCS 4079, pp. 270–284, 2006.

compiler perspective, it might be a step towards tools that can generate truly optimal code, which could have an impact on many areas, especially resource-critical environments such as embedded systems and high performance computing.

This paper presents the results of the first phase of the TOAST project, with the infrastructure complete and three machine architectures implemented. At present, off-the-shelf solvers are used without any domain-specific optimisations, so the results we present provide not only useful benchmarks for TOAST, but also for the answer set solvers themselves.

2   The Problem Domain

Before describing the TOAST system and how it uses answer set technology, it is important to consider the problem that it seeks to solves and how this fits into the larger field of compiler design.

2.1   Compilers and Optimisation

Optimisation, as commonly used in the field of compiler research and implementation, is something of a misnomer. A typical compiler targeting assembly language or machine code will include an array of code improvement techniques, from the relatively cheap and simple (such as identification of common sub-expressions and constant folding) [10] to the costly and esoteric (such as auto-vectorisation and inter-function register allocation) [11]. However, none of these generate optimal code; the code that they output is only improved (though often to a significant degree). All of these techniques identify and remove specific inefficiencies, but it is impossible to guarantee that the code could not be further improved.

Further confusion between code improvement and the generation of optimal code is created by complications in defining optimality. In the linear case, a shorter instruction sequence is quite clearly better[1]. However, if the code branches, but is acyclic, a number of definitions are possible: shortest average path, shortest over all sequences, etc. For code containing cycles, it is not possible to define optimality in the general case. To do so would require calculating how many times the body of the loop would be executed – a problem equivalent to the halting problem. To avoid this and other problem areas, such as equivalence of floating point operations, this paper only considers optimality in terms of the number of instructions used in acyclic, integer-based code.

It is also important to consider the scale of savings that are likely to be achieved. The effect of improvements in code generation for an average program have been estimated as a 4% speed increase per year[2] [12]. In this context, a saving of just one or two

---

[1] Although the TOAST approach could be easily generalised to handle them, this paper ignores complications such as pipelining, caching, pre-fetching, variable-instruction latency and super-scalar execution.

[2] This may seem very low in comparison with the increase in processing power created by advances in processor manufacture. However, it is wise to consider the huge disparity in research spending in the two areas, as well as the link between them: most modern processors would not achieve such drastic improvements without advanced compilers to generate efficient code for them.

instructions is significant, particularly if the technique is widely applicable or can be used to target 'hot spots', CPU-intensive sections of code.

2.2 Superoptimisation

Superoptimisation is a radically different approach to code generation, first described by Massalin [9]. Rather than starting with crudely generated code and improving it, a superoptimiser starts with the specification of a function and performs an exhaustive search for a sequence of instructions that meets this specification. Clearly, as the length of the sequence increases, the search space potentially increases at an exponential rate. This makes the technique unsuitable for use in normal compiler toolchains, though for improving the code generators of compilers and for targeting key sections of performance critical functions, the results can be impressive.

A good example of superoptimisation is demonstrated by the sign function [9], which returns the sign of a binary integer, or zero if the input is zero:

```
int signum(int x)
{
    if (x > 0)       return 1;
    else if (x < 0)  return -1;
    else             return 0;
}
```

A simple compilation of this function would generate ten or so instructions, including at least two conditional branch instructions. A skilled assembler programmer might manage to implement it in four instructions with only one conditional branch. Current state of the art compilers can normally achieve the same. However, superoptimisation of this function (here for the SPARC-V7 architecture) gives the following sequence of three instructions:

```
! input in %i0
addcc   %i0 %i0 %l1
subxcc  %i0 %l1 %l2
addx    %l2 %i0 %o1
! output in %o1
```

Not only is this sequence shorter, it does not require any conditional branches, a significant saving on modern pipelined processors. This example shows another interesting property of code produced by superoptimisation: it is not obvious that this computes the sign of a number or how it does so. The pattern of addition and subtraction 'cancels out', with the actual computation being done by how the carry flag is set and used by each instruction (instructions whose names include cc set the carry flag, likewise x denotes instructions that use the carry flag). Such inventive uses of the processor's features are common in superoptimised sequences; when the GNU Superoptimizer (GSO) [13] was used to superoptimise sequences for the GCC port to the POWER architecture, it produced a number of sequences that were shorter than the processor's designers thought possible!

Despite significant potential, superoptimisation has received relatively little attention within the field of compiler research. Following Massalin's work, the next superoptimising implementation was GSO, a portable superoptimiser developed to improve the GCC toolchain. It advanced on Massalin's search strategy by attempting to apply constraints while generating elements of the search space, rather than generating all possible sequences and then skipping those that were marked as clearly redundant. The most recent work on superoptimisation have been from the Denali project [14,15]. Their approach was much closer to that of the TOAST project, using automatic theorem proving technology as an 'intelligent' approach to handling the large search spaces.

2.3   Analysis of Problem Domain

Superoptimisation naturally decomposes into two sub-problems: searching for sequences that meet some limited criteria and then verifying which of these candidates are fully equivalent to the input function.

The search space of possible sequences of a given length is very large, at least the number of instructions available to the power of the length of the sequences (thus growing at least exponentially as the length rises). However, a number of constraints exist that reduce the amount of the space that has to be searched. For example, if a subsequence is known to be non-optimal, then anything that includes it will also be non-optimal and thus can be discarded. Handling the size and complexity of this space is the current limit on superoptimiser performance.

Verifying that two code sequences are equivalent also involves a large space of possibilities (for a sequence with a single input it is 2^w, where w is the word length (the number of bits per register) of the machine architecture). However, it is a space that shows a number of unusual properties. Firstly, the process is a reasonably simple task for human experts, suggesting there may be a set of strong heuristics. Secondly, sequences of instructions that are equivalent on a reasonably small subset of the space of possible inputs tend to be equivalent on all of it. Both Massalin's superoptimiser and GSO handled verification by testing the new sequence for correctness on a representative set of inputs and declaring it equivalent if it passed. Although non-rigorous, this approach seemed to work in practise [9,13].

Due to the problems in producing accurate, formal models of the search space of instruction sequences the complexity of superoptimisation is currently unknown.

3   Answer Set Programming

Answer set programming is a form of declarative programming oriented towards solving difficult combinatorial search problems, which has emerged from research on the semantics of logic programming languages and non-monotonic reasoning [16,17]. The answer set semantics have developed into an intuitive system for 'real-world reasoning'. For reasons of compactness, this paper only includes a brief summary of answer set semantics, though a more in-depth description can be found in [18].

Answer set semantics are defined with respect to *programs*, sets of Horn clause-style rules composed of literals. Two forms of negation are described: negation as failure and explicit (or classical) negation. The first (denoted as *not*) is interpreted as not knowing that the literal is true, while the second (denoted as $\neg$) is knowing that the literal is not true. For example:

$$a \leftarrow b, not\ c.$$
$$\neg b \leftarrow not\ a.$$

is interpreted as "a is known to be true if b is known to be true and c is not known to be true. b is known to be not true if a is not known to be true" (the precise declarative meaning is an area of ongoing work, see [19] for a further discussion). Constraints are also supported, which allow conjunctions of literals to be deemed inconsistent. Answer sets are sets of literals that are consistent (i.e. do not contain both a or $\neg a$), not constrained (do not contain the bodies of any constraints) and supported (every literal has at least one acyclic way of concluding its truth). A given program may have zero or more answer sets.

Answer set programming is describing a problem as a program under the answer set semantics in such a way that the answer sets of the program correspond to the solutions of the problem. In many cases, this is simply a case of encoding the description of the problem domain and the description of what constitutes a solution. Thus, solving the problem is reduced to computing the answer sets of the program.

Computing an answer set of a program is an NP-complete task, but there are a number of sophisticated tools (known as answer set solvers) that can perform this computation. The first generation of efficient solvers (such as SMODELS [1] and DLV [20]) use a DPLL-style [21] algorithm. Before computation, the answer set program is *grounded* (an instantiation process that creates copies of the rules for each usable value of each variable) by using tools such as LPARSE [22], to remove variables. The answer sets are then computed using a backtracking algorithm; at each stage the sets of literals that are known to be true and not known to be true are expanded according to simple rules (similar to unit propagation in DPLL), then a branching literal is chosen according to heuristics and both possible branches (asserting the literal to be known to be true or not) are explored. An alternative approach is to use a SAT solver to generate candidate answer sets and then check whether these meet all criteria. This is the approach used by CMODELS [23] and ASSAT [24]. More recent work has investigated using 'Beowulf'-style parallel systems to explore possible models in parallel [25].

4   Total Optimisation Using Answer Set Technology

The TOAST system consists of a number of components that generate answer set programs and parse answer sets, with a 'front end' which uses these components to produce a superoptimised version of an input function. Data is passed between components either as fragments of answer set programs or in an architecture-independent, assembly language-like format. An answer set solver is then used as a 'black box' tool (currently any solver that supports LPARSE syntax).

ASP was chosen because the structure of the rules simplifies the modelling of the bitwise operation of instructions, while also allowing the modelling of complex constraints.

4.1 System Components

Four key components provide most of the functionality of the TOAST system:

pickVectors
> *input*: variable specification
> *output*: ASP vectors
> Given the specification of the inputs to an instruction sequence, a representative set of inputs (known as input vectors) are generated in ASP.

execute
> *input*: ASP vectors, program
> *output*: ASP constraints
> Takes the input vectors (as generated by *pickVectors* or *verify*) and emulates running an instruction sequence with that input, giving constraints on the instruction sequence's outputs.

search
> *input*: search space, ASP vectors, ASP constraints
> *output*: program fragments
> Takes ASP fragments giving 'start' and 'end' values (from *pickVectors/verify* and *execute* respectively) and searches for all instruction sequences of a given length (the search space) that produce the correct output with the described input.

verify
> *input*: program, program
> *output*: boolean
> Takes two instruction sequences with the same input specification and tests if they are equivalent. If they are not, an input vector on which they differ can be output, in a suitable form for *execute* and *search*.

The TOAST system is fully architecture independent. Architecture-specific information is stored in a description file which provides meta-information about the architecture, as well as which operations from the library of instructions are available. At the time of writing, TOAST supports the following architectures: MIPS [26], SPARC-V7 and SPARC-V8 [27]. Porting to a new architecture is simple and takes between a few hours and a week, depending on how many of the instructions used have already been modelled.

4.2 System Architecture

The key observation underlying the design of the TOAST system is that any super-optimised sequence will necessarily be returned by using *search* on the appropriate instruction length. However, not everything that *search* returns is necessarily a correct answer. Thus, to generate superoptimised sequences the front end uses *pickVector* and *execute* on the input instruction sequence to create criteria for *search*. Instruction sequence lengths from one, up to one less than the length of the input sequence, are then searched sequentially. If any answers are given, another criteria set is created and the same length searched again. The two sets are then intersected, as any correct answer must appear in both. This process is repeated until either the intersection is empty, in which case the search moves on to the next length, or until the intersection stops getting any smaller. *verify* can then be used to check members of this set for equivalence to the original input program.

4.3 The Answer Set Programs

All of the answer sets programs created in the system consist of a number of basic components.

Flow control rules define which instruction will be 'executed' at a given time step by controlling the `pc` (program counter) literal. An example set of flow control rules are given in Figure 1. The rules are fairly self-explanatory, for example, an instruction that asserts `jump(C,T,J)`, moves the program's execution on `J` instructions, otherwise it will just move forward by one. As ASP programs may need to simultaneously model multiple independent code streams (for example, when trying to verify their equivalence), all literals are 'tagged' with an abstract property called colour. The inclusion of the `colour(C)` literal in each rule then allows copies to be created for each code stream during instantiation. In most cases, when only one code stream is used, only one value of `colour` is defined and only one copy of each set of rules is produced; the overhead involved is negligible.

```
haveJumped(C,T)   :- jump(C,T,J), jumpSize(C,J),
                     time(C,T), colour(C).

pc(C,PCV+J,T+1)   :- pc(C,PCV,T), jump(C,T,J), jumpSize(C,J),
                     time(C,T), colour(C), position(C,PCV).

pc(C,PCV+1,T+1)   :- pc(C,PCV,T), not haveJumped(C,T),
                     time(C,T), colour(C), position(C,PCV).

pc(C,1,1).
```

Fig. 1. Flow Control Rules in ASP

Flag control rules model the setting and maintenance of processor flags such as carry, overflow, zero and negative. Although generally only used for controlling conditional branches and multi-word arithmetic, these flags are a source of many superoptimised sequences and are thus of prime importance when modelling a processor.

```
value(C,T,B)   :- istream(C,P,lxor,R1,R2,none), pc(C,P,T),
                  value(C,R1,B), -value(C,R2,B),
                  register(R1), register(R2), colour(C),
                  position(C,P), time(C,T), bit(B).

value(C,T,B)   :- istream(C,P,lxor,R1,R2,none), pc(C,P,T),
                  -value(C,R1,B), value(C,R2,B),
                  register(R1), register(R2), colour(C),
                  position(C,P), time(C,T), bit(B).

-value(C,T,B)  :- istream(C,P,lxor,R1,R2,none), pc(C,P,T),
                  not value(C,T,B), register(R1), register(R2),
                  colour(C), position(C,P), time(C,T), bit(B).

symmetricInstruction(lxor).
```

Fig. 2. Modelling of a Logical XOR Instruction in ASP

The *instruction sequence* itself is represented as a series of facts, or in the case of *search*, a set of choice rules (choice rules are a syntactic extension to ASP, see [1]). These literals are then used by the *instruction definitions* to control the value literals that give the value of various registers within the processor. If the literal is in the answer set, the given bit is taken to be a 1, if the classically-negated version of the literal is in the answer set then it is a 0. An example instruction definition, for a logical XOR (exclusive or) between registers, is given in Figure 2. Note the use of negation as failure to reduce the number of rules needed and the declaration that lxor is symmetric, which is used to reduce the search space.

Input vectors and *output constraints* are the program fragments created by *pickVectors* and *execute* respectively. None of the ASP programs generated require disjunction, aggregates or any other non-syntactic extensions to answer set semantics.

5 Testing

In this section we present preliminary results on using ASP as a tool for superoptimisation, also showing some interesting properties of the different answer set solvers used in the tests.

5.1 System and Solvers

Tests were run on a Beowulf-style cluster of sixteen 800MHz Intel Celeron, 512MB RAM machines connected by 100Mb Ethernet, running SuSE Linux 9.2. Results are given for SMODELS-2.28 (denoted s), SURYA [28] (denoted u), NOMORE++ 1.4 [29] (denoted m) and the MPI version of PLATYPUS running on n nodes (denoted p/n). CMODELS, ASSAT and LPSM were also tested, though concerns over their stability and correctness means the results are not presented. DLV has yet to be tested, as the difference in syntax would require extensive alterations to the input programs. It is hoped that we will soon be able to publish results for these solvers. LPARSE-1.0.17 was used to ground the programs. Times for the sequential solvers were recorded using the system time command, while the MPI wall time was used for PLATYPUS (both given in seconds).

5.2 Test Programs

Three suites of programs were used in the tests. In the first, *search* was used to generate programs that searched the space of SPARC-V7 instructions for candidate optimisations for the following instruction sequence:

```
! input in %i0, %i1
and      %i0 %i1 %l1
add      %i0 %l1 %l2
add      %i0 %l2 %l3
sub    0     %l3 %o1
! output in %o1
```

This sequence was selected as a 'worst case', an example of a sequence that cannot be superoptimised, giving an approximate ceiling on the performance of the system. Programs s1 to s4 are searches over the spaces of 1 to 4 instructions respectively.

The remaining two test suites give different approaches to testing *verify*. In the first case, an older encoding of the search space using choice rules (and thus limiting it to SMODELS and PLATYPUS) was used. The test was to verify the equivalence of:

```
! input in %i0              ! input in %i0
add       %i0 %i0 %o1       umult    %i0  2    %o1
! output in %o1             ! output in %o1
```

using the SPARC-V8[3] architecture, but varying the processor word length (the number of bits per register). This pair of programs were chosen because, although they are clearly equivalent, the modelling and reasoning required to show this is non-trivial. Programs v8 to v24 are variants with word lengths of 8 to 24 bits respectively.

The final test suite for *verify* uses two instruction sequences that differed only on one input, thus creating a program with a single answer set. The size of the search space was altered by simply fixing the value of some of the bits (programs w8 to w24 test for equivalence over 8 to 24 bits). The instruction sequences were:

```
! input in %i0
sra %i1 31 %l1             ! input in %i0
orcc %l1 %l1 %o1          addcc    %i0 %i0 %l1
bne 2                      subxcc   %i0 %l1 %l2
add %l1 1 %o1             addx     %l2 %i0 %o1
! output in %o1           ! output in %o1
```

The programs used in these tests are available online[4] and will be contributed to the Asparagus benchmark collection [30].

5.3   Results

Figure 3 gives the number of atoms, answer sets and rules, along with the sizes of the search spaces, for the programs used in the tests. Timing results for the *search* tests are given in Figure 4, while the results for the two *verify* tests are given in Figures 5 and 7 and graphed in Figures 6 and 8 respectively. Not all tests could be completed due to time constraints, with entries marked $> n$ aborted after n seconds and those marked $-$ not attempted due to estimated compute times. Results for PLATYPUS on a single node are not presented, due to limitations in the current MPI implementation.

5.4   Analysis

The results presented suggest a number of interesting conclusions. Firstly, answer set solvers are capable of handling non-trivial, real-world problems and attempting to solve the problem of generating optimal code with them is viable. Although the compute time for the space of four instructions is prohibitively high, it is worth noting that this is without even obvious constraints (such as the output of each instruction apart from the

---

[3] SPARC-V8 is an later, minimal extension of SPARC-V7 with the addition of the umult instruction.

[4] http://www.bath.ac.uk/~mjb/toast/

Program	Atoms	Rules	Raw search space	Program	Atoms	Rules	Raw search space
v8	975	1755	2^8	w8	2296	12892	2^8
v9	1099	2063	2^9	w9	2296	12894	2^9
v10	1235	2402	2^{10}	w10	2296	12896	2^{10}
v11	1383	2772	2^{11}	w11	2296	12898	2^{11}
v12	1543	3173	2^{12}	w12	2296	12900	2^{12}
v13	1715	3605	2^{13}	w13	2296	12902	2^{13}
v14	1899	4068	2^{14}	w14	2296	12904	2^{14}
v15	2095	4562	2^{15}	w15	2296	12906	2^{15}
v16	2303	5087	2^{16}	w16	2296	12908	2^{16}
v17	2527	5645	2^{17}	w17	2296	12910	2^{17}
v18	2763	6234	2^{18}	w18	2296	12912	2^{18}
v19	3011	6854	2^{19}	w19	2296	12914	2^{19}
v20	3271	7505	2^{20}	w20	2296	12916	2^{20}
v21	3543	8187	2^{21}	w21	2296	12918	2^{21}
v22	3827	8900	2^{22}	w22	2296	12920	2^{22}
v23	4123	9644	2^{23}	w23	2296	12922	2^{23}
v24	4431	10419	2^{24}	w24	2296	12924	2^{24}
s1	6873	1197185	129				
s2	6873	1197184	35862				
s3	6873	1197183	15241350				
s4	6873	1197182	9190534050				

Fig. 3. Program Sizes

Program	s	u	m	$p/2$	$p/4$	$p/8$	$p/16$
s1	42.93	1736.11	60.95	140.327	141.824	139.167	141.167
s2	214.31	66357.55	235.08	256.68	397.393	410.122	461.69
s3	74777.67	> 304401.98	> 407556.46	51580	19523.7	9758.36	7503.68
s4	> 237337.35	-	-	-	-	-	-

Fig. 4. Search Test Times (secs)

Program	s	$p/2$	$p/4$	$p/8$	$p/16$
v8	0.153	0.497732	0.560709	0.633932	0.721136
v9	0.306	0.866704	0.70772	0.808055	0.935053
v10	0.675	1.61512	1.2337	1.16333	1.39326
v11	1.537	3.42153	1.97181	1.93191	2.2948
v12	3.597	7.46042	4.28284	3.53243	3.38788
v13	8.505	15.8174	8.86814	6.25371	6.22179
v14	17.795	34.4004	19.5743	12.38	9.52772
v15	39.651	77.0911	41.1235	27.2365	15.3818
v16	93.141	167.222	71.3785	46.6144	35.3159
v17	217.162	372.57	146.603	99.3623	72.3708
v18	463.025	815.373	384.237	189.690	122.038
v19	1002.696	1738.02	681.673	421.681	262.611
v20	2146.941	3790.84	1514.80	896.705	566.040
v21	4826.837	8206.4	3438.71	1874.36	1244.95
v22	11168.818	17974.8	6683.06	3850.71	2296.87
v23	23547.807	38870.5	15047	7947.95	4833.66
v24	52681.498	83405.1	32561.2	16165.4	10580.4

Fig. 5. First Verify Test (secs)

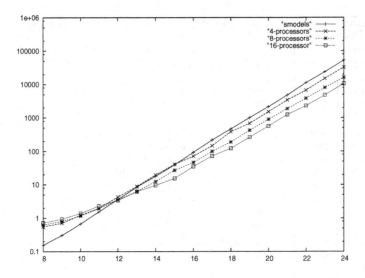

Fig. 6. First Verify Test Timings (log scale)

Program	s	u	m	$p/2$	$p/4$	$p/8$	$p/16$
w8	0.63	10.939	3.05	3.90092	5.31244	5.24863	5.6869
w9	0.75	20.077	4.78	5.18021	5.65978	7.06414	6.04698
w10	1.02	35.487	8.03	6.67866	6.64935	7.29748	7.87806
w11	1.67	72.561	13.83	10.2767	10.0379	10.7023	9.45804
w12	2.79	129.669	25.67	17.4263	15.9894	15.3256	14.996
w13	5.03	248.974	45.83	32.1642	27.4496	27.4135	22.0735
w14	8.99	541.228	88.23	60.5059	54.06	47.4698	40.7822
w15	18.46	1019.908	161.95	118.506	102.141	77.1823	68.1758
w16	32.55	1854.699	303.69	232.18	189.572	174.96	136.873
w17	69.06	3918.655	554.62	460.882	386.886	357.874	252.538
w18	128.03	7245.888	1034.30	910.266	774.498	653.251	467.091
w19	254.43	14235.360	1898.05	1815.91	1602.51	1311.38	885.655
w20	526.03	27028.049	3576.83	3647.52	3012.45	2558.88	1527.01
w21	1035.09	60064.824	6418.55	7306.26	6061.85	4715.55	3378.42
w22	2552.65	109205.951	11910.02	14813.1	11279.8	9499.05	6788.65
w23	4091.70	238583.922	22766.03	-	23948.4	18912.2	11793.5
w24	8730.61	-	43161.32	-	47673.3	37630.4	23156.8

Fig. 7. Second Verify Test (secs)

last must be used, no instruction or argument pair should be repeated, etc), let alone some of the more sophisticated constraints (such as removing all non-optimal pairs and triples). Thus implementing *search* using ASP seems eminently possible. The results for *verify* are less encouraging and suggest that attempting to verify sequences using greater than 32 bits of input is likely to require significant resources given current solver technology.

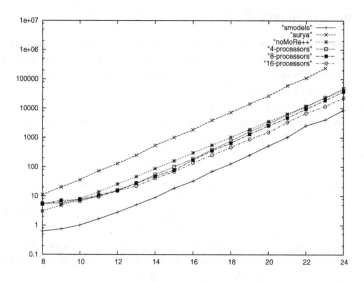

Fig. 8. Second Verify Test Timings (log scale)

The results also suggest a number of interesting points related to solver design and implementation. Firstly, clearly implementation does matter. SURYA implements a slight refinement of the algorithm used in SMODELS, but performs significantly worse in almost all cases. How serious these implementation differences are is not known, but clearly for any solver that is intended to be competitive, implementation details do matter. Another, more subtle issue suggested by these results is the cost of *lookahead*. In the first verify test, the times increase significantly faster that doubling, despite the search space itself only doubling. In the second test, the rate of increase is much closer to doubling. In the first case, the increasing number of atoms, and thus the rising cost of *lookahead* is thought to cause this disparity. This fits with other experiments that have been run using the TOAST programs and explains why NOMORE++ is generally slower than SMODELS. Interestingly, the second verify test also has NOMORE++'s times increasing by less than a factor of two as the search space doubles, suggesting that, although more costly, its branching heuristic is indeed 'smarter'. Again this fits with other tests, which have found degenerate *verify* programs where NOMORE++'s branching heuristic has performed significantly better than any other solver.

Finally, the results suggest some interesting possibilities in the field of distributed solver development. The performance of PLATYPUS on s3 and v16 to v24 demonstrates the power of the technique and that, especially for larger programs, near-linear speed up is possible. However, the performance on s1, s2 and v8 to v15 also shows that, unsurprisingly, on smaller programs the overhead of distribution outweighs the benefits. Why PLATYPUS takes longer than SMODELS on w8 to w24 is not known. Potentially, the smaller number of atoms meant the program's balance between *expand*, *lookahead* and branching were not of the right form to demonstrate the value of distribution or problems with the delegation policy. Parallel solvers are clearly a very powerful advance in solver technology, but one that must be used carefully.

6   Future Development

One of the key targets in the next stage of TOAST development is to reduce the amount of time required in searching. Doing so will also increase the length of instruction sequence that can be found. This requires improving both the programs that are generated and the tools used to solve them.

A key improvement to the generated programs will be to remove all short sequences that are known to be non-optimal. A slight modification to *search* allows it to generate all possible instruction sequences of a given length. By superoptimising each one of these for the smaller lengths, it is then possible to build a set of equivalence classes of instructions. Only the shortest member of each class needs to be in the search space and thus a set of constraints can be added to the programs that *search* generates. This process only ever needs to be done once for each processor architecture the TOAST system is ported to and will give significant improvements in terms of search times. The equivalence classes generated may also be useful to augment *verify*.

The other developments needed to reduce the *search* time are in the tools used. Addressing the amount of memory consumed by LPARSE and attempting to improve the scaling of the SMODELS algorithm are both high priorities.

The performance of *verify* also raises some interesting questions. In its current form, it is usable for some of the smaller, embedded processors, though it is unlikely to scale to high end, 64 bit processors. A number of alternative approaches are being considered, such as attempting to prove equivalence results about the ASP program generated, reducing the instructions to a minimal/pseudo-normal form (an approach first used by Massalin), using some form of algebraic theorem proving (as the Denali project used) or attempting to use the observation that sequences equivalent on a small set of points tend to be equivalent on all of them.

Using the TOAST system to improve the code generated by toolchains such as GCC is also a key target for the project. By implementing tools that translate between the TOAST internal format and processor-specific assembly language, it will be possible to check the output of GCC for sequences that can be superoptimised. Patterns that occur regularly could be added to the instruction generation phase of GCC. The code generators used by JIT (Just In Time) compilers and performance critical system libraries, such as GMP (GNU Multiple Precision Arithmetic Library) could also be application areas.

It is hoped that it will not only prove useful as a tool for optimising sections of performance-critical code, but that the ASP programs could be used as benchmarks for solver performance and the basis of other applications which reason about machine code.

7   Conclusion

This paper suggests that ASP can be used to solve large-scale, real-world problems. Future work will hopefully demonstrate this is also a powerful approach to superoptimisation and thus, perhaps even a 'killer application' for ASP.

However, it is not without challenges. Although savings to both the size of the ASP programs used and their search spaces are possible, this will remain a 'high end' application for answer set solvers. Some of the features it requires, such as the handling of large, sparse search spaces and efficiency in producing all possible answer sets (or traversing the search space of programs without answer sets) are not key targets of current solver development.

The TOAST project demonstrates that answer set technology is ready to be used in large-scale applications, although more work needs to be done to make it competitive.

References

1. I. Niemelä and P. Simons: Smodels: An Implementation of the Stable Model and Well-Founded Semantics for Normal Logic Programs. In: Proceedings of the 4th International Conference on Logic Programing and Nonmonotonic Reasoning (LPNMR'97). Volume 1265 of LNAI., Springer (1997) 420–429
2. Thomas Eiter and Nicola Leone and Cristinel Mateis and Gerald Pfeifer and Francesco Scarcello: The KR System DLV: Progress Report, Comparisons and Benchmarks. In: Proceedings of the 6th International Conference on the Principles of Knowledge Representation and Reasoning (KR'98), Morgan Kaufmann (1998) 406–417
3. WASP: WP5 Report: Model Applications and Proofs-of-Concept. http://www.kr.tuwien.ac.at/projects/WASP/wasp-wp5-web.html (2004)
4. Thomas Eiter and Wolfgang Faber and Nicola Leone and Gerald Pfeifer and Axel Polleres: Using the DLV System for Planning and Diagnostic Reasoning. In: Proceedings of the 14th Workshop on Logic Programming (WLP'99). (2000) 125–134
5. Monica Nogueira and Marcello Balduccini and Michael Gelfond and Richard Watson and Matthew Barry: An A-Prolog Decision Support System for the Space Shuttle. In: Proceedings of the 3rd International Symposium on Practical Aspects of Declarative Languages (PADL'01). Volume 1990 of LNCS., Springer (2001) 169–183
6. De Vos, M., Crick, T., Padget, J., Brain, M., Cliffe, O., Needham, J.: A Multi-agent Platform using Ordered Choice Logic Programming. In: Proceedings of the 3rd International Workshop on Declarative Agent Languages and Technologies (DALT'05). Volume 3904 of LNAI., Springer (2006) 72–88
7. P. Giorgini, F. Massacci, J. Mylopoulos and N. Zannone: Requirements Engineering Meets Trust Management: Model, Methodology, and Reasoning. In: Proceedings of the 2nd International Conference on Trust Management (iTrust 2004). Volume 2995 of LNCS., Springer (2004) 176–190
8. S. Costantini and A. Formisano and E. Omodeo: Mapping Between Domain Models in Answer Set Programming. In: Proceedings of Answer Set Programming: Advances in Theory and Implementation (ASP'03). (2003)
9. Massalin, H.: Superoptimizer: A Look at the Smallest Program. In: Proceedings of the 2nd International Conference on Architectural Support for Programming Languages and Operating Systems (ASPLOS'87), IEEE Computer Society Press (1987) 122–126
10. Aho, A.V., Sethi, R., Ullmann, J.D.: Compilers: Principles, Techniques and Tools. Addison-Wesley (1986)
11. Appel, A.W.: Modern Compiler Implementation in C. Cambridge University Press (2004)
12. Proebsting, T.: Proebsting's Law: Compiler Advances Double Computing Power Every 18 Years. http://research.microsoft.com/~toddpro/papers/law.htm (1998)
13. Granlund, T., Kenner, R.: Eliminating Branches using a Superoptimizer and the GNU C Compiler. In: Proceedings of the ACM SIGPLAN Conference on Programming Language Design and Implementation (PLDI'92), ACM Press (1992) 341–352

14. Joshi, R., Nelson, G., Randall, K.: Denali: A Goal-Directed Superoptimizer. In: Proceedings of the ACM SIGPLAN Conference on Programming Language Design and Implementation (PLDI'02), ACM Press (2002) 304–314

15. Joshi, R., Nelson, G., Zhou, Y.: The Straight-Line Automatic Programming Problem. Technical Report HPL-2003-236, HP Labs (2003)

16. Gelfond, M., Lifschitz, V.: The Stable Model Semantics for Logic Programming. In: Proceedings of the 5th International Conference on Logic Programming (ICLP'88), MIT Press (1988) 1070–1080

17. Gelfond, M., Lifschitz, V.: Classical Negation in Logic Programs and Disjunctive Databases. New Generation Computing 9(3-4) (1991) 365–386

18. Baral, C.: Knowledge Representation, Reasoning and Declarative Problem Solving. Cambridge University Press (2003)

19. Denecker, M.: What's in a Model? Epistemological Analysis of Logic Programming. In: Proceedings of the 9th International Conference on the Principles of Knowledge Representation and Reasoning (KR2004), AAAI Press (2004) 106–113

20. Leone, N., Pfeifer, G., Faber, W., Eiter, T., Gottlob, G., Perri, S., Scarcello, F.: The DLV System for Knowledge Representation and Reasoning. to appear in ACM Transactions on Computational Logic (2006)

21. Davis, M., Logemann, G., Loveland, D.: A Machine Program for Theorem-Proving. Communications of the ACM 5(7) (1962) 394–397

22. Syrjänen, T.: Lparse 1.0 User's Manual. Helsinki University of Technology. (2000)

23. Giunchiglia, E., Lierler, Y., Maratea, M.: SAT-Based Answer Set Programming. In: Proceedings of the 19th National Conference on Artificial Intelligence (AAAI-04), AAAI Press (2004) 61–66

24. Fangzhen Lin and Yuting Zhao: ASSAT: Computing Answer Sets of a Logic Program by SAT Solvers. Artificial Intelligence 157(1-2) (2004) 115–137

25. Enrico Pontelli and Marcello Balduccini and F. Bermudez: Non-Monotonic Reasoning on Beowulf Platforms. In: Proceedings of the 5th International Symposium on Practical Aspects of Declarative Languages (PADL'03). Volume 2562 of LNAI., Springer (2003) 37–57

26. Kane, G.: MIPS RISC Architecture. Prentice Hall (1988)

27. SPARC International, Inc: The SPARC Architecture Manual, Version 8. (1992)

28. Mellarkod, V.S.: Optimizing The Computation Of Stable Models Using Merged Rules. Technical report, Texas Tech University (2002)

29. Anger, C., Gebser, M., Linke, T., Neumann, A., Schaub, T.: The nomore++ Approach to Answer Set Solving. In: Proceedings of Answer Set Programming: Advances in Theory and Implementation (ASP'05). (2005)

30. Asparagus Project Team: Asparagus Benchmark Project. http://asparagus.cs.uni-potsdam.de/ (2004)

Modelling Biological Networks by Action Languages Via Answer Set Programming

Susanne Grell[1], Torsten Schaub[1,*], and Joachim Selbig[1,2]

[1] Institut für Informatik, Universität Potsdam, Postfach 900327, D-14439 Potsdam, Germany
[2] Institut für Biologie, Universität Potsdam, Postfach 900327, D-14439 Potsdam, Germany

Abstract. We describe an approach to modelling biological networks by action languages via answer set programming. To this end, we propose an action language for modelling biological networks, building on previous work by Baral et al. We introduce its syntax and semantics along with a translation into answer set programming. Finally, we describe one of its applications, namely, the sulfur starvation response-pathway of the model plant Arabidopsis thaliana and sketch the functionality of our system and its usage.

1 Introduction

Molecular biology has seen a technological revolution with the establishment of high-throughput methods in the last years. These methods allow for gathering multiple orders of magnitude more data than was procurable before. For turning such huge amounts of data into knowledge, one needs appropriate and powerful knowledge representation tools that allow for modelling complex biological systems and their behaviour. Of particular interest are qualitative tools that allow for dealing with biological and biochemical networks. Since these networks are very large, a biologist can manually deal with a small part of it at once. Among the more traditional qualitative formalisms, we find e.g. Petri Nets [1,2], Flux Balance Analysis [3] or Boolean Networks [4]. As detailed in [5], these approaches lack sufficiently expressive reasoning capacities.

Groundbreaking work addressing this deficiency was recently done by Chitta Baral and colleagues who developed a first *action language* for representing and reasoning about biological networks [6,5]. Action languages were introduced in the 1990s by Gelfond and Lifschitz (cf. [7]). By now, there exists a large variety of action languages, like the most basic language $\mathcal{A}$ and its extensions [8] as well as more expressive action languages like $\mathcal{C}$ [9] or $\mathcal{K}$ [10]. Traditionally, action languages are designed for applications in autonomous agents, planning, diagnosis, etc, in which the explicit applicability of actions plays a dominant role. This is slightly different in biological systems where *reactions* are a major concern. For instance, while an agent usually has the choice to execute an action or not, a biological reaction is often simply triggered by its application conditions. This is addressed in [5] by proposing *trigger* and *inhibition rules* as an addition to the basic action language $\mathcal{A}$; the resulting language is referred to as $\mathcal{A}_T^0$. A further extension, allowing knowledge about event ordering, is introduced in [11].

---

* Affiliated with the School of Computing Science at Simon Fraser University, Burnaby, Canada.

S. Etalle and M. Truszczyński (Eds.): ICLP 2006, LNCS 4079, pp. 285–299, 2006.

The advantages of action languages for modelling biological systems are manifold:

- We get a simplified model. It is not necessary to have any kinetic parameters. The approach can thus already be used in a very early state to verify whether the proposed model of the biological system can or cannot hold.
- Different kinds of reasoning can be used to plan and support experiments. This helps to reduce the number of expensive experiments.
- Further reasoning modes allow for prediction of consequences and explanation of observations.
- The usage of static causal laws allows to easily include background knowledge like environmental conditions, which play an important role for the development of a biological system but are usually difficult to include in the model.
- The approach is elaboration tolerant because it allows to easily extend the model without requiring to change the rest of the model.

We start by introducing our action language $\mathcal{C}_{TAID}$ by building on language $\mathcal{A}_T^0$ [5] and $\mathcal{C}$ [9]. $\mathcal{C}_{TAID}$ extends $\mathcal{C}$ by adding biologically relevant concepts from $\mathcal{A}_T^0$ such as triggers and it augments $\mathcal{A}_T^0$ by providing static causal laws for modelling background knowledge. Moreover, fluents are no longer inertial by definition and the concurrent execution of actions can be restricted. A feature distinguishing $\mathcal{C}_{TAID}$ from its predecessors is its concept of *allowance*, which was motivated by our biological applications. The corresponding *allowance rules* let us express that an action can occur under certain conditions but does not have to occur. In fact, biological systems are characterised by a high degree of incomplete knowledge about the dependencies among different component and the actual reasons for their interaction. If the dependencies are well understood, they can be expressed using triggering rules. However, if the dependencies are only partly known or not part of the model, e.g. environmental conditions, they cannot be expressed appropriately using triggering rules. The concept of allowance permits actions to take place or not, as long as they are allowed (and not inhibited). This introduces a certain non-determinism that is used to model alternative paths, actions for which the preconditions are not yet fully understood, and low reaction rates. Of course, such a non-deterministic construct increases the number of solutions. However, this is a desired feature since we pursue an exploratory approach to bioinformatics that allows the biologist to browse through the possible models of its application.

We introduce the syntax and semantics of $\mathcal{C}_{TAID}$ and give a soundness and completeness result, proved in [12]. For implementing $\mathcal{C}_{TAID}$, we compile specifications in $\mathcal{C}_{TAID}$ into logic programs under answer set semantics [13]. This has been implemented in Java and was used meanwhile in ten different application scenarios at the Max-Planck Institute for Molecular Plant Physiology for modelling metabolic as well as signal transduction networks. Among them we present the smallest application, namely the sulfur starvation response-pathway of the model plant Arabidopsis thaliana.

2 Action Language $\mathcal{C}_{TAID}$

The alphabet of our action language $\mathcal{C}_{TAID}$ consists of two nonempty disjoint sets of symbols: a set of *actions* A and a set of *fluents* F. Informally, fluents describe changing properties of a world and actions can influence fluents. We deal with propositional fluents that are either *true* or *false*. A *fluent literal* is a fluent f possibly preceded by $\neg$.

We distinguish three sublanguages of $\mathcal{C}_{TAID}$: The *action description language* is used to describe the general knowledge about the system, the *action observation language* is used to express knowledge about particular points of time and the *action query language* is used to reason about the described system.

Action Description Language. To begin with, we fix the syntax of $\mathcal{C}_{TAID}$'s action description language:

Definition 1. *A domain description $D(A, F)$ in $\mathcal{C}_{TAID}$ consists of expressions of the following form:*

$$(a \textbf{ causes } f_1, \ldots, f_n \textbf{ if } g_1, \ldots, g_m)\ (1) \qquad (f_1, \ldots, f_n \textbf{ inhibits } a)\quad (5)$$
$$(f_1, \ldots, f_n \textbf{ if } g_1, \ldots, g_m)\ (2) \qquad (\textbf{noconcurrency } a_1, \ldots, a_n)\quad (6)$$
$$(f_1, \ldots, f_n \textbf{ triggers } a)\ (3) \qquad\qquad\qquad (\textbf{default } f)\quad (7)$$
$$(f_1, \ldots, f_n \textbf{ allows } a)\ (4)$$

where $a, a_1, \ldots, a_n$ are actions and $f, f_1, \ldots, f_n, g_1, \ldots, g_m$ are fluent literals.

Note that $\mathcal{A}_T^0$ consists of expressions of form (1), (3), and (5) only.

A *dynamic causal law* is a rule of form (1), stating that $f_1, \ldots, f_n$ hold after the occurrence of action a if $g_1, \ldots, g_m$ hold when a occurs. If there are no preconditions of the form $g_1, \ldots, g_m$, the if-part can be omitted. Rule (2) is a *static causal law*, used to express immediate dependencies between fluents; it guarantees that $f_1, \ldots, f_n$ hold whenever $g_1, \ldots, g_m$ hold. Rules (3) to (6) can be used to express whether and when an action can or cannot occur. A *triggering rule* (3) is used to state that action a occurs immediately if the preconditions $f_1, \ldots, f_n$ hold, unless it is inhibited. An *allowance rule* of form (4) states that action a can but need not occur if the preconditions $f_1, \ldots, f_n$ hold. An action for which triggering or allowance rules are specified can only occur if one of its triggering or allowance rules, resp., is satisfied. An *inhibition rule* of form (5) can be used to express that action a cannot occur if $f_1, \ldots, f_n$ hold. A rule of the form (6) is a no-concurrency constraint. Actions included in such a constraint cannot occur at the same time. Rule (7) is a *default rule*, which is used to define a default value for a fluent. This makes us distinguish two kinds of fluents: inertial and non-inertial fluents. Inertial fluent change their value only if they are affected by dynamic or static causal laws. Non-inertial fluents on the other hand have the value, specified by a default rule, unless they are affected by a dynamic or static causal law. Every fluent that has no default value is regarded to be inertial. Additionally, we distinguish three groups of actions depending on the rules defined for them. An action can either be a triggered, an allowed or an exogenous action. That means, for one action there can be several triggering or several allowance rules but not both.

As usual, the semantics of a domain description $D(A, F)$ is defined in terms of transition systems. An *interpretation I* of F is a complete and consistent set of fluents.

Definition 2 (State). *A state $s \in S$ of the domain description $D(A, F)$ is an interpretation of F such that for every static causal law $(f_1, \ldots, f_n \textbf{ if } g_1, \ldots, g_n) \in D(A, F)$, we have $\{f_1, \ldots, f_n\} \subseteq s$ whenever $\{g_1, \ldots, g_n\} \subseteq s$.*

Hence, we are only interested in sets of fluents satisfying all static causal laws, i.e. correctly model the dependencies between the fluents.

Depending on the state, it is possible to decide which actions can or cannot occur. Therefore we define the notion of active, passive and applicable rules.

Definition 3. *Let $D(A, F)$ be a domain description and s a state of $D(A, F)$.*

1. *An inhibition rule $(f_1, \ldots, f_n$ **inhibits** $a)$ is active in s, if $s \models f_1 \wedge \ldots \wedge f_n$, otherwise the inhibition rule is passive. The set $A_I(s)$ is the set of actions for which there exists at least one active inhibition rule in s.*
2. *A triggering rule $(f_1, \ldots, f_n$ **triggers** $a)$ is active in s, if $s \models f_1 \wedge \ldots \wedge f_n$ and all inhibition rules of action a are passive in s, otherwise the triggering rule is passive in s. The set $A_T(s)$ is the set of actions for which there exists at least one active triggering rule in s. The set $\overline{A}_T(s)$ is the set of actions for which there exists at least one triggering rule and all triggering rules are passive in s.*
3. *An allowance rule $(f_1, \ldots, f_n$ **allows** $a)$ is active in s, if $s \models f_1 \wedge \ldots \wedge f_n$ and all inhibition rules of action a are passive in s, otherwise the allowance rule is passive in s. The set $A_A(s)$ is the set of actions for which there exists at least one active allowance rule in s. The set $\overline{A}_A(s)$ is the set of actions for which there exists at least one allowance rule and all allowance rules are passive in s.*
4. *A dynamic causal law $(a$ **causes** $f_1, \ldots, f_n$ **if** $g_1, \ldots, g_n)$ is applicable in s, if $s \models g_1 \wedge \ldots \wedge g_n$.*
5. *A static causal law $(f_1, \ldots, f_n$ **if** $g_1, \ldots, g_n)$ is applicable in s, if $s \models g_1 \wedge \ldots \wedge g_n$.*

Observe that point two and three of the definition express that an action has to occur or may occur as long as there is one active triggering or allowance rule respectively. An action cannot occur if either an inhibition rule for the action is active or if all triggering or allowance rules for the action are passive.

The effects of an action are determined by the applicable dynamic causal laws defined for this action. Following [8], the effects of an action a in a state s of domain description $D(A, F)$ are defined as follows:

$$E(a, s) = \{f_1, \ldots, f_n \mid (a \text{ **causes** } f_1, \ldots, f_n \text{ **if** } g_1, \ldots, g_m) \text{ is applicable in } s\}$$

The effects of a set of actions A is defined as the union of the effects of the single actions: $E(A, s) = \bigcup_{a \in A} E(a, s)$. Besides the direct effects of actions, a domain description also defines the consequences of static relationships between fluents. For a set of static causal laws in a domain description $D(A, F)$ and a state s, the set

$$L(s) = \{f_1, \ldots, f_n \mid (f_1, \ldots, f_n \text{ **if** } g_1, \ldots, g_m) \text{ is applicable in } s\}$$

contains the heads of all static causal laws whose preconditions hold in s.

Finally, the way the world evolves according to a domain description is captured by a *transition relation*; it defines to which state the execution of a set of actions leads.

Definition 4. *Let $D(A, F)$ be a domain description and S be the set of states of $D(A, F)$. Then, the transition relation $\Phi \subseteq S \times 2^A \times S$ determines the resulting state $s' \in S$ after executing all actions $B \subseteq A$ in state $s \in S$ as follows:*

$$(s, B, s') \in \Phi \text{ for } \quad s' = \{(s \cap s') \cup E(B, s) \cup L(s') \cup \Delta(s')\}$$

$$\text{where} \quad \Delta(s') = \quad \{\ f \mid (\textbf{default} \quad f) \in D(A, F), \neg f \notin E(B, s) \cup L(s')\}$$
$$\cup \{\neg f \mid (\textbf{default} \neg f) \in D(A, F), \quad f \notin E(B, s) \cup L(s')\}$$

Even if no actions are performed, there can nevertheless be a change of state due to the default values defined by the domain description. Intuitively, if actions occur, the next state is determined by taking all effects of the applicable dynamic and static causal laws and adding the default values of fluents not affected by these actions. The values of all fluents that are not affected by these actions or by default values remain unchanged.

The transition relation determines the resulting state when an action is executed, but it cannot be used to decide whether the action happens at all, since it does not consider triggering, allowance or inhibition rules. This is accomplished by the concept of a *trajectory*, which is a sequence of states and actions that takes all rules in the domain description into account.

Definition 5 (Trajectory). *Let $D(A, F)$ be a domain description.*

A trajectory $s_0, A_1, s_1, \ldots, A_n, s_n$ of $D(A, F)$ is a sequence of actions $A_i \subseteq A$ and states s_i satisfying the following conditions for $0 \leq i < n$:

1. $(s_i, A, s_{i+1}) \in \Phi$
2. $A_T(s_i) \subseteq A_{i+1}$
3. $\overline{A_T}(s_i) \cap A_{i+1} = \emptyset$
4. $\overline{A_A}(s_i) \cap A_{i+1} = \emptyset$
5. $A_I(s_i) \cap A_{i+1} = \emptyset$
6. $|A_i \cap B| \leq 1$
   for all (**noconcurrency** $B) \in D(A, F)$.

A trajectory assures that there is a reason why an action occurs or why it does not occur. The second and third point of the definition make sure that the actions of all active triggering rules are included in the set of actions and that no action for which all triggering rules are passive is included in the set of actions. Point four and five assure that no actions for which all allowance rules are passive and no inhibited actions are included in the set of actions. [1] The definition does not include assertions about the active allowance rules, because they can be, but not necessarily have to be, included in the set of actions. (As detailed above, this is motivated by our biological application.) Point two to four imply that for an action there can either be only triggering rules or only allowance rules defined. The last point of the definition assures that all no-concurrency constraints are correctly applied.

Action Observation Language. The action observation language provides expressions to describe particular states and occurrences of actions:

$$(f \text{ at } t_i) \qquad\qquad (a \text{ occurs\_at } t_i) \qquad\qquad (8)$$

where f is a fluent literal, a is an action and t_i is a point of time. The initial point of time is t_0. For a set of actions $A' = \{a_1, \ldots, a_k\}$ we write $(A' \text{ occurs\_at } t_i)$ to abbreviate $(a_1 \text{ occurs\_at } t_i), \ldots, (a_k \text{ occurs\_at } t_i)$. Intuitively, an expression of form $(f \text{ at } t_i)$ is

---

[1] Allowance rules can be rewritten as inhibition rules, if the corresponding action is declared to be exogenous. But this is inadequate in view of our biological application and results in a significant blow-up in the number of rules obtained after compilation.

used to state that a fluent f is *true* or present at time t_i. If the fluent f is preceded by $\neg$ it states that f is *false* at t_i. An observation of form $(a \ \textbf{occurs\_at} \ t_i)$ says that action a occurs at time t_i. It is possible that action a is preceded by $\neg$ to express that a does not occur at time t_i.

A domain description specifies how the system can evolve over time. By including observations the possibilities of this evolution are restricted. So only when all information, the domain description and the observations, is taken into account, we get an appropriate picture of the world. The combination of domain description and observations is called an *action theory*.

Definition 6 (Action theory). *Let D be a domain description and O be a set of observations. The pair (D, O) is called an action theory.*

Intuitively, trajectories specify possible evolutions of the system with respect to the given domain description. However, not all trajectories satisfy the observations given by an action theory. Trajectories satisfying both, the domain description as well as given observations, are called *trajectory models*:

Definition 7 (Trajectory model). *Let (D, O) be an action theory.*
A trajectory $s_0, A_1, s_1, A_2, \ldots, A_n, s_n$ of D is a trajectory model of (D, O), if it satisfies all observations in O in the following way:

- *if $(f \ \textbf{at} \ t) \in O$, then $f \in s_t$*
- *if $(a \ \textbf{occurs\_at} \ t) \in O$, then $a \in A_{t+1}$.*

The problem that arises here is to find biologically meaningful models. Obviously, such trajectory models often include redundant information, but since this is a common phenomena of biological systems it is not possible to simply exclude such trajectory models. Often, only the minimal trajectories are considered to be of interest, but this is not appropriate for biological systems, since we are not only interested in the shortest path through the transition system, but also in, possibly longer, alternative paths and just as well in models which include the concurrent execution of actions. To decide which actions are redundant is thus a rather difficult problem and the question whether a model is biologically meaningful can only be answered by a biologist, not by an automated reasoner. One way to include additional information which may be derived from data on measurement could be the use of preferences, which is subject to future work.

A question we can already answer is that abut logical consequence of observations.

Definition 8. *Let (D, O) be an action theory. Then,*

- *(D, O) entails fluent observation $(f \ \textbf{at} \ t_i)$, written $(D, O) \models (f \ \textbf{at} \ t_i)$, if $f \in s_i$ for all trajectory models $s_0, A_1, \ldots, s_i, A_{i+1}, \ldots, A_n, s_n$ of (D, O),*
- *(D, O) entails action observation $(a \ \textbf{occurs\_at} \ t_i)$, written $(D, O) \models (a \ \textbf{occurs\_at} \ t_i)$, if $a \in A_{i+1}$ for all trajectory models $s_0, A_1, \ldots, s_i, A_{i+1}, \ldots, A_n, s_n$ of (D, O).*

Action Query Language. Queries are about the evolution of the biological system, i.e. about trajectories. In general, a query is of the form:

$$(f_1, \ldots, f_n \ \textbf{after} \ A_1 \ \textbf{occurs\_at} \ t_1, \ldots, A_m \ \textbf{occurs\_at} \ t_m) \tag{9}$$

where $f_1, ..., f_n$ are fluent literals, $A_1, ..., A_m$ sets of actions, and $t_1, ..., t_m$ time points.

For queries the most prominent question is the notion of logical consequence. Under which circumstances entails an action theory or a single trajectory model a query.

Definition 9. *Let* (D, O) *be an action theory and* Q *be a query of form (9).^{2} Then,*

- *Q is cautiously entailed by* (D, O), *written* $(D, O) \models_c Q$, *if every trajectory model* $s_0, A_1', s_1, A_2', \ldots, A_p', s_p$ *of* (D, O) *satisfies* $A_i \subseteq A_i'$ *for* $0 < i \leq m \leq p$ *and* $s_p \models f_1 \wedge \ldots \wedge f_n$.
- *Q is bravely entailed by* (D, O), *written* $(D, O) \models_b Q$, *if some trajectory model* $s_0, A_1', s_1, A_2', \ldots, A_p', s_p$ *of* (D, O) *satisfies* $A_i \subseteq A_i'$ *for* $0 < i \leq m \leq p$ *and* $s_p \models f_1 \wedge \ldots \wedge f_n$.

While cautiously entailed queries are supported by all models, bravely entailed queries can be used for checking the possible hypotheses.

We want to use the knowledge given as an action theory to reason about the corresponding biological system. Reasoning includes explaining observed behaviour, but also predicting the future development of the system or how the system may be influenced in a particular way. The above notion of entailment is used to verify the different queries introduced in the next sections.

Planning. In planning, we try to find possibilities to influence a system in a certain way. Neither the initial state nor the goal state have to be completely specified by fluent observations. A plan is thus a sequence of actions starting from one possible initial state and ending at one possible goal state. There are usually several plans, taking into account different paths but also different initial and goal states.

Definition 10 (Plan). *Let* (D, O_{init}) *be an a action theory such that* O_{init} *contains only fluent observations about the initial state and let* Q *be a query of form (9).*

If $(D, O_{init}) \models_b Q$, *then* $P = \{(A_1 \text{ occurs\_at } t_1), \ldots, (A_m \text{ occurs\_at } t_m)\}$ *is a plan for* $f_1, \ldots, f_n$.

Note that a plan is always derived from the corresponding trajectory model.

Explanation. Usually, there are not only observations about the initial state but also about other time points and we are more interested in understanding the observed behaviour of a system than in finding a plan to cause certain behaviour of the system.

Definition 11 (Explanation). *Let* (D, O) *be an action theory and let* Q *be a query of form (9) where* $f_1 \wedge \ldots \wedge f_n \equiv true$.

If $(D, O) \models_b Q$, *then* $E = \{(A_1 \text{ occurs\_at } t_1), \ldots, (A_m \text{ occurs\_at } t_m)\}$ *is an explanation for the set of observations* O.

When explaining observed behaviour it is neither necessary to completely define the initial state, nor the final state. The less information is provided the more possible explanation there are, because an explanation is one path from one possible initial state to one possible final state, via some possible intermediate partially defined states given by the observations. The initial state and the explanation are induced by the underlying trajectory model.

---

^{2} Parameters m and n are taken as defined in (9).

Prediction is mainly used to determine the influence of actions on the system; it tries to answer questions about the possible evolution of the system. A query answers the question whether, starting at the current state and executing a given sequence of actions, fluents will hold or not hold after a certain time.

Definition 12 (Prediction). *Let (D, O) be an action theory and let Q be a query of form (9).*

- *If $(D, O) \models_c Q$, then $f_1, \ldots, f_n$ are cautiously predicted,*
- *If $(D, O) \models_b Q$, then $f_1, \ldots, f_n$ are bravely predicted.*

All of the above reasoning modes are implemented in our tool and used in our biological applications. Before describing its usage, we first detail how it is implemented.

3   Compilation

We implemented our action language by means of a compiler mapping C_{TAID} onto logic programs under *answer set semantics* (cf. [14,13]). This semantics associates with a logic program a set of distinguished models, referred to as *answer sets*. This model-based approach to logic programming is different from the traditional one, like Prolog, insofar as solutions are read off issuing answer sets rather than proofs of posed queries. Our compiler uses efficient off-the-self answer set solvers as a back-end, whose purpose is to compute answer sets from the result of our compilation. Since we do not elaborate upon theoretical aspects of this, we refer the reader to the literature for a formal introduction to answer set programming (cf. [14,13]).

Our translation builds upon and extends the one in [6]. We adapt the translation of the language $\mathcal{A}_T^0$ to include new language constructs and we extend the compilation of $\mathcal{A}_T^0$ in order to capture the semantics of static causal laws, allowance and default rules, and of no-concurrency constraints. In what follows, we stick to the syntax of the smodels system [15].

Action Description Language. The expressions defined in a domain description $D(A, F)$ have to be composed of symbols from A an F. When constructing the logic program for $D(A, F)$, we first have to define the alphabet. We declare every fluent $f \in F$ and action $a \in A$, resp., by adding a fact of the form `fluent(f)`, and `action(a)`. We use continuously a variable `T`, representing a time point where $0 \leq T \leq t_{max}$. This range is encoded by the smodels construct `time(0..t_{max})`, standing for the facts `time(0)`,...,`time(t_{max})`. Furthermore, it is necessary to add constraints expressing that f and $\neg f$ are contradictory.

```
:- holds(f,T), holds(neg(f),T), fluent(f), time(T).
```

Whenever clear from the context, we only give translations for positive fluent literals $f \in F$ and omit the dual rule for the negative fluent, viz. $\neg f$ represented as `neg(f)`.

For each inertial fluent $f \in F$, we include rules expressing that f has the same value at t_{i+1} as at t_i, unless it is known otherwise:

```
holds(f,T+1)  :- holds(f,T),not holds(neg(f,T+1)),not default(f),
    fluent(f),time(T),time(T+1).
```

For each non-inertial fluent $f \in F$, we add the fact `default(f)` and include for the default value *true*:

```
holds(f,T) :- not holds(neg(f),T), fluent(f), time(T).
```

For each dynamic causal law (1) in $D(A, F)$ and each fluent $f_i \in F$, we include:

```
holds(fi,T+1) :- holds(occurs(a),T),holds(g1,T),...,holds(gn,T),
    fluent(g1),...,fluent(gn),fluent(fi),action(a),time(T;T+1).
```

For each static causal law (2) in $D(A, F)$ and each fluent $f_i \in F$, we include:

```
holds(fi,T) :- holds(g1,T),...,holds(gn,T),
    fluent(g1), ..., fluent(gn),fluent(fi), time(T).
```

Every triggering rule (3) in $D(A, F)$ is translated as:

```
holds(occurs(a),T) :- not holds(ab(occurs(a)),T),
    holds(f1,T),...,holds(fn,T),
    fluent(f1),...,fluent(fn),action(a),time(T).
```

For each allowance rule (4) in $D(A, F)$, we include:

```
holds(allow(occurs(a)),T) :- not holds(ab(occurs(a)),T),
    holds(f1,T),...,holds(fn,T),
    fluent(f1),...,fluent(fn),action(a),time(T).
```

For every exogenous action $a \in A$, the translation includes a rule, stating that this action can always occur.

```
holds(allow(occurs(a)),T) :- action(a), time(T).
```

Every inhibition rule (5) in $D(A, F)$ is translated as:

```
holds(ab(occurs(a)),T) :- holds(f1,T),...,holds(fn,T),
    action(a),fluent(f1),...,fluent(fn), time(T).
```

For each no-concurrency constraint (6) in $D(A, F)$, we include an integrity constraint assuring that at most one of the respective actions can hold at time t:

```
:- time(T), 2 {holds(occurs(a1),T):action(a1),...,
                        holds(occurs(an),T):action(an)}.
```

Action Observation Language. There are two different kinds of fluent observations. Those about the initial state, (f **at** t_0), and the fluent observations about all other states, (f **at** t_i) for $i > 0$. Fluent observations about the initial state are simply translated as facts: `holds(f,0)`. Because they are just assumed to be true and need no further justification. All other fluent observations however need a justification. Due to this, fluent observations about all states except the initial state are translated into integrity constraints of the form: `:- not holds(f,T),fluent(f),time(T).`

The initial state can be partially specified by fluent observations. In fact, only the translation of the (initial) fluent observations must be given. All possible completions of the initial state are then generated by adding for every fluent $f \in F$ the rules:

```
holds(f,0):- not holds(neg(f),0).
holds(neg(f),0):- not holds(f,0).
```
(10)

When translating action observations of form (8) the different kinds of actions have to be considered. Exogenous actions can always occur and need no further justification. Such an exogenous action observation is translated as a fact: `holds(occurs(a),T)`. Unlike this, observations about triggered or allowed actions must have a reason, e.g. an active triggering or allowance rule, to occur. To assure this justification, the action observation is translated using constraints of the form:

```
:- holds(neg(occurs(a)),T),action(a),time(T).
```

assuring that every answer set must satisfy the observation (*a* **occurs_at** t_i).

Apart from planning (see below), we also have to generate possible combinations of occurrences of actions, for all states. To this effect, the translation includes two rules for every exogenous and allowed action.

$$
\begin{aligned}
&\texttt{holds(occurs(a),T)} \texttt{ :- holds(allow(occurs(a)),T),} \\
&\quad\texttt{not holds(ab(occurs(a)),T), not} \\
&\qquad\texttt{holds(neg(occurs(a)),T),} \\
&\quad\texttt{action(a), time(T), T<}t_{max}. \\
&\texttt{holds(neg(occurs(a)),T) :- not holds(occurs(a),T),} \\
&\quad\texttt{action(a), time(T), T<}t_{max}.
\end{aligned} \tag{11}
$$

Basic correctness and completeness result. The following result provides a basic correctness and completeness result; corresponding results for the specific reasoning modes are either obtained as corollaries or adaptions of its proof.

Theorem 1. *Let* (D, O_{init}) *be an action theory such that* O_{init} *contains only fluent observations about the initial state. Let Q be a query as in (9) and let*

$$A_Q = \{(a \text{ occurs\_at } t_i) \mid a \in A_i, 1 \leq i \leq m\}.$$

Let $\mathcal{T}$ *denote the translation of* $\mathcal{C}_{TAID}$ *into logic programs, described above. Then, we have the following results.*

1. *If* $s_0, A_1, s_1, A_2, \ldots, A_m, s_m$ *is a trajectory model of* $(D, O_{init} \cup A_Q)$, *then there is an answer set X of logic program* $\mathcal{T}(D, O_{init} \cup A_Q)$ *such that we have for all* $f \in F$ *and* $0 \leq k \leq m$
   (a) `holds(f,k)`$\in X$, *if* $s_k \models f$ *and*
   (b) `holds(neg(f),k)`$\in X$, *if* $s_k \models \neg f$.
2. *If X is an answer set of logic program* $\mathcal{T}(D, O_{init} \cup A_Q)$ *and for* $0 \leq k \leq m$

$$s_k = \{f \mid \texttt{holds(f,k)} \in X\} \cup \{\neg f \mid \texttt{holds(neg(f),k)} \in X\}$$

then there is a trajectory model $s_0, A_1, s_1, A_2, \ldots, A_m, s_m$ *of* $(D, O_{init} \cup A_Q)$.

Action Query Language. In the following t_{max} is the upper time bound, which has to be provided when the answer sets are computed.

Planning. Recall that the initial state can be partially specified; it is then completed by the rules in (10) for taking into account all possible initial states. A plan for $f_1, \ldots, f_n$ (cf. Definition 10) is translated using the predicate "achieved". It ensures that the goal holds in the final state of every answer set for the query.

```
:- not achieved.
achieved :- achieved(0).
achieved :- achieved(T+1),not achieved(T),time(T),time(T+1).
achieved(T)  :- holds(f₁,T),...,holds(fₙ,T),
    achieved(T+1),fluent(f₁),...,fluent(fₙ),time(T),time(T+1).
achieved(n)  :- holds(f₁,T),...,holds(fₙ,T),
    fluent(f₁),...,fluent(fₙ),T = tₘₐₓ.
```

Constant t_{max} is the maximum number of steps in which the goals $f_1, \ldots, f_n$ should be achieved. The proposition `achieved(T)` represents the earliest point of time `T` at which the plan is successfully achieved. Once the query is satisfied only triggered actions can occur, all other actions should not occur since that might invalidate the plan. That is why `achieved(T)` occurs in the translation of every allowed and exogenous action.

```
holds(occurs(a),T) :- holds(allow(occurs(a)),T),not achieved(T),
    not holds(ab(occurs(a)),T), not holds(neg(occurs(a)),T),
    action(a),time(T).
holds(neg(occurs(a)),T) :- not holds(occurs(a),T),
    action(a),time(T).
```

These rules are used to generate all possible combinations of occurrences of non-triggered actions. Such actions can only occur as long as the goal is not yet achieved and if they are not inhibited. If there is an answer set X for the planning problem, then we have for a plan P (cf. Definition 10) that $(a \textbf{ occurs\_at } t_i) \in P$ if `holds(occurs(a),i)` $\in X$.

Explanation. The translation of an explanation contains the translation of all action and fluent observations in O, as described above. Since the observations about the initial state are often incomplete the translation contains the rules in (10) to generate all initial states which do not contradict the observations. Also, we have to generate possible combinations of occurrences of actions for all states. To this effect, the translation includes for every exogenous and allowed action the rules in (11). If there exists an answer set X for the explanation problem, then for an explanation E as in Definition 11 we have $(a \textbf{ occurs\_at } t_i) \in E$ if `holds(occurs(a),i)` $\in X$.

Prediction. The translation includes all fluent and action observations in O, as described above. As in explanation, we have to fill in missing information, which is necessary to justify the observed behaviour. That means we have to include for every fluent f two rules of form (10) to generate possible initial states. Moreover the translation includes for every non-triggered action two rules similar to those of an explanation of form (11). The actual prediction for $f_1, \ldots, f_n$ (cf. Definition 12) is translated as:

```
predicted :- holds(f₁,T), ..., holds(fₙ,T),
    fluent(f₁),...,fluent(fₙ),time(T),T >= i.
```

where i is the time of the latest observation. If the atom `predicted` is included in all (some) answer sets, it is a cautious (brave) prediction.

4   Application

Meanwhile, we have used $\mathcal{C}_{TAID}$ in several different application scenarios at the Max-Planck Institute for Molecular Plant Physiology for modelling metabolic as well as signal transduction networks. For illustration, we describe below the smallest such application, namely the sulfur starvation response-pathway of the model plant Arabidopsis thaliana. Sulfur is essential for the plant. If the amount of sulfur it can access is not sufficient to allow a normal development of the plant, the plant follows a complex strategy. First the plant forms additional lateral roots to access additional sources of sulfur and to normalise its sulfur level. However, if this strategy is not successful the plant uses its remaining resources to form seeds.

Normally, the amount of sulfur in a plant is sufficient, but due to external, e.g. environmental conditions, the amount of sulfur can be reduced. A problem, when modelling this network are such environmental conditions, which are not and cannot be part of a model and which might or might not lead to the reduction of sulfur. Once the level of sulfur in the plant is decreased, complex interactions of different compounds are triggered. Genes are activated, which induce the generation of auxin, a plant hormone, playing a key role as a signal in coordinating the development of the plant. This eventually leads to the formation of additional lateral roots. Since this consumes the scarce resources, the development should be stopped, when it becomes apparent that it is not successful (i.e. it takes too long and consumes too many of the plant's resources). This "emergency stop" is triggered by complex interactions that lead, via a surplus of the auxin flux, to the expression of IAA28, a gene which is subject to current research. If IAA28 is expressed and the sulfur level is still low, other processes result in a different physiological endpoint, the production of seeds.

We now show how this biological network can be represented as a domain description $D(A, F)$ in C_{TAID}.

$A = \{$ sulfur_depletion, sulfur_repletion, enhanced_lateral_root_formation,

$\quad\quad\quad$ iaa28_expression, rapid_seed_production $\}$

$F = \{$ normal_sulfur, depleted_sulfur, enhanced_lateral_roots, expressed_iaa28, seeds $\}$

The biologist's knowledge about the biological system, gives rise to the following dynamic causal laws.

(sulfur_depletion **causes** depleted_sulfur **if** normal_sulfur)
(enhanced_lateral_root_formation **causes** enhanced_lateral_roots)
(sulfur_repletion **causes** normal_sulfur)
(iaa28_expression **causes** expressed_iaa28)
(rapid_seed_production **causes** seeds)

Additionally, two static causal laws specify the relationship between *normal sulfur* and *depleted sulfur*. They assure that at most one of the fluents is *true* at all times.

(¬normal_sulfur **if** depleted_sulfur)
(¬depleted_sulfur **if** normal_sulfur)

For two of the actions, we know all the preconditions that have to be satisfied for the actions to occur.

(depleted_sulfur **triggers** enhanced_lateral_root_formation)
(expressed_iaa28, depleted_sulfur **triggers** rapid_seed_production)

For the remaining three actions, it is more difficult to decide whether and when they occur. Whether the action *sulfur depletion* occurs depends on environmental conditions being outside the model. The same holds for the action *sulfur repletion*, which might or might not be successful, depending on the environmental conditions. For the occurrence of action *iaa28 expression* the question is not whether it occurs but when it occurs. The longer it is delayed, the more resources are used to form additional lateral roots.

(*normal_sulfur* **allows** *sulfur_depletion*)
(*depleted_sulfur* **allows** *iaa28_expression*)
(*enhanced_lateral_roots* **allows** *sulfur_repletion*)

There is only one inhibition relation in this example.

(*expressed_iaa28* **inhibits** *enhanced_root formation*)

But only if we add a default value for the fluent *enhanced lateral roots*, the inhibition relation has the desired effect of stopping the formation of additional lateral roots.

(**default** ¬*enhanced_lateral_roots*)

The knowledge that the plant either forms additional lateral roots or produces seeds can be expressed by the following no-concurrency constraint:

(**noconcurrency** *enhanced_lateral_roots formation* , *rapid_seed_production*)

After defining the domain description, let us define a set of observations O. The initial state, where we still have a normal level of sulfur can be described by the following fluent observations:

$O = \{($ *normal_sulfur* **at** $0)$, $(\neg$ *enhanced_lateral_roots* **at** $0)$,
$(\neg$ *expressed_iaa28* **at** $0)$, $(\neg$ *seeds* **at** $0)\}$

Now that we defined our action theory (D, O), we can start to reason about it. Let us first find an explanation for the observed behaviour:

$O_1 = O \cup \{($ *sulfur_depletion* **occurs_at** $0)$, $($ *normal_sulfur* **at** $3)\}$

For a time bound of $t_{max} = 3$ there are already 4 possible explanations. They all have in common that *sulfur depletion* occurs at time point 0, the formation of lateral roots is triggered at time point 1 and the action *sulfur repletion* occurs at time point 2. The explanations differ in whether and when the action *iaa28 expression* and the action *rapid seed production* occurs. One explanation is:

$(D, O_1) \models_b ($ *true* **after** *sulfur_depletion* **occurs_at** 0,
enhanced_lateral_root formation **occurs_at** 1,
enhanced_lateral_root formation **occurs_at** 2, *sulfur_repletion* **occurs_at** 2)

A second explanation is:

$(D, O_1) \models_b ($ *true* **after** *sulfur_depletion* **occurs_at** 0,
enhanced_lateral_root formation **occurs_at** 1,
enhanced_lateral_root formation **occurs_at** 2,
sulfur_repletion **occurs_at** 2, *iaa28_expression* **occurs_at** 2)

Our next question is whether the given observations are sufficient to predict a certain behaviour of the plant.

$(D,O) \models_c$ (seeds **after** sulfur_depletion **occurs_at** 0, iaa28_expression **occurs_at** 1)
$(D,O) \models_b$ (normal_sulfur **after** sulfur_depletion **occurs_at** 0, iaa28_expression
  occurs_at 1)

Using these predictions, we can say that when sulfur is depleted and IAA28 is expressed the plant grows seeds, but it is still possible that it also stabilises its sulfur level.

Finally, we want to find a plan for the action theory (D, O) that results in the production of seeds. For time bound $t_{max} = 3$, there are 4 plans. One possible plan is:

$(D,O) \models_b$ (seeds **after** sulfur_depletion **occurs_at** 0,
  iaa28_expression **occurs_at** 1, enhanced_lateral_root_formation **occurs_at** 1,
  rapid_seed_production **occurs_at** 2, rapid_seed_production **occurs_at** 3)

The number of plans and explanations depend on the number of allowance rules, since the different possibilities for the occurrence of such an allowed action is reflected by different answer sets.

5 Discussion

We proposed the action language $\mathcal{C}_{TAID}$ and showed how it can be used to represent and reason about biological networks. $\mathcal{C}_{TAID}$ is based on the action language $\mathcal{A}_T^0$ introduced in [6]. The latter language provides only minimal features to define dynamic causal laws, triggering and inhibition rules, which turn to be a fruitful basis but insufficient for modelling our biological applications. Moreover, our exploratory approach made us propose the concept of allowance that enables the experimenter to investigate alternative models "in silico". As a consequence, we extended $\mathcal{A}_T^0$ by static causal laws, allowance rules, default rules and no-concurrency constraint which furnish a more appropriate representation of our biological networks. Especially static causal laws and default rules can be used to include background knowledge and other dependencies like environmental conditions which influence the biological system, but are not part of the actual model. Allowance rules are mainly used to express incomplete knowledge about the reasons why an action occurs. This missing information is a common problem for biologists due to the immanent complexity of biological systems.

We fixed the semantics of $\mathcal{C}_{TAID}$ in the standard way by means of transition relations, trajectories and trajectory models. In contrast to $\mathcal{A}_T^0$, for example, default values can enable state changes without the occurrence of an action. Also, Baral et al. guarantee a unique trajectory model and a unique answer set, if the initial state is completely defined by a set of observations. This is not the case in $\mathcal{C}_{TAID}$ because of the nondeterminism introduced by allowance rules that may yield multiple answer sets.

We implemented our action language by means of a compiler mapping $\mathcal{C}_{TAID}$ onto logic programs under answer set semantics. Our translation builds upon and extends the one given in [6]. The resulting tool is implemented in Java and freely available at [16]. Meanwhile, it has been used in ten different application scenarios at the Max-Planck Institute for Molecular Plant Physiology for modelling metabolic as well as signal transduction networks. For illustration, we described the smallest such application, namely, a part of the sulfur starvation response-pathway of model plant Arabidopsis thaliana.

Beyond the traditional approaches mentioned in the introductory section, further logic-based approaches using rule-based languages have emerged recently: Closely related work has been conducted in abductive logic programming where abduction was used in [17] as the principal mode of inference for modelling gene relations from microarray data. A very sophisticated and much more advanced automated reasoning tool for systems biology can be found in the area of constraint programming, namely the BIOCHAM [18] system. BIOCHAM relies on CTL [19] and is thus particularly strong in modelling temporal aspects of systems biology. Unlike our abstract approach, the constraint-based approach offers fine-grained capacities for modelling biochemical processes, including kinetics and reactions.

References

1. Reddy, V., Mavrovouniotis, M., Liebman, M.: Petri net representations in metabolic pathways. Proc. First ISMB (1993) 328–336
2. Pinney, J.W., Westhead, D.R., McConkey, G.A.: Petri net representations in systems biology. Biochem Soc Trans **31**(Pt 6) (2003) 1513–1515
3. Bonarius, H.P.J., Schmid, G., Tramper, J.: Flux analysis of underdetermined metabolic networks: The quest for the missing constraints. Trends Biotechnol **15** (1997) 308314
4. Shmulevich, I., Dougherty, E., Kim, S., Zhang, W.: Probabilistic boolean networks: A rule-based uncertainty model for gene regulatory networks. Bioinformatics **18(2)** (2002) 261–274
5. Baral, C., Chancellor, K., Tran, N., Tran, N., Joy, A., Berens, M.: A knowledge based approach for representing and reasoning about signaling networks. In: ISMB. (2004) 15–22
6. Tran, N., Baral, C.: Reasoning about triggered actions in ansprolog and its application to molecular interactions in cells. In: KR. (2004) 554–564
7. Gelfond, M., Lifschitz, V.: Representing action and change by logic programs. Journal of Logic Programming **17** (1993) 301–321
8. Gelfond, M., Lifschitz, V.: Action languages. Electron. Trans. Artif. Intell. **2** (1998) 193–210
9. Giunchiglia, E., Lifschitz, V.: An action language based on causal explanation: preliminary report. In: AAAI/IAAI, AAAI Press (1998) 623–630
10. Eiter, T., Faber, W., Leone, N., Pfeifer, G., Polleres, A.: Planning under incomplete knowledge. In: CL, Springer (2000) 807–821
11. Tran, N., Baral, C., Shankland, C.: Issues in reasoning about interaction networks in cells: Necessity of event ordering knowledge. In: AAAI, AAAI Press (2005) 676–681
12. Grell, S.: Investigation and analysis of new approaches for representing and reasoning about biological networks using action languages. Diploma thesis, University of Potsdam and Max Planck Institute of Molecular Plant Physiology (2006)
13. Baral, C.: Knowledge Representation, Reasoning and Declarative Problem Solving. Cambridge University Press (2003)
14. Gelfond, M., Lifschitz, V.: Classical negation in logic programs and disjunctive databases. New Generation Computing **9** (1991) 365–385
15. Simons, P., Niemelä, I., Soininen, T.: Extending and implementing the stable model semantics. Artificial Intelligence **138**(1-2) (2002) 181–234
16. (http://bioinformatics.mpimp-golm.mpg.de/bionetreasoning/)
17. Papatheodorou, I., Kakas, A.C., Sergot, M.J.: Inference of gene relations from microarray data by abduction. In: LPNMR, Springer (2005) 389–393
18. Chabrier-Rivier, N., Fages, F., Soliman, S.: The biochemical abstract machine biocham. In: CMSB, Springer (2004) 172–191
19. Clarke, E., Grumberg, O., Peled, D.: Model checking. MIT Press (1999)

Using Answer Set Programming for the Automatic Compilation of Assessment Tests

Petra Schwaiger and Burkhard Freitag

University of Passau, Germany
{Petra.Schwaiger, Burkhard.Freitag}@uni-passau.de

Abstract. Life-long learning is more and more playing a key role for economical, personal and social success. Therefore the management and development of skills and knowledge is of premier importance in industry and, on the other hand, a major expense factor. So called examination management systems assist teachers and trainers through an automatic compilation of documents, in particular assessment tests, based on user defined requirements and constraints and thus help reduce costs.

In this paper we present and discuss a solution of the underlying general problem using Answer Set Programming and show the power and advantages of our approach.

1 Introduction

In industry and service enterprises like financial services and consulting firms the employee training plays an important role. Many companies rely at least partly on electronic support for their qualification programs.

Assessment tests and examinations are a customary way to check the knowledge of applicants and employees. Generally, these tests are compiled from a pool of questions and have to satisfy a number of requirements. These constraints can concern the difficulty level, the coverage of important topics, the distribution of difficulty levels and others.

The development of new media has its influence in education and training, too. Meanwhile some companies use only electronic media in employee qualification. As a consequence, the questions from which assessments can be built are now represented by digital documents. Principally, the generation of a test from a question pool can be supported by a so-called examination management system (e. g. IFIS ASSESSMENT SUITE [12], EXAM BUILDER [8]).

However, today there is no general solution yet to the difficult problem of compiling an assessment test from the available questions in a way that all user defined requirements are respected. Industrial solutions suffer from restrictions and are mostly not satisfying. Depending on the method applied, number restrictions, hierarchical value spaces, transitive relationships, and a multi-dimensional solution space are hard to deal with.

From the general situation described above the use case of our investigation has been derived.

S. Etalle and M. Truszczyński (Eds.): ICLP 2006, LNCS 4079, pp. 300–314, 2006.

In this paper we show that and how Answer Set Programming [9,14] can be used to support the automatic compilation of an electronic examination or assessment test under constraints. It turns out that the representation is very natural and therefore adequate from the modeling point of view. The implementation is immediate and shows a good performance over a wide range of runtime parameters.

In Section 3 we describe the use case informally and present the main components of an adequate abstract model. Subsequently, the transformation of the abstract model into the language of the ASP-Solver SMODELS is presented in Section 4. Finally, in Section 5 we discuss our approach with respect to desirables and principles of software engineering like performance, scalability, adequacy, maintainability and usability. Moreover we outline future perspectives of our approach w.r.t. other application areas like education management systems.

2   Related Work

2.1   Answer Set Programming

The Answer Set Semantics for logic programs has its roots in nonmonotonic logics and the stable model semantics of normal logic programs [10] where rules are of the form

$$H \leftarrow A_1, ..., A_n, not\ B_1, ..., not\ B_m$$

with atomic formulas (atoms) H, $A_1, ..., A_n$, $B_1, ..., B_m$ $(n, m \geq 0)$. A literal is an atom A (positive literal) or its negation $not\ A$ (negative literal) where the operator not denotes the default negation.

There are a lot of publications showing the basic ideas and principles of the Answer Set Programming (ASP) paradigm (among others [9,14]). ASP represents a promising approach to declarative problem solving and knowledge representation. An important feature is the advanced capability of dealing with incomplete information and defaults. The underlying idea in programming with ASP is to represent a problem to be solved in an ASP-program in such way that the solutions of the problem are the stable models (answer sets) of the program.

Several ASP-systems are available; among the most important are SMODELS [17] and DLV [2].

[16,20] propose an extension of the basic ASP-syntax by cardinality and weight constraints: Allowing constraint-, weight- and conditional literals in rules leads to weight constraint rules, choice rules and constraint rules. Weight constraint rules are of the form

$$C_0 \leftarrow C_1, ..., C_n$$

with $n \geq 0$ and weight or constraint literals $C_i, 0 \leq i \leq n$, with the restriction that C_0 does not contain default negation. The associated semantics is an extension of the stable model semantics. For example, to express that at least one and at most three of the questions

```
question(q1). question(q2). question(q3). question(q4).
```

are to be selected (predicate `draw/1`) we can use the constraint literal

```
1 {draw(q1), draw(q2), draw(q3), draw(q4)} 3.
```

or in combination with the shorter conditional literal

```
1 {draw(X) : question(X)} 3.
```

Similarly, a weight literal can be used to constrain the sum of weights assigned to some literals. By

```
#weight drawDuration(X,Y) = Y.
```

we express that `drawDuration/2` assigns weights to some questions (in our use case: available time to work on). The weight literal

```
5 [drawDuration(X,Y) : questionDuration(X,Y)] 13.
```

then restricts the total weight, i.e., total time available, to at least 5 and at most 13 units.

The language of the SMODELS system, here denoted by *smodels*, allows only so called ω-restricted rules in order to guarantee decidability. This means, that every variable in a rule has to occur in a positive domain literal of the body.

In addition to the language extension mentioned above, there are a lot of others providing an increased declarativity, expressiveness and usability of ASP. It should also be mentioned that there are also attempts to integrate answer set generation and constraint solving [1].

Among the great number of applications of Answer Set Programming [6] in the fields of planning [5,15], verification, model checking, configuration [19] as well as diagnostic systems and inconsistency management [4], especially some industrial and innovative application areas [7,11,18] have to be mentioned.

2.2   Application to our Use Case

Our use case – we call it "Generating Examinations under Constraints" – has its origin in an industrial application. In [11] a similar use case is studied. The authors describe the assessment test generation engine of the "EXAM portal", give a system overview and present the internal and formal specification of the underlying problem. They use the ASP system DLV to represent the logical rules. We believe and will try to show that our approach is more general – we present an in-depth investigation of the possible structural preconditions of the use case, define a specification formalism and show how a given problem can be translated into *smodels* programs. With our specification formalism we can formulate a user-friendly description of a problem instance independent of a special engine. Moreover because of the generality of our approach we can specify and solve a wider class of problem instances of the "Generating Examinations under Constraints"-problem.

3   The Use Case "Generating Examinations Under Constraints" and Its Abstract Model

Many organisations in industry and education take advantage from e-learning services. Examination management systems such as [3,8,12] support the compilation and execution of exercises and examinations and assessment tests.

3.1   The Use Case "Generating Examinations Under Constraints"

In the following we give an overview of the main components of the kernel of an examination management system. Figure 1 illustrates the specification-based generation of an examination.

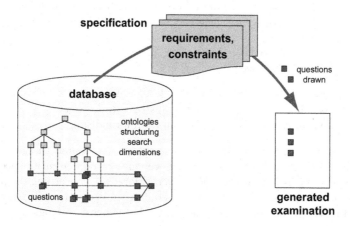

Fig. 1. Automatic Generation of an Examination

As shown in figure 1 the kernel of an examination management system contains a repository which stores and manages a large collection of questions (**question pool/question catalogue**) in an "intelligent" way, some framework for the specification of the desired result, and a mechanism that selects suitable questions and compiles the result, i.e., a set of exercises, an examination, or an assessment test, according to the constraints imposed by the specification.

The representation of a question, e.g. in some XML-format, comprises a *unique identifier*, the question text itself, and all possible answers. For our further investigation, the question text and the answers are not important and will therefore mostly be ignored in the following.

Metadata describe relevant properties of questions. The metadata categories – later also called search dimensions – are described by *attributes* such as topic and duration. The corresponding *attribute values* such as *robotics, medicine* and *1, 5*, respectively, provide the individual description of a single question. To each question at least one vector of metadata has to be attached. It is also possible to use formalized ontologies, for instance a hierarchy of topics, to give the metadata more structure.

Typically, the result, i.e. the collection of questions (**examination**), to be compiled from the pool of available questions has to satisfy certain **user defined requirements**. As an example, a minimal duration of the entire examination could be specified. Or, quite commonly, a maximum number of questions about a specific topic could be defined.

Remark 1 (Valid examination and choice). Each collection of questions – note, that in general there is more than one – selected from the question pool and satisfying the given constraints is a so-called "valid" examination. Normally, from the set of valid examinations only one arbitrarily chosen is needed. Sometimes we call the questions contained in a valid examination the "drawn questions". In this context we speak also about "drawing questions".

Now, based on the description above we explain the main components of an abstract model of our use case. Due to space limitations we have to omit from some of the details.

3.2   An Abstract Model

The rest of this section is devoted to the development of an an abstract model of our use case. The model we present is abstract in the sense that it does not make any assumptions about the representation formalism.

Question Pool and Metadata. From now on we assume that a question is represented by its identifier q and that we can abstract from its specific instance values such as text or possible answers. Moreover, concerning the possible structure of a search dimension, i.e., a metadata category, we will restrict our investigation to tree-shaped hierarchies instead of general ontologies.

Definition 1 (Question Pool, Attributes, Attribute Values, Subordinate Relation). A **question pool** is a finite set $Q = \{q_i \mid i \leq n, n \in \mathbb{N}\}$ of questions. It has attached a finite **sequence of attributes** $\mathcal{A}_{ord} = A_1, \ldots A_m, m \in \mathbb{N}$ which we also consider as the dimensions of our search space.

The **domain** $domain(A_j)$ of an attribute A_j is the set of possible values that can be associated directly or indirectly with a question w.r.t. this attribute. The **range** $range(A_j) \subseteq domain(A_j)$ of attribute A_j is the set of those values that can be associated directly with a question w.r.t. this attribute.

In case of a flat attribute domain we have $range(A_j) = domain(A_j)$, i.e., the elements of $range(A_j)$ are the only A_j-values that can be associated with a question. However, if the domain of attribute A_j is structured by a generalization hierarchy there may be additional attribute values that are indirectly associated with a question by inheritance.

Let attribute A_j have a domain structured by a generalization hierarchy which in turn is represented by a (directed) tree-shaped graph $H_j = (V_j, E_j)$ with V_j finite. The set $hierVal(A_j)$ of **hierarchical attribute values** is defined as $domain(A_j) \setminus range(A_j)$. Therefore the set of vertices of the hierarchy H_j is the disjoint union $V_j = range(A_j) \cup hierVal(A_j)$ and $hierVal(A_j) = \emptyset$ if A_j is not hierarchical.

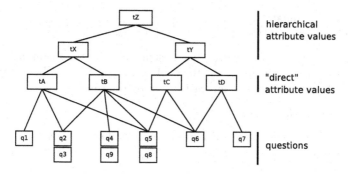

Fig. 2. The hierarchical (and multivalued) attribute topic

Based on the hierarchy H_j and the relation E_j, respectively, we define the **relation subordinate**$_j$, *subordinate*$_j \subseteq domain(A_j) \times hierVal(A_j)$, as follows: $(u, v) \in subordinate_j$ iff there exist a path from v to u in H_j. Therefore *subordinate*$_j$ is the transitive closure of E_j^{-1}.

Example 1 (Hierarchical attribute and subordinate$_j$). As an example of a hierarchical attribute consider the attribute topic shown in figure 2. Assume that the specification of the desired examination prescribes that a certain topic, say tA, has to be covered by a question. When a question q for this topic tA is selected, q covers also the supertopic (tX) and all ancestor-topics up the hierarchy. In this sense q "counts" for these more general topics as well. In our example we have $(tA, tX), (tX, tZ), (tA, tZ) \in subordinate_1$.

The definition of metadata, i.e., the assignment of attribute values to the individual questions, is described by relations.

Definition 2 (Relation meta and Relation matches). The relation $meta \subseteq Q \times \prod_{j=1}^{m} range(A_j)$ formalizes the assignment of *direct* attribute values to the elements of the question pool Q.

However, in the hierarchical case we wish to take into account also the "inherited" attribute values from higher levels in the value hierarchy. Moreover, sometimes it is useful not to specify all attribute values but to insert a "joker" matching any value of a certain attribute. Therefore we extend the relation *meta* to the **relation matches** as follows:

$$matches \subseteq Q \times \prod_{j=1}^{m} (domain(A_j) \cup \{*\}),$$

$$(q, v_1, \ldots, v_m) \in matches :\Leftrightarrow \exists (q, w_1, \ldots, w_m) \in meta : \forall j = 1..m :$$
$$(v_j = *) \vee (w_j = v_j) \vee$$
$$((w_j, v_j) \in subordinate_j(w_j, v_j)).$$

Example 2 (Attributes and Metadata). As a sample attribute sequence with related ranges let

$\mathcal{A}_{ord}$ = topic, duration;
$range(\text{topic}) = \{tA,\ tB,\ tC,\ tD\},\ range(\text{duration}) = \{1,5,10\}.$

Let us assume that the attribute topic is structured by the hierarchy of figure 2 and that question q is about the topic tA as well as tB and the duration is 5 (minutes). The metadata assignment is given by the tuples

$$(q, tA, 5), (q, tB, 5) \in meta.$$

Therefore, in *matches* among others we have the following elements

$$(q, tA, 5), (q, tX, 5), (q, tZ, *), (q, *, *) \in matches.$$

Remark 2 (Different interpretations of a question in an examination in the case of multivalued attributes). Due to multivalued attributes for a single question q there may exist more than one *meta*-tuple meaning that this question can assume different "roles". There are two possibilities to interpret this situation in an examination:

- The question q plays *all the roles* in the examination that the relation *meta* assigns. (Consider example 2: if q is chosen for an examination, q covers topics tA and tB.)
- The question q appears in *only one role* in the examination. In this case it must be decided which of the possible *meta*-tuples shall be considered relevant for q and therefore has to be chosen. (Consider example 2: if q is chosen for an examination, q covers either topic tA or topic tB.)

Remark 3 (Our Assumption). For our further investigation we adopt the second assumption of remark 2, that is, we assume that in an examination a question appears in only one role.

Therefore we define the set of all "singlevalued" metadata based on *meta*.

Definition 3 (The "Singlevalued" Metadata: $meta^s$ and $matches^s$). Given a relation *meta* we define[1]

$$\mathcal{M}_{meta} = \{meta^s \subseteq meta \mid \pi_1 \circ meta^s = \pi_1 \circ meta\ \wedge$$
$$(q, v_1, \ldots, v_m), (q, u_1, \ldots, u_m) \in meta^s \Rightarrow v_i = u_i, i = 1..m\}$$

If there is no multivalued attribute defining the relation *meta* it holds: $\mathcal{M}_{meta} = \{meta\}$. For each $meta^s \in \mathcal{M}_{meta}$ we define the **relation matches**$^{meta^s}$ or simply **relation matches**^{s} in an analogous way – by replacing *meta* with $meta^s$ in the definition of *matches*.

User Defined Requirements. The user can specify requirements about the set $D \subseteq Q$ of questions to be drawn and their attribute values. In this case D must satisfy the conjunction of all requirements. In the following we describe the requirements underlying our implementation. User requirements can be specified

---

[1] π_1 means the projection onto the first component.

with the help of relations. Due to space limitations we only sketch these relations and do not give a formal definition.

- Restriction of the **Absolute Number**
  Let $A_1, \ldots A_m = \mathcal{A}_{ord}$ be the fixed attribute sequence (see Def. 1). The requirement $absConstr(v_1, \ldots, v_m, N_{min}, N_{max})$ specifies that for the number N of questions from D matching the attribute values $v_1, \ldots, v_m$ it must hold that $N_{min} \leq N \leq N_{max}$. (Recall that matching should be understood in the sense of remark 3 and definition 3.) For an illustration consider example 2: The user requirement $absConstr(*, 5, 3, \infty)$ expresses that in the result examination there have to be "at least 3 questions with a duration of 5 minutes".

- Restriction of the **Weighted Sum**
  Let A be a real-valued attribute A which is neither multivalued nor hierarchical. The requirement $weightedSumConstr(A, W_{min}, W_{max})$ expresses that for the total sum S of values of A taken over all questions in D it must hold that $W_{min} \leq S \leq W_{max}$. In the situation of example 2 $weightedSumConstr(\text{duration}, 20, 25)$ expresses that the total "duration of the examination has to lie between 20 and 25 minutes".

- Requirements concerning **Percentage**
  Restrict the percentage of certain attribute values of an attribute.

- **Exclusion** of Questions:
  Specify questions that are not allowed in the result examination.

- **Optimization** of a Goal Function:
  The requirement $optimize(v_1, \ldots, v_m, opt)$ with $opt \in \{min, max\}$ prescribes the number of questions having the given attribute values should be minimized or maximized.

One has to keep in mind that the user expects at least one valid examination that satisfies all requirements. However, there are several reasons, why it might be impossible to find a set of questions that satisfies all requirements:

- Inconsistent set of requirements;
- Instance based inconsistency, i.e., the question pool does not contain enough questions with required attribute values.

4 Implementation

4.1 Main Components of the *smodels*-Program

The logical program implemented in SMODELS consists of three files:

- **Question pool (data.pl)** with facts representing the association of attribute values to questions (metadata).
- **General rules modeling the drawing of questions (draw.lp)**. These rules constitute the invariant core of the implementation.
- **Rules modeling the user defined requirements (constraint.lp)**.

The 5 main components of our *smodels*-based system core implement the following functionality:

- provide metadata describing the questions;
- draw the required number of questions;
- for each question drawn determine the coverage;
- formalize and store the requirements each represented by one rule;
- compute the answer sets.

Now, we will show in a step by step fashion how the problem "Generating Examination under Constraints" can be translated into *smodels* programs. For details of the problem description see section 3.

4.2   Question Pool and Metadata

Because we do not need knowledge about the specific attribute names we only need to state that there is a sequence of abstract attributes $A_{ord} = A_1, \ldots, A_m$ which can be represented by m facts `attribute(1). ... attribute(m).` or shorter by the fact `attribute(1..m).` For each tuple $(q, v_1, \ldots, v_j, \ldots, v_m) \in meta$ we define a rule `question_prop(q, v_1, \ldots, v_j, \ldots, v_m).` The information that A_j is hierarchical can be expressed by a fact `hier_attr(j)..` In this case each edge $(v_1, v_2) \in E_j$ of the hierarchy graph H_j is represented by a fact `direct_subord(j, v_2, v_1)..` Rules computing the transitive closure (`subord/3`) of the `direct_subord/3`-facts represent the information given by the relation $subordinate_j$.

The direct and hierarchical attribute values of an attribute A_j are represented by atoms `attr_val(j, V)` and the following rules:

```
attr_val(j,Vj) :- question_prop(Q,V1,...,Vj,...,Vm),
attr_val(A,V)  :- direct_subord(A,X,V),
attr_val(A,V)  :- direct_subord(A,V,X).
```

4.3   User Defined Requirements

Exclusion of Questions. For each "forbidden" question q_u we add a fact `used(q_u).`

Allowed Questions. Allowed questions are those that are not explicitly forbidden:

```
question(Q) :- question_prop(Q,V1,...,Vm).
allowed(Q)  :- question(Q), not used(Q).
```

Question Drawing. The selection of at least N_{min} and at most N_{max} questions from the set of allowed questions is formalized by the constraint literal

$$N_{min} \ \{ \ \texttt{draw(Q)} \ : \ \texttt{allowed(Q)} \ \} \ N_{max}.$$

This rule represents the user defined requirement $absConstr(*, \ldots, *, N_{min}, N_{max})$. In case that none such requirement exists, N_{min} and N_{max} are omitted in the constraint literal above. If $N_{max} = \infty$ only N_{max} is omitted in the rule.

Determining the Coverage. As mentioned in remark 2 each selected question appears in exactly one role in the examination. This general setting can be modeled with an additional predicate: We define that exactly one sequence of direct attribute values should be assigned to each question q drawn by

$$1 \ \{\texttt{draw\_prop(Q,V1,}\ldots\texttt{,V}m\texttt{)} \ : \ \texttt{question\_prop(Q,V1,}\ldots\texttt{,V}m\texttt{)}\} \ 1 \ \texttt{:-}$$
$$\texttt{draw(Q), allowed(Q)}.$$

Absolute Number Requirements. We have to distinguish between hierarchical and non-hierarchical attribute values when representing the user defined requirement $absConstr(v_1,\ldots,v_m,N_{min},N_{max})$.

The *non-hierarchical case*: If none of the attributes is hierarchical we can use the following rules:

$$\texttt{cons}(i) \ \texttt{:-} \ N_{min} \ \{ \ \texttt{draw\_prop(Q,}v_1,\ldots,v_m\texttt{)}$$
$$\texttt{: question\_prop(Q,}v_1,\ldots,v_m\texttt{)} \ \} \ N_{max}.$$
$$\texttt{active\_rule}(i).$$

By "$\texttt{active\_rule}(i)$." the i-th rule is set "active", i.e. switched on. Note, that a wildcard $v_j = *$ is substituted by a "fresh" variable $\texttt{V}j$.

The *hierarchical case*: If $v_1,\ldots,v_m$ contains at least one hierarchical attribute value we need further auxiliary rules. In the following we assume that only attribute A_1 is hierarchical. The rules

$$\texttt{trans\_prop\_1(Q,V1,}\ldots\texttt{,V}m\texttt{)} \qquad \texttt{:- question\_prop(Q,V1,}\ldots\texttt{,V}m\texttt{)}.$$
$$\texttt{trans\_prop\_1(Q,V1H,V2,}\ldots\texttt{,V}m\texttt{)} \ \texttt{:- question\_prop(Q,V1,V2,}\ldots\texttt{,V}m\texttt{)},$$
$$\texttt{subord(A,V1,V1H), hier\_attr(A)}.$$

define the transitive closure of the question properties. These properties are "applied" to the questions drawn by

$$\texttt{draw\_trans\_prop\_1(Q,V1H,}\ldots\texttt{,V}m\texttt{)} \qquad \texttt{:- draw\_prop(Q,V1,}\ldots\texttt{,V}m\texttt{)},$$
$$\texttt{trans\_prop\_1(Q,V1H,V2,}\ldots\texttt{,V}m\texttt{), subord(A,V1,V1H)}.$$

The constraint can be asserted – analogously to the non-hierarchical case – by:

$$\texttt{cons}(i) \ \texttt{:-} \ N_{min} \ \{ \ \texttt{draw\_trans\_prop\_1(Q,}v_1,\ldots,v_m\texttt{)}$$
$$\texttt{: question\_trans\_prop(Q,}v_1,\ldots,v_m\texttt{)} \ \} \ N_{max}.$$
$$\texttt{active\_rule}(i).$$

Weighted Sum Requirements. We must take into account that SMODELS operates with integers. The requirement $weightedSumConstr(A_j, W_{min}, W_{max})$ with $range(A_j) \subset \mathbb{N}$ can be directly translated into *smodels* programs as shown below.

If only one (direct) attribute's sum is restricted we can use the following rules. First, we assign a weight to $\texttt{draw\_prop}$ by

$$\texttt{\#weight draw\_prop(Q,V1,}\ldots\texttt{,V}m\texttt{)} \ \texttt{=} \ \texttt{V}j.$$

Then we formalize the restriction of the sum by

```
cons(i) :- W_min [ draw_prop(Q,V1,...,Vm)
                    : question_prop(Q,V1,...,Vm) ] W_max.
active_rule(i).
```

If we want to restrict the weighted sum *for more than one attribute*, we need two additional rules:

```
question_prop(Q,j,Vj) :- question_prop(Q,V1,...,Vm).
draw_prop(Q,j,Vj)      :- question_prop(Q,V1,...,Vm),
                          draw_prop(Q,V1,...,Vm).
```

In an analogous way as above, we can formulate the weight-assignment and the restriction to the sum.

Percentage Requirements. The basic idea is to reduce this problem to the case of the restriction of the number of questions with certain properties. The procedure is similar to those we have already explained.

Optimization of a Goal Function. The optimization of a goal function is only possible in a restricted way in SMODELS. The commands #minimize and #maximize optimize the number of atoms with certain properties [21, p.48f], but their semantics is not very intuitive.

Combining the User Defined Requirements. All rules for user defined requirements that have been "activated" by a fact "active_rule(i)." are combined using the following three rules:

```
incons(R)   :- not cons(R), active_rule(R).
someincons :- incons(R), active_rule(R).
allcons    :- not someincons.
```

We ensure that the atom allcons/0 is true only in stable models satisfying the active requirements. The command to compute n stable models is

```
#compute n { allcons }.
```

For $n = 0$ *all* stable models are computed. If the requirements cannot be satisfied, no stable models containing the atom allcons will be found. In this case it is desired to get an indication of what caused the error.

Checking Inconsistency. If inconsistency is to be checked SMODELS tries to maximize the number of "valid requirements" (cons/1-atoms).

```
#maximize { cons(R) : active_rule(R) }.
#compute 0 { }.
```

If the last stable model contains the atom allcons/0, then all user defined requirements are satisfied. Otherwise the incons/1-atoms represent the requirements causing the inconsistency. Applying this method it is not possible to check the consistency of the user defined requirements without a question pool.

5   Discussion

5.1   Adequacy

In section 4 we have shown that it is straightforward to translate the specification (section 3) into *smodels*-rules. To a certain extend the system is generic: The core implementation using SMODELS corresponds closely to the intuition behind question drawing. No knowledge is necessary about the specific attribute names and domains. Solely, in case of hierarchical attributes the generalization hierarchy, i.e. the underlying ontology, has to be specified. The entire system is specialized to a particular application via the user requirements as described in section 3.2. As could be seen in section 4 the user requirements can be directly translated into corresponding *smodels*-rules.

5.2   Extensibility and Maintainability

Assuming that the system core, i.e. question drawing, is stable the extensibility and maintainability of the system is rather good because only local changes are required in all important cases. Extensions to the specification of valid examinations can be obtained by simply adding further requirements (cf. section 3.2). Equally well, requirements can be dropped if not needed any longer. Mandatory questions can be specified by adding appropriate facts or computing the stable models with the mandatory questions as an input. It should be mentioned that as few as about 100 lines of code are necessary for our moderately complex use case. The size of the code is linear in the number of requirements.

5.3   Usability

The system kernel as presented in this paper is certainly not suitable for the average end-user. A separate presentation layer is required to provide user-friendly interaction and support the convenient specification of requirements. However, this task can be performed without too much effort. In case of an inconsistent set of requirements SMODELS will not find a stable model. With the current SMODELS-implementation it is not possible to check the consistency of the user defined requirements without a question pool. Therefore we verify only the instance-based consistency (see section 3.2). Errors can be localized and error messages can be forwarded to the user. But in some cases this could cost performance because numerous stable models have to be computed (see section 4). A small change in the program allows to compute those models that maximize the number of requirements satisfied. In this variant the stable models contain the identifiers of the requirements that could not be satisfied. Note that this modification causes longer runtime.

5.4   Performance and Scalability

In this paper we can show only a few results of our runtime tests. To allow for comparison with another logic-based state-of-the-art implementation we com-

Table 1. Asymptotic runtime complexity w.r.t. a variety of parameters

Parameter		SMODELS	ECLiPSe
Question pool size	$|Q|$	exponential	linear
Num. of questions to draw	$|D|$	slight dependency	slight dependency
Num. of attributes	$|\mathcal{A}|$	linear	exponential
Num. of attribute values $|range(A_1)|$		hier.: exponential non-hier: linear	mval.: exponential non-mval.: no dependency
Num. of mval attr. values		linear	binomial distrib.
Size of hierarchy		linear	exponential
Num. of abs. constr.		linear decr./incr.	slight dependency
Num. of perc. constr.		linear	slight dependency

pare the SMODELS-implementation with an implementation based on the constraint logic programming system ECLiPSe. Clearly, the absolute runtime results may depend on the chosen implementations.

While the runtimes of the SMODELS-implementation behave rather well for most parameters, the size of the question pool, i.e. the number of questions is critical. Runtimes increase exponentially depending on the number of questions. Nevertheless, the absolute times (not shown here) suggest that SMODELS can be used in practice. However, "just-in-time"-applications, for instance designing an examination "online" by trial and error, should be avoided. Realistic industrial question pools contain about 2000 or 3000 questions. Academic question pools tend to be smaller but more specific. Larger question pools can often be separated into smaller disjoint subsets or pre-filtered according to the specific requirements.

For a question pool containing 3000 questions the absolute runtimes range from a few seconds in the case of only singlevalued non-hierarchical attributes to a few minutes in the case of multivalued hierarchical attributes. In any case, the time needed to prepare an examination could be significantly reduced as compared to the usual manual preparation by human trainers.

5.5   New Applications

Academic education becomes more and more international today. Also, quite a number of bachelor and master programs with rather complex regulations and manifold interrelationships between course modules have emerged. In this situation students are often left alone with their course planning and need better assistance. In the course of their ongoing efforts towards service quality improvement universities try to build a better personal and technical infrastructure for student assistance and advisory services. However, facing exploding costs, the number of human advisors is limited and therefore additional instruments have to be developed. In particular, a computer-aided advisory system and a means for checking the adequacy of regulations in terms of consistency and applicability are desirable. Actually, these goals are part of the mission of a major ongoing project [13] which aims at developing a state-of-the-art campus management system.

A first investigation revealed that the essential requirements as formulated in the official regulations governing the bachelor and master programs can easily be represented using the *smodels* language. Some requirements are rather similar to those of our use case "Generating Examinations under Constraints". As an example consider the typical requirement "from the module group B one has to take 5 to 7 courses with a sum of at least 37 credit points". The models, i.e. the answer sets, of the ASP program representing the regulations contain just the courses and exams a student has to take and pass to pursue a regular course of study as prescribed by the regulations. Once the regulations or at least the course plan has been represented it is also possible to give a student highly personalized advice, e.g. about the courses recommended for the next semester.

Of course, a lot of work remains to be done. However, we are very optimistic that Answer Set Programming is a good choice for implementing the "automatic validation of study regulations" and the "automatic student advisory" problems.

Acknowledgement

We would like to thank Christoph Pirkl for implementing the benchmark-framework and running the benchmarks.

References

1. S. Baselice, P. A. Bonatti, and M. Gelfond. Towards an integration of answer set and constraint solving. In M. Gabbrielli and G. Gupta, editors, *ICLP*, volume 3668 of *Lecture Notes in Computer Science*, pages 52–66. Springer, 2005.
2. F. Calimeri, W. Faber, N. Leone, S. Perri, and G. Pfeifer. DLV - declarative problem solving using answer set programming. In *Proceedings of the Seventh Congress of the Italian Association for Artificial Intelligence AI*IA 2001*, Bari, Italy, 2001.
3. DEAKIN KM KNOWLEDGE PRESENTER Homepage. http://www.deakinkm.com.
4. T. Eiter, W. Faber, N. Leone, and G. Pfeifer. The diagnosis frontend of the dlv system. In *AI Communications – The European Journal on Artificial Intelligence*, volume 12, pages 99–111, 1999.
5. T. Eiter, W. Faber, N. Leone, G. Pfeifer, and A. Polleres. A logic programming approach to knowledge-state planning, II: the small DLV^K system. *Artificial Intelligence*, 144(1-2):157–211, March 2003.
6. E. Erdem. *Theory and applications of answer set programming*. PhD thesis, Technische Universität Wien, 2002.
7. E. Erdem, V. Lifschitz, and D. Ringe. Temporal phylogenetic networks and logic programming. *Theory and Practice of Logic Programming*, 2005.
8. EXAM BUILDER e-learning solutions for professionals Homepage. http://www.exambuilder.com.
9. M. Gelfond and N. Leone. Logic programming and knowledge representation — the A-Prolog perspective. *Artificial Intelligence*, 138(1–2):3–38, 2002.
10. M. Gelfond and V. Lifschitz. The stable model semantics for logic programming. In R. A. Kowalski and K. Bowen, editors, *Proceedings of the Fifth International Conference on Logic Programming*, pages 1070–1080, Cambridge, Massachusetts, 1988. The MIT Press.

11. G. Ianni, C. Panetta, and F. Ricca. Specification of assessment-test criteria through ASP specifications. In M. D. Vos and A. Provetti, editors, *Answer Set Programming*, volume 142 of *CEUR Workshop Proceedings*. CEUR-WS.org, 2005.

12. IFIS. Homepage ASSESSMENT.SUITE. http://www.assessment-suite.de/.

13. InteLeC. Homepage INTELEC. http://im.uni-passau.de/intelec/.

14. V. Lifschitz. Introduction to answer set programming. Unpublished draft.

15. V. Lifschitz. Action languages, answer sets and planning. In *The Logic Programming Paradigm*, 1999.

16. I. Niemelä and P. Simons. Extending the Smodels system with cardinality and weight constraints. In J. Minker, editor, *Logic-Based Artificial Intelligence*, chapter 21, pages 491–521. Kluwer Academic Publishers, 2000.

17. I. Niemelä, P. Simons, and T. Syrjänen. Smodels: a system for answer set programming. In *Proceedings of the 8th International Workshop on Non-Monotonic Reasoning (cs.AI/0003073)*, Breckenridge, Colorado, USA, April 2000. cs.AI/0003033.

18. M. Nogueira, M. Balduccini, M. Gelfond, R. Watson, and M. Barry. An A-Prolog decision support system for the Space Shuttle. In *PADL '01: Proceedings of the Third International Symposium on Practical Aspects of Declarative Languages*, volume 1990, pages 169–183, London, UK, 2001. Springer-Verlag.

19. T. Soininen, I. Niemelä, J. Tiihonen, and R. Sulonen. Representing configuration knowledge with weight constraint rules. In *Proc. AAAI Spring Symp. on Answer Set Programming: Towards Efficient and Scalable Knowledge*, 2001.

20. T. Syrjänen. Cardinality constraint programs. In J. J. Alferes and J. Leite, editors, *The 9th European Conference on Logics in Artificial Intelligence (JELIA'04)*, pages 187–200. Springer-Verlag, September 2004.

21. T. Syrjänen. *Lparse 1.0 – User's Manual*.

Compositional Semantics
for the Procedural Interpretation of Logic

Maarten H. van Emden

Department of Computer Science
University of Victoria

Abstract. Semantics of logic programs has been given by proof theory, model theory and by fixpoint of the immediate-consequence operator. If clausal logic is a programming language, then it should also have a compositional semantics. Compositional semantics for programming languages follows the abstract syntax of programs, composing the meaning of a unit by a mathematical operation on the meanings of its constituent units. The procedural interpretation of logic has only yielded an incomplete abstract syntax for logic programs. We complete it and use the result as basis of a compositional semantics. We present for comparison Tarski's algebraization of first-order predicate logic, which is in substance the compositional semantics for his choice of syntax. We characterize our semantics by equivalence with the immediate-consequence operator.

1   Introduction

This paper concerns the semantics of the part of Prolog that remains when the built-in predicates have been removed and when unification is enhanced by the occurs check. Let us call this part "pure Prolog". It can be regarded as the result of Kowalski's procedural interpretation of positive Horn clauses [14,13,8]. The semantics of pure Prolog has been given by proof theory, by model-theory, and by a fixpoint method [22,16,1]. All three approaches follow the syntax of clausal form. As a result, the procedural interpretation has been ignored. The purpose of the present paper is to remedy this defect.

One of the symptoms of the current deficiency in the semantics of Prolog is that procedures can only be recognized in an informal way. As it stands, the procedural interpretation does not provide procedure-valued expressions that can be substituted for the procedure symbol in a procedure call. Procedures are not "first-class citizens" the way functions can be in functional programming [20].

Compositional semantics does provide this possibility. According to this method, programs are expressions, consisting, if composite, of an operation and its operand(s). The value of the composite expression is the result of the operation on the values of its operands. The method is taken for granted when doing school-room sums: the value of $(4 \div 2) \times (1 + 1)$ is 4 because the value of $4 \div 2$ and $1 + 1$ are both 2 and because $2 \times 2 = 4$. In the late sixties Landin [15] and Scott and Strachey [19] applied the method to expressions that are programs.

S. Etalle and M. Truszczyński (Eds.): ICLP 2006, LNCS 4079, pp. 315–329, 2006.

In logic programming, compositional semantics seems to have been used only for elucidating how the union of two logic programs affects the definition of a predicate [6,4]. In this paper we identify the compositions that occur within a clause and give a compositional semantics for these.

There are several advantages to a compositional semantics for a programming language. One is that it guides implementation. In fact, "syntax-directed compilation" [12], a widely used implementation technique, is compositional semantics *avant la lettre*. The compositional semantics presented here decomposes logic programs down to single procedure symbols, which take relations as value. This accommodates relations that are not defined in the logic program itself.

Another advantage of compositional semantics is that it forces *a language to be modular*. For example, in a functional language with compositional semantics $E_0 E_1$ is the result of applying the value of E_0, which must be a function, to the value of E_1, which may or may not be a function. The result can be a function, but need not be.

Compositionality requires that the value of $E_0 E_1$ does not change when E_0 is replaced by a different expression with the same value. This forces modularity in the sense that names of auxiliary functions occurring in E_0 do not affect its value, hence are local. Compositional semantics endows logic programs with the same property. The value of a procedure call $p(t_0, \ldots, t_{n-1})$ is obtained by an operation on the value of p (which is a relation) and the argument tuple $\langle t_0, \ldots, t_{n-1} \rangle$. Again, the result depends on the value of the relational expression substituted for p, not on the expression itself.

Contributions of this paper. When one attempts a compositional semantics for the procedural interpretation of logic, it becomes apparent that it needs development beyond Kowalski's original formulation. This is done in Section 3.

Section 4 contains no contributions. It needs to be included because cylindric set algebras are a compositional semantics for first-order predicate logic and hence are a candidate for compositional semantics for the procedural interpretation of logic. This section includes enough to show why these algebras are not suitable. We do find, however, an interesting connection between the tables introduced here and the cylinders of Tarski (see Theorem 2).

Tables, their operations and some of their properties are described in Section 5. This is the basis on which the compositional semantics of Section 6 rests. Implications for modularity are discussed in Section 7.

2   Notation and Terminology

In this section we collect terminology and notation that may differ between authors.

2.1   General Terminology

Definition 1 (tuple, function, index set, type, restriction, subtuple).

- *A* tuple *is a function t that maps every index i to $t(i)$, which is called the tuple's component at i.*

- A function *is a triple consisting of a set that is its* domain, *a set that is its* co-domain, *and a* mapping *that associates with every element of the domain a unique element of the co-domain.*
- *If the function is a tuple, then the domain is usually called "index set".*
- *The set of all functions with domain S and co-domain T is denoted $S \to T$. This set is often referred to as the* type *of the functions belonging to it.*
- *Let f be a function in $S \to T$ and let S' be a subset of S. $f \downarrow S'$ is the* restriction *of f to S'. It has S' as domain, T as co-domain and its mapping associates $f(x) \in T$ with every $x \in S'$.*
- *If t is a tuple with index set I and if I' is a subset of I, then $t \downarrow I'$ is the* subtuple *of t defined by I'.*

Definition 2 (relation). *A* relation *with index set I and co-domain T is a set of tuples that have I as index set and T as co-domain. An n-ary relation is a relation that has as index set the set $\{0, \ldots, n-1\}$ of integers.*

Note that a relation need not be an n-ary relation. Indeed, *any set can be the index set of a relation.*

Definition 3 (projection, cylindrification). *Let r be a relation that has I as index set. Let I' be a subset of I. The* projection *$\pi_{I'}(r)$ of r on I' is $\{t \downarrow I' \mid t \in r\}$.*

The cylinder *in I on a relation r' with index set I' is denoted $\pi_I^{-1}(r')$ and is the greatest relation with index set I and co-domain T that has r' as its projection on I'; that is*

$$\pi_I^{-1}(r') = \cup\{\rho \mid \pi_{I'}(\rho) = r' \text{ and } \rho \text{ has index set } I \text{ and co-domain } T\}.$$

2.2 Mathematical Objects Arising in Connection with the Semantics of Logic Programs

To serve as semantic objects, three basic objects are defined independently of another; all three are mutually disjoint sets:

- $\mathcal{H}$, an Herbrand universe
- $\mathcal{V}$, a set of variables
- $\mathcal{P}$, a set of predicate symbols, also called "procedure symbols"

From the three basic objects the following are derived:

- $\mathcal{T}_V$, the set of terms that contain no function symbols or constants other than those occurring in $\mathcal{H}$ and no variables other than those occurring in a subset V of $\mathcal{V}$. We write $\mathcal{T}$ for $\mathcal{T}_{\mathcal{V}}$.
- Substitutions, each of which is a tuple of type $V \to \mathcal{T}_V$, for some subset V of $\mathcal{V}$. If θ is a substitution and $\theta(x) = t$, then we say that θ *substitutes t for x.* We may equate θ with the set $\{x = t \mid \theta(x) = t \text{ and } x \in V\}$ of term equations.

- *Term equations* are equations of the form $t_0 = t_1$, where t_0 and t_1 are terms belonging to $\mathcal{T}$. A set of term equations is said to be in *solved form* if every left-hand side is a variable, and if all these variables are different, and if all variables in the right-hand sides also occur as a left-hand side. If a set of term equations has a solution, then it has a solution in solved form.
  We will not distinguish between term equations in solved form, substitutions, and tuples of elements of $\mathcal{T}$ with a subset of $\mathcal{V}$ as index set.
- Relations consisting of tuples of elements of $\mathcal{H}$ that are indexed by $\{0, \dots, n-1\}$. To distinguish these from the next item, we refer to them as *integer-indexed relations*.
- Relations consisting of tuples of elements of $\mathcal{H}$ that are indexed by a subset V of $\mathcal{V}$ that is characteristic of the relation. We refer to these as *variable-indexed relations*.
- The *Herbrand base*, which is the set of ground atoms.
- *Herbrand interpretations*, which are subsets of the Herbrand base.
- *Relational interpretations*, which are tuples of integer-indexed relations indexed by $\mathcal{P}$.

2.3   Compositional Semantics

Compositional semantics assigns the *value* $\mathcal{M}(E)$ to the *expression* E. We are interested in expressions that are programs. In this case the value is the behaviour of the program. As "value" and "behaviour" do not match very well, we often use "meaning" instead of "value" as a more neutral term. It also happens to fit well with "semantics".

Compositionality of the semantics means that if E is composed of subexpressions E_0 and E_1, then $\mathcal{M}(E)$ is the result of an operation on $\mathcal{M}(E_0)$ and $\mathcal{M}(E_1)$. A well-known example illustrates the compositional semantics of binary numerals. It specifies how integers are assigned as meanings to binary numerals:

$$\mathcal{M}(0) = 0; \mathcal{M}(1) = 1; \mathcal{M}(\mathtt{N0}) = 2\mathcal{M}(\mathtt{N}); \mathcal{M}(\mathtt{N1}) = 2\mathcal{M}(\mathtt{N}) + 1$$

3   The Procedural Interpretation of Positive Horn Clauses

3.1   The Original Procedural Interpretation

Kowalski [14] gives the procedural interpretation of positive Horn clauses as follows:

> "A Horn clause $B \leftarrow A_1, \dots, A_m$, with $m \geq 0$, is interpreted as a *procedure* whose *body* $\{A_1, \dots, A_m\}$ is a set of procedure calls A_i. Top-down derivations are *computations*. Generation of a new goal statement from an old one by matching the selected procedure call with the *name* B of a procedure $B \leftarrow A_1, \dots, A_m$ is a *procedure invocation*.
> A *logic program* consists of a set of Horn clause procedures and is activated by an initial goal statement."

Its semantics can be given by the fact that a ground substitution θ is included in a result of activating program P with goal G iff $P \cup \{G\theta\}$ is false in all Herbrand interpretations. A more general characterization exists.

3.2   A Complete Procedural Interpretation

The procedural interpretation of logic can be formalized by expressing it as an *abstract procedural syntax*. Kowalski proposed, in effect, $B \leftarrow A_0, \ldots, A_{m-1}$ as an alternative syntax in the form of a decomposition of $\{B, \neg A_0, \ldots, \neg A_{m-1}\}$ into a procedure heading and a procedure body. This omits several decomposition steps: (1) the clause may be but one of several several that can respond to the same procedure call, so it is really a *partial* procedure, (2) a body needs to be decomposed into calls, and (3) each call needs to be decomposed into its predicate symbol and its argument tuple. To make the procedural interpretation not only formal, but also to complete it, we propose Definition 4 as the abstract syntax needed for compositional semantics.

Definition 4 (procedural program)

1. *A procedural program is a tuple of procedures with index set* $\mathcal{P}^1$.
2. *A n-ary procedure is a set of n-ary clauses.*
3. *An n-ary clause is a pair consisting of a parameter tuple of order n and a procedure body.*
4. *A procedure body is a set of procedure calls.*
5. *A procedure call is a pair consisting of an n-ary procedure symbol and an argument tuple of order n.*
6. *A parameter tuple of order n and an argument tuple of order n are both n-tuples of terms.*

Let us consider as example a set $\mathcal{P} = \{\texttt{app},\texttt{mem}\}$ of procedure symbols and the procedural program in Figure 1; let us call it p. As p is a tuple with $\mathcal{P}$ as index set, and as a tuple is a function, p can be specified by

$p(\texttt{app}) = \{(\texttt{nil},\texttt{y},\texttt{y}) \;\texttt{:-}\; \{\}, \;(\texttt{u.x},\texttt{y},\texttt{u.z}) \;\texttt{:-}\; \{\texttt{app}(\texttt{x},\texttt{y},\texttt{z})\}\}$
$p(\texttt{mem}) = \{(\texttt{x},\texttt{y}) \;\texttt{:-}\; \{\texttt{app}(\texttt{u},\texttt{x.v},\texttt{y})\}\}$

By itself, Definition 4 defines *some* procedural language. It is only of interest in so far as it is related to clausal logic. Similarly, the relational interpretations for procedural programs need to be related to Herbrand interpretations. Hence the following definition.

Definition 5 (correspondence between logic and procedural programs).
An Herbrand interpretation I and a relational interpretation R correspond to each other ($I \sim R$) iff the following holds:

$R(p) = \{\langle a_0, \ldots, a_{n-1}\rangle \mid p(a_0, \ldots, a_{n-1}) \in I\}$ *for all* $p \in \mathcal{P}$ *and*
$I = \{p(a_0, \ldots, a_{n-1}) \mid p \in \mathcal{P} \text{ and } \langle a_0, \ldots, a_{n-1}\rangle \in R(p)\}$

---

[1] The procedure symbols in $\mathcal{P}$ index only one procedure. This differs from Prolog where predicate symbols include an arity.

```
app(nil,y,y).                        {app{(nil,y,y) :- {}
app(u.x,y,u.z) :- app(x,y,z).           ,(u.x,y,u.z) :- {app(x,y,z)}
                                        }
mem(x,y) :- app(u,x.v,y).            ,mem{(x,y) :- {app(u,x.v,y)}}
                                     }
```

Fig. 1. A Prolog program (left) and an equivalent procedural program (right)

Let S be a sentence consisting of positive Horn clauses (for which we assume Kowalski's notation). Let P be a procedural program. S and P correspond to each other (S ∼ P) iff the following holds:

$P(p) = \{partuple :\text{-} body \mid p(partuple) \leftarrow body \in S\}$ *for all $p \in P$ and*
$S = \{p(partuple) \leftarrow body \mid \exists p \in \mathcal{P}$ *such that partuple* $:\text{-} body \in P(p)\}.$

Each of the syntactical rules of Definition 4 specifies that a certain type of expression is composed of sub-expressions. Compositional semantics then assigns to each of syntactical rules a semantical rule that specifies the corresponding operation on meanings of the constituent sub-expressions.

The next section introduces the mathematical objects that are suitable meanings. Section 6 describes the semantical rules.

Before starting on this we give an informal idea of what is involved. Let us work through the items in Definition 4, starting at the bottom.

Rule 5. Consider the atoms $p(x, v, w)$ and $p(u, w, y)$. Although both involve the same relation p, they are different calls and typically have different meanings. These meanings are the result of a binary operation with the relation p and the tuple of arguments as operands.

   The meaning of the entire call can be viewed as a selection from the tuples that constitute relation p. The selection is specified by the argument tuple, and selects the tuples from the relation that match the argument tuple. Each such match takes the form of a substitution for the variables in the argument tuple. Therefore the result of the operation, which we call *filtering*, is a set of such substitutions.

   As such sets are best presented in tabular form, we call the result of the filtering operation on a relation and an argument tuple a *table* (see Definition 6).

Rule 4. We define the *product* operation on tables (see Definition 8) by means of which procedure bodies obtain values. These values are tables. Theorem 2 shows how product is related to the semantic counterpart of conjunction in Tarski's cylindric set algebra.

Rule 3. The meaning of a *clause* is the n-ary relation that results from an operation on the meanings of the constituents of the clause: the parameter tuple and the body. As a parameter tuple has itself as meaning, we define an operation, which we call *projection*, on a parameter tuple of order n and a table (see Definition 11). The operation yields an n-ary relation.

This completes the preview of the novel semantic operations: filtering, product, and projection. The remaining operations, those arising from Rules 1 and 2, will not require any explanation beyond the following few lines. In Rule 2, a procedure symbol is combined with a set of clauses. As the meaning of a clause is an n-ary relation, a set of such clauses denotes the union of these relations, that is, an n-ary relation again. Rule 2 merely creates a pair consisting of a procedure symbol and a relation.

Rule 1 combines into a set a number of procedures, each of which is a pair of a procedure symbol and a relation. The semantic object corresponding to a program is therefore a tuple of procedures indexed by $\mathcal{P}$, the set of procedure symbols.

4   Compositional Semantics for Logic

Though there does not seem to exist any compositional semantics for the procedural interpretation of logic, one does exist for logic that is parsed in the conventional way. It is called *algebraic logic*, which would be called compositional semantics if it would concern a programming language. It is therefore a good starting point for a compositional semantics of logic programs.

Algebraic logic assigns elements of an algebra as meanings to formulas of logic; it assigns operations of the algebra as meaning to the connectives that compose logical formulas. The more widely known approach to algebraic is based on the cylindric set algebras of Tarski [9,21] of which we give a brief sketch here. Tarski's approach is based on the algebraic interpretation of propositional logic due to Boole [2].

4.1   Propositional Logic and Boolean Algebra

In general, a Boolean algebra is any algebra that satisfies certain defining axioms. A Boolean *set* algebra is a special case. It is described as the tuple $\langle S, \cup, \cap, \sim, \emptyset, U \rangle$ where S is a set of subsets of U that contains $\emptyset$ and U and is closed under union, intersection, and complementation (here denoted as $\sim$).

A special case of a Boolean set algebra is the one where U is the Cartesian product D^n, for some given non-empty set D. Recall that the Cartesian product D^n is the set of all n-tuples of elements of D. We can further specify the Boolean set algebra by choosing $U = D^0 = \{\langle\rangle\}$ and $S = \{\{\}, \{\langle\rangle\}\}$. As a result, the algebra has two elements: $\{\}$ and $\{\langle\rangle\}$. Boolean addition, multiplication, and complementation then become set union, set intersection, and set complement, respectively. Let $\mathcal{M}$ be the mapping from propositional formulas to the elements of the Boolean algebra. We have that $\mathcal{M}(p_0 \vee p_1) = \mathcal{M}(p_0) \cup \mathcal{M}(p_1)$, $\mathcal{M}(p_0 \wedge p_1) = \mathcal{M}(p_0) \cap \mathcal{M}(p_1)$, and $\mathcal{M}(\neg p) = \sim \mathcal{M}(p)$ when we define $\mathcal{M}(true) = \{\langle\rangle\}$ and $\mathcal{M}(false) = \{\}$.

4.2   Predicate Logic and Cylindric Set Algebra

Tarski sought an algebra that would do for first-order predicate logic what Boolean algebra does for propositional logic. The result was cylindric set algebra [21,9].

In model theory, formulas correspond to relations. If this intuitively attractive feature is to be retained, a puzzle needs to be solved. Consider $\mathcal{M}(p(x,y) \wedge p(y,z))$. As the formula has three free variables, this should be a ternary relation. As conjunction means the same in predicate logic as in propositional logic, this ternary relation should be the result of set intersection. But the arguments of the set intersection are derived from binary predicates.

Another part of the puzzle is that $p(x,y)$ and $p(y,z)$ should both denote binary relations, but these should be different and cannot both be the relation denoted by p.

Tarski solved these conundrums by mapping every formula to a relation consisting tuples indexed by *all* the variables in the language. He assumed a countable infinity of variables in the language, in a given order. In this way he could identify each variable with a natural number. Thus this meaning algebra has as elements relations that are subsets of the Cartesian product D^ω.

The choice of the two 0-ary relations on D for the two elements of the Boolean algebra for propositional logic is now clear: the number of variables in a propositional formula is 0.

A first-order predicate logic formula without free variables is either true or false. It is mapped accordingly to the full or empty ω-ary relation over D; that is, to D^ω or $\emptyset$. At first sight it might seem right to map a formula $F[x_0, \ldots, x_{n-1}]$ with free variables $x_0, \ldots, x_{n-1}$ to the relation that consists of all the tuples $\langle a_0, \ldots, a_{n-1} \rangle$ such that $F[a_0, \ldots, a_{n-1}]$ is true. By mapping instead this formula to the *cylinder* on this relation with respect to all variables, Tarski ensured that $\mathcal{M}(p_0 \vee p_1) = \mathcal{M}(p_0) \cup \mathcal{M}(p_1)$ and $\mathcal{M}(p_0 \wedge p_1) = \mathcal{M}(p_0) \cap \mathcal{M}(p_1)$, just as in the case of propositional logic.

Going back to the above puzzle, we see that $\mathcal{M}(p(x,y))$ and $\mathcal{M}(p(y,z))$ are not binary relations but ω-ary relations that are cylinders on a binary relation. Though the binary relation denoted by p in these formulas is the same, the cylinders on $\mathcal{M}(p(x,y))$ and $\mathcal{M}(p(y,z))$ are different. In this way $\mathcal{M}(p(x,y)) \cap \mathcal{M}(p(y,z))$ is a cylinder on a ternary relation.

Thus Tarski devised a compositional semantics for first-order predicate logic. He simplified the language to contain as connectives only conjunction, disjunction, and negation. The presence of the negation connective makes it possible to do with a single quantifier, the existential one. There are no function symbols. An atomic formula can be of the form $x = y$.

For this language a suitable algebra for a compositional semantics is the *cylindric set algebra* $\langle S, \cup, \cap, \sim, \emptyset, D^\omega, C_k, \delta_{i,j} \rangle$ for all natural numbers i, j, and k. This algebra is a Boolean algebra (for the first six items). In addition, there are $\delta_{i,j}$, the (i,j) diagonal relations: the subsets of D^ω consisting of the tuples where the elements indexed by i and j are equal. The specification of cylindric set algebras also includes for all $k \in \omega$ the cylindrification operations C_k, which are defined by $C_k r$ being the subset of D^ω consisting of the tuples that differ from a tuple in r in at most the k-th component.

S is the set that contains $\emptyset$, D^ω, as well as all the diagonal relations $\delta_{i,j}$ and that is closed under the Boolean operations as well as under C_k.

4.3 Cylindric Set Algebra for the Compositional Semantics of Procedural Programs?

Cylindric set algebra interprets formulas as relations; relations are a suitable model for the procedures of a procedure-oriented language. These facts might suggest that cylindric set algebras be used for a compositional semantics for the procedural interpretation of logic.

The following are reasons not to do so.

- Tarski's choice of language for first-order predicate logic is no more procedure-oriented than clausal form is.
- Tarski's semantics does not specify by what operation, for example, the binary relation $\mathcal{M}(p(x, y, x))$ arises from the ternary relation p and the argument tuple $\langle x, y, x \rangle$. That is, his compositionality stops short of the atomic formula.

Accordingly, we create an independent alternative, centered around the concept of *table*. Surprisingly, one of the operations on tables reflects the way Tarski uses cylinders to algebraize the logical connectives.

5 Tables

Some of the semantic objects for the procedural programs of Definition 4 are familiar; they have been introduced in Section 2. This section is devoted to the one novel type of semantic object.

Definition 6 (table). *A table on a subset V of $\mathcal{V}$ is a set of tuples each of which has type $V \to \mathcal{T}_V$. If the set of tuples is empty, then we have the* null *table, which we write as $\bot$. If V is empty and the set of tuples is not, then the table is the* unit *table, which we write as $\top$.*

As there is only one function of type $\{\} \to \mathcal{T}_V$ for any subset V of $\mathcal{V}$, we have that $\top = \{\langle\rangle\}$.

To every table there corresponds a unique variable-indexed relation, which we call the result of *grounding* the table.

Definition 7 (grounding, table equivalence). *Let t be a table with tuples of type $V \to \mathcal{T}_V$. $\Gamma(t)$, the result of grounding t, is the variable-indexed relation consisting of the tuples of type $V \to \mathcal{H}$ each of which is a ground instance of a tuple in t.*

Tables t_0 and t_1 are equivalent if $\Gamma(t_0) = \Gamma(t_1)$.

In this section we define and discuss the product, filtering, and projection operations. These operations are adapted from [10], where filtering is called "application".

5.1 Product

As we will see, compositional semantics assigns tables as values to the calls in a procedure body as well as to the body itself. The co-occurrence of calls in a body corresponds to the *product* operation of the corresponding tables. An example will be given in Section 6.1.

Definition 8 (product). *Let τ_0 and τ_1 be tables consisting of tuples with index sets V_0 and V_1, respectively. The* product $\tau_0 * \tau_1$ *of these tables is defined as a table with $V_0 \cup V_1$ as index set. The product table $\tau_0 * \tau_1$ contains a tuple t if and only if there is a tuple t_0 in τ_0 and a tuple t_1 in τ_1 such that the set of equations $t_0 \cup t_1$ is solvable and has t as solved form.*

Theorem 1. − *Product is commutative and associative.*
  − *The null table $\perp$ is an absorbing element: $\perp * \tau = \tau * \perp = \perp$ for all tables τ.*
  − *The top table $\top$ is a unit: $\top * \tau = \tau * \top = \tau$ for all tables t.*
  − *$\tau * \tau$ and τ are equivalent.*

Commutativity and associativity give the obvious meaning to $*S$, where S is a set of tables, assuming that $*\{\} = \top$.

Definition 9 (cylinder on table). *The cylinder $\pi^{-1}(T)$ on a table T with index set $V \in \mathcal{V}$ is a table where $\mathcal{V}$ is the index set and where every tuple t' is obtained from a tuple t in T by defining $t'(v) = t(v)$ for every $v \in V$ and $t'(v) = v$ for every $v \in \mathcal{V} \setminus V$.*

This definition of "cylinder" is independent of Tarski's notion, which is the one in Definition 3. The two notions are connected as follows.

Lemma 1. *Let T be a table with index set V, a subset of $\mathcal{V}$. We have that $\Gamma(\pi^{-1}(T)) = \pi^{-1}(\Gamma(T))$. The first occurrence of π^{-1} is the cylindrification on tables from Definition 9; the second one is the cylindrification on relations in Definition 3.*

The distinguishing feature of Tarski's use of cylindric set algebra as semantics for first-order predicate logic is that conjunction in logic simply translates to intersection in the algebra. And this is the case even though the conjunction may be between two formulas with sets V_0 and V_1 of free variables. There is no restriction on these sets: they may be disjoint, one may be a subset of the other, or neither may be the case. Tarski's device works because the intersection is not between relations with V_0 and V_1 as index sets, but between *cylinders* on these relations in the set of all variables. This crucial idea reappears in the product of tables defined here. The connection is made apparent by the following theorem.

Theorem 2. *Let τ_i be a table with set V_i of variables, for $i \in \{0, 1\}$. $\Gamma(\tau_0 * \tau_1) = \pi_{V_0 \cup V_1}(\pi_\mathcal{V}^{-1}(\Gamma(\tau_0)) \cap \pi_\mathcal{V}^{-1}(\Gamma(\tau_1)))$.*

5.2   Filtering: From Relations to Tables

Just as in a functional programming language a function is applied to the n-tuple of its arguments, we think of the combination of a procedure symbol with its argument tuple as a binary operation. Consider therefore a call consisting of a procedure symbol and an argument tuple of order n. The procedure symbol has as value an integer-indexed relation of order n. It combines with the argument tuple to produce a table. This is the operation we call *filtering*. An example of this operation can be found in Section 6.1.

Definition 10 (filtering). *Let p be an integer-indexed relation of order n and let t be an n-tuple of terms with V as set of variables. The result of the filtering $p : t$ is a table where V is the index set of the tuples. For every tuple $\langle a_0, \ldots, a_{n-1} \rangle$ in p for which the set $\{t_0 = a_0, \ldots, t_{n-1} = a_{n-1}\}$ of equations is solvable, the table contains a tuple that is the solved form of these equations.*

In functional programming, an expression $E_0 E_1$ denotes function application. Here E_0 is an expression that evaluates to a function, and it is this function that is applied. Filtering is the relational counterpart: in $p : t$ the first operand p has a relation as value; it is filtered by the tuple t; the result is a table.

5.3   Projection: From Tables to Integer-Indexed Relations

Finally, a clause is a contribution to a procedure, which is an integer-indexed relation of order n. This relation, which is the clause's value, is somehow produced by a combination of the parameter tuple of the clause and the table that is the value of its body. We call this operation *projection*. An example of this operation can be found in Section 6.1.

Definition 11 (projection). *Let T be a table consisting of tuples whose index set is a subset V of $\mathcal{V}$. The result of projecting T on an n-tuple of terms, denoted $\langle t_0, \ldots, t_{n-1} \rangle / T$, is an integer-indexed relation consisting of n-tuples of ground terms. The relation contains such a tuple if and only if it is a ground instance of $\langle t_0\theta, \ldots, t_{n-1}\theta \rangle$, for some θ in T.*

6   Compositional Semantics

The operations of product, filtering, and projection are intended to be the semantical counterparts of the way in which procedural programs are put together syntactically. But so far only the intention exists.

The definition below formalizes this intention. It defines the meaning $\mathcal{M}(P)$ of a procedural program P, where P is regarded as a tuple with index set $\mathcal{P}$ of integer-indexed relations. This meaning depends on a relational interpretation I (Definition 5) that assigns relations to the procedure symbols in $\mathcal{P}$. We indicate this dependence by a subscript, as in $\mathcal{M}_I$.

Definition 12 gives the compositional semantics for procedural programs. As Definition 5 shows, a procedural program is just another way of writing a set of positive Horn clauses. The semantics of these has been defined in three equivalent ways: model-theoretically, proof-theoretically, and by means of fixpoints. The main theorem (3) of this paper relates the compositional semantics of procedural programs to the established semantics of the corresponding clausal sentences.

Definition 12.   *1. For every procedural program prog, $\mathcal{M}_I(prog)$ is the tuple with index set $\mathcal{P}$ such that for every $prsym \in \mathcal{P}$ the prsym-component is $\mathcal{M}_I(prog(prsym))$.*

   2. For every procedure proc, $\mathcal{M}_I(proc) = \cup\{\mathcal{M}_I(clause) \mid clause \in proc\}$

3. *For every clause with pars as parameter tuple and B as body,*
   $\mathcal{M}_I(pars \text{ :- } B) = pars/\mathcal{M}_I(B)$ *(use of projection)*
4. *For every procedure body B, we have $\mathcal{M}_I(B) = *\{\mathcal{M}_I(call) \mid call \in B\}$ (use of product)*
5. *For every call with prsym as procedure symbol and args as argument tuple,*
   $\mathcal{M}_I(prsym\ args) = \mathcal{M}_I(prsym) : args$ *(use of filtering)*
6. *For every $prsym \in \mathcal{P}$ we have that $\mathcal{M}_I(prsym) = I(prsym)$*

Here the numbering follows that of the syntactical rules of Definition 4.

Theorem 3. *Let I be a relational interpretation and I' the corresponding (Definition 5) Herbrand interpretation. Let P be a procedural program and P' the corresponding (Definition 5) set of positive Horn clauses. We have*

$$T_{P'}(I') \sim \mathcal{M}_I(P),$$

where T is the immediate-consequence operator for logic programs.

We only know a cumbersome, though straightforward, proof of this theorem.

T has a unique least fixpoint [22,16,1]. The partial order among Herbrand interpretations (set inclusion) translates according to the correspondence in Definition 5 to a partial order among relational interpretations (component-wise inclusion). Hence there is, for each procedural program P, a unique least relational interpretation I such that $I = \mathcal{M}_I(P)$.

Definition 13. $\mathcal{M}(P) = \mathcal{M}_{I_m}(P)$ *where I_m is the least relational interpretation I such that $I = \mathcal{M}_I(P)$.*

Theorem 4. *Let P' be a logic program and let P be the corresponding procedural program. Then we have $lfp(T_{P'}) \sim \mathcal{M}(P)$.*

This relates the compositional semantics of procedural programs to the mutually equivalent least fixpoint, proof-theoretical, and model-theoretical semantics of logic programs.

6.1   An Example

Consider the procedural program clause $(f(y), z) \text{ :- } \{p(x, f(y)), p(f(x), z)\}$. Here $\mathcal{M}(p)$ is an integer-indexed relation with $\{0, 1\}$ as index set. Let us assume that $\mathcal{M}(p) = \begin{array}{c||c|c|c|c} 0 & a & f(a) & f(a) & f(b) \\ \hline 1 & f(b) & b & f(b) & f(a) \end{array}$. Here the four 2-tuples, indexed by $\{0, 1\}$, are displayed vertically.

The value of a call is a table; that is, a variable-indexed relation.

$$\mathcal{M}(p(x, f(y))) = \mathcal{M}(p) : \langle x, f(y) \rangle = \begin{array}{c||c|c|c} x & a & f(a) & f(b) \\ \hline y & b & b & a \end{array}.$$

Similarly, $\mathcal{M}(p(f(x), z)) = \mathcal{M}(p) : \langle f(x), z \rangle = \begin{array}{c||c|c|c} x & a & a & b \\ \hline z & b & f(b) & f(a) \end{array}.$

The value of the body is the product of the above two tables:

$$\mathcal{M}(p(x, f(y)), p(f(x), z)) = \mathcal{M}(p(x, f(y))) * \mathcal{M}(p(f(x), z)) = \begin{array}{c|c|c} x & a & a \\ \hline y & b & b \\ z & b & f(b) \end{array}.$$

Finally, the meaning of the entire clause

$(f(y), z) :\!\!- p(x, f(y)), p(f(x), z)$ is obtained by projection:

$$\langle f(y), z \rangle / \mathcal{M}(p(x, f(y)), p(f(x), z)) = \begin{array}{c|c|c} 0 & f(b) & f(b) \\ \hline 1 & b & f(b) \end{array}.$$

7   Implications for Modularity

Suppose P and P' are procedural programs with the same Herbrand universe. If $p(t_0, \ldots, t_{n-1})$ is a call in P, then the meaning of p is $(\mathcal{M}(P))(p)$. But p is a special case of an expression that has an n-ary integer-indexed relation as value. Such an expression could also be $(\mathcal{M}(P'))(p')$ if p' is a procedure symbol in P' paired with an n-ary procedure. The value of this expression is a set of n-tuples of ground terms. This value is independent of the procedure symbols occurring in P'. Hence these symbols are "encapsulated" in the expression $(\mathcal{M}(P'))(p')$.

This only addresses the semantics of a module mechanisms. It leaves open the syntax that indicates which set of clauses is a module and which procedure symbol is exported.

8   Related Work

Modules for logic programs can be obtained via proof theory [18,17] or via higher-order logic [5]. A different approach is to base it on decompositions of the immediate-consequence operator as done by Brogi et al. [3]. It is baffling that the various approaches to modularity are so difficult to relate. Several more are mentioned by Brogi et al. [3], who also seem at a loss in relating them to their own work.

Additional details about the operations on tables and relations, there called "table-relation algebra", can be found in [10,11].

9   Concluding Remarks

The procedural programs of Definition 4 are the result of the desire to give a procedural interpretation not only of an entire clause, but also of the composition of head and body within a clause as well as of the compositions that can be recognized in the body. Thus procedural programs are but another way of parsing a set of positive Horn clauses.

But suppose that in 1972 one had never heard of clausal logic and that the motivation was to characterize in what way languages with procedures, such as Algol, are of a higher level than their predecessors. A higher level of programming in such languages is achieved by using procedure calls as much as possible. That suggests the ultimate altitude in level of programming: procedure bodies contain procedure calls only.

What about data structures for a pure procedural language? Just as Lisp simplified by standardizing all data structures to lists, one could make a similar choice by standardizing on trees. In this way a pure procedure-oriented language would arise that coincides with the procedural programs of Definition 4.

Functional programming languages have an obvious semantics in the form of functions as defined in mathematics. The semantics of Algol-like languages is defined in terms of transitions between computational states. These transitions are specified directly or indirectly in terms of assignments. In this way one might think that procedure-oriented programming languages are of inherently lower level than functional programming languages.

It is not necessary to specify procedures in terms of state transitions. A procedure is more directly specified as the set of all possible combinations of values of the arguments of a call. That is, as a set of tuples of the same arity, which is a relation.

In this way the procedural programs of Definition 4 become as high-level as functional programs and obtain a semantics that is as mathematical.

One might argue that this gives procedural programs a significance that extends beyond logic programming. For example, they may be a way to describe Colmerauer's view [7] that Prolog is not necessarily a logic programming language. In the procedural interpretation described here, the Herbrand universe can be replaced by a sufficiently similar data structure, such as the rational trees.

Acknowledgements

I am grateful to Belaid Moa and the anonymous referees for their suggestions for improvement. This research was supported by the University of Victoria and by the Natural Science and Engineering Research Council of Canada.

References

1. K.R. Apt. *Logic programming.* In *Handbook of Theoretical Computer Science*, 1990.
2. George Boole. *An Investigation of the Laws of Thought.* Dover, 1854. Dover edition not dated.
3. Antonio Brogi, Paolo Mancarella, Dino Pedreschi, and Franco Turini. Modular logic programming. *ACM Transactions on Programming Languages and Systems*, 16:1361–1398, 1994.
4. François Bry. A compositional semantics for logic programs and deductive databases. In *Proc. Joint Int. Conf. Symp. Logic Programming*, 1996.
5. W. Chen, M. Kifer, and D.S. Warren. HILOG: A foundation for higher-order logic programming. *Journal of Logic Programming*, 15:187 – 230, 1993.
6. Michael Codish, Saumya K. Debray, and Roberto Giacobazzi. Compositional analysis of modular logic programs. In *Proc. 20th ACM Symposium on Principles of Programming Languages (POPL)*, 1993.

7. A. Colmerauer. Sur les bases théoriques de Prolog. Technical report, Groupe d'Intelligence Artificielle, Université d'Aix-Marseille II, 1979.

8. A. Colmerauer, H. Kanoui, R. Paséro, and P. Roussel. Un système de communication homme-machine en français. Technical report, Groupe d'Intelligence Artificielle, Université d'Aix-Marseille II, 1972.

9. Leon Henkin, J. Donald Monk, and Alfred Tarski. *Cylindric Algebras, Parts I, II*. Studies in Logic and the Foundations of Mathematics. North-Holland, 1985.

10. H. Ibrahim and M.H. van Emden. Towards applicative relational programming. Unpublished draft; available from the Computing Research Repository (http://arxiv.org/corr/home), 1991.

11. Husain Ibrahim. Applicative expressions for relational programming. Master's thesis, University of Victoria, 1992.

12. Edgar T. Irons. A syntax-directed compiler for Algol 60. *Communications of the ACM*, 4:51–55, 1961.

13. R.A. Kowalski. Predicate logic as programming language. In *Proc. IFIP 74*, pages 569–574, 1974.

14. R.A. Kowalski. *Logic for Problem-Solving*. Elsevier North-Holland, 1979.

15. P. Landin. The mechanical evaluation of expressions. *Computer Journal*, 6:308–320, 1963.

16. J.W. Lloyd. *Foundations of Logic Programming*. Springer-Verlag, 2nd edition, 1987.

17. Francis G. McCabe. *Logic and Objects*. Prentice Hall, 1992.

18. Dale Miller. A logical analysis of modules in logic programming. *Journal of Logic Programming*, 6:79 – 108, 1989.

19. Dana Scott and Christopher Strachey. Toward a mathematical semantics for computer languages. In *Proceedings of the Symposium on Computers and Automata*, pages 19–46, Polytechnic Institute of Brooklyn, 1971.

20. Joseph E. Stoy. *Denotational Semantics: The Scott-Strachey approach to Programming Language Theory*. MIT Press, 1977.

21. A. Tarski. A representation theorem for cylindric algebras. *Bull. Amer. Math. Soc.*, 58:65 – 66, 1952.

22. M.H. van Emden and R.A. Kowalski. The semantics of predicate logic as a programming language. *Journal of the ACM*, 23(4):733–742, 1976.

Coinductive Logic Programming

Luke Simon, Ajay Mallya, Ajay Bansal, and Gopal Gupta

Department of Computer Science
University of Texas at Dallas, Richardson, TX 75080

Abstract. We extend logic programming's semantics with the semantic dual of traditional Herbrand semantics by using greatest fixed-points in place of least fixed-points. Executing a logic program then involves using *coinduction* to check inclusion in the greatest fixed-point. The resulting *coinductive logic programming language* is syntactically identical to, yet semantically subsumes logic programming with rational terms and lazy evaluation. We present a novel formal operational semantics that is based on *synthesizing a coinductive hypothesis* for this coinductive logic programming language. We prove that this new operational semantics is equivalent to the declarative semantics. Our operational semantics lends itself to an elegant and efficient goal directed proof search in the presence of rational terms and proofs. We describe a prototype implementation of this operational semantics along with applications of coinductive logic programming.

But look! What was that? One of the snakes had seized hold of its own tail, and the form whirled mockingly before my eyes.

—Friedrich A. Kekule, 1864

1 Introduction

The traditional declarative and operational semantics for logic programming (LP) is inadequate for various programming practices such as programming with infinite data structures and *corecursion* [2]. While such programs are theoretically interesting, their practical applications include improved modularization of programs as seen in lazy functional programming languages, rational terms, and applications to model checking as discussed in section 5. For example, we would like programs such as the following program, which describes infinite binary streams, to be semantically meaningful and finitely derivable.

```
bit(0).
bit(1).
bitstream([H | T]) :- bit(H), bitstream(T).
| ?- X = [0, 1, 1, 0 | X], bitstream(X).
```

We would like the above query to return a positive answer in finite time, however, aside from the `bit` predicate, the least fixed-point (lfp) semantics of the above

S. Etalle and M. Truszczyński (Eds.): ICLP 2006, LNCS 4079, pp. 330–345, 2006.

program is null, and no finite SLD derivation exists for the query. Hence the problems are two-fold. The Herbrand universe does not allow for infinite terms such as X and the least Herbrand model does not allow for infinite proofs, such as the proof of `bitstream(X)`. However, the traditional declarative semantics of LP can be extended in order to give declarative semantics to such infinite structures and properties, as seen in numerous accounts of rational terms and infinite derivations [14,10,12,11]. Furthermore, the operational semantics must be extended, so as to be able to finitely represent an otherwise infinite derivation. This paper proposes such an operational semantics which is based on synthesizing a coinductive hypothesis, and discusses its implementation and applications. We refer to this variation of logic programming as "coinductive logic programming".[1] The work reported in this paper is a culmination of authors' previous work [18,5,13,6,7]. The novel contribution of our work is the development of an efficient top-down operational semantics for computing the greatest fixed-point of a logic program.

2   Syntax and Semantics

Traditionally, declarative semantics for LP has been given using the notions of Herbrand universe, Herbrand base, and minimal model [12]. Each is defined as a least fixed-point, and the set is manifested in traditional set theory. The declarative semantics of coinductive LP, on the other hand, takes the dual of each of these notions, in hyperset theory with the *axiom of plenitude* [2]. This variation of the declarative semantics of a logic program has appeared before [14,10,12,11] in order to describe rational trees and infinite SLD derivations. However, here it is used to finitely describe potentially infinite derivations in our new operational semantics, which we call co-SLD in section 2.4.

2.1   Induction and Coinduction

A naive attempt to prove a property of the natural numbers involves demonstrating the property for 0, 1, 2, ... In order for such a proof to be comprehensive, it must be infinite. However, since an explicitly infinite proof cannot written, the principle of proof by induction can be used to represent such an infinite proof in a finite form. This is precisely what the operational semantics of coinductive LP does as well. That is, coinductive LP uses the principle of proof by coinduction for representing infinite proofs or derivations in a finite form. The difference between induction and coinduction will be made more obvious later.

Following the account given in Barwise [2] and Pierce [15], we briefly review the set theoretic notions of induction and coinduction, which are defined in terms of monotonic functions on sets and least and greatest fixed-points, which

---

[1] Note that coinductive LP defined in this paper is not at all related to *inductive* LP which is the common term used to refer to LP systems for learning rules. In fact, sometimes we'll use the term inductive LP itself to refer to traditional SLD (or OLDT) resolution-based LP.

exist and are unique according to Theorem 1. For the remaining discussion, it is assumed that all objects such as elements, sets, and functions are taken from the universe of hypersets with the axiom of plenitude. Details can be found in [2].

Definition 1. *A function Γ on sets is monotonic if $S \subseteq T$ implies $\Gamma(S) \subseteq \Gamma(T)$. Such functions are called generating functions.*

Generating functions can be thought of as a definition for creating objects, such as terms and proofs. The following example demonstrates one such definition.

Example 1. Let Γ_N be a function on sets: $\Gamma_N(S) = \{0\} \cup \{succ(x) \mid x \in S\}$. Obviously, Γ_N is a monotonic function, and intuitively, it defines the set of natural numbers, as will be demonstrated below.

Definition 2. *Let S be a set.*

1. *S is Γ-closed if $\Gamma(S) \subseteq S$; S is Γ-justified if $S \subseteq \Gamma(S)$.*
2. *S is a fixed-point of Γ if S is both Γ-closed and justified.*

A set S is Γ-closed when every object created by the generator Γ is already in S. Similarly, a set S is Γ-justified when every object in S is created or justified by the generator. Theorem 1 shows that a generating function Γ can be used for giving a precise definition of a set of objects in terms of the least or greatest fixed-point of Γ, as these fixed-points are guaranteed to exist, and are unique.

Theorem 1. *(Knaster-Tarski) Let Γ be a generating function. The least fixed-point of Γ is the intersection of all Γ-closed sets. The greatest fixed-point (gfp) of Γ is the union of all Γ-justified sets.*

Since these fixed-points always exist and are unique, it is customary to define unary operators μ and ν for manifesting either of these fixed-points.

Definition 3. *$\mu\Gamma$ denotes the lfp of Γ, and $\nu\Gamma$ denotes the gfp.*

Example 2. Let Γ_N be defined as in example 1. The definition of the natural numbers N can now be unambiguously invoked via theorem 1, as $N = \mu\Gamma_N$, which is guaranteed to exist and be unique. Note that this definition is equivalent to the standard "inductive" definition of the natural numbers, which is written: Let N be the smallest set such that $0 \in N$ and if $x \in N$, then $x + 1 \in N$.

Hence what is sometimes referred to as an inductive definition, is subsumed by definition via least fixed-point. This is further generalized by creating the dual notion of a definition by greatest fixed-point, termed a coinductive definition.

Example 3. Γ_N from example 1 also unambiguously defines another set, that is, $N' = \nu\Gamma_N = N \cup \{\omega\}$, where $\omega = succ(\omega)$, that is, $\omega = succ(succ(succ(...)))$ an infinite application of *succ*.

Corollary 1. *The principle of induction states that if S is Γ-closed, then $\mu\Gamma \subseteq S$, and the principle of coinduction states that if S is Γ-justified, then $S \subseteq \nu\Gamma$.*

Definition 4. *Let $Q(x)$ be a property. Proof by induction demonstrates that the characteristic set $S = \{x \mid Q(x)\}$ is Γ-closed, and then invokes the principle of induction to prove that every element x of $\mu\Gamma$ has the property $Q(x)$.*

Similarly, proof by coinduction demonstrates that the characteristic set S is Γ-justified, and then invokes the principle of coinduction to prove that every element x that has property $Q(x)$ is also an element of $\nu\Gamma$.

Example 4. The familiar proof by induction can be instantiated with regards to the set $\mathcal{N}$ defined in the previous example. Let $Q(x)$ be some property, and let $S = \{x \mid Q(x)\}$. In order to show that every element x in $\mathcal{N}$ has property $Q(x)$, by induction it is sufficient to show that $\Gamma_{\mathcal{N}}(S) \subseteq S$, which is equivalent to showing that $0 \in S$, and if $x \in S$, then $succ(x) \in S$.

Proof by coinduction is used in many areas of computer science. e.g., bisimilarity proofs for process algebras such as the π-calculus. Our soundness proof of the operational semantics of coinductive LP also relies on coinduction [20].

2.2 Syntax

A coinductive logic program is syntactically identical to a traditional logic program, i.e., a coinductive logic program is a finite set of definite clauses. Syntactic terms and atoms have their traditional inductive definitions. However, coinductive LP also makes use of infinite terms and atoms in its semantics. These generalizations of syntactic terms and atoms have a straightforward definition as the greatest fixed-points of the same respective generating functions used to define syntactic terms and atoms. Finally, we assume that there is at least one constant and one unary function symbol in a coinductive logic program.

2.3 Declarative Semantics

The declarative semantics of a coinductive logic program is the "across the board" dual of the traditional minimal model Herbrand semantics [12,1], i.e., the model of a coinductive logic program P, written $M^{co}(P)$, is the maximal infinitary Herbrand model of a program P. The maximal infinitary Herbrand model is the greatest fixed-point of T_P with atoms ranging over the infinitary Herbrand base. The details can be found in [14,10,12]. As demonstrated in [14,10,12,11], this allows the universe of terms, called the infinitary Herbrand universe, to contain infinite terms, in addition to the traditional finite terms, and similarly for the infinitary Herbrand base, which contains finite and infinite atoms. It also allows for the model to contain ground goals that have either finite or infinite proofs. The difference here is that we define such goals as true, and in the next section we provide a new operational semantics that yields *finite* derivations for goals with an *infinite* (rational) proof.

Definition 5. *A possibly infinite atom A is true in program P iff the set of all groundings of A, with substitutions ranging over the infinitary Herbrand universe, is a subset of $M^{co}(P)$.*

Example 5. Let P_1 be the following program.

```
from(N, [N|T]) :- from(s(N), T).
| ?- from(0, _).
```

The coinductive semantics are derived as follows. The infinitary Herbrand universe is $U^{co}(P_1) \supseteq N \cup \Omega \cup L$ where $N = \{0, s(0), s(s(0)), \ldots\}$, $\Omega = \{s(s(s(\ldots)))\}$, and L is the set of all finite and infinite lists of elements in N, Ω, L. Therefore the maximal infinitary Herbrand model $M^{co}(P_1) = \{from(t, [t, s(t), s(s(t)), \ldots]) \mid t \in U^{co}(P_1)\}$, which is the meaning of the program and obviously not null, as was the case with traditional LP. Furthermore $from(0, [0, s(0), s(s(0)), \ldots]) \in M^{co}(P_1)$ implies that the query returns "yes".

The model characterizes semantics in terms of truth, that is, the set of ground atoms that are true. This set is defined via a generator T_P, and in section 2.6, we discuss the way in which the generator is applied in order to include an atom in the model. For example, the generator is only allowed to be applied a finite number of times for any given atom in the minimal model, while it can be applied an infinite number of times for an atom in the maximal infinitary Herbrand model. We characterize this by recording the application of the generator in the elements of a new fixed-point. We call these elements "idealized proofs".

Definition 6. *Let $node(A, L)$ be a constructor of a tree with root A and subtrees L, where A is an atom and L is a list of trees. Let $G^{co}(P)$ be the set of ground instances of clauses of a program P. The set of idealized proofs for program P is $\nu \Sigma_P$, where*

$$\Sigma_P(S) = \{node(C, [T_1, \ldots, T_n]) \mid \\ C \leftarrow D_1, \ldots, D_n \in G^{co}(P) \wedge \text{ the root of } T_i \in S \text{ is } D_i\}$$

Again, this is nothing more than a reformulation of the maximal infinitary Herbrand model, which records the applications of the generator in the elements of the fixed-point itself, as the following theorem demonstrates.

Theorem 2. *Let $S = \{A \mid \exists T \in \nu \Sigma_P . A \text{ is the root of } T\}$, then $S = M^{co}(P)$.*

Hence any element in the model has an idealized proof and anything that has an idealized proof is in the model. A similar theorem exists, equating the minimal model with the least fixed-point of Σ_P restricted to finite terms, i.e., the minimal model consists of all ground atoms that have a finite idealized proof. This formulation of the declarative semantics in terms of idealized proofs will be used in section 2.6.

2.4   Operational Semantics

This section defines the operational semantics for coinductive logic programming. This requires some infinite tree theory. However, this section only states a few definitions and theorems without proof. Details can be found in [4].

The operational semantics given for coinductive LP is defined in a manner similar to SLD, and is therefore called co-SLD. Where SLD uses sets of syntactic atoms and syntactic term substitutions for states, co-SLD uses finite trees of syntactic atoms along with systems of equations. Of course, the traditional goals of SLD can be extracted from these trees, as the goal of a tree is simply the set of leaves of the tree. Furthermore, where SLD only allows program clauses as state transition rules, co-SLD also allows an implicit *coinductive hypothesis rule* for providing atoms that have an infinite proof, with a finite derivation. As is the case with SLD, it is up to the underlying search strategy to find a sequence of transition rules that prove the original query.

Definition 7. *A tree is rational if the cardinality of the set of all its subtrees is finite. An object such as a term, atom, or idealized proof is said to be rational if it is modeled as a rational tree.*

Definition 8. *A substitution is a finite mapping of variables to terms. A substitution is syntactic if it only substitutes syntactic terms for variables. A substitution is said to be rational if it only substitutes rational terms for variables.*

Definition 9. *A term unification problem is a finite set of equations between terms. A unifier for a term unification problem is a substitution that satisfies every equation in the problem. σ is a most general unifier (mgu) for a term unification problem, if any other solution σ' can be defined as the composition $\sigma'' \circ \sigma$.*

Note that terms are possibly infinite. So it is possible for a unification problem to lack a syntactic unifier, while at the same time the problem has a solution: a rational unifier. However, objects of an operational semantics should be finite. Hence we define a standard finite representation of rational substitutions called a system of equations.

Definition 10. *A system of equations E is a term unification problem where each equation is of the form $X = t$, s.t. X is a variable and t a syntactic term.*

Theorem 3. *(Courcelle) Every system of equations has a mgu that is rational.*

Theorem 4. *(Courcelle) For every rational substitution σ with domain V, there is a system of equations E, such that the mgu σ' of E is equal to σ when restricted to the domain V.*

Without loss of generality, the previous two theorems allow for a solution to a term unification problem to be simultaneously a substitution as well as a system of equations. Note that given a substitution specified as a system of equations E, and a term A, the term $E(A)$ denotes the result of applying the substitution E to A.

Now the operational semantics can be defined. The semantics implicitly defines a state transition system. Systems of equations are used to model part of the state of coinductive LP's semantics. They effectively denote the current state of unification of terms. The current state of the pending goals is modeled using a finite tree of atoms, as it is necessary to recognize cycles in the sequence of pending goals, that is, the ancestors of a goal are memo-ed in order to recognize a cycle in the proof.

Definition 11. *A state S is a pair (T, E), where T is a finite tree with nodes labeled with syntactic atoms, and E is a system of equations.*

Note that the states of the operational semantics only allow for rational terms in any given state, while the declarative semantics allows for irrational terms, i.e., infinite terms that are not rational. This is due to the fact that at any given state of the computation, a term must be finitely representable. In the current operational semantics, irrational terms only exist "in the limit" of an infinite derivation. Future work involves extending the operational semantics presented in this paper so that subgoals that cannot fail can be suspended and resumed via coroutining, which will allow for a finite representation of irrational terms in a manner similar to functional programming's lazy data structures. This discrepancy manifests in the completeness proof, which must be restricted to atoms that have a rational idealized proof, as atoms with irrational idealized proofs do not necessarily have finite co-SLD derivations.

Definition 12. *A transition rule R of a coinductive logic program P is an instance of a clause in P, with variables standardized apart, i.e., consistently renamed for freshness, or R is a coinductive hypothesis rule of the form $\nu(n)$ (defined below), where n is a natural number.*

Definition 13. *A state (T, E) transitions to another state (T', E') by transition rule R of program P whenever:*

1. R is a definite clause of the form $p(t'_1, \ldots, t'_n) \leftarrow B_1, \ldots, B_m$ and E' is the mgu for $\{t_1 = t'_1, \ldots, t_n = t'_n\} \cup E$, and T' is obtained from T according to the following case analysis of m:
   (a) $m = 0$ implies T' is obtained from T by removing a leaf labeled $p(t_1, \ldots, t_n)$ and the maximum number of its ancestors, such that the result is still a tree.
   (b) $m > 0$ implies T' is obtained from T by adding children $B_1, \ldots, B_m$ to a leaf labeled with $p(t_1, \ldots, t_n)$.
2. R is of the form $\nu(m)$, a leaf N in T is labeled with $p(t_1, \ldots, t_n)$, the proper ancestor of N at depth m is labeled with $p(t'_1, \ldots, t'_n)$, E' is the mgu for $\{t_1 = t'_1, \ldots, t_n = t'_n\} \cup E$, then T' is obtained from T by removing N and the maximum number of its ancestors, such that the result is still a tree.

The part of the previous definition that removes a leaf and a maximum number of its ancestors can be thought of as a successful call returning and therefore deallocating memo-ed calls on the call stack. This involves successively removing ancestor nodes of the leaf until an ancestor is reached, which still has other children, and so removing any more ancestors would cause the result to no longer be a tree, as children would be orphaned. Hence the depth of the tree is bounded by the depth of the call stack.

Definition 14. *A transition sequence in program P consists of a sequence of states $S_1, S_2, \ldots$ and a sequence of transition rules $R_1, R_2 \ldots$, such that S_i transitions to S_{i+1} by rule R_i of program P.*

A transition sequence denotes the trace of an execution. Execution halts when it reaches a terminal state: either all goals have been proved or the execution path has reached a dead-end.

Definition 15. *The following are two distinguished terminal states:*

1. An accepting state is of the form $(\emptyset, E)$, where $\emptyset$ denotes an empty tree.
2. A failure state is a non-accepting state lacking any outgoing edges.

Without loss of generality, we restrict queries to be single syntactic atoms. A query containing multiple atoms can be modeled by adding a new predicate with one clause to the program. Finally we can define the execution of a query as a transition sequence through the state transition system induced by the input program, with the start state consisting of the initial query.

Definition 16. *A co-SLD derivation of a state (T, E) in program P is a state transition sequence with the first state equal to (T, E). A derivation is successful if it ends in an accepting state, and a derivation has failed if it reaches a failure state. We say that a syntactic atom A has a successful derivation in program P, if $(A, \emptyset)$ has a successful derivation in P.*

2.5   Examples

In addition to allowing infinite terms, the operational semantics allows for an execution to succeed when it encounters a goal that unifies with an ancestor goal. While this is somewhat similar to tabled LP in that called atoms are recorded so as to avoid unnecessary redundant computation, the difference is that coinductive LP's memo-ed atoms represent a coinductive hypothesis, while tabled logic programming's table represents a list of results for each called goal in the traditional inductive semantics. Hence we call the memo-ed atoms the dynamic coinductive hypothesis. An example that demonstrates the distinction is the following program.

```
p :- p.
| ?- p.
```

Execution starts by checking the dynamic coinductive hypothesis for an atom that unifies with **p**, which does not exist, so **p** is added to the hypothesis. Next, the body of the goal is executed. Again, the hypothesis is checked for an atom that unifies with **p**, which is now already included in the hypothesis, so the most recent call succeeds and then since no remaining goals exist, the original query succeeds. Hence, according to the operational semantics of coinductive LP, the query has a successful derivation, and hence returns "yes", while traditional (tabled) LP returns "no".

Now for a more complicated example involving function symbols. Consider the execution of the following program, which defines a predicate that recognizes infinite streams of natural numbers and ω, that is, infinity.

```
stream([H | T]) :- number(H), stream(T).
number(0).
number(s(N)) :- number(N).
| ?- stream([0, s(0), s(s(0)) | T ]).
```

The following is an execution trace, for the above query, of the memoization and unmemoization of calls by the operational semantics:

1. MEMO: stream([0, s(0), s(s(0)) | T])
2. MEMO: number(0)
3. UNMEMO: number(0)
4. MEMO: stream([s(0), s(s(0)) | T])
5. MEMO: number(s(0))
6. MEMO: number(0)
7. UNMEMO: number(0)
8. UNMEMO: number(s(0))
9. MEMO: stream([s(s(0)) | T])
10. MEMO: number(s(s(0)))
11. MEMO: number(s(0))
12. MEMO: number(0)
13. UNMEMO: number(0)
14. UNMEMO: number(s(0))
15. UNMEMO: number(s(s(0)))

The next goal call is stream(T), which unifies with memo-ed ancestor (1), and therefore immediately succeeds. Hence the original query succeeds with

    T = [0, s(0), s(s(0)) | T]

The user could force a failure here, which would cause the goal to be unified with the next matching memo-ed ancestor, if such an element exists, otherwise the goal is memo-ed and the process repeats—generating additional results (T = [0, s(0), s(s(0)) | R], R = [0 | R], etc.). Note that excluding the occurs check is necessary as such structures have a greatest fixed-point interpretation and are in the infinitary Herbrand universe. We will see that this is in fact one of the benefits of coinductive LP. Traditional LP's least Herbrand model semantics requires SLD resolution to unify with occurs check (or lack soundness), which adversely affects performance in the common case. Coinductive LP, on the other hand, has a declarative semantics that allows unification without doing occurs check in an efficient manner as seen in rational tree unification, and in addition, coinductive LP allows for programs to reason about rational terms generated by rational tree unification in a manner that is impossible in traditional LP, as traditional LP would diverge into an infinite derivation, where coinductive LP would yield a finite derivation thanks to the dynamic synthesis of a coinductive hypothesis via memoization.

2.6   Correctness

We next prove the correctness of the operational semantics by demonstrating its correspondence with the declarative semantics via soundness and completeness theorems. Completeness, however, must be restricted to atoms that have a rational proof. Section 6 discusses an extension of the operational semantics, so as to improve its completeness. The soundness and completeness theorems are stated below, their proofs are omitted and can be found elsewhere [20].

Theorem 5. *(soundness) If atom A has a successful co-SLD derivation in program P, then $E(A)$ is true in program P, where E is the resulting variable bindings for the derivation.*

Theorem 6. *(completeness) If $A \in M^{co}(P)$ has a rational idealized proof, then A has a successful co-SLD derivation in program P.*

3   Related Work

Most of the work in the past has been focused on allowing for infinite data structures in LP, or it has dealt with mathematically describing infinite derivations. However, these stop short of providing both a declarative semantics as well as finite derivations for atoms that have infinite idealized proofs. Logic programming with rational trees [3,10] allows for finite terms as well as infinite terms that are rational trees, that is, terms that have finitely many distinct subterms. Coinductive LP as defined in Section 2, on the other hand, allows for finite terms, rational infinite terms, but unlike LP with rational trees, the declarative semantics of coinductive LP also allows for irrational infinite terms. Furthermore, the declarative semantics of LP with rational trees corresponds to the minimal infinitary Herbrand model. On the other hand, coinductive LP's declarative semantics is the maximal infinitary Herbrand model. Also, the operational semantics of LP with rational trees is simply SLD extended with rational term unification, while the operational semantics of coinductive LP corresponds to SLD only via the fact that both are implicitly defined in terms of state transition. Thus, LP with rational trees does not allow for finite derivations of atoms that have infinite idealized proofs, while coinductive LP does. Finally, LP with rational trees can *only* create infinite terms via unification (without occurs check), while coinductive LP can create infinite terms via unification (without occurs check) *as well as via user-defined coinductively recursive (or corecursive) predicates*, as demonstrated by the bit stream example in the introduction.

It is also well known that atoms with infinite SLD derivations are contained in the maximal model [14,10,12,11]. However, the novel contribution of coinductive LP is co-SLD's use of memoization for synthesizing a coinductive hypothesis, which allows for the invocation of co-SLD's coinductive hypothesis rule for recognizing atoms that have an infinite idealized proof. For example, the work of [14,10,12,11] doesn't provide an effective means, i.e., an operational semantics, for answering the bit stream query in the introduction. In their operational semantics, such a query would simply not terminate, while in coinductive logic programming such a query terminates in finite time because it has a successful, finite co-SLD derivation.

Jaffar et al's coinductive tabling proof method [9] uses coinduction as a means of proving infinitary properties in model checking, as opposed to using it in defining the semantics of a new declarative programming language, as is the case with coinductive LP presented in this paper. Jaffar et al's coinductive tabling proof method is not assigned any declarative, model-theoretic semantics, as is the case with coinductive logic programming presented in this paper, which has a declarative semantics, operational semantics, and a correctness proof showing the correspondence between the two. Coinductive logic programming, when extended with constraints, can be used for the same applications as Jaffar et al's coinductive tabling proof method (see [20]).

Lazy functional LP (e.g., [8]) also allows for infinite data structures, but it encodes predicates as Boolean functions, while in comparison, coinductive LP defines predicates via Horn clauses; the difference in the semantics of the two is quite pronounced.

4   Implementation

A prototype implementation of coinductive LP is being realized by modifying the YAP Prolog system [17]. The general operational semantics described above allows for a coinductively recursive call to terminate (coinductively succeed) if it *unifies* with a call that has been seen earlier. However, in the current prototype, a coinductive call terminates only if it is a *variant* of an ancestor call.

The implementation of coinductive LP is reasonably straightforward, and is based on the machinery used in the YAP system for realizing OLDT style tabling [17]. Predicates have to be declared coinductive via the directive:

```
:- coinductive p/n.
```

where p is the predicate name and n its arity. When a coinductive call is encountered for the first time, it is recorded in the memo-table that YAPTAB [17] uses for implementing standard tabled LP. The call is recorded again in the table after head unification, but this time it is saved as a solution to the tabled call. The variables in the recorded solution are interpreted w.r.t. the environment of the coinductive call (so effectively the closure of the call is saved). When a variant call is encountered later, it is unified with the solution saved in the table and made to succeed. Note that everything recorded in the memo-table for a specific coinductive predicate p will be deleted, when execution backtracks over the first call of p. Consider the example program:

```
:- coinductive p/1.
p(f(X)) :- p(X).
| ?- p(Y).
```

When the call p(Y) is made, it is first copied (say as p(A)) in the table as a coinductive call. Next, a matching rule is found and head unification performed (Y is bound to f(X)). Next, p(Y) (i.e., p(f(X))) is recorded as a solution to the call p(A). The variable X in the solution refers to the X in the rule matching the coinductive call (i.e., it points to the variable X in the environment allocated on the stack). When the coinductive call p(X) is encountered in the body of the rule, it is determined to be a variant of the call p(A) stored in the memo-table, and unified with the solution p(f(X)). This results in X being bound to f(X), i.e., X = f(X), producing the desired solution $f^\omega(..)$.

5   Applications

Coinductive LP augments traditional logic programming with rational terms and rational proofs. These concepts generalize the notions of rational trees and lazy predicates. Coinductive LP has practical applications in concurrent LP, bisimilarity, model checking, and many other areas. Furthermore, it appears that the concept of ancestors in the co-SLD semantics can be used to give a top-down operational semantics to a restricted form of ASP programs (work is in progress). Coinductive LP also allows type inference algorithms in functional programming to be implemented directly and elegantly.

Infinite Terms and Properties: As previously stated, coinductive LP subsumes logic programming with rational trees of Jaffar et al [10] and Colmerauer [3]. However, because LP with rational trees has semantics ascribed by the minimal infinitary Herbrand model, applying predicates to infinite trees is rather limited. Doing so typically results in nontermination. Coinductive LP removes this limitation by ascribing the semantics in terms of *maximal* infinitary Herbrand model and it provides an operational semantics that provides finite derivations for atoms with infinite idealized proofs. This is demonstrated by the traditional definition of append, which, when executed with coinductive logic programming's semantics, allows for calling the predicate with infinite arguments. This is illustrated below. As an aside, note that irrational lists also make it possible to directly represent an infinite precision irrational real number as an infinite list of natural numbers.

```
append( [], X, X ).
append( [H|T], Y, [H|Z] ) :- append( T, Y, Z ).
```

Not only can the above definition append two finite input lists, as well as split a finite list into two lists in the reverse direction, it can also append infinite lists under coinductive execution. It can even split an infinite list into two lists that when appended, equal the original infinite list. For example:

```
| ?- Y = [4, 5, 6, | Y], append([1, 2, 3], Y, Z).
      Answer: Z = [1, 2, 3 | Y], Y = [4, 5, 6, | Y]
```

More generally, the coinductive append has interesting algebraic properties. When the first argument is infinite, it doesn't matter what the value of the second argument is, as the third argument is always equal to the first. However, when the second argument is infinite, the value of the third argument still depends on the value of the first. This is illustrated below:

```
| ?- X = [1, 2, 3, | X], Y = [3, 4 | Y], append(X, Y, Z).
      Answer: Z = [1, 2, 3 | Z]
| ?- Z = [1, 2 | Z], append(X, Y, Z).
      Answers: X = [], Y = [1, 2 | Z]; Z = [1, 2 | Z]
               X = [1], Y = [2 | Z]; Z = [1, 2 | Z]
               X = [1, 2], Y = Z; Z = [1, 2 | Z]
```

Lazy Evaluation of Logic Programs: Coinductive LP also allows for lazy evaluation to be elegantly incorporated into Prolog. Lazy evaluation allows for manipulation of, and reasoning about, cyclic and infinite data structures and properties. In the presence of coinductive LP, if the infinite terms involved are rational, then given the goal p(X), q(X) with coinductive predicates p/1 and q/1, then p(X) can coinductively succeed and terminate, and then pass the resulting X to q(X). If X is bound to an infinite irrational term during the computation, then p and q must be executed in a coroutined manner to produce answers. That is, one of the goals must be declared the producer of X and the other the consumer of X, and the consumer goal must not be allowed to bind X. Consider the (coinductive) lazy logic program for the sieve of Eratosthenes:

```
:- coinductive sieve/2, filter/3, member/2.
primes(X) :- generate_infinite_list(I), sieve(I,L), member(X, L).
sieve([H|T], [H|R]) :- filter(H,T,F), sieve(F,R).
filter(H,[],[]).
filter(H,[K|T],[K|T1]) :- R is K mod H, R > 0,filter(H,T,T1).
filter(H,[K|T],T1) :- 0 is K mod H, filter(H,T,T1).
```

In the above program `filter/3` removes all multiples of the first element in the list, and then passes the filtered list recursively to `sieve/2`. If the predicate `generate_infinite_list(I)` binds I to a rational list (e.g., X = [2, .., 20 | X], then filter can be `completely` processed in each call to `sieve/2`. However, in contrast, if I is bound to an irrational infinite list as in:

```
:- coinductive int/2.
int(X, [X|Y]) :- X1 is X+1, int(X1, Y).
generate_infinite_list(I) :- int(2,I).
```

then in the `primes/1` predicate, the calls `generate_infinite_list/1`, `sieve/2` and `member/2` should be co-routined, and, likewise, in the `sieve/2` predicate, the calls `filter/3` and the recursive call `sieve/2` must be coroutined.

Model Checking and Verification: Model checking is a popular technique used for verifying hardware and software systems. It works by constructing a model of the system defined in terms of a finite state Kripke structure and then determining if the model satisfies various properties specified as temporal logic formula. The verification is performed by means of systematically searching the state space of the Kripke structure for a counter-example that falsifies the given property. The vast majority of properties that are to be verified can be classified into *safety* properties and *liveness* properties. Intuitively, safety properties are those which assert that 'nothing bad will happen' while liveness properties are those that assert that 'something good will eventually happen.'

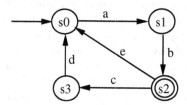

Fig. 1. Example Automata

An important application of coinductive LP is in directly representing and verifying properties of Kripke structures and ω-automata (automata that accept infinite strings). Just as automata that accept finite strings can be directly programmed using standard LP, automata that accept infinite strings can be directly represented using coinductive LP (one merely has to drop the base case). Consider the automata (over finite strings) shown in Figure 1 which is represented by the logic program below.

```
automata([X|T], St) :- trans(St, X, NewSt), automata(T, NewSt).
automata([], St) :- final(St).
trans(s0, a, s1).                    trans(s1, b, s2).
trans(s2, c, s3).                    trans(s3, d, s0).
trans(s2, e, s0).                    final(s2).
```

A call to | ?- automata(X, s0). in a standard LP system will generate all finite strings accepted by this automata. Now suppose we want to turn this automata into an ω-automata, i.e., it accepts infinite strings (an infinite string is accepted if states designated as final state are traversed infinite number of times), then the (coinductive) logic program that simulates this automata can be obtained by simply dropping the base case.[2]

```
automata([X|T], St) :- trans(St, X, NewSt), automata(T, NewSt).
```

Under coinductive semantics, posing the query | ?- automata(X, s0). will yield the solutions:

---

[2] We'll ignore the requirement that final-designated states occur infinitely often; this can be checked by introducing a coinductive definition of member/2 and checking that member(s2, X) holds for all accepting strings.

```
X = [a, b, c, d | X];
X = [a, b, e | X];
```

This feature of coinductive LP can be leveraged to directly verify liveness properties in model checking, multi-valued model checking, for modeling and verifying properties of timed ω-automata, checking for bisimilarity, etc.

Verifying Liveness Properties: It is well known that safety properties can be verified by reachability analysis, i.e, if a counter-example to the property exists, it can be finitely determined by enumerating all the reachable states of the Kripke structure. Verification of safety properties amounts to computing least fixed-points and thus is elegantly handled by standard LP systems extended with tabling [16]. Verification of liveness properties under such tabled LP systems is however problematic. This is because counterexamples to liveness properties take the form of infinite traces, which are semantically expressed as greatest fixed-points. Tabled LP systems [16] work around this problem by transforming the temporal formula denoting the property into a semantically equivalent least fixed-point formula, which can then be executed as a tabled logic program. This transformation is quite complex as it uses a sequence of nested negations.

In contrast, coinductive LP can be directly used to verify liveness properties. Liveness verification merely becomes the dual of safety verification. Coinductive LP can directly compute counterexamples using greatest fixed-point temporal formulae without requiring any transformation. Intuitively, a state is not live if it can be reached via an infinite loop (cycle). Liveness counterexamples can be found by (coinductively) enumerating all possible states that can be reached via infinite loops and then by determining if any of these states constitutes a valid counterexample.

This direct approach to verifying liveness properties also applies to *multi-valued model checking* of the μ-calculus [13]. Coinductive LP can also be used to check for *bisimilarity*. Bisimilarity is reduced to coinductively checking if two ω-automata accept the same set of rational infinite strings. We do not give details due to lack of space.

Verifying Properties of Timed Automata: Timed automata are simple extensions of ω-automata with stopwatches, and are easily modeled as coinductive logic programs with CLP(R) [6]. Timed automata can be modeled with coinductive logic programs together with constraints over reals for modeling clock constraints. The system can be queried to enumerate all the infinite strings that will be accepted by the automata and that meet the time constraints. Safety and liveness properties can be checked by negating those properties, and checking that they fail for each string accepted by the automata with the help of coinductively defined member/2, append/3 predicates (similar to [6]; see [20]).

6   Conclusions and Future Work

In this paper we presented a comprehensive theory of coinductive LP, demonstrated its practical applications as well as reported on its preliminary implementation on top of YAP Prolog. Current work involves obtaining an implementation of full coinductive LP that works both for infinite outputs as well as infinite inputs. Current work [19] also involves extending coinductive logic programming to allow for finite derivations in the presence of irrational terms and proofs, that is, infinite terms and proofs that do not have finitely many distinct subtrees. Our current approach is to allow the programmer to annotate predicate definitions with pragmas, which can be used to decide at run-time when a semantic cycle in the proof search has occurred, however, in the future we intend to infer these annotations by using static analysis.

Acknowledgments. We are grateful to Vítor Santos Costa and Richardo Rocha for help with YAP, and Srividya Kona for comments.

References

1. K. R. Apt. Logic programming. Ch. 15. Handbook of Theoretical Computer Science, 493-574. MIT Press, 1990.
2. J. Barwise, L. Moss. *Vicious Circles: On the Mathematics of Non-Wellfounded Phenomena.* CSLI Publications, 1996.
3. A. Colmerauer. Equations and inequations on finite and infinite trees. In *Proc. FGCS-84*: pages 85–99, Tokyo, 1984.
4. B. Courcelle. Fundamental properties of infinite trees. *TCS*, pp:95–212, 1983.
5. G. Gupta. Verifying Properties of Cyclic Data-structures with Tabled Unification. Internal Memo. New Mexico State University. February 2000.
6. G. Gupta, E. Pontelli. Constraint-based Specification and Verification of Real-time Systems. In *Proc. IEEE Real-time Symposium '97.* pp. 230-239.
7. G. Gupta. Next Generation of Logic Programming Systems. Technical Report UTD-42-03, University of Texas, Dallas. 2003.
8. M. Hanus. Integration of functions into LP. *J. Logic Prog.*, 19 & 20:583–628, 1994.
9. J. Jaffar, A. E. Santosa, R. Voicu. A CLP proof method for timed automata. In *RTSS*, pages 175–186, 2004.
10. J. Jaffar, P. J. Stuckey. Semantics of infinite tree LP. *TCS*, 46(2–3):141–158, 1986.
11. M. Jaume. Logic Programming and Co-inductive Definitions CSL, 2000.
12. J.W. Lloyd. *Foundations of LP.* Springer, 2nd. edition, 1987.
13. A. Mallya. Deductive Multi-valued Model Checking, ICLP'05, Springer LNCS 3368. pp. 297-310.
14. M. A. Nait-Abdallah. On the Interpretation of Infinite Computations in Logic Programming *Proc. ICALP 1984.* pp. 358-370.
15. B. Pierce. *Types and Programming Languages.* MIT Press, Cambridge, MA, 2002.
16. Y. Ramakrishna, C. R. Ramakrishnan, I. V. Ramakrishnan, D. S. Warren, et al. Efficient Model Checking Using Tabled Resolution. *CAV 1997.* pp. 143-154.
17. R. Rocha, F. Silva, V. S. Costa Theory and Practice of Logic Programming 5(1-2). 161-205 (2005) Tabling Engine That Can Exploit Or-Parallelism. ICLP 2001: 43-58
18. L. Simon. Coinductive LP. Internal memo, UT Dallas, March 2004.
19. L. Simon, A. Mallya, A. Bansal, and G. Gupta. Co-Logic Programming: Extending Logic Programming with Coinduction. Tech. Report, UT Dallas, UTDCS-21-06.
20. L. Simon, A. Mallya, A. Bansal, and G. Gupta. Coinductive Logic Programming. Technical Report, UT Dallas, UTDCS-11-06, Mar 2006.

Analysing and Extending Well-Founded and Partial Stable Semantics Using Partial Equilibrium Logic

Pedro Cabalar[1], Sergei Odintsov[2], David Pearce[3], and Agustín Valverde[4],[*]

[1] Corunna University, Corunna, Spain
cabalar@udc.es
[2] Sobolev Institute of Mathematics, Novosibirsk, Russia
odintsov@math.nsc.ru
[3] Universidad Rey Juan Carlos, Madrid, Spain
davidandrew.pearce@urjc.es
[4] University of Málaga, Málaga, Spain
a_valverde@ctima.uma.es

Abstract. In [4] a nonmonotonic formalism called *partial equilibrium logic* (PEL) was proposed as a logical foundation for the well-founded semantics (WFS) of logic programs. PEL consists in defining a class of minimal models, called *partial equilibrium* (p-equilibrium), inside a non-classical logic called HT^2. In [4] it was shown that, on normal logic programs, p-equilibrium models coincide with Przymusinki's partial stable (p-stable) models. This paper begins showing that this coincidence still holds for the more general class of disjunctive programs, so that PEL can be seen as a way to extend WFS and p-stable semantics to arbitrary propositional theories. We also study here the problem of strong equivalence for various subclasses of p-equilibrium models, investigate transformation rules and nonmonotonic inference, and consider a reduction of PEL to equilibrium logic. In addition we examine the behaviour of PEL on nested logic programs and its complexity in the general case.

1 Introduction

Of the various proposals for dealing with default negation in logic programming the *well-founded semantics* (WFS) of Van Gelder, Ross and Schlipf [20] has proved to be one of the most attractive and resilient. Particularly its favourable computational properties have made it popular among system developers and the well-known implementation XSB-Prolog[1] is now extensively used in AI problem solving and applications in knowledge representation and reasoning.

Closely related to WFS is the semantics of *partial stable models* due to Przymusinski [15]. Partial stable (henceforth p-stable) models provide a natural generalisation of stable models [8] to a multi-valued setting and on normal logic

---

[*] This research was partially supported by CICyT project TIC-2003-9001-C02.

[1] See http://www.cs.sunysb.edu/~sbprolog/xsb-page.html

S. Etalle and M. Truszczyński (Eds.): ICLP 2006, LNCS 4079, pp. 346–360, 2006.

programs capture the well-founded model as a special (minimal model) case. Although the newly developing area of *answer set programming* (ASP) has focused mainly on (2-valued) stable models, there has also been a steady stream of interest in the characterisation and computation of p-stable models, eg [17,18,6,7,9].

Recently [4] proposed a solution to the following long-standing problem in the foundations of WFS: which (non-modal) logic can be considered adequate for WFS in the sense that its minimal models (appropriately defined) coincide with the p-stable models of a logic program? This problem is tackled in a similar spirit to the way in which the so-called logic of *here-and-there*, *HT*, has been used to capture ordinary stable models and led to the development of a general nonmonotonic formalism called *equilibrium logic*, [13]. While 2-valued stable models can be characterised using the 3-valued Kripke frames of *HT*, for p-stable models one requires a more complex notion of frame of a kind studied by Routley [16]. These are generalisations of *HT* frames, referred to as HT^2 frames, and characterised by a 6-valued logic, whose negation is different from that of intuitionistic and minimal logic. To capture p-stable models in this setting a suitable notion of minimal, total HT^2 model is defined, which for obvious reasons can be called *partial equilibrium (p-equilibrium) model*. On normal logic programs, these models were shown [4] to coincide with p-stable models and so the resulting *partial equilibrium logic* (PEL) was proposed as a logical foundation for WFS and p-stable semantics. In addition [4] axiomatises the logic of HT^2-models and proves that it captures the strong equivalence of theories PEL.

The aim of the present paper is to extend the work of [4] beyond the area of normal programs treated previously. In particular we examine the case of disjunctive logic programs and show that also here p-equilibrium models coincide with p-stable models. Thus PEL can be seen also as yielding a suitable foundation for p-stable semantics and as a natural means to extend it beyond the syntax of disjunctive programs, eg to so-called nested logic programs or to arbitrary propositional theories. In summary, we shall treat the following topics. §2 describes the basic logic, HT^2, and defines partial equilibrium models. We review the main results of [4] and show that PEL captures p-stable semantics for disjunctive programs. In §3 we extend previous results on the strong equivalence of theories to special subclasses of models: the well-founded models defined in [4] and the classes of L-stable and M-stable models studied in [7]. §4 looks briefly at some of the general properties of PEL as a nonmonotonic inference relation, while §5 considers syntactic transformations of disjunctive programs, distinguishing between those preserving equivalence and those preserving strong equivalence. §6 considers the transformation technique of [9] that captures p-stable models via stable models and extends this method to PEL in general. §7 studies the behaviour of nested logic programs under PEL and some valid unfolding techniques. Finally, §8 studies the main complexity classes for PEL over propositional theories, showing that complexity is the same as that of p-stable semantics for disjunctive programs [7], while §9 concludes the paper with some open problems for future study.

2   Logical Preliminaries: The Logics HT^2 and PEL

We introduce the logic HT^2 and its semantics, given in terms of HT^2 *frames*, and we define *partial equilibrium logic* (PEL) in terms of minimal HT^2 models. Formulas of HT^2 are built-up in the usual way using atoms from a given propositional signature At and the standard logical constants: $\land, \lor, \to, \neg$. A set of HT^2 formulae is called a *theory*. The axiomatic system for HT^2 is described in two stages. In the first stage we include the following inference rules:

$$\frac{\alpha,\ \alpha \to \beta}{\beta} \text{ (Modus Ponens)} \qquad \frac{\alpha \to \beta}{\neg\beta \to \neg\alpha}$$

plus the axiom schemata of *positive logic* together with:

A1. $\neg\alpha \land \neg\beta \to \neg(\alpha \lor \beta)$ A2. $\neg(\alpha \to \alpha) \to \beta$ A3. $\neg(\alpha \land \beta) \to \neg\alpha \lor \neg\beta$

Thus, both De Morgan laws are provable in HT^2. Moreover, axiom A2 allows us to define intuitionistic negation, '$-$', in HT^2 as: $-\alpha := \alpha \to \neg(p_0 \to p_0)$. In a second stage, we further include the rule $\frac{\alpha \lor (\beta \land \neg\beta)}{\alpha}$ and the axioms schemata:

A4. $-\alpha \lor -{-}\alpha$
A5. $-\alpha \lor (\alpha \to (\beta \lor (\beta \to (\gamma \lor -\gamma))))$
A6. $\bigwedge_{i=0}^{2}((\alpha_i \to \bigvee_{j\neq i}\alpha_j) \to \bigvee_{j\neq i}\alpha_j) \to \bigvee_{i=0}^{2}\alpha_i$
A7. $\alpha \to \neg\neg\alpha$
A8. $\alpha \land \neg\alpha \to \neg\beta \lor \neg\neg\beta$
A9. $\neg\alpha \land \neg(\alpha \to \beta) \to \neg\neg\alpha$
A10. $\neg\neg\alpha \lor \neg\neg\beta \lor \neg(\alpha \to \beta) \lor \neg\neg(\alpha \to \beta)$
A11. $\neg\neg\alpha \land \neg\neg\beta \to (\alpha \to \beta) \lor (\beta \to \alpha)$

HT^2 is determined by the above inference rules and the schemata A1-A11.

Definition 1. *A (Routley) frame is a triple $\langle W, \leq, * \rangle$, where W is a set, $\leq$ a partial order on W and $* : W \to W$ is such that $x \leq y$ iff $y^* \leq x^*$. A (Routley) model is a Routley frame together with a valuation V ie. a function from $At \times W \longrightarrow \{0, 1\}$ satisfying:*

$$V(p, u) = 1\ \&\ u \leq w \ \Rightarrow\ V(p, w) = 1 \tag{1}$$

The valuation V is extended to all formulas via the usual rules for intuitionistic (Kripke) frames for the positive connectives $\land, \lor, \to$ where the latter is interpreted via the $\leq$ order:

$$V(\varphi \to \psi, w) = 1 \text{ iff for all } w' \text{ such that } w \leq w', \ \ V(\varphi, w') = 1 \Rightarrow V(\psi, w') = 1$$

The main difference with respect to intuitionistic frames is the presence of the $*$ operator that is used for interpreting negation via the following condition:

$$V(\neg\varphi, w) = 1 \text{ iff } V(\varphi, w^*) = 0.$$

A proposition φ is said to be *true* in a model $\mathcal{M} = \langle W, \leq, *, V \rangle$, if $V(\varphi, v) = 1$, for all $v \in W$. A formula φ is *valid*, in symbols $\models \varphi$, if it is true in every model. It is easy to prove by induction that condition (1) above holds for any formula φ, ie

$$V(\varphi, u) = 1 \ \& \ u \leq w \Rightarrow V(\varphi, w) = 1. \tag{2}$$

Definition 2 (*HT^2 model*). *An HT^2 model is a Routley model $\mathcal{M} = \langle W, \leq, R, V \rangle$ such that (i) W comprises 4 worlds denoted by h, h', t, t', (ii) $\leq$ is a partial ordering on W satisfying $h \leq t$, $h \leq h'$, $h' \leq t'$ and $t \leq t'$, (iii) the $*$ operation is determined by $h^* = t^* = t'$, $(h')^* = (t')^* = t$, (iv) V is a-valuation.*

The diagram on the right depicts the $\leq$-ordering among worlds (a strictly higher location means $\geq$) and the action of the $*$-mapping using arrows:

Truth and validity for HT^2 models are defined analogously to the previous case and from now on we let $\models$ denote the truth (validity) relation for HT^2 models. One of the main results of [4] is the following completeness theorem[2]:

Theorem 1 ([4]). *HT^2 is complete for HT^2 models, ie $\models \varphi$ iff φ is a theorem of HT^2.*

2.1 Minimal Models and Relation to Logic Programs

Now, consider an HT^2 model $\mathcal{M} = \langle W, \leq, ^*, V \rangle$ and let us denote by H, H', T, T' the four sets of atoms respectively verified at each corresponding point or world h, h', t, t'. More succinctly, we can represent $\mathcal{M}$ as the pair $\langle \mathbf{H}, \mathbf{T} \rangle$ so that we group each pair of unprimed/primed worlds as $\mathbf{H} = (H, H')$ and $\mathbf{T} = (T, T')$. Notice that $H \subseteq H'$ and $T \subseteq T'$ by construction of $\mathcal{M}$ and, as a result, both $\mathbf{H}$ and $\mathbf{T}$ can be seen as 3-valued interpretations. Although the representation as a (consistent) set of literals is perhaps more frequent in the logic programming literature, a 3-valued interpretation $\mathbf{I}$ can be alternatively described by a pair of sets of atoms $I \subseteq I'$ with I containing the true atoms and I' the non-false ones. Let us use the set $\{0, 1, 2\}$ to respectively denote the possible values of atom p: *false* ($p \notin I'$), *undefined* ($p \in I' \setminus I$) and *true* ($p \in I$). As we have two 3-valued interpretations $\langle \mathbf{H}, \mathbf{T} \rangle$ we could define the possible "situations" of a formula in HT^2 by using a pair of values xy with $x, y \in \{0, 1, 2\}$. Condition (2) restricts the number of these situations to the following six $00 := \emptyset$, $01 := \{t'\}$, $11 := \{h', t'\}$, $02 := \{t, t'\}$, $12 := \{h', t, t'\}$, $22 := W$ where each set shows the worlds at which the formula is satisfied. Thus, an alternative way of describing HT^2 is by providing its logical matrix (see [4]) in terms of a 6-valued logic.

The truth-ordering relation among 3-valued interpretations $\mathbf{I}_1 \leq \mathbf{I}_2$ is defined so that $\mathbf{I}_1$ contains less true atoms and more false ones (wrt set inclusion) than $\mathbf{I}_2$. Note that by the semantics, if $\langle \mathbf{H}, \mathbf{T} \rangle$ is a model then necessarily $\mathbf{H} \leq \mathbf{T}$,

---

[2] The first stage alone defines a logic complete for the general Routley frames.

since it is easy to check that this condition is equivalent to $H \subseteq T$ and $H' \subseteq T'$. Moreover, for any theory Π note that if $\langle \mathbf{H}, \mathbf{T} \rangle \models \Pi$ then also $\langle \mathbf{T}, \mathbf{T} \rangle \models \Pi$.

The ordering $\leq$ is extended to a partial ordering $\trianglelefteq$ among models as follows. We set $\langle \mathbf{H_1}, \mathbf{T_1} \rangle \trianglelefteq \langle \mathbf{H_2}, \mathbf{T_2} \rangle$ if (i) $\mathbf{T_1} = \mathbf{T_2}$; (ii) $\mathbf{H_1} \leq \mathbf{H_2}$. A model $\langle \mathbf{H}, \mathbf{T} \rangle$ in which $\mathbf{H} = \mathbf{T}$ is said to be *total*. Note that the term *total* model does not refer to the absence of undefined atoms. To represent this, we further say that a total partial equilibrium model is *complete* if $\mathbf{T}$ has the form (T, T).

We are interested here in a special kind of minimal model that we call a partial equilibrium (or p-equilibrium) model. Let Π be a theory.

Definition 3 (Partial equilibrium model). *A model $\mathcal{M}$ of Π is said to be a* partial equilibrium *model of Π if (i) $\mathcal{M}$ is total; (ii) $\mathcal{M}$ is minimal among models of Π under the ordering $\trianglelefteq$.*

In other words a p-equilibrium model of Π has the form $\langle \mathbf{T}, \mathbf{T} \rangle$ and is such that if $\langle \mathbf{H}, \mathbf{T} \rangle$ is any model of Π with $\mathbf{H} \leq \mathbf{T}$, then $\mathbf{H} = \mathbf{T}$. *Partial equilibrium logic* (PEL) is the logic determined by truth in all p-equilibrium models of a theory. Formally we can define a nonmonotonic relation of PEL-inference as follows.

Definition 4 (entailment). *Let Π be a theory, φ a formula and $\mathcal{PEM}(\Pi)$ the collection of all p-equilibrium models of Π. We say that Π entails φ in PEL, in symbols $\Pi \hspace{1pt}\vdash\hspace{-6pt}\sim\hspace{2pt} \varphi$, if either (i) or (ii) holds: (i) $\mathcal{PEM}(\Pi) \neq \emptyset$ and $\mathcal{M} \models \varphi$ for every $\mathcal{M} \in \mathcal{PEM}(\Pi)$; (ii) $\mathcal{PEM}(\Pi) = \emptyset$ and φ is true in all HT^2-models of Π.*

In this definition, therefore, we consider the skeptical or cautious entailment relation; a credulous variant is easily given if needed. Clause (ii) is needed since, as Theorem 2 below makes clear, not all consistent theories have p-equilibrium models. Again (ii) represents one possible route to understanding entailment in the absence of intended models; other possibilities may be considered depending on context.

We turn to the relation between PEL and logic programs. A *disjunctive logic program* is a set of formulas (also called *rules*) of the form

$$a_1 \wedge \ldots \wedge a_m \wedge \neg b_1 \wedge \ldots \wedge \neg b_n \rightarrow c_1 \vee \ldots \vee c_k \qquad (3)$$

where $m, n, k \geq 0$. For simplicity, given any rule r like (3) above, we will frequently use the names $B^+(r), B^-(r)$ and $Hd(r)$ to denote the corresponding sets $\{a_1, \ldots, a_m\}$, $\{b_1, \ldots, b_n\}$ and $\{c_1, \ldots, c_k\}$, respectively. By abuse of notation, we will also understand $B^+(r)$ as the conjunction of its atoms, whereas $B^-(r)$ and $Hd(r)$ are understood as the respective disjunctions of their atoms (remember de Morgan laws hold for negation). As usual, an empty disjunction (resp. conjunction) is understood as the constant $\bot$ (resp. $\top$). As a result, when r has the form (3) it can be represented more compactly as $B^+(r) \wedge \neg B^-(r) \rightarrow Hd(r)$. Additionally, the body of a rule r is defined as $B(r) := B^+(r) \wedge \neg B^-(r)$.

The definition of the p-stable models of a disjunctive logic program Π is given as follows. Given a 3-valued interpretation $\mathbf{I} = (I, I')$, Przymusinski's valuation[3]

---

[3] We have just directly adapted the original definitions to the current representation of 3-valued interpretations.

of formulas consists in interpreting conjunction as the minimum, disjunction as the maximum, and negation and implication as:

$$\mathbf{I}(\neg\varphi) := 2 - \mathbf{I}(\varphi) \qquad\qquad \mathbf{I}(\varphi \to \psi) := \begin{cases} 2 & \text{if } \mathbf{I}(\varphi) \le \mathbf{I}(\psi) \\ 0 & \text{otherwise} \end{cases}$$

The constants $\perp$, $\mathbf{u}$ and $\top$ are respectively valued as 0, 1 and 2. We say that $\mathbf{I}$ is a *3-valued model* of a formula φ, written $\mathbf{I} \models_3 \varphi$, when $\mathbf{I}(\varphi) = 2$. The *reduct* of a program Π wrt $\mathbf{I}$, denoted as $\Pi^{\mathbf{I}}$, consists in replacing each negative literal $\neg b$ in Π by the constant corresponding to $\mathbf{I}(\neg b)$. A 3-valued interpretation $\mathbf{I}$ is a *p-stable* model of Π if $\mathbf{I}$ is a $\le$ −minimal model of $\Pi^{\mathbf{I}}$.

By inspection of HT^2 and Przymusinski's interpretations of disjunctive rules it is relatively simple to check that:

Lemma 1. *For any disjunctive program Π and any HT^2 interpretation $\langle \mathbf{H}, \mathbf{T} \rangle$:* $\langle \mathbf{H}, \mathbf{T} \rangle \models \Pi$ *iff* $\mathbf{H} \models_3 \Pi^{\mathbf{T}}$ *and* $\mathbf{T} \models_3 \Pi^{\mathbf{T}}$.

Theorem 2. *A total HT^2 model $\langle \mathbf{T}, \mathbf{T} \rangle$ is a p-equilibrium model of a disjunctive[4] program Π iff the 3-valued interpretation $\mathbf{T}$ is a p-stable model of Π.*

Proof. Let $\langle \mathbf{T}, \mathbf{T} \rangle$ be a p-equilibrium model of Π. Suppose $\mathbf{T}$ is not p-stable. By Lemma 1, $\mathbf{T} \models \Pi^{\mathbf{T}}$, and so there must exist a smaller $\mathbf{H} < \mathbf{T}$ such that $\mathbf{H} \models_3 \Pi^{\mathbf{T}}$. But then $\langle \mathbf{H}, \mathbf{T} \rangle$ forms an HT^2 interpretation and, again by Lemma 1, $\langle \mathbf{H}, \mathbf{T} \rangle \models \Pi$, contradicting that $\langle \mathbf{T}, \mathbf{T} \rangle$ is in p-equilibrium. Now, let $\mathbf{T}$ be a p-stable model of Π. Then $\mathbf{T} \models \Pi^{\mathbf{T}}$ and is minimal. From Lemma 1 on $\langle \mathbf{T}, \mathbf{T} \rangle$ we conclude $\langle \mathbf{T}, \mathbf{T} \rangle \models \Pi$. Assume there exists a model $\langle \mathbf{H}, \mathbf{T} \rangle$ of Π such that $\mathbf{H} < \mathbf{T}$. By Lemma 1, $\mathbf{H} \models_3 \Pi^{\mathbf{T}}$ contradicting the minimality of $\mathbf{T}$. □

We define a further partial ordering on total models by $\langle \mathbf{T}_1, \mathbf{T}_1 \rangle \preceq \langle \mathbf{T}_2, \mathbf{T}_2 \rangle$ if both $T_1 \subseteq T_2$ and $T_2' \subseteq T_1'$. Then we say that a total HT^2 model that is $\preceq$-minimal among the p-equilibrium models of a theory Γ is a *well-founded model* of Γ. This terminology is justified by:

Theorem 3 ([4]). *If Π is a normal logic program, the unique $\preceq$-minimal p-equilibrium model of Π coincides with the well-founded model of Π in the sense of [20].*

3 Strong Equivalence of Theories wrt Different Classes of Partial Equilibrium Models

The notion of *strong equivalence* (SE) is important both conceptually and as a potential tool for simplifying nonmonotonic programs and theories and optimising their computation. For stable semantics strong equivalence can be completely captured in the logic HT [10] and in ASP this fact has given rise to a lively programme of research into defining and computing different equivalence concepts

---

[4] For normal programs the theorem is proved in [4].

[5,22]. In the case of WFS and p-stable semantics, however, until recently there have been no studies of strong equivalence and related notions.

Here we recall the main result of [4] on strong equivalence in PEL and then consider several special classes of models. Specifically, we look at strong equivalence wrt the class of well-founded models, defined above, and the classes of L-stable and M-stable models as described by [7]. Later on we shall see that, as in the case of stable and equilibrium models, the problem of checking SE in PEL is computationally simpler than that of checking ordinary equivalence.

In the present context we say that two propositional theories Γ_1 and Γ_2 are *equivalent*, in symbols $\Gamma_1 \equiv \Gamma_2$, if they have the same p-equilibrium models and *strongly equivalent*, in symbols $\Gamma_1 \equiv_s \Gamma_2$, if for any theory Γ, theories $\Gamma_1 \cup \Gamma$ and $\Gamma_2 \cup \Gamma$ have the same p-equilibrium models.

Theorem 4 ([4]). *Theories Γ_1 and Γ_2 are strongly equivalent iff Γ_1 and Γ_2 are equivalent as HT^2 theories.*

Recall that a total model $\langle \mathbf{T}, \mathbf{T} \rangle$ is a well-founded model of Γ if it is $\preceq$ minimal in the class of all p-equilibrium models of Γ.

Definition 5. *Two HT^2 theories Γ_1 and Γ_2 are WF equivalent if for any HT^2 theory Γ, each well founded model of $\Gamma_1 \cup \Gamma$ is a well founded model of $\Gamma_2 \cup \Gamma$ and vice versa.*

Theorem 5. *Theories Γ_1 and Γ_2 are WF equivalent iff Γ_1 and Γ_2 are equivalent as HT^2 theories.*

The 'if' direction is easy. For the non-trivial converse direction we use

Lemma 2. *If theories Γ_1 and Γ_2 have different classes of p-equilibrium models, then there is a theory Γ such that theories $\Gamma_1 \cup \Gamma$ and $\Gamma_2 \cup \Gamma$ have different classes of well founded models.* □

Corollary 1 (of Lemma 2). *For every HT^2 theory Γ, there is an extension Γ_1 having at least one well founded model.*

We then use Lemma 2 as follows. Assume that Γ_1 and Γ_2 are not equivalent as HT^2 theories. The latter means by Theorem 4 that there is a theory Γ such that $\Gamma_1 \cup \Gamma$ and $\Gamma_2 \cup \Gamma$ have different classes of p-equilibrium models. Now we can apply Lemma 2 to obtain a theory Γ' such that $\Gamma_1 \cup \Gamma \cup \Gamma'$ and $\Gamma_2 \cup \Gamma \cup \Gamma'$ have different classes of well founded models.

Some other classes of partial stable model different from $\preceq$ minimal stable models were considered in the literature. We define the corresponding classes of p-equilibrium models.

Definition 6. *Let Γ be an HT^2 theory and $\mathcal{M} = \langle \mathbf{T}, \mathbf{T} \rangle$ a p-equilibrium model of Γ. Then (i) $\mathcal{M}$ is said to be an M -equilibrium model of Γ if it is $\preceq$ maximal in the class of all p-equilibrium models of Γ; (ii) $\mathcal{M}$ is said to be an L -equilibrium model of Γ if for any p-equilibrium model $\langle \mathbf{T_1}, \mathbf{T_1} \rangle$ of Γ the inclusion $T_1' \setminus T_1 \subseteq T' \setminus T$ implies the equality $T_1' \setminus T_1 = T' \setminus T$.*

Since the difference $T' \setminus T$ is a measure of indefiniteness of a model $\langle \mathbf{T}, \mathbf{T} \rangle$, L-equilibrium models are minimal in the class of p-equilibrium models wrt indefiniteness. Taking into account the equivalence of p-equilibrium and p-stable models of disjunctive logic programs (see Theorem **??**) we immediately obtain

Proposition 1. *Let Π be a disjunctive logic program and $\langle \mathbf{T}, \mathbf{T} \rangle$ a model of Π. Then $\langle \mathbf{T}, \mathbf{T} \rangle$ is an M (L)-equilibrium model of Π iff $\mathbf{T}$ is an M (L)-stable model of Π in the sense of [7].*

For additional motivation for L-stable and M-stable models, see [7]. The latter for example coincide on normal programs with the regular models of [23].

Definition 7. *Two HT^2 theories Γ_1 and Γ_2 are M(L)-equivalent if for any HT^2 theory Γ, each M(L)-equilibrium model of $\Gamma_1 \cup \Gamma$ is an M(L)- equilibrium model of $\Gamma_2 \cup \Gamma$ and vice versa.*

Theorem 6. *Theories Γ_1 and Γ_2 are M(L)-equivalent iff Γ_1 and Γ_2 are equivalent as HT^2 theories.*

As before the proofs of these propositions rely on the following lemma:

Lemma 3. *If theories Γ_1 and Γ_2 have different classes of p-equilibrium models, then (i) there is a theory Γ such that theories $\Gamma_1 \cup \Gamma$ and $\Gamma_2 \cup \Gamma$ have different classes of M-equilibrium models; (ii) there is a theory Γ' such that theories $\Gamma_1 \cup \Gamma'$ and $\Gamma_2 \cup \Gamma'$ have different classes of L-equilibrium models.*

4   Some Properties of Partial Equilibrium Inference

We consider some of the properties of $\mathrel{\vnsim}$ as a nonmonotonic inference relation. Generally speaking the behaviour of PEL entailment is fairly similar to that of equilibrium logic or stable model inference; however $\mathrel{\vnsim}$ fails some properties preserved by stable inference. Consider the following properties of inference:

$$\varphi \in \Pi \Rightarrow \Pi \mathrel{\vnsim} \varphi \qquad \text{reflexivity}$$
$$\forall i \in I, \Pi \mathrel{\vnsim} \psi_i, \Pi \cup \{\psi_i : i \in I\} \mathrel{\vnsim} \varphi \Rightarrow \Pi \mathrel{\vnsim} \varphi \qquad \text{cut}$$
$$\Pi \mathrel{\vnsim} \varphi, \Pi \mathrel{\vnsim} \psi \Rightarrow \Pi \cup \varphi \mathrel{\vnsim} \psi \qquad \text{cautious monotony}$$
$$\Pi \cup \varphi \mathrel{\vnsim} \alpha, \Pi \cup \psi \mathrel{\vnsim} \alpha \Rightarrow \Pi \cup (\varphi \vee \psi) \mathrel{\vnsim} \alpha \qquad \text{disj. in antecedent}$$
$$\Pi \cup \varphi \mathrel{\vnsim} \alpha, \Pi \cup \neg\varphi \mathrel{\vnsim} \alpha \Rightarrow \Pi \mathrel{\vnsim} \alpha \qquad \text{truth by cases}$$
$$\Pi \cup \varphi \mathrel{\vnsim} \psi \Rightarrow \Pi \mathrel{\vnsim} \varphi \to \psi \qquad \text{conditionalisation}$$
$$\Pi \mathrel{\vnsim} \psi, \Pi \cup \varphi \mathrel{\not\vnsim} \psi \Rightarrow \Pi \mathrel{\vnsim} \neg\varphi \qquad \text{rationality}$$
$$\Pi \mathrel{\vnsim} \psi, \Pi \cup \varphi \mathrel{\vnsim} \neg\psi \Rightarrow \Pi \mathrel{\vnsim} \neg\varphi \qquad \text{weak rationality}$$
$$\Pi \mathrel{\vnsim} \varphi \to \psi, \Pi \mathrel{\vnsim} \neg\psi \Rightarrow \Pi \mathrel{\vnsim} \neg\varphi \qquad \text{modus tollens}$$

Proposition 2. *Partial equilibrium inference fails cautious monotony, truth by cases, conditionalisation, rationality and weak rationality.*

For the first condition we do however have a special case:

Proposition 3 (cautious monotony for negated formulas). *For any theory Γ, if $\Gamma \mathrel{\vnsim} \neg\varphi$ then Γ and $\Gamma \cup \{\neg\varphi\}$ have the same partial equilibrium models.*

Proposition 4. *Partial equilibrium inference satisfies reflexivity, cut, disjunction in the antecedent and modus tollens.*

5 Syntactic Transformation Rules for Disjunctive Programs

Following Brass and Dix [3], there has been considerable discussion of syntactic transformations rules that preserve the semantics of programs. For example it is well-known that while the disjunctive semantics D-WFS of [3] preserves the rule of unfolding or GPPE (see below), p-stable semantics does not. More recently [12,5] have studied for (2-valued) stable semantics the difference between transformation rules that lead to equivalent programs and those that lead to strongly equivalent (or even uniformly equivalent) programs. With the help of HT^2 and PEL, this distinction can also be made for p-stable (p-equilibrium) semantics over disjunctive programs, or for WFS over normal programs as a special case. We consider here the situation with respect to the principal rules considered in [5]. In table 2, equivalence and strong equivalence are denoted as before by by $\equiv$, $\equiv_s$. The rules themselves are summarised in Table 1. In addition to the rules normally studied for p-stable semantics, we consider also the weaker form of unfolding, WGPPE, discussed in [5] and the rule S-IMP of Wang and Zhou [21] whose meaning is explained below.

We first give an example to show that although p-stable semantics does not obey the GPPE rule, it is not actually weaker than D-WFS.

Example 1 (from [21]). Consider the program Π comprising two rules $\neg p \rightarrow b \vee l$ and $p \vee l$. Neither b nor $\neg b$ can be derived from Π under D-WFS and the STATIC semantics. The p-equilibrium models are $\langle \{l\}, \{l\} \rangle$ and $\langle \{p\}, \{p\} \rangle$ and so $\Pi \hspace{-0.3em}\mid\hspace{-0.9em}\sim \neg b$.

In fact, D-WFS just allows one to derive the minimal pure disjunction $l \vee p$, whereas p-equilibrium models further derive $\neg b$. So, in this example, PEL is *strictly stronger* than D-WFS. From this and the well-known behaviour of p-stable semantics wrt GPPE, we conclude the following.

Proposition 5. *D-WFS and PEL are not comparable (even when restricted to pure disjunctions).*

Proposition 6. *Transformation WGPPE preserves strong equivalence, $\equiv_s$. In fact:* $\{(p \wedge A \rightarrow B), (C \rightarrow p \vee D)\} \vdash A \wedge C \rightarrow B \vee D$.

We turn now to the rule S-IMP, due to [21] and discussed in [5]. As in the case of NONMIN this is a kind of subsumption rule allowing one to eliminate a rule that is less specific than another rule belonging to the program. By definition, r stands in the S-IMP relation to r', in symbols $r \lhd r'$, iff there exists a set $A \subseteq B^-(r')$ such that (i) $Hd(r) \subseteq Hd(r') \cup A$; (ii) $B^-(r) \subseteq B^-(r') \backslash A$; (iii) $B^+(r) \subseteq B^+(r')$. For stable or equilibrium inference S-IMP is a valid rule, even preserving strong equivalence [5]. This is not so for PEL. Another rule, CONTRA, valid for stable inference, also fails in PEL.

Table 1. Syntactic transformation rules from [5].

Name	Condition	Transformation
TAUT	$Hd(r) \cap B^+(r) \neq \emptyset$	$P' = P \setminus \{r\}$
RED$^+$	$a \in B^-(r_1)$, $\not\exists r_2 \in P : a \in Hd(r_2)$	$P' = P \setminus \{r_1\} \cup \{r'\}^\dagger$
RED$^-$	$Hd(r_2) \subseteq B^-(r_1)$, $B(r_2) = \emptyset$	$P' = P \setminus \{r_1\}$
NONMIN	$Hd(r_2) \subseteq Hd(r_1)$, $B(r_2) \subseteq B(r_1)$	$P' = P \setminus \{r_1\}$
GPPE	$a \in B^+(r_1)$, $G_a \neq \emptyset$, for $G_a = \{r_2 \in P \mid a \in Hd(r_2)\}$	$P' = P \setminus \{r_1\} \cup G_a'^\ddagger$
WGPPE	same condition as for GPPE	$P' = P \cup G_a'^\ddagger$
CONTRA	$B^+(r) \cap B^-(r) \neq \emptyset$	$P' = P \setminus \{r\}$
S-IMP	$r, r' \in P$, $r \lhd r'$	$P' = P \setminus \{r'\}$

† $r' : Hd(r_1) \leftarrow B^+(r_1) \cup not\,(B^-(r_1) \setminus \{a\})$.
‡ $G_a' = \{Hd(r_1) \cup (Hd(r_2) \setminus \{a\}) \leftarrow (B^+(r_1) \setminus \{a\}) \cup not\,B^-(r_1) \cup B(r_2) \mid r_2 \in G_a\}$.

Table 2. Syntactic transformations preserving equivalence

Eq.	TAUT	RED$^+$	RED$^-$	NONMIN	GPPE	WGPPE	CONTRA	S-IMP
$\equiv$	yes	yes	yes	yes	no	yes	no	no
$\equiv_s$	yes	no	yes	yes	no	yes	no	no

Proposition 7. *The rules S-IMP and CONTRA are not sound for p-stable (p-equilibrium) inference.*

6 Translating Partiality by Atoms Replication

A promising approach to implementating p-stable models for disjunctive programs has been developed by Janhunen *et al* [9]. They provide a method to capture p-stable models by (2-valued) stable models using a linear-time transformation of the program. We show here that their transformation can be extended to arbitrary propositional theories such that PEL can be reduced to ordinary equilibrium logic. Furthermore it provides an encoding of the underlying logics, of HT^2 into HT. This offers the possibility to check strong equivalence of arbitrary PEL theories by applying first this transformation, and using afterwards a satisfiability checker for arbitrary HT theories like [19].

The translation of a theory Γ, denoted $Tr(\Gamma)$, consists of a formula $p \to p'$ where p' is a new atom per each atom p occurring in Γ plus, for each $\alpha \in \Gamma$, the formula $[\alpha]$ recursively defined as follows:

$$[\varphi \to \psi] := \big([\varphi] \to [\psi]\big) \wedge [\varphi \to \psi]' \qquad [\varphi \to \psi]' := [\varphi]' \to [\psi]'$$
$$[\neg\varphi] := \neg\,[\varphi]' \qquad\qquad\qquad [\neg\varphi]' := \neg\,[\varphi]$$
$$[\varphi \oplus \psi] := [\varphi] \oplus [\psi] \qquad\qquad [\varphi \oplus \psi]' := [\varphi]' \oplus [\psi]'$$
$$[p] := p \qquad\qquad\qquad\qquad [p]' := p'$$
$$[\epsilon] := \epsilon \qquad\qquad\qquad\qquad [\epsilon]' := \epsilon$$

where $\oplus \in \{\wedge, \vee\}$ and $\epsilon \in \{\top, \bot\}$.

Example 2. The translation $\varphi = \neg(a \to \neg b) \to c$ consists of the formulas $a \to a'$, $b \to b'$, $c \to c'$ and $\neg(a' \to \neg b) \to c) \wedge (\neg((a \to \neg b') \wedge (a' \to \neg b)) \to c'$. □

It is quite easy to see that for any disjunctive rule r like (3), its translation $[r]$ has the form $(a_1 \wedge \ldots \wedge a_m \wedge \neg b'_1 \wedge \ldots \wedge \neg b'_n \to c_1 \vee \ldots \vee c_k) \wedge$ $(a'_1 \wedge \ldots \wedge a'_m \wedge \neg b_1 \wedge \ldots \wedge \neg b_n \to c'_1 \vee \ldots \vee c'_k)$ so that $Tr(\Pi)$ amounts to Janhunen et al's transformation [9] when Π is a disjunctive logic program.

We prove next that the present generalisation of Janhunen et al's transformation works not only for representing PEL into equilibrium logic, but is actually correct at the monotonic level, i.e., it allows encoding HT^2 into HT. Let us extend first the $[\cdot]'$ notation to any set of atoms S so that $[S]' := \{p' \mid p \in S\}$.

Proposition 8. *An HT^2 interpretation $\mathcal{M}_1 = \langle(H, H'), (T, T')\rangle$ is an HT^2 model of Γ iff $\mathcal{M}_2 = \langle H \cup [H']', T \cup [T']'\rangle$ is an HT model of $Tr(\Gamma)$.*

Proposition 9. *A total HT^2 interpretation $\langle(T, T'), (T, T')\rangle$ is a partial equilibrium model of Γ iff $\langle T \cup [T']', T \cup [T']'\rangle$ is an equilibrium model of $Tr(\Gamma)$.*

7   Nested Logic Programs

The term *nested logic program* refers to the possibility of nesting default negation, conjunction and disjunction, both in the heads and bodies of the program rules. At least in what refers to rule bodies, this feature is, in fact, quite common in most Prolog interpreters, including XSB which relies on well-founded semantics. In this way, for instance, a possible XSB piece of code could look like a :- \+ (b; c, \+ (d, \+ e)) or using logical notation:

$$\neg(b \vee c \wedge \neg(d \wedge \neg e)) \to a \qquad (4)$$

The semantics for nested expressions under stable models was first described in [11]. In that paper, it was also shown that nested expressions can actually be unfolded until obtaining a non-nested program (allowing negation and disjunction in the head) by applying the following HT-valid equivalences:

(i) $F \wedge G \leftrightarrow G \wedge F$ and $F \vee G \leftrightarrow G \vee F$.
(ii) $(F \wedge G) \wedge H \leftrightarrow F \wedge (G \wedge H)$ and $(F \vee G) \vee H \leftrightarrow F \vee (G \vee H)$.
(iii) $F \wedge (G \vee H) \leftrightarrow (F \wedge G) \vee (F \wedge H)$ and $F \vee (G \wedge H) \leftrightarrow (F \vee G) \wedge (F \vee H)$.
(iv) $\neg(F \vee G) \leftrightarrow \neg F \wedge \neg G$ and $\neg(F \wedge G) \leftrightarrow \neg F \vee \neg G$.
(v) $\neg\neg\neg F \leftrightarrow \neg F$.
(vi) $F \wedge \top \leftrightarrow F$ and $F \vee \top \leftrightarrow \top$.
(vii) $F \wedge \bot \leftrightarrow \bot$ and $F \vee \bot \leftrightarrow F$.
(viii) $\neg\top \leftrightarrow \bot$ and $\neg\bot \leftrightarrow \top$.
(ix) $(F \wedge G \leftarrow H) \leftrightarrow (F \leftarrow H) \wedge (G \leftarrow H)$.
(x) $(F \leftarrow G \vee H) \leftrightarrow (F \leftarrow G) \wedge (F \leftarrow H)$.
(xi) $(F \leftarrow G \wedge \neg\neg H) \leftrightarrow (F \vee \neg H \leftarrow G)$.
(xii) $(F \vee \neg\neg G \leftarrow H) \leftrightarrow (F \leftarrow \neg G \wedge H)$.

Proposition 10. *The formulas (i)-(x) are valid in HT^2.*

Transformations (xi) and (xii), however, are not valid in HT^2. As a result the occurrence of double negation cannot be reduced in the general case to a disjunctive logic program format as shown by:

Proposition 11. *The theory $\{\neg\neg p \to p\}$ is not HT^2-equivalent to any disjunctive logic program Π (even allowing negation in the head) for signature $\{p\}$.*

One might object that this behaviour is peculiar to HT^2 and not the expected one for a well-founded semantics for nested expressions. Consider, however, the following example due to V. Lifschitz. Take the programs $\Pi_1 = \{\neg\neg p \to p\}$ and $\Pi_2 = \{p \vee \neg p\}$ which, by (xi) are HT-equivalent. Intuitively, if we could not use double negation or negation in the head, we could replace $\neg p$ by an auxiliary atom $\bar{p}$ and "define" this atom with a rule like $\bar{p} \leftarrow \neg p$. As a result, Π_1 would become $\Pi_1' = \{(\neg\bar{p} \to p), (\neg p \to \bar{p})\}$ whereas Π_2 would be now $\Pi_2' = \{(p \vee \bar{p}), (\neg p \to \bar{p})\}$. The normal program Π_1' is a typical example where p and $\bar{p}$ should become undefined in WFS. On the other hand, for Π_2' one would expect two complete models, one with p true and $\bar{p}$ false, and the symmetric one. If we remove the auxiliary atom, these two different behaviours agree, in fact, with the results in PEL for Π_1 and Π_2.

Although Proposition 11 observes that we cannot generally get rid of double negation without extending the signature, we show next that the auxiliary atom technique used in the example is in fact general enough for dealing with double negation in rule bodies, and so, thanks to transformations (i)-(x), provides a method for unfolding bodies with nested expressions.

A *disjunctive logic program with double negation* is a set of rules of the form:

$$a_1 \wedge \cdots \wedge a_n \wedge \neg b_1 \wedge \cdots \wedge \neg b_m \wedge \neg\neg c_1 \wedge \cdots \wedge \neg\neg c_s \to d_1 \vee \cdots \vee d_t \quad (5)$$

with $m, n, s, t \geq 0$. We extend the previously defined notation so that, given a rule r like (5) $B^{--}(r)$ denotes the set of atoms $\{c_1, \ldots, c_s\}$ or, when understood as a formula, their conjunction.

Proposition 12. *Let Π be a disjunctive logic program with double negation for alphabet V. We define the disjunctive program Π' consisting of a rule*

$$\neg c \to \bar{c} \quad (6)$$

for each double-negated literal $\neg\neg c$ occurring in Π, where $\bar{c}$ is a new atom, plus a rule r' for each rule $r \in \Pi$ where: $B^+(r') := B^+(r)$, $B^-(r') := B^-(r) \cup \{\bar{c} \mid c \in B^{--}(r)\}$ and $Hd(r') := Hd(r)$. Then Π and Π' are strongly equivalent modulo the original alphabet At, that is, $\Pi \cup \Gamma$ and $\Pi' \cup \Gamma$ have the same partial equilibrium models for any theory Γ for alphabet At. $\qquad \square$

Example 3. Take the program consisting of rule (4). Applying transformations (i)-(x) we get that it is strongly equivalent to the pair of rules $\neg b \wedge \neg c \to a$ and $\neg b \wedge \neg\neg d \wedge \neg e \to a$ which by Proposition 12 are strongly equivalent to

$$\neg d \to \bar{d} \qquad \neg b \wedge \neg c \to a \qquad \neg b \wedge \neg\bar{d} \wedge \neg e \to a$$

modulo the original alphabet.

8   Complexity Results for HT^2 and PEL

We denote by SAT_{CL} and VAL_{CL} the classes of satisfiable formulas and valid formulas respectively in Classical Logic, and SAT_{HT^2} and VAL_{HT^2} the classes of satisfiable formulas and valid formulas respectively in HT^2 logic.

Theorem 7. SAT_{HT^2} *is NP-complete and* VAL_{HT^2} *is coNP-complete.*

For finite-valued logics it is straightforward that the satisfiability and validity problems are at most NP-hard and coNP-hard respectively. Let φ be a formula over $\{\neg, \rightarrow, \wedge, \vee\}$ and consider the formula φ' obtained by replacing every variable p in φ by $\neg(p \rightarrow \neg p)$. The formula φ' has the following properties: every HT^2-assignment, V, verifies that $V(\varphi) \in \{00, 22\}$; if φ is satisfiable, then it has a model satisfying $V(p) \in \{00, 22\}$ for every variable p in φ'; if $W(\varphi) = 00$ for some assignment W, then there exists an assignment V such that $V(\varphi) = 00$ and $V(p) \in \{00, 22\}$ for every variable p in φ'. Finally, we have also: $\varphi \in SAT_{CL}$ if and only if $\varphi' \in SAT_{HT^2}$ and $\varphi \notin VAL_{CL}$ if and only if $\varphi' \notin VAL_{HT^2}$. Thus, the polynomial transformation of φ in φ' reduce the satisfiability and validity in classical logic to the corresponding problems in HT^2 and therefore SAT_{HT^2} is NP-complete and VAL_{HT^2} is coNP-complete.

Corollary 2. *The problem of checking the strong equivalence of theories is coNP-complete.*

Theorem 8. *The problem of deciding whether a formula in HT^2 has partial equilibrium models, partial equilibrium consistency, is Σ_2^P-hard.*

It is straightforward from the finite-valued semantics of HT^2 that the complexity is at most Σ_2^P. To prove that the complexity is in fact Σ_2^P we use that the equilibrium consistency is Σ_2^P-hard. Given a formula φ in HT, we define

$$\varphi' = \varphi \wedge \bigwedge_{p \text{ occurs in } \varphi} (\neg p \vee \neg\neg p)$$

The formula φ' has the following properties: any HT^2-model of φ', V, verifies $V(p) \in \{00, 02, 12, 22\}$ for every variable p in φ; if V is a model of φ such that $V(p) \in \{00, 02, 12, 22\}$, then the assignment V' defined as follows is also a model of φ: $V'(p) = 12$ if $V(p) = 02$ and $V'(p) = V(p)$ otherwise (this fact can be proved easily by inspection of the truth tables). So, for the formula φ', we can "forget" the value 02 and the bijection $00 \leftrightarrow 0$, $12 \leftrightarrow 1$, $22 \leftrightarrow 2$ lets us conclude that φ has equilibrium models if and only if φ' has partial equilibrium models. Thus, the polynomial transformation of φ in φ' reduces the equilibrium consistency to partial-equilibrium consistency and so this problem is Σ_2^P-hard.

Corollary 3. *The decision problem for equilibrium entailment is Π_2^P-hard.*

9   Conclusions and Future Work

Until recently, the well-founded and p-stable semantics have lacked a firm logical foundation of the kind that the logic of here-and-there provides for stable semantics and ASP[5]. Partial equilibrium logic supplies such a foundation and opens the way to extending these semantics beyond the syntax of normal and disjunctive programs. Here we have seen that PEL captures p-stable semantics for disjunctive programs and we have examined its behaviour on nested logic programs. An open problem for future work is whether this semantics agrees with implementations of WFS such as XSB-Prolog which allow nested expressions in rule bodies. We have also seen here how various special classes of p-stable (p-equilibrium) models, including the L-stable and M-stable models, possess a strong equivalence theorem. Moreover our complexity results for HT^2 and PEL show that testing strong equivalence in the general case (ie. PEL over theories) is computationally simpler than testing ordinary equivalence. In this respect there is agreement with the case of stable models. A major open problem is the question of strong equivalence for normal and disjunctive programs. Clearly if such programs are equivalent in HT^2 they are strongly equivalent; but, if not, it remains to be seen whether in general the addition of new formulas in the form of program rules is sufficient to establish non-strong equivalence.

The technique of [9] for capturing p-stable semantics over disjunctive programs via a reduction to ordinary stable models has been shown here to extend to arbitrary formulas and thus provide a reduction of PEL to equilibrium logic. We have seen however that nonmonotonic inference in PEL lacks several properties enjoyed by ordinary stable inference. Similarly we observed that some of the equivalence-preserving syntactic transformations applicable in ASP are no longer sound for PEL. Our results here show that PEL, like p-stable semantics, is non-comparable with extensions of WFS such as D-WFS and STATIC. However the situation wrt to the semantics WFDS of [21] is still unclear: PEL is evidently not stronger (since S-IMP fails in it), but is not yet proven to be weaker.

We hope to have shown here how PEL can provide a conceptual foundation as well as a practical tool for investigating extensions of WFS and p-stable semantics. Future work will explore the above open questions besides further issues such as how to add strong or explicit negation to PEL (and capture the WFSX semantics [14]) and how to construct a complete proof theory.

References

1. J. Alcantara, C. Damasio & L. M. Pereira. A Frame-based Characterisation of the Paraconsistent Well-founded Semantics with Explicit Negation. Unpublished draft, available at http://centria.di.fct.unl.pt/~jfla/publications/
2. A. Bochman. A logical foundation for logic programming I: Biconsequence relations and nonmonotonic completion, II: Semantics for logic programs. *Journal of Logic Programming*, 1998, 35: 151-170 & 171-194.

---

[5] The approach of [2] has a more proof theoretic flavour, while that of [1] is semantical but lacks a clear logical axiomatisation.

3. S. Brass & J. Dix. A disjunctive semantics based on unfolding and bottom-up evaluation. In *IFIP'94 Congress, Workshop FG2: Disjunctive Logic Programming and Disjunctive Databases*, 1994, pp. 83–91.
4. P. Cabalar, S. Odintsov & D. Pearce. Logical Foundations of Well-Founded Semantics in *Proceedings KR 2006*, to appear.
5. T. Eiter, M. Fink, H. Tompits and S. Woltran. Simplifying Logic Programs under Uniform and Strong Equivalence V. Lifschitz & I. Niemela (eds.), *Proceedings LPNMR 2004*, Springer, LNAI 2923, 2004.
6. T. Eiter, N. Leone & D. Saccà. On the Partial Semantics for Disjunctive Deductive Databases. *Ann. Math, & Artificial Intelligence* 17 (1997), 59-96.
7. T. Eiter, N. Leone & D. Saccà. Expressive Power and Complexity of Partial Models for Disjunctive Deductive Databases. *Theoretical Computer Science* 206 (1998), 181-218.
8. M. Gelfond and V. Lifschitz. The stable model semantics for logic programming. In *Proc. of ICLP'88*, pp. 1070–1080, 1988. The MIT Press.
9. T. Janhunen, I. Niemelä, D. Seipel, P. Simons, and J.-H. You. Unfolding partiality and disjunctions in stable model semantics. *ACM Transactions on Computational Logic*, to appear.
10. V. Lifschitz, D. Pearce, and A. Valverde. Strongly equivalent logic programs. *ACM Transactions on Computational Logic*, 2(4):526–541, October 2001.
11. V. Lifschitz, L.R. Tang, and H. Turner. Nested expressions in logic programs. *Annals of Mathematics and Artificial Intelligence*, 25(3–4):369–389, 1999.
12. M. Osorio, J. Navarro & J. Arrazola. Equivalence in Answer Set Programming. in *Proc. LOPSTR 2001*, LNCS 2372, Springer, 2001, pp. 57-75.
13. D. Pearce. A new logical characterization of stable models and answer sets. In *Proc. of NMELP 96*, LNCS 1216, pp. 57–70. Springer, 1997.
14. L. M. Pereira & J. J. Alferes, Well Founded Semantics for Logic Programs with Explicit Negation, in: *European Conference on Artificial Intelligence*, B. Neumann (ed.), John Wiley & Sons 1992, pp.102-106
15. Przymusinski, T. Stable semantics for disjunctive programs. *New Generation Computing* 9 (1991), 401-424.
16. R. Routley and V. Routley. The Semantics of First Degree Entailment. *Noûs*, 6, 335–359, 1972.
17. C. Ruiz & J. Minker. Compuing Stable and Partial Stable Models of Extended Disjunctive Logic Programs. In *Nonmonotonic Extensions of Logic Programming*, Springer LNCS 927, 1995, 205-229.
18. D. Seipel, J. Minker & C. Ruiz. A Characterization of the Partial Stable Models for Disjunctive Deductive Databases. in *Int. Logic Programming Symp.*, MIT Press, 1997, 245-259.
19. A. Valverde. `tabeql`: A Tableau Based Suite for Equilibrium Logic. *Proc. of JELIA'04*, LNAI 3229, pp.734–737, 2004.
20. A. van Gelder, K.A. Ross, and J.S. Schlipf. Unfounded sets and well-founded semantics for general logic programs. *JACM*, 38(3):620–650, 1991
21. K. Wang & L. Zhou. Comparisons and computation of well-founded semantics for disjunctive logic programs. *ACM Transactions on Computational Logic*, 6(2): 295-327, 2005.
22. S. Woltran. Characterizations for Relativized Notions of Equivalence in Answer Set Programming. In J. J. Alferes & J. Leite (eds), *Proc. of JELIA'04*, Springer, LNAI 3229, 2004.
23. J. You & L. Y. Yuan. Three-valued formalization of logic programming: is it needed? in *Proc. PODS 90*, ACM, 1990, 172-182.

The Semantics of Nominal Logic Programs

James Cheney

University of Edinburgh
jcheney@inf.ed.ac.uk

Abstract. Nominal logic programming is a form of logic programming with "concrete" names and binding, based on nominal logic, a theory of α-equivalence founded on swapping and freshness constraints. Previous papers have employed diverse characterizations of the semantics of nominal logic programs, including operational, denotational, and proof-theoretic characterizations; however, the formal properties and relationships among them have not been fully investigated. In this paper we give a uniform and improved presentation of these characterizations and prove appropriate soundness and completeness results. We also give some applications of these results.

1 Introduction

Nominal logic is an extension of first-order logic that provides support for programming with abstract syntax with names and binding modulo α-equivalence. It is similar in spirit to higher-order logic programming languages and logical frameworks that provide *higher-order abstract syntax* facilities for encoding variables and binding in object languages; however, nominal logic is semantically much closer to first-order logic. Nominal logic axiomatizes α-equivalence in terms of an invertible renaming operation ("name-swapping") and the freshness (or "not-free-in") relation; it also includes a novel self-dual *nominal* quantifier N which quantifies over "fresh" names.

In previous work, Cheney and Urban [1] have presented αProlog, a logic programming language inspired by nominal logic, which employs a simple backchaining proof search technique like that of Prolog, but uses Urban, Pitts, and Gabbay's *nominal unification* [16] algorithm instead of first-order (that is, purely syntactic) unification. In addition, αProlog permits the N-quantifier in both goal formulas and clauses. The N-quantifier can be used to write some programs more easily than in higher-order abstract syntax, specifically programs that involve inequalities among names (for example, closure conversion).

This paper is concerned with establishing the relationships among operational, proof-theoretic, and denotational semantics of nominal logic programs. Because nominal logic involves both equality and freshness constraints, constraint logic programming (CLP) provides an appropriate and well-understood starting point. Nominal logic can be presented as a theory of first-order logic [15]; indeed, the N-quantifier can be defined in terms of the existential (or equivalently universal) quantifiers and the freshness relation (#):

$$\mathsf{N}\mathsf{a}.\phi(\mathsf{a}, \overline{X}) \iff \exists A.A \,\#\, \overline{X} \wedge \phi(A, \overline{X}) \iff \forall A.A \,\#\, \overline{X} \supset \phi(A, \overline{X})$$

S. Etalle and M. Truszczyński (Eds.): ICLP 2006, LNCS 4079, pp. 361–375, 2006.

Moreover, as shown in a separate paper [4], nominal logic has a well-behaved Herbrand model theory and nominal terms form a well-behaved constraint domain. Consequently, we can view Horn clause nominal logic programming as an instance of the Constraint Logic Programming Scheme [9], by translating И-quantified goal subformulas to equivalent existential formulas and И-quantified program clauses to universal formulas.

While this approach suffices to define a semantics for nominal logic programs, it is unsatisfactory in some respects. First, the syntactic translation that removes И may increase the size of the program by a quadratic factor, impeding analyses formulated in terms of the semantics of CLP. Second, from prior work on the proof theory of nominal logic [8,3], we know that both И-goals and program clauses can be read as a proof search operation "generate a fresh name and proceed to solve goal G (or refine clause D)". However, the translation of И obscures this proof-search reading. Finally, nominal constraint solving is NP-complete [2], whereas Urban, Pitts, and Gabbay's nominal unification algorithm solves a polynomial time special case. This algorithm relies on the use of "atoms" (special name-constants which correspond to И-quantified names in nominal logic programs). Translating atoms to ordinary first-order variables precludes the use of this efficient constraint solving algorithm. We believe that these facts justify the investigation of more direct approaches to the semantics of nominal logic programs.

Several such direct semantics have been presented in previous papers on nominal logic and αProlog, including an operational semantics [1], a denotational semantics [5, Chapter 6] and two proof-theoretic semantics [8,17]. In [5], soundness, algebraic completeness, and logical completeness results for the denotational and operational semantics paralleling Jaffar, Maher, Marriott, and Stuckey's semantics of constraint logic programming [9] were developed. However, except for this work, the relationships among the approaches have not been studied carefully.

The purpose of this paper is to fill this gap, by giving a uniform presentation of the denotational, proof-theoretic, and operational semantics and proving appropriate soundness and completeness theorems among them. Section 2 reviews nominal logic and nominal Horn clause programs. Section 3 presents the denotational semantics; Section 4 the proof-theoretic semantics; and Section 5 the operational semantics. Appropriate soundness and completeness theorems are proved along the way. Section 6 sketches two applications of these results, and Sections 7 and 8 discuss related and future work and conclude.

2   Background

The syntax of nominal logic types σ, contexts Σ, terms t, constraints C, and formulas ϕ is shown in Figure 1. We assume fixed countable sets $\mathbb{V}$ of *variables* $X, Y, Z, \ldots$ and $\mathbb{A}$ of *names* a, b, c, $\ldots$ (also known as *atoms* [16]). A *language* $\mathcal{L}$ consists of a set of *data types* δ, *name types* ν, *constants* $c : \delta$, *function symbols* $f : \overline{\sigma} \to \delta$, and *relation symbols* $p : \overline{\sigma} \to o$ (where o is the type of propositions). The novel term constructors include names a $\in \mathbb{A}$, name-abstractions $\langle a \rangle t$ denoting α-equivalence classes, and name-swapping applications $(a\ b) \cdot t$. The atomic formula $a \mathbin{\#} t$ is called *freshness*, and intuitively means that the name a is not free in the term t. Well-formed terms and atomic

$$
\begin{array}{llll}
\text{(Types)} & \sigma ::= \nu \mid \delta \mid \langle \nu \rangle \sigma \\
\text{(Contexts)} & \Sigma ::= \cdot \mid \Sigma, X{:}\sigma \mid \Sigma \# \mathsf{a}{:}\nu \\
\text{(Terms)} & t ::= \mathsf{a} \mid \mathsf{c} \mid f(\overline{t}) \mid x \mid (\mathsf{a}\ \mathsf{b}) \cdot t \mid \langle \mathsf{a} \rangle t \\
\text{(Constraints)} & C ::= t \approx u \mid \mathsf{a} \# t \mid C \wedge C' \mid \exists X{:}\sigma.C \mid \mathsf{Иa}{:}\sigma.C \\
\text{(Formulas)} & \phi ::= \top \mid \bot \mid p(\overline{t}) \mid C \mid \phi \supset \psi \mid \phi \wedge \psi \mid \phi \vee \psi \mid \forall X{:}\sigma.\phi \mid \exists X{:}\sigma.\phi \mid \mathsf{Иa}{:}\nu.\phi
\end{array}
$$

Fig. 1. Syntax of nominal logic

$$
\dfrac{\mathsf{a}:\nu \in \Sigma}{\Sigma \vdash \mathsf{a}:\nu} \quad
\dfrac{x:\sigma \in \Sigma}{\Sigma \vdash x:\sigma} \quad
\dfrac{c:\delta \in \mathcal{L}}{\Sigma \vdash c:\delta} \quad
\dfrac{f:\overline{\sigma} \to \delta \in \mathcal{L} \quad \Sigma \vdash \overline{t}:\overline{\sigma}}{\Sigma \vdash f(\overline{t}):\delta} \quad
\dfrac{\Sigma \vdash \mathsf{a}:\nu \quad \Sigma \vdash t:\sigma}{\Sigma \vdash \langle \mathsf{a} \rangle t:\langle \nu \rangle \sigma}
$$

$$
\dfrac{\Sigma \vdash \mathsf{a}:\nu \quad \Sigma \vdash \mathsf{b}:\nu \quad \Sigma \vdash t:\sigma}{\Sigma \vdash (\mathsf{a}\ \mathsf{b}) \cdot t:\sigma} \quad
\dfrac{\Sigma \vdash t,u:\sigma}{\Sigma \vdash t \approx u:o} \quad
\dfrac{\Sigma \vdash \mathsf{a}:\nu \quad \Sigma \vdash t:\sigma}{\Sigma \vdash \mathsf{a} \# t:o}
$$

$$
\dfrac{}{\Sigma \vdash \top, \bot:o} \quad
\dfrac{\Sigma \vdash \phi, \psi:o}{\Sigma \vdash \phi \wedge \psi, \phi \vee \psi, \phi \supset \psi:o} \quad
\dfrac{\Sigma, X{:}\sigma \vdash \phi:o}{\Sigma \vdash \forall X{:}\sigma.\phi, \exists X{:}\sigma.\phi:o} \quad
\dfrac{\Sigma \# \mathsf{a}{:}\nu \vdash \phi:o}{\Sigma \vdash \mathsf{Иa}{:}\nu.\phi:o}
$$

Fig. 2. Well-formedness for nominal terms and formulas

$$
\begin{array}{ll}
(\mathsf{a}\ \mathsf{b}) \cdot \mathsf{a} = \mathsf{b} & (\mathsf{a}\ \mathsf{b}) \cdot \mathsf{c} = \mathsf{c} \\
(\mathsf{a}\ \mathsf{b}) \cdot \mathsf{b} = \mathsf{a} & (\mathsf{a}\ \mathsf{b}) \cdot f(\overline{t}) = f((\mathsf{a}\ \mathsf{b}) \cdot \overline{t}) \\
(\mathsf{a}\ \mathsf{b}) \cdot \mathsf{a}' = \mathsf{a}' \quad (\mathsf{a} \neq \mathsf{a}' \neq \mathsf{b}) & (\mathsf{a}\ \mathsf{b}) \cdot \langle \mathsf{a}' \rangle t = \langle (\mathsf{a}\ \mathsf{b}) \cdot \mathsf{a}' \rangle (\mathsf{a}\ \mathsf{b}) \cdot t
\end{array}
$$

$$
\dfrac{(\mathsf{a} \neq \mathsf{b})}{\vDash \mathsf{a} \# \mathsf{b}} \quad
\dfrac{}{\vDash \mathsf{a} \# \mathsf{c}} \quad
\dfrac{\bigwedge_{i=1}^{n} \vDash \mathsf{a} \# t_i}{\vDash \mathsf{a} \# f(t_1^n)} \quad
\dfrac{\vDash \mathsf{a} \# \mathsf{b}}{\vDash \mathsf{a} \# \langle \mathsf{b} \rangle t} \quad
\dfrac{\vDash \mathsf{a} \# t}{\vDash \mathsf{a} \# \langle \mathsf{a} \rangle t}
$$

$$
\dfrac{}{\vDash \mathsf{a} \approx \mathsf{a}} \quad
\dfrac{}{\vDash \mathsf{c} \approx \mathsf{c}} \quad
\dfrac{\bigwedge_{i=1}^{n} \vDash t_i \approx u_i}{\vDash f(t_1^n) \approx f(u_1^n)} \quad
\dfrac{\vDash t \approx u}{\vDash \langle \mathsf{a} \rangle t \approx \langle \mathsf{a} \rangle u} \quad
\dfrac{\vDash \mathsf{a} \# u \quad \vDash t \approx (\mathsf{a}\ \mathsf{b}) \cdot u}{\vDash \langle \mathsf{a} \rangle t \approx \langle \mathsf{b} \rangle u}
$$

Fig. 3. Swapping, freshness, and equality for ground nominal terms

formulas are defined in Figure 2. Contexts include ordinary typed variables $\Sigma, X{:}\sigma$ and name-typed names $\Sigma \# \mathsf{a}{:}\nu$. Quantification over types mentioning o is not allowed.

Figure 3 defines the swapping, freshness, and equality operations on ground terms. Swapping exchanges two syntactic occurrences of a name in a term (including occurrences such as a in $\langle \mathsf{a} \rangle t$.) The freshness relation defines what it means for a name to be "not free in" (or *fresh* for) a term. Intuitively, a name a is fresh for a term t (that is, a $\#\ t$) if every occurrence of a in t is enclosed in an abstraction of a. Finally, the equality relation on nominal terms is defined using freshness and swapping. The only interesting cases are for abstractions; the second rule for abstractions is equivalent to more standard forms of α-renaming, as has been shown elsewhere [15].

We sometimes refer to the set of "free" names of a term $supp(t) = \mathbb{A} - \{\mathsf{a} \mid \mathsf{a} \# t\}$ as its *support*. Also, swapping and support are extended to formulas by setting $(\mathsf{a}\ \mathsf{b}) \cdot QX.\phi[X] = QX.(\mathsf{a}\ \mathsf{b}) \cdot \phi[X]$ for $Q \in \{\forall, \exists\}$ and $(\mathsf{a}\ \mathsf{b}) \cdot \mathsf{Иa}'.\phi = \mathsf{Иa}'.(\mathsf{a}\ \mathsf{b}) \cdot \phi$, provided $\mathsf{a}' \notin \{\mathsf{a}, \mathsf{b}\}$; thus, using α-renaming, we have $(\mathsf{a}\ \mathsf{b}) \cdot \forall X.\mathsf{Иa}.p(\mathsf{a}, \mathsf{b}, X) = \mathsf{Иa}'.\forall X.p(\mathsf{a}', \mathsf{a}, X)$.

$\mathcal{H} \vDash \top$

$\mathcal{H} \nvDash \bot$

$\mathcal{H} \vDash A \quad \Longleftrightarrow \quad A \in \mathcal{H}$

$\mathcal{H} \vDash t \approx u \quad \Longleftrightarrow \quad \vDash t \approx u$

$\mathcal{H} \vDash a \mathbin{\#} u \quad \Longleftrightarrow \quad \vDash a \mathbin{\#} u$

$\mathcal{H} \vDash \phi \wedge \psi \quad \Longleftrightarrow \quad \mathcal{H} \vDash \phi \text{ and } \mathcal{H} \vDash \psi$

$\mathcal{H} \vDash \phi \vee \psi \quad \Longleftrightarrow \quad \mathcal{H} \vDash \phi \text{ or } \mathcal{H} \vDash \psi$

$\mathcal{H} \vDash \phi \supset \psi \quad \Longleftrightarrow \quad \mathcal{H} \vDash \phi \text{ implies } \mathcal{H} \vDash \psi$

$\mathcal{H} \vDash \forall X{:}\sigma.\phi \quad \Longleftrightarrow \quad \text{for all } t : \sigma, \mathcal{H} \vDash \phi[t/X]$

$\mathcal{H} \vDash \exists X{:}\sigma.\phi \quad \Longleftrightarrow \quad \text{for some } t : \sigma, \mathcal{H} \vDash \phi[t/X]$

$\mathcal{H} \vDash \mathsf{N}a{:}\nu.\phi \quad \Longleftrightarrow \quad \text{for fresh } b : \nu \notin supp(\mathsf{N}a{:}\nu.\phi),$
$\qquad\qquad\qquad\qquad\quad \mathcal{H} \vDash (b\,a) \cdot \phi.$

Fig. 4. Term model semantics of nominal logic

Likewise, swapping can be extended to sets of terms or formulas by setting $(a\,b) \cdot S = \{(a\,b) \cdot t \mid t \in S\}$.

For the purposes of this paper, it suffices to restrict attention to *term models* of nominal logic in which the domain elements are nominal terms with equality and freshness defined as in Figure 3. We write $B_{\mathcal{L}}$ for the *Herbrand base*, that is, the set of all non-constraint atomic formulas. We view an Herbrand model $\mathcal{H}$ as a subset of $B_{\mathcal{L}}$ that is *equivariant*, or closed under swapping (that is, $\mathcal{H} \subseteq (a\,b) \cdot \mathcal{H}$ for any a, b.) The semantics of nominal logic formulas over term models is defined as shown in Figure 4. The only nonstandard case is that for N; it is shown in [4] that this definition of the semantics of N-quantified formulas is correct for term models.

We generalize the satisfiability judgments as follows. Given sets of closed formulas Γ, Δ, we write $\mathcal{H} \vDash \Gamma$ to indicate that $\mathcal{H} \vDash \phi$ for each $\phi \in \Gamma$, and $\Gamma \vDash \Delta$ to indicate that $\mathcal{H} \vDash \Gamma$ implies $\mathcal{H} \vDash \Delta$. We define ground substitutions θ as functions from $\mathbb{V}$ to ground terms. Given a context Σ, we say that a ground substitution θ *satisfies* Σ (and write $\theta : \Sigma$) when $\theta(x) : \Sigma(x)$ for all $x \in \Sigma$, and $a \mathbin{\#} \sigma(x)$ for every subcontext $\Sigma' \mathbin{\#} a$ and every $x \in \Sigma'$. For example, $[X \mapsto a, Y \mapsto b]$ satisfies $\Sigma = a, X \mathbin{\#} b, Y$ but not $X, Y \mathbin{\#} a \mathbin{\#} b$. We write $\Sigma : \theta \vDash \phi$ or $\Gamma, \theta \vDash \Delta$ as shorthand for $\theta : \Sigma$ and $\vDash \theta(\phi)$ or $\theta(\Gamma) \vDash \theta(\Delta)$, respectively. Moreover, we write $\Sigma : \Gamma \vDash \Delta$ to indicate that $\Sigma : \Gamma, \theta \vDash \Delta$ for every $\theta : \Sigma$. Note that, for example, $X \mathbin{\#} a : \cdot \vDash a \mathbin{\#} X$ but $a, X : \cdot \nvDash a \mathbin{\#} X$.

We define the *nominal Horn goal formulas* G and *nominal Horn program clauses* D as follows:

$$G ::= \top \mid A \mid C \mid G \wedge G' \mid G \vee G' \mid \exists X.G \mid \mathsf{N}a.G$$
$$D ::= \top \mid A \mid D \wedge D' \mid G \supset D \mid \forall X.D \mid \mathsf{N}a.D$$

2.1 Examples

We now present two relations definable using nominal logic programs but not easily definable in some other formalisms. For more examples of nominal logic programs, see [1] or [5, Chapter 2]. We use the convention that a formula $A :\!\!- \overline{B}$ abbreviates $\mathsf{N}\overline{a}.\forall \overline{X}. \bigwedge \overline{B} \supset A$, where $\{\overline{a}\} = supp(A, \overline{B})$ and $\{\overline{X}\} = FV(A, \overline{B})$.

Example 1. The first example, tc in Figure 5, performs typechecking for the simply-typed λ-calculus. (The built-in predicate $mem(A, L)$ holds when A is an element of list L). This relation is tricky to implement correctly and declaratively in Prolog because

$$tc(Ctx, var(X), T) \qquad\qquad :- mem((X, T), Ctx).$$
$$tc(Ctx, app(E_1, E_2), U) \qquad\quad :- tc(Ctx, E_1, fn\_ty(T, U)), tc(Ctx, E_2, T).$$
$$tc(Ctx, lam(\langle x \rangle E), fn\_ty(T, U)) :- x \# Ctx, tc([(x, T)|Ctx], E, U)$$

$$qlist(mono\_ty(T), [], T). \quad qlist(all\_ty(\langle a \rangle P), [a|L], T) :- a \# L, qlist(P, L, T).$$

Fig. 5. Example programs

it lacks support for programming modulo α-equivalence. Nominal logic programming provides approximately the same level of convenience and expressiveness as higher-order logic programming for this example.

Example 2. The second example, *qlist* in Figure 5, performs an important step in the implementation of ML-style type inference. It relates a "polytype" $\forall \overline{\alpha}.\tau$ to a suitably α-renamed list of its bound variables and underlying "monotype" τ. It can be run in the forward direction to strip the quantifiers off of a polytype, or in the backward direction to build a closed polytype from monotype and its list of free variables. This relation is difficult to implement in Prolog because of the lack of built-in support for α-renaming, and difficult for higher-order languages because it involves manipulating expressions with unknown numbers of free variables. There are other ways of implementing ML-style type inference in higher-order logic programming, but they are very different from what is usually implemented.

These examples highlight a subtle implementation issue: the impact of using the И-quantifier as a D-formula on the complexity of constraint solving. For example, tc can be rewritten to avoid clausal use of И. As we shall see in Section 6, the simplistic, but efficient proof search performed by αProlog is complete for such programs. However, *qlist* relies essentially on clausal use of И, so executing it appears to require solving intractable nominal constraints. At present, αProlog does not support full nominal constraint solving, so proof search is incomplete for programs such as *qlist*.

3 Denotational Semantics

In this section we define the denotational semantics of nominal logic programs. We show that least Herbrand models exist for nominal Horn clause programs and that the least Herbrand model is the least fixed point of an appropriate continuous one-step deduction operator, following Lloyd's exposition [11]. This section also relies on standard definitions and concepts from lattice theory [7].

3.1 Least Herbrand Models

It is a well-known fact that least Herbrand models exist for Horn clause theories in first-order logic. Building on a previous development of Herbrand models for nominal logic [4], we now show that nominal logic programs also have least Herbrand models.

Theorem 1 (Nominal Herbrand models). *A collection of nominal Horn program clauses is satisfiable in nominal logic if and only if it has an Herbrand model.*

Proof. We note without proof that we can prenex-normalize all ∃ and И quantifiers in goals in *D*-formulas out to the top level as ∀ and И quantifiers respectively. The result forms a И∀-theory in the sense of [4], so has a model iff it has an Herbrand model.

Lemma 1. *Let* Δ *be a set of closed program clauses and* $\mathcal{M}$ *a nonempty set of Herbrand models of* Δ. *Then* $\mathcal{H} = \bigcap \mathcal{M}$ *is also an Herbrand model of* Δ.

Proof. We first note that the intersection of a collection of equivariant sets is still equivariant, so $\mathcal{H}$ is an Herbrand model. To prove it models Δ, we show by mutual induction that

1. For any program clause D, if $\forall M \in \mathcal{M}.M \vDash D$ then $\mathcal{H} \vDash D$; and
2. For any goal formula G, if $\mathcal{H} \vDash G$ then $\forall M \in \mathcal{M}.M \vDash G$.

All the cases are standard except for Иa.G and Иa.D. If $\forall M \in \mathcal{M}.M \vDash$ Иa.D then for each M, $M \vDash$ (b a) · D for any fresh b not in $supp($Иa.D$)$. Without loss of generality we can choose a b $\notin supp($Иa.D$)$ such that $\forall M \in \mathcal{M}.M \vDash$ (b a) · D. Appealing to the induction hypothesis, we obtain $\mathcal{H} \vDash$ (b a) · D, whence $\mathcal{H} \vDash$ Иa.D. The case for Иa.G is similar.

An immediate consequence is that a $\subseteq$-least Herbrand model $\mathcal{H}_\Delta = \bigcap\{\mathcal{H} \mid \mathcal{H} \vDash \Delta\}$ exists for any nominal Horn theory Δ. Moreover, $\mathcal{H}_\Delta$ consists of all ground atoms entailed by Δ, as we now show.

Theorem 2. *Let* Δ *be a set of program clauses. Then* $\mathcal{H}_\Delta = \{A \in B_\mathcal{L} \mid \Delta \vDash A\}$.

Proof. If $A \in \mathcal{H}_\Delta$, then A is valid in every Herbrand model of Δ, so by Theorem 1, A is valid in every model of Δ. Conversely, if $\Delta \vDash A$ then since $\mathcal{H}_\Delta \vDash \Delta$ we have $\mathcal{H}_\Delta \vDash A$; thus $A \in \mathcal{H}_\Delta$.

3.2   Fixed Point Semantics

Classical fixed point theorems assert the existence of a fixed point. However, to ensure that the fixed point of an operator on Herbrand models is still an Herbrand model we need an additional constraint: we require that the operator is also equivariant, in the following sense.

Definition 1. *A set operator* $\tau : \mathcal{P}(B_\mathcal{L}) \to \mathcal{P}(B_\mathcal{L})$ *is called* equivariant *if* (a b)·$\tau(S) = \tau(($a b$) \cdot S)$.

Theorem 3. *Suppose* $\tau : \mathcal{P}(B_\mathcal{L}) \to \mathcal{P}(B_\mathcal{L})$ *is equivariant and monotone. Then* $\mathrm{lfp}(\tau) = \bigcap\{S \in \mathcal{P}(B_\mathcal{L}) \mid \tau(S) \subseteq S\}$ *is the least fixed point of* τ *and is equivariant. If, in addition,* τ *is continuous, then* $\mathrm{lfp}(\tau) = \tau^\omega = \bigcup_{i=0}^\omega \tau^i(\varnothing)$.

Proof. By the Knaster-Tarski fixed-point theorem, $\mathrm{lfp}(\tau)$ is the least fixed point of τ. To show that $\mathrm{lfp}(\tau)$ is equivariant, it suffices to show that $A \in \mathrm{lfp}(\tau) \implies$ (a b) · $A \in \mathrm{lfp}(\tau)$. Let a, b be given and assume $A \in \mathrm{lfp}(\tau)$. Then for any pre-fixed point S of τ (satisfying $\tau(S) \subseteq S$), we have $A \in S$. Let such an S be given. Note that $\tau(($a b$) \cdot S) = ($a b$) \cdot \tau(S) \subseteq ($a b$) \cdot S$, so (a b) · S is also a pre-fixed point of τ. Hence $A \in ($a b$) \cdot S$ so (a b) · $A \in ($a b$) \cdot ($a b$) \cdot S = S$. Since S was an arbitrary pre-fixed point, it follows that (a b) · $A \in \mathrm{lfp}(\tau)$, so $A \in ($a b$) \cdot \mathrm{lfp}(\tau)$.

The second part follows immediately from Kleene's fixed point theorem.

Definition 2. *Let S be an Herbrand interpretation and D a program clause. The one-step deduction operator $\tau_D : \mathcal{P}(B_{\mathcal{L}}) \to \mathcal{P}(B_{\mathcal{L}})$ is defined as follows:*

$$\tau_\top(S) = S$$
$$\tau_{D_1 \wedge D_2}(S) = \tau_{D_1}(S) \cup \tau_{D_2}(S)$$
$$\tau_{G \supset D}(S) = \begin{cases} \tau_D(S) & \text{if } S \vDash G \\ S & \text{otherwise} \end{cases}$$

$$\tau_A(S) = S \cup A$$
$$\tau_{\forall X : \sigma . D}(S) = \bigcup_{t : \sigma} \tau_{D[t/X]}(S)$$
$$\tau_{\mathsf{N}a : \nu . D}(S) = \bigcup_{b : \nu \notin supp(\mathsf{N}a.D)} \tau_{(a\ b) \cdot D}(S)$$

We define τ_Δ as $\tau_{D_1 \wedge \cdots \wedge D_n}$ provided $\Delta = \{D_1, \ldots, D_n\}$ and each D_i is closed.

Lemma 2. *For any program Δ, τ_Δ is monotone and continuous.*

Proof. We prove by induction on the structure of D that τ_D has the above properties. Monotonicity is straightforward. For continuity, the cases for $\top, \wedge, \forall, \mathsf{N}$, and atomic formulas are straightforward. For $G \supset D$, let $S_0, S_1, \ldots,$ be an ω-chain of subsets of $B_{\mathcal{L}}$. Suppose that $A \in \tau_{G \supset D}(\bigcup_i S_i)$. If $\bigcup_i S_i \vDash G$ then $A \in \tau_D(\bigcup_i S_i)$, and by induction $A \in \bigcup_i(\tau_D(S_i)) = \bigcup_i \tau_{G \supset D}(S_i)$. Otherwise, $A \in \bigcup_i(S_i) = \bigcup_i \tau_{G \supset D}(S_i)$. This shows that $\tau_{G \supset D}(\bigcup_i S_i) \subseteq \bigcup_i \tau_{G \supset D}(S_i)$. For the reverse direction, suppose $A \in \bigcup_i \tau_{G \supset D}(S_i)$. Then for some i, $A \in \tau_{G \supset D}(S_i)$. There are two cases. If $S_i \vDash G$, then $A \in \tau_D(S_i) = \tau_{G \supset D}(S_i) \subseteq \tau_{G \supset D}(\bigcup_i(S_i))$. Otherwise, $A \in S_i = \tau_{G \supset D}(S_i) \subseteq \tau_{G \supset D}(\bigcup_i(S_i))$.

Lemma 3. *For any $a, b \in \mathbb{A}$, $(a\ b) \cdot \tau_D(S) = \tau_{(a\ b) \cdot D}((a\ b) \cdot S)$. In particular, if Δ is a closed program with $FV(\Delta) = supp(\Delta) = \varnothing$, then τ_Δ is equivariant.*

Proof. The proof is by induction on the structure of D. The cases for $\top, A, \wedge$ are straightforward; for $\supset$ we need the easy observation that $S \vDash G \iff (a\ b) \cdot S \vDash (a\ b) \cdot G$. For $\forall X : \sigma . D$ formulas, the proof is straightforward once we observe that $(a\ b) \cdot \bigcup_{t:\sigma} \tau_{D[t/X]}(S) = \bigcup_{t:\sigma} \tau_{((a\ b) \cdot D)[(a\ b) \cdot t/X]}((a\ b) \cdot S) = \bigcup_{u:\sigma} \tau_{((a\ b) \cdot D)[u/X]}((a\ b) \cdot S) = \tau_{(a\ b) \cdot \forall X . D}((a\ b) \cdot S)$. For N, the argument is similar.

Theorem 4. $\mathcal{H}_\Delta = \mathrm{lfp}(\tau_\Delta) = \tau_\Delta^\omega$.

Proof. Clearly $\tau_\Delta^\omega = \mathrm{lfp}(\tau_\Delta)$ by Theorem 3. We show that $\mathcal{H}_\Delta \subseteq \tau_\Delta^\omega$ and $\mathrm{lfp}(\tau_\Delta) \subseteq \mathcal{H}_\Delta$.

For $\mathcal{H}_\Delta \subseteq \tau_\Delta^\omega$, it suffices to show that τ_Δ^ω is a model of Δ. We prove by induction on D that if $\tau_D(\mathcal{M}) = \mathcal{M}$ then $\mathcal{M} \vDash D$; from this it follows that $\tau_\Delta^\omega \vDash D$ for each $D \in \Delta$. Cases $D = \top, A, D_1 \wedge D_2, \forall X : \sigma . D$ are straightforward. For $D = \mathsf{N}a : \nu . D'$, note that $\mathcal{M} = \tau_{\mathsf{N}a.D}(\mathcal{M}) = \bigcup_{b : \nu \notin supp(\mathsf{N}a.D)} \tau_{(a\ b) \cdot D'}(\mathcal{M})$ implies $\tau_{(a\ b) \cdot D'}(\mathcal{M}) = \mathcal{M}$ for every fresh b. Hence by the induction hypothesis $\mathcal{M} \vDash (a\ b) \cdot D'$ for every fresh b; consequently $\mathcal{M} \vDash \mathsf{N}a.D'$.

For $\mathrm{lfp}(\tau_\Delta) \subseteq \mathcal{H}_\Delta$, it suffices to show that $\mathcal{H}_\Delta$ is a pre-fixed point of τ_Δ, that is, $\tau_\Delta(\mathcal{H}_\Delta) \subseteq \mathcal{H}_\Delta$. We prove that for any D, if $\mathcal{H}_\Delta \vDash D$ then $\tau_D(\mathcal{H}_\Delta) \subseteq \mathcal{H}_\Delta$, by induction on the structure of D. Cases $D = \top, A, D_1 \wedge D_2, \forall X : \sigma . D$ are straightforward. For $\mathsf{N}a : \nu . D$, by induction $\tau_{(a\ b) \cdot D}(\mathcal{H}_\Delta) \subseteq \mathcal{H}_\Delta$ for any $b \notin supp(\mathsf{N}a.D)$ so $\bigcup_{b : \nu \notin supp(\mathsf{N}a.D)} \tau_{(a\ b) \cdot D}(\mathcal{H}_\Delta) \subseteq \mathcal{H}_\Delta$.

4 Proof-Theoretic Semantics

In proof-theoretic semantics, an approach due to Miller, Nadathur, Scedrov, and Pfenning [14], we characterize well-behaved logic programming languages as those for which *goal-directed* proof search is complete. Goal-directed, or *uniform*, proofs are sequent calculus proofs in which right-decomposition rules are always used to decompose the goal to an atomic formula before any other proof rules are considered. An *abstract logic programming language* is then defined as a collection of terms, goal formulas and program clauses for which uniform proof search is complete. Proof-theoretic semantics has been extended to a variety of settings; most relevant here is work on constraint logic programming in a proof theoretic setting [6,10].

A uniform proof-theoretic approach to nominal logic programming was investigated by Gabbay and Cheney [8]. However, this approach was unsatisfactory in some respects. First, the underlying sequent calculus suggested an approach to proof-search for И-formulas quite unlike the intuitive "generate a fresh name and proceed" approach employed in αProlog. Second, the *freshness rule* in NL_{Seq}, corresponding to the nominal logic axiom $\forall \overline{X}.\exists A.A \ \# \ \overline{X}$, is not goal-directed but cannot be delayed past the $\exists R$ and $\forall L$ rules. Instead, it was necessary to weaken the definition of uniform proof in order to permit applications of the freshness principle before these rules.

The first problem has been addressed by an alternative sequent calculus for nominal logic called $NL^{\Rightarrow}$ [3], in which the И-quantifier rules take a simpler form. We adopt a variation on the $NL^{\Rightarrow}$ approach that also addresses the second problem: specifically, we define an "amalgamated" proof system that separates the term-level constraint-based reasoning (including the freshness rule) from logical reasoning and proof search. This technique was employed by Darlington and Guo [6] and further developed by Leach et al. [10] in studying the semantics of constraint logic programs.

In this section we introduce the amalgamated proof system and relate it to the model-theoretic semantics in the previous section. This system is sound with respect to (intuitionistic) nominal logic; we believe it to be complete for nominal Horn clause programs relative to intuitionistic $NL^{\Rightarrow}$ but have not yet proved this carefully. We also introduce a second *residuated* proof system that explicates the process of reducing a goal to an answer constraint; this system forms an important link between the proof theory and the operational semantics in the next section. Residuated proof search corresponds to ordinary proof search in a natural way. Here and elsewhere, we use Γ for a set of goal formulas, Δ for a set of program clauses, and ∇ for a set of constraints.

The proof rules in Figure 6 describe a proof system that first proceeds by decomposing the goal to an atomic formula, which is then solved by refining a program clause. This system reflects the behavior of an interpreter for nominal logic programs, such as αProlog. The uniform proof judgment $\Sigma : \Delta; \nabla \implies G$ indicates that G is derivable from Δ and ∇ in context Σ, while the focused proof judgment $\Sigma : \Delta; \nabla \xrightarrow{D} A$ indicates that atomic goal A is derivable from Δ and ∇ by refining the program clause D (using Δ to help solve any residual goals). The judgment $\Sigma : \nabla \vDash C$ is the ordinary satisfaction relation defined in Section 2.

These rules are unusual in several important respects. First, the hyp rule requires solving a constraint of the form $A \sim B$, which we define as "there exists a permutation π such that $\pi \cdot A \approx B$". In contrast usually the hypothesis rule requires only

$$\frac{\Sigma : \nabla \vDash C}{\Sigma : \Delta; \nabla \Longrightarrow C}\; con \qquad \frac{\Sigma : \Delta; \nabla \Longrightarrow G_1 \quad \Sigma : \Delta; \nabla \Longrightarrow G_2}{\Sigma : \Delta; \nabla \Longrightarrow G_1 \wedge G_2}\; \wedge R$$

$$\frac{\Sigma : \Delta; \nabla \Longrightarrow G_i}{\Sigma : \Delta; \nabla \Longrightarrow G_1 \vee G_2}\; \vee R_i \qquad \frac{\Sigma : \nabla \vDash \exists X.C \quad \Sigma, X : \Delta; \nabla, C \Longrightarrow G}{\Sigma : \Delta; \nabla \Longrightarrow \exists X{:}\sigma.G}\; \exists R$$

$$\frac{\Sigma : \nabla \vDash \mathsf{V}a.C \quad \Sigma \# a : \Delta; \nabla, C \Longrightarrow G}{\Sigma : \Delta; \nabla \Longrightarrow \mathsf{V}a.G}\; \mathsf{V}R \qquad \frac{\Sigma : \Delta; \nabla \xrightarrow{D} A \quad D \in \Delta}{\Sigma : \Delta; \nabla \Longrightarrow A}\; sel$$

$$\frac{\Sigma : \nabla \vDash A' \sim A}{\Sigma : \Delta; \nabla \xrightarrow{A'} A}\; hyp \qquad \frac{\Sigma : \Delta; \nabla \xrightarrow{D_i} A}{\Sigma : \Delta; \nabla \xrightarrow{D_1 \wedge D_2} A}\; \wedge L_i \qquad \frac{\Sigma : \Delta; \nabla \xrightarrow{D} A \quad \Sigma : \Delta; \nabla \Longrightarrow G}{\Sigma : \Delta; \nabla \xrightarrow{G \supset D} A}\; \supset L$$

$$\frac{\Sigma : \nabla \vDash \exists X.C \quad \Sigma, X : \Delta; \nabla, C \xrightarrow{D} A}{\Sigma : \Delta; \nabla \xrightarrow{\forall X{:}\sigma.D} A}\; \forall L \qquad \frac{\Sigma : \nabla \vDash \mathsf{V}a.C \quad \Sigma \# a : \Delta; \nabla, C \xrightarrow{D} A}{\Sigma : \Delta; \nabla \xrightarrow{\mathsf{V}a.D} A}\; \mathsf{V}L$$

Fig. 6. Uniform/focused proof search for intuitionistic nominal logic

that $A \approx A'$. Our rule accounts for the fact that equivalent atomic formulas may not be syntactically equal as nominal terms, but only equal modulo a permutation. Second, the proof system treats constraints specially, separating them into a context ∇. This is necessary because the role of constraints is quite different from that of program clauses: the former are used exclusively for constraint solving whereas the latter are used in backchaining. Third, the $\mathsf{V}R, \mathsf{V}L, \exists R$ and $\forall L$ rules are permitted to introduce a constraint on the witness name a or variable X rather than providing a witness term. This constraint-based treatment makes it possible to compartmentalize all reasoning about the constraint domain (including the freshness rule) in the judgment $\Sigma : \nabla \vDash C$.

For example, the goal $\mathsf{V}a.\exists X.a \# X$ has the following uniform derivation:

$$\frac{\Sigma \# a : \nabla \vDash \mathsf{V}a.\top \qquad \dfrac{\Sigma \# a : \nabla, \top \vDash \exists X.a \# X \quad \Sigma \# a, X : \Delta; \nabla, \top, a \# X \Longrightarrow a \# X}{\Sigma \# a : \Delta; \nabla, \top \Longrightarrow \exists X.a \# X}\; \exists R}{\Sigma : \Delta; \nabla \Longrightarrow \mathsf{V}a.\exists X.a \# X}\; \mathsf{V}R$$

where $\Sigma \# a : \nabla \vDash \exists X.a \# X$ is clearly valid for any ∇ (take X to be any ground name besides a). In contrast, in previous proof-theoretic approaches, proof search for $\mathsf{V}a.\exists X.a \# X$ requires using a freshness rule before $\exists R$.

We first show (by induction on derivations) that the restricted system is sound with respect to the denotational semantics.

Theorem 5 (Soundness). *If $\Sigma : \Delta; \nabla \Longrightarrow G$ is derivable then $\Sigma : \Delta, \nabla \vDash G$. Similarly, if $\Sigma : \Delta; \nabla \xrightarrow{D} G$ is derivable then $\Sigma : \Delta, D, \nabla \vDash G$.*

We next show a restricted, "algebraic" form of completeness [9]. Since the denotational semantics is classical while the proof theory is constructive, it is too much to expect that classical completeness holds. For example, $A, B : \cdot \vDash A \approx B \vee A \# B$ is valid, but $A, B : \cdot; \cdot \Longrightarrow A \approx B \vee A \# B$ is not derivable (and indeed not intuitionistically valid). Instead, however, we can prove that any valuation θ that satisfies G also satisfies a constraint which entails G.

$$\frac{}{\varSigma:\varDelta \Longrightarrow C \setminus C}\; con \qquad \frac{\varSigma:\varDelta \Longrightarrow G_1 \setminus C_1 \quad \varSigma:\varDelta \Longrightarrow G_2 \setminus C_2}{\varSigma:\varDelta \Longrightarrow G_1 \wedge G_2 \setminus C_1 \wedge C_2}\; \wedge R$$

$$\frac{\varSigma:\varDelta \Longrightarrow G_i \setminus C}{\varSigma:\varDelta \Longrightarrow G_1 \vee G_2 \setminus C}\; \vee R_i \qquad \frac{\varSigma,X:\varDelta \Longrightarrow G \setminus C}{\varSigma:\varDelta \Longrightarrow \exists X{:}\sigma.G \setminus \exists X.C}\; \exists R$$

$$\frac{\varSigma\#\mathsf{a}:\varDelta \Longrightarrow G \setminus C}{\varSigma:\varDelta \Longrightarrow \text{И}\mathsf{a}.G \setminus \text{И}\mathsf{a}.C}\; \text{И}R \qquad \frac{\varSigma:\varDelta \xrightarrow{D} A \setminus G \quad (D \in \varDelta) \quad \varSigma:\varDelta \Longrightarrow G \setminus C}{\varSigma:\varDelta \Longrightarrow A \setminus C}\; back$$

$$\frac{}{\varSigma:\varDelta \xrightarrow{A'} A \setminus A \sim A'}\; hyp \qquad \frac{\varSigma:\varDelta \xrightarrow{D_i} A \setminus G}{\varSigma:\varDelta \xrightarrow{D_1 \wedge D_2} A \setminus G}\; \wedge L_i \qquad \frac{\varSigma:\varDelta \xrightarrow{D} A \setminus G'}{\varSigma:\varDelta \xrightarrow{G \supset D} A \setminus G \wedge G'}\; \supset L$$

$$\frac{\varSigma,X:\varDelta \xrightarrow{D} A \setminus G}{\varSigma:\varDelta \xrightarrow{\forall X{:}\sigma.D} A \setminus \exists X.G}\; \forall L \qquad \frac{\varSigma\#\mathsf{a}:\varDelta \xrightarrow{D} A \setminus G}{\varSigma:\varDelta \xrightarrow{\text{И}\mathsf{a}.D} A \setminus \text{И}\mathsf{a}.G}\; \text{И}L$$

Fig. 7. Residuated uniform/focused proof search

Proposition 1. *For any* $\varSigma, \varDelta, G, D \in \varDelta, i \geq 0$:

1. *If* $\varSigma : \tau_\varDelta^i, \theta \vDash G$ *then for some* ∇, *we have* $\varSigma : \theta \vDash \nabla$ *and* $\varSigma : \varDelta; \nabla \Longrightarrow G$.
2. *If* $\varSigma : \tau_D(\tau_\varDelta^i), \theta \vDash A$ *but* $\varSigma : \tau_\varDelta^i, \theta \nvDash A$ *then for some* ∇, $\varSigma : \theta \vDash \nabla$ *and* $\varSigma : \varDelta; \nabla \xrightarrow{D} A$.

Proof. For the first part, proof is by induction on i and G; most cases are straightforward. For atomic goals A, i must be > 0, and if $\varSigma : \tau_\varDelta^{i-1}; \theta \vDash A$ then we use part (1) of the induction hypothesis with $i - 1$; otherwise $\varSigma : \tau_\varDelta^{i-1}; \theta \nvDash A$ so we unwind $\tau_\varDelta^i$ to $\tau_D(\tau_\varDelta^{i-1})$ for some $D \in \varDelta$, apply part (2), and use rule *sel*. Similarly, the second part follows by induction on i and D, unwinding the definition of τ_D in each case.

Theorem 6 (Algebraic Completeness). *If* $\varSigma : \varDelta, \theta \vDash G$ *then there exists a constraint* ∇ *such that* $\varSigma : \varDelta, \theta \vDash \nabla$ *and* $\varSigma : \varDelta; \nabla \Longrightarrow G$ *is derivable.*

Proof. If $\varSigma : \varDelta, \theta \vDash G$, then there is some n such that $\varSigma : \tau_\varDelta^n, \theta \vDash G$, so Proposition 1 applies.

We can also extend this to a "logical" completeness result [9], namely that if an answer ∇ classically implies G, then there is a finite set of constraints which prove G individually and whose disjunction covers ∇.

Theorem 7 (Logical Completeness). *If* $\varSigma : \varDelta, \nabla \vDash G$ *then there exists a finite set of constraints* $C_1, \ldots, C_n$ *such that* $\varSigma : \nabla \vDash C_1 \vee \cdots \vee C_n$ *and for each* i, $\varSigma : \varDelta; C_i \Longrightarrow G$.

The rules in Figure 6 have the potential disadvantage that an arbitrary constraint C is allowed in the rules $\exists R, \forall R, \text{И}L, \text{И}R$. Figure 7 shows a *residuated* proof system that avoids this nondeterminism. Specifically, the judgment $\varSigma : \varDelta \Longrightarrow G \setminus C$ means that given context $\varSigma$ and program $\varDelta$, goal G reduces to constraint C; similarly, $\varSigma : \varDelta \xrightarrow{D} A \setminus G$ means that goal formula G suffices to prove A from D. We state without

$$(B) \quad \Sigma \langle A, \Gamma \mid \nabla \rangle \longrightarrow \Sigma \langle G, \Gamma \mid \nabla \rangle \quad (\text{if } \exists D \in \Delta. \Sigma : \Delta \xrightarrow{D} A \setminus G)$$

$$(C) \qquad \Sigma \langle C, \Gamma \mid \nabla \rangle \longrightarrow \Sigma \langle \Gamma \mid \nabla, C \rangle \quad (\nabla, C \text{ consistent})$$

$$(\top) \qquad \Sigma \langle \top, \Gamma \mid \nabla \rangle \longrightarrow \Sigma \langle \Gamma \mid \nabla \rangle \; smallskip$$

$$(\wedge) \qquad \Sigma \langle G_1 \wedge G_2, \Gamma \mid \nabla \rangle \longrightarrow \Sigma \langle G_1, G_2, \Gamma \mid \nabla \rangle$$

$$(\vee_i) \qquad \Sigma \langle G_1 \vee G_2, \Gamma \mid \nabla \rangle \longrightarrow \Sigma \langle G_i, \Gamma \mid \nabla \rangle$$

$$(\exists) \qquad \Sigma \langle \exists X{:}\sigma.G, \Gamma \mid \nabla \rangle \longrightarrow \Sigma, X{:}\sigma \langle G, \Gamma \mid \nabla \rangle$$

$$(\mathsf{N}) \qquad \Sigma \langle \mathsf{N}\mathsf{a}{:}\nu.G, \Gamma \mid \nabla \rangle \longrightarrow \Sigma \# \mathsf{a}{:}\nu \langle G, \Gamma \mid \nabla \rangle$$

Fig. 8. Operational semantics transitions for nominal logic programs

proof the following appropriate soundness and completeness properties; their proofs are straightforward inductions.

Theorem 8 (Residuated Soundness)

1. If $\Sigma : \Delta \Longrightarrow G \setminus C$ then $\Sigma : \Delta; C \Longrightarrow G$.
2. If $\Sigma : \Delta; \nabla \Longrightarrow G$ and $\Sigma : \Delta \xrightarrow{D} A \setminus G$ then $\Sigma : \Delta; \nabla \xrightarrow{D} A$.

Theorem 9 (Residuated Completeness)

1. If $\Sigma : \Delta; \nabla \Longrightarrow G$ then there exists a constraint C such that $\Sigma : \Delta \Longrightarrow G \setminus C$ and $\Sigma : \nabla \vDash C$.
2. If $\Sigma : \Delta; \nabla \xrightarrow{D} A$ then there exists goal G and constraint C such that $\Sigma : \Delta \xrightarrow{D} A \setminus G$ and $\Sigma : \Delta \Longrightarrow G \setminus C$ and $\Sigma : \nabla \vDash C$.

5   Operational Semantics

We now give a CLP-style operational semantics for nominal logic programs. The rules of the operational semantics are shown in Figure 8. A program state is a triple of the form $\Sigma \langle \Gamma \mid \nabla \rangle$. The backchaining step is defined in terms of residuated focused proof.

We now state the operational soundness and completeness properties. The proofs are straightforward by cases or induction, so omitted. To simplify notation, we write $\Sigma : \Delta \Longrightarrow \overline{\Gamma} \setminus \overline{C}$ where $\Gamma = \{G_1, \ldots, G_n\}$ and $\overline{C} = \{C_1, \ldots, C_n\}$ to abbreviate $\Sigma : \Delta \Longrightarrow G_1 \setminus C_1, \ldots, \Sigma : \Delta \Longrightarrow G_n \setminus C_n$; also, if $\Sigma \langle G \mid \varnothing \rangle \longrightarrow^* \Sigma; \Sigma' \langle \varnothing \mid C \rangle$, then we abbreviate this as $\Sigma \langle G \rangle \Downarrow \exists \Sigma'[C]$.

Proposition 2 amounts to showing that each operational transition corresponds to a valid manipulation on (multisets of) residuated proofs. Its corollary summarizes the soundness results relating the operational semantics to the others.

Proposition 2 (Transition Soundness). *If* $\Sigma \langle \Gamma \mid \nabla \rangle \longrightarrow \Sigma' \langle \Gamma' \mid \nabla' \rangle$ *and* $\Sigma' : \Delta \Longrightarrow \overline{\Gamma'} \setminus \overline{C'}$ *then there exist* $\overline{C}$ *such that* $\Sigma : \Delta \Longrightarrow \overline{\Gamma} \setminus \overline{C}$ *and* $\Sigma' : \nabla', \overline{C'} \vDash \nabla, \overline{C}$.

Corollary 1 (Operational Soundness). *If* $\Sigma \langle G \rangle \Downarrow \nabla$ *then:*

1. *there exists C such that* $\Sigma : \nabla \vDash C$ *and* $\Sigma : \Delta \Longrightarrow G \setminus C$;
2. $\Sigma : \Delta; \nabla \Longrightarrow G$; *and*
3. $\Sigma : \Delta, \nabla \vDash G$.

The transition completeness property (Proposition 3) states that for any configuration $\Sigma\langle \Gamma \mid \nabla\rangle$ such that the goals Γ have appropriate derivations in the residuated proof system, there is an operational transition step to a new state with appropriately modified derivations. This property can be used to relate the operational semantics to the other approaches, as shown in Corollary 2.

Proposition 3 (Transition Completeness). *For any nonempty Γ and satisfiable $\nabla, \overline{C}$, if $\Sigma : \Delta \Longrightarrow \overline{\Gamma} \setminus \overline{C}$ then for some Σ', ∇', and $\overline{C'}$ we have $\Sigma\langle \Gamma \mid \nabla \rangle \longrightarrow \Sigma'\langle \Gamma' \mid \nabla'\rangle$, $\Sigma' : \Delta \Longrightarrow \overline{\Gamma'} \setminus \overline{C'}$, and $\Sigma' : \nabla, \overline{C} \vDash \nabla', \overline{C'}$.*

Corollary 2 (Operational Completeness)

1. *If $\Sigma : \Delta \Longrightarrow G \setminus C$ and C is satisfiable then for some ∇, we have $\Sigma\langle G\rangle \Downarrow \nabla$ and $\Sigma : C \vDash \nabla$.*
2. *If $\Sigma : \Delta; \nabla \Longrightarrow G$ and ∇ is satisfiable then for some ∇', we have $\Sigma\langle G\rangle \Downarrow \nabla'$ and $\Sigma : \nabla \vDash \nabla'$.*
3. *If $\Sigma : \Delta, \theta \vDash G$ then for some ∇, we have $\Sigma\langle G\rangle \Downarrow \nabla$ and $\Sigma : \theta \vDash \nabla$.*
4. *If $\Sigma : \Delta, C \vDash G$ then for some $\overline{\nabla}$, we have $\Sigma\langle G\rangle \Downarrow \overline{\nabla}$ and $\Sigma : C \vDash \nabla_1 \vee \cdots \vee \nabla_n$.*

6   Applications

Correctness of Elaboration. In an implementation, program clauses are often *elaborated* into a normal form $\forall \Sigma[G \supset A]$ which is easier to manipulate. The *elaboration* of a program clause or program is defined as its normal form with respect to the rules:

$$G \supset G' \supset D \rightsquigarrow G \wedge G' \supset D \qquad\qquad G \supset D \wedge D' \rightsquigarrow (G \supset D) \wedge (G \supset D')$$
$$G \supset \forall X.D \rightsquigarrow \forall X.(G \supset D)\, (X \notin FV(G)) \quad G \supset \mathsf{Иa}.D \rightsquigarrow \mathsf{Иa}.(G \supset D)\,(a \notin supp(G))$$
$$\forall X.(D \wedge D') \rightsquigarrow \forall X.D \wedge \forall X.D' \qquad \mathsf{Иa}.(D \wedge D') \rightsquigarrow \mathsf{Иa}.D \wedge \mathsf{Иa}.D'$$
$$G \supset \top \rightsquigarrow \top \qquad D \wedge \top \rightsquigarrow D \qquad \top \wedge D \rightsquigarrow D$$
$$\forall X.\top \rightsquigarrow \top \qquad \mathsf{Иa}.\top \rightsquigarrow \top \qquad \Delta, D \wedge D' \rightsquigarrow \Delta, D, D' \qquad \Delta, \top \rightsquigarrow \Delta$$

It is straightforward to show that this system is terminating and confluent (up to α- and multiset-equality) and that elaborated programs consist only of closed formulas $Q_1 \cdots Q_n[G \supset A]$ or $Q_1 \cdots Q_n[A]$, where $\overline{Q}$ is a sequence of $\forall$- or $\mathsf{И}$-quantifiers. Moreover, this translation preserves the meaning of the program:

Theorem 10. *1. If $\Delta \rightsquigarrow \Delta'$ then $\Sigma : \Delta; \nabla \Longrightarrow G$ iff $\Sigma : \Delta'; \nabla \Longrightarrow G$.*

2. If $\Delta \rightsquigarrow \Delta'$ then $\Sigma : \Delta; \nabla \xrightarrow{D} A$ iff $\Sigma : \Delta', D; \nabla \Longrightarrow A$.

3. If $D \rightsquigarrow D'$ then $\Sigma : \Delta; \nabla \xrightarrow{D} A$ iff $\Sigma : \Delta, D'; \nabla \Longrightarrow A$.

A sublanguage with Tractable Constraints. In general, nominal constraint solving is intractable [2]. However, Urban, Pitts, and Gabbay's nominal unification algorithm (which forms the basis of the αProlog implementation) solves a tractable special case:

Definition 3. *A term, constraint, or formula is simple if in every subterm of the form $a \# t$, $\langle a\rangle t$, or $(a\ b) \cdot t$, the terms a and b are ground names.*

For example, $\langle a \rangle X$ and $(a\ b) \cdot Y$ are *simple*, while $\langle A \rangle X$ and $((A\ B) \cdot C\ (A\ C) \cdot B) \cdot C$ are not. Constraint solving for *simple* problems involving only $\approx$ and $\#$ is decidable in polynomial time [16]. Moreover, it is easy to see that the residuated and operational semantics reduce any satisfiable goal to a *simple* constraint.

Unfortunately, because atomic formulas are equivalent if they are equal modulo a permutation in nominal logic, this is not enough to ensure that *simple* nominal logic programs can be executed efficiently, because constraint solving is **NP**-complete even for *simple* constraints $A \sim B$. Therefore, it is tempting to replace the hyp rule with $hyp_\approx$, in which $\Sigma : \nabla \vDash A \approx B$ is required to to conclude $\Sigma : \Delta; \nabla \xrightarrow{A} B$. We write $\Sigma : \Delta; \nabla \Longrightarrow_\approx G$ and $\Sigma : \Delta; \nabla \xrightarrow{D}_\approx A$ for uniform or focused proofs in which $hyp_\approx$ is used instead of hyp, and call such proofs $\approx$-*backchaining*. The current implementation of αProlog implements $\approx$-backchaining over *simple* programs.

Such proofs only require solving tractable *simple* constraints involving $\approx$ or $\#$. However, proof search is incomplete for this system. For example, there is no proof of $\Sigma : \text{Иa}.p(\mathsf{a}); \nabla \Longrightarrow_\approx \text{Иa}.p(\mathsf{a})$. There are, however, sublanguages of *simple* nominal Horn clauses for which αProlog's $\approx$-backchaining is complete. One interesting example identified by Urban and Cheney [17]. In this language, И is forbidden in goal formulas and program clauses are required to satisfy a well-formedness condition which ensures that every derivation using hyp can be transformed to one using $hyp_\approx$.

We now identify an alternative sublanguage for which αProlog's proof search is complete. We say that a program clause is *И-clause-free* if it contains no D-formula of the form $\text{Иa}.D$. However, И-quantified goals $\text{Иa}.G$ are allowed. All the programs considered well-formed according to Urban and Cheney's definition appear equivalent to *И-clause-free* programs and vice versa; investigating this relationship is future work.

Example 3. Although the tc program of Figure 5 is not *И-clause-free*, its third clause can be replaced by the *И-clause-free* formula

$$tc(Ctx, lam(F), fn\_ty(T, U)) :- \text{Иx}.F = \langle x \rangle E, tc([(x, T)|Ctx], E, U).$$

To prove $\approx$-backchaining complete for *И-clause-free* programs, we first show:

Lemma 4. *Let π be a type-preserving permutation of names in Σ.*

1. *If $\Sigma : \Delta; \nabla \Longrightarrow_\approx G$ then $\Sigma : \Delta; \nabla \Longrightarrow_\approx \pi \cdot G$.*
2. *If $\Sigma : \Delta; \nabla \xrightarrow{D}_\approx A$ then $\Sigma : \Delta; \nabla \xrightarrow{\pi \cdot D}_\approx \pi \cdot A$.*

Proof. By induction on derivations. The cases for quantifiers require some care; for example, in the case for $\forall X.G[X]$, we have subderivation $\Sigma, X : \Delta; \nabla, C[X] \Longrightarrow_\approx \pi \cdot G[\pi \cdot X]$ where $\Sigma : \nabla \vDash \exists X.C[X]$. Since π is invertible, we can substitute $Y = \pi \cdot X$ to obtain $\Sigma, X : \Delta; \nabla, C[\pi^{-1} \cdot Y] \Longrightarrow_\approx \pi \cdot G[Y]$; moreover, clearly, $\Sigma : \nabla \vDash \exists Y.C[\pi^{-1} \cdot Y]$, so we can conclude $\Sigma : \Delta; \nabla \Longrightarrow_\approx \pi \cdot \forall X.G[X]$.

Theorem 11. *If Δ is И-clause-free then*

1. *If $\Sigma : \Delta; \nabla \Longrightarrow G$ is derivable, $\Sigma : \Delta; \nabla \Longrightarrow_\approx G$ is derivable.*
2. *If $\Sigma : \Delta; \nabla \xrightarrow{D} A$ is derivable, then $\Sigma : \Delta; \nabla \xrightarrow{\pi \cdot D}_\approx A$ is derivable for some π.*

Proof. The proof is by induction on derivations. The most interesting cases are *hyp* and *sel*. For *hyp*, from $\Sigma : \Delta; \nabla \xrightarrow{\pi \cdot A} A'$ we have $\Sigma : \nabla \vDash A' \sim A$, which by definition means there exists a π such that $\Sigma : \nabla \vDash \pi \cdot A' \approx A$, so $\Sigma : \Delta; \nabla \xrightarrow{\pi \cdot A}_{\approx} A'$. For *sel*, from $\Sigma : \Delta; \nabla \Longrightarrow A$ we obtain $\Sigma : \Delta; \nabla \xrightarrow{D} A$ for some closed $D \in \Delta$. By induction, for some π, $\Sigma : \Delta; \nabla \xrightarrow{\pi \cdot D}_{\approx} A$. However, since D is closed, $\pi \cdot D = D \in \Delta$ so we may conclude $\Sigma : \Delta; \nabla \Longrightarrow_{\approx} A$ using the *sel* rule again. Other cases follow by arguments similar to those for Lemma 4. The case for $\mathsf{N}L$ is vacuously true: no instance of $\mathsf{N}L$ can occur in a N-*clause-free* program derivation.

Note that Theorem 11 fails if $\mathsf{N}L$ is allowed: specifically, given an instance of $\mathsf{N}L$ deriving $\Sigma : \Delta; \nabla \xrightarrow{\mathsf{N}a.D} A$ from $\Sigma\#a : \Delta; \nabla \xrightarrow{D} A$, we can obtain a derivation of $\Sigma\#a : \Delta; \nabla \xrightarrow{\pi \cdot D}_{\approx} A$ by induction, but since π may mention a, it is not possible in general to conclude $\Sigma : \Delta; \nabla \xrightarrow{\pi \cdot \mathsf{N}a.D}_{\approx} A$.

7   Related and Future Work

Basic results relating the denotational and operational semantics similar to those of Jaffar et al. [9] were first proved in [5, Chapter 6]. Although many of the basic ideas are the same, we believe the definitions and proofs in this paper are cleaner and more extensible. For example, extending the proof-theoretic semantics to hereditary Harrop programs (following [10]), supporting negation-as-failure, or extending the constraint domain to include traditional classes of constraints or additional binding constructs appears straightforward. Another interesting direction to pursue is the possibility of compiling nominal logic programs to ordinary CLP programs with an appropriate nominal constraint solver written using constraint handling rules.

Nominal logic programming is similar in expressive power to restricted forms of higher-order logic programming, such as Miller's L_λ [13], in which all subterms are required to be *higher-order patterns*. The unification problems for nominal terms and higher-order patterns are similar [16], although their syntactic form and semantic motivations appear quite different. The N-*clause-free* fragment seems similar in expressive power to L_λ, except for minor differences such as that goal formulas can be passed as arguments in L_λ. Thus, nominal logic may constitute a logical foundation for L_λ.

8   Conclusions

Nominal logic is an interesting extension of ordinary first-order logic with a constraint and equality theory describing terms with bound names up to α-equivalence. In this paper, we have given three semantics for nominal logic programs: a classical, denotational semantics (based on nominal Herbrand models), a constructive, proof-theoretic semantics, and an operational semantics. Moreover, we have proved appropriate soundness and completeness theorems relating the semantics. These results provide a solid logical foundation for nominal logic programming, provide criteria for judging the correctness and completeness of implementations, and suggest that nominal logic programming can be provided as simply another constraint domain within a full CLP system. In addition, we used the proof-theoretic semantics to prove the correctness of program elaboration and to provide a new characterization of programs for which αProlog-style proof search is complete.

References

1. J. Cheney and C. Urban. Alpha-Prolog: A logic programming language with names, binding and alpha-equivalence. In *Proceedings of the 20th International Conference on Logic Programming (ICLP 2004)*, number 3132 in LNCS, pages 269–283, 2004.
2. James Cheney. The complexity of equivariant unification. In *Proceedings of the 31st International Colloquium on Automata, Languages and Programming (ICALP 2004)*, volume 3142 of *LNCS*, pages 332–344. Springer-Verlag, 2004.
3. James Cheney. A simpler proof theory for nominal logic. In *Proceedings of the 2005 Conference on Foundations of Software Science and Computation Structures (FOSSACS 2005)*, number 3441 in LNCS, pages 379–394. Springer-Verlag, 2005.
4. James Cheney. Completeness and Herbrand theorems for nominal logic. *Journal of Symbolic Logic*, 81(1):299–320, 2006.
5. James R. Cheney. *Nominal Logic Programming*. PhD thesis, Cornell University, Ithaca, NY, August 2004.
6. John Darlington and Yike Guo. Constraint logic programming in the sequent calculus. In *Proceedings of the 1994 Conference on Logic Programming and Automated Reasoning (LPAR 1994)*, volume 822 of *Lecture Notes in Computer Science*, pages 200–214. Springer-Verlag, 1994.
7. B. A. Davey and H. A. Priestley. *Introduction to Lattices and Order*. Cambridge University Press, 2002.
8. M. J. Gabbay and J. Cheney. A sequent calculus for nominal logic. In H. Ganzinger, editor, *Proceedings of the 19th Annual IEEE Symposium on Logic in Computer Science (LICS 2004)*, pages 139–148, Turku, Finland, 2004. IEEE.
9. Joxan Jaffar, Michael J. Maher, Kim Marriott, and Peter J. Stuckey. The semantics of constraint logic programs. *Journal of Logic Programming*, 37(1–3):1–46, 1998.
10. Javier Leach, Susan Nieva, and Mario Rodríguez-Artalejo. Constraint logic programming with hereditary Harrop formulas. *Theory and Practice of Logic Programming*, 1(4):409–445, July 2001.
11. J. W. Lloyd. *Foundations of Logic Programming*. Springer-Verlag, 1987.
12. Spiro Michaylov and Frank Pfenning. Higher-order logic programming as constraint logic programming. In *Position Papers for the First Workshop on Principles and Practice of Constraint Programming*, pages 221–229, Newport, Rhode Island, April 1993.
13. Dale Miller. A logic programming language with lambda-abstraction, function variables, and simple unification. *J. Logic and Computation*, 1(4):497–536, 1991.
14. Dale Miller, Gopalan Nadathur, Frank Pfenning, and Andre Scedrov. Uniform proofs as a foundation for logic programming. *Annals of Pure and Applied Logic*, 51:125–157, 1991.
15. A. M. Pitts. Nominal logic, a first order theory of names and binding. *Information and Computation*, 183:165–193, 2003.
16. C. Urban, A. M. Pitts, and M. J. Gabbay. Nominal unification. *Theoretical Computer Science*, 323(1–3):473–497, 2004.
17. Christian Urban and James Cheney. Avoiding equivariant unification. In *Proceedings of the 2005 Conference on Typed Lambda Calculus and Applications (TLCA 2005)*, number 3461 in LNCS, pages 74–89. Springer-Verlag, 2005.

Macros, Macro Calls and Use of Ensembles in Modular Answer Set Programming

Chitta Baral, Juraj Dzifcak, and Hiro Takahashi

Department of Computer Science and Engineering
Arizona State University
Tempe, AZ 85287
{chitta, juraj.dzifcak, hiro}@asu.edu

Abstract. Currently, most knowledge representation using logic programming with answer set semantics (AnsProlog) is 'flat'. In this paper we elaborate on our thoughts about a modular structure for knowledge representation and declarative problem solving formalism using AnsProlog. We present language constructs that allow defining of modules and calling of such modules from programs. This allows one to write large knowledge bases or declarative problem solving programs by reusing existing modules instead of writing everything from scratch. We report on an implementation that allows such constructs. Our ultimate aim is to facilitate the creation and use of a repository of modules that can be used by knowledge engineers without having to re-implement basic knowledge representation concepts from scratch.

1 Introduction

Currently, most knowledge representation languages are 'flat'. In other words, for the most part they are non-modular. (It is often mentioned that CYC's language [Guha 1990] allows the use of modules. But this is not well published outside CYC.) Our focus in this paper is the knowledge representation language AnsProlog [Gelfond & Lifschitz 1988, Baral 2003] (logic programming with answer set semantics), where most programs are a collection of AnsProlog rules. Although sets of AnsProlog rules in these programs are often grouped together with comments that describe the purpose of those rules, the existing syntax does not allow one to construct libraries of modules that can be used in different programs. Such libraries are commonplace in many of the programming languages such as C++ and Java and recently in domains such as natural language [Miller *et al.* 1990]. The presence of such libraries makes it easier to write large programs without always starting from scratch, by referring and using already written pieces of code (modules, methods, subroutines etc.).

There are many other advantages of using libraries of modules. For example, having higher level modules available enforces code standardization. A module repository also has the benefit of being proven over the years and hence deemed reliable. In addition, modules may be built using multiple languages which lends to an overall application architecture where strengths of a language are fully exploited without having to find a work-around.

There are several ways to introduce modularity into answer set programming. Some of the ways to do that include:

S. Etalle and M. Truszczyński (Eds.): ICLP 2006, LNCS 4079, pp. 376–390, 2006.

(1) Macros: Modules are defined as macros or templates. A macro-call would be re-placed by a collection of AnsProlog rules as specified by a semantics of the macro call. Such an approach with focus on aggregates is used in [Calimeri *et al.* 2004].

(2) Procedure/method calls: A module is an AnsProlog program with well defined input and output predicates. Other programs can include calls to such a module with a specification of the input and a specification of the output. Such an approach is used in [Tari, Baral, & Anwar 2005].

(3) Procedure/method calls with a specified engine: Here a module is also an AnsProlog program with not only well-defined input and output predicates, but also with an as-sociated inference engine. For example, the associated engine could be a top-down engine such as Prolog or Constraint logic programming, or an answer set enumer-ator such as Smodels or DLV. Such an approach with respect to constraint logic programming can be built on the recent work [Baselice, Bonatti, & Gelfond 2005] where answer set programming is combined with constraint logic programming.

In this paper, we will focus on the first way to represent knowledge in a modular way. In our approach there is an initial macro-expansion phase during which macro calls are appropriately replaced by AnsProlog code. The result of the macro-expansion phase is an AnsProlog program which can then be used by an appropriate interpreter. In this paper we will use the Smodels [Niemelä & Simons 1997] interpreter for illustration purposes. The organization of the rest of the paper is as follows. We will first present a simple example of our approach, then we will present the syntax and semantics for our language constructs and then introduce a detailed illustration with respect to planning and reasoning about actions. Finally, we will conclude and discuss related work.

2   A Simple Example: Transitive Closure

Let us consider the simple example of transitive closure. We will illustrate how a simple transitive closure module can be defined once and can then be used in many different ways. A transitive closure module of a binary predicate p is computed by the binary predicate q, and is given as follows.

```
Module_name: Transitive_closure.
Parameters(Input: p(X,Y); Output: q(X,Y);). Types: Z = type X.
Body:   q(X,Y) :- p(X,Y).
        q(X,Y) :- p(X,Z), q(Z,Y).
```

Now, if in a program we want to say that anc [1] is the transitive closure of par [2] then we can have the following macro call in that program:

CallMacro Transitive_closure(**Replace:** p **by** par, q **by** anc, X **by** U, Y **by** V;).

Our semantics of the macro call will be defined in such a way that during the macro-expansion phase the above call will be replaced by the following rules, together with type information about the variable Z.

---

[1] $anc(a, b)$ means that b is an ancestor of a.

[2] $par(a, b)$ means b is a parent of a.

```
anc(U,V)  :- par(U,V).
anc(U,V)  :- par(U,Z), anc(Z,V).
```

Now suppose in another program we would like to define descendants of a, where $descendant(a, b)$ means that a is a descendant of b, then one can include one of the following macro calls:

CallMacro Transitive_closure(**Replace**: p **by** *par*, q **by** *descendant*, Y **by** a; **Unchanged**: X;).

CallMacro Transitive_closure(**Replace**: p **by** *par*, q **by** *descendant*; **Specialize**: $Y = a$; **Unchanged**: X;).

Our semantics of the macro call will be defined in such a way that during the macro-expansion phase the above calls will be replaced by the following rules and type information about Z.

```
descendant(X,a)  :- par(X,a).
descendant(X,a)  :- par(X,Z), descendant(Z,a).

descendant(X,Y)  :- par(X,Y), Y = a.
descendant(X,Y)  :- par(X,Z), descendant(Z,Y), Y = a.
```

A similar example is given in [McCarthy 1993]. There McCarthy gave a context in which above(x,y) is the transitive closure of on(x,y) and wrote lifting rules to connect this theory to a blocks world theory with on(x,y,s) and above(x,y,s).

3   Syntax and Semantics of Modules and Macro Calls

We now present the syntax and semantics of modules and macro calls. We start with the alphabet. Our alphabet has module names, predicate names, variable names, function names and the following set of keywords '**Module_name**', '**Parameters**', '**#domain**', '**Input**', '**Output**', '**Types**', '**type**', '**Body**', '**Callmacro**', '**specializes**', '**generalizes**', '**variant_of**', '**Specialize**', '**Generalize**', '**Unchanged**', '**Replace**', '**by**', '**Add**', '**to**', '**Remove**' and '**from**'. We use the terminology of atoms, literals, naf-literals etc. from [Baral 2003]. Recall that naf-literal is either an atom or an atom preceded by the symbol '**not**'. Besides that, if p is a predicate of arity k, and $V_1, \ldots, V_k$ are terms, then we refer to $p(V_1, \ldots, V_k)$ as a predicate schema. Furthermore, we define a variable domain statement to be of the form $\#domain\ p(V)$, which says that the variable V is of type p. For example $\#domain\ fluent(F)$ means that the variable F is of the type $fluent$.

3.1   Syntax

We start with the syntax of a call-macro statement and then define a module.

Definition 1. A call-macro statement is of the following form:

$Callmacro\ Mname($ **Replace**: p_1 **by** $p'_1, \ldots, p_k$ **by** p'_k, v_1 **by** $v'_1, \ldots, v_l$ **by** v'_l; **Add**: u_1 **to** $q_1, \ldots, u_r$ **to** q_r; **Remove**: w_1 **from** $q'_1, \ldots, w_s$ **from** q'_s; **Specialize**: $S_1, \ldots, S_m$; **Generalize**: $G_1, \ldots, G_n$; **Unchanged**: $x_1, \ldots, x_t$;)

where $Mname$ is a module name, $p_1, \ldots, p_k$, $p'_1, \ldots, p'_k$, $q_1, \ldots, q_r$ and $q'_1, \ldots, q'_r$ are predicate names; $v_1, \ldots, v_l$, $v'_1, \ldots, v'_l$ are terms; $u_1, \ldots, u_r$ are sets of terms; $w_1, \ldots, w_s$ are sets of variables; x_1 to x_t are variables or predicates; S_is and G_js are naf-literals; $\{S_1, \ldots, S_m\} \cap \{G_1, \ldots, G_n\} = \emptyset$. Any of k, l, r, s, m, n or t could be 0. Also, the order in which we specify the keywords does not matter.   □

Definition 2. A *module* is of the form:

Module_Name: $Mname$ sg $Mname'$.
Parameters($P_1 \ldots P_t$; Input: $I_1, \ldots, I_k$; Output: $O_1, \ldots, O_l$;).
Types: $D_0, \ldots D_j$, $L_1 = type\ V_1, \ldots L_o = type\ V_o$.
Body: r_1 $\ldots$ r_m.
        c_1 $\ldots$ c_n.

where, $Mname$, and $Mname'$ are module names; sg is either the keyword 'specializes', the keyword 'generalizes' or the keyword 'variant_of'; P_is, I_is and O_is are predicate schemas; r_is are AnsProlog rules (we also allow for Smodels constructs such as '#const' etc.); c_js are call-macro statements; $L_1, \ldots, L_o$ and $V_1, \ldots, V_o$ are variables; and $D_0, \ldots, D_j$ are variable domain statements. $Mname'$ is optional and in its absence we do not have the sg part.

But if $Mname'$ is there and sg is equal to 'specialize' or 'generalize', then $m = 0$, $n = 1$ and only sg appears in c_1. In other words, if sg is equal to specialize, then there is exactly one call to the module $Mname'$ using specialize and not generalize (similarly for generalize), and there are no other rules or macro calls. The idea of specifying specialize, generalize and variant between modules is to show the connection between the modules and if one is familiar with a module then it becomes easier for him/her to grasp the meaning of a specialization, generalization or variant of that module.

Additionally, we specify the parameters of the module, e.g. predicates and variables that are passed in and out from the module. We may define those in general, or further specify them to be input or output predicates or variables. The input and output labeling is optional, but are useful to express more information about the module. As shown in the upcoming examples, specifying inputs and outputs helps with understanding and usage of the particular module. In cases where $k = 0$ ($l = 0$) we may omit the $Input$ ($Output$) keyword. However, if input or output is present, we require the following conditions to hold:

(i) If p is an input predicate, then there must be a rule r_i whose body has p, or there must be a call-macro statement c_j with p in it.

(ii) If p is an output predicate, then there must be a rule r_i whose head has p, or there must be a call-macro statement c_j with p in it.   □

The above conditions ensure that the input and output predicates play their intended role in a module. Intuitively, a module takes in facts of a set of input predicates and reasons with them to produce a set of facts about output predicates. This is similar to the interpretation of logic programs as lp-functions in [Gelfond & Gabaldon 1997]. The first condition above requires that each of the specified inputs is actually used within the module, while the second one ensures that the module really computes each of the specified outputs.

Let us now take a closer look at the variables in a module and their domains. First, we say a variable is *local*, if it does not appear in any parameter statement of the module. Otherwise, we say the variable is *global*. Our syntax allows for defining the domain of a variable either using '$\#domain$' statement, or by type constraints of the form $V = type$ V' meaning that the type of variable V is the same as the type of V'. We require that domains be only defined for local variables, as global variables get their domain from the macro calls. For example in the transitive closure module, defined in previous section, we do not want to specify the types of X and Y, as X and Y can be person, number, etc. The local variables must have a well-defined type, which is formally defined as follows:

A local variable V has a well-defined type if one of the following holds:

1. The definition of the module $Mname$ contains a statement $\#domain\ p(V)$.
2. The definition of the module $Mname$ contains a statement $V = type\ V'$ where V' is a global variable.
3. The definition of the module $Mname$ contains a statement $V = type\ V'$ where V' has a well-defined type.

In addition, we require the following condition to hold for any macro call:

(iii) If X is a predicate or variable in any parameter schema of $Mname$, then any macro call to the module $Mname$ must contain either a replace, remove, generalize or unchanged statement involving X. Furthermore, a macro call to a module can not refer to any local variable of that module. Finally, although we do not require it, it is advisable to make sure that any variable that is introduced (by the u_i notation of the Add statements) by a macro call to a module is either different from existing variable in that module or if same, has a reason behind it. (In our implementation we will flag such variables.).

3.2   Macro Expansion Semantics

To characterize the expansion of modules we need to consider not just a single module but a collection of modules, as a module may include call-macro statements that call other modules. Given a set of modules S we define the dependency graph G_S of the set as follows: There is an edge from M_1 to M_2 if the body of M_1 has a call-macro statement that calls M_2. In the following we only consider the sets of modules whose dependency graph does not have cycles.

Now given a set of modules its macro expansion semantics is a mapping λ from module names to AnsProlog programs. We define this mapping inductively as follows:

1. If M is a module with no macro calls then $\lambda(M) = \{r_1, \ldots, r_m\}$.
2. If c is a call-macro statement in module $Mname$ of the form

   Callmacro Mname(**Replace:** p_1 **by** $p'_1, \ldots, p_k$ **by** p'_k, v_1 **by** $v'_1, \ldots, v_l$ **by** v'_l; **Add:** u_1 **to** $q_1, \ldots, u_r$ **to** q_r; **Remove:** w_1 **from** $q'_1, \ldots, w_s$ **from** q'_s; **Specialize:** $S_1, \ldots, S_m$; **Generalize:** $G_1, \ldots, G_n$; **Unchanged:** $x_1, \ldots, x_t$;)
   such that $\lambda(M)$ is defined, then $\lambda(c)$ is defined as follows:
   (a) Each rule r in $\lambda(M)$ is replaced by a rule r' constructed from r by applying all of the following(if applicable) changes to r:

    i. (Replace) Let $p_i \in r$, $i = 1, ..., k$. Then p_i is replaced by it's respective predicate p_i' in r'. Similarly, any of the terms v_1 to v_l in any predicate $p \in r$ is replaced by it's respective term v_1' to v_l'.

    ii. (Add) Let $p(t_1, ..., t_i)$ be a predicate of r with it's respective terms. If for any j, $p = q_j$ and $u_j = \{t_1', ..., t_{i'}'\}$, then $p(t_1, ..., t_i)$ is replaced by $p(t_1, ..., t_i, t_1', ..., t_{i'}')$ in r'.

Example 1. Let p be the atom $q(Z, Y)$ of a rule r. Let the call contain the following: **Replace:** q **by** *occurs*; **Add:** $\{A, neq(B)\}$ **to** q; Following the above cases, $q(Z, Y)$ will be replaced by $occurs(Z, Y, A, neg(B))$ in r'. □

    iii. (Remove) Let w be any variable in term t_i from the set w_j for some j. Let q_j' be any predicate of the form $q_j'(t_1, ..., t_i, ...t_a)$ in r (notice that t_i may be equal to w). Then q_j' is replaced by $q_j'(t_1, ..., t_{i-1}, t_{i+1}...t_a)$ in r' assuming $t - 1 \geq 1$ and $t + q \leq a$ Otherwise the respective t_{i-1} or t_{i+1} is not present in p.

    iv. (Unchanged) For any predicate or variable x_i, no change or substitution is performed.

    v. If there exists i, j such that $p_i = p_j$ and $p_i' \neq p_j'$, or $v_i = v_j$ and $v_i' \neq v_j'$ then we say that the set of substitutions is conflicting. If that is the case, we say that the semantics of the call c, $\lambda(c)$ is undefined.

(b) (Specialize, Generalize) $S_1, ..., S_m$ is added to and $G_1, ..., G_n$, if present, are removed from the body of each of the rules of the module.

(c) (Local variables types) For each local variable L of $Mname$, it's type is assigned as follows. The type of L is assigned according to the $\#domain\, p(L)$ statement (if present in $Mname$) or type constraint $L = type\, V$ for some variable V with already defined type (i.e. a global or well-defined local variable). Notice that our syntax requires each local variable to be well-defined. Then, in the first case, the type of L is p, while in the latter case type of L is the same as type of V, where V is a global variable or a well-defined local variable.

(d) If $S_1, ..., S_m$ include evaluable predicates or equality predicates then appropriate simplification is done.

3. For a module M, such that $\lambda(c_1), ..., \lambda(c_n)$ are already defined $\lambda(M)$ is defined as follows:

$$\lambda(M) = \{r_1, ..., r_m\} \cup \lambda(c_1) \cup ... \cup \lambda(c_n)$$

Definition 3. Let S be a set of modules. Two modules M and M' are said to be rule-set equivalent (in S)[3] if $\lambda(M)$ and $\lambda(M')$ have the same set of rules modulo changes in the ordering of naf-literals in the body of a rule.   □

4   Examples of Simple Specialization and Generalization

In this section we illustrate some simple examples of specialization and generalization. We start with a simple module of inertial reasoning which says if F is true in the index T then it must be true in the index T'.

---

[3] When the context is clear we do not mention S explicitly.

```
Module_Name: Inertia.
Parameters(Input: holds(F,T); Output: holds(F,T');).
Body:  holds(F,T')  :- holds(F,T).
```

Consider the following call-macro statement.

CallMacro Inertia(**Replace**: *F* by *G*, *T'* by *res(A, T)*; **Unchanged**: holds, T;).

When the above call-macro statement is expanded we obtain the following:

```
holds(G,res(A,T))  :- holds(G,T).
```

Consider a different call-macro statement.

CallMacro Inertia(**Replace**: *F* by *G*, *T'* by *(T+1)*; **Unchanged**: holds, T;).

When the above call-macro statement is expanded we obtain the following:

```
holds(G,T+1)  :- holds(G,T).
```

Now let us define some modules that specialize the module 'Inertia'.

(i) Inertia1

```
Module_Name: Inertia1 specializes Inertia.
Parameters(Input: holds(F,T); Output: holds(F,T');).
Body:  Callmacro Inertia(Unchanged: holds, F, T, T';
        Specialize: not ~holds(F,T'), not ab(F,T,T');).
```

Proposition 1. The module Inertia1 is rule-set equivalent to Inertia1' below.   □

```
Module_Name: Inertia1'.
Parameters(Input: holds(F,T), ab(F,T,T');Output: holds(F,T');).
Body: holds(F,T')  :- holds(F,T), not ~holds(F,T'),
                  not ab(F,T,T').
```

(ii) Inertia2

```
Module_Name: Inertia2 variant_of Inertia.
Parameters(Input: holds(F,T); Output: holds(F,T');).
Body: Callmacro Inertia(Unchanged: holds, F, T, T';
        Specialize: not ~holds(F,T');).
      Callmacro Inertia(Replace: holds by ~holds;
        Unchanged: F, T, T'; Specialize: not holds(F,T');).
```

Note that in the above module we say 'variant_of' instead of 'specialize'. That is because the body of the above module has two macro calls and when using 'specialize' we only allow for one macro call.

Proposition 2. The module Inertia2 is rule-set equivalent to Inertia2' below.   □

```
Module_Name: Inertia2'.
Parameters(Input: holds(F,T); Output: holds(F,T');).
Body: holds(F,T')   :- holds(F,T), not ~holds(F,T').
      ~holds(F,T')  :- ~holds(F,T),  not holds(F,T').
```

(iii) Inertia3

```
Module_Name: Inertia3 specializes Inertia.
Parameters(Input: holds(F,T); Output: holds(F,T');).
Body: Callmacro Inertia(Unchanged: holds, F, T, T';
                        Specialize: not ab(F,T,T');).
```

Proposition 3. The module Inertia3 is rule-set equivalent to Inertia3' below.   □

```
Module_Name: Inertia3'.
Parameters(Input: holds(F,T), ab(F,T,T');Output: holds(F,T');).
Body: holds(F,T') :- holds(F,T), not ab(F,T,T').
```

(iv) Inertia4

```
Module_Name: Inertia4 generalizes Inertia3.
Parameters(Input: holds(F,T); Output: holds(F,T');).
Body: Callmacro Inertia3(Unchanged: holds, F, T, T';
                         Generalize: not ab(F,T,T');).
```

Proposition 4. The module Inertia4 is rule-set equivalent to the module Inertia.   □

The above modules show how one can define new modules using previously defined modules by generalizing or specializing them. This is similar to class-subclass definitions used in object oriented programming languages. A specialization is analogous to a subclass while a generalization is analogous to a superclass. Now let us consider several call-macro statements involving the above modules.

(a) The statement "CallMacro Inertia2(**Replace**: F by G, T by X, T' by $X+1$; **Unchanged**: holds;)", when expanded [4], gives us the following rules:

```
holds(G,X+1)  :- holds(G,X), not ~holds(G,X+1).
~holds(G,X+1) :- ~holds(G,X), not holds(G,X+1).
```

(b) Similarly, the statement "CallMacro Inertia2(**Replace**: F by G, T by X, T' by $res(A,X)$; **Unchanged**: holds;)" when expanded will result in the following rules:

```
holds(G,res(A,X))  :- holds(G,X), not ~holds(G,res(A,X)).
~holds(G,res(A,X)) :- ~holds(G,X), not holds(G,res(A,X)).
```

The above illustrates how the same module Inertia2 can be used by different knowledge bases. *The first call-macro statement is appropriate to reason about inertia in a narrative while the second is appropriate to reason about inertia with respect to hypothetical situations.*

5 Modules for Planning and Reasoning About Actions

In this section we present several modules that we will later use in planning and reasoning about actions. In the process, we will show how certain modules can be used through appropriate macro calls in different ways.

---

[4] All such statements in the rest of this paper can be thought of as formal results. But since their proofs are straight forward we refrain from adding a whole bunch of propositions.

5.1 Forall

We start with a module called 'Forall' defined as follows:

```
Module_Name: Forall.
Parameters(Input: in(X,S), p(X,T); Output: all(S,T);).
Body: ~all(S,T) :- in(X,S), not p(X,T).
      ~all(S,T) :- in(neg(X),S), not ~p(X,T).
      all(S,T)  :- not ~all(S,T).
```

Intuitively, the above module defines when all elements of S (positive or negative fluents) satisfy the property p at time point T. Now let us consider call-macro statements that call the above module.

- The statement "CallMacro Forall(**Replace:** X **by** F, p **by** *holds*, *all* **by** *holds_set*; **Unchanged:** S, T, in;)" when expanded will result in the following rules:

  ```
  ~holds_set(S,T) :- in(F,S), not holds(F,T).
  ~holds_set(S,T) :- in(neg(F),S), not ~holds(F,T).
  holds_set(S,T)  :- not ~holds_set(S,T).
  ```

- The statement "CallMacro Forall(**Replace:** X **by** F, *in* **by** *finally*, p **by** *holds*;**Remove:** $\{S\}$ **from** *all*, $\{S\}$ **from** *in*, $\{S\}$ **from** p; **Unchanged:** all, T;)" when expanded will result in the following rule:

  ```
  ~all(T) :- finally(F), not holds(F,T).
  ~all(T) :- finally(neg(F)), not ~holds(F,T).
  all(T)  :- not ~all(T).
  ```

The above rules define when all goal fluents (given by the predicate 'finally') are true at a time point T. Although the module specification of 'Forall' has an extra variable S, when the above macro call is expanded, S is removed.

5.2 Dynamic Causal Laws

Now let us consider a module that reasons about the effect of an action. The effect of an action is encoded using $causes(a, f, s)$, where a is an action, f is a fluent literal and s is a set of fluent literals. Intuitively, $causes(a, f, s)$ means that a will make f true in the 'next' situation if all literals in s hold in the situation where a is executed or a is to be executed.

```
Module_name: Dynamic1.
Parameters(Input: causes(A,F,S), holds_set(S,T);
           Output: holds(F,T');).
Body: holds(F,T')  :- causes(A,F,S), holds_set(S,T).
      ~holds(F,T')  :- causes(A,neg(F),S), holds_set(S,T).
```

Now let us consider call-macro statements that call the above module.

- The statement "CallMacro Dynamic1(**Replace**: F **by** G, T **by** X, T' **by** $X+1$; **Specialize**: *occurs(A,X)*; **Unchanged**: A, S, holds, causes, holds_set;)" when expanded will result in the following rules:

```
holds(G,X+1)   :- occurs(A,X), causes(A,G,S), holds_set(S,X).
~holds(G,X+1) :- occurs(A,X), causes(A,neg(G),S),
                 holds_set(S,X).
```

- The statement "CallMacro Dynamic1(**Replace**: F **by** G, T **by** X, T' **by** *res(A,X)*; **Unchanged**: A, S, holds, causes, holds_set;)" when expanded will result in the following rules:

```
holds(G,res(A,X))   :- causes(A,G,S), holds_set(S,X).
~holds(G,res(A,X)) :- causes(A,neg(G),S),holds_set(S,X).
```

- The statement "CallMacro Dynamic1(**Replace**: F **by** G, T **by** X, T' **by** $X+D$; **Specialize**: *occurs(A,X)*, *duration(A,D)*; **Unchanged**: A, S, holds, causes, holds_set;)" when expanded will result in the following rules:

```
holds(G,X+D)   :- causes(A,G,S), holds_set(S,X),
                  occurs(A,X), duration(A,D).
~holds(G,X+D) :- causes(A,neg(G),S), holds_set(S,X),
                  occurs(A,X), duration(A,D).
```

The above illustrates how the module Dynamic1 can be used in three different ways: when reasoning about narratives where each action has a unit duration, when reasoning about hypothetical execution of actions, and when reasoning about narratives where each action has a duration that is given.

5.3 Enumeration

```
Module_Name: Enumerate1.
Parameters(Input: r(X), s(Y);Output: q(X,Y);). Types:Z=type X.
Body: ~q(X,Y) :- q(Z,Y), X!=Z, s(Y).
       q(X,Y)   :- r(X), s(Y), not ~q(X,Y).
```

The statement "CallMacro Enumerate1(**Replace**: *r* **by** *action*, *s* **by** *time*, *q* **by** *occurs*, *X* **by** *A*, *Y* **by** *T*;)" when expanded will result in the following rules:

```
~occurs(A,T) :- occurs(Z,T), A!=Z, time(T).
occurs(A,T)   :- action(A), time(T), not ~occurs(A,T).
```

5.4 Initialize

```
Module_Name: Initialize.
Parameters(Input: initially(F); Output: holds(F,0);).
Body: holds(F,0)   :- initially(F).
       ~holds(F,0) :- initially(neg(F)).
```

6 Planning

In this section we show how we can specify a planning program (and also a planning module) using call-macro statements to modules defined in the previous section.

6.1 An AnsProlog Planning Program in Smodels Syntax

We start with a program that does planning. In the following program we have two actions a and b, and two fluents f and p. The action a makes f true if p is true when it is executed, while the action b makes p false if f is true when it is executed. Initially p is true and f is false and the goal is to make f true and p false.

```
initially(neg(f)).  initially(p).       causes(a,f,s).
in(p,s).            set(s).             causes(b, neg(p), ss).
in(f,ss).           set(ss).            action(a).
action(b).          fluent(p).          fluent(f).
finally(f).         finally(neg(p)).    #const length = 1.
time(0..length).    #domain fluent(F).  #domain set(S).
#domain action(A).  #domain time(T).    #show holds(X,Y).
#show occurs(X,Y).


holds(F,0)         :- initially(F).
~holds(F,0)        :- initially(neg(F)).
holds(F, T+1)      :- holds(F,T), not ~holds(F,T+1).
~holds(F, T+1)     :- ~holds(F,T), not holds(F,T+1).
holds(F,T+1)       :- occurs(A,T), causes(A,F,S), holds_set(S,T).
~holds(F,T+1)      :- occurs(A,T),causes(A,neg(F),S),holds_set(S,T).
~holds_set(S,T)    :- in(F,S), not holds(F,T).
~holds_set(S,T)    :- in(neg(F),S), not ~holds(F,T).
holds_set(S,T)     :- not ~holds_set(S,T).
o_occurs(A,T)      :- occurs(Z,T), A!=Z, time(T).
occurs(A,T)        :- action(A), time(T), not o_occurs(A,T).
~allgoal           :- finally(F), not holds(F,length+1).
~allgoal           :- finally(neg(F)), not ~holds(F,length+1).
allgoal            :- not ~allgoal.
                   :- not allgoal.
```

6.2 A Planning Module That Calls Several Macros

We now define a planning module that has many call-macro statements calling macros defined in the previous section.

```
Module_name: Simple_Planning.
Parameters(Input: initially(F), causes(A,F,S), finally(F),
    in(F,S), action(A), length, holds(F, T), holds_set(S, T),
    time(T); Output: occurs(A,T), allgoal;).
Body: Callmacro Initialize(Unchanged: initially, holds, F;).
      Callmacro Inertia2(Replace: T' by T+1;
                         Unchanged: holds, F, T;).
```

```
Callmacro Dynamic1(Replace: T' by T+1;
                        Specialize: occurs(A,X);
             Unchanged: causes, holds_set, holds, A, F, S, T;).
   Callmacro Forall(Replace: X by F, p by holds, all by holds_set;
                    Unchanged: in, S, T).
   Callmacro Enumerate1(Replace: X by A, Y by T, r by action,
                        s by time, q by occurs;).
   Callmacro Forall(Replace: X by F, in by finally, p by holds,
                    all by allgoal; Remove: {S, T} from all,
                    {S} from in, {T} from p; Add: {length+1} to p;).
:- not allgoal.
```

6.3   A Planning Program That Calls the Planning Module

A planning program that calls the planning module in Section 6.2 and which when expanded results in the planning program in will consist of the declaration (first 9 lines) of the module in Section 6.1 and the following call:

```
Callmacro Simple_Planning(Unchanged: F, S, initially, causes,
    finally, in, action, length, holds, holds_set, time, occurs,
    allgoal;).
```

7   Ensembles and Associated Modules

So far in this paper we have focused on macros and macro expansions. To take the reuse and independent development of modules in an object-oriented manner further we propose that modules be grouped together under a "heading". This is analogous to object-oriented languages such as Java where methods that operate on the objects of a class are grouped under that class. In other words the "headings" in Java are class names under which methods are grouped.

Before we elaborate on what we propose as "headings" for our purpose here, we first consider some examples from Java. A typical class in Java (from Chapter 3 of [Horstman 2005]) is *BankAccount*. Associated with this class are the methods *deposit*, *withdraw* and *getBalance*. A subclass of *BankAccount* (from Chapter 13 of [Horstman 2005]) is the class *SavingsAccount*. In Java, in the *SavingsAccount* class definition one only specifies new methods as it automatically inherits all methods from the *BankAccount* class. An example of a new method for the class *SavingsAccount* is *addInterest*.

The questions we would now like to address are: How are modules, as defined in this paper, organized? If they are grouped, how are they grouped and under what "headings"? If they are grouped, how do inheritance and polymorphism manifest themselves?

We propose that the modules be grouped under "headings". That allows one to locate a module more easily, compare modules that are similar, notice duplicate modules, etc. In regards to what "headings" we should use for grouping the modules, we notice that a module has predicates specified in its parameters and each positions of these predicates have an associate class. Thus we define a notion of an *ensemble* as a pair consisting of a set of classes S and a set of relation schemas R and propose to use ensembles as "headings" under which modules are grouped.

An example of an ensemble is a set $S = \{action, fluent, time\}$ and $R = \{initially(fluent\text{-}literals), causes(action, fluent\text{-}literals, set\ of\ fluent\ literals), finally(fluent\text{-}literals)\}$. Associated with each ensemble are a set of modules about those classes and relation schemas.

Similar to the notion of classes and sub-classes in Java we define the notion of sub-ensembles as follows. Let $E = (S, R)$ be an ensemble and $E' = (S', R')$ be another ensemble. We say E' is a sub-ensemble of E if there is a total one-to-one function f from S to S' such that for all class $c \in S$, $f(c)$ is a sub-class of c and $R \subseteq R'$.

By $F(S)$ we denote the subset of S given by $\{f(c) \mid c \in S\}$. Let us assume S and S' are of the same cardinality and $R = R'$. In that case E' basically has specialized subclasses for the various classes in E. Thus E' inherits the original modules (in the absence of overriding) that are in E and it may have special modules. For example S' may have the class $move\_actions$ which are a sub-class of $actions$ [Lifschitz & Ren 2006] and thus E' may have additional modules about such a sub-class of actions.

The above definition allows more relation schemas in E' than E. On the surface of it this may be counter-intuitive, but the intuition becomes clear when we assume $S = S'$. In that case E' has more relation schemas, so it can have more modules than in E. Thus E' can inherit all modules that correspond to E and can have more modules. In addition E' may have some module of the same name as E. In that case when one is in E' the module definition there overrides the module of the same name in E. E' can also have more classes than E and the intuition behind it is similar to the above and becomes clear when one assumes $S \subseteq S'$.

Macro calls can be used inside modules. When calling modules one then needs to specify the ensemble name from where the module comes from. This is analogous to class.methods calls in Java.

When developing a large knowledge base we will have an ensemble which will consist of a set of class names and a set of relation schemas. It will have its own modules. This ensemble will automatically inherit (when not overridden by its own modules) from various of its super-ensembles. One needs to deal with the case when an ensemble has say two super-ensembles each of which have a module of the same name.

For a knowledge base, exactly one of its module will be the "main" module. This is analogous to the "main" method in Java. This module may contain rules as well as macro calls to other modules that are defined or inherited. The set of rules of this module, after macro expansion will be the program that will be run to obtain answer sets or used to answer queries.

8   Conclusion, Related Work and Software Availability

In this paper we have introduced language constructs – syntax and semantics, that allows one to specify reusable modules for answer set programming. We illustrate our approach with respect to the planning example, and present several modules that can be called from a planning program. We also hint at how some of those modules, such as inertia, can be used by a program that does hypothetical reasoning about actions. In particular, while the statement "CallMacro Inertia2(**Replace**: F by G, T by X, T' **by** $X+1$; **Unchanged**: holds;)" can be used in a planning program or a program that reasons with narratives the statement "CallMacro Inertia2(**Replace**: F **by** G, T **by** X, T' **by** $res(A,X)$; **Unchanged**: holds;)" can be used for hypothetical reasoning about actions. Note that both of them call the same module Inertia2. This is what we earlier referred to as reuse of code.

Among other works, our work is close to [Calimeri *et al.* 2004], [Gelfond 2006], [Lifschitz & Ren 2006]. In [Calimeri *et al.* 2004] 'templates' are used to quickly introduce new predefined constructs and to deal with compound data structures. The approach in [Gelfond 2006] is similar to us, and in [Lifschitz & Ren 2006] modular action theories are considered. Our use of "Replace" and the resulting simpler parameter matching – than in our earlier version of the paper in AAAI'06 spring symposium, is inspired by [Lifschitz & Ren 2006], which was also presented in the same symposium. Earlier, Chen et al. [Chen, Kifer, & Warren 1993] proposed the language of Hi-log that allows specification similar to our transitive closure modules. Other works in logic programming that discuss modularity include [Bugliesi *et al.* 1994, Eiter *et al.* 1997, Etalle & Gabbrielli 1996] and [Maher 1993].

Besides the above and CYC [Guha 1990] most recent efforts on resources for large scale knowledge base development and integration have focused on issues such as ontologies [Niles & Pease 2001], ontology languages [Dean *et al.* 2002], [Horrocks *et al.* 2003], [rul 2005], [Boley *et al.* 2004], [Grosof *et al.* 2003], and interchange formats [Genesereth & Fikes 1992, com]. Those issues are complementary to the issue we touch upon on this paper.

An initial implementation of an interface and interpreter of modules and macro calls is available at http://www.baral.us/modules/. As this is being written, we are still fine tuning the implementation.

Acknowledgements

We thank Michael Gelfond, Joohyung Lee, John McCarthy, Steve Maiorano, other participants of the 2006 AAAI spring symposium and anonymous reviewers for their suggestions. This work was supported by a DOT/ARDA contract and NSF grant 0412000.

References

[Baral 2003]   Baral, C. 2003. *Knowledge representation, reasoning and declarative problem solving*. Cambridge University Press.

[Baselice, Bonatti, & Gelfond 2005] Baselice, S.; Bonatti, P.; and Gelfond, M. 2005. Towards an integration of answer set and constraint solving. In *Proc. of ICLP'05*.

[Boley *et al.* 2004] Boley, H.; Grosof, B.; Kifer, M.; Sintek, M.; Tabet, S.; and Wagner, G. 2004. Object-Oriented RuleML. http://www.ruleml.org/indoo/indoo.html.

[Bugliesi *et al.* 1994] Bugliesi, M.; Lamma, E.; Mello, P. 1994. Modularity in logic programming. In *Journal of logic programming*, Vol. 19-20, 443–502.

[Calimeri *et al.* 2004] Calimeri, F.; Ianni, G.; Ielpa, G.; Pietramala, A.; and Santoro, M. 2004. A system with template answer set programs. In *JELIA*, 693–697.

[Chen, Kifer, & Warren 1993] Chen, W.; Kifer, M.; and Warren, D. 1993. A foundation for higher-order logic programming. *Journal of Logic Programming* 15(3):187–230.

[com]   Common Logic Standard. http://philebus.tamu.edu/cl/.

[Dean *et al.* 2002] Dean, M.; Connolly, D.; van Harmelen, F.; Hendler, J.; Horrocks, I.; McGuinness, D.; Patel-Schneider, P.; and Stein, L. 2002. OWL web ontology language 1.0 reference. http://www.w3.org/TR/owl-ref/.

[Eiter *et al.* 1997] Eiter, T.; Gottlob, G.; Veith, H. 1997. Modular logic programming and generalized quantifiers. In *Proc. 4th international conference on Logic programming and non-monotonic reasoning*, 290–309. Springer

[Etalle & Gabbrielli 1996] Etalle, S.; Gabbrielli M. 1996. Transformations of CLP modules. In *Theoretical computer science*, Vol. 166, 101–146.

[Gelfond & Gabaldon 1997] Gelfond, M., and Gabaldon, A. 1997. From functional specifications to logic programs. In Maluszynski, J., ed., *Proc. of International symposium on logic programming*, 355–370.

[Gelfond & Lifschitz 1988] Gelfond, M., and Lifschitz, V. 1988. The stable model semantics for logic programming. In Kowalski, R., and Bowen, K., eds., *Logic Programming: Proc. of the Fifth Int'l Conf. and Symp.*, 1070–1080. MIT Press.

[Gelfond 2006] Gelfond, M. 2006. Going places - notes on a modular development of knowledge about travel. In *Proceedings of AAAI 06 Spring Symposium: Formalizing and Compiling Background Knowledge and Its Applications to Knowledge Representation and Question Answering*.

[Genesereth & Fikes 1992] Genesereth, M., and Fikes, R. 1992. Knowledge interchange format. Technical Report Technical Report Logic-92-1, Stanford University.

[Grosof *et al.* 2003] Grosof, B.; Horrocks, I.; Volz, R.; and Decker, S. 2003. Description Logic Programs: Combining Logic Programs with Description Logic. In *Proceedings of 12th International Conference on the World Wide Web (WWW-2003)*.

[Guha 1990] Guha, R. 1990. Micro-theories and Contexts in Cyc Part I: Basic Issues. Technical Report MCC Technical Report Number ACT-CYC-129-90.

[Horrocks *et al.* 2003] Horrocks, I.; Patel-Schneider, P.; Boley, H.; Tabet, S.; Grosof, B.; and Dean, M. 2003. SWRL: A Semantic Web Rule Language Combining OWL and RuleML. http://www.daml.org/2003/11/swrl/.

[Horstman 2005] Horstman, C. 2005. *Big java*. John Wiley.

[Lifschitz & Ren 2006] Lifschitz, V. and Ren, W. 2006. Towards a Modular action description language. In *Proceedings of AAAI 06 Spring Symposium: Formalizing and Compiling Background Knowledge and Its Applications to Knowledge Representation and Question Answering*.

[Maher 1993] Maher, M. 1993. A transformation system for deductive databases modules with perfect model semantics. In *Theoretical computer science*, Vol. 110, 377–403.

[McCarthy 1993] McCarthy, J. 1993. Notes on formalizing contexts. In Bajcsy, R., ed., *Proceedings of the Thirteenth International Joint Conference on Artificial Intelligence*, 555–560. San Mateo, California: Morgan Kaufmann.

[Miller *et al.* 1990] Miller, G.; Beckwith, R.; Fellbaum, C.; Gross, D.; and Miller, K. 1990. Introduction to wordnet: An on-line lexical database. *International Journal of Lexicography (special issue)* 3(4):235– 312.

[Niemelä & Simons 1997] Niemelä, I., and Simons, P. 1997. Smodels – an implementation of the stable model and well-founded semantics for normal logic programs. In Dix, J.; Furbach, U.; and Nerode, A., eds., *Proc. 4th international conference on Logic programming and non-monotonic reasoning*, 420–429. Springer.

[Niles & Pease 2001] Niles, I., and Pease, A. 2001. Towards a standard upper ontology. In *Proceedings of the international conference on Formal Ontology in Information Systems*, 2–9.

[rul 2005] 2005. RuleML: The Rule Markup Initiative. http://www.ruleml.org/.

[Tari, Baral, & Anwar 2005] Tari, L.; Baral, C.; and Anwar, S. 2005. A Language for Modular ASP: Application to ACC Tournament Scheduling. In *Proc. of ASP'05*.

Deductive Spreadsheets Using
Tabled Logic Programming

C.R. Ramakrishnan, I.V. Ramakrishnan, and David S. Warren

Dept. of Computer Science, Stony Brook University, Stony Brook, NY 11794-4400
{cram, ram, warren}@cs.sunysb.edu

Abstract. Rule-based specifications in Datalog are used in a number of application areas, such as configuration management, access control and trust management, decision making, etc. However, rules sets are typically hard to maintain; the rules often interact in subtle ways, making them difficult to understand and reason about. This has impeded the wide-spread adoption of rule-based computing. This paper describes the design and implementation of XcelLog, a deductive spreadsheet system (DSS), that permits users to specify and maintain Datalog rules using the popular and easy-to-use spreadsheet interface. The driving idea underlying the system is to treat sets as the fundamental data type and rules as specifying relationships among sets, and use the spreadsheet metaphor to create and view the materialized sets. The fundamental feature that makes XcelLog suitable even for non-programmers is that the user mainly sees the effect of the rules; when rules or basic facts change, the user sees the impact of the change immediately. This enables the user to gain confidence in the rules and their modification, and also experiment with what-if scenarios without any programming. XcelLog is implemented as an add-in to Excel with XSB serving as the rule engine for evaluating Datalog specifications. Preliminary experience with using XcelLog indicates that it is indeed feasible to combine the power of rule-based computing and the elegance and simplicity of the spreadsheet metaphor, so that end users can encode and maintain rule bases with little or no programming.

1 Introduction

The defining problem: Rule-based specifications are used in a wide variety of applications. Examples include business rules (e.g. [19]), authorization rules for scalable access control and distributed trust management (e.g. [11, 16]), and configuration management of complex systems (e.g. system administration [2], security policy configuration [14], and vulnerability analysis [17, 18]). Also automated support for decision making is by and large based on rule-based systems. Usually Datalog [3, 25] and extensions of Datalog are used for rule specifications. However, a major factor that hampers their large-scale adoption is the difficulty of developing, understanding and modifying the (rule-based) specifications. In general, it is not easy to infer the effect of a rule from the way in which it is written. Rule systems need a "programmer" to specify the rules and additional tools to analyze the rules in order to convince the users of their soundness and completeness; a case in point is the SELinux security policies [14] and the variety of tools that have been developed to analyze these policies [6, 7, 23]. This raises the

S. Etalle and M. Truszczyński (Eds.): ICLP 2006, LNCS 4079, pp. 391–405, 2006.

question: How can we simplify the creation of rule-based applications and their maintenance? More interestingly can we empower end-users to develop such applications
with very little or better still with no programming?

Deductive Spreadsheets: The electronic spreadsheet, as exemplified by Excel®, is a
spectacularly popular application program that is widely used by the masses. Every
spreadsheet user effectively creates a program to process data without having to be
trained as a programmer. The large-scale adoption of spreadsheets as a programming
tool by the masses (albeit for particular classes of problems) is mainly because computations are specified by examples. A user specifies an instance of a computation (e.g.
sum of two cells in a row); subsequently by copying and filling, the user specifies that
the other cells (the destination of the filling gesture) are computed in a "similar" manner. This allows the user to not have to think about abstractions and general parameterized operations, but instead concentrate on multiple concrete operations. Moreover, the
spreadsheet user interface shows the results of the computation directly and changes the
results whenever the underlying data changes. This direct interaction with data eliminates the line between code development and testing.

The idea of *deductive spreadsheets* (DSS) is to bring the power of rules-driven computing within the familiar paradigm of spreadsheets — specifically empower end users,
particularly non-programmers to write and maintain rules, not in an ad hoc language,
but in terms of the effect of the rules on an underlying sample of data using the classic
2-D graphical spreadsheet metaphor.

An Example: We illustrate the idea of DSS using a simple example from Trust Management (following [12]).

1. A publisher, PUB, wants to give a discount to their member, which is anyone who
   is both a student and a preferred customer.
2. PUB delegates the authority over the identification of preferred customers to its
   parent organization ORG.
3. ORG has a policy of treating IEEE members as preferred customers.
4. PUB also delegates the authority over the identification of students to accredited
   universities.
5. The identification of accredited universities, in turn, is based on credentials issued
   by the University Accreditation Board, UAB.

These rules, which form a deductive system, have been traditionally written in a
special syntax specific to the trust management system; the meaning of the rules is
usually given in terms of the set of all logical inferences that can be drawn from these
rules. Using a DSS, the same rules can be specified and their impact can be more directly
visualized as in Figure 1.

Following traditional spreadsheets, a DSS is a two dimensional array of cells. However, columns and rows in a DSS are labeled by symbolic values. For instance, rows in
the DSS shown in Figure 1, labeled PUB, ORG, ..., represent entities referenced in the
example. Columns correspond to properties of these entities. The value in a cell at row
r and column c (denoted by $r.c$, or in a functional notation $(c\ r)$) represents the value of
property c of entity r. For instance, the cell "IEEE.member" represents the set of IEEE

	member	preferred	student	univ
PUB	*PUB.preferred* && *PUB.student* /* Rule 1 */ {Amy}	*ORG.preferred* /* Rule 2 */ {Amy, Joe}	*PUB.univ.student* /* Rule 4 */ {Amy, Bob}	*UAB.member* /* Rule 5 */ {ESU, USB}
ORG		*IEEE.member* /* Rule 3 */ {Amy, Joe}		
IEEE	{Amy, Joe}			
UAB	{ESU, USB}			
ESU			{Amy}	
USB			{Bob}	

Fig. 1. Deductive Spreadsheet for Discount Eligibility

members; and the cell "UAB.member" represents the set of universities accredited by UAB. To manipulate multiple interrelated DSSs, we use the notation $s!r.c$ to denote the cell $r.c$ in sheet s.

Note that, unlike in a traditional spreadsheet (and indeed in other logical spreadsheets, e.g. [5, 10]), each DSS cell contains a *set* of values. Cell references correspond to expressions that evaluate to a set. In the figure, expressions (called *intensions*) are shown in *italics* and their values (called *extensions*) are shown in `teletype`. In the figure the cell expressions and comments (enclosed between "/*" and "*/") are shown for illustration only. Following traditional spreadsheets, the user specifies only the intensions; the DSS system computes the extensions, shows only the extensions in the cells, and recomputes them whenever cell values change.

Now consider the encoding of Rule 3 of the example above, which states that every IEEE member is a preferred customer of ORG. This is specified in DSS using a *cell reference*: the cell *ORG.preferred* contains a reference to another cell *IEEE.member*, indicating that whatever occurs in *IEEE.member* must also occur in *ORG.preferred*. This is analogous to the idea in traditional spreadsheets of referring in one cell to the numeric value in another cell. Rules 2 and 5 can be similarly encoded. Rule 4 states that PUB delegates the identification of students to recognized universities. Note that *PUB.univ* contains the set of all universities recognized by PUB and hence $u.student \subseteq PUB.student$ whenever $u \in PUB.univ$. This (rather complex) rule can be specified by "lifting" the dot notation to sets: for example, $a.b.c$ represents $\bigcup y.c$ for every y in $a.b$. In the example, the cell *PUB.student* contains the expression *PUB.univ.student*. Finally, Rule 1 states that *Pub.member* consists of entities that are in both *PUB.preferred* and *PUB.student*.

These two ideas: (1) allowing cells to contain multiple values and (2) permitting cell references that make the statement that a cell must contain all the elements of another cell, bring the power of deduction into a simple spreadsheet framework. Thus they provide the foundation for our vision of DSS.

As a natural consequence of set-valued cells, DSS permits a cell $a.b$ to contain multiple cell references: the meaning of such an expression is that the value of $a.b$ is a set that contains the union of all the values of the referred cells. Moreover, the cell references may be recursive in general. The meaning of recursive references is given in terms of least fixed points [13]. Set-valued cells and recursive definitions provide a powerful platform for encoding complex problems involving deduction. Nevertheless, from an end-user's perspective, these are relatively simple extensions to the traditional spreadsheet paradigm, thereby adding the power of deduction without compromising the simplicity of defining and using spreadsheets. The interesting problem now is to realize a functional DSS system based on the above ideas.

The rest of this paper describes our technical approach to the design and implementation of the DSS system envisioned above. A fundamental design decision was to construct a DSS system as a conservative extension of a traditional spreadsheet system. We thus inherit the advantages of traditional spreadsheets, such as the extensive user base and the availability of data visualization tools. We inherit some of the disadvantages as well: while a spreadsheet is easy to develop using the various intuitive gestures, since the interface shows mainly the intensions, it is usually difficult to comprehend a spreadsheet after it is fully developed. Nevertheless, the enormous popularity of traditional spreadsheet systems indicates that the advantages far outweigh the disadvantages.

The starting point of our technical development is the design of the DSS expression language and intuitive gestures for specifying contents of cells and relationships between them (see Section 2). In general DSS expressions can involve circular references as is typical when computing with logical relations. We give least-model semantics [13] to DSS expressions by translating them into Datalog programs. In Section 3 we describe the implementation of XcelLog, our prototype DSS system, with Excel as it's front-end and our XSB tabled logic programming system as the backend deduction machine [21]. We have encoded problems drawn from a number of application domains including logistics and combinatorial optimization in XcelLog. We illustrate the encoding of one such problem in Section 4. There have been a large number of proposals to combine logic with the spreadsheet metaphor; our approach differs in a fundamental way from the others by supporting set-valued cells and meaningful recursive definitions. In Section 5 we describe related work in more detail. Discussion appears in Section 6.

2   The Deductive Spreadsheet Language

The primary design criterion for the DSS language was simplicity: the users should be able to construct and manipulate deductive spreadsheets with gestures, operators and expressions that are easy to learn and intuitive to use. Abstraction is one of the fundamental aspects of programming, and also one of the most difficult aspects to learn and master. User-level programming in spreadsheets cleverly circumvent this problem by letting the user program by examples (e.g. specifying an expression in a specific cell) and then generalize the program (e.g. by filling cells with expression from another cell). Thus users never deal directly with the notion of variables. We have followed the same philosophy by designing an expression language without variables. The following is a brief summary of the salient aspects of the language.

A deductive spreadsheet contains a grid of cells, each of which contains a set of elements. A spreadsheet may also refer to an external database table. Thus tables, spread-

sheets, cells, and elements are the four classes of entities that will be defined and manipulated by our language. We classify the operators based on the entities they produce,
as follows:

1. *Element operators:* Elements can be atomic values (strings, integers, etc.) or formed
   using *tuple construction, tuple projection, arithmetic, aggregation* (such as SUM,
   MIN, MAX, etc.) and conditional operators. The tuple construction and projection
   operations offer a way to create and access data structures.
2. *Cell operators:* Cell expressions evaluate to sets of elements. The contents of a
   cell may be specified by explicitly listing a set of elements, and/or by expressions
   constructed using *cell reference, selection, difference* and *lifted operators* that lift
   tuple construction, tuple projection, aggregation and conditionals to sets.
3. *Sheet operators* to construct a sheet from other sheets or from database tables.
4. *Abstraction operators:* Copy and paste gestures, extended from those present in
   traditional spreadsheets, permit the user to first specify a computation on concrete
   instances, then copy the specification and "fill" other cells, which causes similar
   specifications to be generated for the destination cells. In particular a user in DSS
   can bulk copy a subset of cells and paste it into a target cell.

These operators are relationally complete. We will illustrate their use in the encoding
exercises later on (in Section 4). As is the case with traditional spreadsheets DSS users
also type in simple expressions either in the cells directly or in the function box f_x.
More complex expressions get created by gestures such as copy, paste and fill.

Semantics: The semantics of a DSS expression is given by translation to Datalog programs, i.e., Prolog programs without function symbols [15]. A Prolog program consists
of rules of the form *head :- body* where *head* is a literal and *body* is a conjunct of literals. The *head* is true whenever the *body* is true. A *head* with an empty *body* is a fact
that is unconditionally true.

A set of spreadsheets defines a 4-ary relation:*sheet(Name,Row,Column,Contents)*,
where *sheet(Sht, Ro, Co, Ent)* is true iff *Ent* is in the cell at the intersection of the row
Ro and column *Co* in sheet *Sht*. For example, the upper left cell in the DSS table named
say 'discount' in Figure 1, is defined by the Prolog rule:

```
sheet(discount,'PUB',discount,X)  :-
      sheet(discount,'PUB',preferred,X),
      sheet(discount,'PUB',student,X).
```

The meaning of the spreadsheet is the least fixed point of the Datalog program defined in this way. The language does include negation (in set difference and in the
aggregation operators), and we require that all uses of negation be stratified.

3   The XcelLog DSS System

A deductive engine becomes a core computational infrastructure component for implementing a DSS system that is predicated on translating DSS expressions into Datalog.

A key requirement for such an engine is that it completely and efficiently evaluate Datalog programs. The XSB Tabled Logic Programming system is well suited for this purpose [21]. It is a high-performance deductive engine that uses tabling to implement a more complete version of resolution-based query answering. In contrast a standard Prolog system would loop infinitely when given cyclic definitions.

We implemented XcelLog, the prototype DSS system, with an Excel front end and XSB with its tabling machinery as the backend deductive engine to correctly and finitely compute the DSS semantics. Below we provide an overview of the XcelLog system. It was engineered as an Excel "add-in", i.e. the implementation of deductive spreadsheets was encapsulated within the Excel environment. This way XcelLog users would continue getting the benefits of traditional Excel along with the added power of deduction.

The architectural schematic of our XcelLog prototype for evaluating DSS expressions is shown in Figure 2. Notice that Excel and the XSB Tabled LP system are the two main components making up the XcelLog Deductive Spreadsheet System. In this architecture users see only the Excel front end. They interact with the system via Excel's familiar interface.

Cells in XcelLog are of two types: traditional Excel cells and DSS (deductive spreadsheet) cells. Deduction expressions are specified only within DSS cells. All DSS expressions are enclosed within "[ ]". E.g. the DSS expression, using functional notation for a cell reference, corresponding to the (intensional) Rule 2 is: [preferred ORG] while the (extensional) set of values computed by this expression in cell at row *PUB* and column *preferred* is the DSS expression: [Amy, Joe]. DSS cell contents of the form [...] are automatically translated for Excel as =DSS("..."). So a DSS expression in Excel's function box f_x is enclosed within "=DSS( )". These correspond to the intensional view of rules associated with DSS cells. The cells themselves display materialized views of the effect of the rules, as in Excel. Note the flexibility afforded by this system combining traditional Excel-style computing (embodied within Excel cells) intermixed with deduction specified in DSS cells.

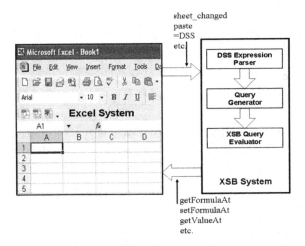

Fig. 2. The XcelLog DSS System

Evaluation of a DSS program in XcelLog requires bi-directional communication between Excel and XSB. This is facilitated via the XLL-Add-in component. The XLL-Add-in component is set up to recognize certain events such as when a cell's content is changed, when DSS expressions are entered into a cell, etc. Whenever such an event occurs, control is passed to XSB via this component, using sheet changed, paste, =DSS operations in Figure 2 (among others). XSB does the needed processing, perhaps using call-back functions that Excel provides (e.g. getFormulaAt, setFormulaAt, getValueAt operations in the figure), and then returns control back to Excel. In the basic operation of materializing a DSS cell, XSB parses the cell expression, translates it to a Prolog goal, and then simply uses `call/1` to invoke the XSB query evaluator to evaluate the goal and produce the extensional values. These are the materialized sets that get displayed in the cells. For example the materialized set corresponding to Rule 1 in Figure 1 (row PUB) and column member) that is computed by XcelLog is {Amy}. Note that in our XcelLog implementation we use the functional notation for cell references so as to be consistent with Excel. So for example "`PUB.preferred`" in functional notation is "`preferred PUB`". More details of the implementation now follows.

3.1 DSS Prototype Implementation in XSB

The DSS prototype is implemented as an addin to Microsoft Excel. The main functionality is provided through 1) a set XSB predicates that are invoked by Excel, and 2) a set of functions that XSB invokes to exchange information with Excel.

The major XSB predicates invoked by Excel are `sheet_changed` and `dss`. `sheet_changed` is called when the formula value of a cell (or set of cells) in the Excel spreadsheet is changed. `dss` is called by Excel to evaluate the user-registered function =DSS. `sheet_changed` performs two functions: it allows a user to enter a DSS expression in square brackets instead of requiring it to be entered in an `=DSS("...")` context, and it notifies Excel to re-evaluate those cells whose values might have changed as a result of the change to this cell. So if the entered value is enclosed in square brackets, Excel is called to replace the cell formula value by a call to the user function =DSS, passing the bracketed string. If the formula value is changed, its value is computed incrementally by XSB using the technique described in [22]. The incremental evaluation procedure maintains dependency information between the cell values. When a cell value is changed, only those cells which depend on the changed value are recomputed.

The other main entry point to the XSB code is through the registered user function =DSS. When =DSS ("dss expression") is the formula value of a cell whose (extensional) value Excel needs, it calls XSB passing the string argument and XSB returns the value. All the main work of DSS is done in this XSB predicate, `dss`. The string representing the DSS expression is parsed and translated into a pair consisting of a goal and a variable. The goal is called and all instantiations of the variable are accumulated, translated to a display string form, and that string is returned to Excel. During the evaluation of such a goal, access may be required to the values of other cells in the spreadsheet. This is managed by the XSB predicate `getXSBValueAt`. `getXSBValueAt` calls Excel to get the formula value of the desired cell, translates it to a goal and variable, calls the goal and returns the values of the variable. A key point is that `getXSBValueAt` is tabled. This allows XSB's tabling mechanism to minimize communication with Excel and to properly handle recursive spreadsheets, i.e. those with cyclic dependencies.

XSB's tabling mechanism transparently handles recursive definitions. The real data dependencies had to be hidden from Excel, since Excel refuses to allow any form of cyclic dependency. From Excel's point of view, the DSS expression passed as a string argument to the =DSS function is opaque.

4   Encoding Exercises in XcelLog

We have encoded a number of problems, drawn from varied areas such as logistics, combinatorial optimization and network security, in XcelLog. Here we illustrate two such problems to demonstrate its deductive power and versatility. The first example deals with directed graphs, and determines, for each node in the graph, the set of all nodes reachable from it. This example shows the need for recursive definitions, and the naturalness of the least fixed point semantics. It also illustrates the example-based mechanism for defining new relations. The second example is a more complex one, of finding optimal purchase strategy in a supply chain. This example illustrates features of XcelLog that were described but not illustrated before: (a) the use of tuple values in cells, (b) aggregation operations over cell values, and (c) abstraction. Moreover, this example also shows the power of XcelLog to encode complex problems of this nature with few relatively simple gestures.

(1) The reachability problem in graphs: The problem here is to compute the set of reachable nodes from every node in the graph in Figure 3(a). This is the canonical transitive closure example that is used for illustrating deduction through recursive rules.

Figure 3(b) depicts a fragment of the encoding in XcelLog. The rows represent the 4 nodes in the graph. The edge column for a row contains the set of nodes directly reachable from that node through some edge. The f_x box associated with a cell show the DSS definitions of the cell contents and the cell itself shows its computed contents of these definitions. In Figure 3(b), the DSS expression =DSS("a,d") in the f_x box is associated with the highlighted cell in row b and column edge. This expression indicates that nodes a and d are targets of edges from node b. The f_x box in Figure 3(c) is the DSS expression associated with the reach cell in row b. The =DSS("edge b, edge reach b") cell expression indicates that there are two ways to get an entry in this highlighted cell: "edge b" indicates that every entry in the cell at column edge and row b must be in this cell; "edge reach b" indicates that we take each entry in the cell at column reach and row b (a node reachable from b), and using that value as the row indicator in column edge, we add the entries in *that* cell to the current cell (i.e. those reachable by taking one more edge). This is an example of a cyclic specification: the reach column of row b contains a cell expression that refers to itself.

The user sees the effect of the rules (which are the materialized sets) rather than the rule itself. In addition when the rules or base facts change the user can immediately see their effect. For example, if we remove the edge from b to a in Figure 3(a) and add the edge from b to c instead, then XcelLog recomputes the new set of reachable nodes (see Figure 3(d)). Thus it provides immediate feedback to "what-if" scenarios.

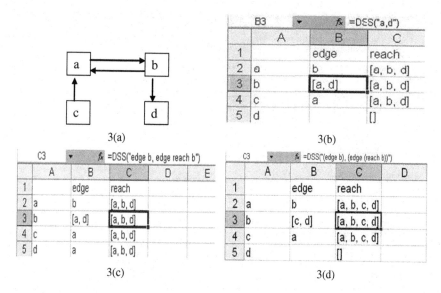

Fig. 3. Reachability problem

It is noteworthy pointing out how the user creates this DSS. First he types in all the entries into the edge column. These are the direct edges between nodes (see the edge column in Figure 3(b)). Next he creates the reach expression for a cell say in row b and column reach (see the f_x box in Figure 3(c)). Then he copies this expression (using DSS copy) and fills (using the DSS paste operation) all the cells in the reach column with the copied expression. The system automatically inserts the appropriate row number into the expression for the corresponding reach cell in that row. This is similar in terms of user experience with traditional spreadsheets. However the idea of allowing set valued cell expressions and cyclic references as illustrated in this example, has enabled the user to perform more complex computations.

The DSS expression in the reach column in Figure 3(c) gets translated to the following left-recursive Datalog rules:

```
graph(b,'reach',X) :- graph(b,'edge',X).
graph(b,'reach',X) :- graph(b,'reach',Y), graph(Y,'edge',X).
```

The XSB system evaluates the recursive rules and passes the computed result (in this case, the set {a, b, d} of reachable nodes) to Excel for displaying at that cell. Note that traditional Prolog systems will go into an infinite loop on this example. XSB's tabling machinery ensures termination in the presence of such recursive definitions.

(2) A complex logistics example: the supply chain problem. The supply chain of a manufacturer is a complex network of suppliers, retailers, distributors, transporters and storage facilities that participate in the sale, delivery and production of finished goods. Analysis of the behavior of the supply chain provides important information to the manufacturer for contingency planning, resource optimization, etc. Such an analysis

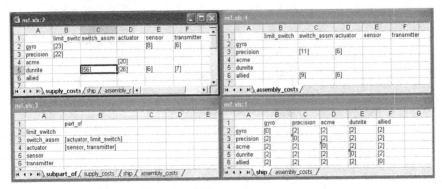

(a) base costs

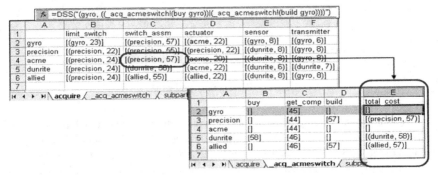

(b) computing acquisition costs

Fig. 4. Supply chain problem

can be facilitated by specifying the rules governing the supply chain parameters and relationships in DSS as illustrated below. A switch assembly consists of two major components: a limit switch and an actuator subassembly; the actuator in turn is made up of a sensor and a transmitter. Each part can either be bought off the shelf or, if a composite part, can be acquired by assembling it from its components. Figure 4(a) shows the DSSs that contain data about (a) the cost of buying a part off the shelf from different vendors (the "supply costs" sheet); (b) the cost of assembling a part (given its components) at different manufacturing sites ("assembly costs" sheet); (c) the cost of shipping a part from one site to another ("ship" sheet); and the composition of a part ("subpart of" sheet).

The purchase policy is to acquire a part from the cheapest source: either off-the-shelf, or by custom assembly. In order to compute the least cost, we create a new sheet (the "acquire" sheet shown in Figure 4(b)) with the different vendors and assemblers as rows, and the parts as columns. The value of a cell *dest.part* in this sheet represents, for a given part and the destination where it should be shipped to, the best price and a supplier that provides the given part at that price. That is, it is a pair *(v, p)* where *p* is the price that *dest* has to pay to acquire the part *part* from vendor *v*. We now describe how the values in this sheet are calculated.

Consider the purchase of the switch assembly from *acme*: this part can either be (i) bought from *dunrite* and shipped to *acme*; or (ii) its parts can be bought, shipped to one of the assemblers (*precision* or *allied*), and the final assembly shipped to *acme*. In order to encode this complex decision process, we create an intermediate sheet "_acq_acmeswitch" to represent the different ways of getting the switch assembly to *acme*. The basic idea behind an intermediate sheet is to specify, step by step, a complex expression that defines a single selected cell's value. In the above example, we use the sheet "_acq_acmeswitch" to define the cell *acme.switch_assm* in the acquire sheet.

The rows of "_acq_acmeswitch" represent all the possible sources and the columns correspond to different kinds of costs. The cells in row *gyro* in this sheet represent the following. The cell at column *buy* represents the cost of purchasing the switch assembly off the shelf from *gyro*. The value of this cell is the sum of the price at which *gyro* sells switch assemblies (i.e. the value at *gyro.switch_assm* cell in the "supply_costs" sheet) and the cost to ship from *gyro* to *acme* (i.e. the value at *gyro.acme* in the "ship" sheet). Note in this case the cell is empty since *gyro* does not sell switch assemblies. For every row **R**, the value of **R**.*buy* is given by the expression *supply_costs!***R**.*switch_assm* + *ship!***R**.*acme*. This "rule" is specified in XcelLog by first specifying an instance for *gyro*, and then filling all the cells in the buy column with the expression in *gyro.buy*.

The cell at column *get_comp* represents the cost of acquiring and sending the components of the switch assembly to *Gyro*. This cell has a more complex definition. We first need to find all the components of the switch assembly. That is given by the value in the cell *switch_assm.part_of* in the "subpart_of" sheet. For each such part **P**, the best way to get that part to *gyro* is in the cell *gyro.***P** in the "acquire" sheet. Hence the expression: "*acquire!gyro.(subpart_of!switch_assm.part_of)*" represents a set of values: each element in the set represents the best way to get some subpart of switch assembly to *gyro.*. Summing over all elements of this set therefore gives the best way to get all the components of the switch assembly. This is done by applying an aggregation operation to reduce a set to a single element (in this case, *sum*).

The cell at *build* adds the cost of assembly at *gyro* to the cost of acquiring the components (it is empty in this row since *gyro* does not assemble switch assemblies). Finally, the cell at *total_cost* represents the sum of all costs of costs for *acme* to get the switch assembly from *gyro*.

Observe that the values in column *total_cost* in "_acq_acmeswitch" sheet represent the best ways of obtaining a switch assembly to *Acme* from different vendors. The minimum over all these values is therefore the best way for *Acme* to acquire a switch assembly. This is specified in XcelLog by selecting the column values and "filling" the cell acme.swiTch_assm in the "acquire" sheet (see the arrow denoting this operation in Figure 4(b)). Note that in traditional spreadsheets, the destination of a "fill" operation must be at least as large as the source. In XcelLog, an entire column (more generally, any rectangular area in a sheet) can be used to fill a single cell. The meaning of this operation is to set the destination cell's value to the union of all the contents of the source cells. In this example, we modify this default meaning by selecting an aggregation operation — *minimum* — to apply to this union.

Consider a cell $r.c$ filled with values from a column, say cells $r_1.c', r_2.c', \ldots, r_2.c'$. Instead of generating $[r_1.c', r_2.c', \ldots, r_n.c']$ as the expression for $r.c$, we generate a more abstract expression $[exists(R, R.c')]$ where R is a variable that ranges over rows, i.e. the set $\{r_1, r_2, \ldots, r_n\}$. This *abstraction* is useful in two contexts. First of all, when the rows of a sheet change (e.g. when a new row is added), the abstraction remains unchanged but still retains the original intention of the user: that the cell shall contain all values in column c'. Note that without the abstraction, the user will have to change the expression of $r.c$ to add the new row. Secondly, the abstraction permits us to have non-materialized sheets. For instance, the sheet "_acq_acmeswitch" is used to compute the values of *acme.switch_assm* in the "acquire" sheet, but there is no such sheet corresponding to the other cells of the "acquire" sheet. Using abstractions with inlining (where a cell reference $r.c$ is replaced by the cell expression at $r.c$) we can compute the values at the other cells of the "acquire" sheet without explicitly creating the corresponding intermediate sheets.

Observe from the above examples that the spreadsheet metaphor was used to create the rules without the user having to specify any expression with variables. The traditional copy and fill gestures are used to abstract "rules" from one instance and to apply them to other instances. In this example, the only cells whose intensions were entered explicitly and not by filling (other than the four base tables) were the four cells in the *gyro* row of the _acq_acmeswitch table. The abstractions may introduce variables into DSS expressions but the user never needs to deal with them directly. Complex rule systems can be constructed with relatively simple interactions. We have thus introduced deduction into spreadsheets without compromising on its basic simplicity and ease-of-use from the end user perspective.

A noteworthy feature is that cell references can be recursive (unlike traditional spreadsheets); this enables the user to specify dynamic programming solutions. In this example, the cheapest cost of a part is defined in terms of the cheapest costs of its subparts. Indeed shortest path in a cyclic graph (with nonnegative edge weights) can be specified easily in a DSS. The specification is example based and yet at a high level: specifying only how the different cell values are related. Moreover, numeric and symbolic computations are seamlessly combined. Finally, the user sees the effect of the specifications directly and immediately; a change in a component's price, for example, would immediately propagate to all the dependent cells (as in a traditional spreadsheet.) This permits the user to experiment with what-if scenarios: e.g. the impact of a supplier ceasing to sell a particular part.

5   Related Work

Spreadsheets based on Logic: There have been a great many proposals for combining the spreadsheet metaphor with logic. A recent survey is available at http://www.ainewsletter.com/newsletters/aix_0505.htm. We will describe in more detail recent approaches that are most similar to ours.

Knowledge-sheet [5] and *PrediCalc* [10] extend traditional spreadsheets by allowing the user to specify constraints on the values of cells. Cells are still required to contain unique values, but those values may be partially (or totally) determined by constraints. In *Knowledgesheet* finite-domain constraints are associated with cells and specify combinatorial problems. On user request, the system converts these constraints into a CLP(FD) program, executes it, and returns the solution as cell values. In *PrediCalc* the constraint-solving engine is more integrated into spreadsheet interaction, and issues addressed include how to handle over-specified (or inconsistent) values and under-specified values. *PrediCalc* is similar to our model in that rows and columns of spreadsheets are given names and individual cells are referenced by providing the sheet name, the row name, and the column name. Our approach differs from these in a fundamental way in that these approaches maintain the functional aspect of traditional spreadsheets, in that each cell contains a unique value. We allow cells to contain sets of values, and cell references specify subset constraints. This means that recursively defined cells don't make sense in their functional framework but are perfectly meaningful in our relational one. *This is what really allows our spreadsheets to support full deduction.* These approaches add constraints to the functional framework, which as they have shown can be very useful, and constraints can also be added to our relational framework. Another interesting combination of rules and spreadsheets is ARulesXL (http://www.arulesxl.com/). ARulesXL allows users to define WHEN rules that specify cell contents using defined variables. The use of logic is interesting, but it retains the functional aspects of traditional spreadsheets and does not support recursive definitions. Deductive spreadsheets can be understood as specifying subset relationships among sets. There have been several proposals for programming languages that support such set specifications [8, 24]. Our DSS might be viewed as a visual interface to a language like that of [8], however the other language is much more powerful than ours; we can define only Datalog programs, whereas the other language is Turing complete. Our focus is less on the power of the underlying language and more on its presentation and usability in the tabular spreadsheet form.

Visual Programming: There are a number of research as well as commercial systems that call themselves "Visual Prolog" or "visual logic programming" systems. We can distinguish these works into two broad categories. The first one describes technologies and systems, mainly commercial ones, which provide an integrated programming environment to develop and debug Prolog programs very much akin to Forte which provides a development environment for Java programming. An example of such a system is in http://www.visual-prolog.com. The second group of works focuses on graphical interfaces to create logic programs. Examples include [1], which provides graphical symbols via which one can create Prolog terms, Prolog clauses and Prolog programs. These kinds of work are more along the lines of visual programming languages. However unlike the vision espoused in DSS, users of such systems are required to be knowledgeable of logic programming. Finally we point out a recent work that describes extensions to the Excel spreadsheet that integrate *user-defined (non-recursive) functions* into the spreadsheet grid, rather than treating them as a "bolt-on" [9]. What they have achieved is a way to specify user defined functions visually with a spreadsheet. But each cell still possesses a unique value. We can lift these point-wise user-defined functions to work over cells representing sets of values as in XcelLog.

6 Discussion

The synergy between spreadsheets and rule-based computing has the potential to put into the hands of end users (ranging from novices to power users) technology to create and manage their own automated decision support applications with the same ease with which they are currently able to create financial applications of varying complexity with traditional spreadsheets. Our XcelLog system demonstrates that technology to create rules-driven applications with the spreadsheet metaphor is feasible. Nevertheless our experience with using XcelLog suggests that there is considerable scope for further research and development. The most immediate one concerns generating and visualizing explanations of the computational behavior of DSS expressions. This is useful not only for debugging the application but also for analyzing "what if scenarios". Our work on generating explanations for deduction [4, 20] and Excel's color-coded outlines denoting cell dependencies offers a suitable starting point for this problem. Another interesting and useful problem that has emerged from our XcelLog encoding exercises is to develop a DSS methodology that will aid end users to conceptualize, and systematically develop DSS encodings for their problems. On the computing infrastructure side efficiency can be improved by using incremental algorithms for (re)evaluating DSS expressions when cell content is changed. We have implemented and integrated incremental algorithms for logic program evaluation [22] for this purpose. Progress on these fronts has the potential to make DSS a practical and easy-to-use tool for rule-based programming.

Acknowledgments

This work was supported by DARPA Contract W31P4Q-05-C-R034 to XSB Inc. We also thank Chris Rued for implementing the Excel-XSB interface.

References

1. J. Augusti, J. Puigsegur, D. Robertson, and W. Schorleme. Visual logic programming through set inclusion and chaining. In *CADE 13 Workshop on Visual Reasoning*, 1996.
2. A. L. Couch and M. Gilfi. It's elementary, dear watson: Applying logic programming to convergent system management processes. In *Proceedings of the 13th USENIX Conference on Systems Administration (LISA)*, pages 123–138, 1999.
3. S. K. Das. *Deductive Databases and Logic programming*. Addison-Wesley, 1992.
4. Y. Dong, C. R. Ramakrishnan, and S. A. Smolka. Evidence explorer: A tool for exploring model-checking proofs. In *Computer Aided Verification (CAV)*, volume 2725 of *LNCS*, pages 215–218. Springer, 2003.
5. G. Gupta and S. F. Akhter. Knowledgesheet: A graphical spreadsheet interface for interactively developing a class of constraint programs. In *Practical Aspects of Declarative Languages (PADL)*, volume 1753 of *LNCS*, pages 308–323, 2000.
6. J. D. Guttman, A. L. Herzog, and J. D. Ramsdell. Information flow in operating systems: Eager formal methods. In *Workshop on Issues in the Theory of Security (WITS)*, 2003.
7. T. Jaeger, R. Sailer, and X. Zhang. Analyzing integrity protection in the selinux example policy. In *USENIX Security Symposium*, 2003.
8. B. Jayaraman and K. Moon. Subset logic programs and their implementation. *Journal of Logic Programming*, 42:71–110, 2000.

9. S. P. Jones, A. Blackwell, and M. Burnett. A user-centered approach to function in excel. In *Intl. Conf. on Functional Programming*, 2003.

10. M. Kassoff, L.-M. Zen, A. Garg, and M. Genesereth. Predicalc: A logical spreadsheet management system. In *31st International Conference on Very Large Databases (VLDB)*, 2005.

11. N. Li, B. Grosof, and J. Feigenbaum. A practically implementable and tractable delegation logic. In *IEEE Symposium on Security and Privacy*, pages 27–42, 2000.

12. N. Li, W. H. Winsborough, and J. C. Mitchell. Distributed credential chain discovery in trust management. *Journal of Computer Security*, 11:35–86, 2003.

13. J. W. Lloyd. *Foundations of Logic Programming*. Springer-Verlag, 1987.

14. P. Loscocco and S. Smalley. Integrating flexible support for security policies into the linux operating system. In *FREENIX track of the 2001 Usenix Annual Technical Conference*, 2001. Available from http://www.nsa.gov/selinx/.

15. D. Maier and D. S. Warren. *Computing with Logic: Logic Programming and Prolog*. Benjamin/Cummings Publishers, Menlo Park, CA, 1988. 535 pp.

16. N.Li, J. Mitchell, and W. Winsborough. Design of a role-based trust-management framework. In *Proceedings of 2002 IEEE Symposium on Security and Privacy*, pages 114–130, May 2002.

17. X. Ou, S. Govindavajhala, and A. W. Appel. Mulval: A logic-based network security analyzer. In *14th Usenix Security Symposium*, 2005.

18. C. R. Ramakrishnan and R. Sekar. Model-based analysis of configuration vulnerabilities. *Journal of Computer Security (JCS)*, 10:189–209, 2002.

19. D. M. Reeves, M. P. Wellman, and B. N. Grosof. Automated negotiation from declarative contract descriptions. In *Proceedings of the Fifth International Conference on Autonomous Agents*, pages 51–58. ACM press, 2001.

20. A. Roychoudhury, C. R. Ramakrishnan, and I. V. Ramakrishnan. Justifying proofs using memo tables. In *Principles and Practice of Declarative Programming (PPDP)*, pages 178–189. ACM Press, 2000.

21. K. Sagonas, T. Swift, D. S. Warren, J. Freirre, and P. Rao. XSB programmers manual, 2001. http://xsb.sourceforge.net/.

22. D. Saha and C. R. Ramakrishnan. Incremental evaluation of tabled prolog: Beyond pure logic programs. In *Practical Aspects of Declarative Languages (PADL)*, volume 3819 of *LNCS*, pages 215–229. Springer, 2006.

23. B. Sarna-Starosta and S. D. Stoller. Policy analysis for security-enhanced linux. In *Workshop on Issues in the Theory of Security (WITS)*, pages 1–12, 2004. Available at http://www.cs.sunysb.edu/~stoller/WITS2004.html.

24. J. T. Schwartz, R. B. Dewar, E. Schonberg, and E. Dubinsky. *Programming with sets; an introduction to SETL*. Springer-Verlag, New York, NY, USA, 1986.

25. S. Tsur and C. Zaniolo. LDL: A logic-based data language. In *VLDB*, pages 33–41, 1986.

Using a Logic Programming Framework to Control Database Query Dialogues in Natural Language

Luis Quintano[1] and Irene Rodrigues[2]

[1] Serviço de Computação
Universidade de Évora, Portugal
ljcq@sc.uevora.pt
[2] Departamento de Informática
Universidade de Évora, Portugal
ipr@di.uevora.pt

Abstract. We present a natural language question/answering system to interface the University of Évora databases that uses clarification dialogs in order to clarify user questions. It was developed in an integrated logic programming framework, based on constraint logic programming using the GnuProlog(-cx) language [2,11] and the ISCO framework [1]. The use of this LP framework allows the integration of Prolog-like inference mechanisms with classes and inheritance, constraint solving algorithms and provides the connection with relational databases, such as PostgreSQL. This system focus on the questions' pragmatic analysis, to handle ambiguity, and on an efficient dialogue mechanism, which is able to place relevant questions to clarify the user intentions in a straightforward manner. Proper Nouns resolution and the pp-attachment problem are also handled.

This paper briefly presents this innovative system focusing on its ability to correctly determine the user intention through its dialogue capability.

Keywords: Natural Language, Logic Programming, Information Systems, Dialog Management, Databases.

1   Overview

IIS-UE (Universidade de Évora Integrated Information System) gathers all kinds of information, relevant for students (enrolled courses, grades, class summaries, etc.), for teachers (courses information, projects, students evaluation, personal data, etc.) and staff (data management, statistics, personal data, etc.). Several applications were built around IIS-UE to "deliver" information to the school community, but sometimes that's not enough. To use these applications one must know how they work. A student may know what information he wants but he doesn't know how to get it from the existent applications.

S. Etalle and M. Truszczyński (Eds.): ICLP 2006, LNCS 4079, pp. 406–420, 2006.
© Springer-Verlag Berlin Heidelberg 2006

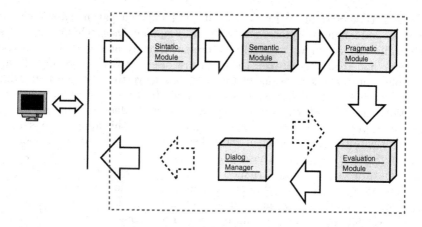

Fig. 1. NL-Ue Architecture

To solve these problems a natural language querying application (NL-Ue) was developed over IIS-UE [1]. Its practical aim is to give to our school community an easy way for retrieving stored information [3] [13].

The information is stored in Postgresql relational databases [10]. To access this data, NL must map the user question to a database query language so that the resulting pragmatic interpretations can be evaluated in the databases.

NL-Ue implementation is based on constraint logic programming using the GnuProlog(-cx) language [11] and the ISCO framework [1].

The system architecture is simple and module-based. The system has five distinct modules which are connected through well defined API's [Fig. 1]. A more detailed description of the system can be found in [18] [17].

In this paper we discuss how pragmatic interpretation is handled by NL-Ue, but the focus will be on its dialog capabilities and how this system is able to clarify the user intentions with effective and precise questions.

Next (section 2) some related work is presented to enhance this application relevance on the dialogue and natural language development context.

In section 3 the pragmatic interpreter is described along with the strategy that was used to generate the pragmatic evaluation rules (which control the flow and the behaviour of the pragmatic interpreter).

Then (section 4) the dialogue mechanism is shown recurring to practical examples and finally some conclusions and future work are presented (section 6).

2   Related Work

Some systems can be found along the last years that touch the problem of relational database querying and clarification dialog. Most of them, as the Precise system, directly generate SQL queries to access relational databases.

---

[1] The system is built for the Portuguese language only interpreting qa and wh-questions.

The Precise System by Etzioni, Kautz and Popescu [20] maps simple english natural language sentences to SQL with graph analysis techniques. Tokens (manually defined - low portability) represent directly attributes of database elements and relations between them. Precise uses a tokenizer to identify all possible complete tokenizations of the question, converting them to SQL with a simple syntactic parser. The system is limited to a restricted set of types of questions. In turn, other systems as Androutsopoulos' Masque/SQL uses an intermediate representation before generating the SQL. This approach is similar to our own, although different in the followed methodology. Androutsopoulos' Masque/SQL [5] [6] system is based on the previous Masque [4] implementation, which in turn was based on Fernando Pereira's CHAT-80 [22].

While Masque maps an english natural language question into Prolog to query a declarative database, Masque/SQL extends it by interfacing directly with relational databases. To do that, Masque/SQL needs some meta-data which has to be reconfigured each time there is a change of working domain. To manage this meta-data Masque/SQL has a domain editor where: (1) the domain entities (represented on the databases) are described (2) the set of "expected words" to appear in the questions and it's logical meaning - Prolog predicates - are describes (3) the connection between each predicate and a database table, view or select is explicitly represented. Once again, portability is one of the main problems of this system.

Although benefiting from the RDBMS SQL optimization, Masque/SQL may sometimes generate redundant SQL queries, decreasing it's efficiency.

Other systems use external integration tools for accessing information repositories. One of them is Katz's START [16] which uses Omnibase [15], a system for heterogeneous database access which uses natural language annotations to describe the data and the kind of questions that can be answered. This system uses the "object-property-value" data model and only works for direct questions about object properties. These annotations are manually built which makes the system's portability difficult.

While the mentioned applications are simple question/answering systems that do not identify wrong interpretations, NL-Ue intends to go a step further adding a clarification dialog capability. Clarification dialogue theory was vastly analyzed by several authors[12] [8] and some works can be found where clarification is applied to open domain or more narrowed domain question answering systems [21].

NL-Ue can be seen as a question/answering dialogue system, identifying erroneous interpretations by means of a clarification dialogue with the user.

3   Pragmatic Interpretation

Syntactic and semantic analysis of this system are generically treated by the VISL parser [7] (syntax) and by an internally built semantic parser to generate DRS structures [14] through first-order logic predicates. At this stage, after syntactic and semantic analysis, the resulting first-order logic predicate (LPO)

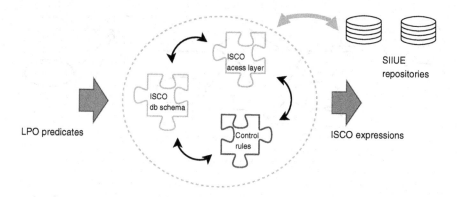

Fig. 2. Pragmatic Interpreter

representation (as seen in Fig. 2) will reach as an input for the pragmatic module. Contextual information is added at this stage.

NL-Ue application context is not only the IIS-UE data but also its structure. This information is added to the interpretation mechanism through a set of pragmatic control rules. To generate these rules, NL-Ue uses ISCO, a logical tool and development framework that enables relational database schema representation and full access to the stored data. This generation is automatic and must be done previously so that the rules are available at interpretation time (runtime).

3.1   Database Representation/Access Framework

ISCO [1] is a logic-based development framework with its roots in the GnuProlog language [11] and is being developed in Universidade de Évora Computer Engineering department. Its use in NL-Ue's pragmatic interpretation adds the system the ability to internally represent and access the IIS-UE relational databases in a logic-based environment.

Figs. 3 and 4 show a fragment of one of IIS-UE's relational databases in entity/relation and SQL representation. It presents the action of "teaching" (lecciona) which relates a teacher (individuo), a course (disciplina) and a curriculum (curso).

The process of pragmatic interpretation needs to know these and other relations structures so that it can "talk" about them. It must also be able to query them to access the stored data and answer to the user question.

The equivalent ISCO representation (Fig. 5) maps each relation/table to a class that can then be accessed through ISCO predicates. Although NL-Ue only uses "select" predicates, ISCO also supports "inserts", "updates" and "deletes" [1].

This declarative description of the relational database schemas is automatically generated. Based on this class description, ISCO (also) automatically generates predicates to access the stored data. These issues increases decisively the portability level of NL-Ue.

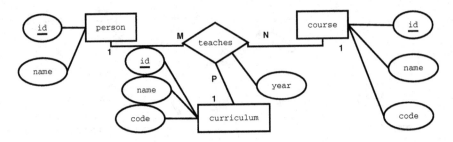

Fig. 3. ER fragment representation

```
create table "person" (
  "id" integer default (nextval ('is__entity_id'))
      primary key,
  "name" text,
  "gender" integer references "gender" ("id"));
create table "teaches" (
  "course" integer references "course" ("id"),
  "year" integer,
  "teacher" integer references "person" ("id"),
  "curriculum" integer references "curriculum" ("id"));
create table "course" (
  "id" integer default (nextval ('is__course_id'))
      primary key,
  "name" text,
  "code" text);
create table "curriculm" (
  "id" integer default (nextval ('is__curriculum_id'))
      primary key,
  "code" integer unique,
  "name" text,);
```

Fig. 4. SQL fragment representation

The goal of the pragmatic interpreter is to map the LPO predicates to these ISCO goals so that IIS-UE databases can be directly queried. For example:

```
person(PERSON, PERSON_NAME, _),
teaches(COURSE, 2005, PERSON, _),
course(333, COURSE_NAME, _).
```

collects all persons (teachers) that teach the course with id 333 in the year of 2005.

NL-Ue also benefits the advantages of the contextual branch of GnuProlog: GnuProlog-cx. This is the context-based variant of the well known GnuProlog language which besides all the base features, also enables contextual goal

```
class person.
  id: serial. key.
  name: text.
  gender: gender.id.
class teaches.
  course: course.id. index.
  year: int. index.
  teacher: person.id. index.
  course: course.id. index.
class course.
  id: serial. key.
  name: text.
  code: text.
class curriculum.
  id: serial. key.
  code: int. unique.
  name: text.
```

Fig. 5. ISCO fragment representation

```
for each CLASS
  build evaluation unit with:
    entity access rules,
    proper nouns rules,
    number rules,
    relation rules
    external domain rules
  end build
end for
```

Fig. 6. Control rules generation algorithm

evaluation [2]. While GnuProlog has a flat predicate namespace, it's contextual variant overrides this problem by defining evaluation units. Each unit has it's own namespace which makes possible to have the same goal definition in distinct units. Contextual goals can be called from other units by means of an explicit contextual call.

This feature is essential for controlling the pragmatic interpretation process because there are numerous interpretation possibilities to consider. Contextual evaluation will restrict these possibilities making the process lighter and more efficient.

3.2 Control Rules

Pragmatic interpretation is guided by a set of control rules. These rules are based on the ISCO description of the IIS-UE repositories, adding contextual information to the user question analysis. ISCO classes, as we've already seen,

```
name(A, PATTERN, []) :-
  check_class_domain(person) :> item(A),
  check_domain(text, PATTERN) :> item(A),
  add_to_context([person(A, _, _)]).
```

collects in A all teachers which have the string PATTERN in its name. This
rule is applied in sentences like: *"the teacher John..."*

Fig. 7. Control rule example for proper nouns: class *person*

represent entities and/or relations. Each one of them will have distinct kinds of
control rules.

Each rule abducts a set of ISCO goals and incrementally builds the evaluation context of the remaining pragmatic interpretation. The final set of abducted
ISCO goals will then be evaluated so that a solution can be found for the user
sentence/question. One evaluation unit is generated for each class (IIS-UE relation). Within these units five distinct types of rules can be found:

- entity access rules - one rule is generated so that the stored data can be
  accessed by NL-Ue for classes that represent entities [2]
- proper noun rules - validate the existence of entities with a specific name in
  a particular context of evaluation [Fig. 7]
- number rules - identify entities that have a property with a specific number
- relation rules - These rules establish wider connections between referents.
  Typically they are the most numerous and they are the main responsible
  for the complexity of pragmatic interpretation. They are also responsible for
  fixing the pp-attachment problem [19] [9]. There are four kinds of such rules:

  - Self relation rules - generated only for entities, they intend to relate two
    referents that refer the same type of entity.
  - Entity relation rules - For each entity (only), these rules associate its pri-
    mary key with each one of its domain restricted arguments (foreign keys).
  - Argument relation rules - Generates a rule for each pair of domain re-
    stricted arguments, considering their relation as a possible interpretation.
  - External relation rules - Establish wider relations not directly within a
    class but mentioning other classes that refer the first one as foreign key.

- External domain rules - For each argument of class C1 that refers a class C2 as
  foreign key, a set of rules for C1 interpretation is added to its evaluation unit.

These rules definition is generic (for any application context), not only for the
IIS-UE domain. Evaluation follows the pragmatic interpretation. After determining the ISCO representation(s) of the user question, they are evaluated by
directly querying IIS-UE's databases. This evaluation will restrain the sentence
referents to the possible instantiations.

---

[2] A class represents an entity if it has a simple primary key.

4   Clarification Mechanism

The sentence pragmatic interpretation may lead to multiple results, reflecting the sentence ambiguity and/or the database structure ambiguity. In this case the system needs to clarify the user intentions by means of a (clarification) dialog.

To show NL-Ue's usage and focus on it's dialogue/clarification mechanism, let's see an example question [3] [Fig. 8].

Que docentes leccionam a disciplina de Gestão?
`(Which teachers lecture the Management course?)`

Fig. 8. Example question

This sentence has one semantic interpretation and one pragmatic interpretation [Fig. 9] which associates all possible teachers of some management course with all possible management courses (that exist within IIS-UE) [4].

Semantics:

`teacher(A), teaches(A, B), course(B), rel(B, C),`
`name('Management',C)`

Pragmatic instantiation:

```
A in [47105..47787] - male/female - plural
B in [188:194:247:259:346:352:486:550:558:835:1053:1108:1210:1270:
      1287:1293:1320:1355:1412:1414:1423..1424:1466:1487:1657:1659:
      1688..1689:1752:1781:1849:1868:1908:1999:2010:2069:2151:2191:
      2249..2252:2441:2479:2525:2534:2588:2598:2698:2754:3107:3134:
      3152:3161:3189:3257:3331:3393:3502:3584:3593:3696:3865:3886:
      3918:3928:4013] - female - singular
C = B
```

Fig. 9. Semantic/Pragmatic interpretation results

Referent A is instantiated with all possible teachers (that exist in IIS-UE) because no other restriction was made to it, while referent B is instantiated with all courses that contain the name *Management*.

The evaluation module will define a set of possible answers. If no ambiguity is found the dialogue manager will directly answer the user with the (only) answer

---

[3] The system was developed for the portuguese language but questions will be translated to english for easier understanding.

[4] This sentence has more pragmatic interpretations , some of them a little bit awkward (at least within the portuguese language). To simplify and because pragmatic disambiguation is not the aim of this paper, we will consider just this one.

```
while not a terminal condition:
    collects properties for each referent
    proceeds with heuristic evaluation
    chooses the best property
    questions the user / receives the answer
    restrains solutions to the question result
end while
```

Fig. 10. Dialogue Manager: clarification algorithm

```
name('Control Management'), name('Computer Management'),
name('Personal Management'), belongs_to('Sociology department'),
belongs_to('Economics department'), lectured_hours(3.5),
lectured_to(Computer Engineering curriculum'), etc.
```

Fig. 11. Properties Set

found. But if more than one possible answer is found, then the dialogue manager enters in a clarification process [Fig. 10].

A `terminal` condition will be reached if only one answer is achieved.

After the evaluation process, possible solutions will be grouped by referent (in our example we have three, referring to `teachers`, `Management` and `course`). This grouping is done to collect the properties of each referent. The best property will be chosen to make a new question.

In wh-questions (which is the case) the referent which is target of the user question (in this case, referent `A`) is excluded from the set of referents to analyze. It makes no sense to make questions referring to what the user wants to know. For each (relevant) referent, different kinds of properties will be collected:

- Class properties: identifies as a referent property its type/class within the scope of IIS-UE - a referent may be a course, a teacher, a student, etc.
- Direct properties: identifies as referent properties direct attributes of its class - if a referent refers to a student, it may have properties as its name, its student number, its gender, etc.
- Indirect properties: identifies as referent properties, attributes of classes that refer the referent class as a foreign key - if a teacher lectures a specific course, then the act of teaching it may be considered as a property of the teacher referent.

After collecting the referent properties [Fig. 11] they will be evaluated with the aim to find the "better one". Heuristic evaluation is used to weight the quality of each property found. The evaluation of a property is a linear sum of three distinct criteria [Fig. 12].

```
∀ properties p: weight(p) = w1(p) + w2(p) + w3(p)
where

  — w1(p) - evaluates the ability that the property has to split equally the
    referents set based on the total number of referents (Rt) and the number
    of those which have the property (Rp): w1(p) = 1 - Rp/Rt.
  — w2(p) - evaluates the semantic potential of the property preferring textual
    (T(p)) to numeric ones: If T(p) then w2(p) = 0.5 else w2(p) = 0.1.
  — w3(p) - evaluates the probability that the user knows this kind of property,
    preferring more generic properties. It assumes the user has more knowledge
    of conceptual properties (C(p)), than specific ones: If C(p) then w3(p)
    = 0.5 else w3(p) = 0.1.
```

Fig. 12. Properties weight heuristics

```
weight(belongs_to('Management department'), 0.987),
weight(lectured_hours(2), 0.987), weight(belongs_to('Economics
department'), 0.696), weight(belongs_to(Mathematics department'),
0.696), etc.
```

Fig. 13. Properties evaluation

After the properties evaluation, each one of them is associated with a specific weight that reflects its potential to generate a relevant question [Fig. 13].[5]

For example the properties belongs_to('Management department') and belongs_to('Mathematics department') are semantically equal (weight 2) and refer to the same concept - department (weight 3) but the first one as a greater ability to split the referents set which gives it a larger weight. While the property belongs_to('Management department') is semantically richer (weight 2), the property lectured_hours(2) has a greater ability to split the referent sets, making both properties to have the same weight.

Having weighted the quality of the properties, they are grouped by type (belongs_to, lectured_hours, name, lectured_to, etc.). Each group inherits the best weight of its members and the best group is chosen to build the question (and the possible answers). Properties are grouped because the clarification process consists of questions with alternative answers, being the alternatives the elements of the chosen group. If the number of alternatives exceeds a previously determined limit, this property is ignored and the system recursively gets the next one. In our example the chosen group is composed by all the belongs_to properties [Fig. 15].

Besides specifying one of the possible alternatives, the user has only one other possibility which is to say "?" meaning "I don't know". In this case the system will recursively get the next "best property" and make a new question.

---

[5] The heuristics shown and the relation between them (relative weights) were incrementally built and based on a set of examples and their evaluation results.

```
"Management course" belongs to:

1) Education department
2) Sociology department
3) Agricultural department
4) Management department

USER: 3
```

Fig. 14. Clarification #1

```
"Management course" is lectured:

1) 2 hours/week
2) 3 hours/week

USER: ?

"Management course" is lectured to:

1) Biophysics curriculum
2) Agriculture Engineering curriculum
3) Computer Engineering curriculum

USER: 2

Answer
Teacher: Francisco João Santos Silva
Course:  Water resources management
```

Fig. 15. Clarification #2

If the user answers one of the alternatives (1-6) the system will restrain and re-evaluate the possible solutions (according to the users answer) and the clarification algorithm returns to its beginning. After re-evaluating the possible solutions, the chosen property referred to the number of lectured hours. As the user didn't knew the answer, the system recurred to the next "best property" and tried to clarify using the curriculums to which the course is lectured, leading to a final solution according to the user additional information.

5   Evaluation

A dialogue/clarification system to query integrated databases in Natural Language should be evaluated from different aspects:

Table 1. Results

Sentence	Context	CPU Time	Real Time	Clarification
Does Mary teaches Databases?	no	0.878	4.970	yes
	yes	0.640	3.285	
Does Mary Higgins teaches the Informatics curriculum?	no	0.910	5.111	no
	yes	0.488	3.164	
Which teachers teach the Management course?	no	5.864	22.324	yes
	yes	3.544	14.225	
Which are the Physics teachers?	no	6.321	20.970	yes
	yes	4.216	12.960	

- Portuguese language coverage: The syntactic analysis is done using VISL [7] which is one of the best portuguese full parsers for portuguese. The semantic coverage is restraint by the databases vocabulary (tables, attributes names and entity names) and a synonym dictionary that can be updated by the users. The dialogue system is able to answer Yes/No and Wh questions.
- The pertinence of the user question pragmatic interpretation: This aspect is reflected in the system clarification dialogues and answers. Our system enables the inference of some relations that clearly natural language forbids due to the rules for pragmatic interpretation of pp-sentences. However, we can state that normally this does not constitutes a problem for our users, since on the average they are able to obtain their answer in 3 dialogue steps.
- The heuristic function quality for choosing the question to clarify user sentence: The evaluation of this aspect must be done using the results of a group test, which isn't done yet. Probably the use of some other heuristics may be more efficient. This is an aspect that must be analyzed in the future.
- The efficiency of the system: How long does the system takes to answer a question? Some results are shown in this section.

The dialog/clarification mechanism is not fully tested but this set of heuristic functions lead the system in 70% of the questions to reach an answer after 3 questions/answers or less.

The results presented in table 1 refer to tests made with the IIS-UE main relational repository, which contains 159 tables with an average of 2281 rows/table. The previously built control rules ascend to the number of 1400 which makes an average of 8 rules for each class. Results are based on distinct sentences[6] representative of possible questions to NL-Ue. No specific treatment is given to questions asked multiple times with slight variations in its structure.[7]

---

[6] Sentences in english may not present the same structure or complexity than in portuguese.

[7] Possible future development which would require the recording of the sentences analysis for future reference.

Times shown (in seconds) refer to the time the system takes from the input of the user to the answer (or to the first clarification question[8]). Further evaluation must be done considering real tests because its conditioned to the clarification process and to the users subjectivity.

Each sentence was tested with and without contextual evaluation. Its use - with GnuProlog-cx - is relevant in the pragmatic interpretation module, minimizing its complexity by reducing the search space. It leads to a gain of efficiency in the order of 80% in more complex sentences and 50% in more simpler ones - cpu time. Yes/no questions (second and third) have a lower cpu processing time than wh. Clarification was needed in three of the sentences.

6   Conclusions and Future Work

Our system aims to be a natural language interpretation system that uses specific tools for increasing efficiency and getting results in real time.

This paper shows how pragmatic interpretation of complex sentences can be handled through a set of contextual control rules which guide the process of interpretation, increasing it's efficiency and without the loss of any results.

The use of the ISCO development framework gives NL-Ue a high level of portability in accessing and querying different sets of databases.

The contextual evaluation strategy (available through the use of Gnuprolog-cx) is applied in the control rule generation and usage, making the pragmatic evaluation process practical and more efficient once the search space is smaller.

NL-Ue is a question/answering system capable of a clarification dialog when needed. It is able to identify the users needs and to extract the desired information from relational databases.

The use of a dedicated development framework and its ability to describe and access distinct data sources in a homogeneous way increased the systems portability rate.

Contextual evaluation gives pragmatic interpretation a more linear and simple treatment decreasing its computational complexity, which can be decisive in systems with large information repositories.

NL-Ue supports yes/no and wh-questions. Besides, it includes a clarification mechanism in which the system dialogues with the user when the desired information is ambiguous.

The clarification/dialogue module uses referent properties to find relevant questions trying to reach an answer the faster it cans. Heuristic evaluation is used to ensure the quality of the questions.

---

[8] This includes: syntactic and semantic analysis; the pragmatic interpretation (each sentence may have more than one interpretation) and finally the evaluation of each sentence interpretation. During this the evaluation, the discourse referents that are constraint variables restrained to a set of database entities, are validated by testing the truth value of the sentence conditions, that are database relations. This way, the process time of a query sentence will depend on the number of database entities associated to each discourse referent. This fact explains why sentence 2 (which has more pragmatic interpretations then sentence 3) takes less time then sentence 3.

Having developed the core mechanism, the next steps will be to confirm the correctness of the followed methodology. For that, the system must be evaluated considering:

− its usefulness (for the users)
− the correctness of pragmatic rules generation
− the types of questions treated
− the heuristic function quality

The system will be available to the public through Universidade de Évora: http://www.uevora.pt

References

1. Salvador Abreu. Isco: A practical language for heterogeneous information system construction. In *Proceedings of INAP'01*, Tokyo, Japan, October 2001. INAP.
2. Salvador Abreu and Daniel Diaz. Objective: In minimum context. In Catuscia Palamidessi, editor, *ICLP*, volume 2916 of *Lecture Notes in Computer Science*, pages 128–147. Springer, 2003.
3. Salvador Pinto Abreu. A Logic-based Information System. In Enrico Pontelli and Vitor Santos-Costa, editors, 2nd *International Workshop on Practical Aspects of Declarative Languages (PADL'2000)*, volume 1753 of *Lecture Notes in Computer Science*, pages 141–153, Boston, MA, USA, January 2000. Springer-Verlag.
4. I. Androutsopoulos. Interfacing a natural language front-end to a relational database, 1992.
5. I. Androutsopoulos, G.D. Ritchie, and P. Thanisch. Natural language interfaces to databases–an introduction. *Journal of Language Engineering*, 1(1):29–81, 1995.
6. Ion Androutsopoulos and Graeme Ritchie. Database interfaces. In H. Moisl R. Dale and H. Somers, editors, *Handbook of Natural Language Processing*, pages 209–240. Marcel Dekker Inc., 2000.
7. Eckhard Bick. A constraint grammar based question answering system for portuguese. In *EPIA*, pages 414–418, 2003.
8. Marco De Boni. An analysis of clarification dialogue for question answering.
9. Michael Collins and James Brooks. Prepositional attachment through a backed-off model. In David Yarovsky and Kenneth Church, editors, *Proceedings of the Third Workshop on Very Large Corpora*, pages 27–38, Somerset, New Jersey, 1995. Association for Computational Linguistics.
10. Development and T. User. The postgresql development team. postgresql user's guide, 1996.
11. D. Diaz. http://www.gnu.org/software/prolog, 1999.
12. J. Ginzburg. Clarifying utterances, 1998.
13. Joaquim Godinho, Luis Quintano, and Salvador Abreu. Universidade de Évora's Integrated Information System: An Application. In Hans Dijkman, Petra Smulders, Bas Cordewener, and Kurt de Belder, editors, *The 9th International Conference of European University Information Systems*, pages 469–473. Universiteit van Amsterdam, July 2003. ISBN 90-9017079-0.
14. H. Kamp and U. Reyle. *From Discourse to Logic*. Kluwer, Dordrecht, 1993.
15. B. Katz, S. Felshin, D. Yuret, A. Ibrahim, J. Lin, G. Marton, A. McFarland, and B. Temelkuran. Omnibase: Uniform access to heterogeneous data for question answering, 2002.

16. Boris Katz and Jimmy J. Lin. Start and beyond.

17. Irene Rodrigues Luis Quintano and Salvador Abreu. Relational Information Retrieval through natural language analysis. In *INAP'01, Tokyo, Japan*, 2001.

18. Irene Rodrigues Luis Quintano, Paulo Quaresma and Salvador Abreu. A Natural Language dialogue manager for accessing databases. In Mamede N. and Ranchhod E., editors, *Proceedings of PorTAL'02, Faro Portugal*, 2002.

19. Paola Merlo. Generalised pp-attachment disambiguation using corpus-based linguistic diagnostics. In *EACL*, pages 251–258, 2003.

20. H. Kautz O. Etzioni and A. Popescu. Towards a theory of natural language interfaces to databases. In *Intelligent User Interfaces (IUI)*, 2003.

21. Ellen M. Voorhees. Overview of the TREC 2001 question answering track. In *Text REtrieval Conference*, 2001.

22. David H. D. Warren and Fernando C. N. Pereira. An efficient easily adaptable system for interpreting natural language queries. *American Journal of Computational Linguistics*, 8(3-4):110–122, 1982.

Declarative Diagnosis of Wrong Answers in Constraint Functional-Logic Programming

Rafael Caballero, Mario Rodríguez Artalejo, and Rafael del Vado Vírseda[*]

Dep. Sistemas Informáticos y Programación, Univ. Complutense de Madrid
{rafa, mario, rdelvado}@sip.ucm.es

Debugging tools are a practical need for diagnosing the causes of erroneous computations. Declarative programming paradigms involving complex operational details, such as constraint solving and lazy evaluation, do not fit well to traditional debugging techniques relying on the inspection of low-level computation traces. As a solution to this problem, *declarative diagnosis* uses *Computation Trees* (shortly, *CTs*) in place of traces. *CTs* are built *a posteriori* to represent the structure of a computation whose top level outcome is regarded as an *error symptom* by the user. Each node in a *CT* represents the computation of some observable result, depending on the results of its children nodes. Declarative diagnosis explores a *CT* looking for a so-called *buggy node* which computes an incorrect result from children whose results are correct; such a node must point to an incorrect program fragment. The search for a buggy node can be implemented with the help of an external *oracle* (usually the user with some semiautomatic support) who has a reliable declarative knowledge of the expected program semantics, the so-called *intended interpretation.*

The generic description of declarative diagnosis in the previous paragraph follows [8]. Declarative diagnosis was first proposed in the field of logic programming [10], and it has been successfully extended to other declarative programming paradigms, including lazy functional programming [9], constraint logic programming [11,4] and functional logic programming [2,3]. In contrast to recent approaches to error diagnosis using *abstract interpretation* [5], declarative diagnosis often involves complex queries to the user. This problem has been tackled by means of various techniques, such as user-given partial specifications of the program's semantics [3], safe inference of information from answers previously given by the user [2], or *CTs* tailored to the needs of a particular debugging problem over a particular computation domain [4]. Current research in declarative diagnosis has still to face many challenges regarding both the foundations and the development of practical tools.

The aim of this work is to present a declarative method for diagnosing wrong computed answers in $CFLP(\mathcal{D})$, a newly proposed generic programming scheme which can be instantiated by any constraint domain $\mathcal{D}$ given as parameter, and supports a powerful combination of functional and constraint logic programming over $\mathcal{D}$ [6]. Borrowing ideas from $CFLP(\mathcal{D})$ declarative semantics we obtain a

---

[*] The authors have been partially supported by the Spanish National Projects MELODIAS (TIC2002-01167), MERIT-FORMS (TIN2005-09207-C03-03) and PROMESAS-CAM (S-0505/TIC/0407).

S. Etalle and M. Truszczyński (Eds.): ICLP 2006, LNCS 4079, pp. 421–422, 2006.

suitable notion of intended interpretation, as well as a convenient definition of proof tree with a sound logical meaning to play the role of CTs. Our aim is to achieve a natural combination of previous approaches that were separately developed for the $CLP(\mathcal{D})$ scheme [11] and for lazy functional logic languages [2]. We have proved theoretical results showing that the proposed debugging method is logically correct for any sound $CFLP(\mathcal{D})$-system [12] whose computed answers are logical consequences of the program in the sense of $CFLP(\mathcal{D})$ semantics. We have implemented a debugging tool called $\mathcal{DDT}$, developed as an extension of previously existing but less powerful tools [1,3] and available at http://toy.sourceforge.net. $\mathcal{DDT}$ implements the proposed diagnosis method for $CFLP(\mathcal{R})$-programming in the $\mathcal{TOY}$ system [7] using the domain $\mathcal{R}$ of arithmetic constraints over the real numbers. Moreover, $\mathcal{DDT}$ provides some facilities for navigating proof trees and avoiding redundant queries to the user. As future work, we plan to develop a formal framework for the declarative diagnosis of *missing answers* in $CFLP(\mathcal{D})$ and we plan several improvements of $\mathcal{DDT}$, such as enabling the diagnosis of missing answers, supporting finite domain constraints, and providing new facilities for simplifying the presentation of queries to the user.

References

1. R. Caballero. *A Declarative Debugger of Incorrect Answers for Constraint Functional-Logic Programs*. Proc. WCFLP'05, ACM SIGPLAN, pp. 8–13, 2005.
2. R. Caballero and M. Rodríguez-Artalejo. *A Declarative Debugging System for Lazy Functional Logic Programs*. ENTCS 64, 63 pages, 2002.
3. R. Caballero and M. Rodríguez-Artalejo. *DDT: A Declarative Debugging Tool for Functional Logic Languages*. Proc. FLOPS'04, Springer LNCS 2998, pp. 70–84, 2004.
4. G. Ferrand, W. Lesaint and A. Tessier. *Towards declarative diagnosis of constraint programs over finite domains*. ArXiv Computer Science e-prints, 2003.
5. M. Hermenegildo, G. Puebla, F. Bueno and P. López-García. *Abstract Verification and Debugging of Constraint Logic Programs*. Proc. CSCLP'02, pp. 1–14, 2002.
6. F.J. López-Fraguas, M. Rodríguez-Artalejo and R. del Vado-Vírseda. *A New Generic Scheme for Functional Logic Programming with Constraints*. To appear in the Journal Higher-Order and Symbolic Computation, 2006. (Extended version of *Constraint Functional Logic Programming Revisited*, WRLA'04, ENTCS 117, pp. 5–50, 2005.)
7. F.J. López-Fraguas, J. Sánchez-Hernández. *TOY: A Multiparadigm Declarative System*. In Proc. RTA'99, Springer LNCS 1631, pp 244–247, 1999. System and documentation available at http://toy.sourceforge.net.
8. L. Naish. *A Declarative Debugging Scheme*. Journal of Functional and Logic Programming, 1997-3.
9. B. Pope and L. Naish. *Practical aspects of declarative debugging in Haskell 98*. Proc. PPDP'03, ACM Press, pp. 230–240, 2003.
10. E.Y. Shapiro. *Algorithmic Program Debugging*. The MIT Press, Cambridge, 1982.
11. A. Tessier and G. Ferrand. *Declarative Diagnosis in the CLP Scheme*. Springer LNCS 1870, Chapter 5, pp. 151–174, 2000.
12. R. del Vado-Vírseda. *Declarative Constraint Programming with Definitional Trees*. In Proc. FroCoS'05, Springer LNAI 3717 pp. 184–199, 2005.

Solving First-Order Constraints in the Theory of the Evaluated Trees

Thi-Bich-Hanh Dao[1] and Khalil Djelloul[2]

[1] LIFO, Bat. 3IA, rue Léonard de Vinci. 45067 Orléans, France
[2] LIF, Parc scientifique et technologique de Luminy. 13288 Marseille, France

Abstract. We describe in this paper a general algorithm for solving first-order constraints in the theory T of the evaluated trees which is a combination of the theory of finite or infinite trees and the theory of the rational numbers with addition, subtraction and a linear dense order relation. It transforms a first-order formula φ, which can possibly contain free variables, into a disjunction ϕ of solved formulas which is equivalent in T, without new free variables and such that ϕ is either *true* or *false* or a formula having at least one free variable and being equivalent neither to *true* nor to *false* in T.

1 Introduction

The theory of finite or infinite trees plays a fundamental role in computer science. There exists algorithms for eliminating quantifiers which can decide the validity of propositions in these theories [7,3]. We have extended this theory by giving a complete first-order axiomatization T of the evaluated trees [6] which are combination of finite or infinite trees with construction operations and the rational numbers with addition, subtraction and a linear dense order relation. This theory reflects essentially to Prolog III and IV which have been modeled using combination of trees, rational numbers, booleans and intervals [2,1]. In this paper we describe a general algorithm for solving first-order constraints in T, i.e. in all models of T. Our aim is not only to decide the validity of the propositions, but to be able to express solutions of constraints in T, which can possibly contain free variables, in a simple and explicit way.

2 Description of the Algorithm

The algorithm is not simply a combination of an algorithm over trees with one over rational numbers, but a powerful mechanism which is able to solve any first-order constraint containing typed/untyped variables and presents the solutions on the free variables in a clear and explicit way. One of the major difficulty resides in the fact that the theory of trees does not accept full elimination of quantifiers and the function symbols $+$ and $-$ of T have two different behaviors whether they are applied on trees or on rational numbers. The main points of the algorithm are (full description of the algorithm can be found in [5]):

S. Etalle and M. Truszczyński (Eds.): ICLP 2006, LNCS 4079, pp. 423–424, 2006.
© Springer-Verlag Berlin Heidelberg 2006

- We define basic formulas, which are conjunctions of formulas of the forms *true*, *false*, *num x*, *tree x*, $x = y$, $x = fy_1...y_n$, $\Sigma_{i=1}^n a_i x_i = a_0 1$, $\Sigma_{i=1}^n a_i x_i < a_0 1$, with x_i, y_j variables and $a_i \in \mathbf{Z}$ and give a mechanism to derive typing constraints in basic formulas.
- We define blocks, which are basic formulas where all the variables are typed and where there is no type conflict and define solved blocks.
- We give the definition of working formulas, which are formulas written by using only existentially quantified blocks and their negation. To be able to control the rewriting rules, which are the heart of the algorithm, we give to each negation symbol ¬ a number, which will present properties of the corresponding working formula. Using these number, we define initial, final working formulas, and solving formulas.
- We give a set of 28 rewriting rules, which transform an initial working formula into a conjunction of final working formulas, which can be directly transformed into a disjunction of solving formulas, which is either *true* or *false* or a formula φ having at least one free variable such that neither $T \models \varphi$ nor $T \models \neg\varphi$. These rules make top-down local solvings and propagations and bottom-up quantifier eliminations and distributions. We show that these rules are correct and terminating.

3 Conclusion

The non-elementarity of the decision in the theory of trees is known [8], i.e the complexity of the decision cannot be bounded by a tower of powers of 2's with a fixed height. Thus our algorithm must not escape this kind of complexity in the worst case. We have programmed a similar algorithm on the theory of trees and nevertheless could be able to solve formulas of winning positions in two partner games, having 160 nested quantifiers [4]. Actually we try to extend our algorithm to any combination of a theory T with the theory of finite or infinite trees.

References

1. Benhamou F, and al. Le manuel de Prolog IV , PrologIA, Marseille, France, 1996.
2. Colmerauer A. An introduction to Prolog III. Comm. of the ACM, 33(7):68–90,1990.
3. Comon H. Résolution de contraintes dans des algèbres de termes. Rapport d'Habilitation, Université de Paris Sud, 1992.
4. Dao T. Résolution de contraintes du premier ordre dans la théorie des arbres finis ou infinis. Thèse d'informatique, Université de la Méditerranée, 2000.
5. Dao TBH, Djelloul K., Solving First-Order Constraints in the Theory of the Evaluated Trees, Rapport de recherche LIFO RR-2006-05, http://www.univ-orleans.fr/lifo/rapports.php
6. Djelloul K. About the combination of trees and rational numbers in a complete first-order theory. 5th Int. Conf. FroCoS 2005, LNAI, vol 3717, P. 106–122.
7. Maher M. Complete axiomatization of the algebra of finite, rational and infinite trees. *Technical report, IBM - T.J.Watson Research Center*, 1988.
8. Vorobyov S. An Improved Lower Bound for the Elementary Theories of Trees, CADE'96, LNAI 1104, pp. 275- 287, 1996.

Relaxation on Optimization Predicates

Hai-Feng Guo[1], Miao Liu[1], and Bharat Jayaraman[2]

[1] Dept. of Computer Science, University of Nebraska, Omaha, NE 68182-0500
{haifengguo, miaoliu}@mail.unomaha.edu
[2] Dept. of Computer Science and Engineering, State University of New York,
Buffalo, NY 14260-2000
bharat@cse.buffalo.edu

Traditional constraint logic programming (CLP) specifies an optimization problem by using a set of constraints and an objective function. In many applications, optimal solutions may be difficult or impossible to obtain, and hence we are interested in finding suboptimal solutions, by either relaxing the constraints or the objective function. Hierarchical constraint logic programming (HCLP) [1] is such a strategy by extending CLP to support required as well as relaxable constraints. HCLP proposed preferences on constraints indicating the relative importance of constraints and organizing them into a hierarchy. Essentially, the solutions of interest must satisfy the required constraints but need not satisfy the relaxable constraints. HCLP has proven to be useful tool in solving the over-constrained applications.

In this paper, we focus on the relaxation problem in preference logic programming (PLP) [2], where an optimization predicate is specified in a declarative way by separating its *general definition* from its *solution preferences*. For instance, a PLP for finding the shortest path may be defined as Example 1, where the optimization predicate path/4 contains a general definition, clauses (1-3), and a solution preference (4), which tells that the path with a shorter distance is preferred. The PLP paradigm is particularly suited to those optimization problems requiring comparison and selection among alternative solutions. Relaxation on optimization predicates in PLP can be achieved in two different ways, by either relaxing the constraints or relaxing the objective function such as a query to an optimization predicate.

Example 1 (Shortest path problem).

$$\text{path(X,X,0,[])} \leftarrow. \tag{1}$$
$$\text{path(X,Y,D,[(X,Y)])} \leftarrow \text{edge(X,Y,D)}. \tag{2}$$
$$\text{path(X,Y,D1+D2,[(X,Z)|P])} \leftarrow \text{edge(X,Z,D1), path(Z,Y,D2,P)}. \tag{3}$$
$$\text{path(X,Y,D1,\_)} \prec \text{path(X,Y,D2,\_)} \leftarrow \text{C2 < C1}. \tag{4}$$

First, relaxable constraints can be properly expressed in solution preferences. Similar to the hierarchy constraints in HCLP, we classify the constraints into required and relaxable ones, and relaxable constraints can be further organized into a constraint hierarchy according to their strengths. Required constraints for an optimization predicate can be specified directly in its general definition, while the constraint hierarchy can be used to compare and order alternative

S. Etalle and M. Truszczyński (Eds.): ICLP 2006, LNCS 4079, pp. 425–426, 2006.
© Springer-Verlag Berlin Heidelberg 2006

solutions by determining how well they satisfy the relaxable constraints, which is consistent to the purpose of solution preferences.

A constraint hierarchy H can be represented as a list $H = [H_1, H_2, \cdots, H_n]$, where $H_1, H_2, \cdots, H_n$ are the constraints in a decreasing strength order. Given a solution S and a constraint hierarchy $H = [H_1, H_2, \cdots, H_n]$, an evaluation predicate $val(S, H, V)$ returns a binary number $V = B_1 B_2 \cdots B_n$ with at most n bits, where the ith bit B_i $(1 \leq i \leq n)$ is 0 if the solution S satisfies the constraint H_i and 1 otherwise. Thus, we can introduce the following solution preference pattern for the alternative solution S1 and S2 with respect to a given constraint hierarchy H:

$$\text{S1} \prec \text{S2} \leftarrow \text{val(S1,H,V1), val(S2,H,V2), V2 < V1.}$$

Secondly, a relaxable query can be expressed in the following form:

$$\leftarrow \text{RELAX } p(\bar{t}) \text{ WRT } c(\bar{u}).$$

where p is an optimization predicate and c is a normal predicate (not an optimization predicate). If the optimal solutions to $p(\bar{t})$ satisfy $c(\bar{u})$, then those are the intended solutions for the relaxable query. Otherwise, the intended solutions are obtained by restricting the feasible solution space of $p(\bar{t})$ using $c(\bar{u})$ as an additional constraint and choosing the best among these solutions.

Consider Example 1. What if we want to find the shortest path P from a to b without going through e (expressed as notin(e,P))? We may not query the system with "← path(a,b,C,P), notin(e,P)" because if all of the shortest paths from a to b go through e, this query returns no solution. Instead, we ought to use a relaxable query:

$$\leftarrow \text{RELAX path(a,b,C,P) WRT notin(e,P).}$$

whose purpose is to treat notin(e,P) as an extra required constraint for the optimization predicate path(a,b,C,P). We use an automatic transformation scheme to properly embed the required constraint into the definition of optimization predicate. Example 2 shows the transformed program, which has successfully captured the semantics of the relaxation query.

Example 2 (Relaxed shortest path problem).

```
relaxed_path(a,b,C,P) ← path1(a,b,C,P), notin(e,P).
relaxed_path(X,Y,C,P) ← (X=/=a; Y=/=b), path1(X,Y,C,P).
relaxed_path(X,Y,C1,_) ≺ relaxed_path(X,Y,C2,_) ← C2 < C1.
path1(X,Y,C,[(X,Y)]) ← edge(X,Y,C).
path1(X,Y,C1+C2,[(X,Z)|P]) ← edge(X,Z,C1), relaxed_path(Z,Y,C2,P).
```

References

1. M. Wilson and A. Borning: Hierarchical Constraint Logic Programming. *Journal of Logic Programming*, 16:277–318, 1993
2. K. Govindarajan, B. Jayaraman, and S. Mantha: Preference Logic Programming. *International Conference on Logic Programming (ICLP)*, pages 731–745, 1995.

Handling Incomplete and Complete Tables in Tabled Logic Programs

(Extended Abstract)

Ricardo Rocha*

DCC-FC & LIACC
University of Porto, Portugal
ricroc@ncc.up.pt

Most of the recent proposals in tabling technology were designed as a means to improve the performance of particular applications in key aspects of tabled evaluation like re-computation and scheduling. The discussion we address in this work was also motivated by our recent attempt [1] of applying tabling to Inductive Logic Programming (ILP) [2]. ILP applications are very interesting for tabling because they have huge search spaces and do a lot of re-computation. Moreover, we found that they are an excellent case study to improve some practical limitations of current tabling execution models. In particular, we next focus on the table space and how to efficiently handle incomplete and complete tables.

Tabling is about storing answers for subgoals so that they can be reused when a repeated call appears. On the other hand, most ILP algorithms are interested in example satisfiability, not in the answers: query evaluation stops as soon as an answer is found. This is usually implemented by *pruning* at the Prolog level. Unfortunately, pruning over tabled computations results in *incomplete tables*: we may have found several answers but not the complete set. Thus, usually, when a repeated call appears we cannot simply trust the answers from an incomplete table because we may loose part of the computation. The simplest approach, and the one that has been implemented in most tabling systems, is to throw away incomplete tables, and restart the evaluation from scratch.

In this work, we propose a more aggressive approach where, by default, we keep incomplete tables around. Whenever a call for an incomplete table appears, we first consume the answers from the table. If the table is exhausted, then we will restart the evaluation from the beginning. Later, if the subgoal is pruned again, then the same process is repeated until eventually the subgoal is completely evaluated. The main goal of this proposal is to avoid re-computation when the already stored answers are enough to evaluate a repeated call. This idea is closer to the spirit of the *just enough tabling (JET)* proposal of Sagonas and Stuckey [3]. Our approach works well in the ILP setting, where queries are often very similar, and thus already stored answers are enough to evaluate a

* This work has been partially supported by Myddas (POSC/EIA/59154/2004) and by funds granted to LIACC through the Programa de Financiamento Plurianual, Fundação para a Ciência e Tecnologia and Programa POSC. We are very thankful to Nuno Fonseca for his support with the April ILP System.

S. Etalle and M. Truszczyński (Eds.): ICLP 2006, LNCS 4079, pp. 427–428, 2006.

repeated call. When this is not the case, we may not benefit from having kept an incomplete table, but we do not pay any cost either.

On the other hand, complete tables can also be a problem. When we use tabling for applications that build very many queries or that store a huge number of answers, we can build arbitrarily very many or very large tables, quickly running out of memory space. In general, we will have no choice but to throw away some of the tables (ideally, the least likely to be used next). A common control implemented in most tabling systems is to have a set of tabling primitives that the programmer can use to dynamically abolish some of the tables. However, this can be hard to implement and difficult to decide what are the potentially useless tables that should be deleted.

In order to allow useful deletion without compromising efficiency, we propose a more suitable approach for large dynamic searches, a memory management strategy based on a *least recently used* algorithm, that dynamically recovers space from the least recently used tables when the system runs out of memory. With our approach, the programmer can still force the deletion of particular tables, but can also rely on the effectiveness of the memory management algorithm to completely avoid the problem of deciding what potentially useless tables should be deleted.

Both proposals have been implemented in the YapTab tabling system [4] with minor changes to the original design. To the best of our knowledge, YapTab is the first tabling system that implements support to handle incomplete and complete tables as discussed above. Preliminaries results using the April ILP system [5] showed very substantial performance gains and a substantial increase of the size of the problems that can be solved by combining ILP with tabling. Despite the fact that we used ILP as the motivation for this work, our proposals are not restricted to ILP applications and can be generalised and applied to any other applications.

References

1. Rocha, R., Fonseca, N., Costa, V.S.: On Applying Tabling to Inductive Logic Programming. In: European Conference on Machine Learning. Number 3720 in LNAI, Springer-Verlag (2005) 707–714
2. Muggleton, S.: Inductive Logic Programming. In: Conference on Algorithmic Learning Theory, Ohmsma (1990) 43–62
3. Sagonas, K., Stuckey, P.: Just Enough Tabling. In: ACM SIGPLAN International Conference on Principles and Practice of Declarative Programming, ACM (2004) 78–89
4. Rocha, R., Silva, F., Santos Costa, V.: YapTab: A Tabling Engine Designed to Support Parallelism. In: Conference on Tabulation in Parsing and Deduction. (2000) 77–87
5. Fonseca, N., Camacho, R., Silva, F., Santos Costa, V.: Induction with April: A Preliminary Report. Technical Report DCC-2003-02, Department of Computer Science, University of Porto (2003)

An External Module for Implementing
Linear Tabling in Prolog
(Extended Abstract)

Cláudio Silva, Ricardo Rocha, and Ricardo Lopes[*]

DCC-FC & LIACC
University of Porto, Portugal
ccaldas@dcc.online.pt, {ricroc, rslopes}@ncc.up.pt

In previous work [1], we have presented a proposal to combine the power of tabling with the Extended Andorra Model (EAM) in order to produce an execution model with advanced control strategies that guarantees termination, avoids looping, reduces the search space, and is less sensitive to goal ordering.

To address the integration between tabling and the EAM, through the BEAM system [2], we have identified several tasks [1]. In particular, to study how tabling interacts with the BEAM, we proposed the ability to use an external module for implementing tabling primitives that provide direct control over the search strategy. This approach may compromise efficiency, if compared to systems that implement tabling support at the low-level engine, but allows tabling to be easily incorporated into any Prolog system. For our work, it will serve as the basis to study and detect in advance the potential integration problems before extending the BEAM system to support tabling running within the EAM environment.

In the past years several alternative mechanisms for tabling have been proposed and implemented in systems like XSB, Yap, B-Prolog, ALS-Prolog and Mercury. In these implementations, we can distinguish two main categories of tabling mechanisms: *delaying-based tabling mechanisms* in the sense that the computation state of suspended tabled subgoal calls has to be preserved, either by freezing the whole stacks or by copying the execution stacks to separate storage; and *linear tabling mechanisms* where a new call always extends the latest one, therefore maintaining only a single SLD tree in the execution stacks. Delaying-based mechanisms can be considered more complicated to implement but obtain better results. The weakness of the linear mechanisms is the necessity of re-computation for computing fix-points.

Implementing tabling through an external module restrict us to linear tabling mechanisms, because external modules cannot directly interact with the execution stacks. Therefore, we have decided to design a module that implements the two available mechanisms that, to the best of our knowledge, implement linear tabling: the SLDT strategy of Zhou *et al.* [3]; and the DRA technique of Guo and Gupta [4]. The key idea of the SLDT strategy is to let a tabled subgoal call

---
[*] This work has been partially supported by Myddas (POSC/EIA/59154/2004) and by funds granted to LIACC through the Programa de Financiamento Plurianual, Fundação para a Ciência e Tecnologia and Programa POSC.

S. Etalle and M. Truszczyński (Eds.): ICLP 2006, LNCS 4079, pp. 429–430, 2006.

execute from the backtracking point of a former variant call if such a call exists. When there are available answers in the table space, the variant call consumes them; otherwise, it uses the predicate clauses to produce answers. Meanwhile, if a call that is a variant of some former call occurs, it takes the remaining clauses from the former call and tries to produce new answers by using them. The variant call is then repeatedly re-executed, until all the available answers and clauses have been exhausted, that is, until a fix-point is reached. The DRA technique is based on dynamic reordering of alternatives with variant calls. This technique tables not only the answers to tabled subgoals, but also the alternatives leading to variant calls, the *looping alternatives*. It then uses the looping alternatives to repeatedly recompute them until a fix-point is reached.

Currently, we have already a preliminary implementation of both approaches in our external module. The module uses the C language interface of the Yap Prolog system to implement external tabling primitives that provide direct control over the search strategies for a transformed program. According to the tabling mechanism to be used, a tabled logic program is first transformed to include the tabling primitives through source level transformations and only then, the resulting program is compiled. Our module is independent from the Yap Prolog's engine which makes it easily portable to other Prolog systems with a C language interface. To implement the table space data structures we use *tries* as originally implemented in the XSB Prolog system [5].

Preliminaries results, on a set of common benchmarks for tabled execution, allows us to make a first and fair comparison between the SLDT and the DRA mechanisms and, therefore, better understand the advantages and weaknesses of each. Starting from these results, we are now working on a new proposal that tries to combine the best features of both in order to produce a more robust and efficient linear tabling mechanism to experiment with the BEAM.

References

1. Rocha, R., Lopes, R., Silva, F., Costa, V.S.: IMPACT: Innovative Models for Prolog with Advanced Control and Tabling. In: International Conference on Logic Programming. Number 3668 in LNCS, Springer-Verlag (2005) 416–417
2. Lopes, R., Santos Costa, V., Silva, F.: A Novel Implementation of the Extended Andorra Model. In: International Symposium on Pratical Aspects of Declarative Languages. Number 1990 in LNCS, Springer-Verlag (2001) 199–213
3. Zhou, N.F., Shen, Y.D., Yuan, L.Y., You, J.H.: Implementation of a Linear Tabling Mechanism. In: Practical Aspects of Declarative Languages. Number 1753 in LNCS, Springer-Verlag (2000) 109–123
4. Guo, H.F., Gupta, G.: A Simple Scheme for Implementing Tabling based on Dynamic Reordering of Alternatives. In: Conference on Tabulation in Parsing and Deduction. (2000) 141–154
5. Ramakrishnan, I.V., Rao, P., Sagonas, K., Swift, T., Warren, D.S.: Efficient Access Mechanisms for Tabled Logic Programs. Journal of Logic Programming **38** (1999) 31–54

Using Combined Static Analysis and Profiling for Logic Program Execution Time Estimation*

Edison Mera[1], Pedro López-García[1], Germán Puebla[1],
Manuel Carro[1], and Manuel Hermenegildo[1,2]

[1] Technical University of Madrid
edison@clip.dia.fi.upm.es,
{pedro.lopez, german, mcarro, herme}@fi.upm.es
[2] University of New Mexico
herme@unm.edu

Motivation. Predicting statically the running time of programs has many applications ranging from task scheduling in parallel execution to proving the ability of a program to meet strict time constraints. A starting point in order to attack this problem is to infer the computational complexity of such programs (or fragments thereof). This is one of the reasons why the development of static analysis techniques for inferring cost-related properties of programs (usually upper and/or lower bounds of actual costs) has received considerable attention.

In most cases such cost properties are expressed using platform-independent metrics: e.g., the number of resolution steps that a procedure will execute as a function of the size of its input data [2, 3]. Although platform-independent costs have been shown to be useful in various applications [4, 6], in distributed execution and mobile/pervasive computation scenarios involving hosts with different computational power, it becomes necessary to express costs in a way that can be instantiated later to different architectures, to accurately reflect execution time.

Approach. With this objective in mind, we have developed a framework which combines cost analysis with profiling techniques in order to infer functions which yield bounds on platform-dependent *execution times* of procedures [7]. In this framework, platform-independent cost functions, parameterized by a certain number of constants, are inferred for each procedure in a given program. These parameters aim at capturing the execution time of certain low-level operations on each platform which is assumed to be independent from data size. Their selection is, obviously, critical. For each execution platform, the value of such constants is determined experimentally by running a set of synthetic benchmarks and measuring their execution time with a profiling toolkit developed in-house. Once such constants are determined, they are substituted into the parametric cost functions to make it possible to predict, with a certain accuracy, actual execution times.

* This work was partly funded by the EU IST FET program, IST-15905 *MOBIUS* project, by the Spanish Ministry of Education under the TIN-2005-09207 *MERIT* project, and the Madrid Regional Government under the *PROMESAS* project. Manuel Hermenegildo is also supported by the Prince of Asturias Chair in Information Science and Technology at UNM.

S. Etalle and M. Truszczyński (Eds.): ICLP 2006, LNCS 4079, pp. 431–432, 2006.

Each selection of parameters for the cost functions determines a cost model. We have implemented this approach in the CiaoPP system [5], and studied a number of cost models in order to determine experimentally which one is more precise. In doing this we have taken into account the trade-off between simplicity of the cost model (which affects the efficiency of the cost analysis and the complexity of the profiling) and the precision of their results. The results achieved show that the combined framework predicts the execution times of programs with a reasonable degree of accuracy and paves the way for more accurate analyses by including additional parameters. We believe this is an encouraging result, since using a one-time profiling for estimating execution times of other, unrelated programs is clearly appealing.

Further Applications. Deducing the expected execution time of programs in a fully automatic way has applications besides the already mentioned, more classical ones. For example, in a Proof-Carrying Code (PCC) framework, producers can send a certificate which includes a platform-independent cost function. The consumer can then, using a calibrating program, compute the values for the constants appearing in the parametric cost functions to obtain certified platform-dependent cost functions. Another application is found in resource-oriented specialization, where refined cost models can be used to help in guiding specialization by taking into account not only the size of the resulting program, but also its expected execution time (and maybe other low-level implementation factors). In particular, they can be used to perform self-tuning specialization in order to compare different specialized versions according to their costs [1].

References

1. S.J. Craig and M. Leuschel. Self-tuning resource aware specialisation for Prolog. In *Proc. of PPDP'05*, pages 23–34. ACM Press, 2005.
2. S.K. Debray and N.W. Lin. Cost analysis of logic programs. *ACM Transactions on Programming Languages and Systems*, 15(5):826–875, November 1993.
3. S.K. Debray, P. López-García, M. Hermenegildo, and N.-W. Lin. Lower Bound Cost Estimation for Logic Programs. In *1997 International Logic Programming Symposium*, pages 291–305. MIT Press, Cambridge, MA, October 1997.
4. M. Hermenegildo, E. Albert, P. López-García, and G. Puebla. Abstraction Carrying Code and Resource-Awareness. In *Proc. of PPDP'05*. ACM Press, July 2005.
5. Manuel V. Hermenegildo, Germán Puebla, Francisco Bueno, and Pedro López-García. Integrated Program Debugging, Verification, and Optimization Using Abstract Interpretation (and The Ciao System Preprocessor). *Science of Computer Programming*, 58(1–2):115–140, October 2005.
6. P. López-García, M. Hermenegildo, and S.K. Debray. A Methodology for Granularity Based Control of Parallelism in Logic Programs. *J. of Symbolic Computation, Special Issue on Parallel Symbolic Computation*, 22:715–734, 1996.
7. E. Mera, P. López-García, G. Puebla, M. Carro, and M. Hermenegildo. Towards Combining Static Analysis and Profiling for Estimating Execution Times in Logic Programs. Technical Report CLIP5/2006.0, Technical University of Madrid (UPM), School of Computer Science, UPM, April 2006.

Towards Region-Based Memory Management for Mercury Programs*

(Extended Abstract)

Quan Phan and Gerda Janssens

Department of Computer Science, K.U. Leuven
Celestijnenlaan, 200A, B-3001 Heverlee, Belgium
{quan.phan, gerda.janssens}@cs.kuleuven.be

Logic programming systems build the terms on the heap. Then automatic memory management for the heap relies on backtracking and runtime garbage collection to reclaim space on the heap. While efficient implementations of garbage collectors for logic programming languages can reuse more than 90% of the heap space, they introduce performance overhead to the execution of a program.

To remedy this shortcoming there has been a lot of research on compile-time memory management techniques, which derive the memory behaviour of a program when compiling and enhance the program with instructions to reuse memory. This static method generally follows two approaches: region-based memory management (RBMM) and compile-time garbage collection (CTGC). The basic idea of RBMM is to divide the heap memory into different regions. The dynamically created terms and their subterms have to be distributed over the regions in such a way that at a certain point in the execution of the program all terms in a region are dead and the region can be removed. RBMM has long been a topic of intensive research for functional programming languages [8, 1, 4] and for procedural languages [3, 2]. For logic programming languages, there has been only one attempt to make RBMM work for Prolog [6, 5]. CTGC detects when allocated memory cells are no longer used and instructs the program to reuse those cells for constructing new terms, reducing memory consumption and in some cases achieving faster code. This idea has been used to reuse memory cells locally in the procedures of the logic programming language Mercury [7].

The ultimate goal of our research is to investigate the possibility and practicality of a hybrid static memory management technique, which combines RBMM and CTGC.

The contribution of our work here is to develop an automated system based on program analysis that adds region annotations to deterministic Mercury programs. The algorithm consists of three phases. First, a region points-to analysis detects the region structure of the memory used by a procedure and represents this information in terms of region points-to graph. Then, live region analysis uses the region points-to graph of each procedure to precisely detect

---

* This work is supported by the project GOA/2003/08 and by FWO Vlaanderen.

S. Etalle and M. Truszczyński (Eds.): ICLP 2006, LNCS 4079, pp. 433–435, 2006.

the lifetime of regions. Finally, based on the information about the lifetime of regions the transformation inserts instructions to create and remove regions into the input program. A prototype analysis has been implemented in Melbourne Mercury Compiler version 0.12.0. The experimental results show that the memory behaviour is promising for several programs and the analysis time is tractable.

Our region analysis and transformation work correctly for deterministic programs in which the condition of if-then-else constructs, if any, can only be a goal that does not require creating or removing any regions inside itself. Note that such a deterministic program can still have different execution paths. There are 2 reasons for these restrictions. Firstly, the region liveness analysis only takes into account forward execution. Therefore the removal and creation of regions are only correct w.r.t. forward execution as we have in deterministic programs. Secondly, even with a deterministic program, we need to be sure that when an execution path of the program is taken all the region instructions on that path are actually executed. A *canfail* goal could cause problems such as created regions would never be removed or a region would be created or removed more than once, and so on. In deterministic programs such *canfail* goals can only appear in the condition of if-then-elses. Therefore, the condition goal of if-then-elses is restricted so that no region instructions occur in this non-deterministic context.

Our approach is a valid starting point for RBMM for general Mercury programs. The authors in [5, 6] describe an enhanced runtime for Prolog with RBMM, which provide the support for nondeterministic goals. The idea of that enhanced runtime is that backtracking is made transparent to the algorithm for deterministic programs by providing a mechanism to undo changes to the heap memory, restoring the heap memory to the previous state at the point to which the program backtracks. We believe that a similar approach can be applied to Mercury and with the runtime support the algorithm presented here can be used unchanged to support full Mercury programs. In future work we will investigate whether static analysis can lessen the support needed at run-time by exploiting the determinism information available to Mercury compiler.

The precision of the current region points-to analysis can be improved and the whole algorithm can be extended to support separate compilation in the context of modules.

References

[1] A. Aiken, M. Fahndrich, and R. Levien. Better static memory management: Improving region-based analysis of higher-order languages. In *PLDI 1995*.

[2] S. Cherem and R. Rugina. Region analysis and Transformation for Java. In *ISMM 2004*, pages 85–96.

[3] D. Grossman, G. Morrisett, T. Jim, M. Hicks, Y. Wang, and J. Cheney. Region-based memory management in Cyclone. In *PLDI 2002*, pages 282–293.

[4] F. Henglein, H Makholm, and H. Niss. A direct approach to control-flow sensitive region-based memory management. In *PPDP 2001*, pages 175–186.

[5] H. Makholm. A region-based memory manager for Prolog. In *ISMM 2000*, pages 25–34.

[6] H. Makholm and K. Sagonas. On enabling the WAM with region support. In *ICLP 2002*.

[7] Mazur N. *Compile-time garbage collection for the declarative language Mercury.* PhD thesis, Computer Science Dept., Katholieke Universiteit Leuven, May 2004.

[8] M. Tofte and J.-P. Talpin. Region-based memory management. *Information and Computation.*, 132(2):109–176, February 1997.

Towards Structured Contexts and Modules
(Extended Abstract)

Salvador Abreu and Vítor Nogueira

Universidade de Évora and CENTRIA FCT/UNL, Portugal
{spa, vbn}@di.uevora.pt

1 Introduction

Contextual Logic Programming was proposed by Monteiro and Porto [4] as a means of bringing modularity to the Prolog language. It was improved upon as a practical extension in a high performance Prolog system by Abreu and Diaz [1], providing a program structuring mechanism as well as fulfilling some of Prolog's shortcomings when used for *programming in-the-large*, namely by enabling an object-oriented programming style without relinquishing the expressiveness and semantic robustness of Logic Programs.

For their dynamically configurable structure, contexts clearly subsume the base mechanisms of most module systems, this being particularly true of the ISO/IEC Prolog Modules standard proposal [2]. This strength is also a weakness: the dynamic nature of a context leads to difficulties in predicting their structure, at compile time, this is particularly true when taking a separate compilation approach. We address these issues by presenting an approach whereby contexts are restricted to statically predictable forms and illustrate the proposal by applying it to implement ISO modules.

2 Structured Contexts

The most obstructive limitation is that a Prolog compilation unit (a CxLP unit) is not self-sufficient for specifying the available set of predicates and their defining clauses. A CxLP program cannot easily be analyzed following a "separate compilation" approach: only a form of inter-unit analysis could be effective to extract properties for a given program.

W.r.t. the proposal of [1] we opt for a different focus on the use of context primitives: we make the context switch operation the default, while still providing the extension operation. This shift promotes the use of explicit contexts over the implicit ones associated with the context extension mechanism. The notation is also revised to provide an easier reading. Moreover, contexts are now specified with the possibility of imposing restrictions on their runtime structure; in particular this can be used to cast ISO modules into CxLP, as briefly discussed in the next section.

S. Etalle and M. Truszczyński (Eds.): ICLP 2006, LNCS 4079, pp. 436–438, 2006.

3   Modules Done with Contexts

Consider the proposed ISO/IEC Prolog standard, part 2, which specifies the module system to be used in compliant implementations. It is feasible to implement the standard using CxLP, by means of a simple preprocessor. Consider example 6.2.6.1 from [2], which defines a `utilities` module that exports `length/2` and `reverse/2`. An equivalent CxLP program can be constructed with two units:

- One called `utilities`, as above, standing for the *interface* unit, i.e. the one in which the publicly accessible predicates reside. This unit will only contain stubs for the "exported" predicates. These will be simple chain rules which resort to a homonym predicate, residing in a private associated unit.
- Another one called `utilities_private`, which will play the role of an *implementation* unit. This unit will contain all the effective program text found in the module definition above.

The essentials of the equivalent CxLP program are:

```
:- unit(utilities).
   length(A, B) :- utilities_private.length(A, B).
   reverse(A, B) :- utilities_private.reverse(A, B).
```

The content of unit `utilities_private` is identical to the module `body` from the ISO Prolog example.

Other aspects such as dealing with operator definitions and meta-predicate declarations are also addressed. The *calling context* as per the ISO definition is interpreted as the topmost unit of the CxLP calling context, i.e. it relies on the unary `:>` operation from [1].

4   Related Work

Although contexts originated as a means of program structuring in terms of composite theories, we prefer to stress the OO reading, as it allows for useful forms of program development.

Several Logic Programming languages include module systems which may relate to contexts. One language which includes a module system with features close to those provided by CxLP is λProlog [3]. CxLP is a language with a purpose very different from that of λProlog, nevertheless, the unit composition mechanism provided by contexts is close to that which would be obtained with the "import" directive of λProlog, as opposed to "accumulate".

References

1. Salvador Abreu and Daniel Diaz. Objective: in Minimum Context. In Catuscia Palamidessi, editor, *Logic Programming, 19th International Conference, ICLP 2003, Mumbai, India, December 9-13, 2003, Proceedings*, volume 2916 of *Lecture Notes in Computer Science*, pages 128–147. Springer-Verlag, 2003. ISBN 3-540-20642-6.

2. ISO/IEC JTC1/SC22/WG17. Information technology – Programming languages – Prolog – Part 2: Modules. Technical Report DIS 13211, ISO, 2000.
3. Dale Miller. A Proposal for Modules in λProlog. In Roy Dyckhoff, editor, *Extensions of Logic Programming*, number 798 in LNAI, pages 206–221. Springer-Verlag, March/April 1993.
4. L. Monteiro and A Porto. Contextual logic programming. In Giorgio Levi and Maurizio Martelli, editors, *Proceedings of the Sixth International Conference on Logic Programming*, pages 284–299, Lisbon, 1989. The MIT Press.

Towards Temporal Contextual Logic Programming

Vítor Nogueira and Salvador Abreu

Universidade de Évora and CENTRIA, Portugal
{vbn, spa}@di.uevora.pt

Abstract. Contextual Logic Programming [3] (CxLP) is a simple and powerful language that extends logic programming with mechanisms for modularization. The importance of temporal representation and reasoning is well known not only in the database community but also in the artificial intelligence one. In this paper we propose a language called Temporal Contextual Logic Programming. Besides giving a brief description of its operational semantics we also present a real-world application.

1 Introduction and Motivation

Contextual Logic Programming [3] (CxLP) is a simple and powerful language that extends logic programming with mechanisms for modularization. Recent work not only presented a revised specification of CxLP together with a new implementation for it but also explained how this language could be seen as a shift into the Object-Oriented Programming paradigm [1]. Finally, CxLP was shown to be a powerful language in which to design and implement Organizational Information Systems [2].

Temporal representation and reasoning is a central part of many Artificial Intelligence areas such as planning, scheduling and natural language understanding. Also in the database community we can see that this is a growing field of research. Although both communities have several proposals for working with time, it seems that we have two types of approaches: one, although very expressive has few connections to practical situations; the other approach is *too practical*, i.e. only allow us to deal with a particular temporal domain.

It is our belief that adding a temporal dimension to CxLP results in a language that besides having all the expressiveness acknowledged to logic programming, easily allow us to establish connections to the real world because of its *contextual structure*. In this article we will introduce the language Temporal Contextual Logic Programming (TCxLP), with a brief description of its operational semantics; we also discuss it in a real–world application: the Portuguese vaccination program.

2 Temporal CxLP

The main point of CxLP is that programs are structured as sets of predicates, *units*, that can be combined in an execution attribute called a *context*. Temporal

S. Etalle and M. Truszczyński (Eds.): ICLP 2006, LNCS 4079, pp. 439–441, 2006.

Contextual Logic Programming is a two–sorted CxLP. A *temporal context* is any list of unit designator term[1], term of the temporal sort or a pair formed by the two elements above.

In an informal way we can say that the time represented by a context is its "first" or topmost temporal term. Moreover, if the context doesn't contains any temporal term, then its time is the *current time*.

2.1   Operational Semantics

Due to the nature of this paper we won't present the complete operational semantics but describe just the main difference towards the semantics of the CxLP, and this happens when the top of the context is a temporally qualified unit, i.e. a unit whose application depends of the time of the context. For that consider the derivation of a goal G in the context $(u, t).C$, where u is a unit designator and t a temporal term. When the time of the context C is unifiable with t and unit u has a rule for goal G, we derive G in the context $u.C$ otherwise we derive it in the context C.

3   Application: Portuguese Vaccination Program

In Portugal, a new National Vaccination Program (PNV) was introduced in 2006. Several changes regarding the previous program (PNV 2000) where made. Although we are going to report our example to the Portuguese case, the reader should notice that not only the vaccination program, but also changes are representative of what happens in other countries. One can easily translate a vaccination program to a TCxLP unit that specify when one given vaccine should be inoculated. For space restrictions we will omit such translation and consider that besides unit pnv_2006 we have a unit person to represent some basic facts about patients. To query, when and what should be the next vaccine of patient whose id is 3 we could have: ?- person(3) :> (item, pnv_2006 :> next(V, D)).. Please, remember that since there is no explicit mention to time, we assume that we are referring to the present time. As mentioned above this program is a substitute for the one of 2000. Unit pnv_2000 and pnv_2006 have different applicability periods: we are going to consider that the former is valid during [2000/1/1, 2005/12/31] and the later after 2006/1/1. Let us see when and what should be the next vaccine of person 1, assuming that the time is 2005/12/20:

```
| ?- date(2005, 12, 20) :> person(1) :> ( item,
          (pnv_2000, [date(2000, 1, 1), date(2005, 12, 31)]) :>
                (pnv_2006, [date(2006, 1, 1), infty])) :> next(V, D)).
```

In this case, we have that the pnv_2000 unit is the one to be considered. If we remove the temporal term date(2005, 12, 20) (i.e. if we are talking about the present time) then unit pnv_2006 is considered instead.

---

[1] A *unit designator* is any instance of the term $u(v_1, \ldots, v_n)$ $(n \geq 0)$, where u is the unit name and $v_1, \ldots, v_n$ are distinct variables called unit's parameters.

4   Conclusions and Future Work

In this paper we presented a temporal extension of CxLP that can be regarded as a two–sorted CxLP. Although we aimed that such extension could be as minimal as possible we also wanted to be as expressive as possible, leading to the notion of units whose applicability depends of the time of the context, i.e. temporally qualified units. Howbeit we presented the operational semantics, we consider that to obtain a more solid foundation there is still need for a declarative approach together with its soundness and completeness proof.

To our understanding the best way to prove the usefullness of this language is by means of a real–world application, and for that purpose we chose the Portuguese vaccination program. Besides this example, we are currently applying this language to the legislation field, namely to represent and reason about the evolution of laws. Finally, it is our goal to show that this language can act as the backbone for construction and maintenance of temporal information systems.

References

1. Salvador Abreu and Daniel Diaz. Objective: in minimum context. In *Proc. Nineteenth International Conference on Logic Programming*, 2003.
2. Salvador Abreu, Daniel Diaz, and Vitor Nogueira. Organizational information systems design and implementation with contextual constraint logic programming. In *IT Innovation in a Changing World – The 10ᵗʰ International Conference of European University Information Systems*, Ljubljana, Slovenia, June 2004.
3. António Porto and Luís Monteiro. Contextual logic programming. In Giorgio Levi and Maurizio Martelli, editors, *Proceedings 6th Intl. Conference on Logic Programming, Lisbon, Portugal , 19–23 June 1989*, pages 284–299. The MIT Press, Cambridge, MA, 1989.

Semantic Property Grammars for Knowledge Extraction from Biomedical Text

Veronica Dahl and Baohua Gu

Simon Fraser University, Burnaby, BC, Canada, V5A 1S6
{veronica, bgu}@cs.sfu.ca

Abstract. We present *Semantic Property Grammars*, designed to extract concepts and relations from biomedical texts. The implementation adapts a CHRG parser we designed for Property Grammars [1], which views linguistic constraints as properties between sets of categories and solves them by constraint satisfaction, can handle incomplete or erroneous text, and extract phrases of interest selectively. We endow it with concept and relation extraction abilities as well.

1 Semantic Property Grammars (SPGs) – An Introduction

Property Grammars (PGs) [2] linguistically characterize sentences not in terms of an explicit, complete parse tree but in terms of seven simple properties between pairs of constituents, for instance, *linearity* (e.g., a determiner must precede a noun) or *unicity* (e.g., a noun can only have one determiner). A directly executable specification of PGs was developed by Dahl and Blache [3], which uses CHRG [4] to combine pairs of constituents according to whether properties between them are satisfied. SPGs are based on an adaptation of this parser which enhances it with concepts and relations gleaned from the substring being parsed. In the example below, for instance, the output gathers in a cat/6 symbol: the phrase's category (noun phrase), its syntactic features (singular, masculine), the parse tree (not needed by the theory, but built for convenience), and the lists of satisfied and unsatisfied properties within this phrase, e.g, prec(prep, np) indicates that the preposition does precede its noun phrase in the embedded prepositional phrase (pp), since it appears in the list of satisfied properties. The unsatisfied property list is empty, since there are no property violations in this np. Finally, the semantic concept list contains the relationship induced by this noun phrase, as well as the concepts its parts intervene in, obtained in consultation with a biomedical ontology.

Input	The activation of NF-kappa-B via CD-28
Output	cat(np,[sing,masc],np(det(the),n(activation),pp(prep(of),np(n('NF-kappa-B'), pp(prep(via)))),np(n('CD-28')))),[prec(prep,sn),unicity(prep),prec(n,pp), unicity(n),exclude(name,n),prec(det,n),unicity(det)],[ ],[protein('NF-kappa-B'), gene('CD-28'),activation('NF-kappa-B','CD-28')])

S. Etalle and M. Truszczyński (Eds.): ICLP 2006, LNCS 4079, pp. 442–443, 2006.

2   Extracting Semantic Information

Extracting Concepts and Relations. The above example shows the simplest and most needed application of our parser to biomedical information extraction, namely, to glean concepts and relations from noun phrases. As shown in the output, we obtain more information than other noun phrase chunkers/parsers available for this task, which only output a parse tree. In addition, we provide semantic output which can further be combined with that of other parts of the sentence, as we shall see below. Although noun phrases are the most common source of wanted concept extraction, we can directly apply the same methodology to extract verb-induced relations, as in the sentence "The retinoblastoma protein negatively regulates transcriptional activation", where the verb *regulate* marks a relation between two concepts *retinoblastoma protein* and *transcriptional activation*. To deal with this type of relation, we extract both concepts from their noun phrases, and link them together into the relationship induced by the verb.

Relating Indirectly Connected Concepts. Once concepts and relations have been extracted from the input, we can infer further concepts by consulting a biomedical ontology (there are several available). This is useful to:

- disambiguate in function of context. For instance, usually *binding site* refers to a DNA domain or region, while sometimes it refers to a protein domain or region. Catching the latter meaning is not trivial since both *c-Myc* and *G28-5* are protein molecules. However, our parser looks for semantic clues from surrounding words in order to disambiguate: in sentence 1) below, *promoters* points to the DNA region binding site, whereas in sentence 2), *ligands* points to the protein meaning of binding site.
- assess a general theme in the (sub)text: since the parser retrieves the semantic classes of objects and relations as it goes along (as shown in section 1), it is a simple matter to assume them as themes. Consuming them when in doubt as to the main theme can assist in further disambiguation as well as in other semantic interpretation tasks.

| 1 | Transcription factors USF1 and USF2 up-regulate gene expression via interaction with an E box on their target **promoters**, which is also a **binding site** for **c-Myc**. |
| 2 | The functional activity of **ligands** built from the **binding site** of **G28-5** is dependent on the size and physical properties of the molecule both in solution and on the cell surfaces. |

References

1. Dahl, V. and Blache, P.: Extracting Selected Phrases through Constraint Satisfaction. Proceeding of ICLP workshop on CSLP, 2005.
2. Blache, P.: Property Grammars: A Fully Constraint-Based Theory", in H. Christiansen et al. (eds), Constraint Solving and NLP, LNCS, Springer, 2005.
3. Dahl, V. and Blache, P.: Directly Executable Constraint Based Grammars. Proc of Journees Francophones de Programmation en Logique avec Contraintes, 2004.
4. Christiansen, H.: CHR Grammars. International Journal on Journal on Theory and Practice of Logic Programming, special issue on CHRs, 2005.

Natural Language Processing
Using Lexical and Logical Combinators

Juan Fernández Ortiz[*] and Jørgen Villadsen[**]

Computer Science, Roskilde University, Building 42.1, DK-4000 Roskilde, Denmark

Abstract. We describe a Prolog implementation of the sequent calculus for the type theory Nabla that can make syntactical and semantical analyses of a fragment of natural language using combinators.

1 Introduction

The multi-dimensional type theory Nabla [3] is a linguistic system based on categorial grammars [1] and with so-called lexical and logical combinators [4,5,6]. We describe a prototype system implemented in Prolog [2].

We here consider only the following logical combinators: $\dot{\mathbf{Q}} \equiv \lambda xy(x = y)$, $\dot{\mathbf{N}} \equiv \lambda a(\neg a)$, $\dot{\mathbf{C}} \equiv \lambda ab(a \wedge b)$, $\dot{\mathbf{O}} \equiv \lambda tu \exists x(tx \wedge ux)$ (overlap), $\dot{\mathbf{I}} \equiv \lambda tu \forall x(tx \Rightarrow ux)$ (inclusion), and $\dot{\mathbf{P}} \equiv \lambda ab(a \Rightarrow b)$ (preservation). See the references for more.

We use the basic category S for sentences, N for proper nouns and G for common nouns with the following lexical category assignments with \ and / for the left- and right-looking type operators ($\bullet$ is the top category for a text):

John Nick Gloria Victoria : N
man woman thief unicorn : G
popular quick : G/G
be : $(N\backslash S)/N$ Multiple categories with
be : $(N\backslash S)/(G/G)$ different semantics.
a every : $(S/(N\backslash S))/G$ $((S/N)\backslash S)/G$ Multiple categories with
also : $S\backslash(S/S)$ same semantics.
so : $S\backslash(\bullet/S)$

The following corresponding lexical combinator definitions give the semantics:

John Nick Gloria Victoria $\equiv$ $\circ$ | J N G V
man woman thief unicorn $\equiv$ $\lambda x(\circ x)$ | M W T U
popular quick $\equiv$ $\lambda tx(\bigcirc(\circ x)(tx))$ | $\dot{\mathbf{C}}$ | P Q
be $\equiv$ $\lambda yx(\bigcirc xy)$ | $\dot{\mathbf{Q}}$
be' $\equiv$ $\lambda fx(f\lambda y(\bigcirc xy)x)$ | $\dot{\mathbf{Q}}$ $\bigcirc$ is place-holder for
a every $\equiv$ $\lambda tu(\bigcirc tu)$ | $\dot{\mathbf{O}}$ $\dot{\mathbf{I}}$ logical combinators.

[*] Erasmus student at Computer Science, Roskilde University, 2005. jfo@lycos.es
[**] Corresponding author, now at IMM/DTU. jv@imm.dtu.dk Sponsored by the IT University of Copenhagen and the CONTROL project: http://control.ruc.dk

S. Etalle and M. Truszczyński (Eds.): ICLP 2006, LNCS 4079, pp. 444–446, 2006.

also ≡ $\lambda ab(\bigcirc ab)$ | $\dot{\mathbf{C}}$ ○ is place-holder for
so ≡ $\lambda ab(\bigcirc ab)$ | $\dot{\mathbf{P}}$ (predicate) constant.

The combinators and constants to be inserted are shown after the | above.

2   From Syntax to Semantics Using Combinators

As a tiny example we consider the following text [2] (i.e. a valid argument):

Every woman is popular. Gloria is a woman. So Gloria is popular.

⤳ **so**

> (**also** (**every woman** (**be′ popular**)) (**a woman** λx(**be** x **Gloria**)))
> (**be′ popular Gloria**)

⤳ $\dot{\mathbf{P}}$

> $(\dot{\mathbf{C}}\ (\dot{\mathbf{I}}\ \lambda x(Wx)\ \lambda x(\dot{\mathbf{C}}\ (Px)\ (\dot{\mathbf{Q}}xx)))\ (\dot{\mathbf{O}}\ \lambda x(Wx)\ \lambda x(\dot{\mathbf{Q}}xG)))$
> $(\dot{\mathbf{C}}\ (PG)\ (\dot{\mathbf{Q}}GG))$

⤳ $\forall x(Wx \Rightarrow Px) \wedge WG \Rightarrow PG$ Which is a valid formula as expected.

The implementation [2] can search for proofs in the sequent calculus:

```
?- analyze([every,woman,be,popular,also,gloria,be,a,woman,
            so,gloria,be,popular],RULES,FORMULA).
FORMULA =
app(app(v(so),app(app(v(also),
  app(app(v(every),v(woman)),app(v(be),v(popular)))),
  app(app(v(a),v(woman)),abs(x,app(app(v(be),v(x)),v(gloria)))))),
  app(app(v(be),v(popular)),v(gloria))),
RULES =
lvL(lvL(rvL(eq,rvL(eq,rvL(eq,eq))),rvL(rvL(eq,lvL(rvR(rvL(eq,
  lvL(eq,eq))),eq)),eq)),rvL(rvL(eq,lvL(eq,eq)),eq))
```

`FORMULA` yields the combinator expression above and `RULES` is the proof structure. For a more substantial natural language fragment with propositional attitudes [4] the combinators change, e.g. $\mathbf{P} \equiv \lambda pq\forall i(pi \Rightarrow qi)$, but the program is unchanged.

References

1. W. Buszkowski, W. Marciszewski, and J. van Benthem, editors. *Categorial Grammar*. John Benjamins Publishing Company, 1988.
2. J. F. Ortiz. *Natural Language Processing Using Lexical and Logical Combinators*. Graduation thesis, Technical University of Madrid, February 2006.
3. J. Villadsen. *Nabla: A Linguistic System based on Multi-dimensional Type Theory*. PhD thesis, Technical University of Denmark, February 1995.

4. J. Villadsen. Combinators for paraconsistent attitudes. In P. de Groote, G. Morrill, and C. Retoré, editors, *Logical Aspects of Computational Linguistics*, pages 261–278. Lecture Notes in Computer Science 2099, Springer-Verlag, 2001.

5. J. Villadsen. Multi-dimensional type theory: Rules, categories, and combinators for syntax and semantics. In H. Christiansen, P. R. Skadhauge, and J. Villadsen, editors, *International Workshop on Constraint Solving and Language Processing*, volume 99 of Roskilde University, Computer Science, Technical Reports, pages 161–165, 2004.

6. J. Villadsen. *Nabla: A Linguistic System based on Type Theory*. LIT Verlag, 2006. Forthcoming in Foundations of Communication and Cognition (New Series).

Learning Semantic Parsers: A Constraint Handling Rule Approach

Dulce Aguilar-Solis

Logic and Functional Programming Group
Department of Computing Science
Simon Fraser University
Burnaby, B.C., Canada
dma@cs.sfu.ca

Semantic parsing is the process of mapping a natural language input into some structure representing its meaning. Even though this process is natural and smooth for human beings, it constitutes a huge problem for a machine. Semantic parsing is a challenging and interesting problem that has been severely understudied. Most of the research in natural language understanding has focused on shallow semantic analysis (i.e. word sense disambiguation, case-role analysis, etc). Previous approaches to semantic parsing are not robust enough or are limited in its applicability because they are applied to simple domains where semantic parsing reduces to filling slots on a frame.

The main problem with semantic parsing is the lack of a universal semantic representation. Formal semantic representations can range from shallow (i.e. case-role analysis) to deeper semantic analysis (i.e. predicate logic, Montague style). Constructing a semantic parser usually involves hand-crafting expert knowledge represented as rules. However, hand-crafted semantic parsers exhibit problems with robustness and incompleteness even for domain specific applications. As the task scales up in size, hand-crafting becomes more and more difficult; this results in applications that are time-consuming and difficult to build and yet perform poorly.

The ultimate goal of this work is to develop a novel constraint handling rule (CHR [1]) approach to learn semantic parsers for mapping natural language sentences to any kind of compositional formal representation. The algorithm will learn a semantic parser given a set of natural language sentences annotated with their correct meaning representations. We assume that the parse tree of each sample sentence is either part of the training data or could be obtained from an unambiguous context-free grammar available for the target meaning-representation language. The only restriction imposed to the semantic representation given in the training data is compositionality: the semantic representation of a sentence can be obtained from the semantic representation of its parts.

As a first step, this work shows how to learn one new semantic rule without going through the process of leaning again the set of known semantic rules. Even though this seems fairly easy, most of the previous work on semantic parsing does not consider a work in progress (an incomplete semantic parser) as input. Also, the final result of previous approaches is some obscure system that can not be

S. Etalle and M. Truszczyński (Eds.): ICLP 2006, LNCS 4079, pp. 447–448, 2006.
© Springer-Verlag Berlin Heidelberg 2006

easily read by an untrained eye. On the other hand, the output of our system is a CHR parser, where each rule is enriched with some self-explanatory actions.

CHR has the advantage of building every single piece of information that can be constructed given the incomplete semantic parser. Even if a semantic rule is missing CHR will not fail and the set of already constructed semantic constraints will be stored for later use (when the semantic parser is completed). Some extensions of CHR, such as Hyprolog, allow the use of assumptions and abductions, which are very useful to build hypothetical scenarios. Another advantage of CHR is its ability to explore all paths without losing information about previously explored paths (all the constraints generated will be stored).

The proposed approach uses CHR and assumptions (Hyprolog [2]) to examine the actual state and the desired state of the semantic representation of a sentence. A series of actions will be inferred to transform the former into the latter:

- *Same variable*: two or more constituents refer to the same variable.
- *Replace variable*: the semantic representation of a constituent is embedded in another constituent. The embedded element could also be a combination of two or more constituents (with or without additional words).
- *Output variable*: a variable not used in the construction of the desired constituent (it usually refers to an upper syntactic category).
- *Main category*: the syntactic category that commands the representation.

Even though the generation of the set of actions will be guided by the input data, the algorithm can explore alternate or additional scenarios. In the event of ambiguities or inconsistencies in the training data, probabilistic CHR will be used. The algorithm is general enough to handle any type of compositional formal semantic representation language, even those with nested structures. Other important features are: the immediate use of the training data as a guide; avoiding generation of spurious answers; avoiding the exhaustive generation of additional examples; allowing the inclusion of additional words when two or more constituents are combined; generating a clear and concise semantic parser as output; and handling noisy training data. Future work includes allowing the system to learn more than one rule at a time. The automatic acquisition of the semantic lexicon will be the last step towards a complete system that learns a semantic parser from examples.

References

1. Fruhwirth, T. W.: Theory and Practice of Constraint Handling Rules. In Journal of Logic Programming 37 (1998) 95–138
2. Christiansen, H., Dahl, V.: HYPROLOG: A New Logic Programming Language with Assumptions and Abduction. Lecture Notes in Computer Science 3668 (2005) 159–173

A Declarative Framework for Security: Secure Concurrent Constraint Programming

Hugo A. López[1], Catuscia Palamidessi[2], Jorge A. Pérez[1], Camilo Rueda[1],
and Frank D. Valencia[3]

[1] Pontificia Universidad Javeriana - Cali
{halopez, japerez, crueda}@cic.puj.edu.co
[2] INRIA and LIX École Polytechnique
catuscia@lix.polytechnique.fr
[3] CNRS and LIX École Polytechnique
frank.valencia@lix.polytechnique.fr

Motivation. Due to technological advances such as the Internet and mobile computing, *Security* has become a serious challenge involving several disciplines of Computer Science. In recent years, there has been a growing interest in the analysis of *security protocols* and one promising approach is the development of formalisms that model communicating processes, in particular *Process Calculi*. The results are so far encouraging although most remains to be done.

Concurrent Constraint Programming (CCP) is a well-established formalism which generalizes *Logic Programming* [Sar93]. In CCP processes interact with each other by telling and asking information represented as *constraints* in a medium, a so-called *store*. One of the most appealing and distinct features of CCP is that it combines the traditional *operational* view of process calculi with a *declarative* one of processes based upon logic. This combination allows CCP to benefit from the large body of techniques of both process calculi and logic. Over the last decade, several reasoning techniques and implementations for CCP have been developed: E.g., denotational models [SRP91], specification logics and proof systems [NPV02], Petri Net interpretations [RM94], and *CCP-based programming languages* [Smo95].

Remarkably, most process calculi for security have strong similarities with CCP. For instance, SPL [CW01], the Spi calculus variants in [ALV03, FA01], and the calculus in [BB02] are all operationally defined in terms of configurations containing information which can only increase during evolution. Such a monotonic evolution of information is akin to the notion of *monotonic store*, which is central to CCP and a source of its simplicity. Also, the calculi in [ALV03, BB02, FA01] are parametric in the underlying logic much like CCP is parametric an underlying *constraint system*. Also, the assertion of (protocol) properties [ALV03] can be formalized as CCP processes imposing constraints. Furthermore, the *notion of unification*, which has been shown useful in [FA01] for the symbolic execution of protocols, is primitive (and more general) in CCP.

Description. Our project *Secure CCP (SCCP)* aims at advancing both the theory and tools of CCP for analyzing and programming security protocols. The main goal is to develop a CCP-based framework for security protocols. The novelty is the combination in one unique formalism of behavioral and logical techniques. In fact, to our best knowledge, there is no work on Security that takes advantage of the reasoning techniques of

S. Etalle and M. Truszczyński (Eds.): ICLP 2006, LNCS 4079, pp. 449–450, 2006.

CCP such as its denotational models, temporal and intuitionistic logics, or Petri Net interpretations. The expected outcome is two-fold. We will advance the CCP theory to deal with new challenging concepts from Security and produce a specification language and tools to model and automatically verify security protocols.

Approach. The approach of the project will be to give a CCP account of a representative calculus for security protocols. We will use CCP *constraint systems* to represent a logic to reason about the information an attacker can deduce from the information accumulated in the monotonic store. The CCP linear-time temporal logic and associated complete inference system in [NPV02] and the verification results in [Val05] can be used to specify and prove safety properties of protocol runs.

Now, most security protocols use mechanisms to allow generation of nonces (or names). Therefore, we shall need to provide CCP with such mechanisms which have been far too little considered in CCP. One approach to this problem will be to use constraint systems based on Nominal Logic [Pit01], a modern logic to reason about *name freshness*. Another possibility is to extend CCP with an operation that provides name generation. To keep the dual operational and declarative view of CCP, the extended language should also have a logic interpretation. In fact, we have recently studied the issue of name generation in [PSVV06] where we proved that existential quantification can replace name generation in a meaningful process calculus.

References

[ALV03]   R. Amadio, D. Lugiez, and V. Vanackere. On the symbolic reduction of processes with cryptographic functions. *TCS: Theoretical Computer Science*, 290, 2003.

[BB02]   M. Boreale and M. Buscemi. A framework for the analysis of security protocols. *Lecture Notes in Computer Science*, 2421, 2002.

[CW01]   F. Crazzolara and G. Winskel. Events in security protocols. In Pierangela Samarati, editor, *Proceedings of the 8th ACM Conference on Computer and Communications Security*, pages 96–105, Philadelphia, PA, USA, November 2001. ACM Press.

[FA01]   M. Fiore and M. Abadi. Computing symbolic models for verifying cryptographic protocols. In *14th IEEE Computer Security Foundations Workshop*, pages 160–173. IEEE Computer Society, 2001.

[NPV02]   M. Nielsen, C. Palamidessi, and F. Valencia. Temporal concurrent constraint programming: Denotation, logic and applications. *Nordic Journal of Computing*, 9(2):145–188, 2002.

[Pit01]   A. Pitts. Nominal logic: A first order theory of names and binding. In *Proc. of TACS 2001*, volume 2215 of *LNCS*. Springer-Verlag, 2001.

[PSVV06] C. Palamidessi, V. Saraswat, B. Victor, and F. Valencia. On the expressiveness of recursion vs replication in the asynchronous pi-calculus. To Appear in LICS'06, 2006.

[RM94]   F. Rossi and U. Montanari. Concurrent semantics for concurrent constraint programming. In *Constraint Programming: Proc. 1993 NATO ASI*, pages 181–220, 1994.

[Sar93]   V. Saraswat. *Concurrent Constraint Programming*. The MIT Press, 1993.

[Smo95]   G. Smolka. The Oz programming model. In Jan van Leeuwen, editor, *Computer Science Today*, volume 1000 of *LNCS*, pages 324–343. Springer-Verlag, 1995.

[SRP91]   V. Saraswat, M. Rinard, and P. Panangaden. The semantic foundations of concurrent constraint programming. In *POPL '91*, pages 333–352, 1991.

[Val05]   F. Valencia. Decidability of infinite-state timed CCP processes and first-order LTL. *Theor. Comput. Sci.*, 330(3):577–607, 2005.

Logic Programming in Knowledge Domains

Andrei Mantsivoda, Vladimir Lipovchenko, and Anton Malykh

Irkutsk State University, Russia
{andrei, lip, malykh}@baikal.ru

Abstract. We propose an approach to combining logic programming and knowledge representation paradigms. This approach is based on the conception of description terms. LP and KR are integrated in such a way that their underlying logics are carefully separated. A core idea here is to push the KR techniques on the functional level. On the LP level the knowledge base is considered as a constraint store, in which special propagation methods are ruling. A constraint logic programming language based on this idea is outlined.

The amalgamation of KR and LP looks promising for many reasons and attracts serious attention. KR formalisms are mostly based on description logics (DLs) [1], which offer flexible tools for knowledge representation. Both DLs and LP are based on *constructive* logical systems. But since they came from the different subsets of the first order logic, their constructive properties have *different* origins. Thus an attempt to mix up LP and DLs within a generalized logical system can make us sacrifice a lot [2].

In [3] we have introduced an approach to knowledge representation, which is based on the notion of a description term. The main idea behind description terms is to move knowledge representation techniques from the logical level to the functional level of terms and objects. As for integration of LP and DL styles, this idea allows us not to mix up the two styles within a joined logical formalism, but keep them separated while preserving tight interconnections between them.

Let Δ be a knowledge domain. A description term t is a term of a special form, which is interpreted as a description of objects $d \in \Delta$. This description includes information about *classes* (concepts) and *properties* (rôles), which characterize d. A description can be incomplete, if it contains only partial data about d. Moreover, one term can describe many objects (for instance, if a term says only that the person's name is John, this term describes all Johns in Δ). Thus, t must be interpreted as the set of those objects $d \in \Delta$, which t describes, that is $t^I \subseteq \Delta$, or more precisely $t^I = \{d \mid t \diamond d, d \in \Delta\}$. Here I is an interpretation, $t \diamond d$ means that d is described by t. Since data in terms is incomplete, it is useful to be able to compare them. We say that t_1 is *approximated* by t_2 ($t_1 \gg t_2$) if all information in t_2 is contained also in t_1. Note that if $t_1 \gg t_2$ then $t_1^I \subseteq t_2^I$, that is, the more precise information t_1 has, the less number of objects it describes.

To incorporate description terms we substitute the standard LP rule with

$$\text{(LPd)} \quad \frac{p(t_1, \ldots, t_k), p_2, \ldots, p_n \qquad p(t'_1, \ldots, t'_k) \mathbin{:-} r_1, \ldots, r_m.}{(r_1, \ldots, r_m, p_2, \ldots, p_n)\Theta}$$

S. Etalle and M. Truszczyński (Eds.): ICLP 2006, LNCS 4079, pp. 451–452, 2006.

if $t_i \Theta \gg t_i' \Theta$ for $i = \overline{1, k}$. Here t_i and t_i' are description terms, the left premise is the goal, the right premise is a rule, r_i and p_i are atoms. In LPd description terms can be parameterized with standard logical variables, and Θ is used to handle them.

The next thing we should do is to establish in our system the knowledge base (KB), which keeps knowledge about the domain Δ. We organize KB in the form of a constraint store, which consists of *naming constraints*. A naming constraint is an expression of the form $id :: t$ where id is the name (identifier) of an object in Δ, and t is its description. This constraint means that an object d of Δ named id is described by t. $id :: t$ is true in an interpretation I, if $id^I \in t^I$.

We also need to incorporate *axioms*, which describe the knowledge domain as a whole. In description logics axioms have the form of inclusions or equivalences, which are satisfied by any element of Δ. The *dual nature* of description terms helps us to introduce axioms in our scheme. On the one hand, in naming constraints description terms describe single objects. On the other hand, since description terms are interpreted as subsets of Δ, we can use them to describe also the sets of objects. So, as axioms we use those description terms, which describe *all* objects of Δ, that is, $t^I = \Delta$.

Application of axioms depends on the inference system and propagation strategies in the naming constraint store. In the general scheme this inference system is not specified, since different entailments can play this role. For instance, it is possible to exploit modifications of tableau algorithms [1].

Now starting with the standard logic programming scheme we (i) substitute ordinary terms by description terms; (ii) replace the standard inference LP-rule with LPd; (iii) establish the constraint store containing axioms and naming constraints, and introduce a propagation scheme based on DL algorithms; (iv) introduce two new built-ins: `axiom/1` (posting an axiom in the constraint store) and `::/2` (posting a naming constraint); (v) introduce special built-ins for retrieval and retraction of information in the constraint store.

Thus we obtain a constraint logic programming language working in knowledge domains. In this language the underling logics of LP and KR do not affect each other. The further steps include investigation of some theoretical problems concerning the inference system and strategies working in the naming constraint store. Also an implementation of the scheme and the design of the corresponding constraint logic programming language are being developed.

References

1. Baader, F., Calvanese, D., McGuinness, D.L., Nardi, D., Patel-Schneider, P.F.: The description logic handbook: theory, implementation, and applications. Cambridge University Press, 2003.
2. Grosof, B.N., Horrocks, I., Volz, R. Description Logic Programs: Combining Logic Programs with Description Logic. Proc. of the Twelfth International World Wide Web, May 2003, ACM, 48–57.
3. A.V. Mantsivoda. Semantic programming for semantic web. Invited Talk. Proc. 9th Asian Logic Conference, August 2005, 17-21.

Logtalk Processing of STEP Part 21 Files*

Paulo Moura[1] and Vincent Marchetti[2]

[1] Dep. of Computer Science, University of Beira Interior, Portugal
pmoura@di.ubi.pt
[2] KShell Analysis
vmarchetti@kshell.com

Abstract. STEP is an international standard for modeling information used in manufacturing activities; Part 21 is a STEP component that standardizes the exchange of this information through text files. We are working on applying logic programming techniques to processing STEP data models. The STEP standard specifies the entities, attributes, consistency rules, and functions used for describing and validating manufacturing information. Most STEP entities and data types are organized into hierarchies, making an object-oriented approach the most straightforward implementation solution. Our work uses Logtalk, an object oriented extension to Prolog, as the primary implementation tool.

Introduction. Our initial work [1] focus on the STEP Application Protocol (AP) 203 — *configuration control design* schema [2,3], which has become a successful vendor neutral file standard for the exchange of Computer Aided Design (CAD) data models, supported by many commercial CAD applications [4]. The conformance validation of data models complements the testing of the geometric validity of design models [5] and is a form of quality control important for the interoperability of CAD and related applications.

Implementing STEP Application Protocols and Data Models. Logtalk [6] provides a flexible object model with a set of features, such as multiple inheritance and multiple instantiation, which are essential for a one-to-one mapping of AP entities and data objects as specified by STEP Part 21. In addition, other Logtalk features, such as support for both classes and prototypes, reflection, and parametric objects, contribute to an easier implementation of AP concepts and application code when compared with other OOP languages.

The Logtalk validation application is divided into three code tiers. The top tier includes the Logtalk compiler and its standard libraries, a library defining a set of meta-classes for AP entities, and a set of prototypes implementing AP-specific data types. The meta-classes provide support for easy validation of a single object, all descendant objects of an AP entity, or all objects on a data-model. The second tier consists of a Logtalk class hierarchy implementing the AP schema entities. Entity attributes are translated into logical predicates: simple facts for explicit attributes and rules for evaluating derived and inverse

---

* Work partially funded by the Instituto de Telecomunicações, Portugal.

S. Etalle and M. Truszczyński (Eds.): ICLP 2006, LNCS 4079, pp. 453–454, 2006.
© Springer-Verlag Berlin Heidelberg 2006

attributes and for conducting entity data consistency tests. This second tier also includes implementations of the AP schema functions. Our practice shows that the techniques of logic programming and the facilities of Logtalk allow the implementation of consistency tests and functions to be more concise and readable than the procedural code used in the AP schema specifications. The code in this second tier is generated by a combination of automated parsing of the AP schema files (using Python scripts) and manual code generation. The third tier corresponds to the data models under processing, specified as instances of the classes defined in the second tier. Instance attributes are defined as ground predicates. This code is automatically generated from a STEP data model file by an open source command-line application written in C++.

Validating STEP Data Models. Validation of a STEP data model is performed by loading the logic model, as defined in the three tiers described above, and then presenting a logical goal to be satisfied. The validation goal leads to a succession of goals testing the validity of the data model at three levels: (1) checking that individual attribute values are valid; (2) checking consistency of each instance as a whole; (3) checking global properties such as the uniqueness of attributes values, constraints involving connections among several data instances, and the acyclicity of hierarchies as specified in the AP schemas. It is worth noting that AP schemas often describe hundreds of entities and that a single data model can contain thousands of objects. To this we must add hundreds of functions and consistency rules used in the validation tests.

Current and Future Work. Current work includes completing the implementation of entity consistency rules and functions, testing our Logtalk implementation across a larger number of data models, and improving validation reports. The tools and techniques developed here are readily extensible to other APs developed under ISO 10303 [2] covering other manufacturing activities such as AP 238 (*cnc machining*) or AP 210 (*electronic printed circuit assembly, design, and manufacturing*). Future work will include development of implementation guidelines for coding other AP schemas. In addition, we are planning a webserver version of our validation application that will allow users to upload and validate data model files.

References

1. STEP Part 21 to Prolog web site http://www.kshell.com/prolog/
2. ISO STEP Standards web site http://www.steptools.com/library/standard/
3. ISO TC184/SC4 web site http://www.tc184-sc4.org/
4. STEP   Software   Products   web   site   http://pdesinc.aticorp.org/step_products.html
5. H. Gu, T. Chase, D. Cheney, T. Bailey, and D. Johnson, "Identifying, Correcting, and Avoiding Errors in Computer-Aided Design Models Which Affect Interoperability", J. Comput. Inf. Sci. Eng. 1(2): 156-166, June, 2001.
6. Logtalk web site http://www.logtalk.org/

Integrating Datalog with OWL: Exploring the AL-log Approach

Edna Ruckhaus[1,3], Vladimir Kolovski[2], Bijan Parsia[3], and Bernardo Cuenca[4]

[1] Universidad Simón Bolívar, Caracas, Venezuela
[2] Univ. of Maryland, Computer Science Dept., MD, USA
[3] Univ. of Maryland, Maryland information and Network Dynamics Lab, MD, USA
[4] Univ. of Manchester, Information Management Group, Manchester, UK

Abstract. We present OWL-log, which is an implementation of the $\mathcal{AL}$-log hybrid knowledge representation system where the Description Logics component is extended to the Web Ontology Language OWL DL. We implemented an OWL-log reasoner coupled to the OWL reasoner *Pellet* and explored different query-answering strategies. We conducted an experimental study using a modified version of the LUBM benchmark in order to evaluate and compare the efficiency of the strategies. Also, to validate OWL-log's usefulness we developed a prototype based on the Web ontology browsing and editing tool *Swoop*.

1 The OWL-Log System

OWL-log is an implementation of the hybrid knowledge representation system $\mathcal{AL}$-log [5] that combines Description Logics (DL) and Datalog components. OWL-log restricts the Datalog atoms to be unary or binary, and the DL component is extended to the Web Ontology Language OWL DL. A constrained OWL-log clause is an axiom in which only OWL DL Class and Datatype predicates are allowed in the antecedent of the rules as constraints. Datalog predicates in an OWL-log clause are limited to being OWL DL classes and properties that are not being used in any of the axioms that belong to the DL component (we define these concepts as *Atomic*). Our approach is to evolve the Web Ontology Language OWL DL toward the Semantic Web Rule Language (SWRL) while retaining practical decidability.

An important application for a system like OWL-log can be Web policies. For instance, we may write a policy rule to specify permissions on a set of services:

$hasPermission(P, S)$:-
    $relatedTo(S, K), participates(O, K), memberOf(P, O),$
    & $K{:}JointProject, S{:}Service, P{:}Person, O{:}Organization.$

Note that to comply with the OWL-log rule definition, the predicates *relatedTo*, *participates* and *memberOf*, will be Atomic concepts (Datalog predicates). On the other hand *JointProject* is a defined class in the DL component:

$JointProject \equiv Project \sqcap \geq 2 \ organizedBy.$

S. Etalle and M. Truszczyński (Eds.): ICLP 2006, LNCS 4079, pp. 455–456, 2006.

Our work differs from other systems that rely on translating the DL and rules components to a common logical language [2,3] and using rule engines for inferencing. OWL-log is a combined approach where both components are kept separately but with an interface handled through the DL atoms in the rules component, and its decision procedure is based on a combination of DL and Datalog reasoners.

2 Implementation and Evaluation

We have developed two different query-answering strategies: *Dynamic* and *Precompilation*. In Dynamic, the method used for answering a query is based on the notions of *constrained SLD-derivation* and *constrained SLD-refutation* [5]. The key idea of Precompilation is to pre-process all of the DL atoms that appear in the Datalog rules, and include them as facts in the Datalog subsystem; once the pre-processing is done, queries can be answered by the Datalog component using any of the known techniques for Datalog query evaluation.

According to [5], constrained SLD-resolution is complete and correct. Thus, Dynamic is a complete and correct procedure. Precompilation is a complete query-answering procedure only for *DL-safe rules*, that is rules in which each variable is bound to individuals that are explicit in the ABox [4].

We conducted an experimental study to compare the performance of the Dynamic and Precompilation query-answering strategies. Our test case of choice was a modified version of the LUBM benchmark [1] with one university and increasing ABox sizes. The performance evaluation results show that Precompilation performs better than Dynamic for queries where there is a large number of results (valid bindings) because in Dynamic, the query-answering time depends on the number of constrained empty clauses. On the other hand, Precompilation does worse than Dynamic when a large number of intermediate predicates are inferred in the Datalog component. Future work includes improving this time with query optimization techniques that include cost-based join-ordering strategies and Magic-Sets rewriting.

References

1. J. Heflin, Z. Pan and Y. Guo. The Lehigh University Benchmark LUBM. http://swat.cse.lehigh.edu/projects/lubm/. 2003.
2. B. Grosof, I. Horrocks, R. Volz and S. Decker. Description Logic Programs: Combining Logic Programs with Description Logic. In *Proceedings of WWW 2003*. 2003.
3. I. Horrrocks, P. Patel-Schneider, S. Bechhofer and D. Tsarkov. OWL Rules. A Proposal and Prototype Implementation. In *Journal of Web Semantics*. Volume 3. 2004.
4. B. Motik, U. Sattler and R. Studer. Query Answering for OWL-DL with Rules. In *Proceedings of ISWC 2004*. 2004.
5. F. Donini, M. Lenzerini, D. Nardi and A. Schaerf. AL-log: Integrating Datalog and Description Logics. In *Journal of Intelligent Information Systems*. Volume 10. 1998.

LMNtal as a Unifying Declarative Language: Live Demonstration

Kazunori Ueda[1], Norio Kato[2], Koji Hara[1], and Ken Mizuno[1]

[1] Dept. of Computer Science, Waseda University, Tokyo, Japan
[2] Center for Verification and Semantics, AIST, Osaka, Japan
`{ueda, n-kato, hara, mizuno}@ueda.info.waseda.ac.jp`

LMNtal (pronounced "*elemental*") is a simple language model based on hierarchical graph rewriting. It features and supports

- rule-based multiset rewriting,
- connectivity of nodes represented using logical variables,
- hierarchy of nodes represented using membranes,
- locality of rewrite rules,
- dynamic migration of processes (= hierarchical graphs) and rewrite rules,
- uniform treatment of processes and data,
- graphical view of computation,

and so on. Figure 1 shows examples of computation that can be encoded into LMNtal straightforwardly.

LMNtal is an outcome of the attempt to unify constraint-based concurrency (also known as concurrent constraint programming) and CHR, but its goal is now much broader: It is intended to be a substrate language of various computational models, especially those addressing concurrency, mobility and multiset rewriting.

Another important goal of LMNtal has been to put hierarchical graph rewriting into practice and demonstrate its versatility. We have given practical considerations to LM-Ntal, and made it into a full-fledged, monolithic programming language, which is available on the web with a number of sample programs.

Language Features. We refer the readers to [1] on LMNtal as a computational model (i.e., the core language). Building on the core, we have made the following extensions:

- term notation for concise description of constants, lists, and trees,
- system rulesets (including arithmetics) that can be extended by programmers,
- guards and typed process contexts for capturing graph structures of specific shapes and/or comparing them,
- randomization of redex and rule selection strategies,
- construct for avoiding infinite application of the same rule to the same subgraph,
- nondeterministic execution mode (exhaustive search),
- modules and foreign-language interface to Java,
- read-eval-print loop (interactive mode),
- visualizer.

S. Etalle and M. Truszczyński (Eds.): ICLP 2006, LNCS 4079, pp. 457–458, 2006.

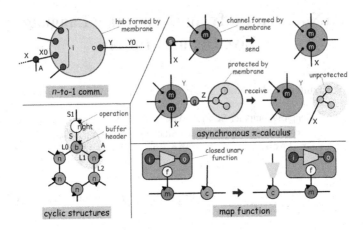

Fig. 1. Diagrammatic representation of computation

Implementation Overview. The current LMNtal system consists of 27,000 lines of Java code. The system compiles an LMNtal source file into intermediate code, and (unless invoked in the interactive mode) translates the intermediate code into a Java program, which in turn is compiled into Java bytecode and packaged into a Java archive file.

LMNtal is a fine-grained concurrent language, but how to implement it correctly and efficiently turns out to be far from obvious because (i) links and membranes may cross each other and (ii) rulesets belonging to different membranes in a lineal relation may attempt to rewrite the same process competitively. We have designed and implemented an execution algorithm that allows asynchronous graph rewriting by multiple tasks. Proper treatment of asynchrony is essential also for interfacing LMNtal with Java's multithreading and GUI.

Examples and Future Directions. We have encoded into LMNtal a wide range of computational models, including the pure and call-by-name lambda calculi, the asynchronous pi-calculus, the ambient calculus, the sequent calculus, all tested on our LMNtal system and ready for demonstration. Some don't use membranes at all, while others make extensive use of membranes for protection, localization, and first-class multisets. Moreover, many (concurrent) logic programs run as LMNtal programs without or with very minor modifications. On a practical side, LMNtal is being applied to declarative graphics, parallel and distributed processing, and verification.

LMNtal has particularly close connections to Bigraphs, Interaction Nets, and CHR. LMNtal and CHR exhibit both commonalities and differences in many respects, including language constructs and intended applications. Clarifying their relationship and promoting cross-fertilization is an important research topic.

Reference

1. Ueda, K. and Kato, N., LMNtal: A Language Model with Links and Membranes. In *Proc. Fifth Int. Workshop on Membrane Computing*, LNCS 3365, Springer, 2005, pp. 110–125.

Declarative Problem Solving Using Answer Set Semantics

Martin Brain

Department of Computer Science
University of Bath
Bath BA2 7AY, UK
mjb@cs.bath.ac.uk

Abstract. My dissertation will make the case that answer set semantics can form the basis of powerful, logical NP problem solving tools. The argument is made in two steps. Firstly a logical programming language, $AnsProlog^{CE}$ is proposed and an efficient, parallel implementation is described. This language is then used to solve a variety of diverse real world problems, demonstrating the power and flexibility of this approach.

Answer set semantics [1] are a formal semantic for logic programs. For a given program, answer sets can be seen as minimal (with respect to deductive closure) sets of literals that are consistent with the program. A summary of the semantics can be found in [2]. Answer set programming (ASP) is a problem solving technique in which a problem is represented as (*modelling*) a logic program under answer set semantics such that when the answer sets are computed (*solving*) they can be mapped to the solutions (*interpretation*).

Within the community of answer set semantics research it is widely believed that ASP is the application / justification of the theoretical research but there has been relatively little work done on it. There are a few [3,4] large scale applications and some comparison [5] and benchmarking [6] works but the case is yet to be made outside of the answer set semantics community. For example, there are questions of use: "What is ASP used for?", "Why not create a procedural solution?" as well as practicality "Roughly how long will this program take to run?" and "How should I develop a program?" that remain difficult to answer.

My thesis should help provide some of the answers to these questions and serve as a bridge from the community of answer set semantics to (and from) the wider community of software developers. The focus of the work is on practicality over, but not at expense of, theory. It is not a finished, 'user friendly' tool, it is proof of concept technology that moves towards this goal. I believe that work of this nature must be conducted to apply the existing research in answer set semantics as well as to uncover the next generation of challenges in solver implementation, program analysis and ultimately the underlying theory.

As a general purpose tool, an answer set solver is unlikely to compute solutions faster than well tuned implementation in a procedural language. So the concept of *time to solution* (the time elapsed between a problem being posed and it being solved) is introduced, evidence is then presented to suggest that ASP has

S. Etalle and M. Truszczyński (Eds.): ICLP 2006, LNCS 4079, pp. 459–460, 2006.

a lower time to solution than other problem solving tools, for some problems. To show that complex problems can be modelled simply and quickly a variety of case studies are presented. If the problem in question requires parallelism to provide sufficient compute power, the time saved in development may be very significant, exceeding the cost of the extra hardware required to make the ASP solution run just as quickly as a procedural one. Then all that remains is to show it is possible to create an implementation that is 'good enough' for this advantage to be significant. (This argument is analogous to the argument for compilers versus assembler; assembler runs faster but the time to solution with compiled languages is less). The first part of my thesis present a tool which is 'good enough' is this sense, the second presents a variety of case studies to support it's design, it's performance versus a variety of other logic programming tools and the expressivity and simplicity of ASP.

First a logical programming language, $AnsProlog^{CE}$ is proposed and given a semantics using a mapping to answer set semantics. Unlike previous solver languages, the constructs and limitations are based on implementation rather than theory. Preliminary results on complexity and the case studies show that these restrictions are not a significant problem. A powerful, parallel implementation is then described – aimed specifically at programs with large search spaces with few, or no answer sets. These are the hardest cases for current solvers and thus provide a good indication of whether solver performance is good enough.

The second part of my thesis then uses the new tools to solve a wide variety of problems demonstrating the scalability, flexibility and versatility of answer set programming. The first set of case studies are simple examples: puzzles such as Su-Doku and Rubik Cube. These help ground some of the theory and have proved to be effective tools for communicating answer set programming. The largest case study is the TOAST (Total Optimisation using Answer Set Technology) project. This is an attempt to generate truly optimal machine code for simple, acyclic functions. This requires extensive modelling of parts of the core of a variety of processors and has already generated some significant and interesting problems.

References

1. Gelfond, M., Lifschitz, V.: The Stable Model Semantics for Logic Programming. In: Proceedings of (ICLP'88), The MIT Press (1988) 1070–1080
2. Baral, C.: Knowledge Representation, Reasoning and Declarative Problem Solving. Cambridge University Press (2003)
3. Nogueira, M., Balduccini, M., Gelfond, M., Watson, R., Barry, M.: An A-Prolog Decision Support System for the Space Shuttle. In: Proceedings of (PADL'01), Springer-Verlag (2001) 169–183
4. Leone, N., Eiter, T., Faber, W., et al.: Boosting information integration: The infomix system. In: Proceedings of (SEBD'05). (2005) 55–66
5. Hietalahti, M., Massacci, F., Niemelä, I.: Des: A challenge problem for nonmonotonic reasoning systems. In: Proceedings of (NMR'00). (2000)
6. Borchert, P., Anger, C., Schaub, T., Truszczynski, M.: Towards systematic benchmarking in answer set programming : The dagstuhl initiative. LNCS **2923** (2003)

The Design and Implementation of the YAP Compiler: An Optimizing Compiler for Logic Programming Languages

Anderson Faustino da Silva and Vítor Santos Costa

Department of Computing and Systems Engineering
Federal University of Rio de Janeiro
Caixa Postal: 68511 – 21941-972 Rio de Janeiro, RJ, Brazil
{faustino, vitor}@cos.ufrj.br

Programming language designers have always searched for programming languages and features that ease the programming process and improve programmer productivity. One promising approach is logic programming. Logic programming languages, such as Prolog, provide programmers with powerful techniques for writing programs quickly and easily.

Aggressive compiler optimization [1] can reduce the overhead imposed by Prolog [2] features. However, the long compilation times introduced by optimizing compilers delay the programming environment's responses to changes in the program. Furthermore, optimization also conflicts with source-level debugging. Thus, programmers have to choose between abstraction and efficiency, and between responsive programming environments and efficiency.

This research proposes to reconcile these seemingly contradictory goals by using dynamic optimization to perform optimizations lazily. Three techniques work together to achieve high performance and high responsiveness in Prolog programs:

1. **Type feedback**[3] achieves high performance by allowing the compiler to compile only the executed path based on information extracted from the runtime system. The main implementation problems of languages that support some form of late binding arise from the paucity of information statically available at compile time. That is, the exact meaning of some operations cannot be determined statically but is dependent on dynamic (i.e., runtime) information. Therefore, it is hard to optimize these late-bound operations statically, based on the program text alone. This problem is solved moving additional runtime information to the compiler. Type feedback works in this manner. The key idea of type feedback is to extract type information from the runtime system and feed it back to the compiler.

2. **Dynamic deoptimization**[4] shields the programmer from the complexity of debugging optimized code by transparently recreating non-optimized code as needed. Dynamic deoptimization shields the debugger from optimizations performed by the compiler by dynamically deoptimizing code on demand. Deoptimization requires the compiler to supply debugging information at discrete interrupt points. Then, the compiler can still perform extensive optimizations between interrupt points without affectingde-

S. Etalle and M. Truszczyński (Eds.): ICLP 2006, LNCS 4079, pp. 461–462, 2006.

buggability. Dynamic deoptimization transforms old compiled code into new versions reflecting the current source-level state.

3. **Adaptive optimization** [5] achieves high responsiveness without sacrificing performance by using a emulator to interpret initial code while automatically compiling heavily used parts of the program with an optimizing compiler. This technique allows that small pieces of code are compiled quickly, and thus small changes to a program can be handled quickly. Using adaptive optimization, the debugging system makes it possible to integrate an optimizing compiler into an exploratory programming environment.

In this research we propose precisely such an approach: we implemented a compilation from Prolog to native code, using dynamic compilation. Our starting point is develop a dynamic optimizing compiler, essentially an high-performance emulator-based system. This facilitates mixing emulated and native code. This new system simultaneously improves execution and compilation speed. The progress made in implementing our system will encourage others to find even better solutions to the implementation challenges posed by logic languages. Our research will contribute to make logic programming environments more popular, as in the past, such systems have often suffered from performance problems that have limited their acceptance.

Our immediate goal is to build an efficient, usable implementation of Prolog. However, we are not willing to compromise Prolog's language semantics and other expressive features. We want to preserve the illusion of the system directly executing the program as the programmer wrote it, with no user-visible optimizations. Our main objective is excellent run-time performance. We wish to make Prolog with similar powerful features competitive in performance with traditional imperative languages such as C and Pascal.

Of course, we do not only wish to implement Prolog efficiently, but also a larger class of logic languages. Fortunately, the techniques used are not specific to the Prolog language. They were applied in languages such as SELF, C++ and Java. In our research we demonstrate how this techniques can be used in logic languages.

References

1. Muchnick, S.S.: Advanced Compiler Design And Implementation. Morgan Kaufmann, San Francisco, CA, USA (1997)
2. Sterling, L., Shapiro, E.: The Art of Prolog. MIT Press, USA (1986)
3. Agesen, O., Holzle, U.: Type Feedback vs. Concrete Type Inference: A Comparison of Optimization Techniques for Object-Oriented Languages. In: Conference on Object-Oriented. (1995) 91–107
4. Hlzle, U., Chambers, C., Ungar, D.: Debugging Optimized Code with Dynamic Deoptimization. In: Proceedings of Conference on Programming Language Design and Implementation, San Francisco, USA (1992) 32–43
5. Holzle, U.: Adaptative Optimization for SELF: Reconciling High Performance with Exploratory Programming. PhD thesis, Stanford University (1994)

Description Logic Reasoning in Prolog

Gergely Lukácsy

Budapest University of Technology and Economics
Department of Computer Science and Information Theory
1117 Budapest, Magyar tudósok körútja 2., Hungary
lukacsy@cs.bme.hu

Abstract. We present a novel Description Logic reasoning approach, which focuses on solving the ABox instance retrieval problem when huge amounts of underlying data are expected. In such cases, traditional description logic theorem proving techniques cannot be used due to performance problems. Our approach is to transform the description logic knowledge base into a set of Horn-clauses forming a Prolog program.

1 Introduction and Problem Description

Description Horn Logic and the related Description Logic Programming (DLP) are a very interesting combination of Logic Programming (LP) and Description Logics (DL) [2]. This hybrid knowledge representation formalism has several advantages over only using DL or LP alone. For example, DLP offers the possibility for the DL based ontology builders to use rules, something which has been a well known shortcoming so far. What is equally important, efficient LP inference algorithms can be used for instance reasoning in DLP.

The motivation for this research comes from our involvement in the development of a knowledge management system for the integration of heterogeneous information sources, using methods and tools based on constraints and logic programming [1]. The main idea is to collect and manage meta-information (i.e models) on the sources to be integrated. Such models are based on the traditional object oriented paradigm as well as on description logics constructs. The models can be used to answer complex queries involving several data sources.

Because of this, we have to query DL concepts where the actual data (the so called ABox) is stored in the underlying databases. We found it practically impossible to use existing DL inference systems for this task. On one hand, these systems are not capable of handling ABoxes stored externally. On the other hand, the existing algorithms are unacceptably inefficient when dealing with huge amounts of data, which is usually the case during information integration.[1]

These performance problems are not because of poor implementation techniques, but the fundamental properties of the algorithms these systems use. Namely, they have to examine the whole content of the ABox to answer a query, which is more or less equivalent of enumerating everything in the databases.

---

[1] Similar problems occur in other important areas where description logic based ontologies are used, for example in the Semantic Web.

S. Etalle and M. Truszczyński (Eds.): ICLP 2006, LNCS 4079, pp. 463–464, 2006.

2   Goals and Current Stage of the Research

In order to do efficient description logic reasoning on large ABoxes we separate the inference algorithm from the actual data storage, e.g. *delegate* as much work as possible to the database systems. We also execute the queries using Prolog's top down evaluation, which normally means that we access the content of the databases in a *focused* way.

In our solution the inference algorithm is divided into two phases. First, from a DL concept to be queried, we create a *query-plan*, as a set of Prolog clauses. Second, data is accessed *dynamically* during the normal Prolog execution of the generated program. With this technique only those pieces of data are accessed which are indeed important for answering the query, i.e. we solve the original problem in a database friendly way.

The first step of our research resulted in a resolution-based transformation of ABox reasoning problems to Prolog [4]. This algorithm is able to answer instance-check and instance-retrieval queries over the DL language $\mathcal{ALC}$ and an empty TBox.

In [4] we have handled the problems due to the so called *open world assumption*. At the same time, we have shown that the Prolog program produced can be viewed as the result of an ABox-independent part of a generic resolution proof. We have also carried out some simple performance analysis, showing that our approach can be several magnitudes faster than the traditional, tableau-based approach.

In paper[3], we examined how ABox reasoning services can be provided with respect to slightly restricted *non-empty* TBox. We generalized the transformation of [2] to include e.g disjunctions. We have written an interpreter which performs the resolution-based proof belonging to instance-check and instance-retrieval queries.

We view the current results as a first step. We plan to extend our algorithm to more elaborate DL languages (such as $\mathcal{SHIQ}$) and to allow full TBox axioms as well. We also work on the optimization of the query plan, considering the use of target language specific elements (like cut, indexing, etc. in Prolog) to make the execution of the query plan more efficient.

References

1. Tamás Benkő, Gergely Lukácsy, Attila Fokt, Péter Szeredi, Imre Kilián, and Péter Krauth. Information integration through reasoning on meta-data. In *Proceedings of the Workshop "AI Moves to IA, Workshop on Artificial Intelligence, Information Access, and Mobile Computing", IJCAI'03, Acapulco, Mexico*, pages 65–77, 2003.
2. Benjamin N. Grosof, Ian Horrocks, Raphael Volz, and Stefan Decker. Description logic programs: Combining logic programs with description logic. In *Proc. of the Twelfth International World Wide Web Conference*, pages 48–57. ACM, 2003.
3. Zsolt Nagy, Gergely Lukácsy, and Péter Szeredi. Description logic reasoning using the PTTP approach. To appear in Proceedings of the International Workshop on Description Logics, 2006.
4. Zsolt Nagy, Gergely Lukácsy, and Péter Szeredi. Translating description logic queries to Prolog. In *Proceedings of PADL, Springer LNCS 3819*, pages 168–182, 2006.

Static Memory Management for Logic Programming Languages

Quan Phan

Department of Computer Science, K.U. Leuven
Celestijnenlaan, 200A, B-3001 Heverlee, Belgium
{quan.phan}@cs.kuleuven.be

Introduction. Logic programming (LP) languages aim to free programmers from procedural details such as memory management tasks. One classical, automatic memory management technique in logic programming is to use a heap memory for all the structured terms and rely on backtracking and on a runtime garbage collector to reclaim memory. While efficient implementation of garbage collectors for LP languages can reuse more than 90% heap space, they introduce performance penalties to the execution of a program because the collectors need to temporarily stop the main program to do their job.

Background Literature. To remedy this shortcoming there has been a lot of research on compile-time memory management techniques, which automatically enhance programs with instructions to reuse memory. This static method generally follows two approaches: region-based memory management (RBMM) and compile-time garbage collection (CTGC). The basic idea of RBMM is to divide the heap memory into different regions. The dynamically created terms and their subterms have to be distributed over the regions in such a way that at a certain point in the execution of the program all terms in a region are dead and the region can be removed. CTGC detects when allocated memory cells are no longer used and instructs the program to reuse those cells to construct new terms, reducing memory consumption and in some cases achieving faster code. RBMM has long been a topic of intensive research for functional programming languages [7, 1, 4] and more recently also for procedural languages [3, 2]. For LP languages, there has been only one attempt to make RBMM work for Prolog [5]. The idea of CTGC has been used to reuse memory cells locally in the procedures of the LP language Mercury [6].

Goal of the Research. RBMM achieves competitive memory consumption for many programs due to timely removal of dead regions and memory management operations are time bound. CTGC can exploit many reuse opportunities. Taking those advantages to have a system in which reusable memory can be reused and non-reusable dead memory can be deallocated timely is the motivation for our current research. The ultimate research goal is to investigate the possibility and practicality of a hybrid static memory management technique, which combines RBMM and CTGC.

S. Etalle and M. Truszczyński (Eds.): ICLP 2006, LNCS 4079, pp. 465–466, 2006.
© Springer-Verlag Berlin Heidelberg 2006

Current Status. Developing an algorithm that combines the nontrivial program analyses of CTGC in [6] and the type-based region inference in [5] has not been straightforward. Its main difficulty comes from the fact that those analyses were developed for different programming languages. The CTGC system is for Mercury, while the RBMM system is originally designed for a first-order subset of ML and extended to work in XSB Prolog. More recently an analysis and transformation algorithm for RBMM, which relies on region points-to graphs and region lifetime analysis, has been reported for Java [2]. We found several similarities in terms of design and the basic concepts used between the algorithm and the analyses in CTGC. This makes it feasible to reformulate the algorithm to work for Mercury and to integrate it later on with CTGC analyses. In the initial step towards the research goal, we have developed an extensible RBMM analysis and transformation algorithm in the context of deterministic Mercury programs. Currently we are working on improving the precision of the algorithm and also on integrating the algorithm into a working Mercury compiler and extending the Mercury runtime to support regions. After having both RBMM and CTGC systems in the context of Mercury the idea of integrating them will have the necessary background to be developed.

Open Issues and Expected Achievements. There are several issues that need further investigation, such as supporting modular region analysis, both the theory and practice of the operation of CTGC when memory is organised in terms of regions, and the interaction of RBMM, CTGC and runtime garbage collection. The combination of RBMM and CTGC may lead to the "reuse inside regions" technique, which is useful when in a program there are procedures containing cells that die but cannot be reused locally by CTGC. We expect that dead, reusable cells can be allocated in separate regions from the regions of dead, non-reusable cells, which can be reclaimed timely by RBMM when they cease to be live.

References

[1] A. Aiken, M. Fahndrich, and R. Levien. Better static memory management: Improving region-based analysis of higher-order languages. In *SIGPLAN Conference on Programming Language Design and Implementation*, pages 174–185, 1995.

[2] S. Cherem and R. Rugina. Region analysis and Transformation for Java. In *Proceedings of the 4th international symposium on Memory management*, pages 85–96. ACM Press., October 2004.

[3] D. Grossman, G. Morrisett, T. Jim, M. Hicks, Y. Wang, and J. Cheney. Region-based memory management in Cyclone. In *Proceedings of the ACM Conference on Programming Language Design and Implementation.*, pages 282–293, 2002.

[4] F. Henglein, H Makholm, and H. Niss. A direct approach to control-flow sensitive region-based memory management. In *Principles and Practice of Declarative Programming.*, pages 175–186, 2001.

[5] H. Makholm and K. Sagonas. On enabling the WAM with region support. In *Proceedings of the 18th International Conference on Logic Programming*, 2002.

[6] Mazur N. *Compile-time garbage collection for the declarative language Mercury.* PhD thesis, Dept. of Computer Science, Katholieke Universiteit Leuven, May 2004.

[7] M. Tofte and J.-P. Talpin. Region-based memory management. *Information and Computation.*, 132(2):109–176, February 1997.

Deductive Databases: Implementation, Parallelism and Applications

Tiago Soares

DCC-FC & LIACC
University of Porto, 4150-180 Porto, Portugal
Tel.: (+351) 226078830; Fax: (+351) 226003654
tiagosoares@ncc.up.pt

1 Research Context and Previous Work

The area of integrating or coupling a database with LP systems in order to obtain a Deductive Database System (DDS) is still of interest and poses many research problems. In particular, the basis for my work is the MySQL Yap Deductive DAtabase System (MYDDAS) [3] which couples the Yap system with the MySQL Relational Database Management System. The connection between these two platforms is achieved by the C foreign language interface that both systems provide.

Fig. 1 shows the three main blocks of the current implementation of MYDDAS: the Yap Prolog compiler, the MYDDAS Interface and the database storage engine. The current effort on the MYDDAS Interface is put on the MySQL C interface rather than on the ODBC C interface. SQL queries are generated by using the generic Prolog to SQL compiler done by Christoph Draxler [1].

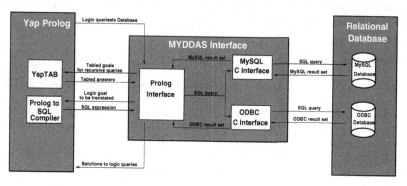

Fig. 1. MYDDAS blueprint

An important drawback of most current Prolog based DDS implementations is the impossibility to declare an action when a *cut operation* occurs. Due to the cut operation semantics, these operations are discouraged when pruning database imported predicates. The problem is that SQL queries *result sets* are

S. Etalle and M. Truszczyński (Eds.): ICLP 2006, LNCS 4079, pp. 467–468, 2006.
© Springer-Verlag Berlin Heidelberg 2006

stored on memory, outside the WAM data structures, therefore needing specific actions to be deallocated when a cut occurs. To solve this problem we have recently proposed a new approach where the cut operation can execute a generic action associated with a given predicate that is being pruned. In a DDS context we use this mechanism to deallocate the result sets associated with database predicates in a efficient manner [4,5].

We are also working on new applications to DDS. Recently, we have started to integrate MYDDAS with Inductive Logic Programming (ILP), and in particular with the APRIL ILP System [2]. The main goal of ILP is to obtain an *intensional representation* (theory) given an *extensional representation of data* (facts). Currently, the complexity of ILP algorithms is very high, making these systems quite slow, especially when computating the coverage of hyphotesis. Preliminary performance results showed that by using a DDS such MYDDAS we are able to significantly reduce the execution time of ILP Systems, and therefore allowing a substantial increase of the size of the problems that can be solved with ILP.

2   Direction and Goal of This Research

The main goal of this research is to improve of the state of the art of current DDS by developing a new DDS which takes advantage of the advanced features of the OPTYAP system. The system should be able to explore tabling and parallelism taking advantage of the or-parallel tabling engine of OPTYap, including the parallel evaluation of recursive queries. We also plan to implement the translation from Prolog to SQL as an automated compilation step, based on program analysis, which takes into account factors such as the size of data, database indexing information and complexity of queries. We aim to use these new evaluation methods to study the advantages of this type of paradigm in several real-world problems.

References

1. C. Draxler. *Accessing Relational and Higher Databases Through Database Set Predicates*. PhD thesis, Zurich University, 1991.
2. N. Fonseca, R. Camacho, F. Silva, and V. Santos Costa. Induction with April: A Preliminary Report. Technical Report DCC-2003-02, Department of Computer Science, University of Porto, 2003.
3. T. Soares, M. Ferreira, and R. Rocha. The MYDDAS Programmer's Manual. Technical Report DCC-2005-10, Department of Computer Science, University of Porto, 2005.
4. T. Soares, R. Rocha, and M. Ferreira. Pruning Extensional Predicates in Deductive Databases. In *Colloquium on Implementation of Constraint and LOgic Programming Systems*, pages 13–24, 2005.
5. T. Soares, R. Rocha, and M. Ferreira. Generic Cut Actions for External Prolog Predicates. In *International Symposium on Practical Aspects of Declarative Languages*, number 3819 in LNCS, pages 16–30. Springer-Verlag, 2006.

Efficient Reasoning About Action and Change in the Presence of Incomplete Information and Its Application in Planning

Phan Huy Tu

Department of Computer Science, New Mexico State University,
PO Box 30001, MSC CS, Las Cruces, NM 88003, USA

Introduction. Many domains that we wish to model and reason about are subject to change due to the execution of actions. Representing and reasoning about dynamic domains play an important role in AI because they serve as a fundamental basis for many applications, including planning, diagnosis, and modelling. Research in the field focuses on the development of formalisms for reasoning about action and change (RAC). Such a formalism normally consists of two components: a representation language and a reasoning mechanism. It has been well known in the field that two criteria for the success of a formalism are its *expressiveness* and *efficiency*. The former means that the representation language is rich enough to describe complicated domains; the latter implies the reasoning mechanism is computationally efficient, making it possible to be implemented on a machine. Besides, in daily life, we have to face the absence of complete information and thus any formalism should take this matter into account.

Most of the existing work on RAC relies on the *possible world approach* [6]. The main weakness of this approach is its high complexity. It was proved in [1], in conformant setting, e.g., the problem of finding a (polynomial length) conformant plan using this approach is Σ_2^P-complete. An alternative is the *approximation-based approach*, adopted by the authors in [4,7]. The main advantage of the approximation-based approach is its lower complexity in reasoning and planning tasks in comparison with the possible world approach as shown in [1]. The price that one has to pay when using an approximation is its incompleteness (w.r.t. the possible world approach). Another limitation of the existing approximations [7,4] is that they do not allow for domain constraints or just allow for a limited class of domain constraints. In a recent paper [10], it is shown that directly handling domain constraints in a planner can indeed improve its performance.

Planning is an important application of RAC. Basically, a planning problem is the problem of finding a structure of actions, called *plan*, that leads to the goal from the initial state. In the absence of complete information, a plan normally exists in two forms: *conformant plan* and *contingent plan*. The former is simply a sequence of actions that leads to the goal from any possible initial state, while the latter is a more sophisticated structure (see [5]). Most of the existing conformant/contingent planners are written in imperative programming languages and their representation languages are somewhat limited – they either do not allow for state constraints or just allow for a limited class of state constraints. There

S. Etalle and M. Truszczyński (Eds.): ICLP 2006, LNCS 4079, pp. 469–470, 2006.
© Springer-Verlag Berlin Heidelberg 2006

has been a very limited effort [2,8] in adding preferences of a plan to planning systems and none of them deals with incomplete information.

Goal of the Research. This research is aimed at developing approximations for action theories in the presence of incomplete information and domain constraints, and building a family of conditional and conformant planners based on the proposed aprpoximations, taking into account preferences and domain knowledge. The approximations may be incomplete but are expected to be strong enough to solve most of the benchmarks in the literature. Logic programming is chosen for the development of planners because of its declarativeness and expressiveness, making it easy to add modules for handling user preferences and exploiting the knowledge of the domain.

Current Results. In [9], we study the completeness of the 0-approximation [7] for action theories with incomplete information and propose a sufficient condition for which an action theory under the 0-approximation semantics is complete. We then suggest a method to modify an action theory in such a way that the modified theory under the 0-approximation is complete with the original theory. This method was implemented in a conformant planner. The planner is sound and complete and our experimental results show that its performance can be competitive with other state-of-the-art conformant planners.

Ongoing and Future Work. The framework in [9], however, is only for action theories without domain constraints. At present, I have an initial proposal for approximations of action theories with domain constraints but there are still open issues: are they strong enough? under what circumstances are they complete? can we modify them so as to be complete? In addition, I am investigating the use of constraint logic programming and constraint handling rules [3] to implement the planners.

References

1. C. Baral, V. Kreinovich & R. Trejo. Computational complexity of planning and approximate planning in the presence of incompleteness. *AI*, 122:241–267, 2000.
2. R. Brafman & Y. Chernyavsky. Planning with goal preferences and constraints. In *ICAPS'05*.
3. T. Frühwirth. Theory and practice of constraint handling rules. *JLP*, 1998.
4. M. Gelfond & R. Morales. Encoding conformant planning in A-PROLOG. *DRT'04*.
5. H. Levesque. What is planning in the presence of sensing? In *Proceedings of the 14th Conference on Artificial Intelligence*, pages 1139–1146. AAAI Press, 1996.
6. R. Moore. A formal theory of knowledge and action. In J. Hobbs and R. Moore, editors, *Formal theories of the commonsense world*. Ablex, Norwood, NJ, 1985.
7. T. Son & C. Baral. Formalizing sensing actions - a transition function based approach. *Artificial Intelligence*, 125(1-2):19–91, January 2001.
8. T. Son & E. Pontelli. Planning with preferences using logic programming. *LP-NMR'04*.
9. T. Son & P. Tu. On the Completeness of Approximation Based Reasoning and Planning in Action Theories with Incomplete Information. In *KR'06*.
10. S. Thiebaux, J. Hoffmann & B. Nebel. In Defense of PDDL Axioms. In *Proceedings of the 18th International Joint Conference on Artificial Intelligence*, 2003.

Deducing Logic Programs

Ka-Shu Wong

National ICT Australia and
School of Computer Science and Engineering
UNSW, Sydney 2052, Australia
kswong@cse.unsw.edu.au

1 Problem Description and Goals

Consider an agent endowed with a logic program which is able to respond to certain questions about the logic program. We would like to answer the question: to what extent can we deduce the logic program from the agent's answers, and how can we do this?

For example, suppose the agent has a logic program with the unique answer set $\{p, q\}$. Supposing that we are only allowed to ask whether a given literal is in an answer set, we may guess that the logic program is $\{p \leftarrow, q \leftarrow\}$. It is clear that this is unlikely to be the actual logic program, however we cannot distinguish between this program and the actual program with only the questions allowed. On the other end of the scale, suppose we are allowed to ask the agent to tell us their logic program. Then it is trivial to determine exactly the logic program of the agent.

Therefore one aspect of the problem that can be investigated is the theoretical limits of this process of deducing logic programs. We would like to know how close we can get to the original logic program, given that we are only allowed questions from a certain class. This can be linked to a notion of "equivalence" of logic programs where two logic programs are considered equivalent if they cannot be distinguished under the class of questions being considered. My research involves a study of the different types of equivalences that arise under the various classes of questions.

Another aspect of the problem is the actual algorithms which can be used for deducing logic programs from answers to questions. For trivial examples such as the one above, it is easy to produce an algorithm which deduces the logic program up to equivalence. For different classes of questions which give rise to finer equivalence classes, the problem may be intractable or may even be computationally impossible. Therefore my research includes exploring the existence of such algorithms relative to the various question classes, with a focus on identifying the question classes for which the problem is tractable, and constructing algorithms to solve the problem in those cases.

My research will be mainly in the context of extended logic programs with answer set semantics [1], however I may also consider other classes of logic programs, such as disjunctive logic programs and nested logic programs [2]. I will also consider situations where we have background knowledge about the agent's

S. Etalle and M. Truszczyński (Eds.): ICLP 2006, LNCS 4079, pp. 471–472, 2006.

logic program. This can be incorporated into the framework as an additional class of questions which can be asked.

2   Related Work

There appears to be little existing work on the topic of deducing logic programs through question-and-answer.

The area of *inductive logic programming* [3,4] (ILP) appears to have superficial similarities to my area of research. Inductive logic programming is about inferring a logic program from a given collection of facts and background knowledge such that the resulting logic program "explains" the given facts. This differs from my research in that ILP is mainly concerned with the facts that can be derived from the logic program, whereas my research is about recovering an agent's logic program, which includes more information than just the facts that can be derived from it. My work is also in a sense broader than ILP, since the questions are not restricted to asking the truth or falsity of certain literals.

3   Research Status and Plan

My research is still at a very early stage. I have settled on my research direction and finalised my thesis proposal, however I have only recently started on the research. The preliminary work that I've done thus far consists of exploring equivalences of extended logic programs under various classes of questions.

The first stage of the project is to define various classes of questions that can be used. I intend to investigate the links between these classes and existing notions of equivalence on logic programs. For each of these classes of questions, I will investigate the existence of syntactical properties of programs which cannot be distinguished under the question class under consideration. This will hopefully result in a way to identify the "simplest" program in each equivalence class. I will consider this on a computational level, with a focus on identifying the classes of questions for which the problem is tractable. Finally, I intend to look at the application of this work to agent negotiation and machine learning. This may involve applying the results obtained in this work to developing negotiation protocols for agents which use logic programs to encode preferences.

References

1. Gelfond, M., Lifschitz, V.: Classical negation in logic programs and disjunctive databases. New Generation Computing 9(3/4) (1991) 365–386
2. Lifschitz, V., Tang, L., Turner, H.: Nested expressions in logic programs. Annals of Mathematics and Artificial Intelligence 25(2-3) (1999) 369–390
3. Shapiro, E.: Inductive inference of theories from facts. In Lassez, J., Plotkin, G., eds.: Computational Logic: Essays in Honor of Alan Robinson. (1991) 199–255
4. Muggleton, S.: Inductive Logic Programming. Academic Press (1992)

Author Index

Lecture Notes in Computer Science

For information about Vols. 1–3988

please contact your bookseller or Springer

Vol. 4037: R. Gorrieri, H. Wehrheim (Eds.), Formal Methods for Open Object-Based Distributed Systems. XVII, 474 pages. 2006.

Vol. 4036: O. H. Ibarra, Z. Dang (Eds.), Developments in Language Theory. XII, 456 pages. 2006.

Vol. 4035: T. Nishita, Q. Peng, H.-P. Seidel (Eds.), Advances in Computer Graphics. XX, 771 pages. 2006.

Vol. 4034: J. Münch, M. Vierimaa (Eds.), Product-Focused Software Process Improvement. XVII, 474 pages. 2006.

Vol. 4033: B. Stiller, P. Reichl, B. Tuffin (Eds.), Performability Has its Price. X, 103 pages. 2006.

Vol. 4032: O. Etzion, T. Kuflik, A. Motro (Eds.), Next Generation Information Technologies and Systems. XIII, 365 pages. 2006.

Vol. 4031: M. Ali, R. Dapoigny (Eds.), Innovations in Applied Artificial Intelligence. XXIII, 1353 pages. 2006. (Sublibrary LNAI).

Vol. 4029: L. Rutkowski, R. Tadeusiewicz, L.A. Zadeh, J. Zurada (Eds.), Artificial Intelligence and Soft Computing – ICAISC 2006. XXI, 1235 pages. 2006. (Sublibrary LNAI).

Vol. 4027: H.L. Larsen, G. Pasi, D. Ortiz-Arroyo, T. Andreasen, H. Christiansen (Eds.), Flexible Query Answering Systems. XVIII, 714 pages. 2006. (Sublibrary LNAI).

Vol. 4026: P.B. Gibbons, T. Abdelzaher, J. Aspnes, R. Rao (Eds.), Distributed Computing in Sensor Systems. XIV, 566 pages. 2006.

Vol. 4025: F. Eliassen, A. Montresor (Eds.), Distributed Applications and Interoperable Systems. XI, 355 pages. 2006.

Vol. 4024: S. Donatelli, P. S. Thiagarajan (Eds.), Petri Nets and Other Models of Concurrency - ICATPN 2006. XI, 441 pages. 2006.

Vol. 4021: E. André, L. Dybkjær, W. Minker, H. Neumann, M. Weber (Eds.), Perception and Interactive Technologies. XI, 217 pages. 2006. (Sublibrary LNAI).

Vol. 4020: A. Bredenfeld, A. Jacoff, I. Noda, Y. Takahashi (Eds.), RoboCup 2005: Robot Soccer World Cup IX. XVII, 727 pages. 2006. (Sublibrary LNAI).

Vol. 4019: M. Johnson, V. Vene (Eds.), Algebraic Methodology and Software Technology. XI, 389 pages. 2006.

Vol. 4018: V. Wade, H. Ashman, B. Smyth (Eds.), Adaptive Hypermedia and Adaptive Web-Based Systems. XVI, 474 pages. 2006.

Vol. 4017: S. Vassiliadis, S. Wong, T.D. Hämäläinen (Eds.), Embedded Computer Systems: Architectures, Modeling, and Simulation. XV, 492 pages. 2006.

Vol. 4016: J.X. Yu, M. Kitsuregawa, H.V. Leong (Eds.), Advances in Web-Age Information Management. XVII, 606 pages. 2006.

Vol. 4014: T. Uustalu (Ed.), Mathematics of Program Construction. X, 455 pages. 2006.

Vol. 4013: L. Lamontagne, M. Marchand (Eds.), Advances in Artificial Intelligence. XIII, 564 pages. 2006. (Sublibrary LNAI).

Vol. 4012: T. Washio, A. Sakurai, K. Nakajima, H. Takeda, S. Tojo, M. Yokoo (Eds.), New Frontiers in Artificial Intelligence. XIII, 484 pages. 2006. (Sublibrary LNAI).

Vol. 4011: Y. Sure, J. Domingue (Eds.), The Semantic Web: Research and Applications. XIX, 726 pages. 2006.

Vol. 4010: S. Dunne, B. Stoddart (Eds.), Unifying Theories of Programming. VIII, 257 pages. 2006.

Vol. 4009: M. Lewenstein, G. Valiente (Eds.), Combinatorial Pattern Matching. XII, 414 pages. 2006.

Vol. 4008: J.C. Augusto, C.D. Nugent (Eds.), Designing Smart Homes. XI, 183 pages. 2006. (Sublibrary LNAI).

Vol. 4007: C. Àlvarez, M. Serna (Eds.), Experimental Algorithms. XI, 329 pages. 2006.

Vol. 4006: L.M. Pinho, M. González Harbour (Eds.), Reliable Software Technologies – Ada-Europe 2006. XII, 241 pages. 2006.

Vol. 4005: G. Lugosi, H.U. Simon (Eds.), Learning Theory. XI, 656 pages. 2006. (Sublibrary LNAI).

Vol. 4004: S. Vaudenay (Ed.), Advances in Cryptology - EUROCRYPT 2006. XIV, 613 pages. 2006.

Vol. 4003: Y. Koucheryavy, J. Harju, V.B. Iversen (Eds.), Next Generation Teletraffic and Wired/Wireless Advanced Networking. XVI, 582 pages. 2006.

Vol. 4001: E. Dubois, K. Pohl (Eds.), Advanced Information Systems Engineering. XVI, 560 pages. 2006.

Vol. 3999: C. Kop, G. Fliedl, H.C. Mayr, E. Métais (Eds.), Natural Language Processing and Information Systems. XIII, 227 pages. 2006.

Vol. 3998: T. Calamoneri, I. Finocchi, G.F. Italiano (Eds.), Algorithms and Complexity. XII, 394 pages. 2006.

Vol. 3997: W. Grieskamp, C. Weise (Eds.), Formal Approaches to Software Testing. XII, 219 pages. 2006.

Vol. 3996: A. Keller, J.-P. Martin-Flatin (Eds.), Self-Managed Networks, Systems, and Services. X, 185 pages. 2006.

Vol. 3995: G. Müller (Ed.), Emerging Trends in Information and Communication Security. XX, 524 pages. 2006.

Vol. 3994: V.N. Alexandrov, G.D. van Albada, P.M.A. Sloot, J. Dongarra, Computational Science – ICCS 2006, Part IV. XXXV, 1096 pages. 2006.

Vol. 3993: V.N. Alexandrov, G.D. van Albada, P.M.A. Sloot, J. Dongarra, Computational Science – ICCS 2006, Part III. XXXVI, 1136 pages. 2006.

Vol. 3992: V.N. Alexandrov, G.D. van Albada, P.M.A. Sloot, J. Dongarra, Computational Science – ICCS 2006, Part II. XXXV, 1122 pages. 2006.

Vol. 3991: V.N. Alexandrov, G.D. van Albada, P.M.A. Sloot, J. Dongarra, Computational Science – ICCS 2006, Part I. LXXXI, 1096 pages. 2006.

Vol. 3990: J. C. Beck, B.M. Smith (Eds.), Integration of AI and OR Techniques in Constraint Programming for Combinatorial Optimization Problems. X, 301 pages. 2006.

Vol. 3989: J. Zhou, M. Yung, F. Bao, Applied Cryptography and Network Security. XIV, 488 pages. 2006.